AWS Certification Books from Sybex

Associate Certifications

AWS Certified SysOps Administrator Study Guide: Associate (SOA-C01) Exam, 2nd Edition — ISBN 978-1-119-56155-2, February 2020

Edition with accompanying online labs — ISBN 978-1-119-75669-9, July 2020

AWS Certified SysOps Administrator Practice Tests: Associate (SOA-C01) Exam — ISBN 978-1-119-62272-7, May 2020

SOA-C01 *Study Guide* and *Practice Tests* also available as a set — ISBN 978-1-119-66410-9, June 2020

AWS Certified Solutions Architect Study Guide with 900 Practice Test Questions: Associate (SAA-C03) Exam, 4th Edition — ISBN 978-1-119-98262-3, October 2022

Edition with accompanying online labs — ISBN 978-1-394-18557-3, December 2022

Foundational Certification

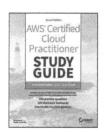

AWS Certified Cloud Practitioner Study Guide: Foundational (CLF-C02) Exam, Second Edition — ISBN 978-1-394-23563-6, December 2023

T0344870

Specialty Certifications

AWS Certified Advanced Networking Study Guide: Specialty (ANS-C01) Exam, 2nd Edition — ISBN 978-1-394-17185-9, December 2023

AWS Certified Data Analytics Study Guide: Specialty (DAS-C01) Exam — ISBN 978-1-119-64947-2, December 2020

Edition with accompanying online labs — ISBN 978-1-119-81945-5, April 2021

AWS Certified Security Study Guide: Specialty (SCS-C01) Exam — ISBN 978-1-119-65881-8, December 2020

AWS Certified Machine Learning Study Guide: Specialty (MLS-C01) Exam — ISBN 978-1-119-82100-7, November 2021

AWS Certified Database Study Guide: Specialty (DBS-C01) Exam — ISBN 978-1-119-77895-0, April 2023

AWS
Certified Developer
Study Guide
Associate (DVA-C02) Exam
Second Edition

Brandon Rich

SYBEX®
A Wiley Brand

About the Author

Brandon Rich is an IT Architect at the University of Notre Dame with over a decade of hands-on experience in AWS. As a leader in Notre Dame's "Cloud First" initiative, he helped advance that institution's mission by automating processes, migrating complex systems, and adopting scalable, managed services. Over his career, Brandon has been responsible for crafting and implementing IT strategy across many areas, including application and integration architecture, cloud strategy, virtual desktop infrastructure, and now, artificial intelligence as Director of AI Enablement. Brandon is also a LinkedIn Learning instructor, focusing on enterprise infrastructure, automation, AI, and AWS technologies. In his spare time, he enjoys traveling, backpacking with his family, and playing music with his Notre Dame bandmates.

Acknowledgments

I'm indebted to many people in the writing of this book. Many thanks to Carole Jelen at Waterside Productions for making connections, finding opportunities, and navigating the details time and time again.

At Wiley, thank you to the team of Kenyon Brown, Krysta Winsheimer, Ashirvad Moses, Magesh Elangovan, and Sara Deichman for shepherding this book through the process and answering many questions along the way.

Thanks to Mike Chapple and Sharif Nijim, who envisioned Notre Dame as a leader in higher education cloud adoption and made it happen. It was your support and encouragement that set me on the path to authorship—first online, and now in print.

To my wife Lauren and our two kids: thank you for your patience, encouragement, and support, and for tolerating a lot of "clicky-clacking." I could not have done it without you.

Thanks to Beckett for walking across the keyboard so often; at least half of this book is his.

Contents at a Glance

Contents

Introduction

Developers bring innovation to life. They transform ideas into reality, imagining, designing, and implementing applications that fulfill a vision, be it for their organizations, their customers, or their own personal projects. For developers, there is no better way to realize those visions in a dynamic, code-forward, flexible, scalable, and automated way than with Amazon Web Services. If you're a developer eager to launch or accelerate your cloud journey, you've come to the right place. From automatic scaling and continuous delivery to event-driven architectures and serverless applications, AWS helps you build amazing things in the cloud, and this book is your guide.

Not only that, but this study guide is also designed to provide you with the knowledge required to obtain the AWS Certified Developer – Associate certification. The guide covers topics relevant to the exam, referencing the exam blueprint throughout each chapter while providing context on how to bring applications to life with the services covered.

Beyond the test, this book can serve as a reference for building highly available applications that run on the AWS Cloud. While we assume you bring prior experience programming in Java, Python, .NET, and other languages, the study guide begins with an introduction to AWS core concepts and provides the knowledge on which the subsequent chapters are built. Because security is a top priority for all applications, the first chapter also describes how to create access keys by using AWS Identity and Access Management (IAM). The rest of the book covers topics ranging from compute services, storage services, databases, encryption, container orchestration, automation pipelines, and serverless-based applications.

The chapters were designed with the understanding that developers learn best by building. To enhance learning through hands-on experience, at the end of each chapter is an "Exercise" section with activities that help reinforce the main topic of the chapter.

Each chapter also contains a "Review Questions" section to assess your understanding of its concepts. Please note that while these review questions focus on chapter-specific content, the actual certification exam will test your ability to synthesize concepts, propose architectures, and evaluate optimal designs from multiple viable options.

To help you determine the level of your AWS knowledge and aptitude before reading the guide, we provide an assessment test with 57 questions at the end of this introduction. Later, you can gauge your readiness to take the certification test with the 91-question practice exam provided online.

By the end of this book, you won't just be ready for the certification exam—you'll be equipped to realize your vision for what's possible in the cloud. Let's begin.

What Does This Book Cover?

This book covers topics that you need to know to prepare for the Amazon Web Services (AWS) Certified Developer – Associate exam.

Chapter 1: Introduction to Amazon Web Services   This chapter provides an overview of how AWS works, including how resources are deployed across regions and availability zones. The chapter includes an introduction to the AWS command-line interface (CLI) and software development kits (SDKs). A review of AWS access keys and how to manage them using AWS Identity and Access Management (IAM) is also included.

Chapter 2: Introduction to Compute and Networking   This chapter reviews compute and networking environments in AWS. It provides an overview of resources such as Amazon EC2, load balancers, security groups, and the network controls exposed through Amazon Virtual Private Cloud (Amazon VPC).

Chapter 3: AWS Data Storage   This chapter covers cloud storage with AWS. It provides an overview of storage fundamentals and the AWS storage portfolio of services, including Amazon Simple Storage Service (Amazon S3), Amazon S3 Glacier, Elastic Block Store (EBS), Elastic File System (EFS) and FSx. The chapter also covers how to tune your storage for performance and choose the right type of storage for a workload.

Chapter 4: AWS Database Services   This chapter provides an overview of the AWS database services as well as a baseline understanding of SQL versus NoSQL. We explore DynamoDB in detail, then dive into Amazon RDS and Amazon Aurora.

Chapter 5: Encryption on AWS   In this chapter, you will explore AWS services that enable you to perform encryption of data at rest using both customer and AWS managed solutions. An overview of each approach and the use case for each is provided. Example architectures are included that show the differences between a customer and an AWS managed infrastructure.

Chapter 6: Deployment Strategies   In this chapter, you will learn about automated application deployment, management, and maintenance using AWS Elastic Beanstalk. You will also learn about the various deployment methodologies and options to determine the best approach for individual workloads.

Chapter 7: Deployment as Code   This chapter describes the AWS code services used to automate infrastructure and application deployments across AWS and on-premises resources. Topics covered include CodeBuild, CodeDeploy, and CodePipeline. You will learn about the differences among continuous integration, continuous delivery, and continuous deployment, in addition to how AWS enables you to achieve each.

Chapter 8: Infrastructure as Code   This chapter focuses on using AWS CloudFormation to create flexible, repeatable templates for a cloud infrastructure. You will learn about the different AWS CloudFormation template components, supported resources, and how to integrate non-AWS resources into your templates using custom resources.

Chapter 9: Secure Configuration and Container Management   This chapter covers AWS's two foundational services for cloud container orchestration: Elastic Container Service (ECS), which is AWS-native and integrates tightly with other services, and Elastic Kubernetes Service (EKS), which lets you launch or migrate Kubernetes workloads to the AWS Cloud with ease. Finally, the chapter delves into two essential services for managing configuration and secret values in Parameter Store and Secrets Manager.

Chapter 10: Authentication and Authorization   This chapter explains the differences between authentication and authorization and how these differences apply to infrastructure and applications running on AWS. You will learn about using Cognito as an identity provider and about integrating third-party identity services, in addition to the differences between the control pane and data pane.

Chapter 11: Refactoring to Microservices   In this chapter, you will learn about microservices and how to refactor large application stacks into small, portable containers. You will also learn how to implement messaging infrastructure to enable communication between microservices running in your environment.

Chapter 12: Serverless Compute   This chapter reviews AWS Lambda as a compute service that you can use to run code without provisioning or managing servers. In this chapter, you will learn about creating, triggering, and securing AWS Lambda functions. You will also learn other features of AWS Lambda, such as versioning and aliases.

Chapter 13: Serverless Applications   This chapter expands on the serverless concepts you learned in Chapter 12, "Serverless Compute," and shows you how to architect full-stack serverless web applications using a variety of serverless AWS resources, including S3, AppSync, ElastiCache, and API Gateway.

Chapter 14: Modern AWS Deployment Frameworks   This chapter showcases some of the higher-level abstractions that AWS provides to create complex architectures in simple ways. Cloud Developer Kit (CDK) lets developers build infrastructure-as-code using code rather than the declarative templates of CloudFormation, while Serverless Application Model provides shortcuts to extend CloudFormation in ways that make building serverless apps easy. Finally, we look at AWS Amplify, a full-stack developer tool for configuring many AWS backends using TypeScript and using them in a variety of popular front-end frameworks.

Chapter 15: Monitoring and Troubleshooting   This chapter discusses how to monitor your applications, alert on changing conditions, and automate your responses. You will learn how to use Amazon CloudWatch to perform log analysis and create custom metrics for ingestion by other tools and for creating visualizations in the dashboard. You'll use CloudTrail to monitor activity in your account and trace changes to users and applications. You'll also see how EventBridge enables the creation of event-driven architectures and learn how to use AWS X-Ray to create visual maps of application components for step-by-step analysis.

Chapter 16: Optimization   This chapter covers some of the best practices and considerations for designing systems that achieve business outcomes at the optimal price. The chapter explores considerations for efficient data transfer, how to use Auto Scaling, and how to realize deep cost savings safely by using Spot Instances and mixed Spot Fleets. The chapter concludes with key AWS tools for managing and monitoring your account's cost and performance.

Interactive Online Learning Environment and Test Bank

The author has worked hard to provide you with some great tools to help you with your certification process. The interactive online learning environment that accompanies the *AWS Certified Developer – Associate Study Guide, Second Edition,* provides a test bank with study tools to help you prepare for the certification exam. This helps you increase your chances of passing it the first time! The test bank includes the following:

Sample Tests

All of the questions in this book, including the 57-question assessment test at the end of this introduction and the review questions that are provided at the end of each chapter. In addition, there is a practice exam available online with 91 questions. Use these questions to test your knowledge of the study guide material. The online test bank runs on multiple devices.

Flashcards

The online test bank includes over a 125 flashcards specifically written to quiz your knowledge of AWS operations. After completing all the exercises, review questions, practice exams, and flashcards, you should be more than ready to take the exam. The flashcard questions are provided in a digital flashcard format (a question followed by a single correct answer). You can use the flashcards to reinforce your learning and provide last-minute test prep before the exam.

Glossary

A glossary of key terms from this book is available as a fully searchable PDF.

 Go to www.wiley.com/go/sybextestprep to register and gain access to this interactive online learning environment and test bank with study tools.

 Like all exams, the Certified Developer – Associate certification from AWS is updated periodically and may eventually be retired or replaced. At some point after AWS is no longer offering this exam, the old editions of our books and online tools will be retired. If you have purchased this book after the exam was retired, or are attempting to register in the Sybex online learning environment after the exam was retired, please know that we make no guarantees that this exam's online Sybex tools will be available once the exam is no longer available.

Exam Objectives

The *AWS Certified Developer – Associate Exam* is intended for individuals who perform in a developer role. This exam validates your proficiency in developing, testing, deploying, and debugging AWS-based applications. Exam concepts that you should understand for this exam include the following:

- Core AWS services, uses, and basic AWS architecture best practices
- Developing, deploying, and debugging cloud-based applications using AWS

  In general, certification candidates should understand the following:
- Using APIs, the CLI, and AWS SDKs to write applications and manipulate AWS resources
- Key features of AWS services
- AWS shared responsibility model
- Application lifecycle management
- CI/CD pipeline to deploy applications on AWS
- Using or interacting with AWS services
- Using cloud-native applications to write code
- Writing code using AWS security best practices (for example, not using secret and access keys in the code, and instead using IAM roles)
- Storing data in the best service for the job
- How to manage data over its life cycle using AWS storage resources
- Writing code for serverless applications
- Using containers in the development process
- Building serverless architectures using AWS-native tools
- Managing configuration values and secrets securely

  The exam covers four different domains, with each domain broken down into individual task statements.

Objective Map

The following table lists each domain and its weighting in the exam, along with the chapters in the book where that domain's objectives and subobjectives are covered.

Domain	Percentage of exam	Chapter(s)
Domain 1: Development with AWS Services	32%	1, 2, 3, 4, 6, 7, 8, 9, 11, 12, 13, 14, 15, 16
Task Statement 1: Develop code for applications hosted on AWS		1, 2, 3, 4, 6, 7, 8, 9, 13, 14, 15, 16

Domain	Percentage of exam	Chapter(s)
Task Statement 2: Develop code for AWS Lambda		12, 13, 14
Task Statement 3: Use data stores in application development		3, 4, 8, 9, 11, 13
Domain 2: Security	26%	1, 2, 3, 4, 5, 9, 10, 12, 13, 14
Task Statement 1: Implement authN and/or AuthZ for apps and AWS services		1, 2, 3, 4, 5, 10, 13, 14
Task Statement 2: Implement encryption by using AWS services		3, 4, 5
Task Statement 3: Manage sensitive data in application code		3, 4, 5, 9, 12
Domain 3: Deployment	24%	6, 7, 8, 9, 12, 14
Task Statement 1: Prepare application artifacts to be deployed to AWS		6, 7, 8, 9, 12, 14
Task Statement 2: Test applications in development environments		6, 12
Task Statement 3: Automate deployment testing		7, 12
Task Statement 4: Deploy code by using AWS CI/CD services		6, 7, 9, 12, 14
Domain 4: Troubleshooting and Optimization	18%	2, 3, 4, 6, 8, 9, 11, 12 13, 15, 16
Task Statement 1: Assist in a root cause analysis		8, 12, 15, 16
Task Statement 2: Instrument code for observability		6, 11, 12, 13, 15, 16
Task Statement 3: Optimize applications by using AWS services and features		2, 3, 4, 8, 9, 11, 12, 13, 15, 16

How to Contact the Publisher

If you believe you have found a mistake in this book, please bring it to our attention. At John Wiley & Sons, we understand how important it is to provide our customers with accurate content, but even with our best efforts an error may occur.

To submit your possible errata, please email it to our Customer Service Team at wileysupport@wiley.com with the subject line "Possible Book Errata Submission."

Assessment Test

1. You have an application running on an Amazon Elastic Compute Cloud (Amazon EC2) instance that needs read-only access to several AWS services. What is the best way to grant that application permissions only to a specific set of resources within your account?

   A. Configure Security Groups to allow the instance to work with the resources it should be able to access.

   B. Launch the EC2 instance, log in, and use `aws configure` to authenticate as an IAM user with appropriate permissions.

   C. Declare the necessary permissions as statements in the AWS SDK configuration file on the EC2 instance.

   D. Launch the EC2 instance with an attached IAM role with custom IAM policies for the permissions.

2. You have identified two Amazon Elastic Compute Cloud (EC2) instances in your account that appear to have the same private IP address. What could be the cause?

   A. These instances are in different Amazon Virtual Private Clouds (VPCs).

   B. The instances are in different subnets.

   C. The instances have different network ACLs.

   D. The instances have different security groups.

3. Your company stores critical documents in Amazon Simple Storage Service (S3), but it wants to minimize cost. Most documents are used actively for only about one month and then used much less frequently after that. However, all data needs to be available within minutes when requested. How can you meet these requirements?

   A. Migrate the data to S3 Reduced Redundancy Storage (RRS) after 30 days.

   B. Migrate the data to S3 Glacier after 30 days.

   C. Migrate the data to S3 Standard – Infrequent Access (IA) after 30 days.

   D. Turn on versioning and then migrate the older version to S3 Glacier.

4. You are changing your application to take advantage of the elasticity and cost benefits provided by AWS Auto Scaling. To horizontally scale, you must no longer store users' session state on your EC2 instances. Which of the following AWS Cloud services is best suited as an alternative for storing session state information?

   A. Amazon DynamoDB

   B. Amazon Redshift

   C. AWS Storage Gateway

   D. Amazon Kinesis

5. Your e-commerce application provides daily and ad hoc reporting to various business units on customer purchases. These operations result in a high level of read traffic to your MySQL Amazon Relational Database Service (RDS) instance. What can you do to scale up read traffic without impacting your database's performance?

   A. Increase the allocated storage for the RDS instance.

   B. Modify the RDS instance to be a multi-AZ deployment.

   C. Create a read replica for an RDS instance.

   D. Change the RDS instance to the DB engine version.

6. Your company has refactored their application to use NoSQL instead of SQL. They would like to use a managed service for running the new NoSQL database. Which AWS service should you recommend?

   A. Amazon Relational Database Service (Amazon RDS)

   B. Amazon Elastic Compute Cloud (Amazon EC2)

   C. Amazon DynamoDB

   D. Amazon AppSync

7. A company is currently using Amazon Relational Database Service (RDS); however, they are retiring a database that is currently running. They have automatic backups enabled on the database. They want to make sure that they retain the last backup before deleting the RDS database. As the lead developer on the project, what should you do?

   A. Delete the database. RDS automatic backups are already enabled.

   B. Create a manual snapshot before deleting the database.

   C. Use the AWS Database Migration Service (DMS) to back up the database.

   D. SSH into the RDS database and perform a SQL dump.

8. You have an Amazon DynamoDB table that has a partition key and a sort key. However, a business analyst on your team wants to be able to query the DynamoDB table with a different partition key. What should you do?

   A. Create a local secondary index.

   B. Create a global secondary index.

   C. Create a new DynamoDB table.

   D. Advise the business analyst that this is not possible.

9. An application is using Amazon DynamoDB. Recently, a developer on your team has noticed that occasionally the application does not return the most up-to-date data after a read from the database. How can you solve this issue?

   A. Increase the number of read capacity units (RCUs) for the table.

   B. Increase the number of write capacity units (WCUs) for the table.

   C. Refactor the application to use a SQL database.

   D. Configure the application to perform a strongly consistent read.

10. A developer on your team would like to test a new idea and requires a NoSQL database. Your current applications are using Amazon DynamoDB. What should you recommend?

A. Create a new table inside DynamoDB.

B. Use DynamoDB Local.

C. Use another NoSQL database on-premises.

D. Create an Amazon Elastic Compute Cloud (EC2) instance, and install a NoSQL database.

11. Amazon Elastic Block Store (EBS) volumes are encrypted by default.

A. True

B. False

12. Which of the following is not part of the AWS Elastic Beanstalk functionality?

A. Notify the account user of language runtime platform changes

B. Display events per environment

C. Show instance statuses per environment

D. Perform automatic changes to AWS Identity and Access Management (IAM) policies

13. What happens to AWS CodePipeline revisions that, upon reaching a manual approval gate, are rejected?

A. The pipeline continues.

B. A notification is sent to the account administrator.

C. The revision is treated as failed.

D. The pipeline creates a revision clone and continues.

14. You have an AWS CodeBuild task in your pipeline that requires large binary files that do not frequently change. What would be the best way to include these files in your build?

A. Store the files in your source code repository. They will be passed in as part of the revision.

B. Store the files in an Amazon Simple Storage Service (S3) bucket and copy them during the build.

C. Create a custom build container that includes the files.

D. It is not possible to include files above a certain size.

15. When you update an `AWS::S3::Bucket` resource, what is the expected behavior if the `Name` property is updated?

A. The resource is updated with no interruption.

B. The resource is updated with some interruption.

C. The resource is replaced.

D. The resource is deleted.

16. What is the preferred method for updating resources created by AWS CloudFormation?

    A. Updating the resource directly in the AWS Management Console

    B. Submitting an updated template to AWS CloudFormation to modify the stack

    C. Updating the resource using the AWS Command Line Interface (CLI)

    D. Updating the resource using an AWS Software Development Kit (SDK)

17. You manage a sales tracking system in which point-of-sale devices send transactions of this form:

    ```
    {"date":"2017-01-30", "amount":100.20, "product_id": "1012", "region":
    "WA", "customer_id": "3382"}
    ```

    You need to generate two real-time reports. The first reports on the total sales per day for each customer. The second reports on the total sales per day for each product. Which AWS offerings and services can you use to generate these real-time reports?

    A. Ingest the data through Amazon Kinesis Data Streams. Use Amazon Kinesis Data Analytics to query for sales per day for each product and sales per day for each customer using SQL queries. Feed the result into two new streams in Amazon Kinesis Data Firehose.

    B. Ingest the data through Kinesis Data Streams. Use Kinesis Data Firehose to query for sales per day for each product and sales per day for each customer with SQL queries. Feed the result into two new streams in Kinesis Data Firehose.

    C. Ingest the data through Kinesis Data Analytics. Use Kinesis Data Streams to query for sales per day for each product and sales per day for each customer with SQL queries. Feed the result into two new streams in Kinesis Data Firehose.

    D. Ingest the data in Amazon Simple Queue Service (SQS). Use Kinesis Data Firehose to query for sales per day for each product and sales per day for each customer with SQL queries. Feed the result into two new streams in Kinesis Data Firehose.

18. You design an application for selling toys online. Every time a customer orders a toy, you want to add an item to the orders table in Amazon DynamoDB and send an email to the customer acknowledging their order. The solution should be performant and cost-effective. How can you trigger this email?

    A. Use an Amazon Simple Queue Service (SQS) queue.

    B. Schedule an AWS Lambda function to check for changes to the orders table every minute.

    C. Schedule a Lambda function to check for changes to the orders table every second.

    D. Use Amazon DynamoDB Streams.

19. A company would like to use Amazon DynamoDB. They want to set up a NoSQL-style trigger. Is this something that can be accomplished? If so, how?

    A. No. This cannot be done with DynamoDB and NoSQL.

    B. Yes, but not with AWS Lambda.

    C. No. DynamoDB is not a supported event source for Lambda.

    D. Yes. You can use Amazon DynamoDB Streams and poll them with Lambda.

20. Which of the following methods does Amazon API Gateway support?

    A. GET

    B. POST

    C. OPTIONS

    D. All of the above

21. A company wants to access the infrastructure on which AWS Lambda runs. Is this possible?

    A. No. Lambda is a managed service and runs the necessary infrastructure on your behalf.

    B. Yes. They can access the infrastructure and make changes to the underlying OS.

    C. Yes. They need to open a support ticket.

    D. Yes, but they need to contact their Solutions Architect to provide access to the environment.

22. Which Amazon services can you use for caching? (Choose two.)

    A. AWS CloudFormation

    B. Amazon Simple Storage Service (S3)

    C. Amazon CloudFront

    D. Amazon ElastiCache

23. Which Amazon API Gateway feature enables you to create a separate path that can be helpful in creating a development endpoint and a production endpoint?

    A. Authorizers

    B. API keys

    C. Stages

    D. Cross-origin resource sharing (CORS)

24. Which authorization mechanisms does Amazon API Gateway support?

    A. AWS Identity and Access Management (IAM) policies

    B. AWS Lambda custom authorizers

    C. Amazon Cognito user pools

    D. All of the above

25. Which tool can you use to develop and test AWS Lambda functions locally?

    A. AWS Serverless Application Model (SAM)

    B. AWS SAM CLI

    C. AWS CloudFormation

    D. None of the above

26. Which AWS service can you use to store user profile information?

    A. Amazon CloudFront

    B. Amazon Cognito

    C. Amazon Kinesis

    D. AWS Lambda

27. Which of the following cache engines does Amazon ElastiCache support? (Choose two.)

    A. Redis

    B. MySQL

    C. Couchbase

    D. Memcached

28. Why would an Amazon CloudWatch alarm report as INSUFFICIENT_DATA instead of OK or ALARM? (Choose two.)

    A. The alarm was just created.

    B. There is an AWS Identity and Access Management (IAM) permission preventing the metric from receiving data.

    C. The alarm's trigger threshold, such as high CPU usage, has not been met.

    D. The alarm has not reached the requisite number of periods to have data.

29. You were asked to develop an administrative web application that consumes low throughput and rarely receives high traffic. Which of the following instance type families will be the most optimized choice?

    A. Memory optimized

    B. Compute optimized

    C. General purpose

    D. Accelerated computing

30. Because your applications are showing a consistent steady-state compute usage, you have decided to purchase an AWS Savings Plan to gain significant pricing discounts. Which of the following is *not* the best purchase option?

    A. All Up-front

    B. Partial Up-front

    C. No Up-front

    D. Pay-as-you-go

31. What is the maximum size of an AWS Lambda deployment package (as a compressed zip or JAR file)?

    A. 25 MB

    B. 50 MB

    C. 100 MB

    D. 250 MB

32. Your application processes transaction-heavy and IOPS-intensive database workloads, often needing over 20,000 IOPS. You need to choose the right Amazon Elastic Block Store (EBS) volume so that application performance is not affected. Which of the following options would you suggest?

    A. HDD-backed storage (st1)

    B. SSD-backed storage (io1)

C. Amazon Simple Storage Service (S3) Intelligent Tier class storage

D. SSD-backed storage (gp3)

33. A legacy financial institution is planning for a huge technical upgrade and planning to go global. The architecture depends heavily on using caching solutions. Which one of the following services does *not* fit into the caching solutions?

A. Amazon ElastiCache for Redis

B. Amazon ElastiCache for Memcached

C. Amazon DynamoDB Accelerator

D. Amazon Elastic Compute Cloud (EC2) memory-optimized

34. Which of the following partition key choices is an inefficient design that leads to poor distribution of the data in an Amazon DynamoDB table?

A. User ID, where the application has many users

B. Device ID, where each device accesses data at relatively similar intervals

C. Status code, where there are only a few possible status codes

D. Session ID, where the user session remains distinct

35. You are planning to build serverless backends by using AWS Lambda to handle web, mobile, Internet of Things (IoT), and third-party API requests. Which of the following are the main benefits in opting for a serverless architecture in this scenario? (Choose three.)

A. No need to manage servers

B. No need to ensure application fault tolerance and fleet management

C. No charge for idle capacity

D. Flexible maintenance schedules

E. Powered for high complex processing

36. A company would like to migrate their existing application to a serverless-based application. They are already using Amazon Simple Storage Service (S3) for their static website, and they have implemented API Gateway and Lambda for their business logic. They would like to be able to set up a serverless database. They are currently running a MySQL database. Which AWS service, which is serverless, could help them?

A. Amazon Aurora

B. Amazon Neptune

C. Amazon DynamoDB

D. Amazon ElastiCache

37. Which AWS service can be used to develop an application sign-in flow automatically, which you can customize if necessary?

A. Amazon Simple Storage Service (S3)

B. Amazon Cognito

C. Amazon Aurora

D. AWS Lambda

38. A company is migrating their web application to a serverless architecture. They are ready to take their static web files and move them to AWS. Which serverless service allows them to host a website?

    A. Amazon Simple Storage Service (S3)

    B. Amazon DynamoDB

    C. Amazon Elastic Compute Cloud (EC2)

    D. AWS Elastic Beanstalk

39. What is the minimum amount of memory that you can allocate to an AWS Lambda function?

    A. 6 MB

    B. 32 MB

    C. 64 MB

    D. 128 MB

40. What is the maximum size of all the code and dependencies for an AWS Lambda function before compression?

    A. 50 MB

    B. 100 MB

    C. 250 MB

    D. 500 MB

41. What is the default setting for Amazon Simple Queue Service (SQS) visibility timeout?

    A. 30 seconds

    B. 1 minute

    C. 1 day

    D. 1 week

42. What are the keys that can be used in an Amazon DynamoDB table? (Choose two.)

    A. Partition key

    B. Sort key

    C. Unique key

    D. Cache key

    E. Master key

43. What feature does Amazon ElastiCache provide?

    A. A highly available and fast indexing service for querying

    B. An Amazon Elastic Compute Cloud (EC2) instance with a large amount of memory and CPU

    C. A managed in-memory caching service

    D. An Amazon EC2 instance with Redis and Memcached already installed

44. Which AWS service can you use to monitor an AWS Lambda function performance?

   A. Lambda is serverless and therefore you cannot monitor its performance.

   B. AWS CloudTrail has metrics about the performance of the Lambda function.

   C. AWS Config stores all configuration details and performance of Lambda functions.

   D. Amazon CloudWatch monitors the performance of Lambda functions.

45. Which launch type in Amazon ECS allows you to run containers without managing EC2 instances?

   A. EC2

   B. On-Premises

   C. Fargate

   D. Lambda

46. AWS Secrets Manager can automatically rotate secrets according to a schedule you define.

   A. True

   B. False

47. What is Amazon Athena primarily used for?

   A. Performing real-time analytics on streaming data

   B. Running SQL queries directly on data stored in Amazon S3

   C. Building machine learning models

   D. Managing relational databases

48. Which of the following scenarios is most appropriate for using Amazon EFS?

   A. Running a high-performance computing (HPC) application that requires low-latency storage

   B. Storing frequently changing website content that needs to be served across multiple EC2 instances

   C. Storing large, infrequently accessed data sets

   D. Backing up data from an RDS instance

49. What is the primary purpose of AWS AppSync?

   A. To host static websites

   B. To deploy and scale container-based applications

   C. To create and manage GraphQL APIs

   D. To keep application configuration consistent between servers

50. AWS API Gateway only supports REST APIs.

   A. True

   B. False

51. Security groups act as a virtual firewall that controls both inbound and outbound traffic for Amazon EC2 instances.

    A. True

    B. False

52. What is the primary purpose of an IAM role?

    A. Associating users with fixed permissions according to their role in the organization

    B. Applying temporary credentials for accessing AWS services

    C. Restricting access to S3 buckets

    D. Managing billing and cost

53. Amazon Aurora is compatible with which two database engines?

    A. Microsoft SQL Server

    B. PostgreSQL

    C. Oracle

    D. MySQL

54. What do EC2 instance types govern?

    A. The operating system of the instance

    B. Hardware characteristics such as CPU, RAM, and Network

    C. The underlying architecture of the virtual machine (e.g., x86 vs. ARM)

    D. Whether the instance uses Spot or On-demand pricing

55. Which deployment strategy in Elastic Beanstalk can minimize downtime by deploying new instances alongside the existing ones before switching traffic?

    A. All at Once

    B. Rolling

    C. Canary

    D. Immutable

56. What happens when you stop an EC2 instance? (Choose two.)

    A. The instance is permanently deleted along with its data.

    B. Any data on instance storage is deleted.

    C. The instance is temporarily shut down, but the attached EBS volumes remain intact.

    D. Attached EBS volumes become unattached.

57. What service best enables you to store and version container images before deploying them?

    A. Elastic Compute Cloud (EC2)

    B. Simple Storage Service (S3)

    C. Elastic Container Registry (ECR)

    D. Elastic Container Service (ECS)

Answers to Assessment Test

1. **D.** Option D is correct. Create a custom IAM policy to configure permissions to a specific set of resources in your account. The `ReadOnlyAccess` IAM policy restricts write access but grants access to all resources within your account. Attaching this to an instance via a role (called attaching an instance profile) allows code running on the instance to access your resources without additional logins. Option A is incorrect because, while security groups may be necessary to open a network path to AWS resources like RDS instances, permissions are granted by IAM, not by security groups. Although feasible, option B is incorrect because AWS IAM roles provide a way to grant permissions directly to instances. Plus, using an IAM user means that any time you rotate credentials, you must update the EC2 host. Option C is incorrect because policies are not configured directly in the SDK.

2. **A.** Option A is correct. Even though each instance in an Amazon VPC has a unique private IP address, you could assign the same private IP address ranges to multiple Amazon VPCs. Therefore, two instances in two different VPCs in your account could end up with the same private IP address. Options B, C, and D are incorrect because within the same VPC, there is no duplication of private IP addresses.

3. **C.** Option C is correct—migrate the data to S3 Standard-IA after 30 days using a life cycle policy. The life cycle policy will automatically change the storage class for objects aged over 30 days. The Standard-IA storage class is for data that is accessed less frequently, but still requires rapid access when needed. It offers the same high durability, high throughput, and low latency of Standard, with a lower per-gigabyte storage price and per-gigabyte retrieval fee. Option A is incorrect because RRS provides a lower level of redundancy. The question did not state that the customer is willing to reduce the redundancy level of the data, and RRS does not replicate objects as many times as standard S3 storage. This storage option enables customers to store noncritical, reproducible data. Option B is incorrect because the fastest retrieval option for S3 Glacier is typically 3–5 hours. The customer requires retrieval in minutes. Option D is incorrect. Versioning will increase the number of files if new versions of files are being uploaded, which will increase cost. The question did not mention a need for multiple versions of files.

4. **A.** Option A is correct. DynamoDB is a NoSQL database store that is a good alternative because of its scalability, high availability, and durability characteristics. Many platforms provide open source, drop-in replacement libraries that enable you to store native sessions in DynamoDB. DynamoDB is a suitable candidate for a session storage solution in a share-nothing, distributed architecture. Option B is incorrect; Redshift is a data warehouse. Option C is incorrect; although it is a storage option, Storage Gateway is designed to let you mount traditional NFS or CIFS filesystems backed by S3 buckets and requires an instance running as the mount point. DynamoDB, being fully serverless, is the better and cheaper option. Option D is incorrect because Kinesis is designed for streaming data events and is not a storage solution.

5. **C.** Option C is correct. RDS read replicas provide enhanced performance and durability for RDS instances. This replication feature makes it easy to scale out elastically beyond the capacity constraints of a single RDS instance for read-heavy database workloads. You can

create one or more replicas of a given source RDS instance and serve high-volume application read traffic from multiple copies of your data, increasing aggregate read throughput. Option A is incorrect because increasing the database's storage will not impact its performance or ability to serve read requests. Option B is incorrect because although a multi-AZ deployment does launch multiple instances, only one is the primary, and the secondary is for failover purposes only. It does not serve requests alongside the primary and therefore will not increase read throughput. Finally, Option D is incorrect because the choice of database engine, though an important one that should be tuned to your use case, is not as clear of a performance improvement as creating a read replica.

6. C. Option C is correct; DynamoDB is the best option. The question states a *managed service*, so this eliminates the EC2 service. Amazon RDS is a database product; AppSync manages GraphQL APIs. The company is looking for a NoSQL product, and DynamoDB is a managed NoSQL service. Option A, Relational Database Service, as its name implies, is for relational databases, not NoSQL. Option B is incorrect because EC2 is not a managed database service (though you can manually run your own databases on an EC2 instance). Option D is incorrect because AppSync is for launching serverless GraphQL APIs.

7. B. Option B is correct; you must take a manual snapshot. Automatic backups do not retain the backup after the database is deleted. Therefore, option A is incorrect. Option C is incorrect. The AWS Database Migration Service is used to migrate databases from one source to another, which isn't what you are trying to accomplish here. Option D is incorrect because you cannot SSH into the Amazon RDS database, which is an AWS managed service.

8. B. Option B is correct. A global secondary index enables you to use a different partition key or primary key in addition to a different sort key. Option A is incorrect because a local secondary index can only have a different sort key. Option C is incorrect. A new DynamoDB table would not solve the issue. Option D is incorrect because it is possible to accomplish this.

9. D. Option D is correct. The application is configured to perform an eventually consistent read, which may not return the most up-to-date data. Option A is incorrect—increasing RCUs does not solve the underlying issue. Option B is incorrect because this is a read issue, not a write issue. Option C is incorrect. There is no need to refactor the entire application, because the issue is solvable.

10. B. Option B is correct. DynamoDB Local is the downloadable version of DynamoDB that enables you to write and test applications without accessing the web service. Option A is incorrect. Although you can create a new table, there is a cost associated with this option, so it is not the best option. Option C is incorrect. Even though you can use another NoSQL database, your team is already using DynamoDB. This strategy would require them to learn a new database platform. Additionally, you would have to migrate the database to DynamoDB after development is done. Option D is incorrect for the same reasons as option C.

11. B. Option B is correct. Encryption of Amazon EBS volumes is optional.

12. D. Option D is correct. Elastic Beanstalk cannot make automated changes to the policies attached to the service roles and instance roles. The capabilities mentioned in options A, B, and C are all part of the Beanstalk service.

13. C. Option C is correct because if a revision does not pass a manual approval transition (either by expiring or by being rejected), it is treated as a failed revision. Successive revisions can then progress past this approval gate (if they are approved). Pipeline actions for a specific revision will not continue past a rejected approval gate, so option A is incorrect. A notification can be sent to an Amazon Simple Notification Service (SNS) topic that you specify when a revision reaches a manual approval gate, but no additional notification is sent if a change is rejected; therefore, option B is incorrect. Option D is incorrect, as AWS CodePipeline does not have a concept of "cloning" revisions.

14. C. Option C is the most appropriate choice, because you can update the build container any time you need to change the files. Option A is not recommended, because storing binary files in a Git-based repository incurs significant storage costs. Option B can work. However, you would have to pay additional data transfer costs any time a build is started. Option D is incorrect, as AWS CodeBuild does not limit the size of files that can be used.

15. C. Option C is correct. Amazon S3 bucket names are globally unique and cannot be changed after a bucket is created. Thus, options A and B are incorrect. Option D is incorrect because the resource is not being deleted, only updated. Option C is correct because you must create a replacement bucket when changing this property in AWS CloudFormation.

16. B. Option B is correct because you can manage resources declared in a stack entirely within CloudFormation by performing stack updates. Manually updating the resource outside of CloudFormation (using the AWS Management Console, AWS CLI, or AWS SDK) will result in inconsistencies between the state expected by CloudFormation and the actual resource state. This can cause future stack operations to fail. Thus, options A, C, and D are incorrect.

17. A. Option A is correct because you want to ingest into Kinesis Data Streams, pass that into Kinesis Data Analytics, and finally feed that data into Kinesis Data Firehose. Option B is incorrect because Data Firehose cannot run SQL queries. Option C is incorrect because Data Streams cannot run SQL queries. Option D is incorrect because Data Analytics cannot run SQL queries against data in SQS.

18. D. Option D is correct because DynamoDB Streams allows DynamoDB to publish a message every time there is a change in a table. This solution is performant and cost-effective. Option A is incorrect because if you add an item to the orders table in DynamoDB, it does not automatically produce messages in SQS. Options B and C are incorrect because if you check the orders table every minute or every second, it will degrade performance and increase costs.

19. D. Option D is correct. Lambda supports DynamoDB event streams as an event source, which can be polled. You can configure Lambda to poll this stream, look for changes, and create a trigger. Option A is incorrect because this can be accomplished with DynamoDB event streams. Option B is incorrect because this can be accomplished with Lambda. Option C is incorrect because DynamoDB is actually a supported event source for Lambda.

20. D. Option D is correct. API Gateway supports all of the methods listed. GET, POST, PUT, PATCH, DELETE, HEAD, and OPTIONS are all supported methods.

21. A. Option A is correct. AWS Lambda uses containers to operate and is a managed service—you cannot access the underlying infrastructure. This is a benefit because your organization does not need to worry about security patching and other system maintenance. Option B is incorrect—you cannot access the infrastructure. Recall that Lambda is serverless. Option C is incorrect. AWS Support cannot provide access to the direct environment. Option D is incorrect—the Solutions Architect cannot provide direct access to the environment.

22. C, D. Options C and D are correct because they are both caching tools. Option A is incorrect because CloudFormation is a service that helps you model and set up your AWS resources. Option B is incorrect because you use S3 as a storage tool for the Internet.

23. C. Option C is the correct answer. You can use stages to create a separate path with multiple endpoints, such as development and production. Option A is incorrect, as authorizers enable you to control access to your APIs by using Amazon Cognito or an AWS Lambda function. Option B is incorrect because API keys are used to provide customers to your API, which is useful for selling your API. Option D is incorrect, as CORS is used to allow one service to call another service.

24. D. Option D is correct. With Amazon API Gateway, you can enable authorization for a particular method with IAM policies, AWS Lambda custom authorizers, and Amazon Cognito user pools. Options A, B, and C are all correct, but option D is the best option because it combines all of them.

25. B. Option B is the correct answer. AWS SAM CLI allows you to test the Lambda function locally. Option A is incorrect. Though AWS SAM is needed for the YAML/JSON template defining the function, it does not allow for testing the AWS Lambda function locally. Option C is incorrect. CloudFormation is used to deploy resources to the AWS Cloud. Option D is incorrect because AWS SAM CLI is the tool to test Lambda functions locally.

26. B. Option B is correct. With Cognito, you can create user pools to store user profile information and store attributes such as user name, phone number, address, and so on. Option A is incorrect. CloudFront is a content delivery network (CDN). Option C is incorrect. Amazon Kinesis is a service that you can implement to collect, process, and analyze streaming data in real time. Option D is incorrect. By using AWS Lambda, you can create custom programming functions for compute processing.

27. A, D. Options A and D are correct because Amazon ElastiCache supports both the Redis and Memcached open source caching engines. Option B is incorrect because MySQL is not a caching engine—it is a relational database engine. Option C is incorrect because Couchbase is a NoSQL database and not one of the caching engines that ElastiCache supports.

28. A, D. Options A and D are correct. For option A, CloudWatch alarms changes to a state other than INSUFFICIENT_DATA only when the alarm resource has had sufficient time to initialize and collect data, so a just-created alarm may have this state. As option D indicates, some alarms may be configured to need a minimum number of polling periods before an alarm is considered active; alarms in this state would show INSUFFICIENT_DATA. Option B is incorrect because permissions for sending metrics to CloudWatch are the responsibility of the resource sending the data. Option C is incorrect because an otherwise operational alarm in this condition would show status OK.

29. C. The answer is C. General-purpose instances provide a balance of compute, memory, and networking resources. T2 instances are a low-cost option that provides a small amount of CPU resources that can be increased in short bursts when additional cycles are available. They are well suited for lower-throughput applications, such as administrative applications or low-traffic websites. For more details on the instance types, see `https://aws.amazon .com/ec2/instance-types`.

30. D. Option D is correct. Pay-as-you-go refers to On-Demand pricing, which does not offer the same cost savings as a Savings Plan. Savings Plans provide significant discounts in exchange for a commitment to consistent usage over a one- or three-year term. Option A is incorrect because the All Up-front payment option offers the largest discount, making it a beneficial choice. Option B is incorrect because the Partial Up-front option still provides a discount with a lower initial payment. Option C is incorrect because the No Up-front option, though offering no initial cost, still provides a discounted hourly rate over the Savings Plan term.

31. B. Option B is correct. As of this writing, the maximum compressed size of a Lambda package is 50 MB compressed, 250 MB unzipped.

32. B. Option B is correct. The performance of the transaction-heavy workloads depends primarily on IOPS; SSD-backed volumes are designed for transactional, IOPS-intensive database workloads, boot volumes, and workloads that require high IOPS. The io1 storage type offers a higher potential IOPS than any of the other options (up to 64,000 IOPS on Nitro-based EC2 instances). Option A is incorrect because a platter-based HDD drive would not meet the performance requirements. Option C is incorrect because S3 is object-based storage, not block. Option D is often a good overall choice for many workloads, but because you need at least 20k IOPS, gp3's max of 16,000 IOPS is insufficient. For more information, see `https://docs.aws.amazon.com/AWSEC2/latest/ UserGuide/AmazonEBS.html`.

33. D. Option D only supplements the setup of your own caching mechanism, and that is not the preferred solution for this scenario. Options A, B, and C help in building a high-speed data storage layer that stores a subset of data. This data is typically transient in nature so that future requests for that data are served up faster than is possible by accessing the data's primary storage location. For more information, see `https://aws.amazon.com/caching/ aws-caching`.

34. C. Option C is correct. The status code option suggests an inefficient partition key, because few possible status codes lead to uneven distribution of data and cause request throttling. Options A, B, and D suggest the efficient partition keys because of their distinct nature, which leads to an even distribution of the data. For more information, see `https://docs.aws .amazon.com/amazondynamodb/latest/developerguide/bp-partition-key- design.html`.

35. A, B, C. Options A, B, and C are correct. Using a serverless approach means not having to manage servers and not incurring compute costs when there is no user traffic. This is achieved while still offering instant scale to meet high demand, such as a flash sale on an e-commerce site or a social media mention that drives a sudden wave of traffic. Option D is incorrect because Lambda runs your code on a high-availability compute infrastructure and performs all the administration of the compute resources, including server and operating system maintenance, capacity provisioning and automatic scaling, code and security patch deployment, and code monitoring and logging. Option E is incorrect because you can configure Lambda functions to run up to 15 minutes per execution. As a best practice, set the timeout value based on your expected execution time to prevent your function from running longer than intended.

36. A. Option A is correct. Aurora has a serverless option that is compatible with MySQL. Option B is incorrect. Neptune is a graph database that is used for applications that have highly connected graph datasets. Option C is incorrect. Although DynamoDB is serverless, it is also NoSQL-based, which means the application would require some refactoring—possibly extensive. Option D is incorrect, as ElastiCache is meant for caching database queries, not a one-for-one replacement.

37. B. Option B is correct. Cognito provides a prebuilt sign-up and sign-in UI to speed up your development process. You can further customize this UI as needed. Option A is incorrect. S3 is used for file object storage. Option C is incorrect. Aurora is a SQL database. Option D is incorrect. Lambda is for developing custom functions, not for building UIs.

38. A. Option A is correct. You can configure S3 to host a static website. Option B is incorrect. DynamoDB is serverless and does store data, but it cannot host a website. Option C is incorrect. EC2 is a virtual machine service. Option D is incorrect. Elastic Beanstalk deploys EC2 instances.

39. D. Option D is correct. As of this writing, the minimum amount of memory is 128 MB.

40. C. Option C is correct. As of this writing, the maximum size of all code and dependencies for a Lambda function is 250 MB. There is also an additional /tmp directory that is available for each Lambda function, which allows for an additional 10 GB of ephemeral storage space.

41. A. Option A is correct as the default setting for SQS visibility timeout is 30 seconds.

42. A, B. Options A and B are correct. Partition and sort keys are the two keys you can use inside DynamoDB. Options C, D, and E are incorrect because these are not valid keys inside DynamoDB.

43. C. Option C is correct. ElastiCache is a managed in-memory caching service. Option A is incorrect because the description aligns more closely to Amazon ES. Option B is incorrect because this is not an accurate description of the ElastiCache service. Option D is incorrect because, as a managed service, ElastiCache does not manage EC2 instances.

44. D. Option D is correct. CloudWatch provides metrics for Lambda. Option A is incorrect because you can use CloudWatch to monitor performance. Option B is incorrect because CloudTrail contains security details about calls made to the API. Option C is incorrect because AWS Config stores configuration information about resources in the environment, not performance.

45. C. Option C is correct. Fargate allows you to run containers without managing any underlying EC2 instances. Option A is incorrect because the EC2 launch type requires self-managing a cluster of EC2 instances. Option B is incorrect because ECS does not support an "On-Premises" launch type. Option D is incorrect because Lambda is not a launch type in ECS.

46. A. The correct answer is A. Secrets Manager can automatically rotate secrets according to a schedule that you define. This best practice leads to better, more hands-off security by regularly updating secrets without requiring manual intervention.

47. B. Option B is correct. Athena is a service that lets you run queries directly on data stored in S3 using standard ANSI SQL. Option A is incorrect because real-time analytics on streaming data is typically handled by services like Amazon Kinesis. Option C is incorrect because Athena is not used for building machine learning models (see Sagemaker for a service that helps with this). Option D is incorrect because Athena is not a database management service (that's RDS, Relational Database Service).

48. B. The correct answer is B. EFS provides highly scalable storage capacity in an NFS-compatible file system interface, making it ideal for shared network storage across multiple EC2 instances. Option A is incorrect; FSx Lustre would be a good option for low-latency HPC storage. Option C is not ideal for EFS, but it would be a perfect case for S3's long-term storage tiers like Standard-Infrequent Access or S3 Glacier. Option D is incorrect, because storage for RDS backups is handled by the RDS service itself in the form of snapshots retained by that service.

49. C. Option C is correct. AWS AppSync is a managed service that allows developers to create and manage GraphQL APIs, an API pattern that allows you to construct queries against a data schema you define. GraphQL is an excellent option for web and mobile backends, especially when paired with DynamoDB storage to create a fully serverless stack. Option A is incorrect; hosting static websites is supported by services like Amazon S3 or AWS Amplify. Option B is incorrect because deploying containers would be a job for Amazon ECS or EKS. Option D sounds correct, given the name, but synchronizing app configuration is not the purpose of AppSync.

50. B. The correct answer is B (false). Although API Gateway does give developers an easy way to scaffold and implement RESTful APIs, it also supports WebSockets. Moreover, because REST is just a design pattern, and API Gateway allows you to define your own HTTP interface for APIs, it is possible to implement your own design that is not specifically REST-oriented.

51. A. The correct answer is A. In AWS, you don't need traditional firewalls with centralized allow and deny lists; instead, you create security groups, which act as firewalls you can attach directly to resources like RDS databases and EC2 instances. Security groups can allow IP ranges or other security groups, giving you flexibility to create role-based networking permissions between resources.

52. B. Option B is correct. IAM roles provide temporary security credentials for AWS services, allowing applications, services, or users to assume these roles and access resources securely. Option A is incorrect because IAM roles are not about assigning fixed permissions to users; that's done by IAM policies. Option C is incorrect because although IAM roles can be used to control access to S3 buckets, that is not their primary purpose. Option D is incorrect because IAM roles do not directly manage billing and costs.

53. B, D. The correct answers are B and D, PostgreSQL and MySQL. Aurora instances can be launched that are compatible with either of those two engines, but not Oracle or SQL Server.

54. B. The correct answer is B. Instance types determine system-level resources such as CPU and RAM. Option A is incorrect because operating system is a separate choice, determined by the AMI (Amazon Machine Image) you choose as the basis for your instance. Option C is incorrect; CPU architecture is also a separate configuration. Finally, Option D is incorrect, because the choice of Spot vs. On-demand pricing relates to how you purchase the instance, not what instance type you choose.

55. D. The correct answer is D. The Immutable deployment policy in Elastic Beanstalk creates new instances with the updated configuration or application version in a new Auto Scaling Group, ensuring that traffic is only switched to the new instances once they are deemed healthy, minimizing downtime and reducing the risk of failed deployments. Option A is incorrect because All at Once forces an update on every compute instance simultaneously, which would result in downtime. Option B is incorrect because a Rolling deployment uses your existing compute infrastructure and does not stand up new instances. Option C is incorrect for the same reason. Also, Beanstalk does not have an explicitly named deployment type called Canary, although it does support the concept of deploying new releases to a small test group via its traffic splitting configuration.

56. B, C. Options B and C are correct. Instance storage, one of the fastest storage options you can get on EC2, depends on the underlying hardware. Starting and stopping an EC2 may relocate it to other hardware, so instance store is lost. Option C is also correct; when the instance shuts down, your EBS volumes stick around. Option A is incorrect, because stopped instances can be restarted. Option D is incorrect because EBS volumes stay attached until you explicitly detach them.

57. C. Option C is correct. ECR lets you create repositories to store and version container images. Option A is incorrect, because EC2 is the virtual machine service in AWS. Option B is incorrect; though S3 can store and even version data, it lacks the integration with container deployment services like ECS that ECR has. Option D is incorrect because ECS is the container orchestration service itself. ECS can pull images directly from ECR for deployment as tasks or services.

Chapter

1

Introduction to Amazon Web Services

**THE AWS CERTIFIED DEVELOPER –
ASSOCIATE EXAM TOPICS COVERED IN
THIS CHAPTER MAY INCLUDE, BUT ARE
NOT LIMITED TO, THE FOLLOWING:**

✓ **Domain 1: Development with AWS Services**

- Task Statement 1: Develop code for applications
hosted on AWS

✓ **Domain 2: Security**

- Task Statement 1: Implement authentication and/or
authorization for applications and AWS services

Introduction to AWS

Amazon Web Services (AWS) is the world's leading provider of cloud infrastructure services, offering compute, storage, networking, and databases, plus a broad set of platform capabilities such as deployment pipelines, analytics, and machine learning, all available on demand with pay-as-you-go pricing.

Think of AWS as a programmable data center. Once upon a time, if you wanted to launch a new web application or provision a database, you started by choosing a server configuration, purchasing it, waiting for it to ship to you, and installing and configuring it on-premises—before you could even begin to log in, configure software, and provide services to your users.

With *infrastructure-as-a-service* (IaaS) provided by AWS, all that can be done in a matter of seconds, with a few clicks or lines of code, freeing you up to focus on delivering value for your users. You can provision virtual servers on demand in minutes and pay only for the compute capacity you use. This ability to tailor capacity and compute costs to demand makes AWS a truly elastic service that can meet your needs however they may vary. Not only that, but AWS operates many data centers worldwide, configured to offer redundancy and high availability, improving the uptime and user experience of your data and services.

In this chapter, you are introduced to AWS and shown how to make your first service calls to build and manage resources. We'll then dive into the infrastructure behind AWS, and you'll learn how to manage the credentials and permissions that you need to securely access these powerful cloud capabilities.

Getting Started with an AWS Account

The AWS Certified Developer – Associate is designed for developers who have hands-on experience working with AWS services. To help you prepare, this book has recommended exercises at the end of each chapter.

To work with AWS, you'll need an account. While you must provide contact and payment information to sign up for an account, you can test many of these services through the *AWS Free Tier*. The AWS Free Tier limits allow you to become familiar with the APIs for the included services without incurring charges.

The AWS Free Tier automatically provides usage alerts to help you stay in control of usage and identify possible charges. You can define additional alerts with AWS Budgets. To best take advantage of the AWS Free Tier and reduce costs, take some time to review the AWS Free Tier limits and make sure to shut down or delete resources when you are done using them.

To create an account, sign up at `aws.amazon.com/free`.

AWS Management Console

After you have created an account, you will be prompted to sign in to the *AWS Management Console*. As part of the sign-up process, you define an email address and password to sign in to the AWS Management Console as the root user for the account.

The AWS Management Console is a web interface where you can create, configure, and monitor AWS resources in your account and explore the functionality of AWS's many services. The console also summarizes your overall monthly spend and provides links to learning materials to help you get started.

Sign in to the AWS Management Console, as shown in Figure 1.1, at `http://signin.aws.amazon.com/console`.

FIGURE 1.1   AWS Management Console

Because all the functionality of AWS is exposed through APIs, AWS provides more than just the web interface for managing resources. For example, the AWS Management Console is also available as a mobile app for iOS and for Android.

After you become familiar with a service, you can manage AWS resources programmatically through either the AWS Command-Line Interface (AWS CLI) or the AWS Software Development Kits (AWS SDKs), as shown in Figure 1.2.

FIGURE 1.2   Options for managing AWS resources

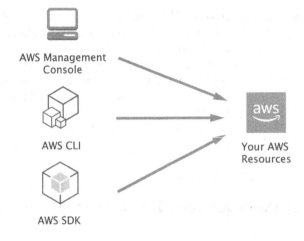

AWS Software Development Kits

AWS software development kits (SDKs) are available in many popular programming languages such as Java, .NET, JavaScript, PHP, Python, Ruby, Go, and C++. AWS also provides specialty SDKs such as its Mobile SDK and Internet of Things (IoT) Device SDK.

Although the instructions for installing and using an AWS SDK vary depending on the operating system and programming language, they share many similarities. In this chapter, the examples are provided in Python, using its SDK, which is named "boto." If Python is already installed on your machine, install boto3 using pip, the Python package manager:

```
pip install boto3 --upgrade –user
```

For documentation on the Python SDK, see `http://boto3.readthedocs.io`.

For more information on SDKs for other programming languages or platforms, see `http://aws.amazon.com/tools/#sdk`.

AWS CLI Tools

In addition to the AWS Management Console and SDKs, AWS provides tools to manage AWS resources from the command line. One such tool is the *AWS Command-Line Interface (CLI)*, which is available on Windows, Linux/UNIX, and macOS.

The AWS CLI allows you to perform actions similar to the SDKs from a terminal. Because the AWS CLI is interactive, it is a good environment for experimenting with AWS features. Also, the AWS CLI and the SDK on the same server can share configuration settings.

If you prefer to manage your resources using PowerShell, use the AWS Tools for Power-Shell instead of the AWS CLI. Other specialty command-line tools are also available, such as the Elastic Beanstalk command-line interface and AWS SAM Local. For more information about these tools and installation, see `http://aws.amazon.com/tools/#cli`.

Once it's installed, you can verify basic functionality of the CLI by typing **aws --version**.

Creating an Administrative IAM User

Before you can use the CLI to work with AWS resources, you configure it with the credentials of the user you wish to use to authenticate and whose permissions will be used by the CLI. While you will have initially logged into AWS as the root user of your account, it is not recommended to act as the root user when performing tasks via the CLI (or SDK). We must create a subuser, or in AWS terms, an *Identity and Access Management (IAM)* user.

Because this book covers so many IAM services, the user we create will be given wide permissions; however, this is still more secure than the root user, which is capable of changing billing information or even closing your account entirely! It's important to protect the root user login information as best you can.

To create an administrative user for use with the CLI or SDK, do the following:

1. Log in to the management console as the root user.
2. Use the Services search bar to navigate to IAM.
3. Click Users in the left-hand menu.
4. Click Create User.
5. For User Details, type **AdminUser**.
6. Select the option Provide User Access To The AWS Management Console. Keep the defaults for Autogenerated Password and "Users must create a new password at next sign-in" options.
7. Click Next.
8. Choose Attach Policies Directly, then filter for and select AdministratorAccess.
9. Click Next.
10. Click Create User.
11. Note the Sign-in Details on this page, including the password, which you can reveal by clicking Show.

From now on, you can use the Console Sign-in URL shown on this page, along with the User Name and Console Password, to log in to the management console. Try it now, logging out as your root user and logging back in with the AdminUser you just created.

Next, we will obtain the access keys for the user, which you can use to configure the CLI.

Obtaining Access Keys for Programmatic Access

Now that you are logged in as AdminUser, let's generate access keys for use with the CLI. Once again, head to the IAM console:

1. Log in to the management console as the root user.

2. Use the Services search bar to navigate to IAM.

3. Click Users in the left-hand menu.

4. Click AdminUser.

5. Select the Security Credentials tab.

6. Scroll to the Access Keys section and click Create Access Key.

7. Choose the use case Command Line Interface, scroll past the recommended alternatives, and select the "I understand the above recommendations" check box.

8. Click Next.

9. Provide the description **Keys for CLI,** and click Next.

On the final page, you will be given a chance to copy two values: the Access Key, which you can always obtain, and the Secret Access Key, which you will not see again.

Make sure to treat these values like passwords and keep them safe.

Configuring the AWS CLI

Now that you have installed the CLI and obtained your access key pair, let's configure the CLI. On your command line, type **aws configure** to initiate a series of prompts for values. You'll be prompted for four values. You have the first two:

- AWS Access Key ID.

- AWS Secret Access Key.

- Default Region Name: You'll learn about these later in this chapter. For now, take the default, us-east-1.

- Default Output Format: Keep the default, json.

The CLI is now configured for this user. You can verify this by running a command that fetches the active account's user details:

```
aws iam get-user
```

For macOS and Linux systems, the AWS CLI stores these values at ~/.aws/ credentials and ~/.aws/config. If you open the credentials file, you will see something like this:

```
[default]
aws_access_key_id = AKIA1234567890
aws_secret_access_key = <secret_string>
```

Similarly, the config file contains your chosen region and format.

CLI Named Profiles

It is possible to configure the AWS CLI to support multiple user profiles at once. First, create another IAM user with different privileges, then choose a profile name. The profile name does not need to correlate with the IAM username you plan to configure; in this example, we use the name "developer." Then run this command:

```
aws configure --profile developer
```

You will be prompted for the configuration values again. From then on, you may append --profile developer to any AWS CLI command to run it as this alternate user.

Using Cloud Shell to Avoid Managing Credentials

AWS provides Cloud Shell, which is another way to get easy CLI access for any user. Log in to the AWS Management Console and locate this button on the toolbar, as shown in Figure 1.3.

FIGURE 1.3   Cloud Shell button

Clicking this button will launch a terminal window in your web browser. This ephemeral environment has no long-term persistent storage, but it comes with the CLI preinstalled and configured for the currently logged-in user. Cloud Shell is a great way to quickly run CLI scripts from any machine without the need to set up a local environment or handle (or even generate) credentials, making it a convenient and secure option.

Using the CLI

While a deep dive into the CLI is outside the scope of this book, you should know that the CLI is capable of programmatically issuing any command that you can perform with your configured user via the Management Console. CLI commands are invoked in the format aws *<service_name>* *<command>*, followed by any additional parameters or flags. For example, you may list details of all S3 buckets in your account with **aws s3 ls** or show details of all EC2 instances using **aws ec2 describe-instances**. To see all services, use **aws help** and to see all commands for a service, use **aws <service_name> help**.

Calling an AWS Service

The CLI is just one way to invoke AWS commands. In this section, you'll use boto, the Python SDK, to make service requests, and learn how to configure the SDK with your user credentials.

 Locate the API reference documentation about the underlying web services and programming language–specific documentation for each SDK at http://aws.amazon.com/documentation.

SDK Example: Hello World

The following example makes a request to *Amazon Polly*. Polly provides text-to-speech services, and it's simple enough to make a great first SDK example.

This Python code example uses boto and Polly to generate an audio clip that says, "Hello World," using made-up credentials to communicate with the AWS service.

```
import boto3

#Explicit Client Configuration
polly = boto3.client('polly',
        region_name='us-west-2',
        aws_access_key_id='AKIAIO5FODNN7EXAMPLE',
        aws_secret_access_key='ABCDEF+c2L7yXeGvUyrPgYsDnWRRC1AYEXAMPLE'
        )

result = polly.synthesize_speech(Text='Hello World!',
                                 OutputFormat='mp3',
                                 VoiceId='Aditi')

# Save the Audio from the response
audio = result['AudioStream'].read()
with open("helloworld.mp3","wb") as file:
    file.write(audio)
```

Behind the scenes, boto maps the SDK function call to an HTTPS request to an Amazon Polly API endpoint that is determined by the region name (`region_name`) parameter.

The SDK also adds authorization information to your request by signing the request using a key derived from the AWS secret access key.

When your request is received at the Amazon Polly API endpoint, AWS authenticates the signature and evaluates IAM policies to authorize the API action.

If authorization succeeds, Amazon Polly processes the request, generates an MP3 audio file, and then returns it to the SDK client as part of the response to the HTTPS request, as shown in Figure 1.4.

FIGURE 1.4   API request and authorization

While it's worth understanding that behind each boto call is an HTTP request to the AWS API, it is not essential to understand. When coding, most developers interact with AWS via an SDK or the CLI and rarely interface directly with the behind-the-scenes API.

Calls to AWS via the SDK or CLI include signatures that incorporate the current date, so make sure your system clock is accurate. AWS requests must be received within 15 minutes of the time stamp in the request to be valid.

SDK Configuration

In the previous example, the AWS region and credentials are provided explicitly in the code:

```
# Explicit Client Configuration
polly = boto3.client('polly',
       region_name='us-west-2',
       aws_access_key_id='AKIAIO5FODNN7EXAMPLE',
       aws_secret_access_key='ABCDEF+c2L7yXeGvUyrPgYsDnWRRC1AYEXAMPLE'
       )
```

This approach of hard-coding credentials is not recommended due to the risk of checking the credentials into a source-control repository, which would expose the keys to everyone who has access to the repository and could even result in public disclosure. Fortunately, you can configure these credentials in other ways that don't require hard-coding.

The SDK and CLI both automatically check several locations for these values when they are not explicitly provided in the code. These locations include environment variables, programming language–specific parameter stores, and local files.

Because we have already configured the AWS CLI, boto can use the default credentials found in ~/.aws/credentials and configuration found in ~/.aws/config.

As a result, we can replace this snippet of code:

```
# Explicit Client Configuration
polly = boto3.client('polly',
      region_name='us-west-2',
      aws_access_key_id='AKIAIO5FODNN7EXAMPLE',
      aws_secret_access_key='ABCDEF+c2L7yXeGvUyrPgYsDnWRRC1AYEXAMPLE'
      )
```

with this line of code, which uses the default CLI credentials:

```
# Implicit Client Configuration
polly = boto3.client('polly')
```

By separating your code from the credentials, you make it easier to collaborate with other developers while making sure that your credentials are not inadvertently disclosed to others.

For code running on an AWS compute environment, such as Amazon Elastic Compute Cloud (Amazon EC2) or AWS Lambda, instead of using local files, assign an IAM role to the environment. This enables the SDK to load the credentials automatically from the role and to refresh the credentials as they are automatically rotated. See the section "Identity and Access Management" in this chapter for more on IAM roles.

Working with Regions

Now we'll take a closer look at what it means to configure the AWS SDK with an *AWS region*. AWS operates facilities in multiple regions across the world, as shown in Figure 1.5. Each region is located in a separate geographic area and maintains its own, isolated copies of AWS services. For many services, you are required to select a specific region in which to provision your resources.

FIGURE 1.5   AWS regions, availability zones, and planned regions (as of May 2024)

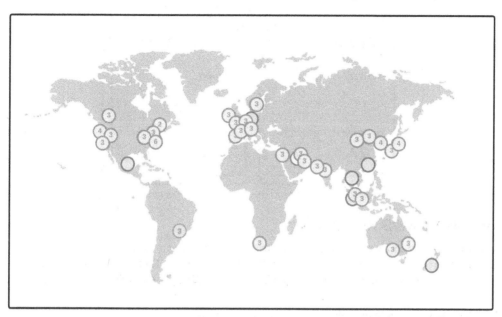

   In this section, you will explore how the structure of a region enables AWS to provide highly available, durable services, and how to choose an appropriate region for your application.

Regions Are Highly Available

Each *AWS region* contains multiple data centers, grouped together to form *availability zones (AZs)*. Availability zones are physically separated from each other and are designed to operate independently from each other in the case of a fault or natural disaster, as shown in Figure 1.6. Even though they are physically separated, AZs are connected via low-latency, high-throughput redundant networking, making multi-AZ architectures a fantastic choice for achieving high availability and scalability in your applications.

   In fact, many AWS services automatically replicate data across multiple AZs within a region to provide high availability and durability of the data. An example of an AWS service that replicates data across AZs within a region is Amazon Simple Storage Service (Amazon S3). S3 enables you to upload files and store those files as objects within a bucket. By default, Amazon S3 automatically replicates objects across a minimum of three AZs within the region hosting the bucket, protecting your data against the loss of any one AZ.

   In the AWS Management Console, you select from a drop-down list to specify your current region. Because so many AWS resources are region-specific, always pay attention to this selection! More than one new AWS developer has been shocked to find their existing resources gone, only to realize they have selected the wrong region.

FIGURE 1.6   Regions and availability zones

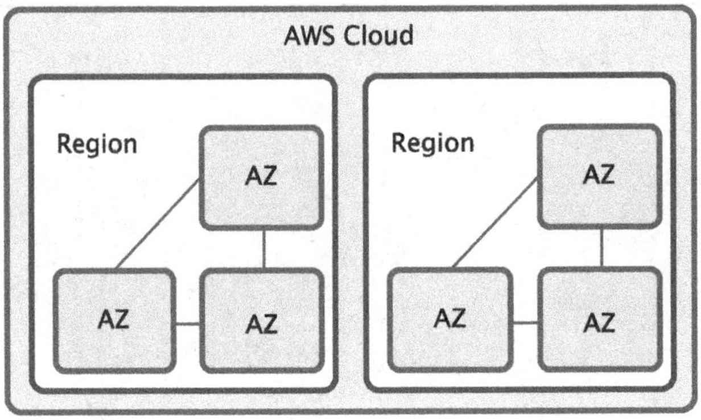

Identifying AWS Regions

When working with AWS Cloud services, the AWS Management Console refers to regions differently from the parameters used in the AWS CLI and SDK. Table 1.1 displays several region names and the corresponding parameters for the AWS CLI and SDK.

TABLE 1.1   Sample of region names and regions

Region name	Region
US East (N. Virginia)	us-east-1
US West (Oregon)	us-west-2
EU (Frankfurt)	eu-central-1
EU (London)	eu-west-2
EU (Paris)	eu-west-3
Asia Pacific (Tokyo)	ap-northeast-1
Asia Pacific (Mumbai)	ap-south-1
Asia Pacific (Singapore)	ap-southeast-1

There are other AWS services, such as *IAM*, that are not limited to a single region. When you interact with these services in the AWS Management Console, the region selector in the top-right corner of the console displays "Global."

Choosing a Region

One factor for choosing an AWS region is the availability of the services required by your application. Other aspects to consider when choosing a region are latency, price, and data residency. Table 1.2 contains selection criteria to include when choosing an AWS region.

TABLE 1.2   Selecting an AWS region

Selection criteria	Description
Service availability	Choose a region that has all or most of the services you intend to use. Each region exposes its own AWS Cloud service endpoints, and not all AWS Cloud services are available in all regions.
Proximity and latency	Choose a region closer to application users, on-premises servers, or your other workloads. This allows you to decrease the latency of API calls.
Data residency	Choose a region that allows you to stay compliant with regulatory or contractual requirements to store data within a specific geographic region.
Business continuity	Choose a pair of regions based on any specific requirements regarding data replication for disaster recovery. For example, you may select a second AWS region as a target for replicating data based on its distance from the primary AWS region.
Price	AWS service prices are set per region. Consider cost when service availability and latency are similar between candidate regions.

Identity and Access Management

You have already seen how to create an IAM user to avoid making calls with the root user and its credentials and how to obtain and configure its security credentials. Now, let's take a closer look at the IAM service and how it gives you powerful controls for handling who can use your account and how.

To manage authentication and authorization, IAM provides users, groups, and roles. IAM authorizes each request to AWS by evaluating the policies associated with the identity and resources affected by the request. This section reviews users, groups, roles, and policies.

Users

IAM user accounts allow you to provision access to other users in your account, assigning credentials to allow AWS Management Console access, programmatic access, or both, as shown in Figure 1.7.

FIGURE 1.7   IAM user long-term credentials

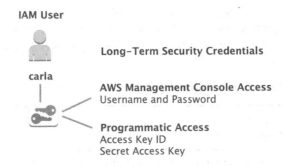

IAM User

carla

Long-Term Security Credentials

AWS Management Console Access
Username and Password

Programmatic Access
Access Key ID
Secret Access Key

AWS Management Console Access

To sign in to the web console, IAM users authenticate with an IAM username and password. When logging in, they provide either the account ID or alias so that IAM usernames only need to be unique within your account. If *multifactor authentication (MFA)* is enabled for an IAM user, they must also provide their MFA code when they attempt to sign in.

> To simplify sign-in, use the special sign-in link in the IAM dashboard that prefills the account field in the console sign-in form.

AWS IAM User API Access Keys

As you saw when configuring the CLI, for *programmatic access to AWS*, we create an access key for the IAM user. An *AWS access key* is composed of two distinct parts:

- Access key ID
- Secret access key

Each user may have up to two active access keys at any time. These access keys are *long-term* credentials and remain valid until you explicitly revoke them.

> Given the importance of the secret access key, you can view or download it only once. If you forget the secret access key, create a new access key and then revoke the earlier key.

Groups

To help you manage the permissions of collections of IAM users, AWS provides *IAM groups*. You can associate users who need the same permissions with a group and then assign policies to the group instead of associating the permissions directly to each user.

For example, all developers working on a specific project could each have their own IAM user. Each of these users can be added to a group, named *developers*, to manage their permissions collectively.

An individual IAM user can be a member of many IAM groups, and each IAM group can have many IAM users associated with the group (see Figure 1.8). IAM users within an IAM group inherit permissions from the policies attached to their group, plus any permissions from policies that are associated directly with that IAM user.

FIGURE 1.8 IAM groups and IAM users

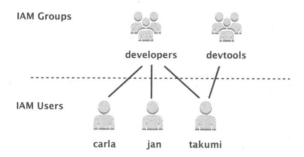

In the example shown in Figure 1.8, *carla* inherits permissions from the IAM user *carla* and from the group *developers*, and *takumi* inherits the union of all policies from *developers* and from *devtools*, in addition to any policies directly associated with *takumi*.

In the case that multiple permissions policies apply to the same API action, any policy that has the effect *deny* will take precedence over any policy that has the effect *allow*. This order of precedence is applied regardless of whether the policies are associated with the user, group, or resource.

Roles

Roles (see Figure 1.9) are a unique feature of AWS IAM. They are similar to users in that you give them a name and assign privileges to them by attaching policies; however, they do not have passwords or credentials and cannot be used to log in.

Instead, the purpose of roles is to give users time-limited, temporary privileges. This can be more secure than assigning persistent privileges to a user, who can *assume* a role momentarily or for a single login session, perform actions allowed by that role, and then switch to a lower-privilege role.

In addition, roles are the mechanism for granting permissions to AWS resources like EC2 instances. The association of a role with an instance, called an *instance profile,* is explored further in Chapter 2, "Introduction to Compute and Networking."

To control access to an IAM role, define a *trust policy* that specifies which *principals* can assume a role. Potential principals include AWS Cloud services and also users who have authenticated using identity federation. Principals could also include users who authenticate with web identity federation, IAM users, IAM groups, or IAM roles from *other* accounts.

FIGURE 1.9   IAM roles

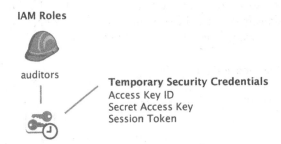

This example trust policy allows Amazon EC2 to request short-term credentials associated with an IAM role:

```
{
  "Version": "2012-10-17",
  "Statement": [
    {
      "Effect": "Allow",
      "Principal": {
        "Service": "ec2.amazonaws.com"
      },
      "Action": "sts:AssumeRole"
    }
  ]
}
```

When a principal assumes a role, AWS provides new short-term security credentials that are valid for a time-limited session through the *AWS Security Token* (AWS STS) service. These credentials are composed of an access key ID, secret access key, and, additionally, a session token with a known expiration date.

This example displays the kind of credentials that are generated when the role is assumed:

```
{
    "AccessKeyId": "ASIAJHP2KG65VIKQU2XQ",
    "SecretAccessKey": "zkvPEbYxCLVVD0seWdRnesc8krNDPHEX1cFMyI5W",
    "SessionToken": "FQoDYXdzEMf//////////wEaDL1b0Wd7VTA3J25cNyL4ARzNSR
czH4U3f8gJwi1W8XiDLWJIE9EdX4l4KXTiST40gPoWc9Do9QkcN2xRHk6/qVT6W23d0
u6+5YFY9C2wnoEeTTmiQBT5SMjqku5MYlhrCDyFQAVbo6RKUeOZXXSG8REshuFGBt
aCNmv95lFF6srCT1b4FZtTtULE7WV3LMcDs6Z2XuN+6aGTawhY50RMnlKRL1w6yHq
++RysQWbBHkuNeK/VqjueDINFODPOje9ZnYePVjR5uLmL8ZARWYVBFrB2tpxG07/
dseUS902q1hMP8DJuEfsbaiK2ASsmXSRA8vOZnuu4AsBq6ERasBw5EcpICP/Ne8zdKO/93tYF",
    "Expiration": "2018-04-18T22:55:59Z"
}
```

While a user assumes a role, their permissions are limited to what the role can do; any permissions the user has directly attached or inherited from a group are not evaluated. Furthermore, you cannot nest IAM roles or add IAM roles to IAM groups, as shown in Figure 1.10.

FIGURE 1.10   IAM roles are distinct from IAM users and groups.

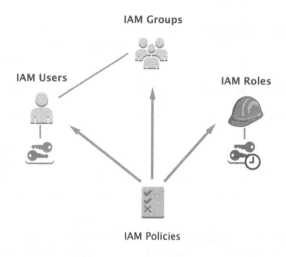

Choosing IAM Identities

The following scenarios will give you an idea of how to apply the right combination of users, roles, and groups for your situation.

Scenario: During Development

IAM users can be a convenient way to share access to an account with your team members or for application code that is running locally. To manage the permissions of collections of IAM users more simply, add those users to IAM groups.

Scenario: When Deploying Code to AWS

Use IAM roles. AWS compute services can be configured to distribute and rotate the role credentials automatically on your behalf, making it easier for you to manage credentials securely.

Scenario: When You Have an Existing External Identity Provider

When you have an external identity provider, such as Active Directory, use IAM roles. That way, team members can use the single sign-on they already use to access AWS without needing to remember an extra password. Also, if a team member leaves, you can easily disable their corporate access in only one place—the external directory.

Use roles in cases in which you need to make AWS service calls from untrusted machines because role credentials automatically expire. For example, use IAM roles for client-side code that must upload data to Amazon S3 or interact with Amazon DynamoDB. Please see Table 1.3 for details on when to use IAM users or roles.

TABLE 1.3   IAM users and IAM roles usage

For code running on . . .	Suggestion
A local development laptop or on-premises server	IAM user
An AWS compute environment such as Amazon EC2	IAM role
An IAM user mobile device	IAM role
Enterprise environments with an external identity provider	IAM role

The exam tests your knowledge of the recommended practices for distributing AWS credentials to your code depending on where that code is running.

Managing Authorization with Policies

You manage permissions for each user, group, or role by assigning *IAM policies* that either *allow* or *deny* permissions to specific actions, as shown in Figure 1.11. Any action is *implicitly denied* unless there is a policy that explicitly allows it. If there is a policy that *explicitly denies* an action, that policy always takes precedence. In this way, AWS defaults to secure operation and errs on the side of protecting the resources in cases where there are conflicting policies.

FIGURE 1.11   IAM identities and IAM policies

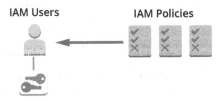

One method of granting permissions is to use *AWS managed policies*. Managed policies are prebuilt, named policies maintained by AWS to support common tasks; they are automatically updated as new services and API operations are added. Earlier in the chapter, we used the managed policy AdministratorAccess to avoid writing our own policy. Other managed policies are clearly named for what privileges they confer, such as AmazonS3 ReadOnlyAccess. Managed policies can always be examined so you may inspect the privileges they grant.

When choosing permissions policies, AWS recommends that you adopt the principle of *least privilege* and grant someone the minimum permissions they need to complete a task.

Take the example of an application that uses Amazon Polly. If the application uses only Amazon Polly to synthesize speech, use the AmazonPollyReadOnlyAccess policy, which grants permissions to Polly actions that do not store any data or modify data stored in AWS. The policy is represented as a JSON document and shown here:

```
{
    "Version": "2012-10-17",
    "Statement": [
        {
            "Effect": "Allow",
            "Action": [
                "polly:DescribeVoices",
                "polly:GetLexicon",
                "polly:ListLexicons",
                "polly:SynthesizeSpeech"
            ],
            "Resource": [
                "*"
            ]
        }
    ]
}
```

If the application needs permission to upload (or delete) a custom lexicon, use the AmazonPollyFullAccess policy. The policy is shown here. Notice that the actions granted by the policy shown here are represented as "polly:*", where the * provides access to all Polly API actions.

```
{
    "Version": "2012-10-17",
    "Statement": [
        {
            "Effect": "Allow",
            "Action": [
                "polly:*"
```

```
        ],
        "Resource": [
            "*"
        ]
    }i
  ]
}
```

Writing Custom Policies

AWS recommends that you use the AWS managed policies whenever possible. However, when you need more control, you can define custom policies.

As shown in the earlier examples, an *IAM policy* is a JSON-style document composed of one or more statements. Each statement has an effect that will either allow or deny access to specific actions on AWS resources. *A deny statement takes precedence over any allow statements.* Use an *Amazon Resource Name (ARN)* to specify precisely the resource or resources to which a custom policy applies.

For example, the following policy authorizes access to the DeleteLexicon action in Polly on the resource specified by the ARN. In this case, the resource is a particular lexicon within a specific account and within a specific region.

```
{
  "Version": "2012-10-17",
  "Statement": [{
      "Sid": "AllowDeleteForSpecifiedLexicon",
      "Effect": "Allow",
      "Action": [
         "polly:DeleteLexicon"],
      "Resource": "arn:aws:polly:us-west-2:123456789012:lexicon/awsLexicon"
      }
  ]
}
```

To allow slightly broader permissions in a similar policy, use *wildcards* in the ARN. For example, to allow a user to delete any lexicon within the specified region and account, replace awsLexicon with an * in the ARN, as shown here:

```
{
  "Version": "2012-10-17",
  "Statement": [{
      "Sid": "AllowDeleteSpecifiedRegion",
      "Effect": "Allow",
```

```
    "Action": [
       "polly:DeleteLexicon"],
    "Resource": "arn:aws:polly:us-east-2:123456789012:lexicon/*"
    }
  ]
}
```

An ARN always starts with `arn:` and can include the following components to identify a particular AWS resource uniquely:

Partition   Usually `aws`. For some regions, such as in China, this can have a different value.

Service   Namespace of the AWS service.

Region   The region in which the resource is located. Some resources do not require a region to be specified.

Account ID   The account in which the resource resides. Some resources do not require an account ID to be specified.

Resource   The specific resource within the namespace of the AWS service. For services that have multiple types of resources, there may also be a resource type.

These are example formats for an ARN:

```
arn:partition:service:region:account-id:resource
arn:partition:service:region:account-id:resourcetype/resource
arn:partition:service:region:account-id:resourcetype:resource
```

Here are some examples of ARNs for various AWS resources:

```
<!-- Amazon Polly Lexicon -->
arn:aws:polly:us-west-2:123456789012:lexicon/awsLexicon


<!-- IAM user name -->
arn:aws:iam::123456789012:user/carla



<!-- Object in an Amazon S3 bucket -->
arn:aws:s3:::bucket-name/exampleobject.png
```

A single policy document can have multiple statements. Additional components to a statement may include an optional *statement ID (Sid)* and condition blocks to restrict when the policy applies. If the policy is attached to a resource rather than to an IAM identity, then the policy must also specify a principal (to whom the policy applies), as shown in Figure 1.12.

FIGURE 1.12   IAM policy elements

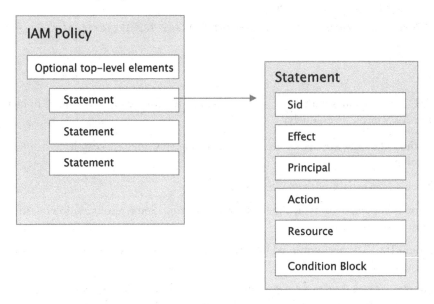

Write custom policies manually or use tools like the *Visual Policy Editor* in the AWS Management Console to generate policies more easily. To help you test the effects of policies, you can also use the IAM policy simulator at http://policysim.aws.amazon.com.

Summary

In this chapter, you learned about the AWS Management Console, the CLI, and the SDKs that you can use to configure and manage resources in the cloud. You learned how to use configuration files, select an AWS region, and manage credentials. The chapter also discussed AWS account root users, IAM, policies, groups, roles, long-term and short-term credentials, the access key ID, and the secret access key.

Exam Essentials

Know the ways to manage AWS resources.   Recall that the AWS SDK, AWS CLI, and AWS Management Console are each an option for managing resources within your account.

Know the importance of AWS regions.   Be able to identify the impact of region selection on your application code, such as the relationship between region selection and user latency. Also recognize how region selection impacts CLI and SDK calls.

Know about IAM users and IAM roles.   Know when it is appropriate to use IAM users or IAM roles for a given application that needs to make AWS calls.

Know how to recognize valid IAM policies.   Identify valid IAM policies and predict the effects of policy statements.

Exercises

EXERCISE 1.1

Signing Up for an Account

In this exercise, you'll sign up for an account.

1. Open your browser and go to `http://aws.amazon.com/free`.

2. Choose Create An AWS Account.

3. Provide personal information.

4. Provide payment Information.

5. Verify your phone number.

6. Select a support plan.

7. Choose Sign In To The Console.

8. Sign in to the console.

You are now signed into the AWS Management Console.

EXERCISE 1.2

Creating an IAM Administrators Group and User

In this exercise, you'll define an Administrators group and then add a user to that group. Generate security keys for this user and call this user `DevAdmin`.

1. Sign in to the AWS Management Console (at `http://signin.aws.amazon.com/console`).

2. Click Services and search for **IAM**. Take note that this is a global service, and region is not selectable.

3. To view the list of IAM groups, select User Groups.

    If this is a new account, the list is empty.

4. Choose Create Group.

5. For Group Name, enter **Administrators**.

6. Under Attach Permissions Policies, select the AdministratorAccess policy.

7. Choose Create Group.

8. To view the list of IAM users, select Users.

    If this a new account, the list is empty.

9. Choose Create User.

10. Set the username to **DevAdmin**.

11. Select Provide User Access To The AWS Management Console. Keep the defaults for all other choices.

12. Click Next.

13. To add this user to the Administrators group, select the Administrators Group option under User Groups.

14. Click Next.

15. On the Review And Create page, scroll down to Tags.

16. Provide a tag with a key of **project** and a value of **dev-study-guide**.

17. Click Create User.

18. Use tags to add customizable key-value pairs to resources so that you can more easily track and manage them.

19. View your password and download the credentials.csv file via the Download .csv File button.

20. Rename the file to **devadmin-credentials.csv**, and move the file to a folder where you would like to keep it.

21. Sign out of the AWS Management Console by clicking your name in the top bar and selecting Sign Out.

You now have a CSV file that contains a username, password, access key ID, secret access key, and console login link. Use the DevAdmin username, password, and console login link to sign into the AWS Management Console for all future exercises unless otherwise noted. Use the access key to configure the SDK in the following exercises.

EXERCISE 1.3

Installing and Configuring the AWS CLI

In this exercise, you'll install and configure the AWS Command-Line Interface. The AWS CLI requires Python2 or Python3. Install Python using pip, the Python installer.

1. Install the AWS CLI using the instructions for your operating system on this page: `http://docs.aws.amazon.com/cli/latest/userguide/getting-started-install.html`.

2. To configure the AWS CLI with a default profile for credentials, run the following command:

    `aws configure`

3. Enter the following values when prompted:

    - `AWS Access Key ID`: Paste the value from the CSV file you downloaded in Exercise 1.2.

    - `AWS Secret Access Key`: Paste the value from the CSV file you downloaded in Exercise 1.2.

    - `Default region name`: Enter **us-east-1**.

    - `Default output format`: Press Enter to leave this blank.

4. Run the CLI command to verify that your CLI is working correctly, and view the available voices for Amazon Polly:

    `aws polly describe-voices --language en-US --output table`

    A table in the terminal lists the available voices for Amazon Polly for the language US English.

EXERCISE 1.4

Downloading the Code Samples

1. If you haven't downloaded the chapter resources from the online test bank, go to www`.wiley.com/go/sybextestprep`.

2. Register to get an access code.

3. Log in and then redeem the access code. The book will be added to the online test bank.

EXERCISE 1.4 *(continued)*

4. Next to Course Dashboard, click Resources.

5. Click Chapter Resources to download the code files.

   You can also download the code files from the book page at

   https://www.wiley.com/en-us/AWS+Certified+Developer+Study+Guide%
   3A+Associate+(DVA-C02)+Exam%2C+2nd+Edition-p-9781394274802

6. Click Downloads to access the online materials for Chapters 1, 2, 11, and 12.

EXERCISE 1.5

Running a Python Script That Makes AWS Cloud API Calls

In this exercise, you'll run the Python script to make an AWS service call.

1. Open a terminal window and navigate to the folder with the book sample code.

2. To install the AWS SDK for Python, run the following command:

   pip install boto3

3. Navigate to the chapter-01 folder where you downloaded the sample code.

4. To generate an MP3 in the chapter-01 folder, run the helloworld.py program:

   python helloworld.py

5. To hear the audio, open the generated file, helloworld.mp3.

6. (Optional) Modify the Python code to use a different voice. See Exercise 1.3 for an AWS CLI command that provides the list of available voices.

You hear "Hello World" when you play the generated audio file. If you completed the optional challenge, you'll also hear the audio spoken in a different voice from the first audio.

EXERCISE 1.6

Working with Multiple Regions

In this exercise, you'll use Amazon Polly to understand the effects of working with different AWS regions.

1. Open a terminal window and navigate to the folder with the book sample code.

2. Navigate to chapter-01 in the folder where you downloaded the sample code.

3. Verify that the region is us-east-1 by running the following command:

    ```
    aws configure get region
    ```

4. Upload aws-lexicon.xml to the Amazon Polly service in the default region, which is US East (N. Virginia):

    ```
    aws polly put-lexicon --name awsLexicon --content file://aws-lexicon.xml
    ```

5. The file helloaws.py is currently overriding the region to be EU (London). Run the Python code and observe the LexiconNotFoundException exception that returns.

    ```
    python.helloaws.py
    ```

6. Upload the lexicon to EU (London) by setting the region to eu-west-2:

    ```
    aws polly put-lexicon --name awsLexicon --content file://aws-lexicon.xml
    --region eu-west-2
    ```

7. Run the following Python script again:

    ```
    python helloaws.py
    ```

    Observe that it executes successfully this time and generates an MP3 file in the current folder.

8. Play the generated helloaws.mp3 file to confirm that it says, "Hello Amazon Web Services."

9. (Optional) Delete the lexicons with the following commands:

    ```
    aws polly delete-lexicon --name awsLexicon
    aws polly delete-lexicon --name awsLexicon --region eu-west-2
    ```

    Even though the text supplied by the API call to synthesize speech was "Hello AWS!" the generated audio file uses the lexicon you uploaded to pronounce it as "Hello Amazon Web Services."

EXERCISE 1.7

Working with Additional Profiles

In this exercise, you'll define a limited user for the account and configure a new profile in the SDK to use these credentials. Notice that the permissions are restrictive for that user, and you need to update the permissions to be more permissive.

1. Sign in to the AWS Management Console using the credentials for DevAdmin from Exercise 1.2.

EXERCISE 1.7 *(continued)*

2. Select Services.

3. Select IAM to open the IAM dashboard.

4. Select Users to view the list of IAM users.

5. Click Create User.

6. Set the username to **DevRestricted**.

7. Select the option Provide User Access To The AWS Management Console.

8. Select I Want To Create An IAM User, leave the other values at the defaults, and click Next.

9. Select Attach Policies Directly.

10. Filter for the AmazonPollyReadOnlyAccess policy.

11. Click Next.

12. Under Tags, define a tag as follows:
    - Key: **project**
    - Value: **dev-study-guide**

13. Click Create User.

14. To configure the SDK in the following exercises, click Download .csv File to download the `credentials.csv` file.

15. Rename the downloaded file to **devrestricted-credentials.csv** and move it to the same folder where you put the CSV file from Exercise 1.2.

16. Open a terminal window and navigate to the folder with the sample code.

17. Navigate to the `chapter-01` folder.

18. (Optional) Review the code in `upload-restricted.py`.

19. Configure the AWS CLI with a new profile called **restricted**. Run the following command:

    `aws configure --profile restricted`

    When prompted, enter the following values:
    - `AWS Access Key ID`: Copy the value from the CSV file you downloaded.
    - `AWS Secret Access Key`: Copy the value from the CSV file you downloaded.
    - `Default region name`: Enter **us-east-1**.
    - `Default output format`: Press Enter to keep this blank.

20. Upload the lexicon.

The upload operation is expected to fail because of the restricted permissions associated with the profile specified in the script. Run the following Python script:

```
python upload-restricted.py
```

21. Return to the AWS Management Console for IAM, and in the left navigation, select Users.

22. To view a user summary page, select DevRestricted User.

23. Choose Add Permissions ➤ Add Permissions.

24. Select Attach Policies Directly.

25. To filter out other policies, in the search box, enter **polly**, and select the AmazonPollyFullAccess policy.

26. Click Next.

27. Click Add Permissions.

28. Repeat step 20 to upload the lexicon.

The upload is successful. After the change in permissions, you did not have to modify the credentials. After a short delay, the new policy automatically takes effect on new API calls from DevRestricted.

29. Delete the lexicon by running the following command:

```
aws polly delete-lexicon --name awsLexicon --region eu-west-2
```

In this exercise, you have configured the SDK and AWS CLI to refer to a secondary credentials profile and have tested the distinction between the AWS managed IAM policies related to Amazon Polly. You have also confirmed that it is possible to change the permissions of an IAM user without changing the access key used by that user.

Review Questions

1. Which of the following is typically used to sign API (CLI or SDK) calls to AWS services?

   A. AWS KMS Key

   B. AWS access key

   C. IAM username and password

   D. Account number

2. When you make calls to AWS services, for most services those requests are directed at a specific endpoint that corresponds to which of the following?

   A. AWS facility

   B. AWS availability zone

   C. AWS region

   D. AWS edge location

3. When you're configuring a local development machine to make AWS calls, which of the following is the simplest secure method of obtaining and using credentials?

   A. Create an IAM user, assign permissions by adding the user to an IAM group with IAM policies attached, and generate an access key for programmatic access.

   B. Sign in with your email and password, and visit My Security Credentials to generate an access key.

   C. Generate long-term credentials for a built-in IAM role.

   D. Use your existing username and password by configuring local environment variables.

4. You have a large number of employees, and each employee already has an identity in an external directory. How might you manage AWS credentials for each employee so that they can interact with AWS for short-term sessions?

   A. Create an IAM user and credentials for each member of your organization.

   B. Share a single password through a file stored in an encrypted Amazon S3 bucket.

   C. Define a set of IAM roles, and establish a trust relationship between your directory and AWS.

   D. Configure the AWS Key Management Service (AWS KMS) to store credentials for each user.

5. You have a team member who needs access to write records to an existing Amazon DynamoDB table within your account. How might you grant write permission to this specific table and only this table?

   A. Write a custom IAM policy that specifies the table as the resource, and attach that policy to the IAM user for the team member.

   B. Attach the `DynamoDBFullAccess` managed policy to the IAM role used by the team member.

   C. Delete the table and re-create it. Permissions are set when the DynamoDB table is created.

   D. Create a new user within DynamoDB, and assign table write permissions.

6. You created a `Movies` DynamoDB table in the AWS Management Console, but when you try to list your DynamoDB tables by using the Java SDK, you do not see this table. Why?

   A. DynamoDB tables created in the AWS Management Console are not accessible from the API.

   B. Your SDK may be listing your resources from a different AWS region in which the table does not exist.

   C. The security group applied to the `Movies` table is keeping it hidden.

   D. Listing tables is supported only in C# and not in the Java SDK.

7. You make a request to describe voices offered by Amazon Polly by using the AWS CLI, and you receive the following error message:

   `Could not connect to the endpoint URL:`
   `https://polly.us-east-1a.amazonaws.com/v1/voices`

   What went wrong?

   A. Your credentials have been rejected.

   B. You have incorrectly configured the AWS region for your call.

   C. Amazon Polly does not offer a feature to describe the list of available voices.

   D. Amazon Polly is not accessible from the AWS CLI because it is only in the AWS SDK.

8. To what resource does this IAM policy grant access, and for which actions?
```
{
  "Version": "2012-10-17",
  "Statement": {
   "Effect": "Allow",
   "Action": "s3:ListBucket",
   "Resource": "arn:aws:s3:::example_bucket"
  }
}
```

   A. The policy grants full access to read the objects in the Amazon S3 bucket.

   B. The policy grants the holder the permission to list the contents of the Amazon S3 bucket called `example_bucket`.

   C. Nothing. The policy was valid only until October 17, 2012 (`2012-10-17`), and is now expired.

   D. The policy grants the user access to list the contents of all Amazon S3 buckets within the current account.

9. When an IAM user makes an API call via the CLI or SDK, that user's long-term credentials are valid in which context?

   A. Only in the AWS region in which their identity resides

   B. Only in the availability zone in which their identity resides

   C. Only in the edge location in which their identity resides

   D. Across multiple AWS regions

10. You have provisioned a user with the managed policy AmazonS3FullAccess. A new feature has been added to the S3 API. What steps do you need to take to ensure that the user has access to use this new feature?

    A. Go to the IAM console, find the AmazonS3FullAccess policy, and click Update.

    B. Remove and reattach the AmazonS3FullAccess policy from the user.

    C. Copy the text of the AmazonS3FullAccess policy and use it to create a custom policy with the new permissions.

    D. Do nothing; AWS updates managed policies automatically when services are updated.

11. You have an on-premises application that needs to sample data from all your Amazon DynamoDB tables. You have defined an IAM user for your application called Table Auditor. How can you give the TableAuditor user read access to new DynamoDB tables as soon as they are created in your account?

    A. Define a custom IAM policy that lists each DynamoDB table. Revoke the access key, and issue a new access key for TableAuditor when tables are created.

    B. Create an IAM user and attach one custom IAM policy per AWS region that has DynamoDB tables.

    C. Add the TableAuditor user to the IAM role DynamoDBReadOnlyAccess.

    D. Attach the AWS managed IAM policy AmazonDynamoDBReadOnlyAccess to the TableAuditor user.

12. The principals who have access to assume an IAM role are defined in which document?

    A. IAM access policy

    B. IAM trust policy

    C. MS grant token

    D. AWS credentials file

13. A new developer has joined your small team. You would like to help your team member set up a development computer for access to the team account quickly and securely. How do you proceed?

    A. Generate an access key based on your IAM user, and share it with your team member.

    B. Create a new directory with AWS Directory Service, and assign permissions in the AWS Key Management Service (AWS KMS).

    C. Create an IAM user, add it to an IAM group that has the appropriate permissions, and generate a long-term access key.

    D. Create a new IAM role for this team member, assign permissions to the role, and generate a long-term access key.

14. You have developed an app that interacts with Amazon S3 using the Python SDK on a Linux server. You are now building a new application in C#, which will run on a separate Windows Server. What is the most straightforward way to enable your new application to work with S3?

   A. Rewrite your existing Python application in .NET to ensure compatibility with the Windows Server environment.

   B. Go to the Amazon S3 service, and change the supported languages to include .NET.

   C. Install the AWS SDK for .NET on your Windows Server.

   D. Implement a proxy service that accepts your API requests, and translate them to Python.

15. You work for a Virginia-based company, and you have been asked to implement a custom application exclusively for customers in Australia. This application has no dependencies on any of your existing applications. What is a method you use to keep the customer latency to this new application low?

   A. Set up an AWS Direct Connect (DX) between your on-premises environment and US East (N Virginia), and host the application from your own data center in Virginia.

   B. Create all resources for this application in the Asia Pacific (Sydney) region, and manage them from your current account.

   C. Deploy the application to the US East (N Virginia) region, and select Amazon EC2 instances with enhanced networking.

   D. It does not matter which region you select, because all resources are automatically replicated globally.

Chapter

2

Introduction to Compute and Networking

THE AWS CERTIFIED DEVELOPER – ASSOCIATE EXAM TOPICS COVERED IN THIS CHAPTER MAY INCLUDE, BUT ARE NOT LIMITED TO, THE FOLLOWING:

✓ **Domain 1: Development with AWS Services**

  ▪ Task Statement 1: Develop code for applications hosted on AWS

✓ **Domain 2: Security**

  ▪ Task Statement 1: Implement authentication and/or authorization for applications and AWS services

✓ **Domain 4: Troubleshooting and Optimization**

  ▪ Task Statement 3: Optimize applications by using AWS services and features

Now that you have an AWS account and you can make API calls from your local machine, it is time to explore how to run code on the AWS Cloud. AWS provides a broad set of compute options through the following services:

- Amazon Elastic Compute Cloud (Amazon EC2)
- Amazon Lightsail
- AWS Elastic Beanstalk
- Amazon Elastic Container Service (Amazon ECS)
- Amazon Elastic Container Service for Kubernetes (Amazon EKS)
- AWS Lambda
- VMWare Cloud
- Amazon app runner

In this chapter, you will explore Amazon Elastic Compute Cloud (Amazon EC2), which allows you to launch virtual machines called *instances*. You will learn about the components of an EC2 instance and explore an example of customizing an instance to run an application. Then, to learn how to customize the network environment for your instances, you will explore the network controls of Amazon Virtual Private Cloud (VPC). Finally, you will review some of the concerns related to managing your compute and networking environments.

Amazon EC2 and Amazon VPC are foundational services, and many of the concepts introduced in this chapter are transferrable to working with other AWS services.

Amazon Elastic Compute Cloud

Amazon Elastic Compute Cloud (EC2) enables you to provision computing environments called *instances*. With Amazon EC2, you have the flexibility to choose the hardware resources you need. You are in control of the operating system and any other software that will run on the instance.

An Amazon EC2 instance is a virtual machine that runs on a host machine within a specific AWS availability zone. This virtualization means that your instance may end up sharing the same physical hardware as that of another AWS customer, but AWS's multitenant architecture ensures that each instance is fully isolated from another.

In addition to virtualized environments, some EC2 instance types offer *bare-metal access.* Bare-metal instances provide your applications with direct access to the processor and memory resources of the underlying server.

Instance Types

With EC2, you choose your hardware resources from a broad set of preconfigured options by selecting a specific instance type and instance size. For example, an instance will have a certain number of virtual CPUs (vCPUs) and a specific amount of RAM. *Instance types* are rated for a certain level of network throughput. Some instance types also include other hardware resources such as high-performance local disks, graphics cards, or chips optimized for machine learning.

Even though AWS presets the hardware allocation for an instance type, a wide variety of instance types and sizes are available so that you can select the right level of resources for your application. For example, a t2.nano instance type allocates a fraction of a virtual CPU and 0.5 GiB of RAM to your instance. On the other end of the size spectrum, an x1e.32xlarge instance type provides 128 virtual CPUs and 3,904 GiB of RAM.

Instance types are also grouped into *instance families* to help you choose the appropriate instance for your application. Instances within a given family share similar characteristics, such as the ratio of vCPU to RAM or access to different types of storage options.

For an overview of the different instance families and their use cases, see Table 2.1.

TABLE 2.1   Amazon EC2 instance families

Amazon EC2 instance family	For applications that require . . .
General purpose	A balanced mix of CPU, RAM, and other resources
Compute optimized	A high amount of CPU, such as high-performance web servers, scientific modeling, and video encoding
Memory optimized	A large amount of RAM, such as in-memory databases and distributed web scale in-memory caches
Storage optimized	A large amount of storage and input/output (I/O) throughput, such as data warehousing, analytics, and big data distributed computing
HPC Optimized	A variety of configurations aimed at specific high-performance computing workloads
Accelerated computing	Dedicated graphics processing unit (GPU) or field-programmable gate array (FPGA) resources, such as 3D rendering, deep learning, genomics research, and real-time video processing

Because EC2 instances are resizable, you need not worry about how to correctly provision your instance the first time, or whether your choice will be sufficient for your future needs. All you need to do to change your hardware configuration is stop the instance, modify the instance type attribute, and then start the instance again.

Storage

Your instance requires storage volumes for both the root volume and any additional storage volumes that you want to configure. You can create persistent storage volumes with *Amazon Elastic Block Store (Amazon EBS)* to provide block storage devices for Amazon EC2 instances. Certain instance types enable you to mount volumes based on an *instance store*, which is temporary storage local to the host machine.

For an overview of the relationship between Amazon EBS volumes, instance store volumes, and the Amazon EC2 instance, see Figure 2.1.

FIGURE 2.1   Amazon EC2 storage

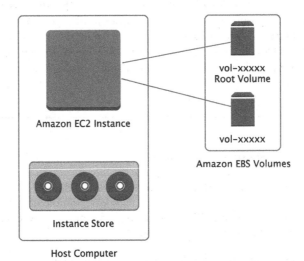

Persistent Storage

For EC2 instances, AWS provides persistent block storage via Elastic Block Store (EBS). EBS volumes can be formatted with a filesystem and mounted by your instance. You attach an EBS volume to a single instance at a time, but you may detach and reattach to instances at your discretion.

EBS volumes exist outside of EC2 and have their own life cycle; they are also replicated within an AZ for high durability and can be backed up on a schedule. Certain EC2 instance types are designated "EBS-optimized," meaning that they are tuned with enhanced network capabilities to achieve low latency when using EBS.

EBS is a highly versatile storage service that is explored in more detail in Chapter 3, "AWS Data Storage."

Temporary Storage

Certain Amazon EC2 instance types also allow you to mount *instance store* volumes—storage local to the physical host that runs your Amazon EC2 instance. This ephemeral storage disappears whenever the instance is stopped, so while its low latency can be effective for transient use cases like caching, it should not be used for any data that needs to persist.

This storage can have a high read/write performance because it is physically attached to the host machine that runs the instance. However, because this storage is local to the host machine, your data persists only while the instance is running on that host machine.

EC2 instance store is also examined in more detail in Chapter 3.

Software Images

When an EC2 instance first boots, it requires an operating system (OS) and the configuration of attached storage volumes. An *Amazon Machine Image (AMI)* provides the template for the OS and applications on the root volume of your instance. AMIs also provide a block device mapping that can specify additional volumes to mount when an instance launches, as shown in Figure 2.2.

FIGURE 2.2 Amazon Machine Images

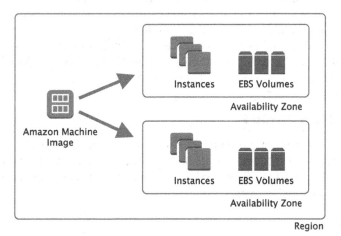

AWS provides a variety of AMIs on different operating systems, some preconfigured with popular software packages. Third parties may also make AMIs available with their own software through the AWS Marketplace. Some third-party AMIs have a cost associated with them.

You can create your own AMIs from an instance that you have previously customized, which is a great way to accelerate boot time for workloads that require specific software configuration. This is a common tactic for use with AWS Auto Scaling groups, where you may need new instances to come online very quickly in response to user demand. AMIs are region-specific but can be shared across regions or even accounts. To control which AWS accounts can use your AMIs, define the launch permissions for your AMI.

In some cases, the cost of software licensing may be included in the hourly rate of the instance in addition to EC2 on-demand runtime costs. Windows Server is one example of an AMI that incorporates software costs into the EC2 costs.

Network Interfaces

Virtual network interfaces called *elastic network interfaces (ENIs)* provide networking for your EC2 instances. Each instance is assigned a *primary network interface* associated with a subnet of a VPC and receives a private IP address to communicate with other resources.

To give your instance a public IP, you may allocate an *Elastic IP* to associate with the machine. Elastic IPs may be detached from one instance and attached to another at any time. While IPv4 addresses have a small monthly cost, IPv6 addresses are free. Keep in mind that merely having a public IP does not make your instance publicly accessible; clients or users still need a path to the machine. This can be achieved, among other ways, by placing the instance in a public subnet, or routing traffic to it with a public load balancer. In addition, the instance's security groups must allow traffic to reach the instance.

Security groups protect traffic entering and exiting an instance's network interface. Security groups act as a stateful firewall. To make network connections to your instance, you must set security group rules to allow the connection.

You can attach additional network interfaces to an EC2 instance, each with its own MAC addresses and IP address associations. Unlike the primary ENI, you can detach a secondary network interface from one instance and later attach it to another.

Accessing Instances

By default, Linux Amazon EC2 instances provide remote access through Secure Shell (SSH), and Windows Amazon EC2 instances provide remote access through the Remote Desktop Protocol (RDP). To connect to these services, you must have the appropriate inbound rules on the security group for the instance.

Default User

The default user for Amazon Linux instances is `ec2-user`. For other Linux operating systems, this default user may vary depending on the AMI provider. For example, the default user for Ubuntu Linux is `ubuntu`.

For Windows instances, the default user is `Administrator`. This account may have a different name depending on the language of the server. For example, if the server is configured with French as the language, the administrator account is localized to `Administrateur`.

Amazon EC2 Key Pairs

In order to connect to an instance via SSH, you must configure SSH key access with a user on the server. AWS allows you to do this at instance creation time by associating an *EC2 key pair* with the default login user.

An EC2 key pair consists of two files: a public key and a private key. When you launch an instance, you may choose to either create a new key pair or use an existing one already on your account to configure SSH access. AWS will associate the public key with the default login user, after which you may use the private key to SSH as that user. When creating a new key pair, AWS allows you to download the private key only once. Treat the private key like a password and keep it secure!

To use SSH to connect to an Amazon Linux instance with your private key, perform the following from a Mac or Linux-based system:

```
chmod 400 /path/to/key
ssh -i /path/to/key ec2-user@<your instance IP>
```

If you do not specify a key pair when you launch the instance, you will be unable to connect via SSH to that instance, unless you use another method to sign in and configure SSH.

Session Manager

Session Manager is a feature of the AWS Systems Manager service that provides a secure browser-based interface to your instances, allowing you to log in without needing to maintain SSH keys or even open inbound ports. By attaching an IAM role with the `Amazon SSMManagedInstanceCore` policy to your instance and making sure the Session Manager agent is running (a default installation on Amazon Linux), you can enable Session Manager and get a shell right in your browser. This tool is particularly useful for instances without public IP addresses or in private subnets, as you can avoid the need to expose the server or create other "jumpbox" instances to reach it.

EC2 Instance Connect

Amazon EC2 Instance Connect provides a secure way to connect to your EC2 instances using SSH. It simplifies key management by allowing you to push a temporary SSH public key to the instance's metadata and connect without needing to manage permanent keys. This is especially useful for providing time-bound, auditable access. As with Session Manager, Instance Connect functionality is enabled by attaching the appropriate IAM role to your instance via its instance profile.

Instance Life Cycle

An Amazon EC2 instance has three primary states: running, stopped, and terminated. Additionally, there are intermediate states of pending, stopping, and shutting down. On-demand Amazon EC2 instances accrue charges for the compute resources only when they are in the running state. However, EBS volumes persist data even when an instance is stopped, so the charges for persistent storage from any EBS volumes accrue independent of the state of the instance.

When you first launch an instance from an AMI, it goes into the pending state until it enters the running state on a host machine.

After an instance is running, for instances with EBS-backed storage, you can stop the instance. If you stop the instance, it enters the stopping state. If the host has an instance store drive, any data residing on that drive will be erased.

When an instance is stopped, you can modify attributes, such as instance type, that cannot be changed while the instance is running. You can also start stopped instances. When you start an instance, it enters the pending state until it is running again.

Typically, each time an instance is started, it is launched on a different physical host machine than before. If the underlying physical host is impaired and requires maintenance, stopping and then starting the EC2 instance moves the instance to a healthy host. This is your first, best troubleshooting move if you find an EC2 instance suddenly unresponsive and unreachable. Keep in mind that a simple reboot will not achieve the same goal.

You can also terminate an instance. It first enters the shutting down state; then eventually it is terminated. The default behavior is to delete the EBS volumes associated with the instance on termination, although this can be configured differently.

To view the life cycle of an Amazon EC2 instance, see Figure 2.3.

FIGURE 2.3   Amazon EC2 instance life cycle

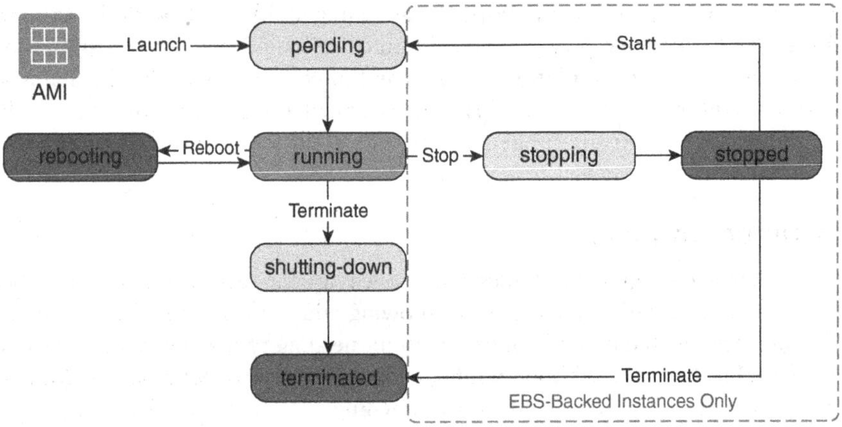

Running Applications on Instances

This section explores some features of EC2 that are useful when you run applications or custom-code on an instance. These include ways of customizing the software on an instance and discovering properties about the instance. An example that ties these features together is provided. Finally, we discuss how you can monitor the status of the instance.

Connecting to Amazon EC2 Instances

With EC2 instances, you have full administrative control to install software packages on your instance and create additional user accounts as needed. As mentioned earlier, you can directly connect to Linux instances via SSH using the private key from the Amazon EC2 key pair, as shown in Figure 2.4.

FIGURE 2.4   Using SSH with an Amazon EC2 instance

```
$ ssh ec2-user@54.234.151.4 -i ~/.ssh/aws-demo-key.pem
      ,      #_
     ~\_  ####_          Amazon Linux 2023
    ~~  \_#####\
    ~~     \###|
    ~~      \#/ ___      https://aws.amazon.com/linux/amazon-linux-2023
     ~~     V~' '->
      ~~~         /
        ~~._.   _/
           _/ _/
          _/m/'
Last login: Tue Mar  5 03:55:36 2024 from 199.16.223.46
[ec2-user@ip-10-0-18-100 ~]$
```

For a Windows instance, the password for the Administrator account is encrypted with the public key. You can decrypt the password by using the associated private key, as illustrated in Figure 2.5 and Figure 2.6.

After you have decrypted the password, you can use Microsoft Remote Desktop to connect to the instance.

Customizing Software with User Data

You can connect to your instance and install any applications you want from an interactive session. However, one of the advantages of moving to the cloud is to automate previously manual steps. Instead of logging in to the instance, another way to customize the software on your instance is to provide *user data* as part of the request to launch the instance. For Linux instances, user data can be a shell script or a *cloud-init* directive. On Windows instances (depending on the version of Windows Server), either EC2Config or EC2Launch will process the user data. By default, commands supplied to user data execute only at first boot of the instance.

Here is an example of installing an Apache web server on an Amazon Linux 2 instance with a shell script that is provided as the user data:

```
#!/bin/bash
yum update -y
yum install httpd -y
systemctl start httpd
systemctl enable httpd
```

FIGURE 2.5   Decrypting a Windows password

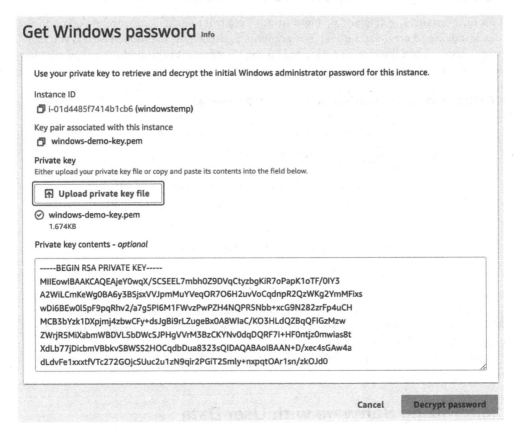

Discovering Instance Metadata

With the *instance metadata service* (IMDS), code running on an Amazon EC2 instance can discover properties about that instance. The IMDS exposes a special IP address, 169.254.169.254, which you can query using HTTP to perform lookups. By first asking the metadata service for a token, then using that token to inquire about the environment, you can query a broad range of metadata attributes, as shown in Figure 2.7. These attributes can include the instance ID, AMI ID, hostname, and much more.

With IMDS, it also possible to retrieve the user data that was used to bootstrap an instance, as shown in Figure 2.8.

Anyone who can access an instance can view its metadata and user data. Do not store sensitive data, such as passwords or access keys, in user data.

FIGURE 2.6   Viewing a Windows password

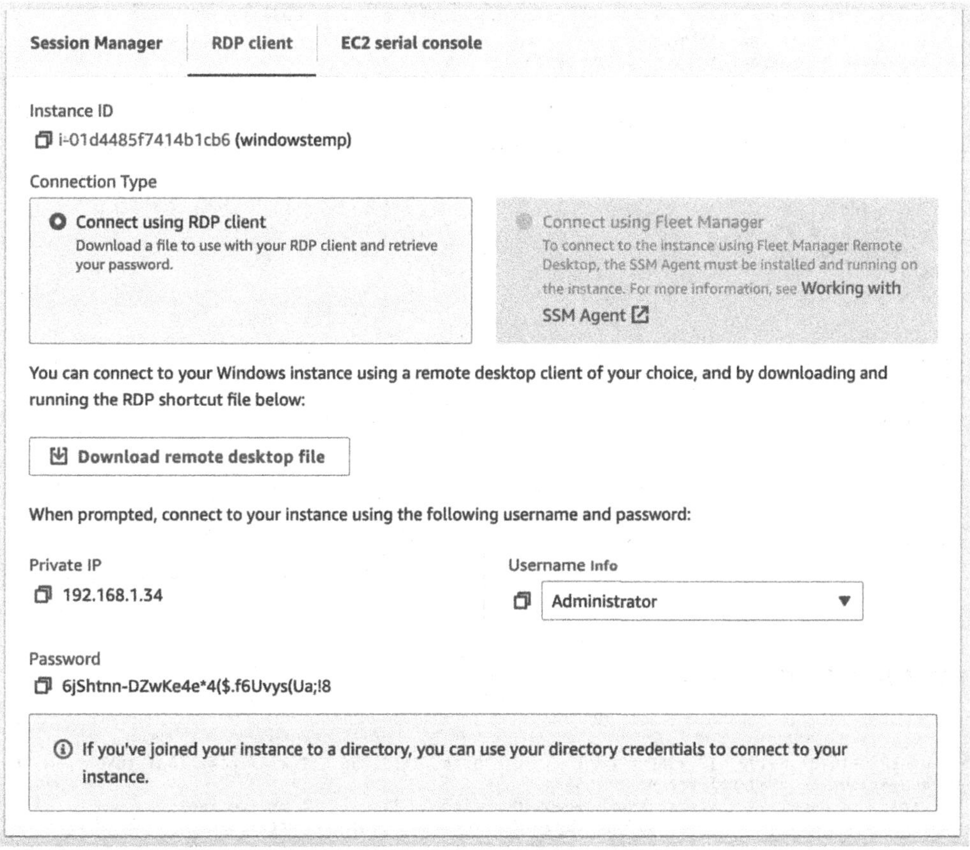

Obtaining AWS Credentials

Usually, when interacting with AWS services via the CLI or various programming language SDKs like boto, you must either explicitly provide AWS credentials in the form of an access key ID and secret access key, or ensure that those values are set in environment variables. However, when calling from an EC2 instance, it is possible to connect to AWS services without any keys at all, using the instance's associated IAM instance profile.

Instance profiles are how you assign an IAM role (with its associated policies) to an instance. When you see "instance profile" as a configurable field on EC2 instances in the console or other parts of AWS, you can think "attached IAM role." A role can be used on many instances at once, but an instance can only have one role at a time. To update the permissions on an instance, you can either update the policies attached to its role or swap the attached role at any time.

FIGURE 2.7   Amazon EC2 metadata attributes

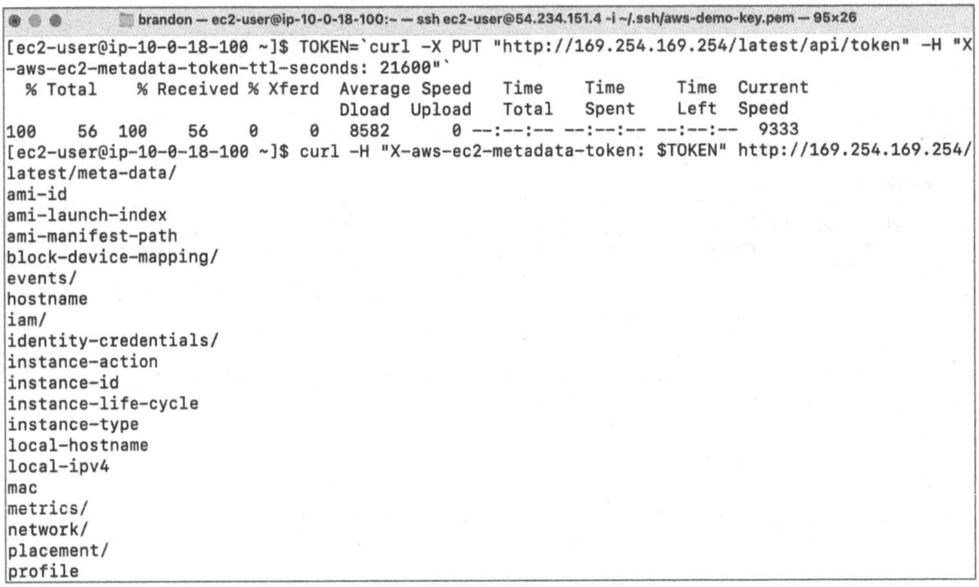

```
●  ●  ●        brandon — ec2-user@ip-10-0-18-100:~ — ssh ec2-user@54.234.151.4 -i ~/.ssh/aws-demo-key.pem — 95×26
[ec2-user@ip-10-0-18-100 ~]$ TOKEN=`curl -X PUT "http://169.254.169.254/latest/api/token" -H "X
-aws-ec2-metadata-token-ttl-seconds: 21600"`
  % Total    % Received % Xferd  Average Speed   Time    Time     Time  Current
                                 Dload  Upload   Total   Spent    Left  Speed
100    56 100    56    0     0   8582      0 --:--:-- --:--:-- --:--:--  9333
[ec2-user@ip-10-0-18-100 ~]$ curl -H "X-aws-ec2-metadata-token: $TOKEN" http://169.254.169.254/
latest/meta-data/
ami-id
ami-launch-index
ami-manifest-path
block-device-mapping/
events/
hostname
iam/
identity-credentials/
instance-action
instance-id
instance-life-cycle
instance-type
local-hostname
local-ipv4
mac
metrics/
network/
placement/
profile
```

FIGURE 2.8   Querying Amazon EC2 user data

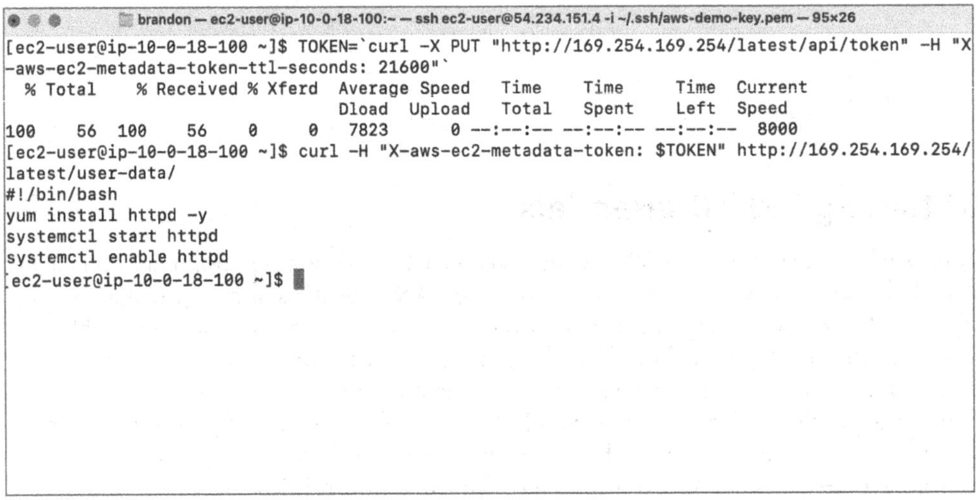

```
●  ●  ●        brandon — ec2-user@ip-10-0-18-100:~ — ssh ec2-user@54.234.151.4 -i ~/.ssh/aws-demo-key.pem — 95×26
[ec2-user@ip-10-0-18-100 ~]$ TOKEN=`curl -X PUT "http://169.254.169.254/latest/api/token" -H "X
-aws-ec2-metadata-token-ttl-seconds: 21600"`
  % Total    % Received % Xferd  Average Speed   Time    Time     Time  Current
                                 Dload  Upload   Total   Spent    Left  Speed
100    56 100    56    0     0   7823      0 --:--:-- --:--:-- --:--:--  8000
[ec2-user@ip-10-0-18-100 ~]$ curl -H "X-aws-ec2-metadata-token: $TOKEN" http://169.254.169.254/
latest/user-data/
#!/bin/bash
yum install httpd -y
systemctl start httpd
systemctl enable httpd
[ec2-user@ip-10-0-18-100 ~]$ █
```

When an IAM role is associated with an instance, the EC2 service makes the necessary calls to the *Security Token Service* automatically to generate short-term credentials for that instance that confer all the capabilities of the attached IAM role. The credentials are exposed to the instance through the Amazon EC2 metadata service, as shown in Figure 2.9.

FIGURE 2.9   Instance profile and IAM role credentials

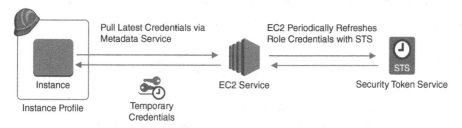

Serving a Custom Web Page

Let's bring this all together in a short demo. This example combines EC2 user data, the EC2 metadata service, and IAM roles to configure an instance with a static web page that shows (and tells!) information about the host.

Entering the following script as the user data of a new Amazon Linux instance generates a static page that displays the instance ID, instance type, availability zone, and public IP address of the instance at the time the script was executed.

The first line of the script declares the type of script. Then the script installs the Apache web server and configures it to run as a service. Because user data runs as root, there is no need to use the sudo command.

Next, the script makes several calls to the Amazon EC2 metadata service and saves the results into environment variables to be used later in the script.

To show how instance profiles confer privileges to the instance that can be used by the CLI, the script makes a call to Amazon Polly to generate an mp3. For this API call to succeed, you must assign the instance an IAM role that allows permissions to the Amazon Polly SynthesizeSpeech action, such as the managed AmazonPollyReadOnlyAccess policy.

Using all these values, the script generates a static HTML page for Apache to serve on port 80. After this script completes, your EC2 instance can respond to HTTP requests and show the customized page. To see this page, you must verify that the EC2 instance has port 80 open in its security group and is assigned a public IP address.

```
#!/bin/bash


# Install Apache Web Server
yum update -y
yum install httpd -y
systemctl start httpd
systemctl enable httpd


# Request and store a session token for the metadata service
TOKEN=`curl -X PUT "http://169.254.169.254/latest/api/token" -H "X-aws-ec2-
metadata-token-ttl-seconds: 21600"`
```

```
# Use the token to retrieve instance metadata
ID=$(curl -H "X-aws-ec2-metadata-token: $TOKEN" \
http://169.254.169.254/latest/meta-data/instance-id)

TYPE=$(curl -H "X-aws-ec2-metadata-token: $TOKEN" \
http://169.254.169.254/latest/meta-data/instance-type)

AZ=$(curl -H "X-aws-ec2-metadata-token: $TOKEN" \
http://169.254.169.254/latest/meta-data/placement/availability-zone)

IPV4=$(curl -f -H "X-aws-ec2-metadata-token: $TOKEN" \
http://169.254.169.254/latest/meta-data/public-ipv4)


# Set up the Web Site
cd /var/www/html

## Make AWS Cloud API calls to generate an audio file
VOICE="Matthew"
aws polly synthesize-speech --region us-west-2 --voice-id $VOICE --text "Hello
from EC2 instance $ID." --output-format mp3 --engine neural instance.mp3

## Generate customized index.html for this instance
echo "<html><body><H1>Welcome to your EC2 Instance</H1><p><p>" > ./index.html
echo "<audio controls>" >> ./index.html
echo '<source src="instance.mp3" type="audio/mp3">' >> ./index.html
echo 'Here is an <a href="instance.mp3"> audio greeting.</a> ' >> ./index.html
echo "</audio><p><p>" >> ./index.html
echo "There are many other instances, but" >> ./index.html
echo "<strong>$ID</strong> is yours.<p><p>" >> ./index.html
echo "This is a <strong>$TYPE</strong> instance" >> ./index.html
echo " in <strong>$AZ</strong>. <p><p>" >> ./index.html
echo "The public IP is <strong>$IPV4</strong>.<p><p>" >> ./index.html
echo "</body></html>" >> ./index.html
```

Monitoring Instances

Now that you have an application running on your instance, you may be interested in understanding how that application performs, watching its resource usage, and ensuring that it stays up and running.

For each of your instances, the EC2 service automatically collects metrics related to CPU utilization, disk reads and writes, network utilization, and instance reachability, and makes them available in *Amazon CloudWatch*. You can supplement these built-in metrics with data from the guest operating system on your instance, such as memory utilization and logs from your application, by installing and configuring the Amazon CloudWatch agent on the instance.

Using Amazon CloudWatch, you can automate actions based on a metric through Amazon CloudWatch alarms. For example, you can configure an Amazon CloudWatch alarm that applies the "recover instance" action if status checks show that the host running the instance is impaired.

Customizing the Network

The out-of-the-box Amazon VPC service offers a straightforward path to launch EC2 instances, but grasping the details of how VPCs work to create software-defined networks is crucial. This section delves into the functionality of VPCs, which lets you establish virtual networks in an AWS region tailored to your computing needs.

Amazon Virtual Private Cloud

Amazon Virtual Private Cloud (VPC) provides logically isolated networks within your AWS account. Although advanced AWS users often adopt multi-VPC architectures, for many users, it's not inaccurate to call a VPC "your data center in the cloud" and think of it as the network container for all your AWS resources. VPC networks can span all the availability zones within a specific AWS region. For each VPC, you have full control over whether the VPC is connected to the Internet, to private on-premises networks, or to other Amazon VPCs. Until you explicitly create these connections, instances in your VPC are able to communicate with other instances in the same VPC.

You define an Amazon VPC with one or more blocks of addresses specified in the Classless Inter-Domain Routing (CIDR) notation. If, for example, you specified 10.0.0.0/16 as the block for a VPC, this means that the VPC includes IP addresses in the range from 10.0.0.0 through 10.0.255.255. For an example of an Amazon VPC spanning multiple availability zones in a region, see Figure 2.10.

Connecting to Other Networks

By default, an Amazon VPC is an isolated network. Instances within an Amazon VPC cannot communicate with the Internet or other networks until you explicitly create connections. Table 2.2 provides an overview of various types of connections that you can establish between an Amazon VPC and other networks.

TABLE 2.2   Amazon VPC connection types

Connection type	Description
Internet Gateway	A highly available connection that allows outbound and inbound requests to the internet from your Amazon VPC
Egress Only Internet Gateway	A special type of internet gateway for IPv6 that allows outbound traffic and corresponding responses but blocks inbound connections
Virtual Private Gateway	Allows you to establish a private connection to your corporate network by using a VPN connection or through Direct Connect (DX)
Amazon VPC Endpoints	Allows traffic from your Amazon VPC to go to specific AWS services or third-party SaaS services without traversing an Internet gateway
Amazon VPC Peering	Privately routes traffic from one Amazon VPC to another Amazon VPC by establishing a peer relationship between this VPC and another VPC
AWS Transit Gateway	Allows you to centrally manage connectivity between many VPCs and an on-premises environment using a single gateway
AWS VPN Cloudhub	Connects multiple remote networks to a central location in AWS using a hub-and-spoke model
AWS Privatelink	Allows private connections from your VPC to AWS services, such as S3, many of which otherwise require outbound internet access

FIGURE 2.10   Amazon VPC overview

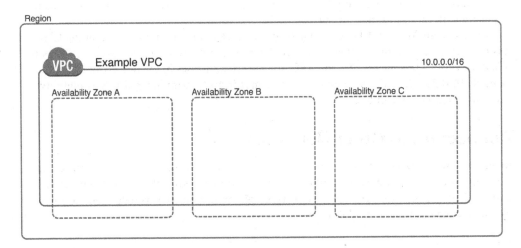

For an example of an Amazon VPC with a connection to an Internet gateway and a VPN connection to an on-premises network provided by a virtual private gateway, see Figure 2.11.

FIGURE 2.11   Amazon VPC with gateway connections

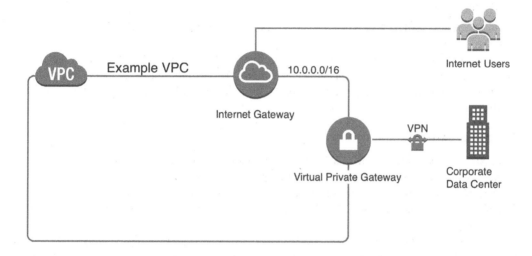

IP Addresses

When working with Amazon VPC, all instances placed within a particular VPC are assigned one or more IP addresses. Several types of IP addresses are available for use with Amazon VPC.

Private IP Addresses

Private IP addresses are IPv4 addresses that are not reachable from the Internet. These addresses are unique within a VPC and used for traffic that is to be routed internally within the VPC, for private communication with connected networks, or for private communication with other VPCs.

When you create a VPC, you assign it one or more blocks of addresses. When an instance is launched, that host is created in a subnet within the VPC and automatically assigned a private IP address from the block associated with that particular subnet. Private IPv4 addresses are free and persist for the life cycle of the instance—even when the instance is stopped.

Public IP Addresses

Whether an EC2 instance is assigned public IP addresses automatically, in addition to the private IP address, depends on the following factors:

- Whether the "public IP" configuration is checked when launching the instance
- Whether the subnet in which that instance is launched is configured to provide public IPs for all instances

Unlike the private IP address, the public IP address is an IPv4 address that is reachable from the Internet.

AWS manages the association between an instance and a public IPv4 address, and the association persists only while the instance is running. You cannot manually associate or disassociate public IP addresses from an instance. All public IPv4 addresses come with a small hourly charge.

Elastic IP Addresses

An *Elastic IP address* is similar to a public IP address in that it is an IPv4 address that is reachable from the Internet. However, unlike public IP addresses, you manage the association between instances and Elastic IP addresses. You control when these addresses are allocated, and you can associate, disassociate, or move these addresses between instances as needed.

You may also assign Elastic IP addresses to infrastructure such as NAT gateways. Like normal public addresses, Elastic IPs incur a small hourly charge, whether associated with an instance or not.

IPv6 Addresses

In addition to IPv4 addresses, you can associate an Amazon-provided block of IPv6 addresses to your VPC. When you enable IPv6 in your VPC, the network operates in *dual-stack mode*, meaning that IPv4 and IPv6 commutations are independent of each other. Your resources can communicate over IPv4, IPv6, or both.

Subnets

Within an Amazon VPC, you define one or more subnets. A subnet is associated with a specific availability zone within the region containing the VPC. Each subnet has its own block of private IP addresses defined using CIDR notation. This block is a subset of the overall IP address range assigned to the VPC and does not overlap with any other subnet in the same VPC.

For example, a subnet may be assigned the CIDR block range 10.0.0.0/24, which would include addresses in the range 10.0.0.0–10.0.0.255. Out of the 256 possible addresses, the VPC reserves the first four IP addresses and the last IP address in the range, leaving 251 IP addresses in the subnet.

When you launch an EC2 instance into a subnet, its primary network interface assigns a private IPv4 address automatically from the CIDR range assigned to the subnet.

Typically, you create at least two types of configurations for subnets in a VPC. The first is for subnets in which you place instances that you want to reach directly from the Internet. This could be an instance running as a web server, for example. Subnets of this type are known as *public subnets*.

The second type of configuration is usually a subnet that backend instances use that must be accessible to your other instances but should not be directly accessible from the Internet. Subnets of this type are known as *private subnets*. For example, if you had an instance that was dedicated to running a database, such as MySQL, you could place that instance in a private subnet. It would be accessible from the web server in the public subnet, but it would not accept traffic from the Internet.

For an example of an Amazon VPC with a public and a private subnet, see Figure 2.12.

FIGURE 2.12   Amazon VPC with public and private subnets

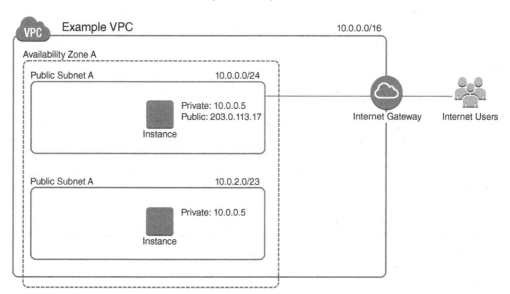

In addition to Amazon EC2 instances, many AWS managed services, such as Amazon Relational Database Service (Amazon RDS) or Amazon ElastiCache, also enable you to expose your resources in specific subnets, including private subnets. You can create these resources and access them privately from instances within your Amazon VPC.

Route Tables

Network traffic exiting a subnet is controlled with routes defined in a route table. A route is composed of two parts: a destination and a target for the network traffic.

Each route table includes a rule called the *local route*. This route is what allows traffic from instances in one subnet within the VPC to communicate with instances in other subnets within the same VPC.

Unless explicitly associated with a specific route table, subnets associate with a default route table called the *main route table*. By default, the main route table includes only the local route. This means that subnets that are associated with the default route table have no connection to the internet. They can route traffic privately only within the Amazon VPC. However, you can modify this table or define additional route tables and rules as required.

For an example of the main route table for an Amazon VPC, see Table 2.3.

TABLE 2.3   Main route table example

Destination	Target
10.0.0.0/16	local

Route tables and the configured rules differentiate public subnets from private subnets. For example, you might create a public subnet by associating the subnet with a route table that includes a rule to route Internet-bound traffic through an Internet gateway. To represent any IP address on the Internet in the rule, you can use the 0.0.0.0/0 CIDR block. The route table would have the rules, as shown in Table 2.4.

TABLE 2.4   Public route table example

Destination	Target
10.0.0.0/16	local
0.0.0.0/0	igw-example123

When you launch an EC2 instance into a public subnet, be sure to assign a public IP address to the instance, whether explicitly upon instance creation, implicitly by the default subnet configuration, or by giving it an Elastic IP. Even though a public subnet will have a route to an Internet gateway, instances are not able to communicate with the Internet without a public IP address. Route table rules are evaluated in order of specificity.

To review a diagram of an Amazon VPC that has a public and a private subnet configured with the route table rules, see Figure 2.13.

FIGURE 2.13   Amazon VPC with public and private subnets with rules

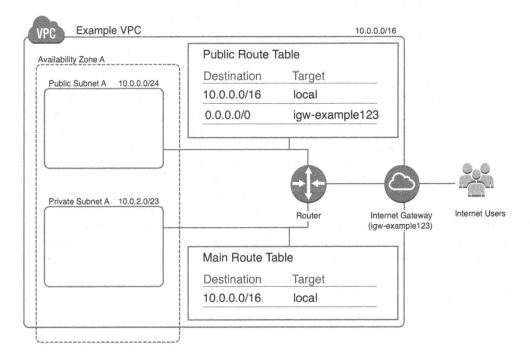

Security Groups

Security groups act as a stateful firewall for resources in your AWS account, from EC2 instances to RDS databases to application load balancers. When you define security group rules, you specify the source or destination of the network traffic along with the protocols and ports that you allow from those sources.

Inbound security group rules let you control the source, protocols, and ports of network traffic that is allowed to reach a resource. For example, you could allow TCP connections originating from the IPv4 address of your home network to connect to EC2 instances via SSH port 22.

Outbound rules allow you to control destination, protocols, and ports of outgoing network traffic. Security groups include a default outbound rule that allows all outbound requests on all protocols and ports to all destinations. To control outbound requests more tightly, you can remove this default rule and add specific outbound rules in its place.

When you use IP addresses or ranges to define a source, your security groups will closely resemble traditional host firewalls, and these are useful, especially when reused for multiple resources. However, the true power of security groups lies in your ability to configure as a source *another security group*.

Consider this scenario. You have two EC2 instances—one instance running a web server, and a second instance running a database. To allow network connections to these instances, you can create two security groups: one for your web server instances called websg and a second security group for your database instances called databasesg.

For websg, you set inbound rules that allow web requests from anywhere. You also allow inbound SSH but only from a specific IP address that your administrator uses. You have not yet modified the default outbound rule for websg, so all outgoing connections are allowed.

For databasesg, you write an inbound rule that allows incoming traffic on TCP port 3306 originating not from any IP range, but from websg. This will allow traffic from any resource bearing this security group—namely, your web tier. The great thing about this is that any additional web host you may create can immediately connect to the database as long as it is given the websg security group. Remove the default outbound rule on data basesg and instead add rules to allow outbound connections to download software updates over HTTP and HTTPS. All other outbound connections from databasesg will be blocked.

To view the diagram of the security groups and rules for this scenario, see Figure 2.14. Also, see Table 2.5, Table 2.6, Table 2.7, and Table 2.8 for the corresponding inbound and outbound rules for these security groups.

FIGURE 2.14   Security groups

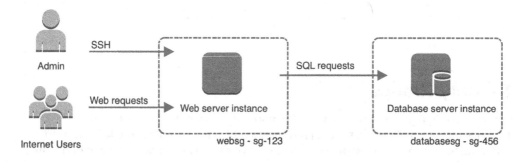

TABLE 2.5   Inbound rules for websg

Protocol	Port	Source	Comments
TCP	80	0.0.0.0/0	Allow incoming HTTP requests from Internet users
TCP	443	0.0.0.0/0	Allow incoming HTTPS requests from Internet users
TCP	22	10.10.0.6/32	Allow incoming SSH only from the administrator's computer

TABLE 2.6 Outbound rules for websg

Protocol	Port	Destination	Comments
All	All	0.0.0.0/0	Allow all outbound IPv4 traffic

TABLE 2.7 Inbound rules for databasesg

Protocol	Port	Source	Comments
TCP	3306	sg-123	Allow inbound SQL queries from the ID of websg

TABLE 2.8 Outbound rules for databasesg

Protocol	Port	Destination	Comments
TCP	80	0.0.0.0/0	Allow all outbound HTTP for updates
TCP	443	0.0.0.0/0	Allow outbound HTTPS requests for updates

*Security groups only support rules to **allow** traffic.* Therefore, if you assign multiple security groups to your instance, that instance receives the cumulative network traffic permissions allowed by all the security group rules.

Network Access Control Lists

In addition to routes, *network access control lists* (network ACLs) allow an administrator to control traffic that enters and leaves a subnet. A network ACL consists of inbound and outbound rules that you can associate with multiple subnets within a specific VPC. Network ACLs act as a stateless firewall for traffic to or from a specific subnet. Whereas security group rules provide only the capability to allow traffic, network ACL rules support the ability to allow or deny specific types of traffic.

However, unlike security groups, network ACLs are stateless and do not track connections and their replies. This means that to allow for a particular traffic flow, both inbound and outbound rules must allow it for that network ACL. For inbound rules, you can specify the protocol, port range, and source IP address range. For outbound rules, you specify the protocol, port range, and destination IP address range. For each rule, you also choose whether the rule allows or denies traffic. Rules in a network ACL are numbered and evaluated in order from the smallest to largest rule number.

If you do not specify a network ACL, the subnet is associated with the default network ACL for the VPC. This network ACL comes with rules that allow all inbound and outbound traffic. Table 2.9 shows an example of the inbound rules for a default network ACL. The final rule for the network ACL, rule 100, is a universal rule that explicitly denies traffic that does not match any other rule. Because there is a rule to allow all traffic and rules are evaluated in order, this universal rule has no effect. However, if you remove or modify rule 100, then the final rule would apply to any traffic that did not match any of the other rules.

TABLE 2.9   Default network ACL inbound rules

Rule number	Type	Protocol	Port range	Source	Allow/deny
100	All traffic	All	All	0.0.0.0/0	Allow
*	All traffic	All	All	0.0.0.0/0	Deny

Table 2.10 shows an example of the outbound rules for the default network ACL for an Amazon VPC. As before, the final rule is a universal rule that denies traffic unless it has been explicitly allowed by a preceding rule.

TABLE 2.10   Default network ACL outbound rules

Rule number	Type	Protocol	Port range	Destination	Allow/deny
100	All traffic	All	All	0.0.0.0/0	Allow
*	All traffic	All	All	0.0.0.0/0	Deny

Figure 2.15 shows an example of an Amazon VPC with security groups protecting Amazon EC2 instances and network ACLs protecting subnets.

Figure 2.16 shows the same Amazon VPC, represented in a different way to highlight the features that control network traffic within an Amazon VPC.

Table 2.11 summarizes key aspects of security groups and network ACLs.

TABLE 2.11   Security groups and network ACLs

Feature	Security group	Network ACL
Applies to	Amazon EC2 instances or elastic network interfaces	Subnets

Feature	Security group	Network ACL
Type of firewall	Stateful: Replies to an allowed traffic flow are automatically allowed	Stateless: Must provide both inbound and outbound rules to allow a specific traffic flow
Rules	Only allow traffic	Allow or deny traffic

FIGURE 2.15   Network ACLs and security groups

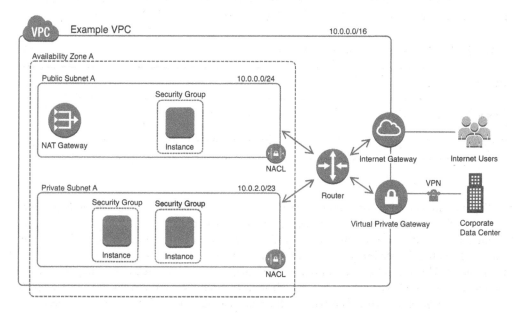

FIGURE 2.16   Controlling network traffic within an Amazon VPC

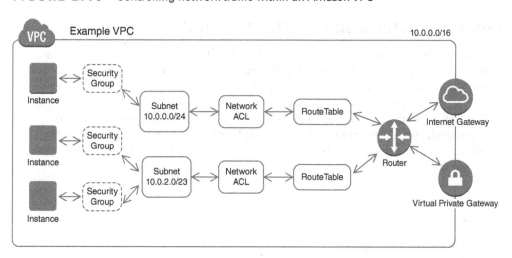

Network Address Translation

Network address translation (NAT) allows for instances in a private subnet to make outbound requests to the Internet without exposing those instances to inbound connections from Internet users, supplying an outgoing public IP to instances that do not have their own. Multiple instances often use the same NAT, which either provides the same shared IP to all outgoing traffic or assigns an IP from a dedicated pool. To achieve this, you can run NAT software on an EC2 instance or use AWS's NAT Gateway service.

For a NAT to perform its job, it must be located in a public subnet that forwards outgoing traffic to the Internet. Make sure that the subnet has a route to an Internet gateway, as previously shown in Table 2.4. To support outbound network requests, you can associate the private subnet with a route table, similar to the one shown in Table 2.12.

TABLE 2.12   Private route table example

Destination	Target
10.0.0.0/16	local
0.0.0.0/0	nat-example456

For the Amazon VPC configuration example, Figure 2.17 shows the corresponding route tables for the public and private subnets using the NAT gateway.

Internet-bound requests route to the NAT gateway through the route table of the private subnet. The NAT, located in a public subnet, then makes a corresponding request out to the Internet. This second outbound request appears to have originated from the public IP assigned by the NAT when the external website receives it. When the website responds, NAT receives the reply and forwards it back to the instance that initiated the original request. Figure 2.18 shows the network flow.

Monitoring Amazon VPC Network Traffic

You can monitor traffic within your Amazon VPC by enabling Amazon VPC Flow Logs, which may be published to Amazon CloudWatch Logs or stored in Amazon S3. You can enable VPC Flow Logs on a particular VPC, on a subnet, or on a specific elastic network interface, such as one associated with an Amazon EC2 instance.

For each network session, Flow Logs capture metadata, such as the source, destination, protocol, port, packet count, byte count, and time interval. The log entry specifies whether the traffic was accepted or rejected. This information helps you debug the network configuration.

FIGURE 2.17   Example of Amazon VPC with NAT

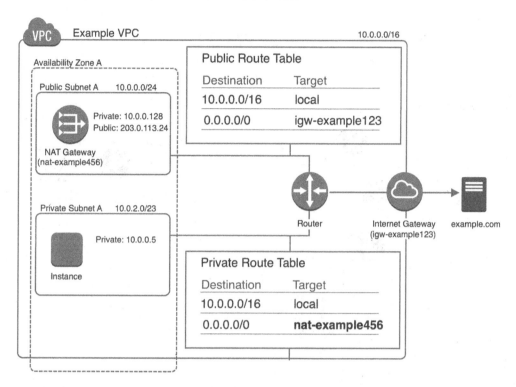

Managing Your Resources

As you've seen, AWS gives you plenty of tools to get started running your data center in the cloud—just enough to be dangerous, if you're not careful! Let's take a closer look at the division of responsibility between you and AWS that will help ensure you're taking care of everything you need to run securely and efficiently.

Shared Responsibility Model

The *Shared Responsibility Model* is AWS's foundational framework for helping customers understand how security is handled in the cloud. In short, the Shared Responsibility Model says that AWS is responsible for the security *of* the cloud, while you are responsible for security *in* the cloud.

FIGURE 2.18   NAT gateway in Amazon VPC

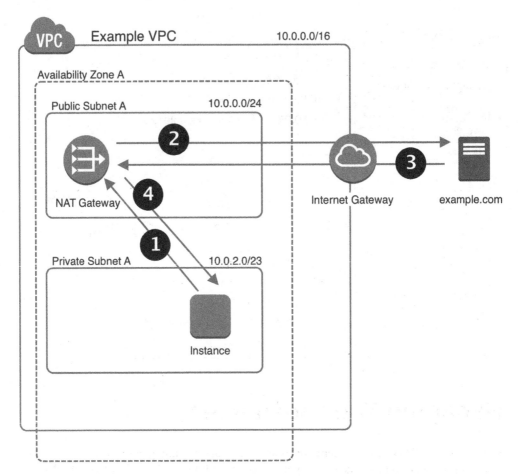

Security *of* the cloud, AWS's part, involves securing physical access to the underlying infrastructure, such as the AWS regions and availability zones, as well as restricting access to the servers, physical networks, and decommissioning of hardware that is no longer useful. As part of securing the cloud infrastructure, AWS is also responsible for maintaining the underlying software for each service provided.

Security *in* the cloud is your responsibility. This includes making secure choices when configuring your infrastructure and developing your applications. These responsibilities can include configuring the relevant encryption options and configuring your firewall rules. Even though this is your responsibility, you can simplify this task by taking advantage of AWS tools for encryption, defining firewall rules, and managing access and authorization to your AWS resources. For a summary of AWS and customer responsibilities, see Figure 2.19.

FIGURE 2.19   Shared responsibility security model

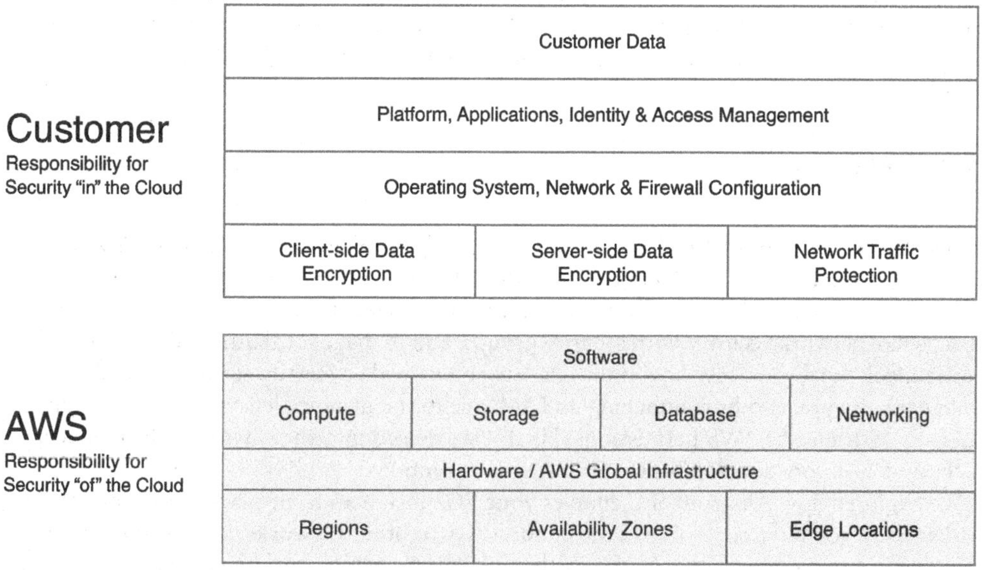

Customer Data		
Platform, Applications, Identity & Access Management		
Operating System, Network & Firewall Configuration		
Client-side Data Encryption	Server-side Data Encryption	Network Traffic Protection

Customer
Responsibility for
Security "in" the Cloud

Software			
Compute	Storage	Database	Networking
Hardware / AWS Global Infrastructure			
Regions	Availability Zones	Edge Locations	

AWS
Responsibility for
Security "of" the Cloud

For example, with EC2, AWS is responsible for the software on the physical host machines up through the virtualization layer. Beyond that, it is your responsibility to ensure that the guest operating system and everything running on it is secured. Your responsibilities include, but are not limited to, the following tasks:

- Making sure that any sensitive data is secured
- Making sure that the operating system is patched regularly
- Managing the operating system's user accounts
- Securing any applications that are installed on that instance
- Controlling network access to and from the instance

AWS provides tools to help you manage these concerns. For example, use AWS Systems Manager to automate the patching of instances on your behalf. You can also use network controls, such as security groups, to restrict access to the instance. In the end, it is your responsibility to configure these features in a way that meets the security requirements for your specific application.

Comparing Managed and Unmanaged Services

Helping AWS users even more is the fact that many AWS services are *managed services*. Managed services automate for customers many of the operational tasks typically involved in securing and maintaining resources and infrastructure. For example, with Amazon RDS, AWS handles the installation and patching of database engines without users ever interacting with the underlying operating system. RDS customers don't need to think about OS patching, and database patches can be scheduled to automatically install on a schedule. With the managed services provided by RDS, the operational burden for security is reduced, and customers can focus on building their own applications and services higher up the stack.

Summary

In this chapter, we explored EC2 instances, the virtual machines populating your AWS data center. With EC2, you have full control over the OS and software, selecting an AMI as the foundation. You control the hardware configuration by selecting an instance type, configure settings like network security with security groups, and manage local attached storage with Elastic Block Store. You saw how user data lets you provide a startup script to install and configure software, and how attaching an IAM role to the instance lets your machine make CLI calls with specific AWS permissions. Finally, we delved into the ways Cloudwatch keeps tracks and monitors details about your instance at runtime.

We explored how Amazon VPC enables your EC2 instances to be placed into isolated networks where you have control over the connectivity to other networks, such as the Internet, on-premises networks, or other VPCs. Within a VPC, the network is segmented into subnets. Instances within a subnet in a VPC are assigned private IPv4 addresses, and can also be given public IPv4 addresses, Elastic IP addresses, or IPv6 addresses.

You saw how routing between subnets is configured using route tables and network ACLs, enabling you to define some subnets as public and others as private. Security groups act as a stateful firewall that protects individual traffic flows at an instance level.

Don't forget: The responsibility for keeping your instances secure is shared between AWS and you, the customer. AWS is responsible for securing access to the infrastructure and providing you with controls that you can use to secure your instances. As an AWS customer, you are responsible for configuring your resources in a way that is secure and that meets your application needs.

Exam Essentials

Know the basics of Amazon EC2, such as resource types, instance types, AMIs, and storage.   Be familiar with launching and connecting to EC2 instances. Understand EC2 instance types and families. Be familiar with the purpose of an AMI in launching an instance. Understand the distinction between persistent and ephemeral storage related to a particular EC2 instance.

Know about user data, instance metadata, and credentials.   Be familiar with using user data to customize the software by executing scripts on instances. Any scripts or code running on an instance can use the EC2 Metadata service to discover the instance configuration. Use IAM roles to provide AWS credentials automatically to code running on an EC2 instance.

Know how EC2 instances communicate within a VPC.   Understand the relationship between an EC2 instance and a VPC network. There may be exam questions that ask you to troubleshoot issues related to connecting to an EC2 instance. Be familiar with how VPCs enable communication between EC2 instances within the same VPC and isolates those instances from other VPCs. Recognize how route tables, network access control lists, and security groups control network traffic.

Know about public and private subnets.   Within a VPC, you must be able to distinguish between public and private subnets. Public subnets allow you to assign public IPv4 addresses to EC2 instances. By contrast, instances in a private subnet have only private IP addresses. The key distinction is that public subnets have a route table entry that forwards Internet-bound traffic to an Internet gateway. Private subnets do not have a direct route to the Internet. Instead, these subnets have a route that forwards Internet-bound traffic through a NAT gateway or NAT instance.

Know about security groups and network ACLs.   Be familiar with security groups and network ACLs. Security groups are used with EC2 instances, acting as stateful firewalls. They provide only rules that allow traffic. In comparison, network ACLs allow traffic between subnets and are stateless. They can allow or deny specific types of traffic.

Know about responsibilities shared between you and AWS.   Be familiar with the separation between AWS responsibility and your responsibility in securing cloud resources. AWS is responsible for providing secure building blocks up until the hypervisor layer for EC2 instances. This includes securing the physical facilities and machines and any hardware decommissioning. You are responsible for patching the guest operating system and applications. You are also responsible for configuring firewall rules, encryption, and access to the instance in a way that meets their requirements.

Exercises

These exercises provide hands-on experience with the fundamentals of working with EC2 and VPC configuration. You will create an isolated network in an AWS account and then launch EC2 instances into that network.

For the following exercises, verify that the region is US West (Oregon). The directions for these exercises assume that you have already completed Exercises 1.1, 1.2, 1.3, and 1.4 in Chapter 1, "Introduction to Amazon Web Services."

You can complete these exercises within the AWS Free Tier, provided that you follow the steps to clean up resources promptly.

The results from these exercises are used in a later chapter, so follow all the activities and directions exactly.

EXERCISE 2.1

Creating an Amazon EC2 Key Pair

In this exercise, you'll generate and save an Amazon EC2 key pair. You are responsible for saving the private key and using it when you want to connect to your Amazon EC2 instances.

1. Sign in to the AWS Management Console using the DevAdmin IAM user you created in Exercise 1.2.

2. To open the Amazon EC2 console, select Services ➤ Compute ➤ EC2.

3. Select Network & Security ➤ Key Pairs.

4. Click Create Key Pair.

5. For Key Pair Name, enter **devassoc**, and then click Create.

   The key pair automatically downloads to your Downloads folder.

6. Move this key to a safe location on your computer. You need it to connect to your Amazon EC2 instances using Secure Shell (SSH) or Remote Desktop Protocol (RDP).

EXERCISE 2.2

Creating an Amazon VPC with Public and Private Subnets

In this exercise, you'll create a virtual private cloud (VPC). Within that Amazon VPC, you will have a public subnet directly connected to the Internet through an Internet gateway. You will also have a private subnet that only has an indirect connection to the Internet using network address translation (NAT).

1. To display the Amazon VPC dashboard, use the Services search bar to find **VPC**.

2. Click Create VPC.

   If a field does not contain an explicit value in these directions, retain the default value.

3. Under Resources To Create, make sure VPC And More is selected.

4. Enter the following details for Amazon VPC:

   a. For Name Tag Auto-Generation, enter **devassoc**.

   b. Keep Number Of Availability Zones, Number Of Private Subnets, and Number Of Public Subnets at 2.

   c. Leave NAT Gateways at None.

5. Click Create VPC.

   The next screen shows the IDs of your newly created VPC and subnets.

6. Copy the VPC ID to a text document.

7. Click the subnet links, which open in another tab. Each subnet's name will indicate whether it is private or public. Note in your text file the Subnet ID of one public and one private subnet.

   Your text document should now look like the following:

   ```
   VPC ID: VPC-06bb2198eaexample
   Public subnet ID: subnet-0625e239a2example
   Private subnet ID: subnet-0e78325d9eexample
   ```

EXERCISE 2.3

Using an IAM Role for API Calls from Amazon EC2 Instances

In this exercise, you'll create an IAM role for the web server. This role enables you to make AWS service calls from code running on the EC2 instance of the web server. To do this, you'll create a new IAM role called devassoc-webserver.

1. Search for **IAM** using the Services menu.

2. Select Roles and click Create Role.

3. Under Trusted Entity Type, select AWS Service, and from the Service Or Use Case drop-down, select EC2. Click Next.

4. Select the following AWS managed policies to attach them to the role and then choose Next: Tags.

   These permissions are required to complete future exercises.

   AmazonPollyReadOnlyAccess grants read-only access to read details about and synthesize speech via the Amazon Polly voice service.

   TranslateReadOnly allows policyholders to detect the dominant language in text, translate text, and list and retrieve custom terminologies.

5. For Role Name, enter **devassoc-webserver** and then click Create Role.

EXERCISE 2.4

Launching an Amazon EC2 Instance as a Web Server

In this exercise, you'll launch an Amazon EC2 instance as a web server and connect to it.

1. Search the Services menu for **EC2**.

2. Select Launch Instance.

3. Name your instance **webserver**.

4. Under Application And OS Images, select Amazon Linux.

5. Under Instance Type, select t2.micro.

6. Under Key Pair, select devassoc.

7. In the Network Settings section, click Edit and do the following:

    - Select VPC ➤ devassoc-vpc.
    - Select Subnet and the public subnet you noted in your text file.
    - Select Auto-Assign Public IP ➤ Enable.
    - Select IAM Role ➤ devassoc-webserver.
    - Under Firewall (security groups), click Create Security Group.
    - For Security Group Name enter **restricted-http-ssh**.
    - For Description, enter **HTTP and SSH from my IP address only**.
    - Update the default SSH rule, changing Source Type to **My IP**.
    - Click Add Security Group Rule.
    - Under Type, choose HTTP and under Source Type, choose **My IP**.

8. Open Advanced Details and under Instance Profile, select devassoc-webserver.

9. Still under Advanced Details, scroll down to User Data and then paste this script:

    ```
    #!/bin/bash
    yum install httpd -y
    systemctl start httpd
    systemctl enable httpd
    ```

    Note: Paste this snippet from chapter-02/server-short.txt, located in the folder in which you downloaded the sample code for this guide.

10. Click Launch Instance.

11. To find your instance, click the instance ID shown on the Success page.

12. In the list of instances, you will see webserver. Wait until the Instance State for your instance reads running and Status Check changes to 2/2 checks passed.

13. Select the check box next to your instance to select it and bring up the Details panel.

14. Copy the Public IPv4 address of the instance to a text document.

15. Paste the IP address of the `webserver` instance into a browser window or click Open Address.

A test web page is displayed. If you do not see a page, wait 30 seconds and then refresh the page.

16. Disable your mobile phone's Wi-Fi and then attempt to access the IP address of the `webserver` instance from your mobile phone with mobile data.

The page fails to load because the security group rule allows HTTP access from only a particular IP address.

Configuring NAT for Instances in the Private Subnet

In this exercise, you'll create a security group for the NAT instance. NAT allows Amazon EC2 instances in a private subnet to make web requests to the Internet, to update software packages, and to make API calls.

1. Select Services ➢ VPC.

2. In the Security section, select Security Groups.

3. Click Create Security Group and configure the properties as follows:

- Set the Security Group Name to **nat-sg**.

- For Description, enter **Allow NAT instance to forward Internet traffic**.

- For VPC, enter **devassoc**.

4. Under Inbound Rules, click Add Rule.

5. Set the following properties for the first rule:

- For Type, select HTTP (80).

- For Source, enter **10.0.0.0/16**.

- For Description, enter **Enable Internet bound HTTP requests from VPC instances**.

6. Click Add Rule, and set the following properties for this rule:

- For Type, select HTTPS (443).

- For Source, enter **10.0.0.0/16**.

- For Description, enter **Enable Internet bound HTTPS. requests from VPC instances**.

7. Click Add Rule, and set the following properties for this rule:

   - For Type, select All ICMP – IPv4.

   - For Source, enter **10.0.0.0/16**.

   - For Description, enter **Enable Internet bound PING requests from VPC instances**.

8. Click Create Security Group.

9. Search Services for **EC2**.

10. Select Instances.

11. Paste the Public subnet ID into the filter box.

    Two results are displayed. The result with an empty name is your NAT instance.

12. To edit the name of the NAT instance, hover over the name field and click the pencil icon.

13. Enter the name **devassoc-nat** and press Enter.

14. Modify the security groups for devassoc-nat to include the nat-sg group as follows:

    - Select the devassoc-nat instance and click Actions.

    - Select Security ≻ Change Security Groups.

    - Select nat-sg. You can clear the default.

    - Click Assign Security Group.

Launching an Amazon EC2 Instance into the Private Subnet

In this exercise, you'll launch an Amazon EC2 instance into the private subnet and then verify that the security group allows HTTP from anywhere. Because this instance is in the private subnet, it does not have a public IP address. Even though the instance can make outbound requests to the Internet through the NAT instance, it is not reachable for inbound connections from the Internet.

1. Search the Services menu for EC2.

2. Select Launch Instance.

3. Name your instance `private-instance`.

4. Under Application and OS Images, select Amazon Linux.

5. Under Instance Type, select t2.micro.

6. Under Key Pair, select `devassoc`.

7. In the Network Settings section, click Edit and then do the following:

- Select VPC ➢ `devassoc-vpc`.

- Select Subnet and the *private* subnet you noted in your text file.

- Select Auto-assign Public IP ➢ Enable.

- Select IAM Role ➢ `devassoc-webserver`.

- Under Firewall (Security Groups), click Create Security Group.

- For Security Group Name, enter **open-http-ssh**.

- For Description, enter **HTTP and SSH from Anywhere**.

8. For the SSH rule, select Source ➢ Anywhere.

9. Click Add Rule and then configure the second rule:

- For Type, select HTTP.

- For Source, select Anywhere.

10. Open Advanced Details and under Instance Profile, choose `devassoc-webserver`.

11. Still under Advanced Details, scroll down to User Data and then paste the code files from the book page at `https://www.wiley.com/en-us/AWS+Certified+ Developer+Official+Study+Guide%3A+Associate+%28DVA+C01%29+Exam- p-9781119508199`. Click Downloads to access the online materials for Chapter 2. Then, from these files, select Choose File ➢ `chapter-02/server-polly.txt`.

12. Click Launch Instance.

13. To find your instance, click the instance ID shown on the Success page.

14. Copy the Private IP of the instance to the text document.

Notice that the instance has no public IP address.

EXERCISE 2.7

Making Requests to a Private Instance

In this exercise, you will explore connectivity to the private instance.

1. From your web browser, navigate to the private IP of the instance. Though the security group is open to requests from anywhere, this will fail because the private IP address is not routable over the Internet.

2. Select Services ➤ EC2.

3. From the list of instances, select webserver.

4. Click Connect and then follow the directions to establish an SSH connection.

5. From within the SSH session, make an HTTP request to the private server with curl. Replace the variable *private-ip-address* with the **private-instance address** that you copied earlier.

   curl *private-ip-address*

6. Download the MP3 audio from the private-instance to webserver using curl as follows:

   curl private-ip-address/instance.mp3 --output instance.mp3

7. Make the file available for download from webserver:

   sudo cp instance.mp3 /var/www/html/instance.mp3

8. In your web browser, enter the following address. Replace *public-ip-of-webserver* with the public IPv4 address of webserver, and listen to the MP3.

   http://*public-ip-of-webserver*/instance.mp3

Though the private web server is not reachable from the Internet, you have confirmed that it is reachable to other instances within the same Amazon VPC. As part of the bootstrapping, the private instance made AWS API calls, which require the ability to make both web requests via the NAT gateway and credentials from an IAM role. You have confirmed that these requests succeeded by downloading the resulting MP3 file from private-instance and placing it on webserver.

EXERCISE 2.8

Performing Partial Cleanup

In this exercise, you will clean up unused instances and keep this Amazon VPC for future use. This partial cleanup reduces costs while providing an environment to complete future exercises. After partial cleanup, you may incur charges related to the Elastic IP address that was allocated for devassoc-nat but is not in use while that instance is stopped.

Complete the following tasks as part of the cleanup:

> `webserver:` Terminate.
>
> `private-instance:` Terminate.
>
> `devassoc-nat:` Stop. You must start this instance again before completing any exercises that require Amazon EC2 to launch or interact with instances in the private subnet.

1. Navigate to Services ➤ EC2.

2. To view your Amazon EC2 instances, select Instances. Clear any filters if they are present.

3. Select `webserver` and `private-instance`.

4. Choose Instance State ➤ Terminate.

5. Clear `public-webserver` and `private-webserver`.

6. Select `devassoc-nat`.

7. Choose Instance State ➤ Stop.

EXERCISE 2.9

(Optional) Complete Cleanup

Note: If you plan to perform future exercises in this guide, this exercise is optional.

In this exercise, you will remove all of the EC2 and VPC resources that remain after Exercise 2.8.

1. Navigate to the Amazon EC2 console, and view the list of running instances.

2. Select `devassoc-nat`.

3. Choose Instance State ➤ Terminate.

4. Confirm by clicking Terminate.

5. To view the Amazon VPC dashboard, select Services ➤ VPC.

6. Navigate to the Elastic IPs list.

7. Select any Elastic IPs that are *not associated with an instance.*

8. To release the Elastic IPs, select Actions, then Release Elastic IP Addresses.

9. Select Release.

EXERCISE 2.9 *(continued)*

10. Select Your VPCs.

11. Select devassoc.

12. Choose Actions ➢ Delete VPC.

13. Click Delete VPC.

If the Amazon VPC deletion fails, wait up to 30 minutes after deleting the Amazon EC2 instances and then try again.

Review Questions

1. When you launch an Amazon Elastic Compute Cloud (Amazon EC2) instance, which of the following is the most specific type of AWS entity in which you can place it?

   A. Region

   B. Availability zone

   C. Edge location

   D. Data center

2. You have saved SSH connection information for an Amazon Elastic Compute Cloud (Amazon EC2) instance that you launched in a public subnet. You previously stopped the instance the last time you used it. Now that you have started the instance, you are unable to connect to the instance using the saved information. Which of the following could be the cause?

   A. Your SSH key pair has automatically expired.

   B. The public IP of the instance has changed.

   C. The security group rules have expired.

   D. SSH is enabled only for the first boot of an Amazon EC2 instance.

3. You are working from a new location today. You are unable to initiate a Remote Desktop Protocol (RDP) to your Windows instance, which is located in a public subnet. What could be the cause?

   A. Your new IP address may not match the inbound security group rules.

   B. Your new IP address may not match the outbound security group rules.

   C. RDP is not available for Windows instances, only SSH.

   D. RDP is enabled only for the first 24 hours of your instance runtime.

4. You have a backend Amazon EC2 instance providing a web service API to your web server instances. Your web servers are in a public subnet. You would like to block inbound requests from the Internet to your backend instance but still allow that backend instance to make API requests over the public Internet. What steps must you take? (Choose two.)

   A. Launch the backend instance in a private subnet and rely on a NAT gateway in a public subnet to forward outbound Internet requests.

   B. Configure the security group for the backend instance to explicitly deny inbound requests from the Internet.

   C. Configure the network access control list (network ACL) for the public subnet to explicitly deny inbound web requests from the Internet.

   D. Modify the inbound security group rules for the backend instance to allow only inbound requests from your web servers.

5. You have launched an Amazon EC2 instance and loaded your application code on it. You have now discovered that the instance is missing applications on which your code depends. How can you resolve this issue?

    A. Modify the instance profile to include the software dependencies.

    B. Create an AWS Identity and Access Management (IAM) user, and sign in to the instance to install the dependencies.

    C. Sign in to the instance as the default user, and install any additional dependencies that you need.

    D. File an AWS Support ticket, and request to install the software on your instance.

6. How can code running on an instance automatically discover its public IP address?

    A. The public IP address is presented to the OS on the instance automatically. No extra steps are required.

    B. The instance can query another Amazon EC2 instance in the same Amazon VPC.

    C. You must use a third-party service to look up the public IP.

    D. The instance can make an HTTP query to the Amazon EC2 metadata service at 169.254.169.254.

7. How can you customize the software of your EC2 instance beyond what the Amazon Machine Image (AMI) provides?

    A. Provide a user data attribute at launch that contains a script or directives to install additional packages.

    B. Additional packages are installed automatically by placing them in a special Amazon Simple Storage Service (Amazon S3) bucket in your account.

    C. You do not have permissions to install new software on Amazon EC2 aside from what is in the AMI.

    D. Unlock the instance using the AWS Key Management Service (AWS KMS) and then sign in to install new packages.

8. You have a process running on an EC2 instance that exceeds the 2 GB of RAM allocated to the instance. This is causing the process to run slowly. How can you resolve the issue?

    A. Stop the instance, change the instance type to one with more RAM, and then start the instance.

    B. Modify the RAM allocation for the instance while it is running.

    C. Take a snapshot of the data and then launch a new instance. You cannot change the RAM allocation.

    D. Send an email to AWS Support to install additional RAM on the server.

9. You have launched an EC2 Windows instance, and you would like to connect to it using the Remote Desktop Protocol. The instance is in a public subnet and has a public IP address. How do you find the password to the Administrator account?

   A. Retrieve the encrypted administrator password from the AWS Management Console, then decrypt it using the private key of the EC2 key pair associated with the instance at launch.

   B. Use the password that you provided when you launched the instance.

   C. Create a new AWS Identity and Access Management (IAM) role, and use the password for that role.

   D. Create an IAM user, and use the password for that user.

10. What steps must you take to ensure that an Amazon EC2 instance can receive web requests from customers on the Internet? (Choose three.)

    A. Assign a public IP address to the instance.

    B. Launch the instance in a subnet where the route table routes Internet-bound traffic to an Internet gateway.

    C. Launch the instance in a subnet where the route table routes Internet-bound traffic to a NAT gateway.

    D. Set the outbound rules for the security group to allow HTTP and HTTPS traffic.

    E. Set the inbound rules for the security group to allow HTTP and HTTPS traffic.

11. Which of the following are true about Amazon Machine Images (AMIs)? (Choose two.)

    A. AMI can be used to launch one or multiple Amazon EC2 instances.

    B. AMI is automatically available in all AWS regions.

    C. All AMIs are created and maintained by AWS.

    D. AMIs are available for both Windows and Linux instances.

12. Which of the following are true about EC2 instance types? (Choose two.)

    A. All Amazon EC2 instance types include instance store for ephemeral storage.

    B. All Amazon EC2 instance types can use EBS volumes for persistent storage.

    C. Amazon EC2 instances cannot be resized once launched.

    D. Some Amazon EC2 instances may have access to GPUs or other hardware accelerators.

13. Which of the following actions are valid based on the Amazon Elastic Compute Cloud (Amazon EC2) instance life cycle? (Choose two.)

    A. Starting a previously terminated instance

    B. Starting a previously stopped instance

    C. Rebooting a stopped instance

    D. Stopping a running instance

14. You have a development EC2 instance where you have installed Apache Web Server and MySQL. How do you verify that the web server application can communicate with the database given that they are both running on the same instance?

    A. Modify the security group for the instance.

    B. Assign the instance a public IP address.

    C. Modify the network access control list (network ACL) for the instance.

    D. No extra configuration is required.

15. What type of route must exist in the associated route table for a subnet to be a public subnet?

    A. A route to a VPN gateway

    B. Only the local route is required

    C. A route to an Internet gateway

    D. A route to a NAT gateway or NAT instance

    E. A route to an Amazon VPC endpoint

16. What type of route must exist in the associated route table for a subnet to be a private subnet that allows outbound Internet access?

    A. A route to a VPN gateway

    B. Only the local route is required

    C. A route to an Internet gateway

    D. A route to a NAT gateway or NAT instance

    E. A route to an Amazon Virtual Private Cloud (Amazon VPC) endpoint

17. Which feature of Amazon Virtual Private Cloud (VPC) enables you to see which network requests are being accepted or rejected in your VPC?

    A. Internet gateway

    B. NAT gateway

    C. Route table

    D. Amazon VPC Flow Log

18. Which AWS service enables you to track the CPU utilization of an Amazon EC2 instance?

    A. AWS Config

    B. AWS Lambda

    C. Amazon CloudWatch

    D. Amazon Virtual Private Cloud (Amazon VPC)

19. What happens to the data stored on an EBS volume when you stop an EC2 instance that is attached to it?

A. The data is moved to Amazon Simple Storage Service (Amazon S3).

B. The data persists in the EBS volume.

C. The volume is deleted.

D. An EBS-backed instance cannot be stopped.

20. Which programming language can you use to write the code that runs on an Amazon EC2 instance?

A. C++

B. Java

C. Ruby

D. JavaScript

E. Python

F. All of the above

21. You have launched an EC2 instance in a public subnet. The instance has a public IP address, and you have confirmed that the Apache web server is running. However, your Internet users are unable to make web requests to the instance. How can you resolve the issue? (Choose two.)

A. Modify the security group to allow outbound traffic on port 80 to anywhere.

B. Modify the security group for the web server to allow inbound traffic port 80 from anywhere.

C. Modify the security group for the web server to allow inbound traffic on port 443 from anywhere.

D. Modify the security group to allow outbound traffic from port 443 to anywhere.

22. Which of the following are the customer's responsibility concerning EC2 instances? (Choose two.)

A. Decommissioning storage hardware

B. Patching the guest operating system

C. Securing physical access to the host machine

D. Managing the sign-in accounts and credentials on the guest operating system

E. Maintaining the software that runs on the underlying host machine

AWS Data Storage

**THE AWS CERTIFIED DEVELOPER –
ASSOCIATE EXAM TOPICS COVERED IN
THIS CHAPTER MAY INCLUDE, BUT ARE
NOT LIMITED TO, THE FOLLOWING:**

✓ **Domain 1: Development with AWS Services**

- Task Statement 1: Develop code for applications
  hosted on AWS

- Task Statement 3: Use data stores in application development

✓ **Domain 2: Security**

- Task Statement 1: Implement authentication and/or
  authorization for applications and AWS services

- Task Statement 2: Implement encryption by using AWS
  services

- Task Statement 3: Manage sensitive data in application code

✓ **Domain 4: Troubleshooting and Optimization**

- Task Statement 3: Optimize applications by using AWS
  services and features

Cloud storage is a critical component of cloud computing. After all, much of the power of cloud computing lies in running your compute as close as possible to your storage. In this chapter, we will walk through the vast array of storage services offered by AWS.

The Internet era poses new challenges for data storage and processing, as the scale and velocity of data creation grows ever higher. Out of the need to manage new data storage, new types of data stores arose—complex, distributed systems optimized for particular types of tasks at particular scales. Because no single data store is ideal for all workloads, you'll need to consider each individual workload or component within your system and choose a data store that is right for it.

The AWS Cloud is a reliable, scalable, and secure location for your data, offering *object storage*, *file storage*, *block storage*, along with data transfer services, which we will explore in this chapter. Figure 3.1 shows three categories of storage services available on AWS.

FIGURE 3.1 The AWS storage portfolio

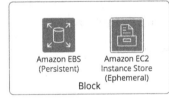
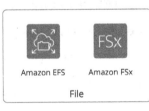

This chapter also covers how to provision storage using just-in-time purchasing, which helps you avoid overprovisioning and paying for unused storage into which you expect to grow eventually.

Storage Fundamentals

Before we explore the various AWS storage services, we should refresh you on a few storage fundamentals. As a developer, you are likely already familiar with block storage and the differences between hot and cold storage. Cloud storage introduces some new concepts, such as object storage, and we will compare these new concepts with the traditional storage concepts with which you are already familiar. If you have been working in the cloud already, these fundamentals are likely a refresher for you.

The goal of this chapter is to produce a mental model that will allow you, as a developer, to make the right decisions for choosing and implementing the best storage options for your applications.

The AWS storage portfolio starts with a few core data services, which include block, file, and object storage. For block storage, AWS has *Amazon Elastic Block Store* (Amazon EBS). For file storage, AWS has *Amazon Elastic File System* (Amazon EFS). For object storage, AWS has *Amazon Simple Storage Service* (Amazon S3) and Amazon Glacier. Figure 3.2 illustrates this set of storage building blocks.

FIGURE 3.2   A complete set of storage building blocks

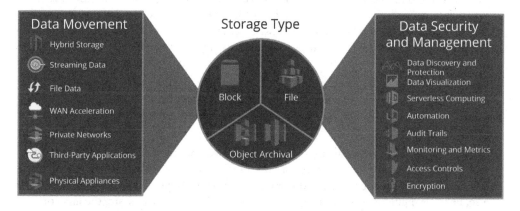

Data Dimensions

Before considering storage options, it's important to take time to evaluate your data and the way you use it. Understanding concepts like data velocity and temperature will help you make informed decisions about what type of storage best suits your data needs.

Think in terms of a data storage mechanism that is most suitable for a particular workload—not a single data store for the entire system. Choose the right tool for the job.

Velocity, Variety, and Volume

The first dimension to consider are the "three Vs" of data: velocity, variety, and volume.

Velocity   *Velocity* is the speed at which data is being read or written, measured in *reads per second* (RPS) or *writes per second* (WPS). The velocity can be based on batch processing, periodic, near-real-time, or real-time speeds.

Variety   *Variety* determines how structured the data is and how many different structures exist in the data. This can range from highly structured to loosely structured, unstructured, or *binary large object* (BLOB) data.

Highly structured data has a predefined schema, such as data stored in relational databases, which we will discuss in Chapter 4, "AWS Database Services." In highly structured data, each entity of the same type has the same number and type of attributes, and the domain of allowed values for an attribute can be further constrained. The advantage of highly structured data is its self-describing nature.

Loosely structured data has *entities*, which have attributes/fields. Aside from a field uniquely identifying an entity, however, the attributes are not required to be the same in every entity. This data is more difficult to analyze and process in an automated fashion, putting more of the burden of reasoning about the data on the consumer or application.

Unstructured data has no structure whatsoever. It has no entities or attributes. Unstructured data typically includes a wide variety of file types, such as text documents, emails, videos, audio recordings, social media posts, web pages, and sensor data, along with images and complex datasets that do not fit neatly into traditional relational databases. It can contain useful information, but it must be extracted by the consumer of the data.

BLOB data is useful as a whole, but there is often little benefit in trying to extract value from a piece or attribute of a BLOB. Therefore, the systems that store this data typically treat it as a black box and only need to be able to store and retrieve a BLOB in its entirety.

Volume   *Volume* is the total size of the dataset. Two common uses for data are developing valuable insights and storage for later use. When getting insights from data, having more data is often preferable to using better models. When keeping data for later use, be it for digital assets or backups, the more data that you can store, the less you need to guess what data to keep and what to throw away. These two uses prompt us to collect as much data as we can store, process, and afford to keep.

Typical metrics that measure the ability of a data store to support volume are maximum storage capacity and cost (such as $/GB).

Storage Temperature

Data temperature is another useful way of looking at data to determine the right storage for your application. It helps us understand how "lively" the data is: how much is being written or read and how soon it needs to be available.

Hot   *Hot data* is being worked on actively; that is, new ingests, updates, and transformations are actively contributing to it. Both reads and writes tend to be single-item. Items tend to be small (up to hundreds of kilobytes). Speed of access is essential. Hot data tends to be high-velocity and low-volume.

Warm   *Warm data* is still being actively accessed, but less frequently than hot data. Often, items can be as small as in hot workloads but are updated and read in sets. Speed of access, while important, is not as crucial as with hot data. Warm data is more balanced across the velocity and volume dimensions.

Cold   *Cold data* still needs to be accessed occasionally, but updates to this data are rare and so reads can tolerate higher latency. Items tend to be large (tens of hundreds of megabytes or gigabytes). Items are often written and read individually. High durability and low cost are essential. Cold data tends to be high-volume and low-velocity.

Frozen   *Frozen data* needs to be preserved for business continuity or for archival or regulatory reasons, but it is not being worked on actively. While new data is regularly added to this data store, existing data is never updated. Reads are extremely infrequent (known as "write once, read never") and can tolerate very high latency. Frozen data tends to be extremely high-volume and extremely low-velocity.

The same data can start as hot and gradually cool down. As it does, the tolerance of read latency increases, as does the total size of the dataset. Later in this chapter, we explore individual AWS Cloud services and discuss which services are optimized for the dimensions that we have discussed so far.

Data Value

Although we would like to extract useful information from all the data we collect, not all data is equally important to us. Some data must be preserved at all costs, and other data can be easily regenerated as needed or even lost without significant impact on the business. Depending on the value of data, we may be more or less willing to invest in additional durability.

 To optimize cost and/or performance further, segment data within each workload by value and temperature, and consider different data storage options for different segments.

Transient Data   *Transient data* is often short-lived. The loss of some subset of transient data does not significantly impact the system as a whole. Examples include click-stream or data on X (formerly Twitter). We often do not need high durability of this data because we expect it to be quickly consumed and transformed further, yielding higher-value data. If we lose a tweet or a few clicks, this is unlikely to affect our sentiment analysis or user behavior analysis.

Not all streaming data is transient, however. For example, for an *intrusion detection system* (IDS), every log entry may be a valuable part of investigating a potential breach.

Reproducible Data   *Reproducible data* contains a copy of useful information that is often created to improve performance or simplify consumption, such as adding more structure or altering a structure to match consumption patterns. Although the loss of some or all of this data may affect a system's performance or availability, this will not result in data loss because the data can be reproduced from other data sources.

Examples include data warehouse data, read replicas of OLTP (online transaction processing) systems, and many types of caches. For this data, we may invest a bit in durability to reduce the impact on system's performance and availability, but only to a point.

Authoritative Data   *Authoritative data* is the source of truth. Losing this data will have significant business impact because it will be difficult, or even impossible, to restore or replace it. For this data, we are willing to invest in additional durability. The greater the value of this data, the more durability we will want.

Critical/Regulated Data   *Critical or regulated data* is data that a business must retain at almost any cost. This data tends to be stored for long periods of time and needs to be protected from accidental and malicious changes—not just data loss or corruption. Therefore, in addition to durability, cost and security are equally important factors.

One Tool Does Not Fit All

Despite the many applications of a hammer, one cannot replace a screwdriver or pair of pliers. Likewise, there is no one-size-fits-all solution for data storage. Analyze your data and understand the dimensions that we have discussed. Once you have done that, then you can move on to reviewing the different storage options available on AWS to find the right tool to store and access your files.

For the exam, know the availability, level of durability, and cost factors for each storage option and how they compare.

Block, Object, and File Storage

There are three types of cloud storage: block, object, and file. Each offers its own unique advantages.

Block Storage

Some enterprise applications, like databases or *enterprise resource planning systems* (ERP systems), can require dedicated, low-latency storage for each host. This is analogous to *direct-attached storage* (DAS) or a *storage area network* (SAN). Block-based cloud storage solutions like Amazon EBS are provisioned with each Amazon Elastic Compute Cloud (Amazon EC2) instance and offer the ultra-low latency required for high-performance workloads.

Object Storage

Applications developed on the cloud often take advantage of object storage's vast scalability and metadata characteristics. Object storage solutions like Amazon S3 are ideal for building modern applications from scratch that require scale and flexibility and can also be used to import existing data stores for analytics, backup, or archive.

Cloud object storage makes it possible to store virtually limitless amounts of data in its native format.

File Storage

Many applications need to access shared files and require a file system. This type of storage is often supported with a *network-attached storage* (NAS) server. File storage solutions like Amazon EFS provide Network File System (NFS) or Common Internet File System (CIFS) interfaces and are ideal for use cases such as large content repositories, development environments, media stores, or user home directories.

AWS Shared Responsibility Model and Storage

It's important to understand how the AWS Shared Responsibility Model relates to cloud storage. While AWS is responsible for securing the storage services themselves, as a developer and customer, you are responsible for securing access to and using encryption on the artifacts you create or objects you store.

AWS makes this model simpler for you by allowing you to inherit certain compliance factors and controls, but you must still ensure that you are securing your data and files in the cloud. Always use the principle of least privilege as part of your responsibility for using AWS Cloud storage. For example, ensure that only those who need access to the file have access and ensure that read and write access are separated and controlled.

AWS Block Storage Services

Let's begin with the storage to which you are most likely already accustomed as a developer—block storage.

Amazon Elastic Block Store

Amazon EBS presents your data to your Amazon EC2 instance as a disk volume, providing the lowest-latency access to your data from single Amazon EC2 instances.

EBS provides durable and persistent block storage volumes for use with EC2 instances. Each EBS volume is automatically replicated within its availability zone to protect your information from component failure, offering high availability and durability. EBS volumes offer the consistent and low-latency performance needed to run your workloads. With EBS, you can scale your usage up or down within minutes, while paying only for what you provision.

Typical use cases for EBS include the following:

- Boot volumes on EC2 instances
- Relational and NoSQL databases

- Stream and log processing applications
- Data warehousing applications
- Big data analytics engines (like the Hadoop/HDFS [Hadoop Distributed File System] ecosystem and Amazon EMR clusters)

EBS is designed to achieve the following:

- Availability of 99.999 percent
- Durability of replication within a single availability zone
- *Annual failure rate* (AFR) of between 0.1 and 0.2 percent

EBS volumes are 20 times more reliable than typical commodity disk drives, which fail with an AFR of around 4 percent.

Amazon EBS Volumes

Amazon EBS volumes exist independently of the life cycle of EC2 instances. EBS volumes like physical hard drives; they can be attached to an instance, then later detached and reattached to another. You may choose to keep and persist the data on these volumes even if their original EC2 hosts are terminated.

EBS volumes are flexible. For current-generation volumes attached to current-generation instance types, you can dynamically increase size, modify provisioned input/output operations per second (IOPS) capacity, and change the volume type on live production volumes without service interruptions.

EBS provides the following volume types, which differ in performance characteristics and price so that you can tailor your storage performance and cost to the needs of your applications:

SSD-Backed Volumes   *Solid-state drive (SSD)–backed volumes* are optimized for transactional workloads involving frequent read/write operations with small I/O size, where the dominant performance attribute is IOPS.

SSDs are available in two volume types: *gp2*, and the newer, more flexible *gp3*. The biggest distinction is that gp3 decouples IOPS and throughput from volume size, whereas these performance features scale with size on gp2. The newer gp3 also provides better baseline performance. The older gp2 is still available mostly for backward-compatibility reasons; new AWS users should choose gp3 when selecting EBS storage types.

HDD-Backed Volumes   *Hard disk drive (HDD)–backed volumes* are standard magnetic drives optimized for large streaming workloads where throughput (measured in MiB/s) is a better performance measure than IOPS.

SSD vs. HDD Comparison

Table 3.1 and Table 3.2 show a comparison of EBS SSD- and HDD-backed volumes.

Table 3.3 shows the most common use cases for the different types of EBS volumes.

TABLE 3.1 SSD volume comparison

	SSD general purpose		SSD provisioned IOPS	
Storage type	gp3	gp2	io2	io1
Max volume size	16 TiB	64 TiB	64 TiB	16 TiB
Max IOPS/volume	16,000	16,000	256,000	64,000
Max throughput/volume	1,000 MiB/s	250 MiB/s	4,000 MiB/s	1,000 MiB/s

TABLE 3.2 HDD volume comparison

	HDD	
	Throughput optimized	Cold
Storage type	st1	sc1
Max volume size	125 TiB	125 TiB
Max IOPS/volume	500	250
Max throughput/volume	500 MiB/s	250 MiB/s

TABLE 3.3 EBS volume use cases

SSD		HDD	
General-purpose	**Provisioned IOPS**	**Throughput-optimized**	**Cold**
<ul><li>Recommended for most workloads</li><li>System boot volumes</li><li>Virtual desktops</li><li>Low-latency interactive</li><li>Apps</li><li>Development and test environments</li></ul>	<ul><li>I/O-intensive workloads</li><li>Relational DBs</li><li>NoSQL DBs</li></ul>	<ul><li>Streaming workloads requiring consistent, fast throughput at a low price</li><li>Big data</li><li>Data warehouses</li><li>Log processing</li><li>Cannot be a boot volume</li></ul>	<ul><li>Throughput-oriented storage for large volumes of data that is infrequently accessed</li><li>Scenarios where the lowest storage cost is important</li><li>Cannot be a boot volume</li></ul>

Elastic Volumes

Elastic Volumes is a feature of Amazon EBS that allows you to dynamically increase storage capacity, tune performance, and change the type of storage volumes live, without interruption to the systems using them. Elastic volumes let you start with the capacity and performance you need when first deploying your application, knowing that you can modify your volume configuration in the future, saving hours of planning and preventing overprovisioning.

Amazon EBS Snapshots

You can protect your data by creating point-in-time snapshots of EBS volumes, which are backed up to S3 for long-term durability. The volume does not need to be attached to a running instance to take a *snapshot*.

As you continue to write data to a volume, periodically create a snapshot of the volume to use as a baseline for new volumes. These snapshots can be used to create multiple new Amazon EBS volumes or move volumes across availability zones.

If you are taking snapshots at regular intervals, such as once per day, you may be concerned about the cost of the storage. Snapshots are incremental backups, meaning that only the blocks on the volume that have changed after your most recent snapshot are saved, making this a cost-effective way to back up your block data. For example, if you have a volume with 100 GiB of data, but only 5 GiB of data have changed since your last snapshot, only the 5 GiB of modified data is written to S3.

Knowing that snapshots are incremental, you may wonder whether it's safe to delete past snapshots, since they may depend on one another. Don't worry—AWS manages all this behind the scenes, so it's safe to treat each snapshot as if it is fully self-contained. AWS won't ever leave you with a partial snapshot.

Amazon EBS Encryption

All EBS volume types support encryption, allowing you to meet a wide range of data-at-rest encryption requirements for regulated/audited data and applications.

EBS encryption uses 256-bit *Advanced Encryption Standard* (AES-256) algorithms and the Amazon-managed key infrastructure *AWS Key Management Service* (AWS KMS). The encryption occurs on the server that hosts the EC2 instance, providing encryption of data in transit from the EC2 instance to EBS storage.

You can encrypt using an AWS KMS–generated key, or you can choose to select a *customer-managed key* (CMK) that you create separately using AWS KMS.

You can also encrypt your files prior to placing them on the volume. Snapshots of encrypted EBS volumes are automatically encrypted. EBS volumes that are restored from encrypted snapshots are also automatically encrypted.

Amazon EBS Performance

To achieve optimal performance from your EBS volumes in a variety of scenarios, use the following best practices:

Use EBS-optimized instances.   The dedicated network throughput that you get when you request EBS-optimized support will make volume performance more predictable and consistent, and your EBS volume network traffic will not have to contend with your other instance traffic because they are kept separate.

Understand how performance is calculated.   When you measure the performance of your EBS volumes, it is important to understand the units of measure involved and how performance is calculated.

Understand your workload.   There is a relationship between the maximum performance of your EBS volumes, the size and number of I/O operations, and the time it takes for each action to complete. Each of these factors affects the others, and different applications are more sensitive to one factor or another.

On a given volume configuration, certain I/O characteristics drive the performance behavior for your EBS volumes. *SSD-backed volumes*, *general-purpose SSD*, and *provisioned IOPS SSD* deliver consistent performance whether an I/O operation is random or sequential. *HDD-backed volumes*, *throughput-optimized HDD*, and *cold HDD* deliver optimal performance only when I/O operations are large and sequential.

To understand how SSD and HDD volumes will perform in your application, it is important to understand the connection between demand on the volume, the quantity of IOPS available to it, the time it takes for an I/O operation to complete, and the volume's throughput limits.

Understand volume initialization and fast snapshot restore.   New EBS volumes receive their maximum performance the moment they are available and do not require initialization (formerly known as *pre-warming*).

Storage blocks on volumes that were restored from snapshots, however, must be initialized (pulled down from S3 and written to the volume) before you can access the block. This preliminary action takes time and can cause a significant increase in the latency of an I/O operation the first time each block is accessed. Performance is restored after the data is accessed once.

For most applications, amortizing this cost over the lifetime of the volume is acceptable. For some applications, however, this performance hit is not acceptable. If that is the case, you may avoid a performance hit by accessing each block prior to putting the volume into production, perhaps with a script. This process is called *initialization*.

EBS can automate this process for you with an option called Fast Snapshot Restore (FSR). For a small per-snapshot, per-AZ cost, EBS can be configured to pre-initialize snapshots in availability zones of your choosing, allowing you to launch new volumes from backup with immediate maximum I/O performance.

Be aware of factors that can degrade HDD performance.   When you create a snapshot of a throughput-optimized HDD or cold HDD volume, performance may drop as far as the volume's baseline value while the snapshot is in progress. This behavior is specific only to these volume types.

Other factors that can limit performance include the following:

- Driving more throughput than the instance can support
- The performance penalty encountered when initializing volumes restored from non-FSR snapshots
- Excessive amounts of small, random I/O on the volume

Increase read-ahead for high-throughput, read-heavy workloads. Some workloads are read-heavy and access the block device through the operating system *page cache* (for example, from a file system). In this case, to achieve the maximum throughput, we recommend you configure the read-ahead setting to 1 MiB. This is a per-block-device setting that should be applied only to your HDD volumes.

Use RAID 0 to maximize utilization of instance resources. Some instance types can drive more I/O throughput than what you can provision for a single EBS volume. You can join multiple volumes of certain instance types together in a *RAID 0* configuration to use the available bandwidth for these instances.

Track performance with Amazon CloudWatch. *Amazon CloudWatch*, a monitoring and management service, provides performance metrics and status checks for your EBS volumes.

Instance Store

An *Amazon EC2 instance store* is *ephemeral* block-level storage using the storage of the actual disks physically attached to an EC2 instance's host computer (unlike EBS volumes, which are network-attached).

 If your data does not need to be resilient to *reboots*, *restarts*, or *autorecovery*, then your data may be a candidate for using an instance store, but you should exercise caution.

Instance Store Volumes

An *instance store* should not be used for persistent storage needs. It is ephemeral (short-lived) storage that does not persist if the instance fails or is terminated.

Because an instance store is on the host of your EC2 instance, it will provide the lowest-latency storage to your instance other than RAM. Instance store volumes can be used when incurring large amounts of I/O for your application at the lowest possible latency. You need to ensure that you have another source of truth for your data, however, and that the only copy is not placed on an instance store. For data that needs to be durable, we recommend using EBS volumes instead.

Not all instance types come with available instance store volume(s), and the size and type of volumes vary by instance type. When you launch an instance, the instance store is available at no additional cost, depending on the instance type. However, you must enable these volumes when you launch an EC2 instance, as you cannot add instance store volumes to an EC2 instance once it has been launched.

After you launch an instance, the instance store volumes are available to the instance, but you cannot access them until they are mounted. Refer to the AWS documentation for Amazon EBS to learn more about mounting these volumes on different operating systems.

Many customers will use a combination of instance stores and Amazon EBS volumes with their instances. For example, you may choose to place your scratch data, *tempdb*, or other temporary files on instance store while your root volume is on EBS.

 Do not use instance stores for any production data.

AWS Object Storage Services

Object storage is a modern data storage architecture that manages data as distinct units called objects. Unlike traditional file systems, which organize data in a hierarchy of folders and files, or block storage, which manages data in fixed-sized blocks, object storage treats each piece of data as a distinct element, annotated with metadata. These objects, stored in a flat address space, are identified by a unique identifier, allowing them to be retrieved efficiently. This architecture is highly scalable and ideal for handling large volumes of unstructured data, like photos, videos, and files, with a high degree of accessibility and durability.

Amazon Simple Storage Service (Amazon S3)

One of Amazon's first-ever cloud services, *Simple Storage Service* (S3) offers software developers a highly scalable, reliable, and low-latency object storage infrastructure at low cost. It is incredibly durable, offers nearly infinite storage, and is a critical component of a large variety of online companies' core infrastructure. AWS has seen enormous growth with S3, and AWS currently has customers who store exabytes of data on this ubiquitous service.

 Amazon S3 is featured in many of AWS's certifications because it is a core enabling service for many applications and use cases.

Before beginning to develop with S3, you must understand a few basic concepts.

Buckets

A *bucket* is a container for objects stored in S3. Every object is contained in a bucket.

 By default, you can only create up to 100 buckets per account, but this limit can be increased up to 1,000 buckets by requesting a quota increase.

Universal Namespace

A bucket name must be unique across all existing bucket names in S3 across all of AWS—not just within your account or within your chosen AWS region. You must comply with *Domain Name System* (DNS) naming conventions when choosing a bucket name.

The rules for DNS-compliant bucket names are as follows:

- Bucket names must be at least 3 and no more than 63 characters long.

- A bucket name can only contain lowercase letters, numbers, periods (.), and hyphens (-).

- Each label must start and end with a lowercase letter or number.

- Bucket names must not be formatted like *IP addresses* (for example, 192.168.5.4).

- Although they are allowed, AWS recommends that you do not use periods (.) in bucket names. When using virtual hosted-style buckets with *Secure Sockets Layer* (SSL), or when using S3 Transfer Acceleration, using dots can disrupt expected functionality.

S3 bucket names must be universally unique.

Table 3.4 shows examples of invalid bucket names.

TABLE 3.4   Invalid bucket names

Bucket name	Reason
.myawsbucket	The bucket name cannot start with a period (.).
myawsbucket.	The bucket name cannot end with a period (.).
my..examplebucket	There cannot be more than one period in a row.

The following code snippet is an example of creating a bucket using Java:

```
private static String bucketName     = "*** bucket name ***";
public static void main(String[] args) throws IOException {
AmazonS3 s3client = new AmazonS3Client(new ProfileCredentialsProvider());
s3client.setRegion(Region.getRegion(Regions.US_WEST_1));
if(!(s3client.doesBucketExist(bucketName))){
    // Note that CreateBucketRequest does not specify region. So bucket is
    // created in the region specified in the client.
     s3client.createBucket(new CreateBucketRequest(bucketName));
    }
```

```
// Get location.
String bucketLocation = s3client.getBucketLocation(new GetBucketLocationRequest
(bucketName));
System.out.println("bucket location = " + bucketLocation);
```

Versioning

Versioning lets you preserve, retrieve, and restore every version of every object stored in your S3 bucket, including recovering deleted objects. With versioning, you can easily recover from both unintended user actions and application failures.

Versioning is turned off by default. When you turn on versioning, S3 will create new versions of your object every time you overwrite an object.

In Figure 3.3, you can see that we have uploaded the same image multiple times, and all the previous versions of those files have been maintained.

FIGURE 3.3   Amazon S3 versioning

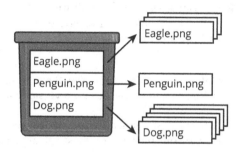

You can later retrieve any past version using GET on the object key name and the particular version number.

S3 versioning also protects against unintended deletes. If you issue a delete command against an object in a versioned bucket, AWS places a delete marker on that object, which means that if you perform a GET on it, you will receive an error as if the object does not exist. However, an administrator, or anyone else with the necessary permissions, can remove the delete marker and access the data.

You can also enable a feature of versioned buckets, MFA Delete, which adds additional protections against accidental deletion. MFA Delete is discussed later in this chapter.

Figure 3.4 illustrates a versioned bucket containing two versions of the same file. You can see that the bucket contains two objects with the same key, but different version IDs—photo.gif (version 111111) and photo.gif (version 121212). Users browsing this bucket would only see one object, but would have the ability to browse its past versions.

Later in this chapter, we will cover *life cycle policies*. You can use versioning in combination with life cycle policies to configure retention policies for objects, deleting past versions after a certain amount of time, and ensuring that versioning does not unnecessarily balloon your storage consumption in S3.

FIGURE 3.4   S3 object version IDs

Key = photo.gif
ID = 121212
Key = photo.gif
ID = 111111

Versioning Enabled

It is easy to set up a life cycle policy to control the amount of data that's being retained when you use versioning on a bucket.

You cannot disable versioning on a bucket. You may suspend versioning, but past object versions accumulated while versioning was enabled will still exist. If you need to fully discontinue versioning, you must first copy all of your objects to a new bucket that has versioning disabled, and then use that bucket going forward.

Once you enable versioning on a bucket, it can never return to an unversioned state. You can, however, suspend versioning on that bucket.

It is important to be aware of the cost implications of the bucket that is versioning-enabled. When calculating cost for your bucket, you must calculate as though every version is a completely separate object that takes up the same space as the object itself. As you can probably guess, this option might be cost prohibitive for things like large media files or when you'll be performing many updates on objects.

Region

S3 creates buckets in a region that you specify. Choose an *AWS region* that is geographically close to you or your users to optimize latency, minimize costs, or address regulatory requirements.

Objects belonging to a bucket that you create in a specific AWS region never leave that region unless you explicitly transfer them to another region.

Operations on Buckets

There are a number of different operations (API calls) that you can perform on S3 buckets. We will summarize a few of the most basic operations in this section. For more comprehensive information on all the different operations that you can perform, refer to the S3 API

Reference document available in the AWS Documentation repository at `https://docs` `.aws.amazon.com`. In this section, we show you how to create a bucket, list buckets, and delete a bucket.

Create a Bucket

This sample Python code shows how to create a bucket:

```python
import boto3

s3 = boto3.client('s3')
s3.create_bucket(Bucket='my-bucket')
```

List Buckets

This sample Python code demonstrates getting a list of all of the buckets in your account:

```python
import boto3

# Create an S3 client
s3 = boto3.client('s3')

# Call S3 to list current buckets
response = s3.list_buckets()

# Get a list of all bucket names from the response
buckets = [bucket['Name'] for bucket in response['Buckets']]

# Print out the bucket list
print("Bucket List: %s" % buckets)
```

Delete a Bucket

The following sample Java code shows you how to delete a bucket. Buckets must be empty before you can delete them, unless you use a `--force` parameter.

```java
import java.io.IOException;

import com.amazonaws.AmazonServiceException;
import com.amazonaws.SdkClientException;
import com.amazonaws.auth.profile.ProfileCredentialsProvider;
import com.amazonaws.services.s3.AmazonS3;
import com.amazonaws.services.s3.AmazonS3ClientBuilder;
import com.amazonaws.services.s3.model.DeleteObjectRequest;

public class DeleteObjectNonVersionedBucket {
```

```
public static void main(String[] args) throws IOException {
    String clientRegion = "*** Client region ***";
    String bucketName = "*** Bucket name ***";
    String keyName = "*** Key name ****";

    try {
        AmazonS3 s3Client = AmazonS3ClientBuilder.standard()
                .withCredentials(new ProfileCredentialsProvider())
                .withRegion(clientRegion)
                .build();

        s3Client.deleteObject(new DeleteObjectRequest(bucketName,
keyName));
    }
    catch(AmazonServiceException e) {
        // The call was transmitted successfully, but Amazon S3
couldn't process
        // it, so it returned an error response.
        e.printStackTrace();
    }
    catch(SdkClientException e) {
        // Amazon S3 couldn't be contacted for a response, or the client
        // couldn't parse the response from Amazon S3.
        e.printStackTrace();
    }
}
}
```

AWS Command-Line Interface

The following is a sample *AWS Command-Line Interface* (AWS CLI) command that will delete a bucket and will use the `--force` parameter to remove a nonempty bucket. This command deletes all objects first and then deletes the bucket—unless the objects have versions, in which case this method will fail.

```
$ aws s3 rb s3://bucket-name --force
```

Objects

You can store an unlimited number of objects within Amazon S3, but an object can only be between 1 byte to 5 TB in size. The largest object that can be uploaded in a single PUT is 5 GB (gigabytes). For objects larger than 100 MB, you should consider using multipart upload (discussed later in this chapter). For any objects larger than 5 GB, you must use multipart upload.

An object consists of the following facets:

Key   The *key* is the name that you assign to an object. Each key must be unique within a bucket. Although S3 buckets are a flat namespace, and no folder truly exists, AWS allows you to simulate folders by using forward-slashes in object names. For instance, two objects may have keys /photos/dog.jpeg and /photos/cat.jpg. While these are just string values and both objects reside at the "root" of the bucket, AWS visually interprets the common /photos part in both keys as a folder in the web console.

Version ID   Within a bucket, a key and *version ID* uniquely identify an object. If versioning is turned off, you have only a single version. If versioning is turned on, you may have multiple versions of a stored object.

Value   The *value* is the actual content that you are storing. An object value can be any sequence of bytes, and objects can range in size from 1 byte up to 5 TB.

Metadata   *Metadata* is a set of name-value pairs with which you can store information regarding the object. You can assign metadata, referred to as *user-defined metadata*, to your objects. S3 also assigns system metadata to these objects, which it uses for managing objects.

Access Control Information   You can control access to the objects you store in S3, which supports *resource-based access control*, such as ACLs, *bucket policies*, and *user-based access control*.

Object Tagging

Object tagging enables you to annotate your objects with metadata in the form of key-value pairs. Consider the following tagging examples.

Suppose an object contains *protected health information* (PHI) data. You can tag the object using the following key-value pair:

PHI=True

or

Classification=PHI

> **WARNING**   While it is acceptable to use tags to label objects containing confidential data (such as personally identifiable information [PII] or PHI), the tags themselves should not contain any confidential information.

Suppose that you store project files in your S3 bucket. You can tag these objects with a key called Project and a value, as shown here:

Project=Blue

You can add multiple tags to a single object, such as the following:

Project=SalesForecast2018
Classification=confidential

You can tag new objects when you upload them, or you can add them to existing objects. Note the following limitations when working with tagging:

- You can associate 10 tags with an object, and each tag associated with an object must have unique tag keys.

- A tag key can be up to 128 Unicode characters in length, and tag values can be up to 256 Unicode characters in length.

 Keys and values are case sensitive.
 In addition to data classification, tagging offers other benefits as follows:

- Object tags enable fine-grained access control of permissions. For example, you could grant an AWS Identity and Access Management (IAM) user permissions to read only objects with specific tags.

- Object tags enable fine-grained object life cycle management in which you can specify a tag-based filter, in addition to key name prefix, in a life cycle rule.

- When using Amazon S3 analytics, you can configure filters to group objects together for analysis by object tags, by key name prefix, or by both prefix and tags.

- You can also customize CloudWatch metrics to display information by specific tag filters. The following sections provide details.

Cross-Origin Resource Sharing

Cross-origin resource sharing (CORS) defines a way for client web applications that are loaded in one domain to interact with resources in a different domain. With CORS support in S3, you can build client-side web applications with S3 and selectively allow cross-origin access to your S3 resources while avoiding the need to use a proxy.

Cross-Origin Request Scenario

Suppose that you are hosting a website in an S3 bucket named *website* on S3. Your users load the website endpoint: `http://website.s3-website-us-east-1` `.amazonaws.com`.

Your website will use JavaScript on the web pages that are stored in this bucket to be able to make authenticated GET and PUT requests against the same bucket by using the Amazon S3 API endpoint for the bucket: `my-website-data.s3.amazonaws.com`.

A browser would normally block JavaScript from allowing those requests, but with CORS, you can configure your bucket to enable cross-origin requests explicitly from `website` `.s3-website-us-east-1.amazonaws.com`.

Suppose that you host a web font from your S3 bucket. Browsers require a CORS check (also referred as a *preflight check*) for loading web fonts, so you would configure the bucket that is hosting the web font to allow any origin to make these requests.

Operations on Objects

There are several operations (API calls) that you can perform on S3 buckets. We will summarize a few of the most basic operations in this section. For more comprehensive information on all the different operations that you can perform, refer to the S3 API Reference document available in the AWS Documentation at `https://docs.aws.amazon.com/s3`.

Write an Object

This sample Python code shows how to add an object to a bucket. Please note that the S3 client can be created without providing a secret access key or access key ID, as long as these values are defined in the environment. Otherwise, supply them as additional parameters to the client constructor on line 3.

```python
import boto3

# Create an S3 client
s3 = boto3.client('s3')

filename = 'file.txt'
bucket_name = 'my-bucket'

# Uploads the given file using a managed uploader, which will split up large
# files automatically and upload parts in parallel.
# The third parameter is the intended key name of the uploaded object
s3.upload_file(filename, bucket_name, filename)
```

Reading Objects

The following Python code example demonstrates downloading an object to a local file:

```python
import boto3
s3 = boto3.client('s3')
object_key = 'file.txt'
bucket_name = 'my-bucket'
local_filename = 'my_local_file.txt'

s3.download_file(bucket_name, object_key, local_filename)
```

Deleting Objects

The following Java sample demonstrates deleting an object by providing the bucket name and key name:

```java
AmazonS3 s3client = new AmazonS3Client(new ProfileCredentialsProvider());
s3client.deleteObject(new DeleteObjectRequest(bucketName, keyName));
```

This next Java sample demonstrates deleting a versioned object by providing a bucket name, object key, and a version ID:

```
AmazonS3 s3client = new AmazonS3Client(new ProfileCredentialsProvider());
s3client.deleteObject(new DeleteVersionRequest(bucketName, keyName,
versionId));
```

List Keys   The following Java code example lists object keys in a bucket:

```
private static String bucketName = "***bucket name***";
AmazonS3 s3client = new AmazonS3Client(new ProfileCredentialsProvider());
System.out.println("Listing objects");
        final ListObjectsV2Request req = new
ListObjectsV2Request().withBucketName(bucketName).withMaxKeys(2);
        ListObjectsV2Result result;
        do {
            result = s3client.listObjectsV2(req);

            for (S3ObjectSummary objectSummary :
                result.getObjectSummaries()) {
                System.out.println(" - " + objectSummary.getKey() + "  " +
                    "(size = " + objectSummary.getSize() +
                    ")");
                }
System.out.println("Next Continuation Token : " + result
.getNextContinuationToken());

req.setContinuationToken(result.getNextContinuationToken());
        } while(result.isTruncated() == true );
```

S3 Batch Operations

When you want to take action on a large number of objects in one or more buckets at one time, S3 offers an alternative to scripting your own batch updates using Python or Java. *S3 batch operations* allow you to provide a list of S3 objects on which to perform certain mass transformations, including updating or deleting object tags, restoring archived objects, placing object locks, invoking Lambda functions on each object, and more, all from an interactive wizard in the AWS console. Object lists may be provided in the form of a CSV file you create or a `manifest.json` file, which S3 can generate on a schedule using the Inventory Configurations feature on a bucket's Management tab.

This feature is found in the S3 management console, and it can save you plenty of time you'd otherwise spend developing custom code for common batch tasks.

Storage Classes

There are several storage classes from which to choose when using S3. Your choice will depend on your level of need for durability, availability, and performance for your application in addition to desired spend. While buckets can define a default storage class (or "tier"), this decision can be made on a per-object basis.

Amazon S3 Standard

Amazon S3 Standard offers high durability, high availability, and high-performance object storage for frequently accessed data. Because it delivers low latency and high throughput, S3 Standard is ideal for a wide variety of use cases, including the following:

- Cloud applications
- Dynamic websites
- Content distribution
- Mobile and gaming applications
- Big data analytics

S3 Standard is designed to achieve durability of 99.999999999 percent of objects (designed to sustain the loss of data in two facilities) and availability of 99.99 percent over a given year (which is backed by the Amazon S3 service level Agreement). This data is replicated into at least three availability zones by S3.

S3 Express One Zone

S3 Express One Zone offers the fastest, lowest-latency S3 storage experience possible at the expense of availability. Although your objects are still replicated to multiple drives, as this tier's name suggests, all those drives are located in the same availability zone, making them vulnerable to an AZ outage. This tier offers up to 10x faster reads and writes than S3 Standard.

Amazon S3 Standard-Infrequent Access (S3 Standard-IA)

Amazon S3 Standard-Infrequent Access (S3 Standard-IA) is an S3 storage class for data that is accessed less frequently but requires rapid access when needed. It offers the same high durability, throughput, and low latency of S3 Standard, but it has a lower per-gigabyte storage price and per-gigabyte retrieval fee.

The ideal use cases for using Standard-IA include the following:

- Long-term storage
- Backups
- Data stores for disaster recovery

Standard-IA is set at the object level and can exist in the same bucket as S3 Standard, allowing you to use life cycle policies to transition objects automatically between storage classes without any application changes.

Standard-IA is designed to achieve availability of 99.9 percent (but low retrieval time) and durability of 99.999999999 percent of objects over a given year (the same as S3 Standard).

Amazon S3 One Zone-Infrequent Access (S3 One Zone-IA)

Amazon S3 One Zone-Infrequent Access (S3 One Zone-IA) is similar to S3 Standard-IA. The difference is that the data is stored only in a single availability zone instead of a minimum of three availability zones. Because of this, storing data in S3 One Zone-IA costs 20 percent less than storing it in Standard-IA. Because of this approach, however, any data stored in this storage class will be permanently lost in the event of an availability zone destruction.

Reduced Redundancy Storage

Reduced Redundancy Storage (RRS) is an S3 storage option that Amazon created for customers to store noncritical, reproducible data at lower levels of redundancy than S3 Standard storage. However, over time, newer tiers of storage became available with better price-performance ratios and similar behavior characteristics, so this tier, while still in existence, is no longer recommended. For such use cases, use S3 Standard instead.

S3 Intelligent Tiering

For use cases with objects whose temperature changes over time, or for users who simply wish for S3 to manage the movement of data between tiers for them, there is S3 Intelligent Tiering. For a small fee, S3 will monitor the access patterns around your data and move objects into a series of storage classes unique to Intelligent Tiering: Frequent Access, Infrequent Access, and Archive Instant Access. These three tiers offer lower levels of durability and availability in exchange for lower costs.

Each of these Intelligent Tiering levels offers instantaneous, synchronous reads; however, it is possible to enable two additional Intelligent Tiering classes—Archive Access and Deep Archive Access— that provide asynchronous data access at even lower costs. Asynchronous access means that you cannot directly download an object; rather, you must put in a request for that object, and receive notification when it is available to download.

Amazon S3 Glacier

Amazon S3 Glacier and *S3 Glacier Deep Archive* are secure, durable, and extremely low-cost S3 storage classes for data archiving that offer the same high durability as Standard S3 at very low cost, making them ideal for infrequently accessed data and uses cases that can sustain longer retrieval times, such as archival data or regulated compliance storage.

Retrieval Times

The S3 Glacier tier provides flexible retrieval options that range from instantaneous to several hours, known as *Glacier Instant Retrieval* and *Glacier Flexible Retrieval*, respectively. Deep Archive is designed for data that is accessed even less often, providing the lowest cost storage option in AWS, with retrieval times typically within 12 hours. These options allow you to tailor your storage solution to meet specific recovery time objectives (RTO) for backups and disaster recovery plans.

Glacier as a Stand-alone Service

For years, Glacier was offered only as a stand-alone service, distinct from S3. Now, Glacier storage tiers are part of S3 itself and can be used like any other storage tier, as a direct destination for uploaded objects or the target of a life cycle policy.

However, Glacier as a separate service is still available and accessible via API, SDK, or CLI calls. Stand-alone Glacier is not deprecated as of this writing and retains some useful, unique features. In the stand-alone service, objects are stored in *vaults,* and vaults can have policies set that apply *vault locks.* Vault locks can enforce "write once" policies that ensure no one, even the policy writer, is able to alter archived data, which can be useful in compliance scenarios.

For most use cases, the S3 tiers of Glacier are sufficient and cost-effective, but for certain use cases, the original Glacier service may be ideal. Consult AWS documentation for details on pricing and on how to interact with this service.

WARNING   Amazon Glacier provides a management console for creating and deleting vaults. However, all other interactions with Glacier require that you use the AWS CLI or write code.

Restoring Objects from Glacier

Outside of Glacier Instant Retrieval, objects in the S3 Glacier storage classes are not immediately accessible once they have been moved to Glacier. Instead, you must initiate a restoration, then return to download the retrieved object when the restore is complete.

Glacier charges a retrieval fee for retrieving objects. When you restore an archive, you pay for both the archive and the restored copy. Because there is a storage cost for the copy, restore objects only for the duration that you need them.

Storage Class Comparison

Table 3.5 shows a comparison of selected S3 storage classes. The table's comparisons can help you make the right choice for your use case, in addition to understanding trade-offs when choosing a data store for an application.

TABLE 3.5   Amazon S3 storage class comparison

	S3 Standard	S3 Standard-IA	S3 Express One Zone	S3 One Zone-IA	Amazon S3 Glacier Flexible Retrieval
Designed for durability	99.999999999%*				
Designed for availability	99.99%	99.9%	99.5%	99.5%	99.99%
Availability SLAs	99.9%	99%	99.9%	99%	99.9%

TABLE 3.5   Amazon S3 storage class comparison *(continued)*

	S3 Standard	S3 Standard-IA	S3 Express One Zone	S3 One Zone-IA	Amazon S3 Glacier Flexible Retrieval
Availability zones	≥3		1		≥3
Minimum capacity charge per object	N/A		128KB*		N/A
Minimum storage duration charge	N/A	30 days	1 hour	30 days	90 days
Retrieval fee	N/A	Per GB retrieved*	N/A	Per GB retrieved*	
First byte latency	milliseconds		Single-digit milliseconds	millisec-onds	Minutes or hours*
Storage type	Object				
Life cycle transitions	Yes				

* Because Amazon S3 One Zone-IA stores data in a single AWS availability zone, data stored in this storage class will be lost in the event of availability zone destruction. Standard-IA has a minimum object size of 128 KB. Smaller objects will be charged for 128 KB of storage. Glacier allows you to select from multiple retrieval tiers based on your needs.

S3 Strong Consistency

Prior to 2020, Amazon S3 operated with an *eventual consistency* model, meaning that applications did not have any guarantee of being able to read a write immediately after making that write. Now, however, S3 provides *strong read-after-write consistency* for writes, as well as strong consistency for list operations without impacting performance or availability. This means that any changes to S3 objects are immediately reflected in subsequent reads, eliminating a source of potential complexity for applications and users.

Presigned URLs

A *presigned URL* is a way to grant temporary access to an object. Developers use presigned URLs to allow users to upload or download objects without granting them direct access to S3 or the account.

For example, if you need to send a document hosted in an S3 bucket to an external reviewer who is outside of your organization, and you do not want to grant them access using IAM to your bucket, you may generate a presigned URL for the object and send that to the user to download your file.

Another example is allowing someone external to your organization to upload a file. Maybe a media company is designing the graphics for the website you are developing. You can create a presigned URL for them to upload their artifacts directly to S3 without granting them access to your S3 bucket or account.

Anyone with valid security credentials can create a presigned URL. For you to upload an object successfully, however, the presigned URL must be created by someone who has permission to perform the operation upon which the presigned URL is based.

The following Java code example demonstrates generating a presigned URL:

```
AmazonS3 s3Client = new AmazonS3Client(new ProfileCredentialsProvider());

java.util.Date expiration = new java.util.Date();
long msec = expiration.getTime();
msec += 1000 * 60 * 60; // Add 1 hour.
expiration.setTime(msec);

GeneratePresignedUrlRequest = new GeneratePresignedUrlRequest(bucketName,
objectKey);
generatePresignedUrlRequest.setMethod(HttpMethod.PUT);
generatePresignedUrlRequest.setExpiration(expiration);

URL s = s3client.generatePresignedUrl(generatePresignedUrlRequest);

// Use the pre-signed URL to upload an object.
```

 Amazon S3 presigned URLs cannot be generated within the AWS Management Console, but they can be generated using the AWS CLI or AWS SDKs.

Encryption

As a best practice, all sensitive data stored in S3 should be encrypted both at rest and in transit.

You can protect *data in transit* by using S3 SSL API endpoints, which ensures that all data sent to and from S3 is encrypted using the *HTTPS protocol* while in transit.

For *data at rest* in S3, you can encrypt it using different options of *server-side encryption (SSE)*. Your objects in S3 are encrypted at the object level as they are written to disk in AWS data centers and then decrypted for you when you access the objects using AES-256. This process, called *seamless encryption*, is automatic and invisible to the user.

You can also use client-side encryption, with which you encrypt the objects before uploading to S3 and then decrypt them after you have downloaded them. Some customers, for some workloads, will use a combination of both server-side and client-side encryption for extra protection.

Server-Side Encryption (SSE)

You have three, mutually exclusive options for how you choose to manage your encryption keys when using SSE with Amazon S3.

SSE-S3 (Amazon S3-Managed Keys)   With this option, objects in your bucket are encrypted at rest using an AES-256 key owned and managed by S3.

SSE-C (Customer-Provided Keys)   With this option, you must provide your own AES-256 encryption key. Whenever you upload an object to S3, you also provide this key, which S3 uses to encrypt the file and subsequently deletes. When you retrieve this object from S3, you must provide the same encryption key in your request in order to decrypt the retrieved object.

SSE-KMS (AWS KMS-Managed Encryption Keys)   You can encrypt your data in S3 by defining an AWS KMS key within your account. Similar to SSE-S3, this encryption method is seamless; S3 automatically encrypts objects when they are uploaded and decrypts them when they are retrieved. However, this method does provide additional safeguards, as you may use IAM policies to control which users have access to the KMS key used for encryption.

Note also that unlike SSE-S3 and SSE-C, using SSE-KMS does incur a small additional charge associated with the creation and maintenance of the KMS key. Refer to the AWS KMS pricing page on the AWS website at `https://docs.aws.amazon.com/kms` for more information.

For maximum simplicity and ease of use, use SSE with AWS-managed keys (SSE-S3 or SSE-KMS). Also, know the difference between SSE-S3, SSE-KMS, and SSE-C for SSE.

Client-Side Encryption

Client-side encryption refers to encrypting your data before sending it to S3. You have two options for using data encryption keys.

Client-Side Key

The first option is to use a client-side key of your own. When uploading an object, you provide a client-side key to the Amazon S3 encryption client (for example,

`AmazonS3EncryptionClient` when using the AWS SDK for Java). The client uses this key only to encrypt the data encryption key (DEK), which it generates randomly and uploads alongside the object.

When downloading an object, the client first downloads the encrypted object from S3 along with its metadata, which contains the DEK. Then, the client uses the original key to decrypt the DEK and uses that key to decrypt the object.

The client-side key that you provide can be either a symmetric key or a public/private key pair. It's essential that you do not lose it; otherwise, neither you nor AWS will be able to decrypt your objects.

AWS KMS-Managed CMK

The second client-side encryption option is to use an AWS KMS-managed customer-managed key (CMK), so named because while you create and manage the key itself, it lives on infrastructure managed by AWS, and you use KMS console functionality to control access, rotation, and other key lifecycle events. It is a similar process to using a client-provided key, but the key is managed by and retrieved from KMS, subject to appropriate IAM policies.

Know the difference between CMK and client-side master keys for client-side encryption.

Access Control

By default, all Amazon S3 resources—buckets, objects, and related sub-resources, such as life cycle configuration and website configuration—are private. Only the creator, the *resource owner*, can access the resource. The resource owner can optionally grant access permissions to others by writing an access policy.

Access policies that you attach to your resources (buckets and objects) are referred to as *resource-based policies*. For example, bucket policies and ACLs are resource-based policies. You can also attach access policies to users in your account. These are called *user policies*. You can choose to use resource-based policies, user policies, or some combination of both to manage permissions to your S3 resources. The following sections provide general guidelines for managing permissions.

Using Bucket Policies and User Policies

Bucket policy and user policy are two of the access policy options available for you to grant permissions to your S3 resources. Both use a JSON-based access policy language, as do all AWS Cloud services that use policies.

A *bucket policy* is attached only to S3 buckets, and it specifies what actions are allowed or denied for whichever principals on the bucket to which the bucket policy is attached (for instance, allow user Alice to `PUT` but not `DELETE` objects in the bucket).

A *user policy* is attached to IAM users to perform or not perform actions on your AWS resources. For example, you may choose to grant an IAM user in your account access to one of your buckets and allow the user to add, update, and delete objects. You can grant them access with a user policy.

Both IAM policies and S3 bucket policies are used for access control, and they are both written in JSON using the AWS access policy language. However, unlike S3 bucket policies, IAM policies specify what actions are allowed or denied on what AWS resources (such as allow `ec2:TerminateInstance` on the EC2 instance with `instance_id=i8b3620ec`). You attach IAM policies to IAM users, groups, or roles, which are then subject to the permissions that you have defined. Instead of attaching policies to the users, groups, or roles, bucket policies are attached to a specific resource, such as an S3 bucket.

Managing Access with Access Control Lists

Access control lists (ACLs) are resource-based access policies that you can use to manage access to your buckets and objects, including granting basic read/write permissions to other accounts. Their capabilities are limited, especially compared to the breadth of control enabled by IAM policies, and are therefore not recommended over the use of IAM.

Defense in Depth—Amazon S3 Security

S3 provides comprehensive security and compliance capabilities that meet the most stringent regulatory requirements, and it gives you flexibility in the way that you manage data for cost optimization, access control, and compliance. With this flexibility, however, comes the responsibility of ensuring that your content is secure.

You can use an approach known as *defense in depth* in S3 to secure your data. This approach uses multiple layers of security to ensure redundancy if one of the multiple layers of security fails.

Figure 3.5 represents defense in depth visually. It contains several S3 objects (A) in a single S3 bucket (B). You can encrypt these objects on the server side or the client side, and you can also configure the bucket policy such that objects are accessible only through CloudFront, which you can accomplish through an origin access identity (C). You can then configure CloudFront to deliver content only over HTTPS in addition to using your own domain name (D).

To meet defense in depth requirements on S3:

- Data must be encrypted at rest and during transit.
- Data must be accessible only by a limited set of public IP addresses.
- Data must not be publicly accessible directly from an S3 URL.
- A domain name is required to consume the content.

You can apply policies to S3 buckets so that only users with appropriate permissions are allowed to access the buckets. Anonymous users and authenticated users without the appropriate permissions are prevented from accessing the buckets.

Hosting a Static Website

If your website contains static content and optionally client-side scripts, then you can host your *static website* directly in S3 without the use of web-hosting servers.

FIGURE 3.5   Defense in depth on S3

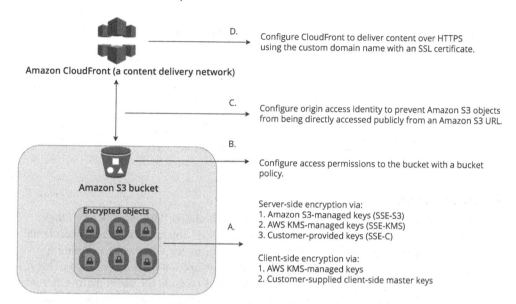

Amazon CloudFront (a content delivery network)

D. Configure CloudFront to deliver content over HTTPS using the custom domain name with an SSL certificate.

C. Configure origin access identity to prevent Amazon S3 objects from being directly accessed publicly from an Amazon S3 URL.

Amazon S3 bucket

Encrypted objects

B. Configure access permissions to the bucket with a bucket policy.

A.
Server-side encryption via:
1. Amazon S3-managed keys (SSE-S3)
2. AWS KMS-managed keys (SSE-KMS)
3. Customer-provided keys (SSE-C)

Client-side encryption via:
1. AWS KMS-managed keys
2. Customer-supplied client-side master keys

To host a static website, you configure an S3 bucket for website hosting, then upload your website content to the bucket. The website is then available at the AWS region–specific website endpoint of the bucket in one of the following formats:

```
<bucket-name>.s3-website-<AWS-region>.amazonaws.com
<bucket-name>.s3-website.<AWS-region>.amazonaws.com
```

Once your static hosting is established on S3, you may use *Amazon Route 53* to point your own domain to this content. Note that S3 does not support server-side scripting or dynamic content. We discuss other AWS options for that throughout this study guide.

    Static websites can be hosted in S3.

MFA Delete

MFA (Multifactor Authentication) Delete is another way to control deletes on your objects in S3. It does so by requiring a unique code from a token or an authentication device (virtual or hardware) in order to delete objects. Figure 3.6 shows what would be required for a user to execute a delete operation on an object when MFA Delete is enabled.

FIGURE 3.6   MFA Delete

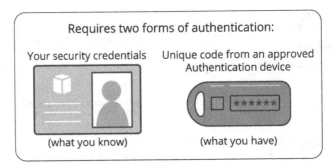

S3 Object Lock

For files that absolutely should not be deleted or even modified, AWS provides *S3 Object Lock*. This feature, configurable at the bucket or individual object level, prevents accidental deletion or overwriting of objects for a set period of time or for all time. By preventing writes as well as deletes, Object Lock provides greater protection than MFA Delete. This feature requires versioning to be enabled on the bucket. It is suitable for use in many different scenarios, including legal holds and compliance with regulatory frameworks like Financial Industry Regulatory Authority (FINRA).

Cross-Region Replication

Cross-region replication (CRR) is a bucket-level configuration that enables automatic, asynchronous copying of objects across buckets in different AWS regions. We refer to these buckets as the *source* bucket and the *destination* bucket. These buckets can be owned by different accounts.

To activate this feature, add a replication configuration to your source bucket to direct S3 to replicate objects according to the configuration. In the replication configuration, provide information, including the following:

- The destination bucket or buckets
- The objects that need to be replicated
- Optionally, the destination storage class (otherwise the source storage class will be used)

The replicas that are created in the destination bucket will have these same characteristics as the source objects:

- Key names
- Metadata
- Storage class (unless otherwise specified)
- Object ACL

All data is encrypted in transit across AWS regions using SSL.

Normally, after S3 replicates an object, the object will not be replicated again until the source object changes. For instance, deleting the replicated object in the destination bucket will not result in another replication. However, it is possible to configure replication bidirectionally between two buckets, so that changes in the destination end up reflected in the source, and vice versa.

> After S3 replicates an object using CRR, the object cannot be replicated again (such as to another destination bucket).

Requirements for CRR include the following:

- Versioning must be enabled for both the source and destination buckets.
- Source and destination buckets must be in different AWS regions.
- Amazon S3 must be granted appropriate permissions to replicate files.

> CRR requires that versioning be enabled for *both* source and destination buckets.

VPC Endpoints

Under normal circumstances, traffic to S3 from your VPC leaves your VPC to traverse the public network. Although this traffic is encrypted in transit via SSL, you may wish to ensure that traffic to S3 stays within your VPC. A *Virtual Private Cloud (VPC) endpoint* enables you to connect your VPC privately to Amazon S3 without requiring an Internet gateway, *network address translation (NAT)* device, *virtual private network (VPN)* connection, or *AWS Direct Connect* connection.

With VPC endpoints, EC2 instances running in private subnets of a VPC can have controlled access to Amazon S3 buckets, objects, and API functions that are in the same region as the VPC. You can use an S3 bucket policy to indicate which VPCs and which VPC endpoints have access to your S3 buckets.

Performance

This section offers a few considerations for optimizing performance when working with S3.

Amazon S3 Transfer Acceleration

Amazon S3 Transfer Acceleration optimizes throughput for transferring large objects across geographic distances by using CloudFront edge locations.

With Transfer Acceleration, instead of traversing large distances over the public Internet—say, when transferring across regions—your uploads can upload to the nearest CloudFront edge location before traveling across the AWS network backbone to your destination region. This option can give you a significant performance improvement and better network consistency than the public Internet.

S3 Transfer Acceleration is enabled by performing the following steps:

- Enable transfer acceleration on a bucket that conforms to DNS naming requirements and does not contain periods (.).

- Transfer data to and from the acceleration-enabled bucket by using one of the S3-accelerate endpoint domain names.

There is a small fee for using transfer acceleration. If your speed using transfer acceleration is no faster than it would have been going over the public Internet, however, there is no additional charge.

Multipart Uploads

When you upload a large object to S3 in a single-threaded manner, it can take a significant amount of time to complete. The multipart upload API enables you to upload large objects in part to speed up your upload by doing so in parallel.

To use multipart upload, you first break the object into smaller parts, parallelize the upload, and then submit a manifest file telling S3 that all of the multipart upload has been uploaded. S3 will then assemble all of those individual pieces to a single S3 object.

Multipart upload can be used for objects ranging from 5 MB to 5 TB in size.

Amazon CloudFront

Amazon CloudFront is a content delivery network (CDN) that can distribute S3 objects to nodes all over the world, providing cached content and giving your users lower latency and higher-throughput performance than they would experience interacting with S3 directly. When a user requests data (like images, videos, or files) that is stored in an S3 bucket, Cloud-Front retrieves the content from the bucket and delivers it through the nearest edge location, where it is then cached for an even faster read by the next consumer. This makes CloudFront an excellent service for distributing slowly changing content that needs to load quickly and consistently for all users.

Pricing

With S3, you pay only for what you use. There is no minimum fee, and there is no charge for data transfer into S3.

You pay for the following:

- The storage that you use

- The API calls that you make (PUT, COPY, POST, LIST, GET) whether through SDK, CLI, or API

- Data transfer out of S3

Data transfer out pricing is tiered, so the more you use, the lower your cost per gigabyte. Refer to the AWS website for the latest pricing.

S3 pricing differs from the pricing of Amazon EBS volumes in that if you create an Amazon EBS volume and store nothing on it, you are still paying for the storage space of the volume that you have allocated. With S3, you pay for the storage space that is being used—not allocated.

Object Life Cycle Management

S3's many storage classes offer you ways to maximize your price-to-performance ratio by moving objects to different classes as they traverse the data life cycle—moving from frequently accessed to rarely accessed, and finally a stage when archival storage makes sense. The Intelligent Tiering class can automate some of this for you, but for the most configurable and flexible experience, use object life cycle management. S3 object life cycle management lets you define a set of rules defining actions that S3 applies to a group of objects.

There are two types of actions:

Transition Actions *Transition actions* define when objects transition to another storage class. For example, you might choose to transition objects to the STANDARD_IA (Standard-IA) storage class 30 days after you created them or archive objects to a Glacier storage class one year after creating them.

Expiration Actions *Expiration actions* define when objects expire. S3 deletes expired objects on your behalf.

When Should You Use Life Cycle Configuration?

You should use life cycle configuration rules for objects that have a well-defined life cycle. The following are some examples:

- If you upload periodic logs to a bucket, your application might need them for a week or a month. After that, you may delete them.

- Some documents are frequently accessed for a limited period of time. After that, they are infrequently accessed. At some point, you might not need real-time access to them, but your organization or regulations might require you to archive them for a specific period. After that, you may delete them.

- You can upload some data to S3 primarily for archival purposes—for example, archiving digital media, financial, and healthcare records, raw genomics sequence data, long-term database backups, and data that must be retained for regulatory compliance.

With life cycle configuration rules, you can tell S3 to transition objects to less expensive storage classes or archive or delete them.

Configuring a Life Cycle

An S3 *life cycle configuration* comprises a set of rules with predefined actions that you need S3 to perform on objects during their lifetime. S3 provides a set of operations for managing life cycle configuration on a bucket, and it is stored by S3 as a *life cycle subresource* that is attached to your bucket.

You can configure the life cycle by using the S3 console, the AWS SDKs, or the REST API.

For example, you might specify rules like these that apply to objects with key name prefix logs/. and specifies the following actions:

- Two transition actions

- Transition objects to the Standard-Infrequent Access storage class 30 days after creation
- Transition objects to the S3 Glacier Flexible Retrieval storage class 90 days after creation

- One expiration action that directs S3 to delete objects a year after creation

Figure 3.7 shows an example of a set of S3 life cycle policies in place that move files automatically from one storage class to another as they age out at certain points in time.

FIGURE 3.7   Amazon S3 life cycle policies allow you to delete or move objects based on age.

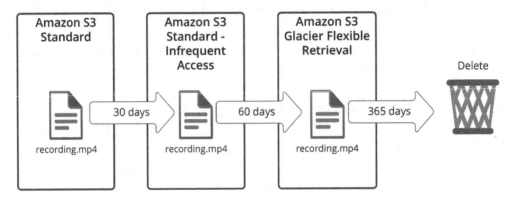

AWS File Storage Services

For file storage that can be shared by multiple users or systems, Amazon offers Elastic File System (EFS), along with managed file servers on Amazon FSx.

Amazon Elastic File System

Amazon Elastic File System (EFS) provides an NFS-based network file system that can be mounted by multiple client systems and can expand up to petabytes of capacity while providing low latency and high throughput. EFS volumes can only be used with non-Windows instances that support NFS volumes.

Consider using EFS instead of S3 or EBS if you have an application (EC2 or on premises) or a use case that requires a file system and any of the following:

- Mounts from multiple systems
- GB/s throughput

- Multi-AZ availability/durability
- Automatic scaling (growing/shrinking of storage)

Customers use EFS for the following use cases today:

- Web serving
- Database backups
- Container storage
- Home directories
- Content management
- Analytics
- Media and entertainment workflows
- Workflow management
- Shared state management

 WARNING   Amazon EFS is not supported on Windows instances.

Creating Your Amazon EFS File system

Two concepts are critical to understanding EFS: the *file system* and *mount targets*.

File System

The *Amazon EFS file system* is the primary resource in EFS, and it is where you store your files and directories.

Mount Target

To access your files ystem from within a VPC, create mount targets in the VPC. A *mount target* is a Network File System (NFS) endpoint within your VPC that includes an IP address and a DNS name, both of which you use in your mount command. A mount target is highly available, and it is illustrated in Figure 3.8.

EFS Storage Classes

Much like S3, EFS offers different tiers of storage that let users determine their optimal price-to-performance ratio.

Regional Storage Types

The first three storage tiers are classified as "Regional" because they are automatically replicated into multiple availability zones. This keeps your data safe from a temporary or permanent outage to an AZ.

FIGURE 3.8   Mount target

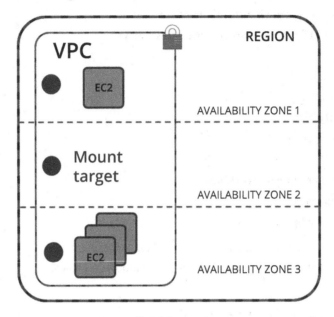

EFS Standard

EFS Standard is EFS's highest-throughput tier, offering sub-millisecond latency suitable for a variety of workloads.

EFS Standard – Infrequent Access

If your workload can sustain a little higher latency than EFS Standard, the EFS Standard-Infrequent Access tier will save you up to 95 percent over Standard, making it a very attractive choice for flexible use cases. Keep in mind, however, that AWS does charge a small per-GB fee for retrieval of data from this tier.

EFS Archive

For your least frequently accessed data (that still needs to be mounted via NFS on multiple machines), EFS Archive offers costs up to 50 percent less than even Infrequent Access tiers, at the expense of the highest latency of any tier. If your archival needs do not require synchronous accessibility, consider the Glacier tiers of S3 instead.

One Zone Storage Types

Much like S3, EFS offers "One Zone" variants on storage that limit replication to just one availability zone.

Even so, your data is replicated multiple times within that AZ, meaning that while your data may be vulnerable to an AZ outage, the high advertised durability and availability of EFS (99.9999999 percent and 99.99 percent, respectively) remains in effect.

Note that, as of this writing, the EFS Archive storage class is not available in a One Zone variant.

EFS One Zone

The standard EFS "One Zone" offering provides the same low latency of EFS Standard at a lower price.

EFS One Zone – Infrequent Access

This tier has the same limitations of both Standard-IA and One Zone storage classes, while offering a significant cost savings. Per-GB retrieval fees do apply.

Managing EFS Life Cycle Policies

Unlike S3, you do not choose EFS storage classes when creating new files. Rather, the storage class for each file is determined by life cycle policies.

When creating an EFS file system, you may establish life cycle rules that automatically transition files from Standard to IA and/or to Archive after a certain number of days idle. At the same time, you can configure EFS to move files back to EFS Standard when they are accessed again. These settings can be updated at any time.

EFS storage classes are largely transparent to the user. To understand more about how EFS is classifying your data, check out the storage class breakdown in AWS Cost Explorer.

Accessing an Amazon EFS File system

There are several different ways that you can access an EFS file system, including using EC2 and AWS Direct Connect.

Using Amazon Elastic Compute Cloud

To access a file system from an EC2 instance, you must mount the file system either by using the standard Linux mount command or the AWS EFS mount helper (a package preinstalled on Amazon Linux), as shown in Figure 3.9. The file system will then appear as a local set of directories and files. An NFS v4.1 client is standard on Amazon Linux AMI distributions.

In your command, specify the file system type (nfs4), the version (4.1), the file system DNS name or IP address, and the user's target directory.

A file system belongs to a region, and your EFS file system spans all availability zones in that region. Once you have mounted your file system, data can be accessed from any availability zone in the region within your VPC while maintaining full consistency. Figure 3.10 shows how you communicate with EC2 instances within a VPC.

Using AWS Direct Connect

You can also mount your on-premises servers to EFS in your VPC using AWS Direct Connect. With *AWS Direct Connect*, you can mount your on-premises servers to EFS using the same mount command used to mount in EC2. Figure 3.11 shows how to use Direct Connect with EFS.

FIGURE 3.9   EFS mounting options

Attach   ✕

Mount your Amazon EFS file system on a Linux instance. Learn more ☑

⦿ Mount via DNS	◯ Mount via IP

Using the EFS mount helper:

```
sudo mount -t efs -o tls fs-56338XXX:/ efs
```

Using the NFS client:

```
sudo mount -t nfs4 -o
nfsvers=4.1,rsize=1048576,wsize=1048576,hard,timeo=600,retrans=2,noresvport fs-
56338XXX.efs.us-east-1.amazonaws.com:/ efs
```

See our user guide for more information. Learn more ☑

Close

FIGURE 3.10   Using EFS

How does it all fit together?

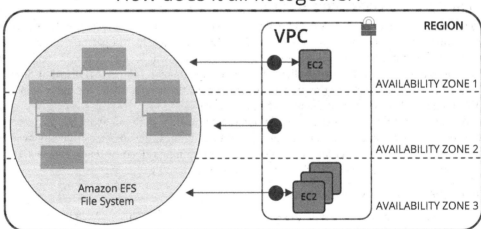

Customers can use EFS combined with Direct Connect for migration, bursting, or backup and disaster recovery.

FIGURE 3.11 Using Direct Connect with EFS

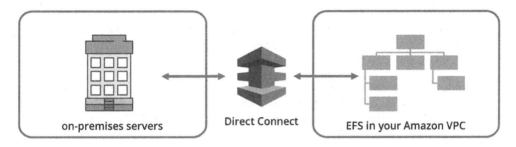

on-premises servers   Direct Connect   EFS in your Amazon VPC

Using *amazon-efs-utils*

For most Linux systems, Amazon makes available a utility called `amazon-efs-utils`. This package, which is preinstalled on Amazon Linux operating systems, provides an easy interface to perform the mounting steps just described. With `amazon-efs-utils` installed, your mount command can be as simple as the following:

```
sudo mount -t efs -o tls fs-my_file_system-number:/ efs
```

For details, click the Attach button in the AWS Management Console after creating a new EFS file system. You'll see instructions on how to use both traditional NFS mounting methods as well as `amazon-efs-utils`.

Syncing Files Using EFS File Sync

Now that you have a functioning EFS file system, you can use *EFS File Sync* to synchronize files from an existing file system to the cloud. EFS File Sync can synchronize your file data and file system metadata such as ownership, time stamps, and access permissions.

To do this, download and deploy a sync agent from the EFS console as either a *virtual machine* (VM) image or as an AMI.

Next, create a sync task and configure your source and destination file systems. Then start your task to begin syncing the files and monitor the progress of the file sync using CloudWatch.

Performance

AWS provides multiple configuration and provisioning options to tune EFS performance to your workload.

Performance Modes

EFS is designed for a wide spectrum of performance needs, including the following:

- High throughput and parallel I/O
- Low latency and serial I/O

To support those two sets of workloads, EFS offers two performance modes, as described here:

General Purpose (Default)   General purpose mode is the default mode, and it is used for latency-sensitive applications and general-purpose workloads, offering the lowest latencies for file operations.

Max I/O   If you are running large-scale and data-heavy applications, then choose the max I/O performance option, which provides you with a virtually unlimited ability to scale out throughput and IOPS, but with a trade-off of slightly higher latencies.

Throughput Modes

EFS also provides three modes that let users shape the throughput characteristics of the file system.

Elastic   Elastic throughput sees AWS automatically scaling throughput for you in response to observed usage of your EFS file system. Amazon recommends this mode when your average-to-peak throughput demands are less than 5 percent.

Provisioned   For spikier workloads whose average-to-peak is regularly higher than 5 percent, AWS allows users to pay for provisioned throughput, which guarantees a certain amount of throughput, paid in advance.

Bursting   Finally, bursting mode, similar to EC2's bursting performance modes, operates by giving you additional throughput just when you need it, based on a system of bursting credits that accumulate when your usage is below a certain base rate.

EFS comes with powerful, yet complex performance configuration options. To compare the fine details and determine the best modes to select for your workload, see the AWS Documentation on Amazon EFS Performance at `https://docs.aws.amazon.com/efs/latest/ug/performance.html`.

Security

You can implement security in multiple layers with EFS by controlling the following:

- Network traffic to and from file systems (mount targets) using the following:
  - VPC security groups
  - Network ACLs
- File and directory access by using POSIX permissions
- Administrative access (API access) to file systems by using IAM Amazon EFS supports:
  - Action-level permissions
  - Resource-level permissions

 Familiarize yourself with the EFS product, details, and FAQ pages. Some exam questions may be answered by components from those pages.

Amazon FSx

Amazon FSx is AWS's suite of managed file system services. With a few clicks, you can spin up highly available, scalable versions of several major file systems. As managed services, these file systems can be automatically provisioned, patched, and backed up. As with EFS, you never see or create instances; you simply request a new file system and start connecting. As of this writing, FSx provides the following file systems:

- NetApp ONTAP
- OpenZFS
- Windows File Server
- Lustre

FSx expands on the capabilities of EFS by providing file systems beyond NFS.

Amazon FSx for Windows File Server

While specially configured Windows clients are capable of connecting to EFS's NFS shares, it is not the default option, and may be incompatible with many Windows features or software. With FSx, Windows clients can connect with their native SMB protocol to the CIFS shares provided by FSx for Windows File Server, making it an ideal choice for Windows home directories and network file sharing in a Windows-based organization.

Amazon FSx for NetApp ONTAP

FSx for *NetApp ONTAP* provides access to the popular file system often used in enterprise settings due to its extensive configurability and unique multiprotocol support. NetApp ONTAP provides NFS, SMB, and iSCSI interfaces, as well as data deduplication and compression. It is an ideal choice for database storage, disaster recovery, and shared network storage.

Amazon FSx for Lustre

Lustre is a high-performance operating system optimized for compute-intensive workloads such as machine learning and media processing. It is often used by researchers that need extremely low latency and whose use cases require scaling to thousands of concurrent clients. With FSx, these users can spin up a file system suitable for high-performance computing (HPC) workloads that also integrate well with other AWS services.

Amazon FSx for OpenZFS

FSx for *OpenZFS* offers a managed version of the popular open source file system used in a variety of workloads. OpenZFS is designed for high reliability, scalability, and performance, and it has a number of advanced features, including data integrity checks, compressions, and copy-on-write. Of course, it's also an excellent choice for anyone already using OpenZFS and looking to migrate easily to the cloud.

Storage Comparisons

This section provides valuable charts that can serve as a quick reference if you are tasked with choosing a storage system for a particular project or application.

Use Case Comparison

Table 3.6 will help you understand the main properties and use cases for each of the cloud storage products on AWS.

TABLE 3.6   AWS Cloud storage products

If you need:	Consider using:
Persistent local storage for EC2, relational and NoSQL databases, data warehousing, enterprise applications, big data processing, or backup and recovery	Amazon EBS
A file system interface and file system access semantics to make data available to one or more EC2 instances for content serving, enterprise applications, media processing workflows, big data storage, or backup and recovery	Amazon EFS
A scalable, durable platform to make data accessible from any Internet location for user-generated content, active archive, serverless computing, big data storage, or backup and recovery	Amazon S3
Highly affordable, long-term storage that can replace tape for archive and regulatory compliance	Amazon S3 Glacier
A hybrid storage cloud augmenting your on-premises environment with AWS Cloud storage for bursting, tiering, or migration	AWS Storage Gateway
A portfolio of services to help simplify and accelerate moving data of all types and sizes into and out of the AWS Cloud	Cloud Data Migration Services
Home directories or network file sharing for a Windows-based office environment	Amazon FSx for Windows File System
High-performance, low latency computing for research clusters	Amazon FSx for Lustre
Backend storage for an enterprise database system	Amazon FSx for NetApp ONTAP

Storage Temperature Comparison

Table 3.7 shows a comparison of instance stores, EBS, S3, and S3 Glacier.

TABLE 3.7   Storage comparison

	Instance store	Amazon EBS	Amazon S3	Amazon S3 Glacier
Average latency	ms		ms, sec, min (~ size)	hrs
Data volume	4 GB to 48 TB	1 GiB to 1 TiB	No limit	
Item size	Block storage		5 TB max	40 TB max
Request rate	Very high		Low to very high (no limit)	Very low (no limit)
Cost/GB per month	Amazon EC2 instance cost	¢¢	¢	
Durability	Low	High	Very high	Very high
Temperature	Hot <--> Cold			

Understanding Table 3.7 will help you make decisions about latency, size, durability, and cost when selecting AWS storage services.

Comparison of S3, EBS, and EFS

Table 3.8 is Amazon's highest-performing file, object, and block cloud storage offerings. This comparison will also be helpful when you're choosing the right data store for the applications that you are developing.

TABLE 3.8 Storage service comparison (EFS, S3, and EBS)

		File Amazon EFS	Object Amazon S3	Block Amazon EBS
Performance	Per-operation latency	Low, consistent	Low, for mixed request types, and integration with CloudFront	Low, consistent
	Throughput scale	Multiple GB per second		Single GB per second
Characteristics	Data Availability/ Durability	Stored redundantly across multiple AZs		Stored redundantly in a single AZ
	Access	One to thousands of EC2 instances or on-premises servers, from multiple AZs, concurrently	One to millions of connections over the web	Single EC2 instance in a single AZ
	Use Cases	Web serving and content management, enterprise applications, media and entertainment, home directories, database backups, developer tools, container storage, big data analytics	Web serving and content management, media and entertainment, backups, big data analytics, data lake	Boot volumes, transactional and NoSQL databases, data warehousing, ETL

Summary

AWS offers a robust, scalable, and highly secure environment for data storage. Essential for cloud computing, cloud storage serves as a repository for the data used by your applications and analytics. This includes big data analytics, data warehousing, Internet of Things projects, and databases, as well as backup and archival solutions. Compared to traditional on-premises storage solutions, cloud storage provides enhanced reliability, scalability, and security, making it a preferred choice for modern data storage needs.

AWS offers a complete range of cloud storage services to support both application and archival compliance requirements. You may choose from object, file, and block storage services and cloud data migration options to start designing the foundation of your cloud IT environment.

EBS provides highly available, consistent, low-latency, persistent local block storage for EC2. It helps you to tune applications with the right storage capacity, performance, and cost.

EFS provides a simple, scalable file system interface and file system access semantics to make data available to one or more EC2 instances via NFS. EFS grows and shrinks capacity automatically and provides high throughput with consistent low latencies. EFS is designed for high availability and durability, and it provides performance for a broad spectrum of workloads and applications.

S3 is a form of object storage that provides a highly scalable, durable platform, allowing you to store and access any type of data with 99.999999999 percent durability. S3 can store tens of trillions of objects, each of which can exist on one of S3's several storage classes that offer varying configurations of price and performance.

S3 Glacier provides extremely low-cost and highly durable object storage for long-term backup and archiving of any type of data. Glacier is a solution for customers who want low-cost storage for infrequently accessed data. It can also replace tape storage and assist with compliance in highly regulated organizations.

Understanding when to use the right tool for your data storage needs is a key component of AWS exams, including data dimension, block versus object versus file storage, data structure, and storage temperature. Be ready to compare and contrast the durability, availability, latency, means of access, and cost of different storage options for a given use case.

Exam Essentials

Know the different data dimensions.   Consider the different data dimensions when choosing which storage option and storage class will be most appropriate for your data. This includes velocity, variety, volume, storage temperature (hot, warm, cold, frozen), data value, transient, reproducible, authoritative, and critical/regulated data.

Know the difference between block, object, and file storage.   Block storage is commonly dedicated, low-latency storage for each host and is provisioned with each instance. Object storage is developed for the cloud, has vast scalability, is accessed over the web, and is not directly attached to an instance. File storage enables accessing shared files as a file system.

Know the AWS Shared Responsibility Model and how it applies to storage.   AWS is responsible for securing the storage services. You are responsible for securing access to the artifacts that you create or objects that you store.

Know what Amazon EBS is and for what it is commonly used.   EBS provides persistent block storage volumes for use with EC2 instances. It is designed for application workloads that benefit from fine-tuning for performance, cost, and capacity. Typical use cases include big data analytics engines, relational and NoSQL databases, stream and log processing applications, and data warehousing applications. EBS volumes also serve as root volumes for EC2 instances.

Know what an Amazon EC2 instance store is and for what it is commonly used.   An instance store provides temporary block-level storage for your instance. It is located on disks that are physically attached to the host computer. An instance store is ideal for temporary storage of information that changes frequently, such as buffers, caches, scratch data, and other temporary content, or for data that is replicated across a fleet of instances, such as a load-balanced pool of web servers. In some cases, you can use instance store–backed volumes. Do not use an instance store (also known as ephemeral storage) for either production data or data that must be kept durable.

Know what S3 is and for what it is commonly used.   S3 is object storage built to store and retrieve any amount of data from anywhere. It is secure, durable, and highly scalable cloud storage using a simple web services interface. S3 is commonly used for backup and archiving, content storage and distribution, big data analytics, static website hosting, cloud-native application hosting, disaster recovery, and as a data lake.

Know the basic concepts of S3.   S3 stores data as objects within resources called *buckets*. You can store as many objects as desired within a bucket, and write, read, and delete objects in your bucket. Objects contain data and metadata and are identified by a user-defined key in a flat file structure. Interfaces to S3 include a native REST interface, SDKs for many languages, the AWS CLI, and the AWS Management Console.

Know how to create a bucket, how to upload, download, and delete objects, how to make objects public, and how to open an object URL.

Understand how security works in S3.   By default, new buckets are private and nothing is publicly accessible. When you add an object to a bucket, it is private by default.

Know how much data you can store in S3.   The total volume of data and number of objects that you can store in S3 are unlimited. Individual S3 objects can range in size from a minimum of 0 bytes to a maximum of 5 TB. The largest object that can be uploaded in a single PUT is 5 GB. For objects larger than 100 MB, consider using the multipart upload capability.

Know the S3 service limit for buckets per account.   One hundred buckets are allowed per account.

Understand the durability and availability of S3.   S3 standard storage is designed for 11 nines of durability and four nines of availability of objects over a given year. Other storage classes differ. The Reduced Redundancy Storage (RRS) storage class is less durable than Standard, and it is intended for noncritical, reproducible data.

Know the S3 storage classes and use cases for each.   S3 Standard is used to store general-purpose data that needs high durability, high performance, and low latency access. S3 Standard-IA is used for data that is less frequently accessed but that needs the same performance and availability when accessed. S3 One Zone-IA is similar to S3 Standard-IA, but it is stored only in a single availability zone, costing 20 percent less. However, data stored with S3 One Zone-IA will be permanently lost in the event of an availability zone destruction. S3 Express One Zone gives the lowest possible latency by trading a degree of availability. Amazon Glacier Flexible Retrieval is used to store rarely accessed archival data at an extremely low cost, when three- to five-hour retrieval time is acceptable under the standard retrieval option. Glacier Instant Retrieval allows immediate access for a higher cost.

Every object within a bucket can be designated to a different storage class.

Know how to enable static web hosting on S3.   The steps to enable static web hosting on S3 require you to do the following:

1. Create a bucket with the website hostname.

2. Upload your static content and make it public.

3. Enable static website hosting on the bucket.

4. Indicate the index and error page objects.

Know how to encrypt your data on Amazon S3.   For server-side encryption, use SSE-SE (S3-managed keys), SSE-C (customer-provided keys), and SSE-KMS (KMS-managed keys). For client-side encryption, choose from a client-side master key or an AWS KMS-managed customer-managed key.

Know how to protect your data on S3.   Know the different options for protecting your data in flight and in transit. Encrypt data in flight using HTTPS and at rest using server-side or client-side encryption. Enable versioning to keep multiple versions of an object in a bucket. Enable MFA Delete to protect against accidental deletion. Use ACLs, S3 bucket policies, and AWS IAM policies for access control. Use presigned URLs for time-limited download access. Use cross-region replication to replicate data to another region automatically.

Know how to use life cycle configuration rules.   Lifecycle rules can be used to manage your objects so that they are stored cost effectively throughout their life cycle. There are two types of actions. Transition actions define when an object transitions to another storage class. Expiration actions define when objects expire and will be deleted on your behalf.

Know what EFS is and for what it is commonly used.   EFS provides simple, scalable, elastic file storage for use with AWS Cloud services and on-premises resources. EFS is easy to use and offers a simple interface that allows you to create and configure file systems quickly and easily. EFS is built to scale elastically on demand without disrupting applications, growing and shrinking automatically as you add and remove files, so your applications have the storage that they need, when they need it. EFS is designed for high availability and durability. EFS can be mounted to multiple EC2 instances at the same time.

Know the basics of S3 Glacier.   S3 Glacier securely encrypts and stores data archives up to 40 terabytes in size. Retrieval can range from immediate to hours, depending on which tier you use, and incurs some cost. Pay attention to minimum storage duration to avoid early retrieval fees.

Know which storage option to choose based on storage temperature.   For hot to warm storage, use an instance store, EBS, or S3. For cold storage, choose S3 Glacier.

Know which storage option to choose based on latency.   Instance stores and EBS are designed for millisecond latency. S3 depends on size, anywhere from milliseconds to seconds to minutes. Glacier is minutes to hours depending on retrieval option.

Know which storage option to choose based on data volume.   Instance stores can be from 4 GB to 48 TB. EBS can be from 1 GiB to 64 TiB. S3 and Glacier have no limit.

Know which storage option to choose based on item size. Instance stores and EBS depend on the size of the block storage and operating system limits. S3 has a 5 TB max size per object, but objects may be split. Glacier has a 40 TB maximum.

Know when you should use EBS, EFS, S3, Glacier, or AWS Storage Gateway for your data. For persistent local storage for EC2, use EBS. For a file system interface and file system access semantics to make data available to one or more EC2 instances, use EFS. For a scalable, durable platform to make data accessible from any Internet location, use S3. For highly affordable, long-term cold storage, use Glacier.

Know when to choose EBS or an EC2 instance store. EBS is most often the default option. However, an instance store may be an option if your data does not meet any of the following criteria:

- Must persist through instance stops, terminations, or hardware failures
- Needs to be encrypted at the full volume level
- Needs to be backed up with EBS snapshots
- Needs to be removed from one instance and reattached to another

Exercises

For assistance in completing the following exercises, refer to the Amazon Simple Storage Service Developer Guide:

`https://docs.aws.amazon.com/AmazonS3/latest/dev/Welcome.html`

We assume that you have performed the exercises in Chapter 1 and Chapter 2 to set up your development environment on your own system with the AWS SDK.

For instructions on creating and testing a working sample, see "Testing the Amazon S3 Java Code Examples" here:

`https://docs.aws.amazon.com/AmazonS3/latest/dev/UsingTheMPJavaAPI`
`.html#TestingJavaSamples`

EXERCISE 3.1

Creating an Amazon S3 Bucket

In this exercise, you will create an Amazon S3 bucket using the AWS SDK for Java. You will use this bucket in the exercises that follow.

For assistance in completing this exercise, copying this code, or for code in other languages, see the following documentation:

`https://docs.aws.amazon.com/AmazonS3/latest/dev/create-bucket-get-`
`location-example.html`

1. Enter the following code in your preferred development environment for Java:

```java
import java.io.IOException;

import com.amazonaws.AmazonServiceException;
import com.amazonaws.SdkClientException;
import com.amazonaws.auth.profile.ProfileCredentialsProvider;
import com.amazonaws.services.s3.AmazonS3;
import com.amazonaws.services.s3.AmazonS3ClientBuilder;
import com.amazonaws.services.s3.model.CreateBucketRequest;
import com.amazonaws.services.s3.model.GetBucketLocationRequest;

public class CreateBucket {

    public static void main(String[] args) throws IOException {
        String clientRegion = "*** Client region ***";
        String bucketName = "*** Bucket name ***";

        try {
            AmazonS3 s3Client = AmazonS3ClientBuilder.standard()
                    .withCredentials(new ProfileCredentialsProvider())
                    .withRegion(clientRegion)
                    .build();

            if (!s3Client.doesBucketExistV2(bucketName)) {
                // Because the CreateBucketRequest object doesn't specify a region, the
                // bucket is created in the region specified in the client.
                s3Client.createBucket(new CreateBucketRequest(bucketName));

                // Verify that the bucket was created by retrieving it and checking its location.
                String bucketLocation = s3Client.getBucketLocation(new GetBucketLocationRequest(bucketName));
                System.out.println("Bucket location: " + bucketLocation);
            }
        }
        catch(AmazonServiceException e) {
            // The call was transmitted successfully, but Amazon S3 couldn't process
            // it and returned an error response.
```

```
                e.printStackTrace();
        }
        catch(SdkClientException e) {
            // Amazon S3 couldn't be contacted for a response, or the client
            // couldn't parse the response from Amazon S3.
            e.printStackTrace();
        }
    }
}
```

2. Replace the static variable values for clientRegion and bucketName. Note that bucket names must be unique across all of AWS. Make a note of these two values, as you will use the same region and bucket name for the exercises that follow in this chapter.

3. Execute the code. Your bucket is created with the name you specified in the region you specified. A successful result shows the following output:

```
Bucket Location: [bucketLocation]
```

Uploading an Object to a Bucket

Now that you have a bucket, you can add objects to it. In this example, you will create two objects. The first object has a text string as data, and the second object is a file. This example creates the first object by specifying the bucket name, object key, and text data directly in a call to AmazonS3Client.putObject(). The example creates a second object by using a PutObjectRequest that specifies the bucket name, object key, and file path. The PutObjectRequest also specifies the ContentType header and title metadata.

For assistance in completing this exercise, copying this code, or for code in other languages, see the following documentation:

https://docs.aws.amazon.com/AmazonS3/latest/dev/UploadObjSingle OpJava.html

1. Enter the following code in your preferred development environment for Java:

```
import java.io.File;
import java.io.IOException;
```

```
import com.amazonaws.AmazonServiceException;
import com.amazonaws.SdkClientException;
import com.amazonaws.auth.profile.ProfileCredentialsProvider;
import com.amazonaws.services.s3.AmazonS3;
import com.amazonaws.services.s3.AmazonS3ClientBuilder;
import com.amazonaws.services.s3.model.ObjectMetadata;
import com.amazonaws.services.s3.model.PutObjectRequest;

public class UploadObject {

    public static void main(String[] args) throws IOException {
        String clientRegion = "*** Client region ***";
        String bucketName = "*** Bucket name ***";
        String stringObjKeyName = "*** String object key name ***";
        String fileObjKeyName = "*** File object key name ***";
        String fileName = "*** Path to file to upload ***";

        try {
            AmazonS3 s3Client = AmazonS3ClientBuilder.standard()
                    .withRegion(clientRegion)
                    .withCredentials(new ProfileCredentialsProvider())
                    .build();

            // Upload a text string as a new object.
            s3Client.putObject(bucketName, stringObjKeyName, "Uploaded String
Object");

            // Upload a file as a new object with ContentType and title
specified.
            PutObjectRequest request = new PutObjectRequest(bucketName,
fileObjKeyName, new File(fileName));
            ObjectMetadata metadata = new ObjectMetadata();
            metadata.setContentType("plain/text");
            metadata.addUserMetadata("x-amz-meta-title", "someTitle");
            request.setMetadata(metadata);
            s3Client.putObject(request);
        }
        catch(AmazonServiceException e) {
            // The call was transmitted successfully, but Amazon S3
couldn't process
```

```
            // it, so it returned an error response.
            e.printStackTrace();
        }
        catch(SdkClientException e) {
            // Amazon S3 couldn't be contacted for a response, or the client
            // couldn't parse the response from Amazon S3.
            e.printStackTrace();
        }
    }
}
```

2. Replace the static variable values for `clientRegion` and `bucketName` used in the previous exercises.

3. Replace the value for `stringObjKeyName` with the name of the key that you intend to create in your S3 bucket, which will upload a text string as a new object.

4. Replace the `Uploaded String Object` text with the text being placed inside the object which you are generating.

5. Replace the `someTitle` text in the code with your own metadata title for the object that you are uploading.

6. Create a local file on your machine and then replace the value for `fileName` with the full path and filename of the file that you created.

7. Replace the `fileObjKeyName` with the key name that you want for the file that you will be uploading. Files can be uploaded with a different name than the file locally.

8. Execute the code. Your bucket is created with the name that you specified in the region that you specified. A successful result without errors will create two objects in your bucket.

EXERCISE 3.3

Emptying and Deleting a Bucket

Now that you have finished with the S3 exercises, you will want to clean up your environment by deleting all the files and the bucket you created. It is easy to delete an empty bucket. However, in some situations, you may need to delete or empty a bucket that contains objects. In this exercise, we show you how to delete objects and then delete the bucket.

For assistance in completing this exercise, copying this code, or for code in other languages, see the following documentation:

https://docs.aws.amazon.com/AmazonS3/latest/dev/delete-or-empty-bucket.html

1. Enter the following code in your preferred development environment for Java:

```java
import java.util.Iterator;

import com.amazonaws.AmazonServiceException;
import com.amazonaws.SdkClientException;
import com.amazonaws.auth.profile.ProfileCredentialsProvider;
import com.amazonaws.services.s3.AmazonS3;
import com.amazonaws.services.s3.AmazonS3ClientBuilder;
import com.amazonaws.services.s3.model.ListVersionsRequest;
import com.amazonaws.services.s3.model.ObjectListing;
import com.amazonaws.services.s3.model.S3ObjectSummary;
import com.amazonaws.services.s3.model.S3VersionSummary;
import com.amazonaws.services.s3.model.VersionListing;

public class DeleteBucket {

    public static void main(String[] args) {
        String clientRegion = "*** Client region ***";
        String bucketName = "*** Bucket name ***";

        try {
            AmazonS3 s3Client = AmazonS3ClientBuilder.standard()
                    .withCredentials(new ProfileCredentialsProvider())
                    .withRegion(clientRegion)
                    .build();

            // Delete all objects from the bucket. This is sufficient
            // for unversioned buckets. For versioned buckets, when you
            attempt to delete objects, Amazon S3 inserts
            // delete markers for all objects, but doesn't delete the object
            versions.
            // To delete objects from versioned buckets, delete all of the
            object versions before deleting
            // the bucket (see below for an example).
            ObjectListing objectListing = s3Client.listObjects(bucketName);
            while (true) {
```

```
                Iterator<S3ObjectSummary> objIter = objectListing
.getObjectSummaries().iterator();
                while (objIter.hasNext()) {
                    s3Client.deleteObject(bucketName, objIter.next()
.getKey());
                }

                // If the bucket contains many objects, the listObjects() call
                // might not return all of the objects in the first listing.
Check to
                // see whether the listing was truncated. If so, retrieve the
next page of objects
                // and delete them.
                if (objectListing.isTruncated()) {
                    objectListing = s3Client.listNextBatchOfObjects
(objectListing);
                } else {
                    break;
                }
            }

            // Delete all object versions (required for versioned buckets).
            VersionListing versionList = s3Client.listVersions
(new ListVersionsRequest().withBucketName(bucketName));
            while (true) {
                Iterator<S3VersionSummary> versionIter = versionList
.getVersionSummaries().iterator();
                while (versionIter.hasNext()) {
                    S3VersionSummary vs = versionIter.next();
                    s3Client.deleteVersion(bucketName, vs.getKey(),
vs.getVersionId());
                }

                if (versionList.isTruncated()) {
                    versionList = s3Client.listNextBatchOfVersions
(versionList);
                } else {
                    break;
                }
            }
```

```
        // After all objects and object versions are deleted, delete
the bucket.
            s3Client.deleteBucket(bucketName);
        }
        catch(AmazonServiceException e) {
            // The call was transmitted successfully, but Amazon S3
couldn't process
            // it, so it returned an error response.
            e.printStackTrace();
        }
        catch(SdkClientException e) {
            // Amazon S3 couldn't be contacted for a response, or the client
couldn't
            // parse the response from Amazon S3.
            e.printStackTrace();
        }
    }
}
```

2. Replace the static variable values for clientRegion and bucketName with the values that you used in the previous steps.

3. Execute the code.

4. When execution is complete without errors, both of your objects and your bucket will have been deleted.

Review Questions

1. Your organization stores a large volume of data on S3, which includes both frequently accessed files and files that are rarely accessed after 30 days. To optimize storage costs while maintaining accessibility, what life cycle policy should you implement?

    A. Move files to S3 Standard-Infrequent Access (S3 Standard-IA) after 30 days, then to S3 Glacier after 90 days.

    B. Keep all files in S3 Standard indefinitely.

    C. Upload files directly to S3 Glacier Deep Archive immediately.

    D. Move files to S3 One Zone-Infrequent Access (S3 One Zone-IA) after 30 days, then delete after 90 days.

2. In what ways does S3 object storage differ from block and file storage? (Choose two.)

    A. Amazon S3 stores data in fixed size blocks.

    B. Objects are identified by a numbered address.

    C. Objects contain both data and metadata.

    D. Objects are stored in buckets.

3. You are restoring an Amazon Elastic Block Store (EBS) volume from a snapshot. How long will it take before the data is available?

    A. It depends on the provisioned size of the volume.

    B. The data will be available immediately.

    C. It depends on the amount of data stored on the volume.

    D. It depends on whether the attached instance is an Amazon EBS–optimized instance.

4. What are some of the key characteristics of Amazon S3? (Choose three.)

    A. All objects have a URL.

    B. Amazon S3 can store unlimited amounts of data.

    C. S3 offers native NFS and CIFS interfaces to mount via EC2 instances.

    D. Amazon S3 offers up to 99.999999999% durability.

    E. You must preallocate the storage in a bucket.

5. Amazon S3 Glacier is well suited to data that is which of the following? (Choose two.)

    A. Infrequently or rarely accessed

    B. Must be immediately available when needed

    C. Can be accessed after a three- to five-hour restore period

    D. Is frequently erased within 30 days

6. You have valuable media files hosted on S3, which should be accessible only for a limited time to users who have successfully authenticated to your web application. What method should you employ to ensure the temporary and secure access to these documents?

   A. Use static web hosting.

   B. Generate presigned URLs for content in the web application.

   C. Use AWS Identity and Access Management (IAM) policies to restrict access.

   D. Use logging to track your content.

7. Which of the following are features of Amazon Elastic Block Store (Amazon EBS)? (Choose two.)

   A. Data stored on EBS is automatically replicated within an availability zone.

   B. EBS data is automatically backed up to tape.

   C. EBS volumes are encrypted transparently to workloads on the attached instance.

   D. Data on an EBS volume is lost when the attached instance is stopped.

8. Which option should you choose for EFS when tens, hundreds, or thousands of EC2 instances will be accessing the file system concurrently?

   A. General-Purpose performance mode

   B. RAID 0

   C. Max I/O performance mode

   D. Change to a larger instance

9. Which of the following must be performed to host a static website in an S3 bucket? (Choose three.)

   A. Configure the bucket for static hosting, and specify an index and error document.

   B. Create a bucket with the same name as the website.

   C. Enable File Transfer Protocol (FTP) on the bucket.

   D. Make the objects in the bucket world-readable.

   E. Enable HTTP on the bucket.

10. You have a workload that requires 1 TB of durable block storage at 1,500 IOPS during normal use. Every night there is an extract, transform, load (ETL) task that requires 3,000 IOPS for 15 minutes. What is the most appropriate volume type for this workload?

   A. Use a provisioned IOPS SSD volume at 3,000 IOPS.

   B. Use an instance store.

   C. Use a general-purpose SSD volume.

   D. Use a magnetic volume.

11. Which statements about S3 Glacier are true? (Choose three.)

    A. Objects may only enter Glacier tiers via S3 life cycle policies.

    B. Objects in Glacier must be a minimum of 1GB in size.

    C. Glacier objects may take multiple hours to restore.

    D. There is a fee for data retrieval.

    E. It can be used as a stand-alone service and as an S3 storage class.

12. You are developing an application that will be running on several hundred EC2 instances. The application on each instance will be required to reach out through a file system protocol concurrently to a file system holding the files. Which storage option should you choose?

    A. Amazon EFS

    B. Amazon EBS

    C. Amazon EC2 instance store

    D. Amazon S3

13. You need to take a snapshot of an EBS volume. How long will the volume be unavailable?

    A. It depends on the provisioned size of the volume.

    B. Volume availability is not affected by taking a snapshot.

    C. It depends on the amount of data stored on the volume.

    D. It depends on whether the attached instance is an EBS-optimized instance.

14. S3 bucket policies can restrict access to an S3 bucket and objects by which of the following? (Choose three.)

    A. Company name

    B. IP address range

    C. AWS account

    D. Country of origin

    E. Objects with a specific prefix

15. Which of the following are *not* appropriate use cases for S3? (Choose two.)

    A. Storing static web content or hosting a static website

    B. Storing an operating system or boot volume for an Amazon EC2

    C. Storing backups for a relational database

    D. Primary storage for a database

    E. Storing logs for analytics

16. Which features enable you to manage access to S3 buckets or objects? (Choose three.)

    A. Enable static website hosting on the bucket.

    B. Create a presigned URL for an object.

    C. Use an Amazon S3 access control list (ACL) on a bucket or object.

    D. Use a life cycle policy.

    E. Use an S3 bucket policy.

17. Your application stores critical data in S3 that must be protected against inadvertent or intentional deletion. How can this data be protected? (Choose two.)

   A. Use cross-region replication to copy data to another bucket automatically.

   B. Set a vault lock.

   C. Enable versioning on the bucket.

   D. Use a life cycle policy to migrate data to Amazon S3 Glacier.

   E. Enable MFA Delete on the bucket.

18. You have a set of users that have been granted access to your Amazon S3 bucket. For compliance purposes, you need to keep track of all files accessed in that bucket. To have a record of who accessed your S3 data and from where, what should you do?

   A. Enable versioning on the bucket.

   B. Enable website hosting on the bucket.

   C. Enable server access logging on the bucket.

   D. Create an AWS Identity and Access Management (IAM) bucket policy.

   E. Enable CloudWatch logs.

19. What are some reasons to enable cross-region replication on an S3 bucket? (Choose three.)

   A. Your compliance requirements dictate that you store data at an even further distance than availability zones, which are tens of miles apart.

   B. You want to minimize latency when your customers are in two geographic regions.

   C. You need a backup of your data in case of accidental deletion.

   D. You have compute clusters in two different AWS regions that analyze the same set of objects.

   E. Your data requires at least five nines of durability.

20. Your company requires that all data sent to external storage be encrypted before being sent. You will be sending company data to S3. Which S3 encryption solution will meet this requirement?

   A. Server-side encryption with AWS-managed keys (SSE-S3)

   B. Server-side encryption with customer-provided keys (SSE-C)

   C. Client-side encryption with customer-managed keys

   D. Server-side encryption with AWS Key Management Service (AWS KMS) keys (SSE-KMS)

21. By default, how is data stored in S3 for high durability?

   A. Data is automatically replicated to other regions.

   B. Data is automatically replicated within a region.

   C. Data is replicated only if versioning is enabled on the bucket.

   D. Data is automatically backed up on tape and restored if needed.

Chapter 4

AWS Database Services

**THE AWS CERTIFIED DEVELOPER –
ASSOCIATE EXAM TOPICS COVERED IN
THIS CHAPTER MAY INCLUDE, BUT ARE
NOT LIMITED TO, THE FOLLOWING:**

✓ **Domain 1: Development with AWS Services**

  ■ Task Statement 1: Develop code for applications
    hosted on AWS

  ■ Task Statement 3: Use data stores in application development

✓ **Domain 2: Security**

  ■ Task Statement 1: Implement authentication and/or
    authorization for applications and AWS services

  ■ Task Statement 2: Implement encryption by using AWS
    services

  ■ Task Statement 3: Manage sensitive data in application code

✓ **Domain 4: Troubleshooting and Optimization**

  ■ Task Statement 3: Optimize applications by using AWS
    services and features

Filesystems and object storage are far from the only way AWS offers you the ability to store data—and that's good news, because many use cases, from web application to data pipelines, require the use of a database. While you can always install and run your own database on an EC2 instance, the real power of AWS for databases comes in the form of managed services—databases that AWS maintains for you, taking the complexity of running, patching, and scaling out of your hands.

AWS Cloud offerings include the following databases:

Managed relational databases for transactional applications

Nonrelational databases for Internet-scale applications

Data warehouse databases for analytics

In-memory data store databases for caching and real-time workloads

Time-series databases for efficiently collecting, synthesizing, and deriving insights from time-series data

Ledger databases for when you need a centralized, trusted authority to maintain a scalable, complete, and cryptographically verifiable record of transactions

Graph databases for building applications with highly connected data

For almost every use case, there is an AWS database service that closely aligns with your needs. Table 4.1 describes each database that AWS offers and indicates the database type.

TABLE 4.1 AWS database service mapping to database type

Product	Type	Description
Amazon Aurora	Relational database	A MySQL- and PostgreSQL-compatible relational database built for the cloud that combines the performance and availability of traditional enterprise databases with the simplicity and cost-effectiveness of open source databases.
Amazon Relational Database Service (Amazon RDS)	Relational database	A managed relational database for MySQL, PostgreSQL, Oracle, SQL Server, and MariaDB. Easy to set up, operate, and scale a relational database in the cloud quickly.

Product	Type	Description
Amazon DynamoDB	NoSQL database	A serverless, managed NoSQL database that delivers consistent single-digit millisecond latency at any scale. Pay only for the throughput and storage you use.
Amazon Redshift	Data warehouse	A fast, fully managed, petabyte-scale data warehouse at one-tenth the cost of traditional solutions. Simple and cost-effective solution to analyze data by using standard SQL and your existing business intelligence (BI) tools.
Amazon ElastiCache	In-memory data store	To deploy, operate, and scale an in-memory data store based on Memcached or Redis in the cloud.
Amazon Neptune	Graph database	A fast, reliable, fully managed graph database to store and manage highly connected datasets.
Amazon Document DB	Nonre-lational database	A fast, scalable, highly available, and fully managed document database service that supports MongoDB workloads.
Amazon Timestream	Time series database	A fast, scalable, fully managed time-series database service for IoT and operational applications that makes it easy to store and analyze trillions of events per day at one-tenth the cost of relational databases.
Amazon Quantum Ledger Database (Amazon QLDB)	Ledger database	A fully managed ledger database that provides a transparent, immutable, and cryptographically verifiable transaction log owned by a central trusted authority.
AWS Database Migration Service (AWS DMS)	Database migration	Help migrate your databases to AWS easily and inexpensively with minimal downtime.

In this chapter, we'll focus on the most relevant services for developers looking to build on AWS. Table 4.2 gives you an idea of which services you might choose for common application types.

TABLE 4.2   Application mapping to AWS database service

Applications	Product
Transactional applications, such as ERP, CRM, and e-commerce to log transactions and store structured data	Amazon Aurora or Amazon RDS
Internet-scale applications, such as hospitality, dating, and ride sharing, to serve content and store structured and unstructured data	Amazon DynamoDB or Amazon DocumentDB
Real-time application use cases that require submillisecond latency such as gaming leaderboards, chat, messaging, streaming, and Internet of Things (IoT)	Amazon ElastiCache

Relational Databases

AWS's primary offering for relational databases, straightforwardly named Relational Database Service (RDS), provides a managed database experience supporting many popular database engines. "Managed services" are a core feature of AWS. In this section, we'll explore what AWS brings to the table in a managed database.

Managed vs. Unmanaged Databases

Managed database services on AWS, such as Amazon RDS, enable you to off-load the administrative burdens of operating and scaling distributed databases to AWS so that you don't have to worry about tasks like:

- Hardware provisioning
- Setup and configuration
- Throughput capacity planning
- Replication
- Software patching
- Cluster scaling

AWS provides several database alternatives for developers. As a managed database, Amazon RDS enables you to run a fully featured relational database while off-loading database administration. By contrast, you can run unmanaged databases on Amazon EC2, which gives you more flexibility on the types of databases that you can deploy and configure, but you are responsible for their administration.

Amazon Relational Database Service

With *Amazon Relational Database Service (Amazon RDS)*, you can set up, operate, and scale relational databases in the AWS cloud. Not only do you not need to install the database software, but Amazon RDS can also manage time-consuming database administration tasks, such as patching and backup, freeing you to focus on your applications and business. RDS makes available several popular database engines, as shown in Figure 4.1.

FIGURE 4.1   Amazon RDS database engines

Amazon RDS assumes many of the difficult or tedious management tasks of a relational database:

Procurement, Configuration, and Backup Tasks

- When you buy a server, you get a central processing unit (CPU), memory, storage, and input/output operations per second (IOPS) all bundled together. With Amazon RDS, these are split apart so that you can scale them independently and allocate your resources as you need them.

- Amazon RDS manages backups, software patches, automatic failure detection, and recovery.

- You can configure automated backups or manually create your own backup snapshot and use these backups to restore a database.

- You can use familiar database products: MySQL, MariaDB, PostgreSQL, Oracle, Microsoft SQL Server, and the MySQL- and PostgreSQL-compatible Amazon Aurora DB engine.

Security and Availability

- RDS instances can be encrypted at rest with AWS-provided or your own customer keys.

- You can get high availability with a primary instance and a synchronous secondary instance that you can fail over to when problems occur. You can also use MySQL, MariaDB, or PostgreSQL read replicas to increase read scaling.

- In addition to the security in your database package, you can use AWS Identity and Access Management (IAM) to define users, and permissions help control who can access your Amazon RDS databases.

- You can manage network access to your databases with the same kinds of security groups that govern access to EC2 instances, which you discovered previously in this book.

- To deliver a managed service experience, RDS does not provide shell access to database (DB) instances, and it restricts access to certain system procedures and tables that require advanced permissions.

When you host databases on RDS, AWS is responsible for the items in Figure 4.2.

FIGURE 4.2   Amazon RDS host responsibilities

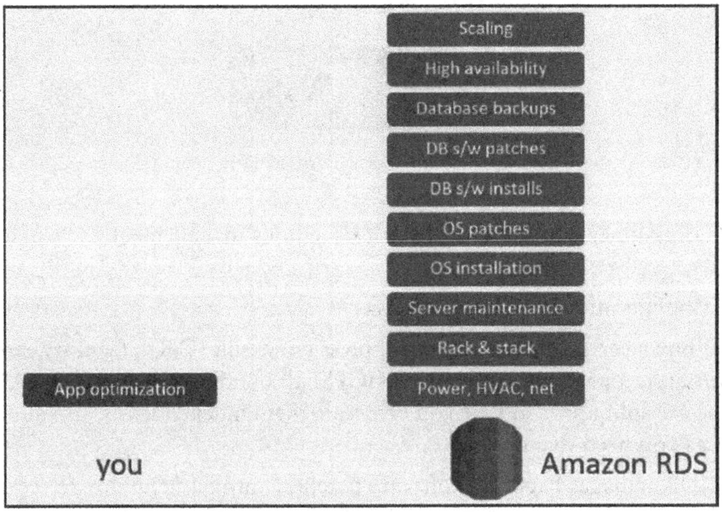

Relational Database Engines on Amazon RDS

Because RDS is a managed service, you gain several benefits and features built right into the Amazon RDS service. These features include, but are not limited to, the following:

- Automatic software patching
- Easy vertical scaling

- Easy storage scaling
- Read replicas
- Automatic backups
- Database snapshots
- Multi-AZ deployments
- Encryption
- IAM DB authentication
- Monitoring and metrics with Amazon CloudWatch

To create an RDS instance, you can run the following command from the AWS CLI:

```
aws rds create-db-instance \
--db-instance-class db.t2.micro \
--allocated-storage 30 \
--db-instance-identifier my-cool-rds-db --engine mysql \
--master-username masteruser --master-user-password masterpassword1!
```

Depending on the configurations chosen, the database may take several minutes before it is active and ready for use. You can monitor the RDS Databases console to view the status. When the status states Available, it is ready to be used, as shown in Figure 4.3.

FIGURE 4.3   RDS Databases console

Automatic Software Patching

Periodically, RDS performs maintenance on RDS resources. Maintenance mostly involves patching the RDS database's underlying operating system or database engine version. Because this is a managed service, RDS handles the patching for you.

When you create an RDS database instance, you can define a maintenance window. A *maintenance window* is where you can define the period in which RDS may apply any updates or downtime to your database instance. You also can enable the automatic minor version upgrade feature, which automatically applies any new minor versions of the database as they are released (see Figure 4.4).

FIGURE 4.4 Maintenance window

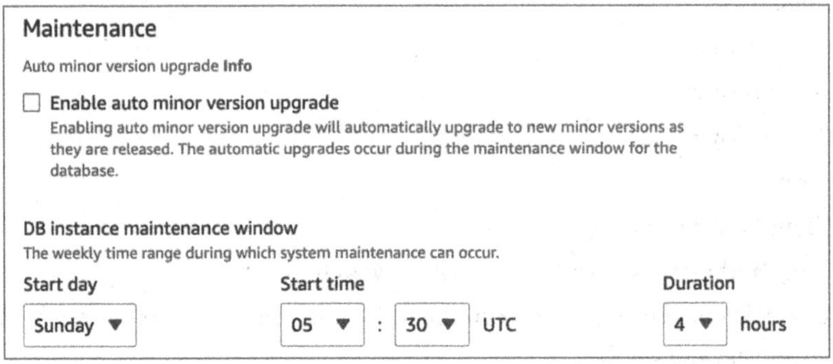

You can select a maintenance window by using the AWS Management Console, AWS CLI, or Amazon RDS API. After selecting the maintenance window, the Amazon RDS instance is upgraded (if upgrades are available) during that time window. You can also modify the maintenance window by running the following AWS CLI command:

```
aws rds modify-db-instance --db-instance-identifer your-db-instance-identifer
--preferred-maintenance-window Mon:07:00-Mon:07:30
```

Vertical Scaling

If your database needs to handle a bigger load, you can vertically scale your RDS instance. There are dozens of available DB instance classes across a wide range of categories, enabling you to choose the number of virtual CPUs, available memory, and network performance in a variety of configurations. To scale the RDS instance vertically, you can use the AWS Management Console, AWS CLI, or AWS SDK to change instance types to something more powerful.

If you are in a single-AZ configuration for your Amazon RDS instance, the database will be unavailable during the scaling operation. However, if you are in a multi-AZ configuration, the standby database is upgraded first and then a failover occurs to the newly configured database. You can also apply the change during the next maintenance window. This way, your upgrade can occur during the normal outage windows expected by your users.

To scale the RDS database by using the AWS CLI, run the following command:

```
aws rds modify-db-instance --db-instance-identifer your-db-instance-identifer
--db-instance-class db.t2.medium
```

Easy Storage Scaling

Storage is a critical component for any database. RDS has the following storage types:

General-Purpose SSD (gp2)   This storage type is for cost-effective storage that is ideal for a broad range of workloads. Gp2 volumes deliver single-digit millisecond latencies and the ability to burst to 3,000 IOPS for extended periods of time. The volume's size determines the performance of gp2 volumes.

General-Purpose SSD (gp3)   This storage type provides scalable performance and cost-effective storage, suitable for various workloads. Unlike gp2, where performance scales with size, gp3 volumes deliver a baseline performance of 3,000 IOPS and allow independent scaling up to 16,000 IOPS for additional costs.

Provisioned IOPS (io1)   This storage type is for input/output-intensive workloads that require low input/output (I/O) latency and consistent I/O throughput. With provisioned IOPS, this storage type can reach 256,000 IOPS!

Magnetic Storage   This storage type is designed for backward compatibility, and AWS recommends that you use General-Purpose SSD or Provisioned IOPS for any new RDS workloads.

To scale your storage, you must modify the RDS DB instance by executing the following AWS CLI command:

```
aws rds modify-db-instance --db-instance-identifer your-db-instance-identifer
--allocated-storage 50 --storage-type io1 --iops 3000
```

This command modifies your storage to 50 GB in size, with a Provisioned IOPS storage drive and a dedicated IOPS of E3,000. Remember, this kind of scaling can incur downtime, unless your RDS instance is configured for high availability.

Read Replicas (Horizontal Scaling)

There are two ways to scale your database tier with RDS: vertical scaling and horizontal scaling. Vertical scaling takes the primary database and increases the amount of memory and vCPUs allocated for the primary database. Alternatively, use horizontal scaling (add another server) to your database tier to improve the performance of applications that are read-heavy as opposed to write-heavy.

Read replicas create read-only copies of your master database, which allow you to off-load any reads (or SQL SELECT statements) to the read replica. The replication from the master database to the read replica is asynchronous. As a result, data queried from the read replica may not be the latest data. If parts of your application require strongly consistent reads, make sure to direct those queries to the primary instance.

As of this writing, RDS supports read replicas in all database engines except IBM Db2.

To create a read replica by using AWS CLI, run the following command:

```
aws rds create-db-instance-read-replica --db-instance-identifier your-db-
instance-identifier --source-db-instance-identifier your-source-db
```

Backing Up Data with Amazon RDS

RDS has two different ways of backing up data of your database instance: *automated backups* and *database snapshots* (DB snapshots).

Automated Backups (Point-in-Time)

With RDS, automated backups offer a point-in-time recovery of your database. When enabled, RDS performs a full daily snapshot of your data that is taken during your preferred backup window. After the initial backup is taken (each day), RDS then captures transaction logs as changes are made to the database.

After you initiate a point-in-time recovery, to restore your database instance, the transaction logs are applied to the most appropriate daily backup. You can perform a restore up to the specific second, as long as it's within your retention period. The default retention period is seven days, but it can be a maximum of up to 35 days.

To perform a restore, you must choose the `Latest Restorable Time`, which is typically within the last five minutes. For example, suppose that the current date is February 14 at 10 p.m., and you would like to do a point-in-time restore of February 14 at 9 p.m. This restore would succeed because the `Latest Restorable Time` is a maximum of February 14 at 9:55 p.m. (which is the last five-minute window). However, a point-in-time restore of February 14 at 9:58 p.m. would fail because it is within the five-minute window.

When you delete an RDS database, you can choose to retain any automated backups that currently exist, giving you the ability to restore a database after deletion. These backups will persist according to the retention period you chose when configuring automated backups.

Database Snapshots (Manual)

Unlike automated backups, database snapshots with RDS are user-initiated and enable you to back up your database instance in a known state at any time. You can also restore to that specific snapshot at any time.

Similar to the other RDS features, you can create the snapshots through the AWS Management Console, with the `CreateDBSnapshot` API, or with the AWS CLI.

DB snapshots are kept until you explicitly delete them. Regardless of the backup taken, storage I/O may be briefly suspended while the backup process initializes (typically a few seconds), and you may experience a brief period of elevated latency. A way to avoid these types of suspensions is to deploy in a multi-AZ configuration. With such a deployment, the backup is taken from the standby instead of the primary database. Before removing any RDS instance, it's a good idea to take a final snapshot.

To create a snapshot of the database from the RDS Databases console, select Actions, then the Take Snapshot option (see Figure 4.5). After a snapshot is taken, you can view all of your snaps from the Snapshots console.

Multi-AZ Deployments

RDS allows you to run your databases in a multi-AZ configuration, giving you a primary and a standby DB instance in two availability zones. Updates to the primary database replicate synchronously to the standby replica. The primary benefit of multi-AZ is realized during certain types of planned maintenance, or in the unlikely event of a DB instance failure or an availability zone failure. RDS automatically fails over to the standby so that you can resume your workload as soon as the standby is promoted to the primary. This means that you can reduce your downtime in the event of a failure.

FIGURE 4.5   Taking an RDS snapshot

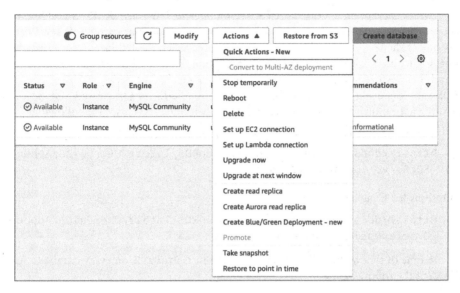

During any instance failure, RDS handles failover automatically by promoting the standby to become the new primary. You never interact directly with the standby, and only ever receive one endpoint connection for the RDS cluster. RDS manages the entire failover event for you.

RDS multi-AZ configuration provides the following benefits:

- Automatic failover; no administration required
- Increased durability in the unlikely event of component failure
- Increased availability in the unlikely event of an availability zone failure
- Increased availability for planned maintenance (automated backups; I/O activity is no longer suspended)

To create an RDS instance in a multi-AZ configuration, you must specify a subnet group that has two different availability zones specified. You can specify a multi-AZ configuration by using AWS CLI by adding the `--multi-az` flag to the AWS CLI command, as follows:

```
aws rds create-db-instance \
--db-instance-class db.t2.micro \
--allocated-storage 30 \
--db-instance-identifier multi-az-rds-db --engine mysql \
--master-username masteruser \
--master-user-password masterpassword1! \
--multi-az
```

Encryption

RDS provides encryption at rest via *AWS Key Management Service (KMS)* for AES-256 encryption, using your AWS account's default primary key or your own KMS key. Encryption is one of the few options that must be configured when the DB instance is created; you cannot modify an RDS database to enable encryption. You can, however, create a DB snapshot and then restore to an encrypted DB instance or cluster.

RDS supports using *Transparent Data Encryption (TDE)* for Oracle and SQL Server. For more information on TDE with Oracle and Microsoft SQL Server, see the following:

- Microsoft SQL Server Transparent Data Encryption Support at:

    ```
    https://docs.aws.amazon.com/AmazonRDS/latest/UserGuide/Appendix
    .SQLServer.Options.TDE.html
    ```

- Options for Oracle DB Instances:

    ```
    https://docs.aws.amazon.com/AmazonRDS/latest/UserGuide/Appendix
    .Oracle.Options.AdvSecurity.html
    ```

At the time of this writing, RDS encryption at rest is available on every database instance type except the following:

- `Db.m1.small`
- `Db.m1.medium`
- `Db.m1.large`
- `Db.m1.xlarge`
- `Db.m2.xlarge`
- `Db.m2.2xlarge`
- `Db.m2.4xlarge`
- `Db.t2.micro`

For encryption in transit, RDS generates a Transport Layer Security (TLS) certificate for each database instance that can be used to connect your application and the RDS instance. For most databases, RDS configures the endpoint to use secure connections via TLS by default. The configuration is unique to each database engine; for more information, see the RDS documentation for your specific database type.

IAM DB Authentication

You can authenticate to your DB instance by using AWS Identity and Access Management (IAM). By using IAM, you can manage access to your database resources centrally instead of storing the user credentials in each database. The IAM feature also encrypts network traffic to and from the database by default using SSL/TLS.

IAM DB authentication is supported only for MariaDB, MySQL, and PostgreSQL. For details on the exact database engines and versions that support this feature, visit:

```
https://docs.aws.amazon.com/AmazonRDS/latest/UserGuide/Concepts
.RDS_Fea_Regions_DB-eng.Feature.IamDatabaseAuthentication.html
```

To enable IAM DB authentication for your RDS instance, run the following command:

```
aws rds modify-db-instance --db-instance-identifier my-rds-db --enable-iam-
database-authentication --apply-immediately
```

Because downtime is associated with this action, you can enable this feature during the next maintenance window. You can do so by changing the last parameter to `--no-apply-immediately`.

Monitoring with Amazon CloudWatch

Amazon CloudWatch allows you to monitor your database and create alarms to notify administrators when there is a failure.

By default, CloudWatch provides some built-in metrics for RDS with a granularity of 5 minutes (600 seconds). If you want to gather metrics in a smaller window of granularity, such as 1 second, enable enhanced monitoring, similar to how you enable these features in EC2.

To view all the RDS metrics that are provided through CloudWatch, select the Monitoring tab in the Amazon RDS console (see Figure 4.6).

FIGURE 4.6 RDS with CloudWatch metrics

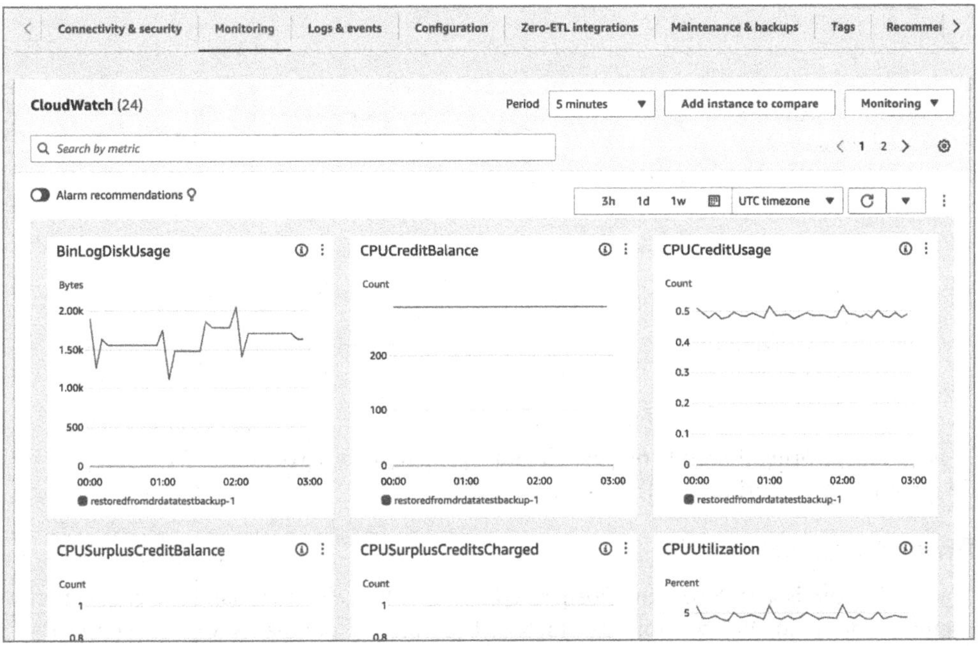

RDS integrates with CloudWatch to send it the following database logs:

- Audit log
- Error log
- General log
- Slow query log

In the RDS console, select the Logs & Events tab to view and download the specified logs, as shown in Figure 4.7.

FIGURE 4.7 RDS with CloudWatch logs

For more information on CloudWatch and its capabilities across other AWS services, see Chapter 15, "Monitoring and Troubleshooting."

Amazon Aurora

Amazon Aurora is a MySQL- and PostgreSQL-compatible relational database engine that combines the speed and availability of high-end commercial databases with the simplicity and cost-effectiveness of open source databases. Aurora is a managed service of RDS.

Amazon Aurora DB Clusters

Aurora is a drop-in replacement for MySQL and PostgreSQL that is cloud-native and built for performance and scalability. You can use the code, tools, and applications that you use today with your existing MySQL and PostgreSQL databases with Aurora.

Like all RDS database engines, with Aurora, time-consuming administration tasks, such as hardware provisioning, database setup, patching, and backups, are automated.

Aurora features a distributed, fault-tolerant, self-healing storage system that automatically scales up to a maximum of 128 TiB per database instance. Aurora delivers high performance and availability with up to 15 low-latency read replicas, point-in-time recovery, continuous backup to S3, and replication across three availability zones. When you create an Aurora instance, you create a DB cluster. A *DB cluster* consists of one or more DB instances and a cluster volume that manages the data for those instances. An Aurora *cluster volume* is a virtual database storage volume that spans multiple availability zones, and each availability zone has a copy of the DB cluster data.

An Aurora DB cluster has two types of DB instances.

Primary Instance   Supports read and write operations and performs all of the data modifications to the cluster volume. Each Amazon Aurora DB cluster has one primary instance.

Amazon Aurora Replica   Supports read-only operations. Each Aurora DB cluster can have up to 15 *Amazon Aurora replicas* in addition to the primary instance. Multiple replicas distribute the read workload, and if you locate Aurora replicas in separate availability zones, you can also increase database availability.

Figure 4.8 illustrates the relationship between the cluster volume, the primary instance, and Aurora replicas in an Aurora DB cluster.

FIGURE 4.8   Amazon Aurora DB cluster

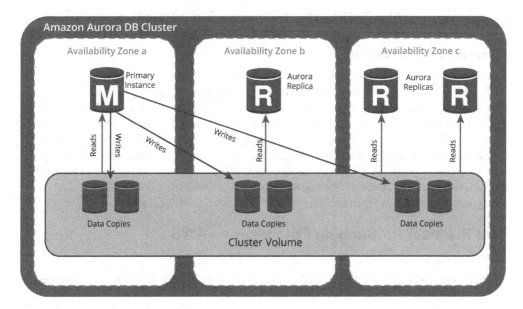

As you can see from Figure 4.8, this architecture is vastly different from the other RDS databases. Aurora is engineered and architected for the cloud. The primary difference is that there is a separate storage layer, called the *cluster volume*, which is spread across multiple availability zones in a single AWS region. This means that the durability of your data is increased.

Additionally, Aurora has one primary instance that writes across the cluster volume. This means that Aurora replicas can be spun up quickly, because they don't have to copy and store their own storage layer; they connect to it. Because the cluster volume is separated in this architecture, the cluster volume can grow automatically as your data increases. This contrasts with how other RDS databases are built, whereby you must define the allocated storage in advance.

Aurora Global Databases

With Aurora, you can also create a multiregional deployment for your database tier. In this configuration, the primary AWS region is where your data is written (you may also do reads from the primary AWS region). Any application performing writes must write to the primary AWS region where the cluster is operating.

The secondary AWS region is used for *reading* data only. Aurora replicates the data to the secondary AWS region with typical latency of less than a second. Furthermore, you can use the secondary AWS region for disaster recovery purposes. You can promote the secondary cluster and make it available as the primary typically in less than a minute. As of this writing, Aurora global databases are available only for certain MySQL or Postgres engine versions and in certain regions, though this selection continues to expand. For details on availability, see:

```
https://docs.aws.amazon.com/AmazonRDS/latest/AuroraUserGuide/
Concepts.Aurora_Fea_Regions_DB-eng.Feature.GlobalDatabase.html
```

Amazon Aurora Serverless

Amazon Aurora Serverless is an on-demand, automatic scaling configuration for Aurora. With Aurora Serverless, the database will *automatically* start up, shut down, and scale capacity up or down based on your application's needs. This means that, as a developer, you can run your database in the AWS Cloud and not worry about managing any database instances. While Aurora Serverless can be more expensive, that additional cost is made up for by its ability to scale down when load decreases. For workloads that have spiky, unpredictable patterns of usage, Aurora Serverless may offer significant savings over provisioned RDS Aurora instances. On the other hand, if your database load stays mostly consistent throughout the day, you may see lower overall costs with the traditional Aurora setup.

Best Practices for Running Databases on AWS

The following are best practices for working with RDS:

> **Follow RDS basic operational guidelines.**   Follow these basic operational guidelines, recommended by Amazon, when working with RDS:

- Monitor your memory, CPU, and storage usage. CloudWatch can notify you when usage patterns change or when you approach the capacity of your deployment so that you can maintain system performance and availability.

- Scale up your DB instance when you approach storage capacity limits. Have some buffer in storage and memory to accommodate unforeseen increases in demand from your applications.

- Enable automatic backups and set the backup window to occur during the daily low in write IOPS.

- If your database workload requires more I/O than you have provisioned, recovery after a failover or database failure will be slow. To increase the I/O capacity of a DB instance, do any or all of the following:

  - Migrate to a DB instance class with high I/O capacity.

  - Convert from standard storage either to general-purpose or provisioned IOPS storage, depending on how much of an increase you need. If you convert to provisioned IOPS storage, make sure that you also use a DB instance class that is optimized for provisioned IOPS.

  - If using gp3 SSD storage, you may pay for increased IOPS by adjusting the Storage IOPS setting in the RDS management console.

  - If you are already using provisioned IOPS storage, provision additional throughput capacity.

- If your client application is caching the Domain Name Service (DNS) data of your DB instances, set a time-to-live (TTL) value of less than 30 seconds. Because the underlying IP address of a DB instance can change after a failover, caching the DNS data for an extended time can lead to connection failures if your application tries to connect to an IP address that no longer is in service.

- Test failover for your DB instance to understand how long the process takes for your use case and to ensure that the application that accesses your DB instance can automatically connect to the new DB instance after failover.

Allocate sufficient RAM to the DB instance.   An RDS performance best practice is to allocate enough RAM so that your working set resides almost completely in memory. Check the ReadIOPS metric by using CloudWatch while the DB instance is under load to view the working set. The value of ReadIOPS should be small and stable. Scale up the DB instance class until ReadIOPS no longer drops dramatically after a scaling operation or when ReadIOPS is reduced to a small amount.

Implement RDS security.   Use AWS IAM accounts to control access to RDS API actions, especially actions that create, modify, or delete RDS resources, such as DB instances, security groups, option groups, or parameter groups, and actions that perform common administrative actions, such as backing up and restoring DB instances, or configuring provisioned IOPS storage.

- Assign an individual IAM account to each person who manages RDS resources. Do not use the AWS root account to manage RDS resources; create an IAM user for everyone, including yourself.
- Grant each user the minimum set of permissions required to perform their duties.
- Use IAM groups to manage permissions effectively for multiple users.
- Rotate your IAM credentials regularly.

Use the AWS Management Console, the AWS CLI, or the Amazon RDS API to change the password for your primary user. If you use another tool, such as a SQL client, to change the primary user password, it might result in permissions being revoked for the user unintentionally.

Use enhanced monitoring to identify operating system issues.   RDS provides metrics in real time for the operating system on which your DB instance runs. You can view the metrics for your DB instance by using the console or consume the Enhanced Monitoring JSON output from CloudWatch Logs in a monitoring system of your choice. Enhanced Monitoring is available for the following database engines:

- MariaDB
- Microsoft SQL Server
- MySQL version 5.5 or later
- Oracle
- PostgreSQL
- Db2

Enhanced monitoring is available for all DB instance classes except for db.m1.small. Enhanced Monitoring is available in all regions except for AWS GovCloud (US).

Use metrics to identify performance issues.   To identify performance issues caused by insufficient resources and other common bottlenecks, you can monitor the metrics available for your RDS DB instance.

Monitor performance metrics regularly to see the average, maximum, and minimum values for a variety of time ranges. If you do so, you can identify when performance is degraded. You can also set CloudWatch alarms for particular metric thresholds.

To troubleshoot performance issues, it's important to understand the baseline performance of the system. When you set up a new DB instance and get it running with a typical workload, you should capture the average, maximum, and minimum values of all the performance metrics at a number of different intervals (for example, one hour, 24 hours, one week, or two weeks) to get an idea of what is normal. It helps to get comparisons for both peak and off-peak hours of operation. You can then use this information to identify when performance is dropping below standard levels.

Use DB parameter groups.   AWS recommends that you apply changes to the DB parameter group on a test DB instance before you apply parameter group changes to your production DB instances. Improperly setting DB engine parameters in a DB parameter group can have unintended adverse effects, including degraded performance and system instability. Always exercise caution when modifying DB engine parameters, and back up your DB instance before modifying a DB parameter group.

Use read replicas.   Use read replicas to relieve pressure on your primary node with additional read capacity. You can bring your data closer to applications in different regions and promote a read replica to a master for faster recovery in the event of a disaster.

 You can use the AWS Database Migration Service to migrate or replicate your existing databases easily to RDS, or to transfer data from one RDS database engine to another.

Nonrelational Databases

Nonrelational databases are commonly used for Internet-scale applications that do not require any complex queries.

NoSQL Database

NoSQL databases are nonrelational databases optimized for scalable performance and schema-less data models. NoSQL databases are also widely recognized for their ease of development, low latency, and resilience.

NoSQL database systems use a variety of models for data management, such as in-memory key-value stores, graph data models, and document stores. These types of databases are optimized for applications that require large data volume, low latency, and flexible data models, which are achieved by relaxing some of the data consistency restrictions of traditional relational databases.

When to Use a NoSQL Database

NoSQL databases are a great fit for many big data, mobile, and web applications that require greater scale and higher responsiveness than traditional relational databases. Because of simpler data structures and horizontal scaling, NoSQL databases typically respond faster and are easier to scale than relational databases. Because they do not use a fixed schema, they are ideal for situations in which data structures may change over time, or when different use cases may result in different fields being saved on an object. If your application requires a flexible schema, NoSQL is a great choice.

Comparison of SQL and NoSQL Databases

Many developers are familiar with SQL databases but might be new to working with NoSQL databases. Relational database management systems (RDBMSs) and nonrelational (NoSQL) databases have different strengths and weaknesses. In RDBMSs, data can be queried flexibly, but queries are relatively expensive and do not scale well in high-traffic situations. In a NoSQL database, you can query data efficiently in a limited number of ways. Table 4.3 shows a comparison of different characteristics of SQL and NoSQL databases.

TABLE 4.3 SQL vs. NoSQL database characteristics

Type	SQL	NoSQL
Data Storage	Rows and columns	Key-value, document, wide-column, graph
Schemas	Fixed	Dynamic
Querying	Using SQL	Focused on collection of documents
Scalability	Vertical	Horizontal
Transactions	Supported	Support varies
Consistency	Strong	Eventual and strong

The storage format for SQL versus NoSQL databases also differs. As shown in Figure 4.9, SQL databases are often stored in a row/column format, whereas NoSQL databases, such as Amazon DynamoDB, have a key-value format that could be in a JSON format, as shown in this example.

FIGURE 4.9 SQL versus NoSQL format comparison

SQL

ISBN	Title	Edition	Format
1119138558	AWS Certified Solutions Architect Study Guide	1	Paperback

NoSQL

```
{
  ISBN: 9182932465265,
  Title: "AWS Certified Solutions Architect Study Guide",
  Edition: "1",
  Format: "Paperback"
}
```

Amazon DynamoDB

Amazon DynamoDB is a fast and flexible NoSQL database service for all applications that need consistent, single-digit millisecond latency at any scale. It is a fully managed cloud database, and it supports both document and key-value store models. Its flexible data model, reliable performance, and automatic scaling of throughput capacity make it a great fit for a variety of use cases, including:

- Mobile

- Gaming

- Adtech (advertising technology)

- Internet of Things (IoT)

- Applications that do not require complex queries

With DynamoDB, you can create database tables that can store and retrieve any amount of data and serve any level of request traffic. You can scale up or scale down your table throughput capacity without downtime or performance degradation. DynamoDB automatically spreads the data and traffic for your tables over enough servers to handle your throughput and storage requirements while maintaining consistent and fast performance. All your data is stored on solid-state disks (SSDs) and automatically replicated across multiple availability zones in an AWS region, providing built-in high availability and data durability. If you want the ultimate high availability assurance, you can use global tables, which keep replicas of your DynamoDB tables in sync across AWS regions.

Core Components of Amazon DynamoDB

The core concepts in DynamoDB are tables, items, and attributes. A *table* is a collection of items, and each item is a collection of *attributes*. DynamoDB uses partition keys to uniquely identify each item in a table, much like the primary key on a relational database record. These can be combined with sort keys to create a kind of composite key to uniquely identify records. Furthermore, secondary indexes can be used to provide more querying flexibility. You can use DynamoDB Streams to capture data modification events in DynamoDB tables.

Figure 4.10 shows the DynamoDB data model, including a table, items, attributes, required partition key, optional sort key, and an example of data being stored in partitions.

Tables

Similar to other database systems, DynamoDB stores data in tables. A table is a collection of items. For example, a table called *People* could be used to store personal contact information about friends, family, or anyone else of interest.

Items

An item in DynamoDB is similar in many ways to rows, records, or tuples in other database systems. Each DynamoDB table contains zero or more items. An *item* is a collection of attributes that is uniquely identifiable for each record in that table. For a *People* table, each item represents a person. There is no limit to the number of items that you can store in a table.

Attributes

Each item is composed of one or more attributes. Attributes in DynamoDB are similar in many ways to fields or columns in other database systems. For example, an item in a *People* table contains attributes called *PersonID*, *Last Name*, *First Name*, and so on.

FIGURE 4.10   Amazon DynamoDB tables and partitions

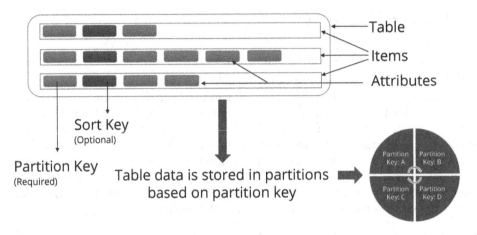

Figure 4.11 shows a table named *People* with items and attributes. Each block represents an item, and within those blocks you have attributes that define the overall item.

In Figure 4.11:

- Each item in the table has a unique identifier, a primary key, or a partition key that distinguishes the item from all others in the table. The primary key consists of one attribute (`PersonID`).

- Other than the primary key, the *People* table is schemaless, which means that you do not have to define the attributes or their data types beforehand. Each item can have its own distinct attributes. This is where the contrast begins to show between NoSQL and SQL. In SQL, you would have to define a schema for a person, and every person would need to have the same attributes. As you can see in Figure 4.11, with NoSQL and DynamoDB, each person can have different attributes.

- Most of the attributes are scalar, so they can have only one value. Strings and numbers are common examples of scalars.

- Some of the items have a nested attribute (`Address`). DynamoDB supports nested attributes up to 32 levels deep.

FIGURE 4.11   DynamoDB table with items and attributes

People

```
{
    "PersonID": 101,
    "LastName": "Smith",
    "FirstName": "Fred",
    "Phone": "555-4321"
}
```

```
{
    "PersonID": 102,
    "LastName": "Jones",
    "FirstName": "Mary",
    "Address": {
        "Street": "123 Main",
        "City": "Anytown",
        "State": "OH",
        "ZIPCode": 12345
    }
}
```

```
{
    "PersonID": 103,
    "LastName": "Stephens",
    "FirstName": "Howard",
    "Address": {
        "Street": "123 Main",
        "City": "London",
        "PostalCode": "ER3 5K8"
    },
    "FavoriteColor": "Blue"
}
```

Primary Key

When you create a table, at a minimum, you are required to specify the table name and primary key of the table. The primary key uniquely identifies each item in the table. No two items can have the same key within a table.

DynamoDB supports two different kinds of primary keys: a partition key and a composite key consisting of a partition key plus a sort key.

Partition Key (Hash Key)   A simple primary key, composed of one attribute, is known as the *partition key*. DynamoDB uses the partition key's value as an input to an internal hash function. The output from the hash function determines the partition (physical storage internal to DynamoDB) in which the item is stored.

No two items in a table can have the same partition key value (unless you are using a sort key; see the next item). For example, in the *People* table, with a simple primary key of PersonID, you cannot have two items with PersonID of 000-07-1075.

The partition key of an item is also known as its *hash attribute*. The term *hash attribute* derives from the use of an internal hash function in DynamoDB that evenly distributes data items across partitions based on their partition key values.

Each primary key attribute must be a scalar (meaning that it can hold only a single value). The only data types allowed for primary key attributes are string, number, or binary.

Partition Key and Sort Key (Range Attribute)   A *composite primary key* is composed of two attributes: *partition key* and the *sort key*.

The *sort key* of an item is also known as its *range attribute*. The term *range attribute* derives from the way that DynamoDB stores items with the same partition key physically close together, in sorted order, by the sort key value.

In a table that has a partition key and a sort key, it's possible for two items to have the same partition key value, but those two items must have different sort key values. You cannot have two items in the table that have identical partition key and sort key values.

For example, if you have a *Music* table with a composite primary key (*Artist* and *Song-Title*), you can access any item in the *Music* table directly if you provide the *Artist* and *SongTitle* values for that item.

A composite primary key gives you additional flexibility when querying data. For example, if you provide only the value for *Artist*, DynamoDB retrieves all the songs by that artist. To retrieve only a subset of songs by a particular artist, you can provide a value for *Artist* with a range of values for *SongTitle*.

As a developer, the attribute you choose for your application has important implications. If there is little differentiation among partition keys, all your data is stored together in the same physical location.

Figure 4.12 shows an example of these two types of keys. In the *SensorLocation* table, the primary key is the SensorId attribute. This means that every item (or row) in this table has a unique SensorId, meaning that each sensor has exactly one location or latitude and longitude value.

Conversely, the *SensorReadings* table has a partition key and a sort key. The SensorId attribute is the partition key and the Time attribute is the sort key, which combined make it a *composite key*. For each SensorId, there may be multiple items corresponding to sensor readings at different times. The combination of SensorId and Time uniquely identifies items in the table. This design enables you to query the table for all readings related to a particular sensor.

Secondary Indexes

DynamoDB tables can be queried by their partition key and sort key. This is all the filtering that can be done server-side; anything further must be done on the client. However, DynamoDB does allow some options to expand on your tables' server-side search capabilities.

FIGURE 4.12   DynamoDB primary keys

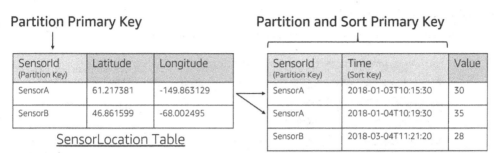

If you want to perform queries on attributes that are not part of the table's primary key, you can create a *secondary index*. By using a secondary index, you can query the data in the table using an alternate key, in addition to querying against the primary key. DynamoDB does not require that you use indexes, but doing so can give you more flexibility when querying your data.

Indexes in DynamoDB are manifested as tables in their own right and kept constantly in sync with the table from which they were derived. As a result, after you create a secondary index on a table, you can then read data from the index in much the same way as you do from the table. DynamoDB automatically creates indexes based on the primary key of a table and automatically updates all indexes whenever a table changes.

A secondary index contains the following:

- Primary key attributes
- Alternate key attributes
- (Optional) A subset of other attributes from the base table (*projected attributes*)

Amazon DynamoDB supports two types of secondary indexes: *local secondary indexes* and *global secondary indexes*. You can define up to five global secondary indexes and five local secondary indexes per table.

Local Secondary Index

A *local secondary index (LSI)* is an index that has the same partition key as the base table, but a different sort key (see Figure 4.13), allowing you to query the table using more than just the original partition and sort key. When creating an LSI, you choose an alternate sort key as well as any other fields you'd like to copy, or *project,* on to the local secondary index. Because LSIs are manifested just like tables, they do incur a storage cost. If you project all the fields, you have essentially replicated the original table with different query options! Try to plan around the types of queries your application will need to perform. LSIs can be created only when you create the primary table; you cannot add, remove, or modify one later.

FIGURE 4.13   Local secondary index

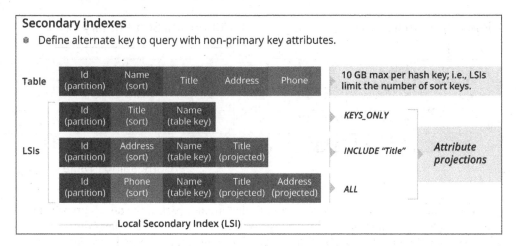

Global Secondary Index

A *global secondary index* is an index with a partition key and a sort key that can be different from those on the base table (see Figure 4.14). It is considered "global" because queries on the index can span all of the data in the base table across all partitions. You can create one during table creation, or you can add, remove, or modify it later.

FIGURE 4.14   Global secondary index

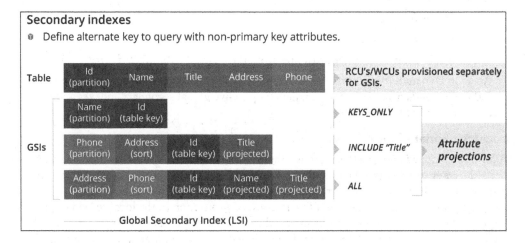

  You can create a global secondary index, not a local secondary index, after table creation.

For example, by using a *Music* table, you can query data items by *Artist* (partition key) or by *Artist* and *SongTitle* (partition key and sort key). Suppose that you also wanted to query the data by *Genre* and *AlbumTitle*. To do this, you could create a global secondary index on *Genre* and *AlbumTitle* and then query the index in much the same way as you'd query the *Music* table.

Figure 4.15 shows the example *Music* table with a new index called *GenreAlbumTitle*. In the index, *Genre* is the partition key, and *AlbumTitle* is the sort key.

FIGURE 4.15   DynamoDB table and secondary index

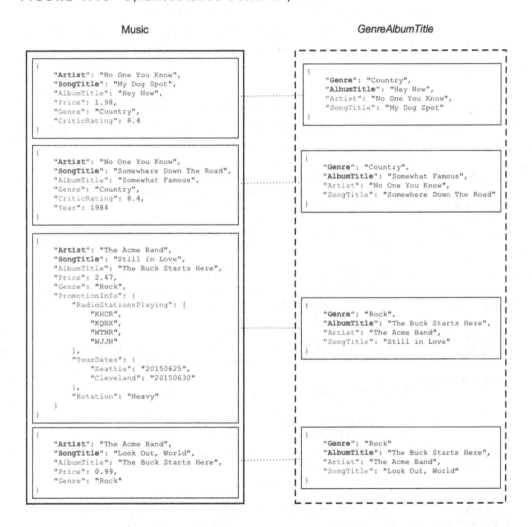

Note the following about the GenreAlbumTitle index:

- Every index belongs to a table, which is called the *base table* for the index. In the preceding example, *Music* is the base table for the GenreAlbumTitle index.

- DynamoDB maintains indexes automatically. When you add, update, or delete an item in the base table, DynamoDB adds, updates, or deletes the corresponding item in any indexes that belong to that table.

- When you create an index, you specify which attributes will be projected from the base table to the index. At a minimum, Amazon DynamoDB projects the key attributes from the base table into the index. This is the case with GenreAlbumTitle, wherein only the key attributes from the *Music* table are projected into the index.

You can query the GenreAlbumTitle index to find all albums of a particular genre (for example, all *Hard Rock* albums). You can also query the index to find all albums within a particular genre that have certain album titles (for example, all *Heavy Metal* albums with titles that start with the letter M).

Comparison of Local Secondary Indexes and Global Secondary Indexes

To determine which type of index to use, consider your application's requirements. Table 4.4 shows the main differences between a global secondary index and a local secondary index.

TABLE 4.4   Comparison of local and global secondary indexes

Characteristic	Global secondary Index	Local secondary index
Query Scope	Entire table, across all partitions.	Single partition, as specified by the partition key value in the query.
Key Attributes	<ul><li>Partition key, or partition and sort key.</li><li>Can be any scalar attribute in the table.</li></ul>	<ul><li>Partition and sort key.</li><li>Partition key of index must be the same attribute as base table.</li></ul>
Projected Attributes	Only projected attributes can be queried.	Can query attributes that are not projected. Attributes are retrieved from the base table.
Read Consistency	Eventual consistency only.	Eventual consistency or strong consistency.
Provisioned Throughput	<ul><li>Separate throughput settings from base table.</li><li>Consumes separate capacity units.</li></ul>	<ul><li>Same throughput settings as base table.</li><li>Consumes base table capacity units.</li></ul>
Life Cycle Considerations	Can be created or deleted at any time.	<ul><li>Must be created when the table is created.</li><li>Can be deleted only when the table is deleted.</li></ul>

Amazon DynamoDB Streams

Amazon DynamoDB Streams is an optional feature that captures data modification events in DynamoDB tables. The data about these events appears in the stream in near real time and in the order that the events occurred.

Each event is represented by a *stream record*. If you enable a stream on a table, DynamoDB Streams writes a stream record whenever one of the following events occurs:

A new item is added to the table: The stream captures an image of the entire item, including all its attributes.

An item is updated: The stream captures the "before" and "after" images of any attributes that were modified in the item.

An item is deleted from the table: The stream captures an image of the entire item before it was deleted.

Each stream record also contains the name of the table, the event time stamp, and other metadata. Stream records have a lifetime of 24 hours; after that, they are automatically removed from the stream.

Figure 4.16 shows how you can use DynamoDB Streams together with AWS Lambda to create a *trigger*—code that executes automatically whenever an event of interest appears in a stream. For example, consider a *Customers* table that contains customer information for a company. Suppose that you want to send a "welcome" email to each new customer. You could enable a stream on that table and then associate the stream with a Lambda function. The Lambda function would execute whenever a new stream record appears, but only process new items added to the *Customers* table. For any item that has an EmailAddress attribute, the Lambda function could invoke *Amazon Simple Email Service (Amazon SES)* to send an email to that address.

 In the example shown in Figure 4.16, the last customer, Craig Roe, will not receive an email because he does not have an EmailAddress.

In addition to triggers, Amazon DynamoDB Streams enables other powerful solutions that developers can create, such as the following:

- Data replication within and across AWS regions
- Materialized views of data in DynamoDB tables
- Data analysis by using *Amazon Kinesis* materialized views

DynamoDB also supports integration with Kinesis Data Streams, enabling events to propagate to even more services within AWS for analysis and processing.

FIGURE 4.16   Example of DynamoDB Streams and AWS Lambda

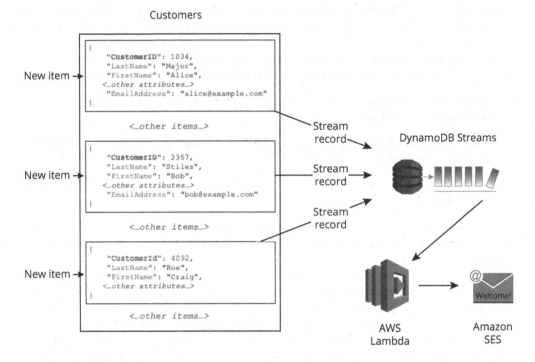

Read Consistency

DynamoDB replicates data among multiple availability zones in a region. When your application writes data to a DynamoDB table and receives an HTTP 200 response (OK), all copies of the data are updated. The data is eventually consistent across all storage locations, usually within one second or less. DynamoDB supports both *eventually consistent* and *strongly consistent* reads.

Eventually Consistent Reads

When you read data from an Amazon DynamoDB table immediately after a write operation, the response might not reflect the results of a recently completed write operation. The response might include some stale data. If you repeat your read request after a short time, the response should return the latest data. DynamoDB uses *eventually consistent reads*, unless you specify otherwise.

Strongly Consistent Reads

When querying data, you can specify whether DynamoDB should return *strongly consistent reads*. When you request a strongly consistent read, DynamoDB returns a response with the most up-to-date data, reflecting updates from all prior write operations that were successful. A strongly consistent read might not be available if there is a network delay or outage.

Comparison of Consistent Reads

As a developer, you must understand the needs of your application. In some applications, eventually consistent reads might be fine, such as a high-score dashboard. In other applications or parts of an application, however, such as a financial or medical system, an eventually consistent read could be an issue. You will want to evaluate your data usage patterns to ensure that you are choosing the right type of reads for each part of your application.

There is an additional cost for strongly consistent reads, and they will have more latency in returning data than an eventually consistent read. Cost and timing should play into your decision.

Read and Write Throughput

When you create a table or index in DynamoDB, you must specify your capacity requirements for read and write activity. By defining your throughput capacity in advance, DynamoDB can reserve the necessary resources to meet the read and write activity your application requires, while ensuring consistent, low-latency performance. Specify your required throughput value by setting the `ProvisionedThroughput` parameter when you create or update a table.

You specify throughput capacity in terms of read capacity units and write capacity units:

- One *read capacity unit* (RCU) represents one strongly consistent read per second, or two eventually consistent reads per second, for an item up to 4 KB in size. If you need to read an item that is larger than 4 KB, DynamoDB will need to consume additional read capacity units. The total number of read capacity units required depends on the item size and whether you want an eventually consistent or strongly consistent read.

- One *write capacity unit* (WCU) represents one write per second for an item up to 1 KB in size. If you need to write an item that is larger than 1 KB, DynamoDB must consume additional write capacity units. The total number of write capacity units required depends on the item size.

For example, suppose you create a table with five read capacity units and five write capacity units. With these settings, your application could do the following:

- Perform strongly consistent reads of up to 20 KB per second (4 KB × 5 read capacity units)

- Perform eventually consistent reads of up to 40 KB per second (twice as much read throughput)

- Write up to 5 KB per second (1 KB × 5 write capacity units)

If your application reads or writes larger items (up to the DynamoDB maximum item size of 400 KB), it consumes more capacity units.

Please note that DynamoDB read/write capacity calculations always round up to the nearest 4 KB. If you need one strongly consistent read per second at 1 KB, you will consume a full RCU (rounding up to 4). If you need a strongly consistent read per second at 5 KB, that will consume two RCUs (rounding up to 8 KB). The same is true of write capacity units (WCUs), which round up to the nearest 1 KB.

If your read or write requests exceed the throughput settings for a table, DynamoDB can throttle that request. DynamoDB may also thottle read requests on an index. Throttling prevents your application from consuming too many capacity units. When a request is throttled, it fails with an HTTP 400 code (Bad Request) and a ProvisionedThroughputExceededException. The AWS SDKs have built-in support for retrying throttled requests, so you do not need to write this logic yourself.

Amazon DynamoDB provides the following mechanisms for managing throughput as it changes:

DynamoDB Autoscaling DynamoDB automatic scaling actively manages throughput capacity for tables and global secondary indexes. With autoscaling, you define a range (upper and lower limits) for read and write capacity units. You can even choose to autoscale only for reads or writes alone. You also define a target utilization percentage within that range. DynamoDB automatic scaling seeks to maintain your target utilization, even as your application workload increases or decreases.

Provisioned Throughput If you aren't using DynamoDB autoscaling, you must define your throughput requirements manually. As discussed, with this setting you may run into a ProvisionedThroughputExceededException if you are throttled.

Reserved Capacity You can purchase *reserved capacity* in advance, where you pay a one-time upfront fee and commit to a minimum usage level over a period of time. You may realize significant cost savings compared to on-demand provisioned throughput settings, but make sure not to overprovision for your needs.

On-Demand It can be difficult to plan capacity, especially if you aren't collecting metrics or perhaps are developing a new application and you aren't sure what type of performance you require. With On-Demand mode, your DynamoDB table will automatically scale up or down to any previously reached traffic level. If a workload's traffic level reaches a new peak, DynamoDB rapidly adapts to accommodate the workload. While this method requires the least forethought, be aware that it is the most expensive option.

Partitions and Data Distribution

When you are using a table in DynamoDB, the data is placed on multiple partitions (depending on the amount of data and the amount of throughput allocated to it; recall that throughput is determined by RCUs and WCUs). When you allocate RCUs and WCUs to a table, those RCUs and WCUs are split evenly among all partitions for your table.

For example, suppose that you have allocated 1,000 RCUs and 1,000 WCUs to a table, and this table has 10 partitions allocated to it. Then each partition would have 100 RCUs and 100 WCUs for it to use. If one of your partitions consumes all the RCUs and WCUs for the table, you may receive a ProvisionedThroughputExceededException error because one of your partitions is hot. To deal with hot partitions, DynamoDB has two features: *burst capacity* and *adaptive capacity*.

Burst Capacity

The previous example discussed how you had 10 partitions, each with 100 RCUs and 100 WCUs allocated to them. One of your partitions begins to become hot and now needs to consume more than 100 RCUs. Under normal circumstances, you may receive the ProvisionedThroughputExceededException error. However, with burst capacity, whenever your partition is not using all of its total capacity, DynamoDB reserves a portion of that unused capacity for later *bursts* of throughput to handle any spike your partition may experience.

As of this writing, DynamoDB currently reserves up to 300 seconds (5 minutes) of unused read and write capacity, which means that your partition can handle a peak load for five minutes over its normal expected load. Burst capacity is enabled and runs in the background.

Adaptive Capacity

Adaptive capacity is when it is not always possible to distribute read and write activity to a partition evenly. In the example, a partition is no longer only experiencing peak demand but consistent demand over and above its normal 100 RCU and 100 WCUs. Suppose that now this partition requires 200 RCUs instead of 100 RCUs.

DynamoDB adaptive capacity enables your application to continue reading and writing to hot partitions without being throttled, provided that the total provisioned capacity for the table is not exceeded. DynamoDB allocates additional RCUs to the hot partition, in this case, 100 more. Once adaptive capacity allocates the RCUs to the partition, DynamoDB is able to sustain the new higher throughput for your partition and table. Adaptive capacity is on by default, and there is no need to enable or disable it.

Retrieving Data from DynamoDB

Two primary methods are used to retrieve data from DynamoDB: Query and Scan.

Query

In DynamoDB, you perform Query operations directly on the table or index. To run the Query command, you must specify, at a minimum, a primary key. If you are querying an index, you must specify both TableName and IndexName.

The following is a query on a *Music* table in DynamoDB using the Python SDK:

```
import boto3
import json
import decimal

# Helper class to convert a DynamoDB item to JSON.
class DecimalEncoder(json.JSONEncoder):
    def default(self, o):
        if isinstance(o, decimal.Decimal):
            if o % 1 > 0:
                return float(o)
```

```
        else:
            return int(o)
    return super(DecimalEncoder, self).default(o)


dynamodb = boto3.resource('dynamodb', region_name='us-east-1')


table = dynamodb.Table('Music')


print("A query with DynamoDB")


response = table.query(
    KeyConditionExpression=Key('Artist').eq('Sam Samuel')
)


for i in response['Items']:
    print(i['SongTitle'], "-", i['Genre'], i['Price'])
```

The query returns all the songs by the artist Sam Samuel in the *Music* table.

Scan

The Scan operation reads every item in a table or a secondary index. Although you can provide a FilterExpression along with the command, any filtering is performed after the full table scan, so you always incur the full cost of reading every item in the table.

If the total number of scanned items exceeds the maximum dataset size limit of 1 MB, the scan stops, and the results are returned to the user as a LastEvaluatedKey value to continue the scan in a subsequent operation. The results also include the number of items exceeding the limit.

A single Scan operation reads up to the maximum number of items set (if using the Limit parameter) or a maximum of 1 MB of data and then applies any filtering to the results by using FilterExpression. If LastEvaluatedKey is present in the response, you must paginate the result set.

Scan operations proceed sequentially; however, for faster performance on a large table or secondary index, applications can request a parallel Scan operation by providing the Segment and TotalSegments parameters.

Scan uses eventually consistent reads when accessing the data in a table; therefore, the result set might not include the changes to data in the table immediately before the operation began. If you need a consistent copy of the data, as of the time that the Scan begins, you can set the ConsistentRead parameter to true.

The following is a scan on a *Movies* table with the Python SDK:

```
// Return all of the data in the index
import boto3
import json
import decimal
```

```
# Create the DynamoDB Resource
dynamodb = boto3.resource('dynamodb', region_name='us-east-1')

# Use the Music Table
table = dynamodb.Table('Music')

# Helper class to convert a DynamoDB decimal/item to JSON.
class DecimalEncoder(json.JSONEncoder):
    def default(self, o):
        if isinstance(o, decimal.Decimal):
            if o % 1 > 0:
                return float(o)
            else:
                return int(o)
        return super(DecimalEncoder, self).default(o)

# Specify some filters for the scan
# Here we are stating that the Price must be between 12 - 30
fe = Key('Price').between(12, 30)
pe = "#g, Price"
# Expression Attribute Names for Projection Expression only.
ean = { "#g": "Genre", }

#
response_scan = table.scan(
    FilterExpression=fe,
    ProjectionExpression=pe,
    ExpressionAttributeNames=ean
    )

# Print all the items
for i in response_scan['Items']:
    print(json.dumps(i, cls=DecimalEncoder))

while 'LastEvaluatedKey' in response:
    response = table.scan(
        ProjectionExpression=pe,
        FilterExpression=fe,
```

```
    ExpressionAttributeNames= ean,
    ExclusiveStartKey=response['LastEvaluatedKey']
    )
for i in response['Items']:
    print(json.dumps(i)
```

As you can see from the Python code, the scan returns all records with a price of between 12 and 30 and the genre and the price. The LastEvaluatedKey property is included to continue to loop through the entire table.

Global Tables

With global tables, DynamoDB performs all the necessary tasks to create copies of your tables in multiple regions and propagate ongoing data changes to all of them, giving you global high availability and low latency options for users in other regions. Figure 4.17 shows an example of how global tables can work with a global application and globally dispersed users.

FIGURE 4.17   Global tables

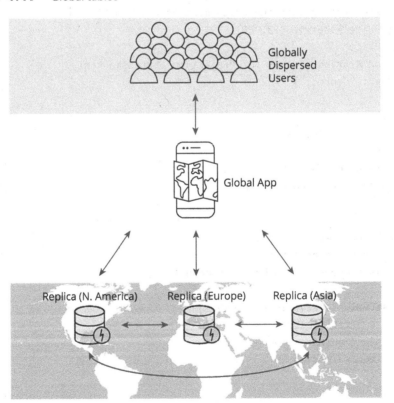

A *global table* is a collection of one or more Amazon DynamoDB tables, all owned by a single AWS account, identified as replica tables. A *replica table* (or replica, for short) is a single DynamoDB table that functions as a part of a global table. Each replica stores the same set of data items. Any given global table can have only one replica table per region, and every replica has the same table name and the same primary key schema. Changes made in one replica are recorded in a stream and propagated to other replicas, as shown in Figure 4.18.

FIGURE 4.18   Replication flow in global tables

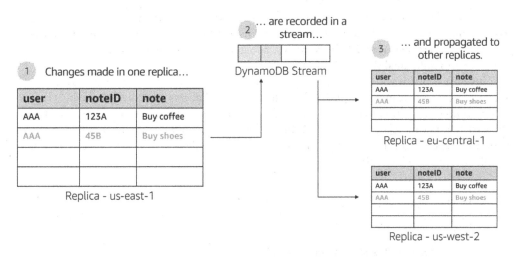

If your application requires strongly consistent reads, then it must perform all its strongly consistent reads and writes in the same region. DynamoDB does not support strongly consistent reads across AWS regions.

Conflicts can arise if applications update the same item in different regions at about the same time (concurrent updates). To ensure eventual consistency, DynamoDB global tables use a "last writer wins" conflict resolution mechanism, wherein all replicas agree on the latest update and converge toward a state in which they all have identical data.

To create a DynamoDB global table, perform the following steps:

1. Create an ordinary DynamoDB table in an AWS region.

2. Click into the details of the new table and select the Global Tables tab.

3. Click Create Replica and choose the AWS regions where you want to replicate the table's data.

DynamoDB will automatically create replica tables in the selected regions with the same table name, partition key, sort key (if applicable), and stream settings.

Amazon DynamoDB Local

DynamoDB Local is the downloadable version of DynamoDB that lets you write and test applications by using the DynamoDB API without accessing the actual live service. Instead, the database is self-contained on your computer.

Having this local version helps you save on provisioned throughput, data storage, and data transfer fees while you build your application. Even better, you don't need an Internet connection while you're developing with DynamoDB Local.

IAM and Fine-Grained Access Control

You can use AWS IAM to grant or restrict access to DynamoDB resources and API actions. For example, you could allow a user to execute the GetItem operation on a *Books* table, but not on others. DynamoDB also supports fine-grained access control so that you can control access to individual data items and attributes.

This means that if you have a *Users* table and you want each user to have access to their data only, you can accomplish this with fine-grained access control. By using a LeadingKeys condition, you can limit the user so that they can access only the items where the partition key matches their userID. In the following example in the *Users* table, you want to restrict who can view the profile information to only the user to which the data or profile information belongs:

```
{
    "Version": "2012-10-17",
    "Statement": [
        {
            "Sid": "LeadingKeysExample",
            "Effect": "Allow",
            "Action": [
                "dynamodb:GetItem",
                "dynamodb:BatchGetItem",
                "dynamodb:Query",
                "dynamodb:PutItem",
                "dynamodb:UpdateItem",
                "dynamodb:DeleteItem",
                "dynamodb:BatchWriteItem"
            ],
            "Resource": [
                "arn:aws:dynamodb:us-east-1:accountnumber:table/UserProfiles"
            ],
            "Condition": {
                "ForAllValues:StringEquals": {
                    "dynamodb:LeadingKeys": [
                        "${www.amazon.com:user_id}"
                    ],
```

```
                "dynamodb:Attributes": [
                    "UserId",
                    "FirstName",
                    "LastName",
                    "Email",
                    "Birthday"
                ]
            },
            "StringEqualsIfExists": {
                "dynamodb:Select": "SPECIFIC_ATTRIBUTES"
            }
        }
    }
  ]
}
```

As you can see in the IAM policy, only the specific user is allowed to access a subset of the total attributes that are defined in the Attributes section of the policy. Furthermore, the SELECT statement specifies that the application must provide a list of specific attributes to act upon, preventing the application from requesting all attributes.

Backup and Restore

You can create on-demand backups and enable point-in-time recovery for your DynamoDB tables.

On-demand backups create full backups of your tables or restore them on-demand at any time. These actions execute with zero impact on table performance or availability and without consuming any provisioned throughput on the table.

Point-in-time recovery helps protect your DynamoDB tables from accidental write or delete operations. For example, suppose that a test script accidentally writes to a production DynamoDB table. With point-in-time recovery, you can restore that table to any point in time during the last 35 days.

Encryption with Amazon DynamoDB

DynamoDB offers fully managed encryption at rest, enabled by default, using AWS KMS. By default, DynamoDB uses an AWS-owned KMS key; however, you can also specify your own customer-managed key (CMK) that you have created. For more information on AWS KMS, see Chapter 5, "Encryption on AWS."

DynamoDB Best Practices

Now that you understand what DynamoDB is and how you can use it to create a scalable database for your application, let's review some best practices for using DynamoDB.

Distribute Workload Evenly

The primary key or partition key portion of a table's primary key determines the logical partitions in which the table's data is stored. This logical partition also affects the underlying physical partitions. While DynamoDB's Adaptive Capacity feature acts quickly to redistribute read and write capacity to avoid overloading any one partition, developers should still strive to distribute workloads across partitions as evenly as possible, reducing the number of "hot" partition issues that may arise.

Table 4.5 compares common partition key schemas and whether they are good for DynamoDB.

TABLE 4.5   Amazon DynamoDB partition key recommended strategies

Partition key value	Uniformity
User ID, where the application has many users	Good
Status code, where there are only a few possible status codes	Bad
Item creation date, rounded to the nearest time period (for example, day, hour, or minute)	Bad
Device ID, where each device accesses data at relatively similar intervals	Good
Device ID, where even if there are many devices being tracked, one is by far more popular than all the others	Bad

In-Memory Data Stores

In-memory data stores are used for caching and real-time workloads. AWS provides a variety of in-memory, key-value database options. You can operate your own nonrelational key-value data store in the cloud on EC2 and EBS, work with AWS solution providers, or take advantage of fully managed nonrelational services such as *Amazon ElastiCache*.

Caching

In computing, the data in a *cache* is generally stored in fast-access hardware, such as *random-access memory (RAM)*, and is intended to increase data retrieval performance by reducing the need to access the underlying slower storage layer.

Trading off capacity for speed, a cache typically stores a subset of data transiently, in contrast to databases whose data is usually complete and durable.

Benefits of Caching

A cache provides high-throughput, low-latency access to commonly accessed application data by storing the data in memory, improving users' experience with your application as your code avoids time-consuming database queries I/O bottlenecks. Even write-intensive applications normally perform enough reads to see the benefits of caching. Benefits of caching include the following:

- Improved application performance
- Reduced database cost
- Reduced load on the backend database tier
- More predictable performance
- Fewer database hotspots
- Increased read throughput (IOPS)

Consider caching your data if the following conditions apply to a dataset:

- It is slow or expensive to acquire when compared to cache retrieval.
- It is accessed with sufficient frequency.
- It changes infrequently.

Caching Strategies

Two of the most common cache implementation methods are *lazy loading* and *write through*.

Lazy Loading   *Lazy loading* is a caching strategy that loads data into the cache only when necessary. When your application requests data, it first makes the request to the cache. If the data exists in the cache (a cache hit), it is retrieved from the cache, but if it does not or has expired (a cache miss), the data is retrieved from your data store and *then* stored in the cache. The advantages of lazy loading are that only requested data is cached; on the other hand, a cache miss has a high penalty, resulting in three trips:

1. Initial request to the cache request.
2. If there is a cache miss, you must query the database.
3. After data retrieval, the cache is updated.

Write-Through   The *write-through* strategy adds data or updates in the cache whenever data is written to the database. The advantage of write-through is that the data in the cache is never stale. The disadvantage is that there is a write penalty because every write involves two trips: a write to the cache and a write to the database. Another disadvantage is that your application ends up storing almost everything in its cache, whether or not it is ever read. In addition, if your data is updated frequently, the cache may be updated often, causing cache churn.

In-Memory Key-Value Store

An *in-memory key-value store* is a NoSQL database optimized for read-heavy application workloads (such as social networking, gaming, media sharing, and Q&A portals) or compute-intensive workloads (such as a recommendation engine). In-memory caching improves application performance by storing critical pieces of data in memory for low-latency access. Cached information may include the results of I/O-intensive database queries or the results of computationally intensive calculations.

Benefits of In-Memory Data Stores

The strict performance requirements imposed by real-time applications mandate more efficient databases. Traditional databases rely on disk-based storage. A single user action may consist of multiple database calls. As these calls accumulate, latency increases. In contrast, in-memory data stores provide higher throughput and lower latency—sometimes one to two orders of magnitude faster than disk-based databases.

As a NoSQL data store, in-memory data stores do not share the architectural limitations found in traditional relational databases; NoSQL data stores are built to be scalable. Using managed cloud services also eliminates the need to administer infrastructure.

Benefits of Distributed Cache

A caching layer not only improves throughput for read-heavy applications, it is also more cost effective. Using a distributed caching layer lets you scale your cache independently of your application or database tier. This architecture helps save money when you need to increase read performance, as you can pay to scale relatively inexpensive cache nodes instead of costly database nodes.

Amazon ElastiCache

Amazon ElastiCache is a web service that makes it easy to deploy, operate, and scale an in-memory cache in the AWS Cloud. The service improves the performance of web applications by allowing you to retrieve information from fast, managed, in-memory caches instead of relying entirely on slower disk-based databases.

ElastiCache manages its own infrastructure and scaling, automatically detecting and replacing failed nodes, providing a resilient system that mitigates the risk of overloaded cloud databases.

ElastiCache currently supports two different open source in-memory key-value caching engines: Redis and Memcached. Each engine provides certain advantages.

Redis

Redis is an increasingly popular open source key-value store that supports advanced data structures such as sorted sets, hashes, and lists. Unlike Memcached, Redis has disk persistence built in, meaning that you can use it for long-lived data. Redis also supports replication, which can be used to achieve multi-AZ redundancy.

Memcached

Memcached is a widely adopted in-memory key store. ElastiCache's implementation is protocol-compliant with Memcached, and it is designed to work with popular tools that you use today with existing Memcached environments. Memcached is also multithreaded, meaning that it makes good use of larger EC2 instance sizes with multiple cores.

Comparison of Memcached and Redis

Although both Memcached and Redis appear similar on the surface, they are quite different in practice. Because of the replication and persistence features of Redis, ElastiCache manages Redis more as a relational database. Redis ElastiCache clusters are managed as stateful entities that include failover, similar to how RDS manages database failover.

Conversely, because Memcached is designed as a pure caching solution with no persistence, ElastiCache manages Memcached nodes as a pool that can grow and shrink, similar to an EC2 Auto Scaling group. Individual nodes are expendable, and ElastiCache provides additional capabilities here, such as automatic node replacement and Auto Discovery.

Use Memcached if you require one or more of the following:

- Object caching is your primary goal, for example, to off-load your database.
- You are interested in as simple a caching model as possible.
- You plan to run large cache nodes and require multithreaded performance with use of multiple cores.
- You want to scale your cache horizontally as you grow.

Use Redis if you require one or more of the following:

- You are looking for more advanced data types, such as lists, hashes, and sets.
- Sorting and ranking datasets in memory help you, such as with leaderboards.
- Your application requires publish and subscribe (pub/sub) capabilities.
- Persistence of your key store is important.
- You want to run in multiple availability zones (multi-AZ) with failover.
- Transactional support, which lets you execute a group of commands as an isolated and atomic operation.

Amazon DynamoDB Accelerator

Amazon DynamoDB Accelerator (DAX) is a fully managed, highly available, in-memory cache for DynamoDB that delivers up to a 10x performance improvement—from milliseconds to microseconds—even at millions of requests per second. DAX does all of the heavy lifting required to add in-memory acceleration to your DynamoDB tables, without requiring developers to manage cache invalidation, data population, or cluster management.

With DAX, you do not need to modify application logic, because DAX is compatible with existing DynamoDB API calls.

Cloud Database Migration

Data is the cornerstone of successful cloud application deployments. Amazon offers a suite of tools to help you move data via networks, roads, and technology partners.

This chapter focuses on the AWS Database Migration Service (AWS DMS) and the AWS Schema Conversion Tool (AWS SCT). Customers also use other AWS services and features that are discussed in Chapter 3, "AWS Data Storage."

AWS Database Migration Service

AWS Database Migration Service (AWS DMS) helps you migrate databases to AWS quickly and securely. The source database remains fully operational during the migration, minimizing downtime to applications that rely on the database. AWS DMS can migrate your data to and from the most widely used commercial and open source databases.

The service supports *homogenous database migrations*, such as Oracle to Oracle, in addition to *heterogeneous migrations* between different database platforms, such as Oracle to Amazon Aurora or Microsoft SQL Server to MySQL. You can also stream data to Amazon Redshift, DynamoDB, and S3 from any of the supported sources, such as Amazon Aurora, PostgreSQL, MySQL, MariaDB, Oracle Database, SAP ASE, SQL Server, IBM DB2 LUW, and MongoDB, enabling consolidation and easy analysis of data in a petabyte-scale data warehouse. You can also use DMS for continuous data replication with high availability.

Figure 4.19 shows an example of both heterogeneous and homogenous database migrations.

To perform a database migration, DMS connects to the source data store, reads the source data, and formats the data for consumption by the target data store. It then loads the data into the target data store. Most of this processing happens in memory, though large transactions might require some buffering to disk. Cached transactions and log files are also written to disk.

At a high level, when setting up DMS, you will complete the following tasks:

1. Create a replication server.

2. Create source and target endpoints that have connection information about your data stores.

3. Create one or more tasks to migrate data between the source and target data stores.

FIGURE 4.19   Homogenous database migrations using DMS

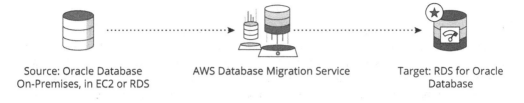

Source: Oracle Database   AWS Database Migration Service   Target: RDS for Oracle
On-Premises, in EC2 or RDS   Database

Source: MySQL Database   AWS Database Migration Service   Target: Amazon Aurora
On-Premises, in EC2 or RDS   Database

A task can consist of three major phases:

- The full load of existing data
- The application of cached changes
- Ongoing replication

AWS Schema Conversion Tool

For heterogeneous database migrations, DMS uses the *AWS Schema Conversion Tool* (AWS SCT). AWS SCT makes heterogeneous database migrations predictable by automatically converting the source database schema and a majority of the database code objects, including views, stored procedures, and functions, to a format compatible with the target database. Any objects that cannot be automatically converted are clearly marked so that they can be manually converted to complete the migration.

SCT can also scan your application source code for embedded SQL statements and convert them as part of a database schema conversion project. During this process, SCT performs cloud-native code optimization by converting legacy Oracle and SQL Server functions to their equivalent AWS service, thus helping you modernize the applications at the same time of database migration.

After the schema conversion is complete, SCT can help migrate data from a range of data warehouses to Redshift by using built-in data migration agents.

Your source database can be on-premises, in RDS or in EC2, and the target database can be in either RDS or EC2. SCT supports a number of different heterogeneous conversions.

Summary

In this chapter, you learned the basic concepts of different types of databases, including relational, nonrelational, and in-memory databases. From there, you learned about the various managed database services available on AWS. These included RDS, DynamoDB, and ElastiCache. Finally, you looked at how to perform homogenous database migrations using the AWS Database Migration Service (DMS). For heterogeneous database migrations, you learned that DMS can use the AWS Schema Conversion Tool (AWS SCT).

Exam Essentials

Know what a relational database is.   A relational database consists of one or more tables. Communication to and from relational databases usually involves simple SQL queries, such as "Add a new record" or "What is the cost of product x?"

Know what a nonrelational database is.   Nonrelational databases do not have a hard-defined data schema. They can use a variety of models for data management, such as in-memory key-value stores, graph data models, and document stores. These databases are optimized for applications that have a large data volume, require low latency, and have flexible data models. In nonrelational databases, there is no concept of foreign keys.

Understand the database options available on AWS.   You can run all types of databases on AWS. You should understand that there are managed and unmanaged options available, in addition to relational, nonrelational, caching, graph, and data warehouses.

Understand which databases Amazon RDS supports.   Amazon RDS currently supports six relational database engines:

- Microsoft SQL Server
- MySQL
- Oracle
- PostgreSQL
- MariaDB
- Amazon Aurora
- Db2

Understand the operational benefits of using Amazon RDS.   Amazon RDS is an AWS managed service. AWS is responsible for patching, antivirus, and the management of the underlying guest OS for RDS. RDS greatly simplifies the process of setting a secondary slave with replication for failover and setting up read replicas to offload queries.

Remember that you cannot access the underlying OS for RDS DB instances. You cannot use Remote Desktop Protocol (RDP) or SSH to connect to the underlying OS. If you need to access the OS, install custom software or agents. If you want to use a database engine that RDS does not support, consider running your database on an EC2 instance instead.

Understand that Amazon RDS handles multi-AZ failover for you. If your primary Amazon RDS instance becomes unavailable, AWS fails over to your secondary instance in another availability zone automatically. This failover is done by pointing your existing database endpoint to a new IP address. You do not have to change the connection string manually; AWS handles the DNS changes automatically.

Remember that RDS read replicas are used for scaling out and increased performance. This replication feature makes it easy to scale out your read-intensive databases. Read replicas are currently supported in RDS for MySQL, PostgreSQL, and Amazon Aurora. You can create one or more replicas of a database within a single AWS region or across multiple AWS regions. RDS uses native replication to propagate changes made to a source DB instance to any associated read replicas. RDS also supports cross-region read replicas to replicate changes asynchronously to another geography or AWS region.

Know how to calculate throughput for DynamoDB. Remember that one read capacity unit (RCU) represents one strongly consistent read per second or two eventually consistent reads per second for an item up to 4 KB in size. For writing data, know that one write capacity unit (WCU) represents one write per second for an item up to 1 KB in size. Be comfortable performing calculations to determine the appropriate setting for the RCU and WCU for a table.

Know that DynamoDB spreads RCUs and WCUs across partitions evenly. Recall that when you allocate your total RCUs and WCUs to a table, DynamoDB spreads these across your partitions evenly. For example, if you have 1,000 RCUs and you have 10 partitions, then you have 100 RCUs allocated to each partition.

Know the differences between a local secondary index and a global secondary index. Remember that you can create local secondary indexes only when you initially create the table; additionally, know that local secondary indexes must share the same partition key as the parent or source table. Conversely, you can create global secondary indexes at any time, with different partitions keys or sort keys.

Know the difference between eventually consistent and strongly consistent reads. Know that with eventually consistent reads, your application may retrieve data that is stale, but with strongly consistent reads, the data is always up-to-date.

Understand the purpose of caching data and which related services are available. Know why caching is important for your database tier and how it helps to improve your application performance. Additionally, understand the differences between the caching methods (lazy loading and write-through) and the corresponding AWS services (DynamoDB Accelerator (DAX), ElastiCache for Redis, and ElastiCache for Memcached).

Exercises

In the following exercises, you will launch two types of databases: the first database is a SQL database on RDS, and the second is DynamoDB (NoSQL). For these sets of exercises, you will use the Python 3 SDK. You can download the Python 3 SDK at http://aws.amazon.com/sdk-for-python.

EXERCISE 4.1

Creating a Security Group for the Database Tier on Amazon RDS

Before you can create your first RDS database, you must create a security group so that you can allow traffic from your development server to communicate with the database tier. To do this, you must use an EC2 client to create the security group. Categorized as part of the EC2 service, security groups are used throughout AWS to govern network traffic between resources.

To create the security group allowing MySQL/MariaDB traffic on port 3306, run the following script:

```
# Excercise 4.1
import boto3
import json
import datetime


# Let's create some variables we'll use throughout these Exercises in
Chapter 4
# NOTE: Here we are using a CIDR range for incoming traffic. We have set it to
0.0.0.0/0 which means
# ANYONE on the internet can access your database if they have the username
and the password
# If possible, specify your own CIDR range. You can figure out your CIDR range
by visiting the following link
# https://www.google.com/search?q=what+is+my+ip
# In the variable don't forget to add /32!
# If you aren't sure, leave it open to the world


# Variables
sg_name = 'rds-sg-dev-demo'
sg_description = 'RDS Security Group for AWS Dev Study Guide'
my_ip_cidr = '0.0.0.0/0'
```

```
# Create the EC2 Client to create the Security Group for your Database
ec2_client = boto3.client('ec2')


# First we need to create a security group
response = ec2_client.create_security_group(
    Description=sg_description,
    GroupName=sg_name)
print(json.dumps(response, indent=2, sort_keys=True))
# Now add a rule for the security group
response = ec2_client.authorize_security_group_ingress(
    CidrIp=my_ip_cidr,
    FromPort=3306,
    GroupName=sg_name,
    ToPort=3306,
    IpProtocol='tcp'
    )
print("Security Group should be created! Verify this in the AWS Console.")
```

After running the Python code, verify that the security group was created successfully from the AWS Management Console. You can find this confirmation under the VPC or EC2 service.

EXERCISE 4.2

Spinning Up the MariaDB Database Instance

Use the Python SDK to spin up your MariaDB database hosted on RDS.

To spin up the MariaDB database, run the following script and update the Variables section to meet your needs:

```
# Excercise 4.2
import boto3
import json
import datetime


# Just a quick helper function for date time conversions, in case you want to
print the raw JSON
def date_time_converter(o):
    if isinstance(o, datetime.datetime):
```

```
        return o.__str__()

# Variables
sg_name = 'rds-sg-dev-demo'
rds_identifier = 'my-rds-db'
db_name = 'mytestdb'
user_name = 'masteruser'
user_password = 'mymasterpassw0rd1!'
admin_email = 'myemail@myemail.com'
sg_id_number = ''
rds_endpoint = ''


# We need to get the Security Group ID Number to use in the creation of the
RDS Instance
ec2_client = boto3.client('ec2')
response = ec2_client.describe_security_groups(
    GroupNames=[
        sg_name
    ])

sg_id_number = json.dumps(response['SecurityGroups'][0]['GroupId'])
sg_id_number = sg_id_number.replace('"','')


#   Create the client for Amazon RDS
rds_client = boto3.client('rds')


# This will create our MariaDB Database
# NOTE: Here we are hardcoding passwords for simplicity and testing purposes
only! In production
# you should never hardcode passwords in configuration files/code!
# NOTE: This will create a MariaDB Database. Be sure to remove it when you
are done.
response = rds_client.create_db_instance(
    DBInstanceIdentifier=rds_identifier,
    DBName=db_name,
    DBInstanceClass='db.t2.micro',
    Engine='mariadb',
    MasterUsername='masteruser',
```

```
        MasterUserPassword='mymasterpassw0rd1!',
        VpcSecurityGroupIds=[
            sg_id_number
        ],
        AllocatedStorage=20,
        Tags=[
            {
                'Key': 'POC-Email',
                'Value': admin_email
            },
            {
                'Key': 'Purpose',
                'Value': 'AWS Developer Study Guide Demo'
            }
        ]
    )


    # We need to wait until the DB Cluster is up!
    print('Creating the RDS instance. This may take several minutes...')
    waiter = rds_client.get_waiter('db_instance_available')
    waiter.wait(DBInstanceIdentifier=rds_identifier)

    print('Okay! The Amazon RDS Database is up!')
```

After the script has executed, the following message is displayed:

```
Creating the RDS instance. This may take several minutes.
```

After the Amazon RDS database instance has been created successfully, the following confirmation is displayed:

```
Okay! The Amazon RDS Database is up!
```

You can also view these messages from the RDS console.

EXERCISE 4.3

Obtaining the Endpoint Value for the RDS Instance

Before you can start using the RDS instance, you must first specify your endpoint. In this exercise, you will use the Python SDK to obtain the value.

To obtain the Amazon RDS endpoint, run the following script:

```python
# Exercise 4.3
import boto3
import json
import datetime


# Just a quick helper function for date time conversions, in case you want to
print the raw JSON
def date_time_converter(o):
    if isinstance(o, datetime.datetime):
        return o.__str__()

# Variables
rds_identifier = 'my-rds-db'

#  Create the client for Amazon RDS
rds_client = boto3.client('rds')

print("Fetching the RDS endpoint...")
response = rds_client.describe_db_instances(
    DBInstanceIdentifier=rds_identifier
)

rds_endpoint = json.dumps(response['DBInstances'][0]['Endpoint']['Address'])
rds_endpoint = rds_endpoint.replace('"','')
print('RDS Endpoint: ' + rds_endpoint)
```

After running the Python code, the following status is displayed:

```
Fetching the RDS endpoint.. RDS Endpoint:<endpoint_name>
```

If the endpoint is not returned, from the AWS Management Console, under the RDS service, verify that your RDS database instance was created.

EXERCISE 4.4

Creating a SQL Table and Adding Records to It

You now have all the necessary information to create your first SQL table by using RDS. In this exercise, you will create a SQL table and add a couple of records. Remember to update the variables for your specific environment.

To update the variables, run the following script:

```
# Exercise 4.4
import boto3
import json
import datetime
import pymysql as mariadb


# Variables
rds_identifier = 'my-rds-db'
db_name = 'mytestdb'
user_name = 'masteruser'
user_password = 'mymasterpassw0rd1!'
rds_endpoint = 'my-rds-db.****.us-east-1.rds.amazonaws.com'

# Step 1 - Connect to the database to create the table
db_connection = mariadb.connect(host=rds_endpoint, user=user_name,
password=user_password, database=db_name)
cursor = db_connection.cursor()
try:
    cursor.execute("CREATE TABLE Users (user_id INT NOT NULL AUTO_INCREMENT,
user_fname VARCHAR(100) NOT NULL, user_lname VARCHAR(150) NOT NULL, user_email
VARCHAR(175) NOT NULL, PRIMARY KEY (`user_id`))")
    print('Table Created!')
except mariadb.Error as e:
    print('Error: {}'.format(e))
finally:
    db_connection.close()


# Step 2 - Connect to the database to add users to the table
db_connection = mariadb.connect(host=rds_endpoint, user=user_name,
password=user_password, database=db_name)
cursor = db_connection.cursor()
try:
```

```
    sql = "INSERT INTO `Users` (`user_fname`, `user_lname`, `user_email`)
VALUES (%s, %s, %s)"
    cursor.execute(sql, ('CJ', 'Smith', 'casey.smith@somewhere.com'))
    cursor.execute(sql, ('Casey', 'Smith', 'sam.smith@somewhere.com'))
    cursor.execute(sql, ('No', 'One', 'no.one@somewhere.com'))
# No data is saved unless we commit the transaction!
    db_connection.commit()
    print('Inserted Data to Database!')
except mariadb.Error as e:
    print('Error: {}'.format(e))
    print('Sorry, something has gone wrong!')
finally:
    db_connection.close()
```

After running the Python code, the following confirmation is displayed:

```
Table Created! Inserted Data to the Database!
```

Your RDS database now has some data stored in it.

In this exercise, you are hard-coding a password into your application code for demonstration purposes only. In a production environment, refrain from hard-coding application passwords. Instead, use services such as AWS Secrets Manager to keep your secrets secure.

Querying the Items in the SQL Table

After adding data to your SQL database, in this exercise you will be able to read or query the items in the *Users* table.

To read the items in the SQL table, run the following script:

```
# Exercise 4.5
import boto3
import json
import datetime
import pymysql as mariadb
```

```
# Variables
rds_identifier = 'my-rds-db'
db_name = 'mytestdb'
user_name = 'masteruser'
user_password = 'mymasterpassw0rd1!'
rds_endpoint = 'my-rds-db.*****.us-east-1.rds.amazonaws.com'

db_connection = mariadb.connect(host=rds_endpoint, user=user_name,
password=user_password, database=db_name)
cursor = db_connection.cursor()
try:
    sql = "SELECT * FROM `Users`"
    cursor.execute(sql)
    query_result = cursor.fetchall()
    print('Querying the Users Table...')
    print(query_result)
except mariadb.Error as e:
    print('Error: {}'.format(e))
    print('Sorry, something has gone wrong!')
finally:
    db_connection.close()
```

After running the Python code, you will see the three records that you inserted in the previous exercise.

EXERCISE 4.6

Removing RDS Databases and Security Groups

You've created an RDS DB instance and added data to it. In this exercise, you will remove a few resources from your account. Remove the RDS instance first.

To remove the RDS instance and the security group, run the following script:

```
# Exercise 4.6
import boto3
import json
import datetime
```

```
# Variables
rds_identifier = 'my-rds-db'
sg_name = 'rds-sg-dev-demo'
sg_id_number = ''

# Create the client for Amazon RDS
rds_client = boto3.client('rds')

# Delete the RDS Instance
response = rds_client.delete_db_instance(
    DBInstanceIdentifier=rds_identifier,
    SkipFinalSnapshot=True)

print('RDS Instance is being terminated...This may take several minutes.')

waiter = rds_client.get_waiter('db_instance_deleted')
waiter.wait(DBInstanceIdentifier=rds_identifier)

# We must wait to remove the security groups until the RDS database has been
deleted, this is a dependency.
print('The Amazon RDS database has been deleted. Removing Security Groups')


# Create the client for Amazon EC2 SG
ec2_client = boto3.client('ec2')

# Get the Security Group ID Number
response = ec2_client.describe_security_groups(
    GroupNames=[
        sg_name
    ])
sg_id_number = json.dumps(response['SecurityGroups'][0]['GroupId'])
sg_id_number = sg_id_number.replace('"','')

# Delete the Security Group!
response = ec2_client.delete_security_group(
```

```
        GroupId=sg_id_number
    )

print('Cleanup is complete!')
```

After running the Python code, the following message is displayed:

```
Cleanup is complete!
```

The RDS database and the security group are removed. You can verify this from the AWS Management Console.

EXERCISE 4.7

Creating a DynamoDB Table

DynamoDB is a managed NoSQL database. Unlike with RDS, we will not specify an instance type or launch any compute resources in the VPC. All we need to do to get started is to create a table.

To create the table, run the following script:

```
# Exercise 4.7
import boto3
import json
import datetime

dynamodb_resource = boto3.resource('dynamodb')

table = dynamodb_resource.create_table(
    TableName='Users',
    KeySchema=[
        {
            'AttributeName': 'user_id',
            'KeyType': 'HASH'
        },
        {
            'AttributeName': 'user_email',
            'KeyType': 'RANGE'
        }
    ],
```

```
    AttributeDefinitions=[
        {
            'AttributeName': 'user_id',
            'AttributeType': 'S'
        },
        {
            'AttributeName': 'user_email',
            'AttributeType': 'S'
        }
    ],
    ProvisionedThroughput={
        'ReadCapacityUnits': 5,
        'WriteCapacityUnits': 5
    }
)


print("The DynamoDB Table is being created, this may take a few
minutes…")
table.meta.client.get_waiter('table_exists').wait(TableName='Users')
print("Table is ready!")
```

After running the Python code, the following message is displayed:

```
Table is ready!
```

From the AWS Management Console, under DynamoDB, verify that the table was created.

Adding Users to the DynamoDB Table

With DynamoDB, there are fewer components to set up than there are for RDS. In this exercise, you'll add users to your table. Experiment with updating and changing some of the code to add multiple items to the database.

```
To add users to the DynamoDB table, run the following script: # Exercise 4.8
import boto3
import json
import datetime
```

```
# In this example we are not using uuid; however, you could use this to
autogenerate your user IDs.
# i.e. str(uuid.uuid4())
import uuid


# Create a DynamoDB Resource
dynamodb_resource = boto3.resource('dynamodb')
table = dynamodb_resource.Table('Users')


# Write a record to DynamoDB
response = table.put_item(
    Item={
        'user_id': '1234-5678',
        'user_email': 'someone@somewhere.com',
        'user_fname': 'Sam',
        'user_lname': 'Samuels'
    }
)


# Just printing the raw JSON response, you should see a 200 status code
print(json.dumps(response, indent=2, sort_keys=True))
```

After running the Python code, you receive a 200 HTTP Status Code from AWS. This means that the user record has been added.

From the AWS Management Console, under DynamoDB, review the table to verify that the user record was added.

EXERCISE 4.9

Looking Up a User in the DynamoDB Table

In this exercise, you look up the one user you've added so far.

To look up users in the DynamoDB table, run the following script:

```
# Exercise 4.9
import boto3
from boto3.dynamodb.conditions import Key
import json
import datetime
```

EXERCISE 4.9 *(continued)*

```
# Create a DynamoDB Resource
dynamodb_resource = boto3.resource('dynamodb')
table = dynamodb_resource.Table('Users')

# Query some data
response = table.query(
    KeyConditionExpression=Key('user_id').eq('1234-5678')
)

# Print the data out!
print(json.dumps(response['Items'], indent=2, sort_keys=True))
```

After running the Python code, the query results are returned in JSON format showing a single user.

EXERCISE 4.10

Writing Data to the Table as a Batch Process

In this exercise, you will write data to the table through a batch process.

To write data using a batch process, run the following script:

```
# Exercise 4.10
import boto3
import json
import datetime
import uuid

# Create a DynamoDB Resource
dynamodb_resource = boto3.resource('dynamodb')
table = dynamodb_resource.Table('Users')

# Generate some random data
with table.batch_writer() as user_data:
    for i in range(100):
        user_data.put_item(
            Item={
```

```
                    'user_id': str(uuid.uuid4()),
                    'user_email': 'someone' + str(i) + '@somewhere.com',
                    'user_fname': 'User' + str(i),
                    'user_lname': 'UserLast' + str(i)
                }
            )
        print('Writing record # ' + str(i+1) + ' to DynamoDB Users Table')
    print('Done!')
```

After running the Python code, the output reads as follows:

```
Writing record # 300 to DyanmoDB Users Table Done!
```

From the AWS Management Console, under DynamoDB Table, verify that the users were written to the table.

EXERCISE 4.11

Scanning the DynamoDB Table

In this exercise, you will scan the entire table.

To scan the entire table, run the following script:

```
# Exercise 4.11
import boto3
import json
import datetime
import uuid

# Create a DynamoDB Resource
dynamodb_resource = boto3.resource('dynamodb')
table = dynamodb_resource.Table('Users')

# Let's do a scan!
response = table.scan()

print('The total Count is: ' + json.dumps(response['Count']))
print(json.dumps(response['Items'], indent=2, sort_keys=True))
```

As you learned in this chapter, scans return the entire dataset located in the table. After running the script, all of the users are returned.

EXERCISE 4.12

Removing the DynamoDB Table

In this exercise, you will remove the DynamoDB table that you created in Exercise 4.7.

To remove the table, run the following script:

```
# Exercise 4.12
import boto3
import json
import datetime
import uuid

# Create a DynamoDB Resource
dynamodb_client = boto3.client('dynamodb')

# Delete the Table
response = dynamodb_client.delete_table(TableName='Users')
print(json.dumps(response, indent=2, sort_keys=True))
```

The DynamoDB table is deleted, or it is in the process of being deleted. Verify the deletion from the AWS Management Console, under the DynamoDB service.

Review Questions

1. Which of the following does Relational Database Service (RDS) manage on your behalf? (Choose three.)

   A. Database settings

   B. Database software installation and patching

   C. Query optimization

   D. Hardware provisioning

   E. Backups

2. What is the recommended way to ensure your RDS instance stays up-to-date and patched with the least impact on availability?

   A. Enable automatic minor version upgrades for your RDS instance and schedule maintenance windows during low-traffic periods.

   B. Regularly take snapshots of your RDS instance.

   C. Create an AWS Lambda function to apply patches from via boto.

   D. Always keep a warm RDS instance online for patching, and swap the active instance after upgrades.

3. You are designing an e-commerce web application that will scale to potentially hundreds of thousands of concurrent users. Which database technology is best suited to hold the session state for large numbers of concurrent users?

   A. Relational database by using RDS

   B. NoSQL database table by using DynamoDB

   C. Data warehouse by using Redshift

   D. MySQL on EC2

4. When using DynamoDB, how many read capacity units (RCUs) do you need to support 25 *strongly consistent* reads per second of 15 KB?

   A. 100 RCUs

   B. 25 RCUs

   C. 10 RCUs

   D. 15 RCUs

5. When using DynamoDB, how many read capacity units (RCUs) do you need to support 25 *eventually consistent* reads per second of 15 KB?

   A. 10 RCUs

   B. 25 RCUs

   C. 50 RCUs

   D. 15 RCUs

6. When using DynamoDB, how many write capacity units (WCUs) are needed to support 100 writes per second of 512 bytes?

   A. 129 WCUs

   B. 25 WCUs

   C. 10 WCUs

   D. 100 WCUs

7. Your company is currently using DynamoDB, and they would like to implement a write-through caching mechanism. They would like to get everything up and running in only a few short weeks. Additionally, your company would like to refrain from managing any additional servers. You are the lead developer on the project; what should you recommend?

   A. Build your own custom caching application.

   B. Implement Amazon DynamoDB Accelerator (DAX).

   C. Run Redis on EC2.

   D. Run Memcached on EC2.

8. Your company would like to implement a highly available caching solution for its SQL database running on Amazon RDS. Currently, all of its services are running in AWS. As their lead developer, what should you recommend?

   A. Implement your own caching solution on-premises.

   B. Implement ElastiCache for Redis.

   C. Implement ElastiCache for Memcached.

   D. Implement DynamoDB Accelerator (DAX).

9. Your organization runs an app using a PostgreSQL database on RDS. You are tasked with significantly enhancing its read performance and introducing high availability. What is your best option?

   A. Add read replicas to your RDS PostgreSQL instance and configure multi-AZ deployment for high availability.

   B. Migrate the PostgreSQL database to Aurora to leverage its performance and scalability capabilities.

   C. Increase the instance size of your RDS database and add a caching layer with ElastiCache.

   D. Rebuild your PostgreSQL database on an EC2 instance with provisioned IOPS SSD storage to achieve faster disk reads.

10. A company is experiencing an issue with DynamoDB whereby the data is taking longer than expected to return from a query. You are tasked with investigating the problem. After looking at the application code, you realize that a Scan operation is being called for a large DynamoDB table. What should you do or recommend?

A. Implement a query instead of a scan, if possible, as queries are more efficient than a scan.

B. Do nothing; the problem should go away on its own.

C. Implement a strongly consistent read.

D. Increase the write capacity units (WCUs).

E. Add more read capacity units (RCUs).

Encryption on AWS

THE AWS CERTIFIED DEVELOPER – ASSOCIATE EXAM TOPICS COVERED IN THIS CHAPTER MAY INCLUDE, BUT ARE NOT LIMITED TO, THE FOLLOWING:

✓ **Domain 2: Security**

- Task Statement 1: Implement authentication and/or authorization for applications and AWS services

- Task Statement 2: Implement encryption by using AWS services

- Task Statement 3: Manage sensitive data in application code

AWS delivers a secure, scalable cloud computing platform with high availability, offering the flexibility for you to build a wide range of applications. If you require an additional layer of security for the data you store in the AWS Cloud, you have several options for encrypting data at rest. These options range from automated AWS encryption solutions to manual, client-side options. Choosing the right solution depends on which AWS service you're using and your requirements for key management. This chapter provides an overview of various methods for encrypting data at rest in AWS. Specifically, it covers three options and compares and contrasts the advantages of each option.

Before exploring the different ways you can use encryption in AWS, the following section describes two services you can use for your encryption strategy: AWS Key Management Service and AWS CloudHSM.

AWS Key Management Service

AWS Key Management Service (KMS) makes it easy to create and manage keys to encrypt data across a wide range of AWS services and in your applications. KMS employs hardware security modules (HSMs), which are FIPS 140-2 validated cryptographic modules, to safeguard your primary keys. The Federal Information Processing Standards (FIPS) are responsible for defining security requirements for cryptographic modules. For more information about FIPS 140-2 validation, see `https://nvlpubs.nist.gov/nistpubs/FIPS/NIST.FIPS.140-2.pdf`.

KMS offers the following features:

- Centralized key management
- Integration with other AWS services
- Auditing capabilities and high availability
- Custom key store
- Compliance

Centralized Key Management

AWS KMS provides you with a centralized view of your encryption keys. You can create a *customer key* to control access to your data encryption keys (data keys) and to encrypt and decrypt your data. KMS uses an Advanced Encryption Standard (AES) in 256-bit mode to encrypt and secure your data.

You can use KMS to create keys in one of three ways: by using AWS KMS, by using AWS CloudHSM, or by importing your own key material. Regardless of the method you use to store your keys, you can manage them with KMS through the AWS Management Console or by using the SDK or the CLI. KMS also automatically rotates your keys once a year, without having to reencrypt data that was previously encrypted.

Integration with Other AWS Services

KMS provides seamless integration with nearly every AWS service, offering the ability to encrypt data at rest using AWS-managed KMS keys. For instance, selecting this option for services like S3 gives you server-side encryption with no manual configuration needed.

Auditing Capabilities and High Availability

If CloudTrail is enabled for your AWS account and region, API requests and other activity in your account are recorded to log files. With CloudTrail, you can see who has used a particular KMS key, the API call that was sent, and when they attempted to use that particular key.

Like S3, AWS KMS keys are stored in systems designed for 99.999999999 percent durability; they also do not leave the CloudHSM instances. Your keys are stored securely within the AWS region so that no one, including AWS employees, can retrieve your plaintext keys. KMS uses FIPS 140-2 validated HSMs to protect your keys and to help ensure the confidentiality and integrity of your data.

Custom Key Store

You can create your own custom key store in an AWS CloudHSM cluster that you control, enabling you to store your KMS keys in a single-tenant environment that is not shared with other AWS customers. The use of a custom key store incurs an additional cost for the AWS CloudHSM cluster.

Compliance

Achieving compliance for your applications can be a lengthy and difficult process. Along with many other AWS services, KMS has been validated and certified in a number of industry-specific compliance and regulatory standards. For a full list of compliance standards that have been met, see https://aws.amazon.com/compliance/services-in-scope.

AWS CloudHSM

AWS CloudHSM offers third-party, validated FIPS 140-2, level 3 hardware security modules in the AWS Cloud. The hardware security module is a computing device that provides a dedicated infrastructure to support cryptographic operations. Before getting into more detail, we'll explore your various options for managing cryptographic keys, then highlight how AWS KMS and CloudHSM can simplify operations significantly.

Controlling the Access Keys

Encryption on any system requires three components: data to encrypt, a method to encrypt the data using a cryptographic algorithm, and the use of encryption keys with the data and the algorithm. Most modern programming languages provide libraries with a wide range of available cryptographic algorithms, such as the Advanced Encryption Standard (AES).

Managing the security of encryption keys is often performed using a *key management infrastructure* (KMI). A KMI is composed of two components: the storage layer that protects the plaintext keys and the management layer that authorizes key use. A common way to protect keys in a KMI is to use a hardware security module. An HSM is a dedicated storage and data processing device that performs cryptographic operations using keys on the device. An HSM typically provides tamper evidence, or resistance, to protect keys from unauthorized use. A software-based authorization layer controls who can administer the HSM and which users or applications can use which keys in the HSM.

As you deploy encryption for various data classifications in AWS, it is important to understand exactly who has access to your encryption keys or data and under what conditions. As shown in Figure 5.1, there are three different options for how you and AWS provide the encryption method and the KMI.

FIGURE 5.1   Encryption options in AWS

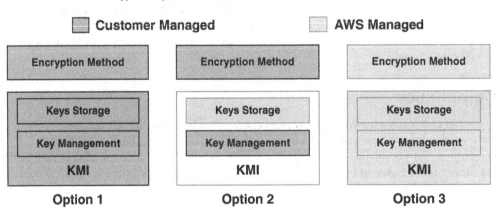

- You control the encryption method and the entire KMI.
- You control the encryption method; AWS provides the storage component of the KMI, and you provide the management layer of the KMI.
- AWS controls the encryption method and the entire KMI.

Option 1: You Control the Encryption Method and the Entire KMI

In this option, you use your own KMI to generate, store, and manage access to keys in addition to controlling all the encryption methods in your applications. This physical location of the KMI and the encryption method can be outside of AWS or on an EC2 instance in your account. The encryption method can be a combination of open source tools, AWS SDKs, or third-party software and hardware. The important security property of this option is that you have full control over the encryption keys and the execution environment that uses those keys in the encryption code. AWS has no access to your keys and cannot perform encryption or decryption on your behalf. You are responsible for the proper storage, management, and use of keys to ensure the confidentiality, integrity, and availability of your data. You can encrypt data in AWS services, as described in the following sections.

Amazon S3

You can encrypt data by using any encryption method you want and then upload the encrypted data using the Amazon S3 API. Most programming languages include libraries that enable you to encrypt data. After you have encrypted an object and safely stored the key in your KMI, you can upload the encrypted object to S3. Any time you retrieve that data, you'll have to decrypt it locally.

AWS provides an alternative to this do-it-yourself approach with the *Amazon S3 encryption client*, a feature of the AWS SDK that lets you supply a key from your KMI to encrypt and decrypt your data as you make calls to S3. The SDK takes your symmetric or asymmetric key as input and encrypt the object before uploading it to S3. The process is reversed when the SDK is used to retrieve an object.

If you're using the S3 encryption client on-premises, AWS does not have access to your keys or unencrypted data. If you're using the client in an application running in EC2, a best practice is to pass keys to the client by using secure transport (i.e., an SSH session) from your KMI to help ensure confidentiality. Figure 5.2 shows an example of S3 client-side encryption from an on-premises system compared with encryption within an EC2 application.

FIGURE 5.2   Amazon S3 client-side encryption

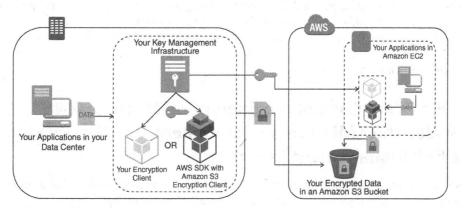

Amazon EBS

Amazon Elastic Block Store (Amazon EBS) provides block-level storage volumes for use with EC2 instances. EBS volumes are network-attached and persist independently from the life of an instance.

System-Level or Block-Level Encryption   Because EBS volumes are presented to an instance as a block device, you can leverage most standard encryption tools for filesystem-level or block-level encryption, such as *dm-crypt*. Tools like this operate below the filesystem layer, using kernel space device drivers to perform the encryption and decryption of data. These tools are useful when you want all data written to a volume to be encrypted regardless of what directory the data is stored in.

Filesystem Encryption   You can use filesystem-level encryption, which works by stacking an encrypted filesystem on top of an existing filesystem. This method is typically used to encrypt a specific directory. *eCryptfs* and *EncFs* are two Linux-based open source examples of filesystem-level encryption tools.

These solutions require you to provide keys either manually or from your KMI. An important caveat with both block-level and filesystem-level encryption tools is that you can use them only to encrypt data volumes that are not EBS boot volumes. This is because these tools do not allow you to make a trusted key available automatically to the boot volume at startup.

AWS Storage Gateway

AWS Storage Gateway is a service connecting an on-premises software appliance with S3. You can expose it to your network as an iSCSI disk to facilitate copying data from other sources. Data on disk volumes attached to the Storage Gateway are automatically uploaded to S3 based on policy. You can encrypt source data on the disk volumes before it is written to the disk. To encrypt all the data on the disk volume, you can also use a block-level encryption tool, such as BitLocker or dm-crypt/LUKS, on the iSCSI endpoint exposed by Storage Gateway.

Amazon RDS

To encrypt data in *Amazon Relational Database Service* (RDS) on the client side, first consider how you want data queries to work. Because RDS does not expose the attached disk it uses for data storage, transparent disk encryption using techniques described in the previous EBS section are not available. You can always encrypt data in your application before writing it to RDS but be aware that clients will need to decrypt the data after they fetch it. This approach can limit your ability to easily query the database, as your values will not be searchable as plaintext.

Option 2: You Control the Encryption Method, AWS Provides the KMI Storage Component, and You Provide the KMI Management Layer

This option is similar to option 1 in that you manage the encryption method, but it differs from option 1 in that the keys are stored in a CloudHSM appliance rather than in a key storage system that you manage on-premises. While the keys are stored in the AWS environment, they are inaccessible to any employee at AWS because only you have access to the cryptographic partitions within the dedicated HSM to use the keys.

The CloudHSM appliance is a FIPS 140-2 level 3 HSM that has both physical and logical tamper-detection mechanisms that trigger *zeroization* of the appliance. Zeroization erases the HSM's volatile memory where any decrypted keys were stored and destroys the key that encrypts stored objects, effectively causing all keys on the HSM to be inaccessible and unrecoverable.

AWS CloudHSM

When deciding if CloudHSM fits your needs, understand that an HSM generates and stores keys and performs cryptographic operations, but it doesn't manage key life cycle events such as access policies and rotation. You'll likely need a separate KMI in addition to Cloud-HSM. The KMI, which you can deploy on-premises or in EC2, securely communicates with CloudHSM over SSL to protect keys and data.

Amazon Virtual Private Cloud

To use CloudHSM, your applications must run in an Amazon VPC and have the CloudHSM client installed. The client communicates with the CloudHSM appliance to encrypt data from your application before sending it to other AWS services for storage. Figure 5.3 shows how the CloudHSM solution works with your applications running on EC2 in a VPC.

FIGURE 5.3   Deploying AWS CloudHSM in an Amazon VPC

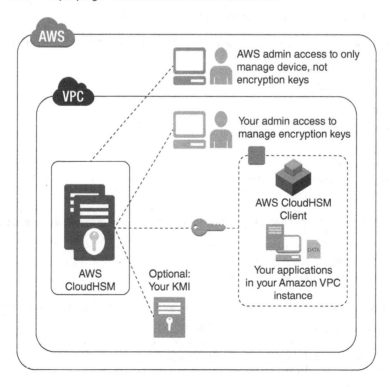

To achieve the highest availability and durability of keys in your CloudHSM appliance, AWS recommends deploying multiple CloudHSM applications across different availability zones.

Option 3: AWS Controls the Encryption Method and the Entire KMI

With this approach, AWS provides server-side encryption of your data, transparently managing the encryption method and keys.

AWS Key Management Service

AWS Key Management Service (KMS) is a managed encryption service that lets you provision and use keys to encrypt your data. AWS KMS keys are similar to keys in an HSM in that they never leave the service itself. Rather, you send data to the KMS service to be encrypted or decrypted with a specific KMS key. This centralized approach allows users to more easily manage and audit access to these keys.

KMS is natively integrated with many other AWS services, including EBS, S3, and Redshift, to simplify encryption of your data within those services. AWS SDKs are integrated with KMS to enable you to encrypt data in your custom applications. KMS provides global availability, low latency, and a high level of durability for your keys.

KMS and other services that encrypt your data directly use a method called *envelope encryption* to balance performance and security. Figure 5.4 describes the flow of envelope encryption.

FIGURE 5.4   Flow of envelope encryption

1. A data key is generated by the AWS service at the time you request your data to be encrypted.

Key
Generator   Data Key

2. Data key is used to encrypt your data.

Plaintext   Data Key   Encrypted
Data   Data

3. The data key is then encrypted with a key-encrypting key unique to the service storing your data.

Data Key   Existing Key   Encrypted Data
               Encrypting Key   Key

4. The encrypted data key and the encrypted data are then stored by the AWS storage service on your behalf.

Encrypted Data   Encrypted   AWS Storage
Key   Data   Services

The key-encrypting keys that are used to encrypt data keys are stored and managed separately from the data and the data keys. Strict access controls are placed on the encryption keys to prevent unauthorized use by AWS employees. When you need access to your plaintext data, this process is reversed. The encrypted data key is decrypted using the key-encrypting key; the data key is used to decrypt your data.

The following section explores how multiple AWS services offer encryption features through integration with KMS.

Amazon S3

There are three ways to encrypt your data in S3 using server-side encryption.

Server-Side Encryption   As discussed in a previous chapter, S3 offers seamless server-side encryption. When you select this option for a bucket, each object is encrypted with a unique data key that is itself encrypted with a periodically rotated key managed by S3. S3 server-side encryption uses 256-bit Advanced Encryption Standard (AES) for its keys.

Server-Side Encryption Using Customer-Provided Keys   S3 also allows you to use your own encryption key when uploading an object. S3 uses your provided key to encrypt the object with AES-256, then deletes the key. To retrieve the object, you must supply the same encryption key in your CLI or SDK retrieval request. S3 verifies the key matches, decrypts the object, and returns it to you.

Server-Side Encryption Using AWS KMS   You can encrypt your data in Amazon S3 by defining an AWS KMS key within your account. This primary key is used to encrypt the unique *object key* (referred to as a data key, as shown in Figure 5.4) that ultimately encrypts your object.

When you upload your object, a request is sent to AWS KMS to create an object key. KMS generates this object key and encrypts it using the primary key that you specified earlier; KMS returns this encrypted object key along with the plaintext object key to S3. The S3 web server encrypts your object using the plaintext object key, stores the now encrypted object (with the encrypted object key), and deletes the plaintext object key from memory.

To retrieve this encrypted object, S3 sends the encrypted object key to KMS. KMS decrypts the object key using the correct primary key and returns the decrypted (plaintext) object key to S3. With the plaintext object key, S3 decrypts the encrypted object and returns it to you.

S3 also enables you to define a default encryption policy. You can specify that all objects are encrypted when stored. You can also define a bucket policy that rejects uploads of unencrypted objects.

Amazon EBS

When creating a volume in EBS, you can choose to encrypt it using an AWS KMS key. This key is used to encrypt a unique *volume key* that, in turn, encrypts your EBS volume.

First, EC2 asks KMS to create a volume key. KMS generates this volume key, encrypts it using the AWS KMS key, and returns the plaintext volume key and the encrypted volume key to the EC2 service. Then, the plaintext volume key is stored in memory to encrypt and decrypt all data going to and from your attached EBS volume.

When the encrypted volume (or any encrypted snapshots of that volume) needs to be reattached to an instance, EC2 asks KMS to decrypt the encrypted volume key. KMS decrypts this encrypted volume key with the correct AWS KMS key and returns the decrypted volume key to EC2.

Encryption and Compliance

These server-side encryption features across multiple services in AWS enable you to encrypt your data easily by setting the configuration in the AWS Management Console by making a CLI or API request for the given AWS service. AWS automatically and securely manages the authorized use of encryption keys. These systems are verified by third-party audits to achieve security certifications, including SOC 1, 2, and 3; PCI-DSS; and FedRAMP.

Summary

If you take all responsibility for the encryption method and the KMI, you can have granular control over how your applications encrypt data. However, that granular control comes at a cost—both in terms of deployment effort and an inability to have AWS services tightly integrate with your applications' encryption methods. Instead, consider AWS's managed encryption services, enabling easier deployment and tighter integration with other parts of AWS. This option offers encryption for several services that store your data and gives you control over your own keys, secured storage for those keys, and auditability on all data access attempts.

Exam Essentials

Know how to define key management infrastructure (KMI).   A KMI consists of two infrastructure components. The first component is a storage layer that protects plaintext keys. The second component is a management layer that authorizes use of stored keys.

Understand the available options for how you and AWS provide encryption using a KMI, such as AWS Key Management Service (KMS) and AWS CloudHSM.   With the first option, you control the encryption method in addition to the entire KMI. In the second option, you control the encryption method and the management layer of the KMI, and AWS provides the storage layer. In the third option, AWS controls the encryption method and both components of the KMI, offering managed services like KMS for key management and encryption.

Understand the maintenance trade-offs of each key management option.   For any options that involve customers managing the components of the KMI or encryption method, maintenance increases significantly. The increased maintenance also reduces your ability to take advantage of built-in integrations between KMS and other services. For options that involve using built-in AWS functionality, additional maintenance is required only when migrating legacy applications to take advantage of new features.

Understand the encryption options available in Amazon S3.   Regardless of the key management tools and process, you can encrypt any objects before uploading them to an S3 bucket. However, any custom encryption logic adds to processing overhead for the encryption and decryption of the data. AWS provides the S3 encryption client to help streamline this process. When encrypting data on-premises, AWS has no visibility into the encryption keys or mechanisms used. For server-side encryption, S3 supports AWS-managed keys, customer-managed keys, and encryption using KMS.

Understand the encryption options available in Amazon EBS.   Like any on-premises block storage, EBS supports both block-level and filesystem encryption. However, an important caveat with block-level and filesystem encryption tools is that you cannot use them to encrypt the boot volume of an EC2 instance. EBS supports encryption by using customer-managed keys and KMS.

Understand the encryption options available in Amazon RDS.   Because RDS does not expose the underlying filesystem of databases, block-level and filesystem encryption options are not available. However, standard libraries for encryption of database fields are fully supported. It is important to evaluate the types of queries that will be run against a database before selecting an encryption process, as this could affect the ability to run queries on encrypted data.

Exercises

EXERCISE 5.1

Configuring an Amazon S3 Bucket to Deny Unencrypted Uploads

In this exercise, you will enforce object encryption for an S3 bucket by using a bucket policy to reject PUT requests without encryption headers.

1. Sign in to the AWS Management Console, and open the S3 console.

2. Create a new bucket with a name of your choice.

3. Apply the following policy to the bucket:

```
{
  "Version": "2012-10-17",
  "Statement": [
    {
      "Sid": "DenyIncorrectEncryption",
      "Effect": "Deny",
      "Principal": "*",
      "Action": "s3:PutObject",
      "Resource": "arn:aws:s3:::<bucket_name>/*",
```

```
      "Condition": {
        "StringNotEquals": {
          "s3:x-amz-server-side-encryption": "AES256"
        }
      },
      {
        "Sid": "DenyMissingEncryption",
        "Effect": "Deny",
        "Principal": "*",
        "Action": "s3:PutObject",
        "Resource": "arn:aws:s3:::<bucket_name>/*",
        "Condition": {
          "Null": {
            "s3:x-amz-server-side-encryption": true
          }
        }
      }
    ]
  }
```

4. From the AWS Identity and Access Management (IAM) console, open the policy simulator.

5. Select an existing policy with access to the bucket that you created.

6. Test the `PutObject` Amazon S3 action with and without the `x-amz-server-side-encryption` header.

When you are uploading a new object or making a copy of an existing object, you can specify whether you want S3 to encrypt your data by adding the header to the API request.

Creating and Disabling an AWS Key Management Service (AWS KMS) Key

In this exercise, you will create a customer KMS key in the AWS Management Console and then disable it. You can disable and reenable the KMS keys that you manage.

1. Sign in to the AWS Management Console and search the Services list for the AWS Key Management Service (AWS KMS) console.

2. Click Create A Key.

3. Select Symmetric Key and for Key Usage, Encrypt And Decrypt. Click Next.

4. Provide values for the key alias, description, and tag(s), and then click Next.

    Note: The alias name cannot begin with aws. The aws prefix is reserved by AWS to represent AWS-managed customer keys in your account.

5. Select one or more IAM users who can administer the KMS key and then click Next. Be sure to select your IAM user.

6. Select one or more IAM users to use the KMS key for cryptographic operations. Be sure to select your IAM user.

7. Click Finish to create the KMS key.

8. Locate the key in the AWS KMS console.

9. Select the check box next to the alias of the KMS key that you want to disable.

10. Choose Key Actions ➤ Disable.

If you disable a KMS key, you cannot use it to encrypt or decrypt data until you reenable it. You may also delete the KMS key with a mandatory waiting period.

EXERCISE 5.3

Creating a customer KMS Key with the Python SDK

In this exercise, you will create a new customer KMS key using the AWS Command-Line Interface (AWS CLI). You will use Python as one of the supported programming languages.

1. To create the AWS KMS key, run the following Python script:

```python
import boto3
import json

kms_client = boto3.client('kms', region_name='us-west-1')

response = kms_client.create_key(
    Description='My KMS Key',
    KeyUsage='ENCRYPT_DECRYPT',
    Origin='AWS_KMS',
    Tags=[
        {
            'TagKey': 'KeyPurpose',
            'TagValue': 'dev-on-aws-key'
        },
```

```
    ]
)

print(response)
```

2. To list the customer keys and describe the available keys, run the following script:

```
import boto3
import json
# List the KMS Keys by ID
kms_client = boto3.client('kms', region_name='us-west-1')
try:
    response = kms_client.list_keys()
except ClientError as e:
    logging.error(e)

print(json.dumps(response, indent=4, sort_keys=True))
```

3. To describe the keys inside AWS KMS, run the following script:

```
import boto3
import json
# List the KMS Keys by ID
kms_client = boto3.client('kms', region_name='us-west-1')

# Describe the Keys
for key in response['Keys']:
    try:
        key_info = kms_client.describe_key(KeyId=key['KeyArn'])
        key_id = key_info['KeyMetadata']['KeyId']
        key_arn = key_info['KeyMetadata']['Arn']
        key_state = key_info['KeyMetadata']['KeyState']
        key_description = key_info['KeyMetadata']['Description']
        print('Key ID: ' + key_id)
        print('Key ARN: ' + key_arn)
        print('Key State: ' + key_state)
        print('Key Description: ' + key_description)
        print('------------------------------------')
    except ClientError as e:
        logging.error(e)
```

4.   To delete the AWS KMS key, run the following script:

```
import boto3

kms_client = boto3.client('kms', region_name='us-west-1')
response = kms_client.schedule_key_deletion(
    KeyId='fasdf1-2451b-151-bea2-easdfg8',
    PendingWindowInDays=7
)

print(response, indent=4, sort_keys=True)
```

Review Questions

1. Which components are required in an encryption system? (Choose three.)
   A. A user to upload data
   B. Data to encrypt
   C. A database to store encryption keys
   D. A method to encrypt data
   E. A cryptographic algorithm

2. Which are the components of key management infrastructure (KMI)? (Choose two.)
   A. Storage layer
   B. Data layer
   C. Management layer
   D. Encryption layer

3. Which of the following are methods for you and AWS to provide an encryption method and key management infrastructure (KMI)? (Choose three.)
   A. You control the encryption method and key management, and AWS provides the storage component of the KMI.
   B. You control the storage component of the KMI, and AWS provides the encryption method and key management.
   C. You control the encryption method and KMI.
   D. AWS controls the encryption method and the entire KMI.
   E. None of the above.

4. Which option uses AWS KMS to manage keys to provide server-side encryption to S3?
   A. S3 managed encryption keys (SSE-S3)
   B. Customer-provided encryption keys (SSE-C)
   C. Use client-side encryption
   D. None of the above

5. Which AWS encryption service provides asymmetric encryption capabilities?
   A. AWS Key Management Service (AWS KMS).
   B. AWS CloudHSM.
   C. AWS does not provide asymmetric encryption services.
   D. Both A and B.

6. Which AWS encryption service provides symmetric encryption capabilities? (Choose two.)

    A. AWS Key Management Service (AWS KMS).

    B. AWS CloudHSM.

    C. AWS does not provide symmetric encryption services.

    D. None of the above.

7. An organization using S3 would like to ensure that all objects stored in S3 are encrypted. However, it does not want to be responsible for managing any of the encryption keys. As their lead developer, which service and feature should you recommend?

    A. Server-side encryption with AWS Key Management Service (SSE-KMS).

    B. Customer-provided encryption keys (SSE-C).

    C. Amazon S3 managed encryption keys (SSE-S3).

    D. This is not possible in AWS.

8. Which feature of AWS KMS enables you to use an AWS CloudHSM cluster for the storage of your encryption keys?

    A. Centralized key management

    B. CloudHSM

    C. Custom key stores

    D. S3DistCp

9. An organization is using KMS to support encryption and would like to encrypt EBS volumes. It wants to encrypt its volumes quickly, with little development time. As their lead developer, what should you recommend?

    A. Encrypt the EBS volumes using an AWS KMS key.

    B. Use open source or third-party encryption tooling.

    C. Use CloudHSM.

    D. AWS does not provide a mechanism to encrypt EBS volumes.

10. Which of the following AWS services does not integrate with KMS?

    A. EBS

    B. S3

    C. Redshift

    D. None of the above

Chapter

6

Deployment Strategies

**THE AWS CERTIFIED DEVELOPER –
ASSOCIATE EXAM TOPICS COVERED IN
THIS CHAPTER MAY INCLUDE, BUT ARE
NOT LIMITED TO, THE FOLLOWING:**

✓ **Domain 1: Development with AWS Services**

- Task Statement 1: Develop code for applications on AWS

✓ **Domain 3: Deployment**

- Task Statement 1: Prepare application artifacts to be deployed to AWS

- Task Statement 2: Test applications in development environments

- Task Statement 4: Deploy code by using AWS CI/CD services

✓ **Domain 4: Troubleshooting and Optimization**

- Task Statement 2: Instrument code for observability

AWS provides a range of services that accelerate and simplify the deployment of web applications by automating the provisioning of infrastructure and configuration of runtime environments, simplifying monitoring and scaling, and enabling you to create pipelines that build and deploy code in a single continuous flow.

Deployments on the AWS Cloud

AWS's powerful software deployment services are best viewed through the lens of the software release life cycle. Let's look at some of the most common phases in this cycle to better understand what happens in each stage.

Phases of the Release Life Cycle

While every organization is different, nearly all traditional release life cycles are composed of five major phases, as shown in Figure 6.1: Source, Build, Test, Deploy, and Monitor. Each phase of the cycle provides increased confidence that the code will work as intended for customers. This also translates to a release life cycle implemented in an AWS environment.

FIGURE 6.1   Major phases of the release life cycle

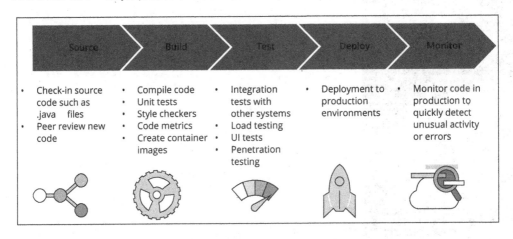

Source Phase

During the *Source phase*, developers check changes into a source code repository. Many teams require feedback on code changes before delivering code to production or target environments. This is often achieved by a combination of automated testing, static code analysis, manual testing, and peer code reviews.

Build Phase

During the *Build phase*, an application's source code is built, and the quality of the code is tested on the build machine. The most common types of quality checks are automated tests that can be executed in a test environment. Some teams extend their quality tests to include code metrics, style checks, and linters. If an application's code needs to be compiled or packaged before deployment, that step takes place at this stage.

Test Phase

The goal of the *Test phase* is to perform tests that cannot be done during the Build phase and that require the software to be deployed to production-like stages. Often, these tests include testing integration with other live systems, load testing, user interface (UI) testing, and penetration testing. Teams deploy to preproduction stages where their application interacts with other systems to ensure that the newly changed software works in an integrated environment. This is also the phase where many teams solicit human feedback on code updates.

Deployment Phase

Finally, code is deployed to production. In the *Deployment phase*, different teams have different deployment strategies, though it is common to set goals to reduce risk when deploying new changes and minimize the impact when a bad change is rolled into production.

Monitor Phase

During the Monitor phase, you must observe the status and performance of the application and its infrastructure to quickly detect and alert any unusual activities and errors.

Software Development Life Cycle with AWS Cloud

Traditional deployment processes often involve many manual steps that introduce the possibility of errors. Developers can limit risk while accelerating time to value by automating steps into a seamless chain of events known as a continuous integration/continuous deployment (CI/CD) pipeline.

Continuous Integration/Continuous Deployment

CI/CD pipelines help developers implement continuous builds, tests, and code deployments that activate in response to changes pushed to version control by developers.

Continuous integration (CI) is the software development practice in which developers push code changes into a shared branch of a central repository, where they may be merged with other developers' contributions. This practice enables developers to verify code changes frequently, validating quality with automated build and test processes.

By implementing CI practices, teams become more productive and develop new features more quickly, as conflicts and errors in in-progress changes are discovered early before they are released to customers.

Continuous delivery (CD) is the software development practice in which all code changes are automatically prepared and made deployable at a single step.

Continuous delivery extends continuous integration to include testing production-like stages and running verification testing against those deployments. Although CD can extend to a production deployment, it requires manual intervention between a code check-in and when that code is available for customer use.

Practicing continuous delivery means that teams gain a greater level of certainty that their software will work in production.

Continuous deployment extends continuous delivery and is the automated release of software to customers, from check-in through production, without human intervention. Continuous deployment helps customers gain value quickly from the code base, with the development team getting faster feedback on the changes made.

 An important distinction between continuous delivery and continuous deployment is that in continuous deployment, changes are automatically released to production after build/test stages; there is no manual approval step.

Figure 6.2 displays the CI/DI pipeline.

FIGURE 6.2   CI/DI pipeline

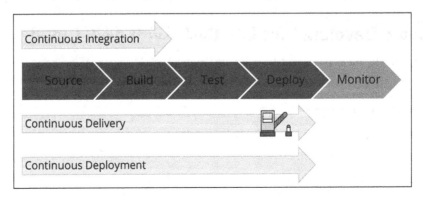

The CI/DI pipeline integrates with other AWS Code services, as illustrated in Figure 6.3.

AWS CodeCommit   *AWS CodeCommit* is a secure, highly scalable, managed source-control service that hosts private GIT repositories. It enables you to store and manage assets (such as documents, source code, and binary files) privately in the AWS Cloud.

AWS CodeBuild   *AWS CodeBuild* executes your commands in a serverless environment to compile source code, run tests, and produce ready-to-deploy software packages.

AWS CodeDeploy   *AWS CodeDeploy* automates code deployments to AWS compute resources. It handles the complexity of updating your applications, which avoids downtime during application deployment. It deploys to Amazon EC2 or on-premises servers, Amazon Lambda, or Amazon Elastic Container Service, in any language and on any operating system. It also integrates with third-party services.

AWS CodePipeline   *AWS CodePipeline* is a service for orchestrating all of the above, letting you create automated CI/CD pipelines triggered by a variety of sources. CodePipeline organizes your source, build, and deploy steps into stages with the ability to inject manual authorization steps. It works with many different AWS and third-party services, letting you automate new or existing CI/CD processes with a simple interface.

We will explore each of these services in detail in Chapter 7.

Deploying Highly Available and Scalable Applications

When your application starts to receive more traffic than one compute instance can handle, you have two options. The first is to scale *vertically* by increasing the resources of the machine, such as CPU or RAM. This approach cannot be scaled indefinitely and requires downtime as you restart your instance into a more capable type. The second approach is to scale *horizontally*, which involves launching additional copies of your application on multiple instances. To achieve horizontal scaling, you must ensure that your application doesn't depend on any local state, such as storing user data on the filesystem. You must also provide

FIGURE 6.3   AWS Code services

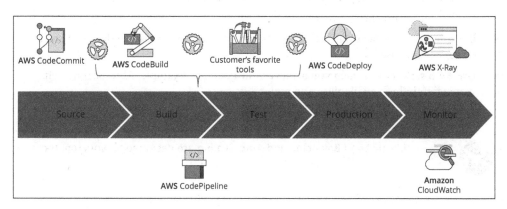

users with a single entry point that can distribute traffic over multiple instances. That entry point is a load balancer.

AWS provides two primary load-balancing options, application load balancers and network load balancers, as well as a legacy offering known as classic load balancers. You select a load balancer based on your application needs.

- The *application load balancer (ALB)* provides advanced request routing targeted at delivering modern application architectures, including microservices and container-based applications. It simplifies and improves the security of your application by ensuring that the latest Secure Sockets Layer (SSL)/Transport Layer Security (TLS) ciphers and protocols are used at all times. The ALB operates at the request level (Layer 7) to route HTTP/HTTPS traffic to its targets: EC2 instances, containers, and IP addresses based on the content of the request. It is ideal for advanced load balancing of HTTP and HTTPS traffic and includes the ability to make intelligent routing decisions based on HTTP headers, URL patterns, and more. By filtering traffic based on URL, one ALB can serve as the entry point for multiple backend applications.

- The *network load balancer (NLB)* operates at the transport layer to route TCP traffic to targets: EC2 instances, containers, and IP addresses based on IP protocol data. It is the best option for load balancing of TCP traffic because it's capable of handling millions of requests per second while maintaining ultra-low latencies. The NLB is optimized to handle sudden and volatile traffic patterns while using a single static IP address per availability zone. It is integrated with other popular AWS services, such as Auto Scaling, EC2, and CloudFormation.

- The *classic load balancer* is a legacy option that provides basic load balancing across multiple EC2 instances and operates at both the request level and the connection level. The classic load balancer is intended for applications that were built within the EC2-Classic network. When using a VPC, AWS recommends the ALB for Layer 7 and the NLB for Layer 4.

Figure 6.4 displays the flow for deploying highly available and scalable applications. When architecting for high availability, consider the following:

- Deploy to multiple availability zones and AWS regions.

- Implement health checks and failover mechanisms.

- Build stateless applications that store session state and other critical data in a cache server or database.

- Use AWS services that help you achieve your goal. For example, Auto Scaling helps you maintain high availability and scalability.

   Elastic Load Balancing and Auto Scaling are designed to work together.

FIGURE 6.4   Deploying highly available and scalable applications

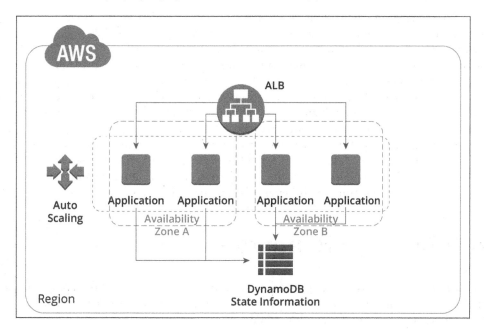

Deploying and Maintaining Applications

AWS provides several services to manage your application and resources. With *AWS Elastic Beanstalk*, you do not have to worry about managing the infrastructure for your application. AWS provides the compute layer, complete with certain supported application stacks. For instance, choosing the Ruby platform ensures that Beanstalk will provision an instance for your Beanstalk deployment that comes with Ruby and Rails dependencies preinstalled. From there, Elastic Beanstalk takes care of scaling and managing your infrastructure. We'll go more in-depth on this service in the next section, "AWS Elastic Beanstalk."

Automatically Adjust Capacity

AWS Auto Scaling is a service that allows you to launch identical compute instances, such as EC2 instances, in a group, automatically adjusting capacity to maintain steady, predictable performance. You can build scaling plans to manage multiple types of resources, including EC2 instances and Spot Fleets, Elastic Container Service (ECS) tasks, DynamoDB tables and indexes, and Aurora Replicas.

AWS Auto Scaling makes scaling simple, with recommendations that allow you to optimize performance, costs, or balance between them. If you are already using EC2 Auto Scaling to scale your EC2 instances dynamically, you can now combine it with AWS Auto Scaling to scale additional resources for other AWS services. With AWS Auto Scaling, your applications have the right resources at the right time.

Auto Scaling Groups

An Auto Scaling group contains a collection of EC2 instances that share similar characteristics. For example, if a single application operates across multiple instances, you might want to increase the number of instances in that group to improve the performance of the application or decrease the number of instances to reduce costs when demand is low.

An Auto Scaling group launches enough EC2 instances to meet its desired capacity. The Auto Scaling group maintains this number of instances by performing periodic health checks on the instances in the group. If an instance becomes unhealthy, the group terminates the unhealthy instance and launches another instance to replace it.

You can use scaling policies to dynamically increase or decrease the number of instances in your group to meet changing conditions. When the scaling policy is in effect, the Auto Scaling group adjusts the desired capacity of the group and launches or terminates the instances as needed. You can also manually scale or scale on a schedule.

AWS Elastic Beanstalk

AWS Elastic Beanstalk is Amazon's *platform-as-a-service* that allows you to deploy and scale applications without worrying about infrastructure. Beanstalk supports deployments using Java, .NET, PHP, Node.js, Python, Ruby, and Go.

Elastic Beanstalk charges only for the resources you use to run your application.

Not only does Elastic Beanstalk provide pre-provisioned compute instances with your platform software of choice, but it also manages the deployment and management of such related services as Auto Scaling groups, load balancers, Route 53 domain configuration, and RDS database instances, to name a few. Behind the scenes, Beanstalk leverages CloudFormation to manage all the resources for your app in a single stack, making Beanstalk environments easy to create and delete.

Figure 6.5 displays Elastic Beanstalk's underlying technologies.

As we've seen, AWS and its customers share responsibility for managing and securing services in the cloud. With Beanstalk, AWS takes on more of this responsibility, managing features up the stack by providing not just compute infrastructure, but the application platform layer, such as Python or .NET versions. Furthermore, Beanstalk automatically applies patch and minor updates for an Elastic Beanstalk–supported platform version.

Figure 6.6 displays Elastic Beanstalk's responsibilities.

FIGURE 6.5 Elastic Beanstalk's underlying technologies

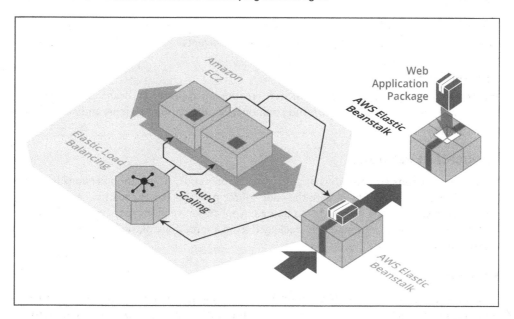

FIGURE 6.6 Responsibilities of AWS Elastic Beanstalk

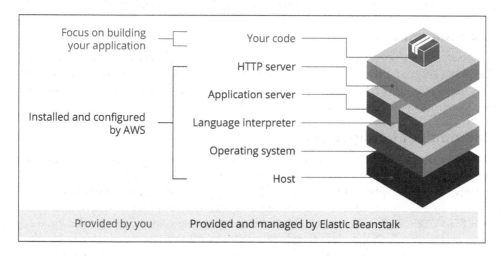

Concepts

Elastic Beanstalk enables you to manage all the resources that run your application as environments. Here are some key Elastic Beanstalk concepts.

Application

The first step in any Beanstalk deployment is creating an application, Beanstalk's logical container for environment variables and components, application versions, and environment configurations.

Application Versions

Application versions are iterations of your application's code. Application versions in Elastic Beanstalk point to an S3 object with the code source package. An application can have many versions, with each version being unique. Application versions may be uploaded to S3 directly, or they can be automatically packaged from source control, such as GitHub or AWS CodeCommit.

Environment

Within an application, Beanstalk users define *environments*: distinct sets of infrastructure components that run a unique instance of your application. For example, you might wish to define dev, test, and production environments within your Beanstalk application, each one comprising an AWS-managed load balancer, auto-scaling group, and database.

Environment Tier

To launch an environment, you must first choose an environment tier. The selection of tier shapes the kinds of resources Beanstalk will provision for your application. A *web server* tier is set up to accept HTTP requests and serve content, whereas a *web worker* tier pulls tasks from Amazon Simple Queue Service (SQS) for execution without a user interface.

Environment Configuration

You can change your environment to create, modify, delete, or deploy resources and change the settings for each. Your environment configuration saves to a configuration template exclusive to each environment and is accessible by either the Elastic Beanstalk application programming interface (API) calls or the service's command-line interface (EB CLI).

In Elastic Beanstalk, you can run either a web server environment or a worker environment. Figure 6.7 displays an example of a web server environment running in Elastic Beanstalk with Amazon Route 53 as the domain name service (DNS) and Elastic Load Balancing to route traffic to the web server instances.

Figure 6.8 shows a worker environment architecture, where AWS Beanstalk creates and provisions resources like SQS queues, Auto Scaling groups, security groups, and EC2 instances, as well as IAM roles to manage your worker applications.

FIGURE 6.7   Application running on Elastic Beanstalk

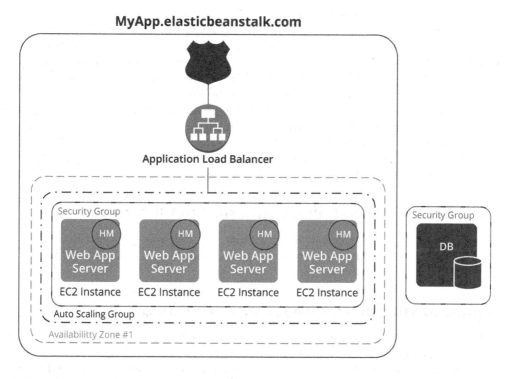

MyApp.elasticbeanstalk.com

FIGURE 6.8   Worker tier on Elastic Beanstalk

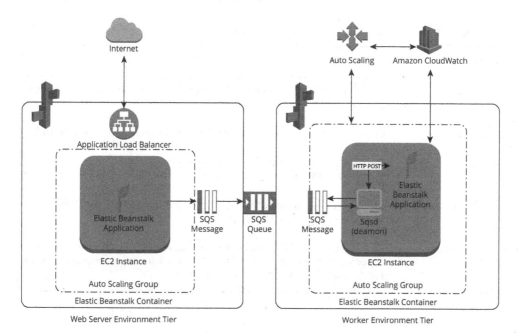

Docker Containers

You can also use Elastic Beanstalk to run applications using Docker. Docker containers are instances of self-contained images that include all the configuration and software that you specify for your application to run. When you choose to deploy your applications with Docker containers, your infrastructure is provisioned with capacity provisioning, load balancing, scaling, and health monitoring, much like a non-container environment. You can continue to manage your application and the AWS resources you use.

With Beanstalk, Docker containers may be deployed individually to an EC2 instance, or as multicontainer applications running on an ECS cluster.

For more sophisticated container orchestration, AWS offers Elastic Container Service (ECS) and Elastic Kubernetes Service (EKS). These options are covered in more detail in Chapter 9, "Secure Configuration and Container Management."

AWS Elastic Beanstalk Command-Line Interface

Elastic Beanstalk has its own command-line interface separate from the AWS CLI tool. To create deployments from the command line, you download and install the AWS Elastic Beanstalk CLI (EB CLI). Table 6.1 lists common EB CLI commands.

Customizing Environment Configurations

Although Beanstalk environments come pre-provisioned with much of the requirements you need for your chosen application stack, you may need to extend the baseline configuration with your own setup. That's where .ebextensions comes in. By creating a specifically formatted YAML configuration file in the .ebextensions file, you can perform many basic

TABLE 6.1   Common AWS Elastic Beanstalk commands

Command	Definition
eb init application-name	Sets default values for Elastic Beanstalk applications with the EB CLI configuration wizard
eb create	Creates a new environment and deploys an application version to it
eb deploy	Deploys the application source bundle from the initialized project directory to the running application
eb clone	Clones an environment to a new environment so that both have identical environment settings
eb codesource	Configures the EB CLI to deploy from an AWS CodeCommit repository, or disables AWS CodeCommit integration and uploads the source bundle from your local machine

host configuration steps, such as defining environment variables, configuring users and groups, transferring files, installing packages, and running other arbitrary scripts. In addition to customizing EC2 instances, .ebextensions files can be used to configure resources in the Beanstalk stack, such as the desired capacity of the stack's autoscaling group.

The .ebextensions folder may contain as many config files as you wish, named however you like. They will be executed with each deployment in lexical order (i.e., alphanumeric order).

The following example configures the environment by first setting some environment variables under the option_settings section, then using the packages section to install GIT and nodeJS via yum. In the files section, some inline content is written to populate an nginx configuration file (note that AWS requires six digits for the file permission mode here). Finally, some additional commands are run under container_commands, where we've chosen to name the steps with prefixes 01 and 02 to ensure their run order.

```
# .ebextensions/example.config
option_settings:
  aws:elasticbeanstalk:application:environment:
    APP_ENV: production
    DB_HOST: my-database.example.com
    DB_PORT: 5432

packages:
  yum:
    git: []
    nodejs: []

files:
  "/etc/nginx/conf.d/proxy.conf" :
    mode: "000644"
    owner: root
    group: root
    content: |
      client_max_body_size 10M;
      client_body_buffer_size 128k;

container_commands:
  01_migrate_db:
    command: "python manage.py migrate"
  02_reload_nginx:
    command: "service nginx reload"
    runas: root
```

For more details on the powerful capabilities of .ebextensions, see the AWS documentation:

https://docs.aws.amazon.com/elasticbeanstalk/latest/dg/ ebextensions.html

You can view Elastic Beanstalk stacks in AWS CloudFormation, but always use the Elastic Beanstalk service and .ebextensions to make modifications. This way, you avoid the risk of configuration drift.

Elastic Beanstalk generates logs specific to your application platform selection and makes them available for download either through the web console or with the EB CLI command eb logs.

Integrating with Other AWS Services

Elastic Beanstalk automatically integrates or manages other AWS services with application code to provision efficient working environments. However, you might find it necessary to add additional services, such as S3 for content storage or DynamoDB for data records, to work with an environment. To grant access between any integrated service and Elastic Beanstalk, you must configure permissions in IAM.

Amazon S3

S3 is a great location for storing static content associated with your applications. By making sure to apply an IAM role with appropriate S3 permissions to your Beanstalk compute instances, your apps can access S3 content via CLI or SDK commands.

Amazon CloudFront

You can integrate your Elastic Beanstalk environment with Amazon CloudFront, which provides content delivery and distribution through the use of edge locations throughout the world. This can decrease the time in which your content is delivered to end users, as the content is cached and routed through the closest edge location serving you. After you deploy your application on Elastic Beanstalk, use the CloudFront content delivery network (CDN) to cache static content from your application. To identify the source of your content in CloudFront, you can use URL path patterns to cache your content and then retrieve it from the cache. This approach serves your content more rapidly and off-loads requests directly sourced from your application.

Amazon RDS

Beanstalk provides an interface to create RDS databases for your application directly in the Beanstalk console. When configured via Beanstalk, the creation of a database will introduce new environment variables to your Beanstalk environment, giving your application access to the endpoint URL, username, and password of your new RDS instance. See Beanstalk documentation for your chosen RDS database engine to learn more about the exact configuration options available and the environment variables you can expect.

You have two choices when creating the RDS database instance. If you create it from the RDS console, its life cycle will exist independently of your Beanstalk app, but you will need to update your Beanstalk environment with RDS environment variables (i.e., username and password) on your own. Alternatively, you can create your database from within the Beanstalk console. By default, this injects all necessary environment variables into your Beanstalk application, and the RDS database will terminate along with your Beanstalk environment. If you want the database to persist beyond the life cycle of the Beanstalk app, make sure to select the option that specifies the database should be retained after termination of the Beanstalk environment.

AWS Identity and Access Management Roles

Elastic Beanstalk integrates with AWS Identity and Access Management (IAM) roles to enable access to the services you require to run your architecture.

When you launch the service to create an environment, a default service role and instance profile are created for you through the service API. Managed policies for resources permissions are also attached, including policies for Elastic Beanstalk instance health monitoring within your infrastructure and platform updates that can be made on behalf of the service. These policies, called AWSElasticBeanstalkEnhancedHealth and AWSElasticBeanstalkService, attach to the default service role and enable the default service role to specify a trusted entity and trust policy.

When you use commands from the EB CLI, the role allows automatic management of the AWS Cloud that services your run. The service creates an environment if you don't identify it specifically, creates a service-linked role, and uses it when you spin up a new environment. The CreateServiceLinkedRole policy must be available in your IAM account to create the environment successfully.

 For IAM to manage the policies for the account better, create policies at the account level.

Deployment Strategies

A *deployment* is the process of copying content and executing scripts on instances in your deployment group. To accomplish this, AWS CodeDeploy performs the tasks outlined in the AppSpec configuration file. For both EC2 on-premises instances and AWS Lambda functions, the deployment succeeds or fails based on whether individual AppSpec tasks complete successfully.

After you have created a deployment, you can update it as your application or service changes. You can update a deployment by adding or removing resources from a deployment, thus updating the properties of existing resources in a deployment.

A serverless application is typically a combination of AWS Lambda and other AWS services.

Deployment Strategies

To give developers flexibility to control downtime, CodeDeploy and Elastic Beanstalk provide multiple deployment strategies that influence how new code is rolled out to your infrastructure.

In-Place Deployments

When you perform an *in-place deployment*, CodeDeploy stops currently running applications on the target instance, deploys the latest revision, restarts applications, and validates successful deployment. In-place deployments can support the automatic configuration of a load balancer. In this case, the instance is deregistered from the load balancer before deployment and registered again after the deployment processes successfully.

In-place updates are also available for your platform updates, such as a coding-language platform update for a web server. Select the new platform and then run the update from the AWS Management Console or command line directly as a platform update.

The *all-at-once deployment* applies updates to all your instances at once. When you execute this strategy, your app will experience downtime, as all instances receive the change at the same time.

AWS Lambda does not support in-place deployments.

Rolling Deployments

A *rolling deployment* applies changes to all your instances by rolling the updates from one instance to another. Elastic Beanstalk can deploy configuration changes in batches. This approach reduces possible downtime during implementation of the change and allows available instances to run while you deploy.

As updates are applied in a batch, the affected instances will be out of service for a short period while the changes propagate and then relaunch with the new configuration. When the change is complete, the service moves on to the next batch of instances to apply the changes. With this strategy, you can implement both periodic changes and pauses between updates. For example, you might specify a time to wait between health-based updates so that instances must pass health checks before moving on to the next batch. If the rolling update fails, the service begins another rolling update for a rollback to the previous configuration.

With Elastic Beanstalk deployments, you can select *rolling* or *rolling with additional batch* strategies. When using *rolling with additional batch*, Beanstalk launches a new batch of instances before you begin to take instances out of service for your rolling updates. This option provides an available batch for rollback from a failed update. After the deployment is successfully executed, Elastic Beanstalk terminates the instances from the additional batch. This is helpful for a critical application that must continue running with less downtime than the standard rolling update.

Blue/Green Deployment

When high availability is critical for applications, you may want to choose a *blue/green deployment* model, where you always maintain two compute environments, and swap between them as deployments occur. In this setup, the running production environment is considered the *blue environment*, and the newer environment with your update is considered the *green environment*. When your changes are ready and have gone through all tests in your green environment, you (or your chosen AWS service) can update the configuration of your load balancer to switch to the new group of updated instances. This strategy provides an instantaneous update with typically zero downtime, and it provides a quick way to fall back from failed deployments, because your original compute stays unaltered.

When you deploy to AWS Lambda functions, blue/green deployments publish new versions of each function. Traffic shifting then routes requests to the new functioning versions according to the deployment configuration you define.

Immutable Deployment

An *immutable deployment* is best when an environment requires a total replacement of instances rather than updates to an existing part of an infrastructure. Similar to a blue/green deployment, this approach deploys code to separate compute instances from what is currently running; the distinction is that these are always completely new instances. Elastic Beanstalk achieves this by creating a temporary Auto Scaling group behind your environment's load balancer to contain the new instances with the updates you apply. If the update fails, the rollback process terminates the Auto Scaling group.

During this type of deployment, your capacity doubles for a short duration between the updates and terminations of instances. Before you use this strategy, verify that your instances have a low on-demand limit and enough capacity to support immutable updates.

See Table 6.2 for feature comparisons between all deployment strategies. The check mark indicates options that the deployment strategy supports.

TABLE 6.2   Deployment strategies

Method	Impact of failed deployment	Deploy time	Zero downtime	No DNS change	Rollback process	Code deployed to
All-at-once	Downtime	🕐		✓	Redeploy	Existing instances
In-place	Downtime	🕐		✓	Redeploy	Existing instances
Rolling	Single batch out of service; any successful batches before failure running new application version	🕐 🕐	✓	✓	Redeploy	Existing instances
Rolling with additional batch	Minimal if first batch fails, otherwise, similar to rolling	🕐 🕐 🕐	✓	✓	Redeploy	New and existing instances
Blue/ Green	Minimal	🕐 🕐 🕐 🕐	✓		Swap URL	New instances
Immutable	Minimal	🕐 🕐 🕐 🕐	✓	✓	Redeploy	New instances

Container Deployments

In addition to allowing developers to deploy application code directly to EC2 instances pre-provisioned with specific application platform dependencies, such as Java or Go, Elastic Beanstalk supports the deployment of container-based applications to two different target platforms. Developers can deploy single Docker containers or multicontainer Docker apps using Docker Compose. These containers may be deployed either to EC2 instances running the Docker engine or to Elastic Container Service (ECS) clusters, which are also based on EC2. Like other Beanstalk deployment platforms, Elastic Beanstalk manages the infrastructure associated with these Docker deployments. This management includes creating the EC2 instances that directly run Docker or establishing the EC2 instances that compose an ECS cluster for ECS-based deployments.

Monitoring and Troubleshooting

You can monitor statistics and view information about the health of your Beanstalk application, its environment, and specific services from the AWS Management Console. Beanstalk also creates alerts that trigger at established thresholds to monitor your environment's health. Metrics gathered by the resources in your environment are published to CloudWatch in five-minute intervals. Figure 6.9 shows an example of the metrics and graphs that you can view.

Basic Health Monitoring

To access the health status from the AWS Management Console, select the Elastic Beanstalk service and then select the tab for your specific application environment. An environment overview shows your architecture's instance status details, resource details, and filter capabilities. Health statuses are indicated in four distinct colors.

To access the health status from the EB CLI, enter the **eb health** command. The output shows the environment and the health of associated instances. Enhanced health reporting

FIGURE 6.9   Metrics for monitoring on Elastic Beanstalk

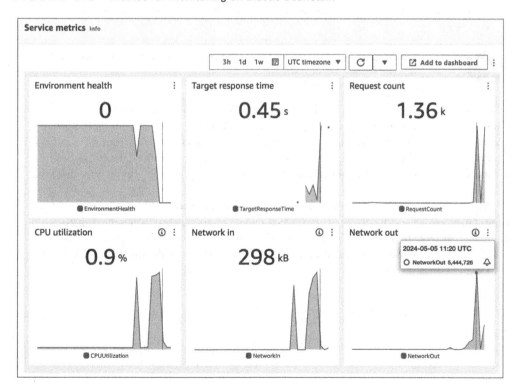

also provides seven health statuses, which are single-word descriptors that provide a better indication of the state of your environment.

```
ok    warning   degraded   severe   info   pending   unknown
```

You can also use the `eb status` command in the EB CLI to retrieve the health status for an environment. You can check the health of the overall environment or the individual services of EC2 or load balancers.

For GET requests with the load balancer, `200 OK` is the default success code and indicates a healthy status. You can also configure a custom static page response to display when health checks fail.

Elastic Beanstalk also reports missing configurations or other issues that could affect the health of the application environment.

Enhanced Health Monitoring

Beanstalk's enhanced health reporting feature gathers additional resource data and displays graphs and statistics of environment health in greater detail. This is important when you deploy multiple versions of your application and when you need to analyze factors that could be degrading your application's availability or performance. You can view these details in the AWS Elastic Beanstalk Monitoring page in the AWS Management Console. These reports require the creation of two IAM roles: a *service role* to allow access between the services and Elastic Beanstalk and an *instance profile* to write logs into an S3 bucket.

> Enhanced health reports provide data directly to Elastic Beanstalk and do not run through CloudWatch.

By default, health monitoring on Elastic Beanstalk does not publish metrics to CloudWatch, so you are not charged for the metrics. There are also custom metrics, which you can run and view that are not charged a fee. You can also enable custom metrics from CloudWatch, but these incur additional charges. To save costs, use the default metrics on the Elastic Beanstalk service, or enable the custom metrics that you need, paying only for what you use.

You can monitor recent health events that you have enabled on Elastic Beanstalk in real time. There are several health event types that can change as an environment transitions from the create state to the run state. Figure 6.10 displays the health events available in the AWS Elastic Beanstalk Monitoring page and examples of the details that allow you to respond to issues identified.

FIGURE 6.10 Events on AWS Elastic Beanstalk

Time	Type	Details
May 4, 2024 15:50:11 (UTC-4)	⚠ WARN	Environment health has transitioned from Pending to Severe. Command failed on all instances. ELB processes are not healthy on all instances. Initialization completed 56 seconds ago and took 4 minutes. ELB health is failing or not available for all instances.
May 4, 2024 15:49:05 (UTC-4)	ⓘ INFO	Command execution completed on all instances. Summary: [Successful: 0, Failed: 1].
May 4, 2024 15:48:11 (UTC-4)	ⓘ INFO	Added instance [i-098e3c80dd8c8eaeb] to your environment.
May 4, 2024 15:47:41 (UTC-4)	ⓘ INFO	Created Load Balancer listener named: arn:aws:elasticloadbalancing:us-east-1:218705140181:listener/app/awseb--AWSEB-Bc4wDXvTOFdF/2cf857a798ddffd7/ef37beed2db7c004
May 4, 2024 15:47:41 (UTC-4)	ⓘ INFO	Created load balancer named: arn:aws:elasticloadbalancing:us-east-1:218705140181:loadbalancer/app/awseb--AWSEB-Bc4wDXvTOFdF/2cf857a798ddffd7

Summary

In this chapter, you learned about the features of Elastic Beanstalk, how to automate deployments for your multitier architectures, and different deployment strategies. You also discovered options for configuring your environments and managing your resources with services such as IAM, Amazon VPC, Amazon EC2, and Amazon S3.

Exam Essentials

Know how to deploy Elastic Beanstalk.   Know how to deploy an application to Elastic Beanstalk and what platforms it supports. To complete the exam successfully, you should also understand how the architectures and services interact with the web, application, and database tiers. Focus on foundational services and how you create and work with Elastic Beanstalk.

Know about .ebextensions.   Understand .ebextensions files and the part they play in service configuration. Be able to recognize the stacks you create and how to change them.

Be familiar with Elastic Beanstalk resources.   Understand how to manage resources with Elastic Beanstalk, including IAM. Understand the definitions and differentiate between the functions of the default IAM service role and the instance profile, both of which are automatically created. Understand permissions for your AWS resources in your environment.

Know Elastic Beanstalk deployment strategies.   Understand what deployment strategies you can use, their differences, and which ones would be best for different use cases and other resources. Know which strategy offers less downtime and which is best suited for complex changes.

Know about Elastic Beanstalk components.   Understand all the components of Elastic Beanstalk, including applications, environments, versions, configurations, and the AWS resources it launches and with which it integrates. Know how to retain or dispose of resources as needed.

Know about Elastic Beanstalk different environment tiers.   Know the differences between the single-instance tier and the web-server environment tier and when to choose one over the other. Understand the services and features used for both.

On the test itself, do not get sidetracked with small details about Elastic Beanstalk. Focus your understanding on how it works as a whole and interacts with other services.

Exercises

EXERCISE 6.1

Deploying Your Application

In this exercise, you will sign up for an AWS account:

1.   Verify that your source code is packaged as a ZIP file and is ready to be retrieved from either your source repository directory or an S3 bucket.

2.   Launch the AWS Management Console.

3.   Navigate to the Elastic Beanstalk service.

4.   Click Create Application. This option takes you through a wizard of guided steps to launch your first application.

5.   Select Web Server Environment and enter an application name.

6.   For Environment Name, enter **development**.

7.   Under Platform, select the application platform for your code.

8.   For Platform Branch and Platform Version, select the preconfigured platform that matches your app. If uploading your own app, be sure to align your code's version requirements to those offered by Beanstalk.

9.   Under Application Code, choose Sample Application, or click Upload Your Code and either upload a ZIP archive or provide a public S3 URL to your archive.

10. Under Presets, choose High Availability. This will create a configuration with a load balancer, allowing for horizontal scaling.

11. Click Next.

12. Under Service Access, click Create And Use New Service Role.

13. Click Next.

14. Under VPC, choose your account's default VPC.

15. Under Instance Settings, choose Activated for Public IP and select at least one subnet.

16. In the Database section, select at least two subnets and click Enable Database. Keep the default selections for the database engine and version.

17. Enter a username and password for the database.

18. Click Next.

19. On the Configure Instance Traffic And Scaling page, keep all defaults, and select the security group that allows HTTP from the world.

20. Keep all defaults for the load balancer configuration, and click Next.

21. On this page, configure logging as desired and enter any environment variable values you need.

22. Click Next.

23. Review your choices and click Submit.

You now have successfully deployed an application on Elastic Beanstalk.

EXERCISE 6.2

Deploying a Blue/Green Solution

In this exercise, you will deploy a blue/green solution.

1. Sign in to your AWS account.

2. Navigate to your existing Elastic Beanstalk environment and application or upload the sample.

You can launch a sample application from this location:

```
https://docs.aws.amazon.com/elasticbeanstalk/latest/dg/
tutorials.html
```

3. Clone your environment or launch a new environment with your new version.

4. Deploy the second application version to the new environment. Test that the new version is running.

5. From the New Environment dashboard, select Actions ➤ Swap Environment Domain.

6. Under Select An Environment To Swap, select the current environment name.

7. Click Swap.

8. The Elastic Beanstalk service swaps the CNAME records between the two environments.

9. On the dashboard, under Recent Events, verify the swap.

You have successfully deployed a blue/green solution on Elastic Beanstalk.

EXERCISE 6.3

Changing Your Environment Configuration on AWS Elastic Beanstalk

In this exercise, you will change your environment configuration on Elastic Beanstalk. Use an existing application that is running on Elastic Beanstalk.

1. Sign in to your AWS account.

2. Navigate to your existing Elastic Beanstalk environment and application.

3. Click Configuration.

4. In the Instance Traffic And Scaling section, click Edit.

5. Under Auto Scaling Group, change Max to **4** and Min to **2**.

6. Scroll down and click Apply.

   The environment might take a few minutes to update. After your environment is updated, verify your changes.

7. Navigate to the Amazon EC2 service dashboard.

8. Click Load Balancers.

9. Check for the instance-id value that matches your Elastic Beanstalk environment instance-id value and view the load balancers.

You have successfully changed an environment configuration on AWS Elastic Beanstalk.

EXERCISE 6.4

Updating an Application Version on AWS Elastic Beanstalk

In this exercise, you will update an application version on Elastic Beanstalk from the AWS Management Console.

1. Sign in to your AWS account.

2. Upload a second version of your application that matches the configuration for your current running environment.

   If you are using a sample solution application, you can find other versions at the following address:

   https://docs.aws.amazon.com/elasticbeanstalk/latest/dg/ GettingStarted.html#GettingStarted.Walkthrough.DeployApp

3. On the Elastic Beanstalk service home page, select your existing application.

4. Select your environment

5. Click Upload And Deploy.

6. Click Choose File and upload the next version of your source bundle that you created or downloaded.

   The console is automatically populated with the version label based on the name of the archive that you upload. For later deployments, if you use a source bundle with the same name, you must type a unique version label.

7. Click Deploy. Elastic Beanstalk deploys your application to your EC2 instances.

   You can view the status of the deployment on the environment's dashboard. The Environment Health status turns gray while the application version is being updated. When deployment is complete, Elastic Beanstalk executes an application health check. The status reverts to green when the application responds to the health check. The environment dashboard shows the new running version as the new version label. Your new application version is added to the table of application versions.

8. To view the table, click Application Versions.

You have updated an application version on AWS Elastic Beanstalk.

Review Questions

1. Which of the following AWS services enables you to automate your build, test, deploy, and release process every time there is a code change?

    A. AWS CodeCommit

    B. AWS CodeDeploy

    C. AWS CodeBuild

    D. AWS CodePipeline

2. Which of the following statements is true about AWS Elastic Beanstalk?

    A. Elastic Beanstalk automatically handles capacity provisioning, load balancing, and application health monitoring.

    B. Developers need to manually manage the underlying infrastructure when deploying applications with Elastic Beanstalk.

    C. Elastic Beanstalk supports only a single programming language for application development.

    D. Applications deployed using Elastic Beanstalk cannot be integrated with other AWS services.

3. Which of the following languages is not supported by AWS Elastic Beanstalk?

    A. Java

    B. Node.js

    C. Objective C

    D. Go

4. What does the Elastic Beanstalk service do?

    A. Deploys applications and architecture

    B. Stores static content

    C. Directs user traffic to EC2 instances

    D. Works with dynamic cloud changes as an IP address

5. Instances in your Elastic Beanstalk application need several operating system packages installed before the app can run. For the fastest possible scaling times, how should you provision this configuration?

    A. Use the `container_commands` section of a `.ebextensions` file to install package via a shell script.

    B. Edit the launch configuration of the application's Auto Scaling group to add package installations to user data.

    C. Install the packages on an instance, create an AMI, and use that AMI in the launch configuration.

    D. Use `.ebextensions` to download the packages from S3.

6. Which of the following components can Elastic Beanstalk deploy? (Choose three.)

   A. EC2 instances with write capabilities to an DynamoDB table

   B. A worker application using SQS

   C. An ECS task

   D. A mixed fleet of Spot and Reserved Instances with four applications running in each environment

   E. A mixed fleet of Reserved Instances scheduled between 9 a.m. and 5 p.m. and On-Demand Instances used for processing data workloads when needed randomly

7. Which of the following operations can Elastic Beanstalk do? (Choose two.)

   A. Access an S3 bucket

   B. Connect to an RDS database

   C. Install agents for the GuardDuty service

   D. Create and manage Amazon WorkSpaces

8. Which service can be used to restrict access to Elastic Beanstalk resources?

   A. AWS Config

   B. Amazon RDS

   C. AWS IAM

   D. Amazon S3

9. Which IAM entities are used when creating an environment? (Choose two.)

   A. Federated role

   B. Service role

   C. Instance profile

   D. Profile role

   E. Username and access keys

10. Which of the following describes how customers are charged for Elastic Beanstalk?

   A. A monthly fee based on an hourly rate for use.

   B. A one-time upfront cost for each environment running.

   C. No additional charges.

   D. A fee is charged only when scaling to support traffic changes.

11. What two AWS resources must be configured to achieve horizontal scaling of a web app on EC2 instances?

   A. An Auto Scaling group and a VPC

   B. An application load balancer (ALB) and Route 53

   C. An application load balancer and an Auto Scaling group

   D. An Auto Scaling group and an Internet gateway

Chapter 7

Deployment as Code

**THE AWS CERTIFIED DEVELOPER –
ASSOCIATE EXAM TOPICS COVERED IN
THIS CHAPTER MAY INCLUDE, BUT ARE
NOT LIMITED TO, THE FOLLOWING:**

✓ **Domain 1: Develop with AWS Services**

- Task Statement 1: Develop code for applications
  hosted on AWS

✓ **Domain 3: Deployment**

- Task Statement 1: Prepare application artifacts to be
  deployed to AWS

- Task Statement 3: Automate deployment testing

- Task Statement 4: Deploy code using AWS CI/CD services

In the previous chapter, you learned about using AWS Elastic Beanstalk to deploy applications to highly available, fault-tolerant infrastructure. As a platform-as-a-service offering, Beanstalk simplifies deployments by providing a selected range of platform options with several predetermined configurations. However, as your experience with AWS deployment increases over time, you may need to customize your workflow further than what is supported natively on Beanstalk. You need deployment services designed for flexibility, empowering customers with complex infrastructure and application deployment requirements.

For users who wish for more control over their deployments, Amazon provides the AWS "Code" services. This set of features lays the foundation to deploy code, infrastructure, and configuration automatically, starting from a source repository.

AWS CodeCommit is such a repository, acting as the initialization point of your deployment process. *AWS CodeBuild* allows you to pull code and packages from various sources to create publishable build artifacts. *AWS CodeDeploy* allows you to deploy compiled artifacts to infrastructure in your environment. Finally, *AWS CodePipeline* brings it all together, allowing users to chain these services together into *continuous integration/continuous deployment pipelines* (CI/CD) that can build, test, configure, and deploy your applications automatically. Not only that, but CodePipeline can provision, configure, and manage infrastructure as well.

With AWS code services, a single commit to a source repository can kick off such processes, like those shown in Figure 7.1.

Use AWS CodePipeline to Automate Deployments

AWS CodePipeline is a continuous integration and continuous delivery service that lets you orchestrate sequences of events using AWS and other provider services.

In Figure 7.2, the developer team is responsible for committing changes to a source repository. CodePipeline automatically detects and moves into the source stage. The code change (revision) passes to the build stage, where changes are built into a package or product ready for deployment. A staging deployment is done where users can manually review the functionality that the changes introduce or modify. Before final production release, an authorized user provides a manual approval. After production release, further code changes can reliably pass through the same pipeline.

FIGURE 7.1   Branch view

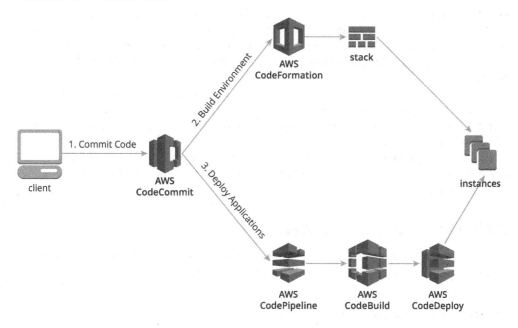

FIGURE 7.2   AWS CodePipeline workflow

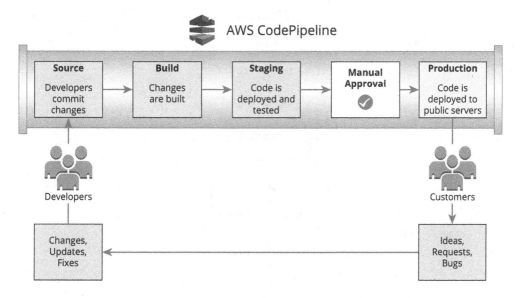

CodePipeline provides several built-in integrations to other AWS services, such as Cloud-Formation, CodeBuild, CodeCommit, AWS CodeDeploy, Amazon Elastic Container Service (ECS), Elastic Beanstalk, Lambda, and Amazon Simple Storage Service (Amazon S3). Some partner tools include GitHub (`https://github.com`) and Jenkins (`https://jenkins.io`). Customers may also create their own integrations, which provides a great degree of flexibility.

You define workflow steps through a visual editor within the AWS Management Console or via a JSON file when using the AWS CLI/SDKs. Access to create and manage release workflows is controlled by IAM permissions, which control what actions users may perform and on which workflows.

CodePipeline provides a dashboard where you can review real-time progress of revisions, attempt to retry failed actions, and review version information about revisions that pass through the pipeline.

AWS CodePipeline Concepts

Several components make up CodePipeline and the workflows (*pipelines*) created by customers. Figure 7.3 displays the AWS CodePipeline concepts.

FIGURE 7.3   Pipeline structure

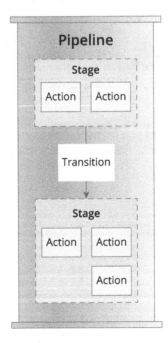

Pipeline

A *pipeline* is the overall workflow that defines what transformations software changes will undergo.

 You cannot change the name of a pipeline. If you would like to change the name, you must create a new pipeline.

Revision

A *revision* is the work item that passes through a pipeline. It can be a change to your source code stored in CodeCommit or GitHub or a change to the version of an archive in Amazon S3. A pipeline can have multiple revisions flowing through it at the same time, but a single stage can process one revision at a time. A revision is immediately picked up by a Source action when a change is detected in the source itself (such as a commit to a CodeCommit repository).

 If you use Amazon S3 as a source action, you must enable versioning on the bucket.

Details of the most recent revision to pass through a stage are kept within the stage itself and are accessible from the console or AWS CLI. To see the last revision that was passed through a source stage, for example, you can select the revision details at the bottom of the stage, as shown in Figure 7.4.

FIGURE 7.4   Source stage

Stage

A *stage* is a group of one or more actions. Each stage must have a unique name. Should any one action in a stage fail, the entire stage fails for this revision.

Action

An *action* defines the work to perform on the revision. You can configure pipeline actions to run in series or in parallel. If all actions in a stage complete successfully for a revision, it passes to the next stage in the pipeline. However, if one action fails in the stage, the revision will not pass further through the pipeline. At this point, the stage that contains the failed action can be retried for the same revision, or a new revision may pass through the stage.

> *A pipeline must have two or more stages.* The first stage includes one or more source actions only. Only the first stage may include source actions.

> Every action in the same stage must have a unique name.

Source

The *source* action defines the location where you store and update source files. Modifications to files in a source repository or archive trigger deployments to a pipeline. CodePipeline source system options include:

- Amazon S3
- AWS CodeCommit
- GitHub
- Amazon ECR (Elastic Container Registry)
- GitLab
- Bitbucket

> *A single pipeline can contain multiple source actions.* If a change is detected in one of the sources, all source actions will be invoked.

To use GitHub or other external repositories as a source provider for CodePipeline, you must authenticate to that service when you create the pipeline. Details vary by provider, but GitHub allows you to configure this connection for all repos or selected repos only. When connecting to external services like this, AWS recommends that you create a service account user so that the life cycle of personal accounts is not tied to the link between CodePipeline and GitHub.

Build

You use a *build* action to define tasks such as compiling source code, running unit tests, and performing other tasks that produce output artifacts for later use in your pipeline. For example, you can use a build stage to import large assets that are not part of a source bundle into the artifact to deploy it to EC2 instances, or to compile a Java application into a JAR file. For build actions, CodePipeline supports AWS CodeBuild and Jenkins.

Test

You can use *test* actions to run various tests against source and compiled code, such as `lint` or syntax tests on source code, and unit tests on compiled, running applications. CodePipeline support for test integrations includes:

- AWS CodeBuild
- BlazeMeter
- Ghost Inspector
- StormRunner Load
- Runscope

Deploy

The *deploy* action is responsible for taking compiled or prepared assets and installing them on instances, on-premises servers, serverless functions, or deploying and updating infrastructure using CloudFormation templates. The following services are supported as deploy actions:

- AWS CloudFormation
- AWS CodeDeploy
- Amazon Elastic Container Service
- AWS Elastic Beanstalk

Approval

An *approval* action is a manual gate that controls whether a revision can proceed to the next stage in a pipeline. Further progress by a revision is halted until a manual approval by an AWS IAM user or IAM role occurs.

 Specifically, the codepipeline:PutApprovalResult action must be included in the AWS IAM policy.

Upon approval, CodePipeline approves the revision to proceed to the next stage in the pipeline. However, if the revision is not approved (rejected or the approval expires), the change halts and will stop progress through the pipeline. The purpose of this action is to allow manual review of the code or other quality assurance tasks prior to moving further down the pipeline.

 Approval actions cannot occur within source stages.

You must approve actions manually within seven days; otherwise, CodePipeline rejects the code. When an approval action rejects, the outcome is equivalent to when the stage fails.

You can retire the action, which initiates the approval process again. Approval actions provide several options that you can use to provide additional information about what you choose to approve.

Publish Approval Notifications   Amazon Simple Notification Service (SNS) sends notices to one or more targets that approval is pending.

Specify a Universal Resource Locator (URL) for Review   You can include a URL in the approval action notification—for example, to review a website published to a fleet of test instances.

Enter Comments for Approvers   You can add additional comments in the notifications for the reviewer's reference.

Invoke

Invoke actions allow you to execute external actions via AWS Lambda or Step Functions, which allows arbitrary code to be run as part of the pipeline execution. Uses for custom actions in your pipeline can include the following:

- Backing up data volumes, Amazon S3 buckets, or databases
- Interacting with third-party products, such as posting messages to Slack channels
- Running through test interactions with deployed web applications, such as executing a test transaction on a shopping site
- Updating IAM roles to allow permissions to newly created resources

> When you deploy changes to multiple AWS Elastic Beanstalk environments, for example, you can use AWS Lambda to invoke a stage to swap the environment CNAMEs (SwapEnvironmentCNAMEs). This effectively implements blue/green deployments via CodePipeline.

Artifact

Artifacts are files that pass between actions and stages in a pipeline to provide a final result or version of the files. For example, with a Java app, a JAR file might be passed as an artifact from a build action to deploy to EC2 during a deploy action. Actions may access output artifacts from any previous stage of a pipeline. Artifacts are kept in an S3 bucket associated with the pipeline.

> Multiple actions in a single pipeline cannot output artifacts with the same name.

For an artifact to transition between stages successfully, you must provide unique input and output artifact names. In Figure 7.5, the output artifact name for the source action must match the input artifact for the corresponding build action.

FIGURE 7.5   Artifact transition

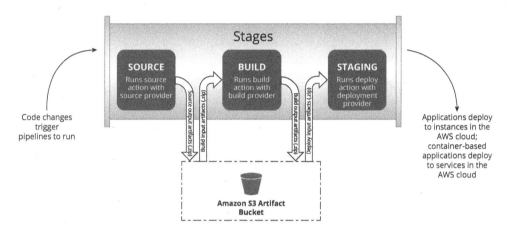

A source action of S3 cannot reference buckets in accounts other than the pipeline account.

Transition

Transitions connect stages in a pipeline and define which stages should transition to one another. When all actions in a stage complete successfully, the revision passes to the next stage(s) in the pipeline.

You can pause pipeline execution by manually disabling the transition between two stages. This causes pipeline revisions to queue until either 30 days elapse and the revisions expire, or you reenable the transition, at which point queued revisions execute sequentially.

Figure 7.6 shows a pipeline with three stages: Source, Build, and Deploy. The Source stage contains a source action referencing a GitHub repository. The source action has already completed and passed the source artifact to Build. In Build, AWS CodeBuild executes some automated tests. When that passes, execution continues to the Deploy stage, where AWS CodeDeploy deploys the application to an Auto Scaling group.

If you deploy revisions to EC2 instances (as with CodeDeploy), you apply a policy to the instance role that allows access to the S3 bucket that the CodePipeline uses in the pipeline account. Additionally, the instance role must also have a policy that allows access to the AWS KMS key.

FIGURE 7.6 Full pipeline

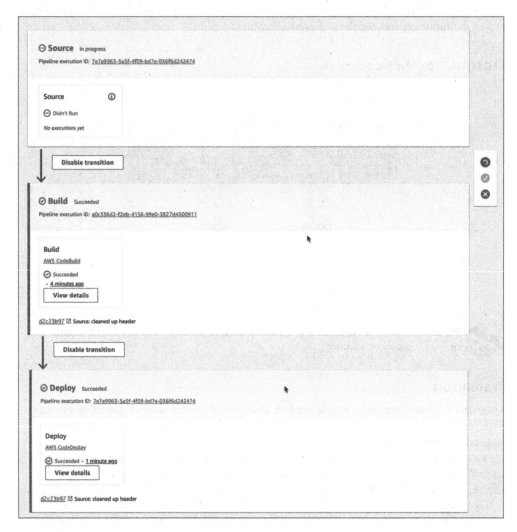

Use AWS CodeCommit as a Source Repository

AWS CodeCommit is a fully managed source control service that makes it easy for companies to host secure and highly scalable private Git repositories.

What Is AWS CodeCommit?

AWS CodeCommit is based on Git and is fully compatible with existing git tooling. While CodePipeline integrates with GitHub, Bitbucket, and many other Git providers as sources, CodeCommit has a few unique features, such as integration with IAM for managing user accounts and the ability to keep all Git traffic private to your VPC, which can be useful in fulfilling certain compliance requirements. CodeCommit can make a great backup mirror for other version control repositories.

Managing Access

CodeCommit users must be created and configured in the IAM console; they are the same as any IAM user, but have policies applied that give them access to CodeCommit repos.

HTTPS

HTTPS connectivity to a Git-based repository requires a username and password, for which IAM users with console access may use their username and password.

SSH

With SSH authentication, users can access repos with an SSH key rather than a username and password. Self-generated SSH keys may be uploaded and attached to the user by an IAM administrator or by users themselves who have the `IAMUserSSHKeys` managed policy.

After uploading a key to an IAM User via the IAM console, AWS assigns it an SSH Key ID, as shown in Figure 7.7.

FIGURE 7.7 SSH Key ID

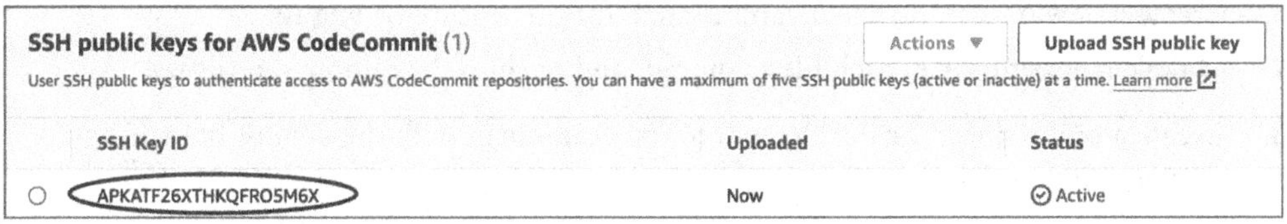

This key must be entered into your local SSH configuration. For Linux or Mac users, edit or create the file **~/.ssh/config** and enter the following:

```
Host git-codecommit.*.amazonaws.com
User YOUR_SSH_KEY_ID_HERE
IdentityFile PATH_TO_YOUR_PRIVATE_KEY_HERE
```

From there, you can clone your CodeCommit repo via SSH or add the CodeCommit SSH URL as a new remote URL to an existing repo as you would normally.

Use the Credential Helper

An alternative to the two methods just described, the credential helper is an AWS CLI feature that lets terminal users authenticate to AWS services like CodeCommit with an IAM user (i.e., with an access ID and secret access key only). With the CLI installed, you may configure Git via the credential helper with the following commands:

```
git config --global \
credential.helper '!aws codecommit credential-helper $@'

git config --global credential.UseHttpPath true
```

Once complete, HTTPS interactions with the AWS CodeCommit repository should work as expected.

 The credential helper authentication method is the only one available for root and federated AWS IAM users.

Repositories

A *repository*, or repo, is the location where you store source code files and track revisions. Like any Git-based system, CodeCommit supports multiple users pushing commits, creating and merging branches, and performing code reviews via pull requests.

Pull Requests

Pull requests allow collaborators to review and comment on changes on a branch before they are merged. The typical workflow pull requests is as follows:

1. Create a new branch off the default branch for the feature or bug fix.

2. Make changes to the branch files, commit, and push to the remote repository.

3. Create a pull request for the changes to integrate them with the default branch, as shown in Figure 7.8.

FIGURE 7.8 Creating a pull request

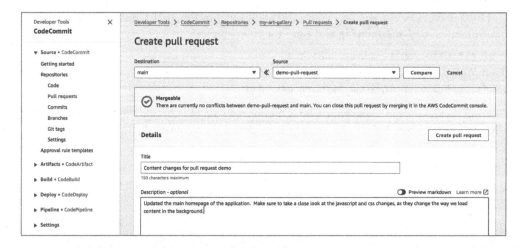

4.   Other users can review the changes in the pull request and provide comments, as shown in Figure 7.9.

FIGURE 7.9   Reviewing changes

5.   You can push any additional changes from user feedback to the same branch to include them in the pull request.

6.   Once all reviewers provide approval, the pull request merges into the default branch and closes. You can close pull requests when you merge the branches locally or when you close the request via the CodeCommit console or the AWS CLI.

Repository Notifications

CodeCommit can be configured to issue CloudWatch events for many types of updates, including pull request creation or closure, comments on code changes, or commits to a branch. This allows for automation opportunities, such as kicking off a Lambda to notify others when a pull request is created.

Repository Triggers

Similar to notifications, *repository triggers* can invoke SNS or Lambda during these events:

- Push to Existing Branch
- Create a Branch or Tag
- Delete a Branch or Tag

Triggers are similar in functionality to webhooks used by other Git providers like GitHub. You can use triggers to perform automated tasks such as starting external builds, notifying administrators of code pushes, or performing unit tests.

Use AWS CodeCommit with AWS CodePipeline

When you select CodeCommit as a source provider in CodePipeline, you must provide a repository name and branch. If you use CodeCommit, it creates a CloudWatch Events rule and an AWS IAM role to monitor the repository and branch for changes, as shown in Figure 7.10.

FIGURE 7.10   Source location

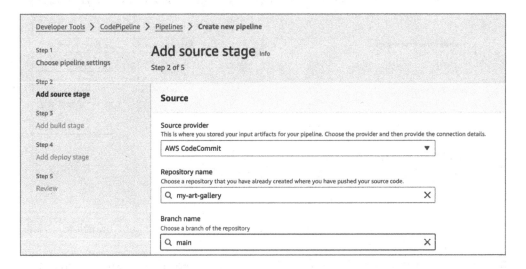

 If your pipeline requires large binary files as source inputs, use versioned S3 buckets instead of a Git repository to store them. By using multiple source stages, you can pull code from CodeCommit and binaries from S3 in one pipeline.

Use AWS CodeBuild to Create Build Artifacts

AWS CodeBuild is a fully managed build service that can compile source code, run tests, and produce software packages that are ready to deploy. Providing serverless build environments in multiple prepackaged or user-specified configurations, CodeBuild scales continuously and processes multiple builds concurrently, so your builds do not wait in a queue. CodeBuild charges by the minute for the compute resources you use.

What Is AWS CodeBuild?

AWS CodeBuild comes with prepackaged build environments for most common workloads and build tools (Apache Maven, Grade, and others), and it allows you to create custom environments for any custom tools or processes.

CodePipeline includes built-in integration with CodeBuild, which can act as a provider for any build or test actions in your pipeline, as shown in Figure 7.11.

FIGURE 7.11   Using CodeBuild in CodePipeline

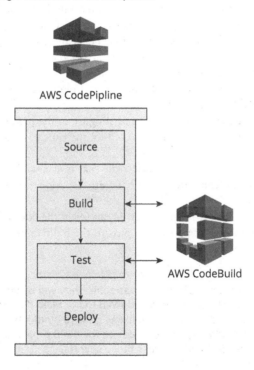

AWS CodeBuild Concepts

CodeBuild initiates build tasks inside a build project, which defines the environmental settings, build steps to perform, and any output artifacts. The build container's operating system, runtime, and build tools make up the build environment.

Build Projects

Build projects define all aspects of a build. This includes the environment in which to perform builds (such as an Ubuntu or Amazon Linux container), any tools to include in the environment, the actual build steps to perform, and outputs to save.

Create a Build Project

When you create a build project, you first select a source provider. CodeBuild supports CodeCommit, S3, GitHub, Bitbucket, GitLab, and more as source providers. When you use an external service like GitHub, a separate authentication flow will be invoked to allow access. GitHub source repositories also support webhooks to trigger builds automatically any time you push a commit to a specific repository and branch, though this can also be achieved through CodePipeline, which you'll see later in this section.

After CodeBuild successfully connects to the source repository or location, you select a *build environment*. CodeBuild provides preconfigured build environments for some operating systems, runtimes, and runtime versions, such as Ubuntu with Java 9.

Next, you will configure the *build specification*. This can be done by inserting build commands in the console or by specifying a `buildspec.yml` file in your source code. The structure of this file is detailed in a moment.

If your build creates artifacts you would like to use in later steps of your pipeline/process, you specify *output artifacts* to save to S3.

CodeBuild supports caching, which you can configure in the next step. Caching saves some components of the build environment to reduce the time to create environments when you submit build jobs.

Every build project requires an IAM service role that is accessible by CodeBuild. When you create new projects, you can automatically create a service role that you restrict to this project only.

After you set the build project properties, you can select the compute type (memory and vCPU settings), any environment variables to pass to the build container, and tags to apply to the project.

When you set environment variables, they will be visible in plaintext in the CodeBuild console and AWS CLI or SDK. If there is sensitive information that you would like to pass to build jobs, consider using *AWS Secrets Manager*. This will require the build project's AWS IAM role to have permissions to access those secrets.

Build Specification (*buildspec.yml*)

The `buildspec.yml` file determines exactly what the CodeBuild project does. Written in YAML, this file controls the environment and actions of a build process using the following format:

```
version: 0.2

env:
```

```
    variables:
      key: "value"
    parameter-store:
      key: "value"
    secrets-manager:
      key: "value"

phases:
  install:
    commands:
      - command
  pre_build:
    commands:
      - command
  build:
    commands:
      - command
  post_build:
    commands:
      - command
artifacts:
  files:
    - location
  discard-paths: yes
  base-directory: location
cache:
  paths:
    - path
```

Version

AWS supports multiple build specification versions; however, AWS recommends you use the latest version whenever possible.

Environment Variables (*env*)

You can add optional environment variables to build jobs. Any key-value pairs that you provide in the `variables` section are available as environment variables in plaintext.

NOTE   Any environment variables that you define here will overwrite those you define elsewhere in the build project, such as those in the container itself or by Docker.

The `parameter-store` mapping specifies parameters to query in AWS Systems Manager Parameter Store, while the `secrets-manager` key allows you to load values from Secrets Manager.

Because you should never store secrets in plaintext or upload plaintext secrets to version control, it is highly recommended to use one of these services for managing secret values outside the BuildSpec file. After saving a value in Secrets Manager, you may reference it in the BuildSpec by loading it into an environment variable:

```
env:
  secrets-manager:
    SECRET_VALUE: SECRET_NAME_OR_ARN:SECRET_KEY_VALUE
```

For instance, let's say you have a database username and password in Secrets Manager. The two key-value pairs are stored under a secret called `MyDatabaseSecrets`, with the keys `dbuser` and `dbpassword`, respectively. After giving the CodeBuild service role the appropriate IAM permissions to access this secret, you may load them into the environment like this:

```
env:
  secrets-manager:
    DATABASE_USER: MyDatabaseSecrets:dbuser
    DATABASE_PASS: MyDatabaseSecrets:dbpassword
```

Your app may then access these values through the environment. For instance, a Bash script can reference `$DATABASE_USER` or a Python script can call `os.getenv('DATABASE_USER')`. The secrets are maintained securely in AWS Secrets Manager and only accessible to your app at runtime.

phases

The `phases` mapping specifies commands to run at each stage of the build job. Phases are only definable in a `buildspec.yml` file, not when defining CodeBuild jobs through the CLI.

install   Commands to execute during installation of the build environment.

pre_build   Commands to be run before the build begins.

build   Commands to be run during the build.

post_build   Commands to be run after the build completes.

 If a command fails in any stage, subsequent stages will not run.

artifacts

The `artifacts` mapping specifies where CodeBuild will place output artifacts, if any. This is required only if your build job produces actual outputs, such as a JAR file resulting from Java code complication. In contrast, unit tests would not produce output artifacts for later use in a pipeline. The `files` list specifies individual files in the build environment that will act as output artifacts. You can specify individual files, directories, or recursive directories.

cache

If you configure caching for the build project, the `cache` mapping specifies which files to upload to S3 for use in subsequent builds.

Build Project Cache

This example sets the JAVA_HOME and LOGIN_PASSWORD environment variables (the latter is retrieved from the AWS Systems Manager Parameter Store), installs updates in the build environment, runs a Maven installation, and saves the JAR output to S3 as a build artifact. For future builds, the content of the /root/.m2 directory (and any subdirectories) is cached to S3.

```
version: 0.2

env:
  variables:
    JAVA_HOME: "/usr/lib/jvm/java-8-openjdk-amd64"
  parameter-store:
    LOGIN_PASSWORD: "dockerLoginPassword"

phases:
  install:
    commands:
      - echo Entered the install phase...
      - apt-get update -y
      - apt-get install -y maven
  pre_build:
    commands:
      - echo Entered the pre_build phase...
      - docker login -u User -p $LOGIN_PASSWORD
  build:
    commands:
      - echo Entered the build phase...
      - echo Build started on `date`
      - mvn install
  post_build:
    commands:
      - echo Entered the post_build phase...
      - echo Build completed on `date`
```

```
artifacts:
  files:
    - target/messageUtil-1.0.jar
  discard-paths: yes
cache:
  paths:
    - '/root/.m2/**/*'
```

Build Environments

A *build environment* is a Docker image with a preconfigured operating system, programming language runtime, and any other tools that CodeBuild uses to perform build tasks and communicate with the service, along with other metadata for the environment, such as the compute settings. CodeBuild maintains its own repository of preconfigured build environments. If these environments do not meet your requirements, you can use public Docker Hub images. Alternatively, you can use container images in Amazon Elastic Container Registry (Amazon ECR).

AWS CodeBuild Environments

CodeBuild provides build environments for Ubuntu and Amazon Linux operating systems, and it supports the following:

- Android
- Docker
- Golang
- Java
- Node.js
- PHP
- Python
- Ruby
- .NET Core

Not all programming languages support both Ubuntu and Amazon Linux build environments.

Environment Variables

CodeBuild provides several environment variables by default, such as AWS_REGION, CODE BUILD_BUILD_ID, and HOME.

When you create your own environment variables, CodeBuild reserves the CODEBUILD_ prefix.

Builds

When you initiate a build, CodeBuild copies the input artifact(s) into the build environment. CodeBuild uses the build specification to run the build process, which includes any steps to perform and outputs to provide after the build completes. Build logs are made available to CloudWatch Logs for real-time monitoring.

Running Builds

When you run builds manually in the CodeBuild console, AWS CLI, or AWS SDK, you have the option to change several properties before you run a build job:

- Source version (Amazon S3)
- Source branch, version, and Git clone depth (AWS CodeCommit, GitHub, and Bitbucket)
- Output artifact type, name, or location
- Build timeout
- Environment variables

Use AWS CodeBuild with AWS CodePipeline

CodePipeline enables you to build jobs for both build and test actions. Both action types require exactly one input artifact and may return zero or one output artifacts. When you create a build or test actions in your pipeline with your build projects, the only input that you require is the build project name. The CodePipeline console also gives you the option to create new build projects when you create the action, as shown in Figure 7.12.

Use AWS CodeDeploy to Deploy Applications

AWS CodeDeploy is a service that automates software deployments to a variety of compute services, such as Amazon EC2, AWS Lambda, and instances running on-premises. Code-Deploy automates software deployments and eliminates the need for error-prone manual operations. The service scales to match your deployment needs, from a single AWS Lambda function to thousands of EC2 instances.

FIGURE 7.12 Build provider

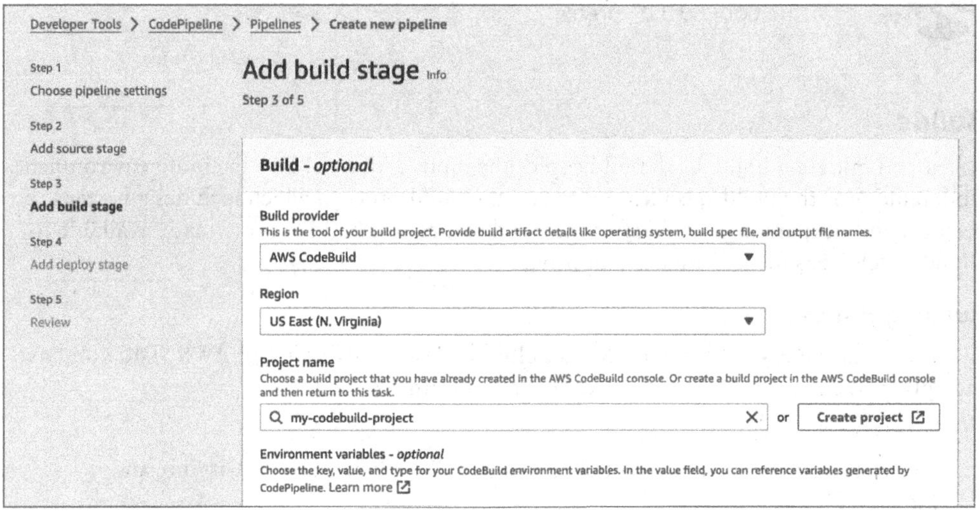

What Is AWS CodeDeploy?

CodeDeploy standardizes and automates deployments of any type of content or configuration to EC2 instances, on-premises servers, or Lambda functions. Because of its flexibility, it is not restricted to deploying only application code, and it can perform various administrative tasks that are part of your deployment process. Additionally, you can create custom deployment configurations tailored to your specific infrastructure needs.

Should deployments fail in your environment, you can configure CodeDeploy with a predetermined failure tolerance. Once this tolerance is breached, deployment will automatically roll back to the last version that works.

You can automate deployment of CodeDeploy with Lambda functions through traffic switching. When updates to functions deploy, CodeDeploy will create new versions of each updated function and gradually route requests from the previous version to the updated function. Lambda functions also support custom deployment configurations, which can specify the rate and percentage of traffic to switch.

AWS CodeDeploy Concepts

Let's explore the key concepts that you need to know to understand how CodeDeploy works.

Revision

A *revision* is an artifact that contains both application files to deploy and an AppSpec configuration file. Application files can include source code, compiled libraries, configuration files, installation packages, static media, and other content. Similar to CodeBuild's BuildSpec file, the AppSpec file specifies what steps CodeDeploy will follow when it performs deployments of an individual revision.

A revision must contain any source files and scripts to execute on the target instance inside a root directory. Within this root directory, the `appspec.yml` file must exist at the topmost level and *not* in any subfolders. For example:

```
/tmp/ or c:\temp (root folder)
  |--content (subfolder)
  |     |--myTextFile.txt
  |     |--mySourceFile.rb
  |     |--myExecutableFile.exe
  |     |--myInstallerFile.msi
  |     |--myPackage.rpm
  |     |--myImageFile.png
  |--scripts (subfolder)
  |     |--myShellScript.sh
  |     |--myBatchScript.bat
  |     |--myPowerShellScript.ps1
  |--appspec.yml
```

When you deploy to Lambda, a revision contains only the AppSpec file. It contains information about the functions to deploy, as well as the steps to validate that the deployment was successful.

CodeDeploy accepts input artifacts from multiple locations, including:

- Amazon S3
- GitHub
- Bitbucket

When you use GitHub or Bitbucket, the source code does not need to be a ZIP archive, as CodeDeploy will package the repository contents on your behalf. S3, however, requires a ZIP archive file.

 Lambda deployments support only S3 buckets as a source repository.

Deployments

A *deployment* is the process of copying content and executing scripts on instances in your deployment group. To accomplish this, CodeDeploy performs the tasks outlined in the AppSpec configuration file. There are two types of deployments supported by AWS CodeDeploy: in-place and blue/green.

In-Place Deployments

In *in-place deployments*, any currently running code is stopped, the new application revision is deployed, and then the application is restarted. While deployment strategies such as phasing out deployments in a load-balanced fleet can minimize downtime, the in-place method does carry the potential for service interruption.

Blue/Green Deployments

Blue/green deployments publish an entirely new instance of a code revision, after which traffic shifting routes requests to the new versions according to the deployment configuration that you define. For example, to achieve blue/green deployments with EC2 as your target, AWS configures a load balancer and two target groups. CodeDeploy publishes code to instances in the inactive target group, confirms its health, and then switches the load balancer to point to the new target group.

> On-premises instances do not support blue/green deployments.

Rollbacks

CodeDeploy achieves automatic rollbacks by redeploying the last working revision to any instances in the deployment group (this will generate a new deployment ID). If you do not configure automatic rollbacks for the application, you can perform a manual rollback by redeploying a previous revision as a new deployment. This will accomplish the same result as an automatic rollback.

During the rollback process, CodeDeploy will attempt to remove any file(s) that were created on the instance during the failed deployment. A record of the created files is kept in the location on your instances.

> By default, CodeDeploy will not overwrite any files that were not created as part of a deployment. You can override this setting for new deployments.

CodeDeploy tracks cleanup files; however, script executions are not tracked. Any configuration or modification to the instance that is done by scripts run on your instance cannot be rolled back automatically by CodeDeploy. As an administrator, you will be responsible for implementing logic in your deployment scripts to ensure that the desired state is reached during deployments and rollbacks.

Test Deployments Locally

If you would like to test whether a revision will successfully deploy to an instance you are able to access, you can use the `codedeploy-local` command in the AWS CodeDeploy agent. This command will search the execution path for an AppSpec file and any content to deploy. If this is found, the agent will attempt a deployment on the instance and provide feedback on the results. This provides a useful alternative to executing the full workflow when you simply want to validate the deployment package.

The following example command attempts to perform a local deployment of an archive file located in S3:

```
codedeploy-local --bundle-location s3://mybucket/bundle.tgz --type tgz
```

 The codedeploy-local command requires the CodeDeploy agent that you install on the instance or on-premises server where you execute the command.

Deployment Group

A *deployment group* is the set of compute targets for a given deployment. With EC2/on-premises deployments, this means a specific instance, group of instances, or Auto Scaling group where your code will run. When you deploy to Lambda functions, this specifies what functions will deploy new versions. For container deployments, a deployment group refers to a specific ECS service. Deployment groups also specify alarms that trigger automatic rollbacks after a specified number or percentage of instances, functions, or tasks fail their deployment.

For Amazon EC2/on-premises deployments, you can add instances to a deployment group based on tag name/value pairs or Auto Scaling group names. An individual application can have one or more deployment groups defined. This allows you to separate groups of instances into environments so that changes can be progressively rolled out and tested before going to production.

When you create deployment groups, you can also configure the following:

Amazon SNS Notifications   Any recipients that subscribe to the topic will receive notifications when deployment events occur. You must create the topic before you configure this notification, and the CodeDeploy service role must have permission to publish messages to the topic.

Amazon CloudWatch Alarms   You can configure alarms to trigger cancellation and rollback of deployments whenever the metric has passed a certain threshold. For example, you could configure an alarm to trigger when CPU utilization exceeds a certain percentage for instances in an Auto Scaling group. If this alarm triggers, the deployment automatically rolls back. For Lambda deployments, you can configure alarms to monitor function invocation errors.

Automatic Rollbacks   You can configure rollbacks to initiate automatically when a deployment fails or based on CloudWatch alarms. To test deployments, you can disable automatic rollbacks when you create a new deployment.

On-Premises Instances

To configure an on-premises instance to work with CodeDeploy, you must complete several tasks. Before you begin, you need to ensure that the instance can communicate with Code-Deploy service endpoints over HTTPS (port 443). You will also need to create an IAM user that has permissions to interact with CodeDeploy.

1. On the host, install and configure the AWS CLI with the IAM user.

2. Register the instance with CodeDeploy via the **aws deploy register** CLI command from the on-premises instance. Provide a unique name with the **--instance-name** property and specify the ARN of the IAM user to associate with the instance:

    ```
    aws deploy register --instance-name AssetTag12010298EX \
    --iam-user-arn arn:aws:iam::8039EXAMPLE:user/CodeDeployUser-OnPrem \
    --region us-west-2
    ```

3. Install the CodeDeploy agent. Run the **aws deploy install** AWS CLI command. By default, this will install a basic configuration file with preconfigured settings.

    After you complete the previous steps, the instance will be available for deployments to the deployment group(s).

Deploy to Auto Scaling Groups

When you deploy to Auto Scaling groups, CodeDeploy will automatically run the latest successful deployment on any new instances created when the group scales out. If the deployment fails on an instance, it updates to maintain the count of healthy instances. For this reason, AWS does not recommend that you associate the same Auto Scaling group with multiple deployment groups (for example, you want to deploy multiple applications to the same Auto Scaling group). If both deployment groups perform a deployment at roughly the same time and the first deployment fails on the new instance, CodeDeploy will terminate. The second deployment, unaware that the instance terminated, will not fail until the deployment times out (the default timeout value is one hour). Instead, consider the use of multiple Auto Scaling groups with smaller instance types.

Deployment Configuration

You use *deployment configurations* to drive how quickly EC2/on-premises instances update by CodeDeploy. You can configure deployments to deploy to all instances in a deployment group at once or subgroups of instances at a time, or you can create an entire new group of instances (*blue/green deployment*). A deployment configuration also specifies the fault tolerance of deployments, so you can roll back changes if a specified number or percentage of instances or functions in your deployment group fail to complete their deployments and signal success back to CodeDeploy.

Amazon EC2/On-Premises Deployment Configurations

When you deploy to EC2/on-premises instances, you can configure either in-place or blue/green deployments.

In-Place Deployments   These deployments deploy revisions on existing instances.

Blue/Green Deployments   These deployments replace currently running instances with sets of newly created instances.

In both scenarios, you can specify wait times between groups of deployed instances (batches). Additionally, if you register the deployment group with a load balancer, newly deployed instances also register with the load balancer and are subject to its health checks.

The deployment configuration specifies success criteria for deployments, such as the minimum number of healthy instances that must pass health checks during the deployment process. CodeDeploy provides three built-in deployment configurations.

CodeDeployDefault.AllAtOnce

For in-place deployments, CodeDeploy will attempt to deploy to all instances in the deployment group at the same time. The success criteria for this deployment configuration requires that at least once instance succeed for the deployment to be successful. If all instances fail the deployment, then the deployment itself fails.

For blue/green deployments, CodeDeploy will attempt to deploy to the entire set of replacement instances at the same time and follow the same success criteria as in-place deployments. Once deployment to the replacement instances succeeds (at least one instance deploys successfully), traffic routes to all replacement instances at the same time. The deployment fails only if all traffic routing to replacement instances fails.

CodeDeployDefault.OneAtATime

For in-place and blue/green deployments, this is the most stringent of the built-in deployment configurations, as it requires all instances to deploy the new application revision successfully, except for the final instance in the deployment. For deployment groups with only one instance, the instance must complete successfully for the deployment to complete.

For blue/green deployments, the same rule applies for traffic routing. If all but the last instance registers successfully, the deployment is successful (with the exception of single-instance environments, where it must register without error).

CodeDeployDefault.HalfAtATime

For in-place deployments, up to half of the instances in the deployment group deploy at the same time (rounded down). Success criteria for this deployment configuration requires that at least half of the instances (rounded up) deploy successfully.

Blue/green deployments use the same rules for the replacement environment, with the exception that the deployment will fail if less than half of the instances in the replacement environment successfully handle rerouted traffic.

AWS Lambda Deployment Configurations

CodeDeploy handles updates to Lambda functions differently than to EC2 or on-premises instances in that only blue/green-style deployments are supported. Lambda deployment configurations specify the traffic switching policy to follow, which stipulates how quickly to route requests from the original function versions to the new versions.

CodeDeploy supports three methods for handling traffic switching in a Lambda environment.

Canary

Canary deployments route a slice of traffic to a new function deployment, only cutting over all traffic when the new version is deemed healthy. CodeDeploy provides a number of built-in canary-based deployment configurations, such as `CodeDeployDefault.Lambda Canary10Percent15Minutes`. If you use this deployment configuration, 10 percent of traffic shifts in the first increment and is monitored for 15 minutes. After this time period, the 90 percent of traffic that remains shifts to the new function version. You can create additional configurations as needed.

Linear

Linear deployments shift traffic in percentage-based increments, with a set number of minutes between each increment. At each step, the requests routed to the new function version must complete successfully for the deployment to continue.

CodeDeploy provides several built-in linear deployment configurations, such as `CodeDeployDefault.LambdaLinear10PercentEvery1Minute`. With this configuration, 10 percent of traffic is routed to the new function version every minute, until all traffic is routed after 10 minutes.

All-at-Once

All traffic is shifted at once to the new function versions.

Application

An *application* is a logical grouping of a deployment group, revision, and deployment configuration.

AppSpec File

The AppSpec configuration file is a JSON or YAML file that manages deployments on instances or functions in your environment. The actual format and purpose of an AppSpec file differs between EC2/on-premises and Lambda deployments.

Amazon EC2/On-Premises AppSpec

For EC2/on-premises deployments, the AppSpec file must be a YAML formatted file named `appspec.yml` and placed in the root of the revision's source code directory.

When you deploy to EC2/on-premises instances, the AppSpec file defines the following:

- A mapping of files from the revision and location on the instance
- The permissions of files to deploy
- Scripts to execute throughout the life cycle of the deployment

The AppSpec file specifies scripts to execute at each stage of the deployment life cycle. These scripts must exist in the revision for CodeDeploy to call them successfully; however, they can call any other scripts, commands, or tools present on the instance. The CodeDeploy agent uses the hooks section of the AppSpec file to reference which scripts must execute at specific times in the deployment life cycle. When the deployment is at the specified stage (such as ApplicationStop), the CodeDeploy agent will execute any scripts in that stage in the hooks section of the AppSpec file. *All scripts must return an exit code of 0 to be successful.*

For any files to place on the instance, the CodeDeploy agent refers to the files section of the AppSpec file, where a mapping of files and directories in the revision dictates where on the instance these files should reside and with what permissions. Here's what an example appspec.yml file looks like:

```
version: 0.0
os: linux
files:
  - source: /
    destination: /var/www/html/WordPress
hooks:
  BeforeInstall:
    - location: scripts/install_dependencies.sh
      timeout: 300
      runas: root
  AfterInstall:
    - location: scripts/change_permissions.sh
      timeout: 300
      runas: root
  ApplicationStart:
    - location: scripts/start_server.sh
    - location: scripts/create_test_db.sh
      timeout: 300
      runas: root
  ApplicationStop:
    - location: scripts/stop_server.sh
      timeout: 300
      runas: root
```

In the previous example, the following events occur during deployment:

- During the install phase of the deployment, all files from the revision (source: /) are placed on the instance in the /var/www/html/WordPress directory.
- The install_dependencies.sh script (located in the scripts directory of the revision) executes during the BeforeInstall phase.
- The change_permissions.sh script executes in the AfterInstall phase.

- The `start_server.sh` and `create_test_db.sh` scripts execute in the `ApplicationStart` phase.
- The `stop_server.sh` script executes in the `ApplicationStop` phase.

The high-level structure of an EC2/on-premises AppSpec file is as follows:

```
version: 0.0
os:
files:
permissions:
hooks:
```

version   Currently the only supported version number is 0.0.

os   The os section defines the target operating system of the deployment group. Either `windows` or `linux` is supported. Note that, unlike with CodeBuild, this directive does not determine your app's runtime environment; the value given here must match the OS of your deployment group instances, where the AppSpec commands will actually run.

files   The `files` section defines the mapping of revision files and their location to deploy on-instance during the install life cycle event. This section is not required if no files are being copied from the revision to your instance. The `files` section supports a list of source/destination pairs:

```
files:
  - source: source-file-location
    destination: destination-file-location
```

The `source` key refers to a file or a directory's local path within the revision (use / for all files in the revision). If `source` refers to a file, the file copies to `destination`, specified as the fully qualified path on the instance. If `source` refers to a directory, the directory contents copy to the instance.

permissions   For any deployed files or directories, the `permissions` section specifies the permissions to apply to files and directories on the target instance. You can also apply permissions to files on the instance by CodeDeploy using the `files` directive of the AppSpec configuration.

```
permissions:
  - object: object-specification
    pattern: pattern-specification
    except: exception-specification
    owner: owner-account-name
    group: group-name
    mode: mode-specification
```

```
acls:
  - acls-specification
context:
  user: user-specification
  type: type-specification
  range: range-specification
type:
  - object-type
```

 Windows instances do not support permissions.

hooks The hooks section specifies the scripts to run at each life cycle event and under what user context to execute them.

One or more scripts can execute for each *life cycle hook*.

ApplicationStop Before the application revision downloads to the instance, this life cycle event can stop any running services on the instance that would be affected by the update. It is important to note that, since the revision has not yet been downloaded, the scripts execute from the previous revision. Because of this, the ApplicationStop hook does not run on the first deployment to an instance.

DownloadBundle The CodeDeploy agent uses this life cycle event to copy application revision files to a temporary location on the instance.

Linux /opt/codedeploy-agent/deployment-root/[deployment-group-id]/
[deployment-id]/deployment-archive

Windows C:\ProgramData\Amazon\CodeDeploy\[deployment-group-id]\
[deployment-id]\deployment-archive

Because your scripts may need to reference these paths, CodeDeploy makes the following special environment variables available during all phases of the deployment life cycle:

- LIFECYCLE_EVENT
- DEPLOYMENT_ID
- APPLICATION_NAME
- DEPLOYMENT_GROUP_NAME
- DEPLOYMENT_GROUP_ID

The DownloadBundle event cannot run custom scripts, as it is reserved for the CodeDeploy agent.

BeforeInstall   Use this event for any preinstallation tasks, such as to clear log files or to create backups.

Install   This event is reserved for the CodeDeploy agent.

AfterInstall   Use this event for any post-installation tasks, such as to modify the application configuration.

ApplicationStart   Use this event to start any services that were stopped during the ApplicationStop event.

ValidateService   Use this event to verify deployment completed successfully.

If your deployment group is registered with a load balancer, additional life cycle events become available. These can be used to control certain behaviors as the instance is registered or deregistered from the load balancer.

BeforeBlockTraffic   Use this event to run tasks before the instance is deregistered from the load balancer.

BlockTraffic   This event is reserved for the CodeDeploy agent.

AfterBlockTraffic   Use this event to run tasks after the instance is deregistered from the load balancer.

BeforeAllowTraffic   Similar in concept to BeforeBlockTraffic, this event occurs before instances register with the load balancer.

AllowTraffic   This event is reserved for the CodeDeploy agent.

AfterAllowTraffic   Similar in concept to AfterBlockTraffic, this event occurs after instances register with the load balancer.

```
hooks:
    deployment-lifecycle-event-name:
      - location: script-location
        timeout: timeout-in-seconds
        runas: user-name
```

In the hooks section, the life cycle name must match one of the non-reserved event names just described. The location property is the relative path in the revision archive where a script is located. You can configure an optional timeout to limit how long a script can run before it is considered failed. (Note that this does not stop the script's execution.) The maximum script duration is 1 hour (3,600 seconds) for each life cycle event. Lastly, the runas property can specify the user to execute the script. This user must exist on the instance and cannot require a password.

Figure 7.13 displays life cycle hooks and their availability for in-place deployments with and without a load balancer.

FIGURE 7.13 Life cycle hook availability with load balancer

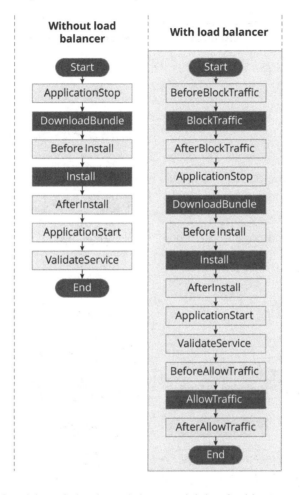

Figure 7.14 displays life cycle hooks and their availability for blue/green deployments.

AWS Lambda AppSpec

When you deploy to Lambda functions, the AppSpec file can be in JSON or YAML format, and it specifies the function versions to deploy as well as other functions to execute for validation testing.

Lambda deployments do not use the CodeDeploy agent.

FIGURE 7.14   Life cycle hook availability with blue/green deployments

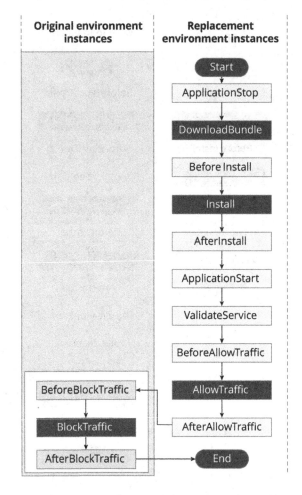

The high-level structure of a Lambda deployment AppSpec file is as follows:

```
version: 0.0
resources:
  lambda-function-specifications
hooks:
  deployment-lifecycle-event-mappings
```

version   Currently the only supported version number is 0.0.

resources   The resources section defines the Lambda functions to deploy.

```
resources:
  - name-of-function-to-deploy:
      type: "AWS::Lambda::Function"
      properties:
        name: name-of-lambda-function-to-deploy
        alias: alias-of-lambda-function-to-deploy
        currentversion: lambda-function-version-traffic-currently-points-to
        targetversion: lambda-function-version-to-shift-traffic-to
```

Name each function in the resources list both as the list item name and in the name property. The alias property specifies the function alias, which maps from the version specified in currentversion to the version specified in targetversion after the update deploys.

hooks   The hooks section specifies the additional Lambda functions to run at specific stages of the deployment life cycle to validate success. The following life cycle events support hooks in AWS Lambda deployments:

> **BeforeAllowTraffic**   For running any tasks prior to traffic shifting taking place
>
> **AfterAllowTraffic**   For any tasks after all traffic shifting has completed

```
hooks:
  - BeforeAllowTraffic: BeforeAllowTrafficHookFunctionName
  - AfterAllowTraffic: AfterAllowTrafficHookFunctionName
```

Figure 7.15 displays the life cycle hook availability for Lambda deployments.

FIGURE 7.15   Life cycle hook availability for Lambda deployments

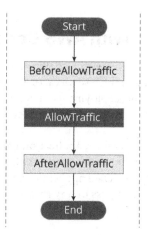

CodeDeploy reserves the Start, AllowTraffic, and End life
cycle events.

For any functions in the hooks section, the function is responsible for notifying Code-
Deploy of success or failure with the PutLifecycleEventHookExecutionStatus
call API from within your validation function. Here's an example for Node.js:

```
CodeDeploy the prepared validation test results.
codedeploy.putLifecycleEventHookExecutionStatus(params, function(err, data) {
    if (err) {
        // Validation failed.
        callback('Validation test failed');
    } else {
        // Validation succeeded.
        callback(null, 'Validation test succeeded');
    }
});
```

AWS CodeDeploy Agent

The *AWS CodeDeploy agent* is responsible for driving and validating deployments on EC2/
on-premises instances, and must be installed and running for any CodeDeploy activity to
succeed on an instance. The agent currently supports Amazon Linux (Amazon EC2 only),
Ubuntu Server, Microsoft Windows Server, and Red Hat Enterprise Linux, and it is available
as an open source repository on GitHub (https://github.com/aws/aws-codedeploy-
agent). It is preinstalled on Amazon Linux instances, and can be installed via the aws
deploy install CLI command, or pushed to instances via the Distributor function of
AWS Systems Manager.

Use AWS CodeDeploy with AWS CodePipeline

CodeDeploy can integrate automatically with CodePipeline as a deployment action to deploy
changes to EC2/on-premises instances, ECS services, or Lambda functions. You can configure
applications, deployment groups, and deployments directly in the CodePipeline console
when you create or edit a pipeline, or you can do this ahead of time with the CodeDeploy
console or the CLI/SDK.

After you define the deployment provider, application name, and deployment group in the
CodePipeline console, the pipeline will automatically configure to pass a pipeline artifact to
CodeDeploy for deployment to the specified application/group, as shown in Figure 7.16.

AWS CodeDeploy monitors the progress of any revisions to deploy and reports success or
failure to CodePipeline.

FIGURE 7.16   Deployment provider

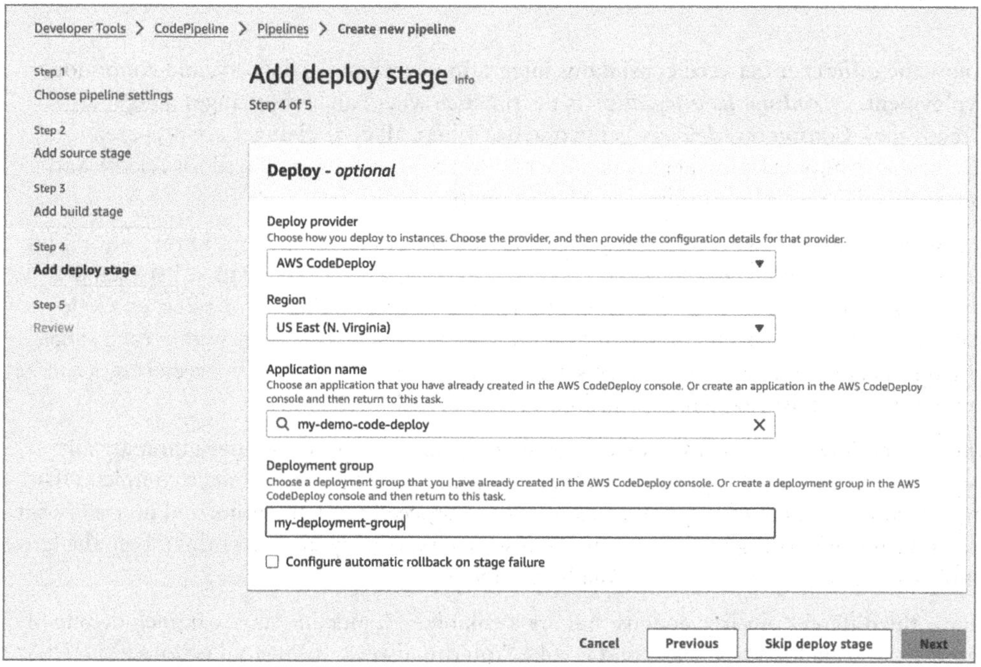

Summary

In this chapter, you learned about these deployment services:

- AWS CodePipeline
- AWS CodeCommit
- AWS CodeBuild
- AWS CodeDeploy

CodePipeline drives application deployments starting with a source repository (Code-Commit), performing builds with CodeBuild, and finally deploying to EC2, an on-premises instance, ECS, or Lambda functions using CodeDeploy. You can use CloudFormation to provision and manage infrastructure in your environment. By integrating this with CodePipeline, you can automate the entire process of creating development, testing, and production environments into a fully hands-off process. In a fully realized enterprise as code, a single commit to a source repository can kick off processes such as those shown in Figure 7.1.

Exam Essentials

Know the difference between continuous integration, continuous delivery, and continuous deployment. *Continuous integration* is the practice where all code changes merge into a repository. *Continuous delivery* is the practice where all code changes are prepared for release. Continuous deployment is the practice where all code is prepared for release and automatically released to production environments.

Know the basics of AWS CodePipeline. CodePipeline contains the steps in the *continuous integration and deployment pipeline* (CI/CD) workflow, driving automation between different tasks after assets have been committed to a repository or saved in a bucket. CodePipeline uses stages, which correspond to different steps in a workflow. Within each stage, different actions can perform tasks in series or in parallel. Transitions between stages can be automatic or require manual approval by an authorized user.

Understand how revisions can move through a pipeline. Revisions move automatically between stages in a pipeline, provided that all actions in the preceding stage complete. If a manual approval is required, the revision will not proceed until an authorized user allows it to do so. When two changes are pushed to a source repository in a short time span, the latest of the two changes will proceed through the pipeline.

Know the different pipeline actions that are available. A pipeline stage can include one or more actions: build, test, deploy, and invoke. You can also create custom actions.

Know the basic concepts of AWS CodeCommit. CodeCommit is a Git-based repository service. It is fully compatible with existing Git tooling. CodeCommit provides various benefits such as encryption in transit and at rest; automatic scaling to handle increases in activity; access control using IAM users, roles, and policies; and HTTPS/SSH connectivity. CodeCommit supports normal Git workflows, such as pull requests.

Know how to use the credential helper to connect to repositories. It is possible to connect to AWS CodeCommit repositories using IAM credentials. The AWS CodeCommit credential helper translates an IAM access key and secret access key into valid Git credentials. This requires the AWS CLI and a Git configuration file that specifies the credential helper.

Understand the different strategies for migrating to AWS CodeCommit. You can migrate an existing Git repository by cloning to your local workstation and adding a new remote URL, pointing to the CodeCommit repository you create. You can push the repository contents to the new remote repo. You can migrate unversioned content in a similar manner; however, you must create a new local Git repository (instead of cloning an existing one). Large repositories can be migrated incrementally because large pushes may fail because of network issues.

Know the basics of AWS CodeBuild. CodeBuild allows you to perform long-running build tasks repeatedly and reliably without having to manage the underlying infrastructure. You are responsible only for specifying the build environment settings and the actual tasks to perform.

Know the basics of AWS CodeDeploy. AWS CodeDeploy standardizes and automates deployments to EC2 instances, on-premises servers, ECS, and Lambda functions. Deployments can include application/static files, configuration tasks, or arbitrary scripts to execute. For EC2/on-premises deployments, a lightweight agent is required.

Understand how AWS CodeDeploy works with Auto Scaling groups. When you deploy to Auto Scaling groups, CodeDeploy will automatically run the last successful deployment on any new instances that you add to the group. If the deployment fails on the instance, it will be terminated and replaced (to maintain the desired count of healthy instances). If two deployment groups for separate CodeDeploy applications specify the same Auto Scaling group, issues can occur. If both applications deploy at roughly the same time and one fails, the instance will be terminated before success/failure can be reported for the second application deployment. This will result in CodeDeploy waiting until the timeout period expires before taking any further action.

Exercises

EXERCISE 7.1

Creating an AWS CodeCommit Repository and Submitting a Pull Request

This exercise demonstrates how to use CodeCommit to submit and merge pull requests to a repository.

1. Create a CodeCommit repository with a name and description. You do not need to configure email notifications for repository events.

2. In the CodeCommit console, choose Add File ➤ Create File to add a simple markdown file to test the repository.

3. Clone the repository to your local machine with HTTPS or SSH authentication using the steps described in this chapter.

4. Create a file locally, commit it to the repository, and push it to test the CodeCommit.

5. Create a feature branch from the main branch in the repository.

6. Edit the file and commit the changes to the feature branch.

7. Use the CodeCommit console to create a pull request. Use the main branch of the repository as the destination and the feature branch as the source.

8. After the pull request successfully creates, merge the changes from the feature branch with the main branch.

The pull request has been merged with the main branch, which can be confirmed by viewing the source code of the markdown file in the main branch.

Creating an Application in AWS CodeDeploy

This exercise demonstrates how to use CodeDeploy to perform an in-place deployment to EC2 instances in your account.

1. Use the sample deployment wizard to create an in-place deployment.

2. Launch a new EC2 instance as part of the application creation process.

3. Download the sample application bundle to your local machine for future updates.

4. Create a deployment group, and verify that the sample application deploys.

5. Update the application code, and submit a new deployment to the deployment group.

6. Verify your changes after the deployment completes.

Creating an AWS CodeBuild Project

This exercise demonstrates how to use CodeBuild to perform builds and the compilation of artifacts prior to deployment to EC2 instances.

1. Create an S3 bucket to hold artifacts.

2. Upload two or more arbitrary files to the bucket.

3. Use the CodeBuild console to create a build project with the following settings:

    Project Name Provide a name of your choice.

    Source Use Amazon S3.

    Bucket Provide the name of the bucket you created.

    S3 Object Key Provide the name of one of the objects you uploaded.

    Environment Image Select the Managed Image type.

    Operating System Use Ubuntu.

    Runtime Use Python.

    Runtime Version Select a version of your choice.

    Service Role Click New Service Role.

    Role Name Provide a name for your service role.

Build Specifications   Click Insert Build Commands.

Build Commands   Select Switch To Editor and enter the following. Replace the S3 object paths with paths to the objects you uploaded to your bucket.

```
version: 0.2

phases:
  build:
    commands:
      - aws s3 cp s3://yourbucket/file1 /tmp/file1
      - aws s3 cp s3://yourbucket/file2 /tmp/file2
artifacts:
  files:
    - /tmp/file1
    - /tmp/file2
```

Artifact Type   Use Amazon S3.

Bucket Name   Select your Amazon S3 bucket.

Artifacts Packaging   Select Zip.

4. Save your build project.

5. Run your build project, and observe the output archive file created in your S3 bucket.

Review Questions

1. You have two AWS CodeDeploy applications that deploy to the same EC2 Auto Scaling group. The first deploys an e-commerce app, while the second deploys custom administration software. You are attempting to deploy an update to one application but cannot do so because another deployment is already in progress. You do not see any instances undergoing deployment at this time. What could be the cause of this?

   A. If both deployment groups reference the same Auto Scaling group, a failure of the first group's deployment can block the second until the deployment times out. Since the instance that failed deployment has been terminated from the Auto Scaling group, the CodeDeploy agent is unable to provide results to the service.

   B. The CodeDeploy agent is not installed on the instances as part of the launch configuration user data script.

   C. If both deployment groups reference the same Auto Scaling group, a failure of the first group's deployment can block the second until the deployment times out. Since the instance that failed deployment has been terminated from the Auto Scaling group, the CodeDeploy service is unable to request status updates from the EC2 API.

   D. The CodeDeploy agent is not installed in the Amazon Machine Image (AMI) being used.

2. If you specify a hook script in the `ApplicationStop` life cycle event of a CodeDeploy `appspec.yml`, will it run on the first deployment to your instance(s)?

   A. Yes.

   B. No.

   C. The `ApplicationStop` life cycle event does not exist.

   D. It will run only if your application is running.

3. If a single pipeline contains multiple sources, such as a CodeCommit repository and an S3 archive, under what circumstances will the pipeline be triggered?

   A. When either a commit is pushed to the repository or the archive is updated, regardless of timing.

   B. When a commit is pushed to the repository and the archive is updated at the same time.

   C. When either a commit is pushed to the repository or the archive is updated, but not when both are updated at the same time.

   D. CodePipeline does not support multiple sources in the same pipeline.

4. If you want to implement a deployment pipeline that deploys both source files and large binary objects to instance(s), how would you best achieve this while taking cost into consideration?

   A. Store both the source files and binary objects in CodeCommit.

   B. Build the binary objects into the AMI of the instance(s) being deployed. Store the source files in CodeCommit.

C. Store the source files in CodeCommit. Store the binary objects in an S3 archive.

D. Store the source files in CodeCommit. Store the binary objects on an Elastic Block Store (Amazon EBS) volume, taking snapshots of the volume whenever a new one needs to be created.

E. Store the source files in CodeCommit. Store the binary objects in S3 and access them from a CloudFront distribution.

5. Your team is building a deployment pipeline to a sensitive application in your environment using CodeDeploy. The application consists of an EC2 Auto Scaling group (ASG) of instances behind an application load balancer. The nature of the application requires as close to 100 percent uptime as possible. The development team wants to deploy changes multiple times per day.

How would this be achieved at the lowest cost and with the fastest deployments?

A. Pre-scale the Auto Scaling group to double capacity, then use rolling deployments with `CodeDeployDefault.HalfAtOnce`.

B. Use rolling deployments on the ASG with the `CodeDeployDefault.AllAtOnce` strategy.

C. Use blue/green deployments.

D. Use parallel branches in CodePipeline to deploy to two Auto Scaling groups at once.

6. What would cause an access denied error when attempting to download an archive file from S3 during a pipeline execution?

A. Insufficient user permissions for the user initiating the pipeline

B. Insufficient role permissions for the CodePipeline service role

C. Insufficient role permissions for the S3 service role

D. Insufficient role permissions for the IAM role of the targeted EC2 instance

7. How do you output build artifacts from CodeBuild to CodePipeline?

A. Write the outputs to `STDOUT` from the build container.

B. Specify artifact files in the `buildspec.yml` configuration file.

C. Upload the files to S3 from the build environment.

D. Output artifacts are not supported with CodeBuild.

8. What would be the most secure means of providing secrets to a CodeBuild environment?

A. Create a custom build environment with the secrets included in configuration files.

B. Upload the secrets to S3 and download the object when the build job runs. Protect the bucket and object with an appropriate bucket policy.

C. Save the secrets in Secrets Manager and load them into the environment using the `env` section of `buildspec.yml`.

D. Include the secrets in the source repository or archive.

9. In which of the pipeline actions can you execute Lambda functions?

    A. Invoke

    B. Deploy

    C. Build

    D. Approval

    E. Test

10. In what ways can pipeline actions be ordered in a stage? (Choose two.)

    A. Series

    B. Parallel

    C. Stages support only one action each

    D. First-in, first-out (FIFO)

    E. Last-in, first-out (LIFO)

11. What can you *not* do with a CodeDeploy AppSpec configuration file?

    A. Scale the number of servers based on load.

    B. Download OS packages needed by your application.

    C. Set permissions for files on Linux hosts.

    D. Execute a script to run at predefined life cycle hooks.

12. How can you connect to a CodeCommit repository without Git credentials?

    A. It is not possible

    B. HTTPS

    C. SSH

    D. AWS CodeCommit credential helper

13. Of the following, which event cannot be used to generate notifications to an SNS topic from CodeCommit without using a trigger?

    A. Pull Request Creation

    B. Commit Comments

    C. Commit Creation

    D. Pull Request Comments

14. Which pipeline action types support AWS CodeBuild projects? (Choose two.)

    A. Invoke

    B. Deploy

    C. Build

    D. Approval

    E. Test

15. You are working on a Java application in GitHub. To release changes, you must compile your code into a JAR file before deploying it to an Auto Scaling group running Tomcat. You wish to automate the entire process. What is the best way to handle the build phase of this deployment?

   A. Create a CodeDeploy job and use the `BeforeInstall` hook of the `appspec.yml` to build the JAR file.

   B. Create a CodeBuild project and configure a webhook to trigger builds on when Git pushes occur. Save the JAR in S3.

   C. Create a CodeBuild project that compiles the JAR, then outputs it as an artifact. Add the CodeBuild project as the Build phase of a CodePipeline, followed by CodeDeploy.

   D. Write a script to compile the JAR locally and push to S3 before invoking CodeDeploy.

16. What is the only deployment type supported by on-premises instances?

   A. In-place

   B. Blue/green

   C. Immutable

   D. Progressive

17. If your CodeDeploy configuration includes creation of a file, `nginx.conf`, but the file already exists on the server (prior to the use of CodeDeploy), what is the default behavior that will occur during deployment?

   A. The file will be replaced.

   B. The file will be renamed `nginx.conf.bak`, and the new file will be created.

   C. The deployment will fail.

   D. The deployment will continue, but the file will not be modified.

18. How does Lambda support in-place deployments?

   A. Function versions are overwritten during the deployment.

   B. New function versions are created, and then version numbers are switched.

   C. Lambda does not support in-place deployments.

   D. Function aliases are overwritten during the deployment.

19. What is the minimum number of stages required by a pipeline in CodePipeline?

   A. 0

   B. 1

   C. 2

   D. 3

20. You are working with a CodePipeline deployment based on CodeCommit. You initiate a deployment by pushing to the branch monitored by the Source stage, but the Deploy stage, using CodeDeploy, fails with an access denied error related to S3. What is the most likely explanation?

   A. Your CodePipeline service role needs access to S3 to push the bundled application revision.

   B. You need to clear your browser's cache.

   C. The instances in your deployment group need an IAM role with S3 access.

   D. The CodeDeploy agent is not running on your deployment group instances.

Chapter 8

Infrastructure as Code

**THE AWS CERTIFIED DEVELOPER –
ASSOCIATE EXAM TOPICS COVERED IN
THIS CHAPTER MAY INCLUDE, BUT ARE
NOT LIMITED TO, THE FOLLOWING:**

✓ **Domain 1: Development with AWS Services**

- Task Statement 1: Develop code for applications hosted on AWS

- Task Statement 3: Use data stores in application development

✓ **Domain 3: Deployment**

- Task Statement 1: Prepare application artifacts to be deployed to AWS

✓ **Domain 4: Troubleshooting and Optimization**

- Task Statement 1: Assist in a root cause analysis

- Task Statement 3: Optimize applications by using AWS services and features

One of the most powerful advantages of cloud computing is the ability to express infrastructure as code. While the AWS Management Console provides users with a helpful user interface, wizards, and guides, it is also the most labor-intensive and error-prone way of building resources in AWS. By using AWS CloudFormation, cloud practitioners can capture all the resource configuration choices they would make in the console and codify them in a reusable template.

CloudFormation templates are an excellent way to manage infrastructure in AWS. Not only do they help avoid errors, but they also act as declarative documents of user intent, clearly depicting in either JSON or YAML a collection of resources, such as EC2 instances, load balancers, security groups, or IAM policies. These templates can be stored in version control systems, giving you all the capabilities associated with keeping code in systems like GitHub: a record of changes with clear attribution, the ability to work collaboratively using pull requests, the ability to jump back to past versions, and more.

Another great aspect of CloudFormation is that the resources created by a single template are managed as a unit (called a *stack*) within AWS. With a single click or SDK command, a stack can be created or torn down all at once. CloudFormation can therefore help group resources that are created for a single purpose, such as all the infrastructure associated with a single web application. At the same time, CloudFormation templates can be parameterized, letting you use the same template to stand up variations on the same stack.

Whether you are managing a small project or an entire fleet of AWS resources, CloudFormation is a fantastic tool to level up your cloud game. Let's dive in.

Use AWS CloudFormation to Deploy Infrastructure

AWS CloudFormation is an essential tool for managing cloud infrastructure, whether for a small project or a large-scale enterprise deployment. Before you deploy your first template, there are a few concepts you need to know.

AWS CloudFormation Concepts

This section details AWS CloudFormation concepts, such as stacks, change sets, permissions, templates, and intrinsic functions.

Stacks

A *stack* is a collection of resources deployed and managed by CloudFormation. When you submit a template, the resources described in the template are provisioned and tagged as being part of that stack. Any modifications to the stack affect the stack's resources. For example, if you remove an `AWS::EC2::Instance` resource from the template and update the stack, CloudFormation causes the referred instance to terminate.

Avoid Stack Drift

Note that nothing in AWS prevents you from modifying resources manually after the stack is provisioned; such changes are known as *drift* because the actual configuration has then "drifted" from its initial state—the state still shown in the CloudFormation template. CloudFormation has a tool to help detect stack drift, but it cannot detect every kind of change you might make. Drift eliminates some of the key advantages of using CloudFormation—namely, the ability to treat the template as the "source of truth" that reflects your actual infrastructure—and it can prevent you from making future changes to your stacks. As a result, best practice is to only make changes to stack resources via Cloud-Formation itself.

Change Sets

There may be times where you would like to see what changes will occur to resources before you update a stack. Instead of submitting an update directly, you can generate a change set. A *change set* describes the changes that will occur to a stack before they are actually executed. You can then review the proposed changes before executing the change set; you can even generate multiple change sets and choose which one to adopt. This feature is especially important in situations where there is a potential for data loss.

Amazon Relational Database Service Instances

There are properties of RDS instances that CloudFormation can modify only by replacing the database instance entirely. If backups are not being taken, data loss will occur. You use a change set to preview the replacement event and take the required precautions before you update the resources.

Permissions

By default, any action that CloudFormation performs is done using the IAM permissions of the executing user. If there is a need to restrict what actions CloudFormation may take, you can provide a service role the stack uses for the create, update, or delete actions. To create a Cloud-Formation service role, make sure that the role as a trust policy allows `cloudformation.amazonaws.com` to assume the role.

As a user, your AWS IAM credentials will need to include the ability to pass the role to CloudFormation, using the `iam:PassRole` permission.

When you create a stack, you can submit a template from a local file or via a URL that points to an object in S3. If you submit the template as a local file, it uploads to S3 on your behalf. Because of this, you must have the appropriate S3 permissions to create a stack.

Template Structure

CloudFormation templates may be written in JSON or YAML. Due to its simpler syntax and support for comments using the # symbol, this chapter will present examples in YAML. The high-level structure of a template is as follows:

```
---
AWSTemplateFormatVersion: '2010-09-09'
Description:
Metadata:
Parameters:
Mappings:
Conditions:
Transform:
Resources:
Outputs:
```

Only the `Resources` section is required. Each property can be in any order, with the exception that `Description` must follow `AWSTemplateFormatVersion`.

AWSTemplateFormatVersion

AWSTemplateFormatVersion is always the literal string "2010-09-09". AWS has never issued a new format version that would demand this line change, so keep it as-is for all your templates!

Resources

Given that the *Resources* section of a CloudFormation template declares the actual AWS resources to be provisioned and their properties, and is the only required section aside from the version line, we'll explore it up front. The `Resources` section follows a standard syntax, where a logical ID acts as the resource key and type/properties subkeys define the actual type of resource to deploy and what properties it should have.

The *logical ID* of the resource allows it to be referenced in other parts of a template. You can refer to `Resources` in other sections of a template, build relationships between interdependent resources, output property values of the resources, and other useful functionality. The `Resource Type` defines the actual type of resource being managed. For example, an S3 bucket type is `AWS::S3::Bucket`. There are too many resource types available to list in this book, and they are updated regularly. Check the CloudFormation documentation for available resource types.

The resource properties section defines what configuration a resource should have. In the same example, the AWS::S3::Bucket resource has an optional property called Bucket Name, which defines the name of the bucket to create.

```
Resources:
  MyBucket:
    Type: AWS::S3::Bucket
    Properties:
      BucketName: MyBucketName1234
```

Resource properties are either optional or required and may be any of the following types:

- String
- List of strings
- Boolean
- References to parameters or pseudoparameters
- Intrinsic functions

It's a good idea to start any new CloudFormation venture by referencing the documentation for the resources you want to build, taking note of required and optional parameters. There are also excellent extensions for Visual Studio Code and other editors that can help in constructing your templates.

Description

The *Description* section allows you to provide a text explanation of the template's purpose or other arbitrary information. The maximum length of the Description field is 1,024 bytes, so be concise.

Metadata

The *Metadata* section of a template allows you to provide structured details about the template. For example, you can provide Metadata about the overall infrastructure to deploy and which sections correspond to certain environments, functional groups, and so on. The Metadata you provide is made available to CloudFormation for reference in other sections of a template or on EC2 instances being provisioned by CloudFormation.

You cannot update template metadata by itself; you must perform an update to one or more resources when you update the Metadata section of a template.

In the Metadata section of the template, you have the ability to specify properties that affect the behavior of different components of the CloudFormation service, such as how template parameters display in the CloudFormation console.

Parameters

You can use *Parameters* to provide inputs into your template, which allows for more flexibility in how the template behaves when you deploy it, as well as the ability to deploy multiple, similar stacks using varied parameter inputs. Parameter values can be set either when you create the stack or when you perform updates.

The `Parameters` section must include a unique logical ID (in the next example, `InstanceTypeParameter`). A parameter must include a value, either a default or one that you provide. Lastly, you cannot reference parameters outside a single template.

AllowedValues

This example defines a String parameter named `InstanceTypeParameter` with a default value of `t2.micro`. The parameter allows `t2.micro`, `m1.small`, or `m1.large`. The `AllowedValues` section specifies what options you can select for this parameter in the CloudFormation console. In the web console, these choices appear in a drop-down menu. If you are calling from the CLI, CloudFormation will throw an error if you add a value not in `AllowedValues`.

```
Parameters:
  InstanceTypeParam:
    Type: String
    Default: t2.micro
    AllowedValues:
    - t2.micro
    - m1.small
    - m1.large
    Description: Enter t2.micro, m1.small, or m1.large. Default is t2.micro.
```

Once you specify a parameter, you can use it within the template using the `Ref` intrinsic function. When CloudFormation evaluates it, the `Ref` statement converts it to the value of the parameter.

```
EC2Instance:
  Type: AWS::EC2::Instance
  Properties:
    InstanceType:
      Ref: InstanceTypeParam
    ImageId: ami-12345678
```

CloudFormation supports the following parameter types:

- String
- Number

- List of numbers
- Comma-delimited list
- AWS-specific parameter types
- AWS Systems Manager Parameter Store (SSM) parameter types

If a parameter value is sensitive, you can add the `NoEcho` property. When this is set, the parameter value displays as asterisks (`***`) for any `cloudformation:Describe*` calls. Within the template itself, the value will resolve to the actual input when making `Ref` calls.

AWS-Specific Parameter Types   When you use *AWS-specific parameter types*, CloudFormation provides Allowed Values lists referencing specific resources within your AWS account. For instance, you might reference EC2 key pair names, IDs of resources, AWS regions/availability zones, or other properties of your account. This can help reduce the risk of an incorrect parameter entry.

AWS SSM Parameter Types   *AWS SSM parameter types* can reference parameters that exist in the AWS Systems Manager Parameter Store. This value is re-queried on each stack update.

Mappings

You can use the `Mappings` section of a template to create rudimentary lookup tables that you can reference in other sections of your template when you create the stack.

A common example of mappings usage is to look up EC2 instance AMI IDs based on the region and architecture type, something not provided by AWS as a built-in parameter. Note that mappings must be nested two layers deep, as in this example with both region and 32- or 64-bit architecture:

```
Mappings:
  RegionMap:
    us-east-1:
      '32': ami-6411e20d
      '64': ami-7a11e213
    us-west-1:
      '32': ami-c9c7978c
      '64': ami-cfc7978a
```

After you declare the `Mappings` section, you can query the values within the mapping with the `Fn::FindInMap` intrinsic function. The example shows an `Fn::FindInMap` call that queries the AMI ID based on region and architecture type (32- or 64-bit). If the region was `us-east-1`, for example, the previous template snippet would resolve to `ami-6411e20d`.

The `AWS::Region` reference is a pseudoparameter; that is, it's a parameter that AWS defines automatically on your behalf. The `AWS::Region` parameter, for example, resolves to the region code where the stack is being deployed (such as `us-east-1`).

```
Resources:
  myEC2Instance:
    Type: AWS::EC2::Instance
    Properties:
      ImageId:
        Fn::FindInMap:
        - RegionMap
        - Ref: AWS::Region
        - '32'
      InstanceType: m1.small
```

Conditions

You can use Conditions in CloudFormation templates to determine when to create a resource or whether a property of a resource is defined.

A common use case for this is to conditionally set an EC2 instance to use a larger instance type if the environment to which you deploy is prod versus dev. In the example, the environment type is input as a template parameter, EnvType, which the conditional statement, CreateProdResources, uses. The conditional statement decides whether to create an additional EBS volume and mount it to the instance with the Condition property of the resource.

 A single condition can reference input parameters, mappings, or other conditions to determine whether the final value is true or false.

```
---
AWSTemplateFormatVersion: '2010-09-09'
Mappings:
  RegionMap:
    us-east-1:
      AMI: ami-7f418316
      TestAz: us-east-1a
    us-west-1:
      AMI: ami-951945d0
      TestAz: us-west-1a
    us-west-2:
      AMI: ami-16fd7026
      TestAz: us-west-2a
Parameters:
  EnvType:
    Description: Environment type.
    Default: test
    Type: String
```

```yaml
      AllowedValues:
      - prod
      - test
Conditions:
  CreateProdResources:
    Fn::Equals:
    - Ref: EnvType
    - prod
Resources:
  EC2Instance:
    Type: AWS::EC2::Instance
    Properties:
      ImageId:
        Fn::FindInMap:
        - RegionMap
        - Ref: AWS::Region
        - AMI
  MountPoint:
    Type: AWS::EC2::VolumeAttachment
    Condition: CreateProdResources
    Properties:
      InstanceId:
        Ref: EC2Instance
      VolumeId:
        Ref: NewVolume
      Device: "/dev/sdh"
  NewVolume:
    Type: AWS::EC2::Volume
    Condition: CreateProdResources
    Properties:
      Size: '100'
      AvailabilityZone:
        Fn::GetAtt:
        - EC2Instance
        - AvailabilityZone
```

You can also use `Conditions` to declare different resource properties based on whether the condition evaluates to true with the `Fn::If` intrinsic function.

Transforms

As templates grow in size and complexity, there may be situations where you use certain components repeatedly across multiple templates, such as common resources or mappings.

Transforms allow you to simplify the template authoring process through a powerful set of macros you use to reduce the amount of time spent in the authoring process. CloudFormation transforms first create a change set for the stack. Transforms are applied to the template during the change set creation process.

There are two types of supported transforms.

AWS::Include Transform AWS::Include Transform acts as a tool to import template snippets from S3 buckets into the template being developed. When the template is evaluated, a change set is created, and the template snippet is copied from its location and is added to the overall template structure. Transforms can be done at the template level, like so:

```
Transform:
  Name: AWS::Include
  Parameters:
    Location: s3://MyAmazonS3BucketName/MyFileName.json
```

Transforms may also be nested in specific resources, such as the Properties section of an AWS::EC2::Instance using this syntax:

```
Fn::Transform:
  Name: AWS::Include
  Parameters:
    Location: s3://MyAmazonS3BucketName/MyFileName.json
```

Any time the stack is updated, the template snippets you reference in any transforms pull from their S3 locations.

CloudFormation does not support nested transforms. If the snippet being imported into a template includes an additional transform declaration, the stack creation or update will fail.

AWS::Serverless Transform The AWS::Serverless transform is used by the AWS Serverless Application Model (AWS SAM), covered elsewhere in this book Chapter 13, "Serverless Applications." The power of transforms to fully redefine a template allows SAM to define its own unique syntax for deploying serverless code based on CloudFormation.

Outputs

Outputs are values that can be made available to use outside a single stack. They can be referenced by other stacks, letting you logically divide up your templates while still maintaining relationships between them. Outputs are also useful in providing meaningful information after a stack has been created or updated successfully, since they show up in the web console. For example, it may be helpful to output a load balancer's URL when a web application stack deploys successfully.

The basic structure for CloudFormation outputs follows. Note the use of Fn::GetAtt to fetch values from the stack's created resources, and the optional Export key to create cross-stack references:

```
Outputs:
  BackupLoadBalancerDNSName:
    Description: The DNSName of the backup load balancer
    Value:
      Fn::GetAtt:
      - BackupLoadBalancer
      - DNSName
    Export:
      Name: MyExportedDNSName
```

Intrinsic Functions

CloudFormation is not a programming language with variables or procedural control structures. Its templates are declarative, intending to be reflective of the infrastructure they create. Still, AWS provides *intrinsic functions* to add some dynamic functionality to CloudFormation templates.

Fn::Base64

The *Fn::Base64* function converts an input string into its Base-64 equivalent. The primary purpose of this function is to pass instructions written in string format to an EC2 instance's UserData property.

```
Fn::Base64: "valueToEncode"
```

Fn::Cidr

The *Fn::Cidr* intrinsic function allows you to convert an IP address block, subnet count, and size mask (optional) into valid CIDR notation—useful when creating VPCs or subnets.

```
"Fn::Cidr": [ ipBlock, count, sizeMask ]
```

Fn::FindInMap

After you create mappings, you use the *Fn::FindInMap* function to query information stored within the mapping table.

```
"Fn::FindInMap": [ "MapName", "TopLevelKey", "SecondLevelKey" ]
```

Consider this Mappings section. The Fn::FindInMap call would return ami-c9c7978c.

```
---
Mappings:
  RegionMap:
    us-east-1:
      32: "ami-6411e20d"
```

```
        64: "ami-7a11e213"
      us-west-1:
        32: "ami-c9c7978c"
        64: "ami-cfc7978a"
      eu-west-1:
        32: "ami-37c2f643"
        64: "ami-31c2f645
```

. . .

```
Fn::FindInMap:
  - "RegionMap"
  - Ref: "AWS::Region"
  - "32"
```

Fn::GetAZs

For each AWS region, different availability zones (with different names) are available. The *Fn::GetAZs* intrinsic function returns a list of availability zones for the account in which the stack is being created.

A common practice is to use the AWS::Region pseudoparameter to return the list of availability zones for the region in which the stack is being created.

```
Fn::GetAZs:
  Ref: "AWS::Region"
```

Fn::Join

In some situations, string values must be concatenated from multiple input strings, as is the case when building Java Database Connectivity (JDBC) connection strings. CloudFormation supports string concatenation with the *Fn::Join* intrinsic function. You can join string values with a predefined delimiter, which you supply to the function along with a list of strings to join.

Fn::Select

If you pass a list of values into your template, there needs to be a way to select an item from the list based on what position (index) it is in the list. *Fn::Select* allows you to choose an item in a list based on the zero-based index.

The Fn::Select intrinsic function does not check for issues such as whether an index is out of bounds or whether the values in a list equal null. You need to verify that the input list does not contain null values and has a known length.

```
"Fn::Select" : [ index, listOfObjects ]
```

Fn::Split

Counter to the Fn::Join intrinsic function, you use *Fn::Split* to create a list of strings by separating a single string by a known delimiter. You can use Fn::Select to access the output list of strings and pass them to an index to select from different substrings.

```
"Fn::Split" : [ "delimiter", "source string" ]
```

Fn::Sub

If you need to build an input string with multiple variables determined at runtime, use the *Fn::Sub* function to populate a template string with input variables from a variable map.

This intrinsic function can also use parameters, resources, and resource attributes already present in your template. Note in this example that two template values are present in the string, but only one mapping value is provided. This is because the AWS::AccountId pseudoparameter will automatically resolve to the account ID where the stack is being created, and AWS::Region automatically resolves to the region ID.

```
Fn::Sub:
  - arn:aws:ec2:${AWS::Region}:${AWS::AccountId}:vpc/${vpc}
  - vpc:
    Ref: MyVPC
```

Ref

You will use the *Ref* intrinsic function frequently within your templates, especially when multiple resources have dependencies and relationships between one another (such as if you create an AWS::EC2::VPC resource with two AWS::EC2::Subnet resources). The behavior of the Ref function can differ slightly depending on the resource type being referenced. In some cases, such as with AWS::S3::Bucket or AWS::AutoScaling::AutoScalingGroup resources, you use Ref to return the resource name (in this situation, either the bucket or AWS Auto Scaling group name). In other cases, different properties such as the resource ARN or physical ID returns. Make sure to check the documentation for the resource type being referenced to verify what data returns.

```
"Ref" : "logicalName"
```

Fn::GetAtt

Resources you create in CloudFormation contain information that you can query in other parts of the same template. Pay attention to AWS documentation to understand what is returned by the Ref function—it can vary from resource to resource. *GetAtt* allows you to be more specific, fetching, for example, either the ARN or public IP of a create EC2 instance. This can be useful when establishing relationships between resources (e.g., while attaching a security group to an instance).

```
Fn::GetAtt:
  - "logicalIDOfResource"
  - "attributeName"
```

Condition Functions

Condition functions are special intrinsic functions that allow you to optionally create resources or set resource properties, depending on whether the condition evaluates to true or false. Use Fn::If, along with logic functions Fn::And, Fn::Equals, Fn:Not, and Fn::Or, to construct Booleans that can shape the functionality of your template. Just be cautious that your templates don't become so dynamic that their effects are difficult for readers to understand.

Configuring the Host with *cfn-init*

AWS CloudFormation comes with some built-in features to help configure the EC2 instances with you build. With these capabilities, you can install packages, create users and groups, and run arbitrary scripts via your template as your instances come online.

AWS::CloudFormation::Init

The cfn-init metadata key offers a powerful set of commands for provisioning EC2 instances as they are created. Similar to configuration management tools like Ansible or Puppet, this section allows you to move files, install packages, set up users and groups, and run commands on an instance after it is created.

One of the benefits of cfn-init over a UserData script alone is the ability to issue updates via CloudFormation. If you update the cfn-init part of a template, the changes will be applied on the instance the next time you issue an update to the stack. The following example shows the basic structure of using AWS::CloudFormation::Init on an EC2 resource:

```
Resources:
  MyInstance:
    Type: AWS::EC2::Instance
    Metadata:
      AWS::CloudFormation::Init:
        config:
          packages:
          groups:
          users:
          sources:
          files:
          commands:
          services:
    Properties:
```

This section has many capabilities that are beyond the scope of this book. For more information, please consult AWS documentation.

Running *AWS::CloudFormation::Init* Metadata

To actually execute AWS::CloudFormation::Init metadata, instances defined in your template must call the cfn-init helper script as part of UserData. When doing so, you must provide the stack name and resource logical ID, as shown next. Remember that UserData is required to be in Base-64 format, so wrap the script in Fn::Base64.

 You must pass UserData to instances in Base-64 format, so call the Fn::Base64 function to convert the text-based script to a Base-64 encoding.

```
UserData:
  Fn::Base64:
    Fn::Join:
    - ''
    - - "#!/bin/bash -xe\n"
      - "# Install the files and packages from the metadata\n"
      - "/opt/aws/bin/cfn-init -v "
      - "         --stack "
      - Ref: AWS::StackName
      - "         --resource WebServerInstance "
      - "         --configsets InstallAndRun "
      - "         --region "
      - Ref: AWS::Region
      - "\n"AWS::CloudFormation::Interface
```

Custom Resources

Sometimes custom provisioning logic is required when creating resources in AWS. Common examples of this include managing resources not currently supported by CloudFormation, interacting with third-party tools, or other situations where more complexity is involved in the provisioning process.

CloudFormation uses *custom resource providers* to handle the provisioning and configuration of custom resources. Custom resource providers may be Lambda functions or SNS topics. When you create, update, or delete a custom resource, either the Lambda function is invoked or a message is sent to the SNS topic you configure in the resource declaration.

In the custom resource declaration, you must provide a service token along with any optional input parameters. The *service token* acts as a reference to where custom resource requests are sent. Any input parameters you include are sent with the request body. After the resource provider processes the request, a SUCCESS or FAILED result is sent to a presigned S3 URL you include in the request body. CloudFormation monitors this bucket location for a response, which it processes once it is sent by the provider. Custom resources can provide outputs back to CloudFormation, which are made accessible as properties of the custom resource. You can access these properties with the Fn::GetAtt intrinsic function to pass the logical ID of the resource and the attribute you desire to query.

AWS Lambda-Backed Custom Resources

AWS Lambda-backed custom resources invoke functions whenever create, update, or delete actions are sent to the resource provider. This resource type is incredibly useful to reference other AWS cloud services and resources that may not support CloudFormation. Also, you can use them to look up data from other resources, such as EC2 instance IDs or entries in a DynamoDB table.

You can include the Lambda function, which acts as a resource provider in the same CloudFormation template that creates the custom resource and adds additional flexibility for stack update events. In this case, you can define the code for the Lambda function itself inline in the template or store it in a separate location such as S3. The following example demonstrates a custom resource, AMIInfo, which makes use of a Lambda function, AMIInfoFunction, as the resource provider. Two additional properties, Region and OSName, provide inputs to the resource provider.

```
AMIInfo:
  Type: Custom::AMIInfo
  Properties:
    ServiceToken:
      Fn::GetAtt:
      - AMIInfoFunction
      - Arn
    Region:
      Ref: AWS::Region
    OSName:
      Ref: WindowsVersion
```

For the Lambda function to execute successfully, you must supply it with an AWS IAM role. If the function will interact with other AWS cloud services, you need the following permissions at minimum:

- `logs:CreateLogGroup`
- `logs:CreateLogStream`
- `logs:PutLogEvents`

Amazon SNS-Backed Custom Resources

Although Lambda functions are incredibly powerful and versatile, they have a limit of 15 minutes of execution time, at which point the function will exit. For custom actions that may take a long time to execute, use *Amazon SNS-backed custom resources*.

With this resource type, notifications are sent to an SNS topic any time the custom resource triggers. As the architect, you are responsible for managing the system that receives notifications and performs processing. For instance, transcoding of long video files may take a longer time than Lambda allows. In these situations, you subscribe an EC2 instance to the SNS topic to listen for requests, consume the input request object, perform the transcoding work, and place an appropriate response.

Custom Resource Success/Failure

For a custom resource to be successful in CloudFormation, the resource provider must return a success response to the presigned S3 URL that you provide in the request. If you do not provide a response, the custom resource will eventually time out. This is especially important with update and delete actions. The custom resource provider will need to respond appropriately to every action type (create, update, delete) for both successful and unsuccessful attempts. If you do not provide a response to an update action, for example, the entire stack update will fail after the custom resource times out, and this results in a stack rollback.

Resource Relationships

By default, CloudFormation will track most dependencies between resources implicitly, any time one resource references another through functions like Ref or GetAtt. There are, however, some exceptions. For example, an application server may not function properly until its backend RDS database is up and running. In this case, you can add a DependsOn attribute to your template to specify the order of creation. The *DependsOn* attribute specifies that creation of a resource should not begin until another completes.

Creation Policies

There may be situations where a dependency is not enough, such as when you install and configure applications on an instance before you attach it to a load balancer. By default, CloudFormation has no way of knowing when this activity is complete. In this case, you can use a CreationPolicy.

A *CreationPolicy* instructs CloudFormation not to mark a resource as CREATE_COMPLETE until the resource itself signals back to the service by calling a helper script called cfn-signal found preinstalled on Amazon Linux EC2 instances. It can also specify that CloudFormation wait for a specific number of signals before proceeding, allowing you to coordinate multiple external actions in sequence.

Wait Conditions

You should use a CreationPolicy any time you are waiting on the completion of User Data. For anything else happening outside the control of CloudFormation, you can use the *WaitCondition* property to insert arbitrary pauses until those activities complete. The WaitCondition property defines a unique URL that you provide to outside processes. When the outside process (say, an AMI creation or the execution of an API call invoked via Lambda) is complete, that script must issue an HTTP PUT call to the URL, letting CloudFormation know of its success or failure, and that it's time to continue.

Stack Create, Update, and Delete Statuses

Whenever you perform an action on a CloudFormation stack, each resource will display a status code as the template executes. These statuses are visible in the CloudFormation console, or if you use the DescribeStacks action.

```
CREATE_COMPLETE

CREATE_IN_PROGRESS
```

```
CREATE_FAILED

DELETE_COMPLETE

DELETE_IN_PROGRESS

DELETE_FAILED

ROLLBACK_COMPLETE

ROLLBACK_IN_PROGRESS

ROLLBACK_FAILED

UPDATE_COMPLETE

UPDATE_IN_PROGRESS

UPDATE_COMPLETE_CLEANUP_IN_PROGRESS

UPDATE_ROLLBACK_COMPLETE

UPDATE_ROLLBACK_IN_PROGRESS

UPDATE_ROLLBACK_COMPLETE_CLEANUP_IN_PROGRESS

UPDATE_ROLLBACK_FAILED
```

These statuses let you know how your stack create, update, or delete action is progressing and are fairly self-explanatory. Just know that by default, failures in resource creation trigger a rollback of the entire stack. If you encounter this (and you will—template creation can be a trial-and-error process), you'll need to inspect the status messages of each resource to determine the cause. These days, AWS helpfully provides a Detect Root Cause button to auto-scroll console users to the offending resource error.

Stack Updates

You may update stacks by modifying the template to add new resources, modify or delete existing ones, or change configuration parameters. CloudFormation will take the appropriate action to update your stack.

Depending on the resource being updated, the result may be:

- Update with no interruption (e.g., changing tags on an EC2 instance)

- Update with some interruption (e.g., updating an EC2 instance's type, resulting in a stop and restart)

- Replacing update (e.g., changing the base AMI of an EC2)

Because some resources cannot be updated directly, they must be torn down and re-created. These replacement updates cause downtime while the existing resource is deleted and a new one is created with a distinct ARN and other physical identifiers, such as RDS endpoint URLs. To know in advance what effect your updates will have, use change sets.

Update Policies

CloudFormation needs a little additional guidance to know how to update certain resources. Use the *UpdatePolicy* field to determine how CloudFormation should process changes to the following resource types:

AWS::AppStream::Fleet

AWS::AutoScaling::AutoScalingGroup

AWS::ElastiCache::ReplicationGroup

AWS::OpenSearchService::Domain

AWS::Elasticsearch::Domain

AWS::Lambda::Alias

Each of these resource types has unique values for UpdatePolicy that influence how configuration changes are executed. For instance, with an Auto Scaling group, changes to the launch configuration (which determines the size and configuration of new instances in the group) may use the UpdatePolicy value AutoScalingReplacingUpdate or AutoScaling RollingUpdate to force updates to happen only when instances are replaced, or on an immediate rolling basis, respectively.

Each of these resource types has specific values and behaviors you can define for updates. For more information, see AWS docs on the UpdatePolicy CloudFormation attribute:

https://docs.aws.amazon.com/AWSCloudFormation/latest/UserGuide/
aws-attribute-updatepolicy.html

Deletion Policies

When you delete a stack, by default all underlying stack resources are also deleted. If this behavior is not desirable, apply the *DeletionPolicy* to resources in the stack to modify their behavior when the stack deletes. You use deletion policies to preserve resources when you delete a stack with DeletionPolicy value Retain.

Some resources, such as AWS::RDS::DBInstance and AWS::EC2::Volume, can instead have a snapshot or backup taken before you delete the resource using DeletionPolicy value Snapshot.

Exports and Nested Stacks

Since CloudFormation enforces limits on how large templates can grow and how many resources, outputs, and parameters you can declare in one template, situations can arise where you will need to manage more infrastructure than a single stack will allow. There are two approaches to manage relationships between multiple stacks. You use *stack exports* to share information between separate stacks or manage CloudFormation stacks themselves as resources in a *nested stack* relationship.

Export and Import Stack Outputs

You can export stack output values to import them into other stacks in the same account and region. This allows you to share data that generates in one stack out to other stacks in your account. If, for example, you create a networking infrastructure such as an Amazon VPC in one stack, you can export the IDs of such resources from this stack and import them into others at a later date.

To export a stack value, update the Outputs section to include an Export declaration for every output you want to share.

```
Outputs:
  Logical ID:
    Description: Information about the value
    Value: Value to return
    Export:
      Name: Value to export
```

 Export values must have a unique name within the AWS account and AWS region.

After you declare the export and the stack creates or updates, it displays in the CloudFormation console on the Exports tab, as shown in Figure 8.1.

FIGURE 8.1   CloudFormation Exports tab

To import this value into another stack, you use the *Fn::ImportValue* intrinsic function. This intrinsic function requires only the export name as an input parameter (the name present in the CloudFormation console).

Nesting with the *AWS::CloudFormation::Stack Resource*

You can manage stacks as resources themselves in CloudFormation. A single parent stack can create one or more AWS::CloudFormation::Stack resources, which act as child stacks that the parent manages. The direct benefits of this are as follows:

- You can work around template limits CloudFormation imposes.

- It provides the ability to separate resources into logical groups, such as network, database, and web application.

- It lets you separate duties. (Each team is responsible only for maintaining their respective child stack.)

You can increase the nesting levels, as shown in Figure 8.2, with the AWS::CloudFormation::Stack resources.

FIGURE 8.2   Nested stack structure

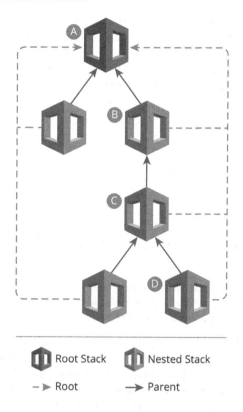

 From a workflow perspective, the "topmost" parent stack should manage all updates to child stacks. In Figure 8.2, if you need to update stack D, you perform the update on stack A, the topmost parent, to accomplish this.

You can share data from each nested stack if you use a combination of stack outputs and the Fn::GetAtt function calls. If there is an output value from a nested stack that you would like to access from its parent, this syntax will let you access stack outputs.

```
Fn::GetAtt:
  - logicalNameOfChildStack
  - Outputs.attributeName
```

 Outputs from stacks created by a nested stack (such as to access outputs in stack C from stack A, as shown in Figure 8.2) can be accessed from the parent stack(s). First, you will need to output the value in the originating stack and then its parent and finally access the output from the parent. To clarify, the output would originate in stack C and be added as an output to stack B, and then stack A references it.

Stack Policies

You can assign a *stack policy* to a stack to allow or deny access to modify certain stack resources, which you can filter by the type of update. Stack policies apply to all users, regardless of their AWS IAM permissions. Please note that stack policies only prevent changes made through CloudFormation itself; they do not protect against changes made directly to a stack's resources, such as deleting an EC2 instance.

```
Statement:
  - Effect: Allow
    Action: Update:*
    Principal: "*"
    Resource: "*"
  - Effect: Deny
    Action: Update:*
    Principal: "*"
    Resource: LogicalResourceId/ProductionDatabase
```

> Stack policies are not a replacement for appropriate access control from an AWS IAM policy. Stack policies are an additional fail-safe to prevent accidental updates to critical resources.

Stack policies protect all resources by default with an implicit deny. To allow access to actions on stack resources, you must apply explicit allow statements to the policy. In the previous example, an explicit allow specifies that you can perform all updates on all resources in the stack. However, the explicit deny for the ProductionDatabase resource prevents update actions to this specific resource. You can specify allow and deny actions for either resource logical IDs or generic resource types. To specify policies for generic resource types, use a condition statement as follows:

```
Statement:
  - Effect: Deny
    Principal: "*"
    Action: Update:*
    Resource: "*"
    Condition:
      StringEquals:
        ResourceType:
          - AWS::EC2::Instance
          - AWS::RDS::DBInstance
```

> Once you apply a stack policy, you cannot remove it. During future updates, the policy must be temporarily replaced.

Once a stack policy has been set, it will need to be overridden during updates to protected resources. To do so, you supply a new, temporary stack policy. You add this stack policy in the console under the `Stack policy` property, as shown in Figure 8.3.

FIGURE 8.3   CloudFormation Stack Policy field

Advanced options
You can set additional options for your stack, like notification options and a stack policy. Learn more 🗗

▼ Stack policy
Defines the resources that you want to protect from unintentional updates during a stack update.

Stack policy - optional
A stack policy is a JSON document that defines the update actions that can be performed on designated resources

⭘ No stack policy   ⦿ Enter stack policy   ⭘ Upload a file

Enter stack policy

JSON formatted text

▼ Rollback configuration
Specify alarms for CloudFormation to monitor when creating and updating the stack. If the operation breaches an alarm threshold, CloudFormation rolls it back.

Monitoring time - optional
Number of minutes after the operation completes that CloudFormation should continue monitoring the specified alarms.

10 Minutes

CloudWatch alarm - optional

arn:aws:cloudwatch:us-east-1:123456789012:alarm:MyAlarmName

When you supply a stack policy during an update, it only modifies the policy for the duration of the update, after which the original policy reinstates.

AWS CloudFormation Command-Line Interface

In addition to letting you execute all the same actions as the web console, the CLI for Cloud-Formation provides several utility functions.

Packaging Local Dependencies

CloudFormation templates can get long. As software developers know, it is sometimes convenient to divide parts of your code into separate files, which you can reference at will. A common example with CloudFormation is AWS Lambda function code. When developing locally, CloudFormation templates can reference other paths on your computer, as shown in the `CodeUri` property here:

```
AWSTemplateFormatVersion: '2010-09-09'
Transform: 'AWS::Serverless-2016-10-31'
Resources:
  MyFunction:
    Type: 'AWS::Serverless::Function'
    Properties:
      Handler: index.handler
      Runtime: nodejs4.3
      CodeUri: /home/user/code/lambdafunction
```

You can use the `aws cloudformation package` command to convert local path references like this to S3 URIs. This action uploads the files and your template in one step, as shown:

```
aws cloudformation package --template /path_to_template/template.json --s3-
bucket mybucket --output json > packaged-template.json
```

When you execute this command, the AWS CLI will package the contents of /home/user/code/lambdafunction into a ZIP archive and upload it to the S3 bucket you specify in the --s3-bucket parameter. After doing so, the template updates to refer to the S3 URI for the archive file and generates the following:

```
AWSTemplateFormatVersion: '2010-09-09'
Transform: 'AWS::Serverless-2016-10-31'
Resources:
  MyFunction:
    Type: 'AWS::Serverless::Function'
    Properties:
      Handler: index.handler
      Runtime: nodejs4.3
      CodeUri: s3://mybucket/lambdafunction.zip
```

Deploy Templates with Transforms

Any CloudFormation template that contains transforms must be deployed via change sets, so users can assess the impact of the transformed template. If you would like to reduce this to a one-step process, the `aws cloudformation deploy` command will generate and execute the change set on your behalf. This is especially useful for rapid iteration during development.

When you use this command, you can override default parameters with the `--parameter-overrides` property.

```
aws cloudformation deploy --template /path_to_template/my-template.json --
stack-name my-new-stack --parameter-overrides Key1=Value1 Key2=Value2
```

AWS CloudFormation Helper Scripts

When you execute custom scripts on EC2 instances as part of your `UserData`, CloudFormation provides several important helper scripts. Use these tools to interact with the stack to query metadata, notify a `CreationPolicy` or `WaitCondition`, and process scripts when CloudFormation detects metadata updates.

cfn-init

Use this script to execute `AWS::CloudFormation::Init` metadata from an `AWS::EC2::LaunchConfiguration` or `AWS::EC2::Instance` resource. It is responsible for installing packages, adding files, creating users and groups, and any other configuration you specify. See the next section for details on how to call this script and convey results back to CloudFormation.

cfn-signal

After `cfn-init` has been called and the `AWS::CloudFormation::Init` metadata has been applied successfully (or unsuccessfully), you can use *cfn-signal* to notify CloudFormation that the instance has completed its configuration. For example, if your template contains a `CreationPolicy` or `WaitCondition` to prevent the setup of a load balancer until instances in an Auto Scaling group have completed some custom setup, `cfn-signal` is the way to perform the notification. The following `UserData` example demonstrates how to call `cfn-init`, then pass the result to `cfn-signal`:

```
UserData:
  Fn::Base64:
    Fn::Join:
    - ''
    - - "#!/bin/bash -x\n"
      - "# Install the files and packages from the metadata\n"
      - "/opt/aws/bin/cfn-init -v "
      - "         --stack "
      - Ref: AWS::StackName
      - "         --resource MyInstance "
      - "         --region "
      - Ref: AWS::Region
      - "\n"
      - "# Signal the status from cfn-init\n"
      - "/opt/aws/bin/cfn-signal -e $? "
      - "         --stack "
      - Ref: AWS::StackName
      - "         --resource MyInstance "
      - "         --region "
      - Ref: AWS::Region
      - "\n"
```

cfn-get-metadata

If your template contains data in the `metadata` section, `cfn-get-metadata` can fetch this information for use on your instance(s).

cfn-hup

Since CloudFormation executes `UserData` only on resource creation, instances do not detect or apply updates to `AWS::CloudFormation::Init` metadata automatically. *cfn-hup* is a script that can run as a daemon on instances and listen for changes to this metadata. Along with its attendant configuration file `hooks.conf`, `cfn-hup` checks for changes to resource metadata, allowing you to perform configuration updates on instances in a stack. For more information on configuring this script and its config files, see AWS documentation.

AWS CloudFormation StackSets

It's common for organizations, once they have migrated to the cloud, to eventually adopt a multi-account strategy. Managing multiple accounts gives you the ability to segment off use cases, resources, and user permissions in a logical way. It can be a great approach for both organization and security, but how do you manage infrastructure as code across accounts?

CloudFormation *StackSets* is that solution, giving users the ability to control, provision, and manage stacks across multiple accounts, as shown in Figure 8.4.

FIGURE 8.4   AWS CloudFormation StackSets structure

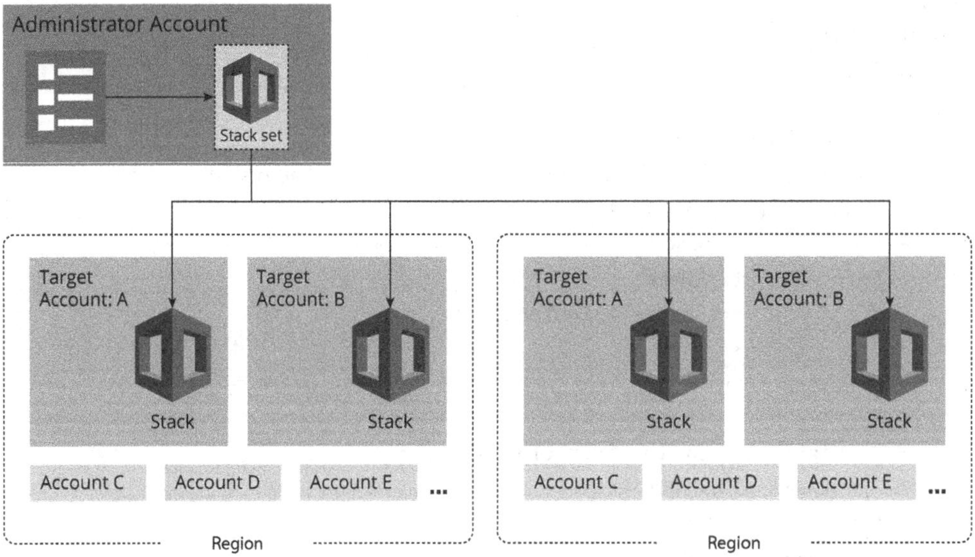

StackSet

A *StackSet* acts as a single point of management for deploying a CloudFormation template across multiple accounts or in multiple regions of the same account.

Stack Instance

Each StackSet contains *stack instances*, an instance of a template applied in a particular target account or region, as shown in Figure 8.5. For example, if a StackSet deploys to four regions in a target account, you create four stack instances. An update to a StackSet propagates to all stack instances in all accounts and regions. Each stack instance has its own life cycle with its own status and can be managed as though it were an individual stack. The difference is that you, as owner of the main account, now have one central point of control for managing their deployment.

FIGURE 8.5   CloudFormation StackSet actions

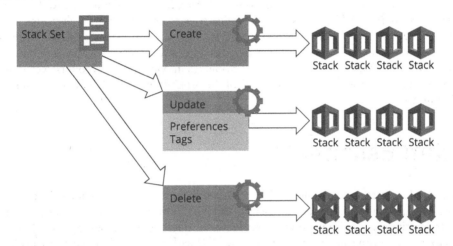

StackSet Permissions

Before you can use StackSets to deploy templates to target accounts, you must create a trust relationship between "parent" and "child" accounts using AWS IAM roles.

The parent, or administrator, account requires an IAM service role with permissions to execute stack set operations and assume an execution role in any target accounts. This service role must have a trust policy that allows cloudformation.amazonaws.com.

Any child, or target, accounts will require an execution role that you create in the administrator account, which the service role can assume. This execution role will require Cloud-Formation permissions and permissions to manage any resources you define in the template being deployed by the StackSet, as shown in Figure 8.6.

FIGURE 8.6   CloudFormation StackSets permissions

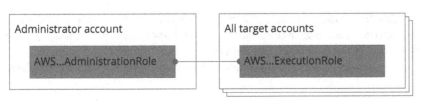

It sounds complicated, but it only takes a few steps, and AWS has documentation to walk you through it. For complete details on how to set up IAM for StackSets, see:
`https://docs.aws.amazon.com/AWSCloudFormation/latest/UserGuide/stacksets-prereqs.html`

Summary

With AWS CloudFormation, cloud practitioners can achieve one of the cloud's biggest benefits: infrastructure as code. By defining your resources, their configuration, and their relationships as JSON or YAML, you gain the ability to capture infrastructure decisions, version them, manage changes over time, and deploy them in a structured, repeatable way. Advanced users can take advantage of intrinsic functions, conditions, custom resources, and template metadata to make the management of resources in one or more accounts even easier, giving you the power to take full advantage of the programmatic nature of cloud computing in AWS.

Exam Essentials

Understand infrastructure as code (IaC).   You model infrastructure as code to automate the provisioning, maintenance, and retirement of complex infrastructure across an organization. The declarative syntax allows you to describe the resource state you desire, instead of the steps to create it. You can version and maintain IaC with the same development workflow as application and configuration code.

Understand the purpose of change sets.   Change sets allow administrators to preview the changes that will take place when a given template deploys to CloudFormation. This includes a description of resources that you will update or replace entirely. You create change sets to help prevent stack updates that could accidentally result in the replacement of critical resources, such as databases.

Know the CloudFormation permissions model.   When you create, update, or delete stacks, CloudFormation will operate with the same permissions as the IAM user or role that performs the stack action. For example, a user who deletes a stack that contains an EC2 instance must also have the ability to terminate instances; otherwise, the stack delete fails. CloudFormation also supports service roles, which you can pass to the service when you perform stack actions. This requires that the user or role have permissions to pass the service role to perform the stack action.

Know the CloudFormation template structure.   You can use these AWS CloudFormation template properties: `AWSTemplateFormatVersion`, `Description`, `Metadata`, `Parameters`, `Mappings`, `Conditions`, `Transform`, `Resources`, and `Outputs`. Templates only require the `Resources` property, and you must define at least one resource in every template.

Know how to use the intrinsic functions.   It is important to understand the AWS CloudFormation templates intrinsic functions, such as these:

- `Fn::FindInMap`
- `Fn::GetAtt`
- `Fn::Join`
- `Fn::Split`
- `Ref`

Understand the purpose of AWS::CloudFormation::Init.   This template section defines the configuration tasks the `cfn-init` helper script will perform on instances that you create individually or as part of AWS Auto Scaling launch configurations. This metadata key allows you to define a more declarative syntax for configuration tasks compared to using procedural steps in the `UserData` property.

Know the use cases for both custom resource types.   You can implement custom resources with Lambda functions or SNS topics. The primary difference between each type is that Lambda-backed custom resources have a maximum execution duration of five minutes. This may not work for custom resources that take a long time to provision or update. In those cases, SNS topics backed by EC2 instances would allow for long-running tasks.

Understand how CloudFormation manages resource relationships.   CloudFormation will automatically order resource provisioning and update steps based on known dependencies. For example, if a template declares a VPC and subnets, the subnets will not be created before the VPC that contains them. However, CloudFormation is not aware of all possible relationships, such as an EC2 instance that needs an RDS database to exist before starting a web app. These kinds of dependencies can be manually declared with the `DependsOn` property.

Understand wait conditions and creation policies.   In some cases, resources in a template should wait for other resources to provision and configure before starting their tasks. For example, you may want to prevent creation of a load balancer resource until instances in an AWS Auto Scaling group have come online. In those cases, you can use either wait conditions or creation policies.

Understand how stack updates affect resources.   When you update a stack, resources may behave differently when properties update. For instance, updating an S3 bucket policy causes no interruption, but renaming a bucket requires replacement of the bucket. Resources can undergo one of three types of updates: update with no interruption, update with some interruption, and replace update.

Know how to use exports and nested stacks to share stacks.   Stack exports allow you to access stack outputs in other stacks in the same region. Exports, however, come with some limitations. For example, you cannot delete stacks that export values until all other stacks that import the exported value have been modified to no longer include the import.

Nested stacks make use of the AWS::CloudFormation::Stack resource type. This way, a single stack can create multiple "child" stacks, which can declare their own resources (including other stacks).

Understand stack policies.   To prevent updates to critical stack resources, you implement stack policies. A stack policy declares what resources you can and cannot update and under what circumstances. A stack containing an RDS instance, for example, can include a stack policy that prevents updates that require replacement of the database instance.

Exercises

EXERCISE 8.1

Writing Your Own AWS CloudFormation Template

Write an AWS CloudFormation template:

1. Create an S3 bucket with a static website configuration that includes references to index and error documents, such as index.html and error.html, respectively.

2. Create an output to the bucket's website URL.

3. Create an output that displays the bucket name.

4. Upload the code as index.html to the root of the bucket for the index document.

    ```html
    <html>
        <body>
            <h1>Hello, World!</h1>
        </body>
    </html>
    ```

5. Upload the code as error.html to the root of the bucket for the error document.

    ```html
    <html>
        <body>
        <h1>Oops! Something went wrong.</h1>
        </body>
    </html>
    ```

6. Access the URL the output provides from your CloudFormation stack to verify the static website works.

EXERCISE 8.2

Troubleshooting a Failed Stack Deletion

1. Deploy the CloudFormation code template, which provisions an S3 bucket in your account.

   ```
   Resources:
     ExampleBucket:
       Type: "AWS::S3::Bucket"
   Outputs:
     BucketName:
       Value:
         Ref: "ExampleBucket
   ```

2. Upload several files and objects to the S3 bucket that the template creates.

3. Delete the stack and monitor progress until it fails. Note the error output by CloudFormation when the stack reaches the DELETE_FAILED state.

4. Delete all files from the S3 bucket.

5. Attempt to delete the stack again, but do not enable the option to retain the bucket.

EXERCISE 8.3

Monitoring Stack Update Activity

1. Deploy the CloudFormation code template, which provisions an Amazon S3 bucket in your account.

   ```
   Resources:
     ExampleBucket:
       Type: "AWS::S3::Bucket"
   Outputs:
     BucketName:
       Value:
         Ref: "ExampleBucket
   ```

2. After the stack is created, make note of the output value. This is the name of your S3 bucket.

3. Use the template code to update the stack, and replace BUCKET_NAME with a name of your choice.

```
Resources:
  ExampleBucket:
    Type: "AWS::S3::Bucket"
    Properties:
      BucketName: "BUCKET_NAME"
Outputs:
  BucketName:
    Value:
      Ref: "ExampleBucket
```

4. Note that a new bucket creates, and the original bucket deletes. This is because you cannot change bucket names after initial creation, so a replacement must be provisioned.

Review Questions

1. Which of the CloudFormation template sections is/are required?

    A. `AWSTemplateFormatVersion`

    B. `Parameters`

    C. `Metadata`

    D. `Resources`

    E. All of the above

2. You are writing a CloudFormation template and would like to create an output value corresponding to your application's website URL. The application is composed of two application servers in a private subnet behind an application load balancer (ALB). The application servers read from an RDS database instance. The logical IDs of the instances are AppServerA and AppServerB. The logical IDs of the load balancer and database are AppLB and AppDB, respectively.

    ```
    Outputs:
      AppEndpoint:
        Description: "URL to access the application"
        Value: "Value to return"
    ```

    Which code correctly completes the previous output declaration?

    A. `'Fn::Join': ['', ['https://', {'Ref': 'AppLB'}, '/login.php']]`

    B. `'Fn::Join': ['', ['https://', {'Fn::GetAtt': ['AppServerA', 'PublicDNSName']}, '/login.php']]`

    C. `'Fn::Join': ['', ['https://', {'Ref': ['AppLB', 'DNSName']}, '/login.php']]`

    D. `'Fn::Join': ['', ['https://', {'Fn::GetAtt': ['AppDB', 'Endpoint.Address']}, '/login.php']]`

    E. `'Fn::Join': ['', ['https://', {'Fn::GetAtt': ['AppLB', 'DNSName']}, '/login.php']]`

3. A CloudFormation template you have written uses a `CreationPolicy` to ensure that video transcoding instances launch and configure before the application server instances so that they are available before users are able to access the website. However, you are finding that the stack always reaches the creation policy's timeout value before the transcoding instances complete setup.

    Why could this be? (Choose three.)

    A. The user data script does not include a call to `cfn-signal`.

    B. The instance could not be launched because of account limits.

    C. The user data script fails before reaching the `cfn-signal` step.

    D. The instance cannot connect to the CloudFormation endpoint when calling `cfn-signal`.

4. Which services may be invoked to implement a CloudFormation custom resource? (Choose two.)

    A. AWS Step Functions

    B. AWS SQS

    C. AWS SNS

    D. AWS ECS tasks

    E. AWS Lambda

5. A Lambda-backed custom resource in your stack creates successfully; however, it attempts to update the resource result in the failure message `Custom Resource failed to stabilize in the expected time`. After you add a service role to extend the timeout duration, the issue still persists. What may also be the cause of this error?

    A. The custom resource defined a function for handling the `CREATE` action but did not do the same for the `UPDATE` action; thus, a success or failure signal was not sent to CloudFormation.

    B. The service role does not have appropriate permissions to invoke the custom resource function.

    C. The custom resource function no longer exists.

    D. All of the above.

6. Which feature of CloudFormation allows users to define templates using the AWS Serverless Application Model (AWS SAM) syntax?

    A. Transforms. The `AWS::Serverless` transform converts SAM syntax to native Cloud-Formation before it is processed.

    B. Includes. SAM pulls translations of serverless code from S3 at runtime.

    C. Custom resources. SAM is not a native CloudFormation feature, so it is implemented as a custom resource.

    D. `WaitConditions`. These ensure the template execution pauses while SAM syntax is resolved.

7. What do the intrinsic functions `Ref` and `GetAtt` have in common with the resource attribute `DependsOn`?

    A. They establish relationships that enforce resource creation order.

    B. They can only be invoked by nested resources.

    C. None of these are valid CloudFormation syntax.

    D. They are all required elements of a Transform task.

8. Which of these helper scripts performs updates to OS configuration when a CloudFormation stack updates?

    A. `cfn-hup`

    B. `cfn-init`

    C. `cfn-signal`

    D. `cfn-update`

9. Which of these options allows you to specify a required number of signals to mark the resource as CREATE_COMPLETE?

   A. Wait Condition

   B. Wait Condition handler

   C. CreationPolicy

   D. WaitCount

10. How would you preview the changes a stack update will make without affecting any resources in your account?

    A. Create a change set.

    B. Perform the stack update, and then manually roll back.

    C. Perform the stack update on a test stack.

    D. Do a manual diff of both templates.

11. How would you access a property of a resource created in a nested stack?

    A. This cannot be done.

    B. In the child stack, declare the resource property as a stack output. In the parent stack, use Fn::GetAtt and pass in two parameters, the child stack logical ID and Outputs .NestedStackOutputName.`

    C. In the child stack, export the resource property. In the parent stack, import the exported value.

    D. Use the cross-stack references.

12. By default, with what permissions will CloudFormation stack operations perform?

    A. Full administrator

    B. The permissions of the user performing the operation

    C. The CloudFormation service role

    D. CloudFormation does not use permissions

13. A CloudFormation template declares two resources: a Lambda function and a DynamoDB table. The function code is declared inline as part of the template and references the table. In what order will CloudFormation provision the two resources?

    A. DynamoDB table, Lambda function

    B. Lambda function, DynamoDB table

    C. This cannot be determined ahead of time

    D. They would be executed simultaneously

14. Which occurs during a replacing update?

    A. The resource becomes unavailable.

    B. The resource physical ID changes.

    C. A new resource is created.

    D. The original resource is deleted during the cleanup phase.

    E. All of the above.

15. Which of the update types results in resource downtime? (Choose two.)

   A. Update with No Interruption

   B. Update with Some Interruption

   C. Replacing Update

   D. Update with No Data

   E. Static Update

16. What must occur before a stack that exports an output can be deleted?

   A. Any stacks importing the exported value must remove the import.

   B. The export must be removed from the stack.

   C. Nothing is required.

   D. The stack must be deleted.

17. What does it mean when a CloudFormation stack is in the UPDATE_COMPLETE_CLEANUP_ IN_PROGRESS state?

   A. The stack has failed to update, and it is removing newly created resources.

   B. The stack has successfully updated, and it is removing old resources.

   C. The stack has successfully updated, and it is removing new resources.

   D. The stack has failed to update, and it is removing old resources.

18. Which of the formats are valid for a CloudFormation template? (Choose two.)

   A. YAML

   B. XML

   C. JSON

   D. Markdown

   E. LaTeX

19. Which is an advantage of using CloudFormation instead of the AWS Management Console, Command-Line Interface (AWS CLI), or software development kits (AWS SDKs) to provision and manage infrastructure?

   A. Reduction of human error

   B. Repeatable infrastructure

   C. Reduced IAM permissions requirements

   D. Versionable infrastructure

   E. All of the above

20. What does a service token represent in a custom resource declaration?

   A. The AWS service that receives the request

   B. The SNS or Lambda resource Amazon Resource Name (ARN) that receives the request

   C. The on-premises server IP address that receives the request

   D. The type of action to take

   E. The commands to execute for the custom resource

21. You are creating a custom resource associated with AWS Lambda that will execute several database functions in an Amazon RDS database instance. As part of this, the functions will return data you would like to use in other resources declared in your CloudFormation template.

How would you best pass this data to the other resources declared in the template?

- **A.** Store the data in a JSON file in S3 bucket, and use the AWS CLI to download the object.
- **B.** Store the output data in the AWS Systems Manager Parameter Store, and query the parameter store using the AWS CLI.
- **C.** Use custom resource outputs to declare the returned data as resource properties. Then, query the properties using the `Fn::GetAtt` intrinsic function.
- **D.** This cannot be accomplished.

Secure Configuration and Container Management

THE AWS CERTIFIED DEVELOPER – ASSOCIATE EXAM TOPICS COVERED IN THIS CHAPTER MAY INCLUDE, BUT ARE NOT LIMITED TO, THE FOLLOWING:

✓ **Domain 1: Development with AWS Services**

- Task Statement 1: Develop code for applications hosted on AWS

- Task Statement 3: Use data stores in application development

✓ **Domain 2: Security**

- Task Statement 3: Manage sensitive data in application code

✓ **Domain 3: Deployment**

- Task Statement 1: Prepare application artifacts to be deployed to AWS

- Task Statement 4: Deploy code by using AWS CI/CD services

✓ **Domain 4: Troubleshooting and Optimization**

- Task Statement 3: Optimize applications by using AWS services and features

In this chapter, we'll delve into two distinct but related topics: management of application configuration and secrets and container orchestration. The former is essential for maintaining the security and portability of your application code, no matter how it is deployed. The latter is a deep dive into container services on AWS. Starting with Elastic Container Service (ECS), we'll explore the most AWS-native way of deploying container-based applications, then take a look at how to run Kubernetes with managed infrastructure and services provided by Elastic Kubernetes Service (EKS).

First, let's take a look at Parameter Store and Secrets Manager, two foundational services that you can use nearly anywhere you interact with AWS to securely manage sensitive values.

Securely Managing Application Configuration and Secrets

As both a security best practice and an invaluable convenience for deployments, it is essential that developers separate application code from configuration and secret values.

Configuration values include items like database URLs, usernames, passwords, API keys, environment names, or any other value that may change from deployment to deployment. Some of these values, like passwords and API keys, are sensitive and must be treated carefully to avoid leaking them to attackers. Others, like environment names or database URLs, may not be sensitive, but are variables that may differ whether you are deploying to a development environment or to production.

Developers who hard-code these values (i.e., by typing them directly in their code bases) run two key risks. First, as part of the code base, hard-coded values must be checked into version control—often on external systems like GitHub—where the risk of exposure is higher, both to unauthorized colleagues and external actors. Second, hard-coded values cannot easily be changed; the code itself must be updated and redeployed again to update a secret.

Instead of hard-coding configuration, developers can store the values in special systems designed to hold them, fetching them at runtime and ensuring that these values never stay in version control. Another benefit is that the same code can then be deployed with a different set of configuration values to different environments.

AWS provides two primary services for externally managing configuration values and secrets: Parameter Store and Secrets Manager.

AWS Parameter Store

As a feature of the larger AWS Systems Manager service, *Parameter Store* allows developers to upload and fetch key-value pairs using the CLI or SDK.

Parameter Store values have three types:

- `String`: A standard plaintext string
- `StringList`: A comma-separated list of values
- `SecureString`: A string value that will be encrypted by a KMS key

In addition, parameters may be standard or advanced. The difference lies primarily in the size and quantity of parameters that may be stored.

Standard vs. Advanced Parameters

Up to 10,000 standard parameters may be stored, free of charge, with each up to 4 KB in size. Advanced parameters cost $0.05 per parameter per month, but can be up to 8 KB in size. You may store 100,000 advanced parameters per account, and unlike standard parameters, they may be shared across accounts. Figure 9.1 shows the creation of standard parameters in Parameter Store.

FIGURE 9.1   AWS Parameter Store

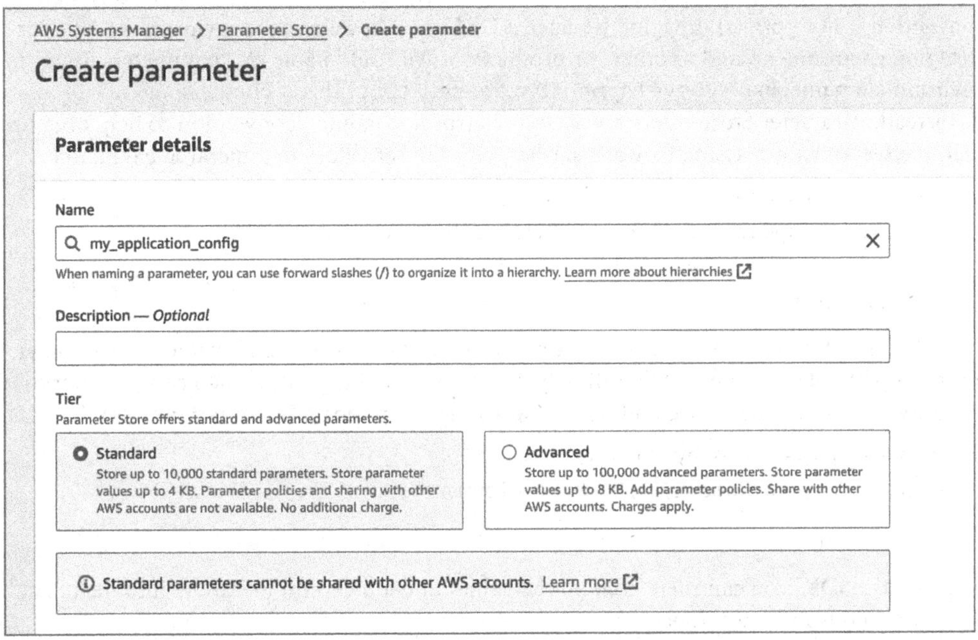

Creating and Fetching Parameters

To create a parameter value, use the AWS Management Console or use the CLI to execute the following command:

```
aws ssm put-parameter \
    --name "MyDatabaseURL" \
    --value "my_url_value" \
    --type String
```

You can then fetch the value by name:

```
aws ssm get-parameter --name "MyDatabaseURL"
```

Storing Encrypted Values

If you give the type `SecureString` when setting the value, Parameter Store will encrypt the data with its default KMS key. In this case, `get-parameter` will retrieve the encrypted value. To fetch the plaintext value, include the command-line parameter `-with-decryption`, as shown here:

```
aws ssm get-parameter --name "MyDatabaseURL" -with-decryption
```

This encryption and decryption is seamless; no special IAM permissions necessary. Provided the caller is allowed to invoke `ssm:GetParameter`, it will be able to fetch and decrypt the value.

Hierarchical Values

In the first code example above, we stored the value `MyDatabaseURL`. However, this naming convention is not optimal. Imagine we have a URL for a development environment, one for a staging environment, and another for production. We could name our parameters using the environment name, like `MyDevelopmentDatabaseURL`, but this is cumbersome.

Instead, Parameter Store offers a way to use a specific naming convention to help organize multiple sets of values. Using forward slashes, you can set values in a hierarchical manner:

```
aws ssm put-parameter \
    --name "MyAppName/Development/DatabaseURL" \
    --value "some_database_url" \
    --type String
```

Then, the CLI command `get-parameters-by-path` will return all values stored under a certain prefix. For example, this call will return any matching value, such as `MyAppName/Development/DatabaseURL` and `MyAppName/Development/DatabasePassword`.

```
aws ssm get-parameters-by-path \
    --path "/MyTeamName/MyAppName/Development"
```

Using the SDK, you can then fetch all the values under a certain hierarchy into memory, as shown in this Python snippet:

```
import boto3
import os


def fetch_and_set_parameters():
```

```python
    # Create a boto3 client for SSM (Systems Manager)
    ssm = boto3.client('ssm')

    # Fetch all parameters under the specified path
    path = '/MyAppName/Development/'
    paginator = ssm.get_paginator('get_parameters_by_path')
    parameters = []

    # Use WithDecryption for SecureString values
    for page in paginator.paginate(Path=path, Recursive=True,
WithDecryption=True):
        parameters.extend(page['Parameters'])

    # Set environment variables
    for param in parameters:
        # Extract the last part of the parameter name as the env var name
        env_var_name = param['Name'].split('/')[-1].upper()
        env_var_value = param['Value']

        # Set the environment variable
        os.environ[env_var_name] = env_var_value
        print(f"Set {env_var_name} = {env_var_value}")

if __name__ == "__main__":
    fetch_and_set_parameters()
```

In addition to helping you organize values, hierarchical naming can help you write IAM policies that let you give permissions based on things like team name, app name, or environment. Imagine the following values:

```
/SalesTeam/MyAppName/Development/DatabaseURL
/SalesTeam/MyAppName/Development/DatabasePassword
/MarketingTeam/MarketingApp/Development/DatabaseURL
```

You can write an IAM policy just for members of the Sales team, allowing them to retrieve only secrets belonging to their team:

```json
{
    "Version": "2012-10-17",
    "Statement": [
        {
            "Effect": "Allow",
            "Action": "ssm:GetParameter",
            "Resource": "arn:aws:ssm:*:*:parameter/SalesTeam/*"
        }
    ]
}
```

Versioning Parameters

Each time you update a Parameter Store value with `put-parameter`, AWS creates a new version of it. You can see this version history with the following command:

```
aws ssm get-parameter-history --name "MyParameterName"
```

To fetch a specific version, add a colon, then the version number to any operation that fetches parameters, like so:

```
aws ssm get-parameter --name "MyDatabaseURL:2" -with-decryption
```

Referencing Parameters from Other Services

In addition to SDK and CLI support, AWS offers ways to fetch Parameter Store values in other AWS services using special syntax. For example, the following CloudFormation code will retrieve a value dynamically from Parameter Store—specifically, version 3 of the value `MyBucketName`:

```
MyS3Bucket:
  Type: 'AWS::S3::Bucket'
  Properties:
    BucketName: '{{resolve:ssm:MyBucketName:3}}'
```

Similarly, the EC2 CLI allows you to reference SSM when naming the AMI on which to base the instance. In this case, we pull the value of a `String` parameter named `MyAMIValue`:

```
aws ec2 run-instances \
    --image-id resolve:ssm:/MyAMIValue \
    --count 1 \
    --instance-type t2.micro \
```

Many other AWS services allow you to use this shorthand for resolving Parameter Store values, so keep on the lookout in AWS documentation, and try to think of ways to use this capability to store configuration outside your code.

Parameter Store is a fantastic option for storing application configuration, and `SecureString` values offer a way to save encrypted secrets. However, for a more complete and secure way of handling sensitive values, AWS has another service: Secrets Manager.

AWS Secrets Manager

AWS Secrets Manager expands on the functionality of Parameter Store by providing features that manage the life cycle of secrets and more tightly integrate with services like RDS.

Rotating Secrets

A best practice for securely handling secret values is to rotate them on a regular basis. For instance, a policy of changing database passwords every 180 days can help limit the impact of inadvertently leaked passwords. Of course, this policy brings complexity, as every client that uses this password must also update how it connects to the database.

Secrets Manager provides two ways of automating this process: managed rotation and rotation by Lambda function.

Managed Rotation

Managed rotation refers to secret rotation that is fully handled by Secrets Manager. These are called *managed secrets,* and many AWS services can take advantage of them, including:

- App Runner
- AWS AppSync
- Amazon Athena
- Amazon Aurora
- AWS CodeBuild
- Amazon Data Firehose
- AWS Elastic Beanstalk
- Amazon Elastic Container Registry
- Amazon Elastic Container Service
- Amazon ElastiCache
- Amazon EventBridge
- Amazon FSx
- Amazon Kinesis Video Streams
- Amazon RDS

Managed rotation refers to any secret whose rotation is fully handled by Secrets Manager.

Fetching Secrets with the Parameter Store API

To help developers transition from Parameter Store to Secrets Manager—or to make it easier to use them in tandem—AWS allows Secrets Manager values to be fetched via the Parameter Store API. If you prefix the secret name with `/aws/reference/secretsmanager`, you can use `get-parameter` as shown here:

```
aws ssm get-parameter \
    --name /aws/reference/secretsmanager/MySecretValue
```

Referencing Secrets from Other Services

As with Parameter Store, Secrets Manager values can be resolved in other AWS services:

```
MyRDSInstance:
  Type: 'AWS::RDS::DBInstance'
  Properties:
    DBName: MyRDSInstance
    AllocatedStorage: '20'
    DBInstanceClass: db.t2.micro
```

```
    Engine: mysql
    MasterUsername: '{{resolve:secretsmanager:MyRDSSecret:SecretString:user
name}}'
    MasterUserPassword: '{{resolve:secretsmanager:MyRDSSecret:SecretString:
password}}'
```

Secrets Manager is supported by many AWS services, making it a great option for securely handling sensitive values in any AWS application scenario.

Container Deployments on AWS

As you have seen, AWS provides an excellent range of tools for automating the provisioning of infrastructure, the deployment of application code, and the configuration of runtime environments.

At the same time, many of these steps can be dramatically simplified by the adoption of container-based deployments. *Docker containers* allow developers to define local environments composed of lightweight, sandboxed operating systems whose configurations (such as packages installed, user groups defined, and files provisioned to the machine) are defined by the developer. On top of this, developers can layer their own application code, after which they can build a Docker *image* that "bakes in" all this configuration.

A *container* is a single instance of a Docker image. They are similar to virtual machines but are more portable, running anywhere that Docker containers may be run. This includes local developer laptops, EC2 instances running the Docker service, and dedicated Docker orchestration environments like the ones provided by AWS. Because so much of the configuration is part of the Docker image, there are many fewer moving parts in a container deployment, meaning troubleshooting can be simplified. Often, issues come down to network access to dependencies (such as a database) or environment variables (such as a database password).

Amazon Elastic Container Registry lets you create repositories where you can upload, version, and tag images for use in AWS services. *Amazon Elastic Container Service (ECS)* allows you to define, schedule, and configure Docker containers for deployment on either a cluster of Amazon EC2 instances or *Fargate*, an AWS-managed, serverless cluster. ECS is Docker orchestration using AWS-native concepts, such as load balancers, security groups, and IAM roles. For those who prefer Kubernetes-based Docker orchestration, *Amazon Elastic Kubernetes Service* automates the deployment of Kubernetes workloads with AWS-native tools. This chapter explores each of these services in detail before concluding with an overview of additional methods to run Docker containers on AWS.

Amazon Elastic Container Registry

Amazon Elastic Container Registry (ECR) is a Docker registry service that is fully compatible with existing Docker CLI tools. Amazon ECR supports resource-level permissions for private repositories and allows you to preserve a secure registry without the need to maintain an additional application. Since it integrates with AWS IAM users and Amazon ECS cluster instances, it can take advantage of AWS IAM users or instance profiles to access and maintain images securely without the need to provide a username and password.

To connect the Docker command-line tool to an ECR repo, use the following command:

```
aws ecr get-login-password --region <region> | docker login --username AWS --password-stdin <YOUR_REPO_URI>
```

The first part of the command generates a password for ECR, which is then piped into the `docker login` command. Subsequent `docker push` commands are directed to your ECR repo. This is demonstrated in the Exercises at the end of this chapter.

Amazon Elastic Container Service

Amazon ECS is a highly scalable, high-performance container orchestration service that supports Docker containers and allows you to easily run and scale containerized applications on AWS. ECS eliminates the need for you to install and operate your own container orchestration software, manage and scale a cluster of virtual machines, or schedule containers on those virtual machines.

With simple API calls, you can launch and stop Docker-enabled applications, query the complete state of your application, and access many familiar features such as IAM roles, security groups, load balancers, Amazon CloudWatch Events, AWS CloudFormation templates, and AWS CloudTrail logs.

Amazon ECS simplifies container management and scheduling across EC2 instance fleets, eliminating the need for separate orchestration or cluster scaling tools. By using an Auto Scaling Group for your cluster, you can even enable ECS to scale its capacity as needed. Fargate further reduces management overhead by deploying containers to a serverless architecture, completely removing cluster management requirements.

To create a cluster and deploy services with ECS, you configure the resource requirements of your containers and specify the desired availability. Amazon ECS handles the rest using an agent running on cluster instances. With AWS Fargate, agent management is unnecessary.

Amazon ECS Concepts

Getting started with ECS requires a high-level understanding of a few concepts. In ECS, individual containers (or an interrelated set of containers) are defined as *tasks*. To scale up and achieve high availability, tasks can be defined as *services* that, like Auto Scaling Groups, automatically maintain a certain number of healthy tasks. Both tasks and services run on a compute layer known as an ECS cluster, which can run on your own EC2 infrastructure or through a serverless, managed service known as Fargate. Each of these concepts is explained in detail next.

Amazon ECS Cluster

Amazon ECS clusters are the foundational infrastructure components on which containers run. EC2-based clusters consist of one or more EC2 instances in your VPC. Each cluster instance must have the ECS agent installed. This agent is responsible for receiving container scheduling/shutdown commands from the ECS service and for reporting the current health status of containers. Figure 9.2 demonstrates an EC2 launch type, where instances make up the ECS cluster.

FIGURE 9.2 Amazon ECS architecture

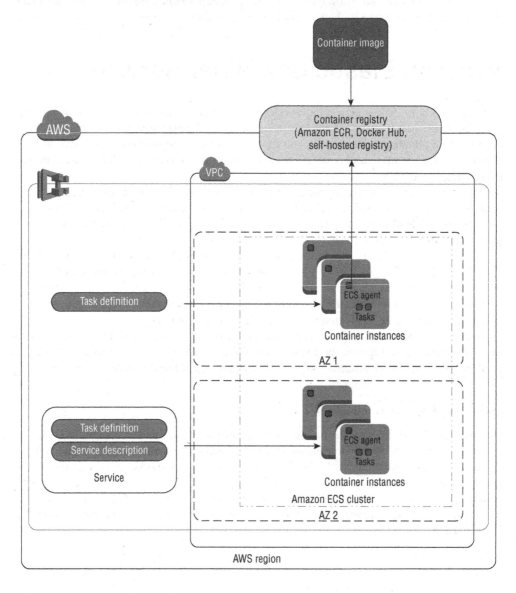

In a Fargate launch type, ECS clusters are no longer made up of EC2 instances. Since the tasks themselves launch on the AWS infrastructure, AWS assigns each one an elastic network interface within a VPC. This provides network connectivity for the container without the need to manage the infrastructure on which it runs. Figure 9.3 demonstrates a Fargate cluster that runs in multiple availability zones (AZs).

FIGURE 9.3   AWS Fargate architecture

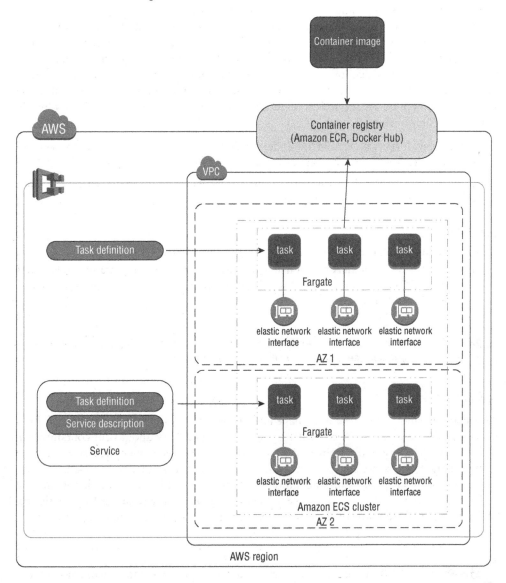

An individual cluster can support both EC2 and Fargate launch types. However, a single cluster instance can belong to only one cluster at a time. EC2 launch types support both on-demand and spot instances, and they allow you to reduce cost for noncritical workloads.

To enable network connectivity for containers that run on your instance, the corresponding task definition must outline port mappings from the container to the host instance. When you create a container instance, you can select the instance type to use. The compute resources available to this instance type will determine how many containers can be run on the instance. For example, if a `t3.micro` instance has one vCPU and 1 GB of RAM, it will not be able to run containers that require two vCPUs.

After you add a container instance to a cluster and you place containers on it, there may be situations where you would need to remove the container from the cluster temporarily, for a regular patch, for example. However, if critical tasks run on a container instance, you may want to wait for the containers to terminate gracefully. Container instance draining can be used to drain running containers from an instance and prevent new ones from being started. Depending on the service's configuration, replacement tasks start before or after the original tasks terminate.

- If the value of `minimumHealthyPercent` is less than 100 percent, the service will terminate the task and launch a replacement.

- If the value is greater than 100 percent, the service will attempt to launch a replacement task before it terminates the original.

Scale Clusters

To make room for additional tasks, you can scale out a cluster with EC2 Auto Scaling Groups. Whether by using an Amazon machine image (AMI) or a user data script, you must ensure that the ECS agent is on every cluster instance. If you terminate instances, any tasks running on them will also halt.

Scaling out a cluster does not also increase the running task count. You use service automatic scaling for this process.

AWS Fargate

AWS Fargate removes the need to manage underlying cluster instances by offering a fully managed, serverless cluster. With Fargate, you only need to think about your container tasks and defining their required resources; AWS takes care of the deployment infrastructure.

With Fargate, there are some restrictions on the types of tasks that you can launch. For example, when you specify a task definition, containers cannot be run in privileged mode. To verify that a given task definition is acceptable by Fargate, use the Requires Capabilities field of the Amazon ECS console or the `--requires-capabilities` command option of the AWS CLI.

AWS Fargate requires that containers launch with the network mode set to awsvpc. This network mode launches within your VPC and assigns an elastic network interface (ENI) to each task, allowing it to have networking properties similar to an EC2 instance.

Containers and Images

 Amazon ECS launches and manages Docker containers. However, Docker is not in scope for the AWS Certified Developer – Associate Exam.

Any workloads that run on Amazon ECS must reside in Docker containers. In a virtual server environment, multiple virtual machines share physical hardware, each of which acts as its own operating system. In a containerized environment, you package components of the operating system itself into containers. This removes the need to run any nonessential aspects of a full-fledged virtual machine to increase portability. In other words, virtual machines share the same physical hardware, while containers share the same operating system.

Container images are similar in concept to AMIs. Images provision a Docker container. You store images in registries, such as a Docker Hub or an Amazon ECR repository.

 You can create your own private image repository; however, AWS Fargate does not support this launch type.

Docker provides mobility and flexibility of your workload to allow containers to be run on any system that supports Docker. Compute resources can be better utilized when you run multiple containers on the same cluster, which makes the best possible use of resources and reduces idle compute capacity. Since you separate service components into containers, you can update individual components more frequently and at reduced risk.

Task Definition

Though you can package entire applications into a single container, it may be more efficient to run multiple smaller containers, each of which contains a subset of functionality of your full application. This is referred to as *service-oriented architecture (SOA)*. In SOA, each unit of functionality for an overall system is contained separately from the rest. Individual services work with one another to perform a larger task. For example, an e-commerce website that uses SOA could have sets of containers for load balancing, credit card processing, order fulfillment, or any other tasks that users require. You design each component of the system as a black box so that other components do not need to be aware of inner workings to interact with them.

A *task definition* is a JSON document that describes what containers launch for your application or system. A single task definition can describe between one and 10 containers and their requirements, referencing images stored in a repository like ECR. Task definitions can also specify compute, networking, and storage requirements, such as which ports to expose to which containers and which volumes to mount.

You should add containers to the same task definition under the following circumstances:

- The containers all share a common life cycle.
- The containers need to run on the same common host or container instance.
- The containers need to share local resources or volumes.

An entire application does not have to deploy with a single task definition. Instead, you should separate larger application segments into separate task definitions. This will reduce the impact of breaking changes in your environment. If you allocate the right-sized container instances, you can also better control scaling and resource consumption of the containers.

After a task definition is created in Amazon ECS, it can be used to launch one or more *tasks*. When you schedule a task, each container defined in the task definition is launched in your cluster via the task scheduler.

Task Definition with Two Containers

The following example demonstrates a task definition with two containers. The first container runs a WordPress installation and binds the container instance's port 80 to the same port on the container. The second container installs MySQL to act as the backend data store of the WordPress container. The task definition also specifies a link between the containers, which allows them to communicate without port mappings if the network setting for the task definition is set to `bridge`.

```
{
  "containerDefinitions": [
    {
      "name": "wordpress",
      "links": [
        "mysql"
      ],
      "image": "wordpress",
      "essential": true,
      "portMappings": [
        {
          "containerPort": 80,
          "hostPort": 80
        }
      ],
      "memory": 500,
      "cpu": 10
    },
    {
      "environment": [
        {
          "name": "MYSQL_ROOT_PASSWORD",
          "value": "password"
```

```
        }
      ],
      "name": "mysql",
      "image": "mysql",
      "cpu": 10,
      "memory": 500,
      "essential": true
    }
  ],
  "family": "hello_world"
}
```

Services

Similar to EC2 Auto Scaling Groups (ASGs), ECS Services are a logical construct that enables you to achieve high availability for your container deployments. Whereas an ASG maintains a certain number of healthy EC2 instances, a service maintains a desired number of healthy ECS tasks. Used in conjunction with a load balancer, ECS Services make your tasks highly available and able to scale up or down in response to load. When creating a *service*, you specify the task definition and number of tasks to maintain at any point in time. Whenever you launch a service, it will create and maintain as many containers as specified in task definition, multiplied by the service's minimum scaling value. If any containers in the task become unhealthy, the service ensures that replacement tasks are launched.

When you define a service, you can also configure deployment strategies to ensure a minimum number of healthy tasks are available to serve requests while other tasks in the service update. The maximumPercent parameter defines the maximum percentage of tasks that can be in the RUNNING or PENDING state. The minimumHealthyPercent parameter specifies the minimum percentage of tasks that must be in a healthy (RUNNING) state during deployments.

For example, say you configure one task for your service, and you would like to ensure that the application is available during deployments. If you set the maximumPercent to 200 percent and minimumHealthyPercent to 100 percent, it will ensure that the new task launches before the old task terminates. If you configure two tasks for your service and some loss of availability is acceptable, you can set maximumPercent to 100 percent and minimumHealthyPercent to 50 percent. This will cause the service scheduler to terminate one task, launch its replacement, and then do the same with the other task. The difference is that the first approach requires double the normal cluster capacity to accommodate the additional tasks.

Load Balancing

You can configure services to run behind a load balancer to distribute traffic automatically to tasks in the service. Amazon ECS supports application load balancers (ALBs) to distribute requests. Of the multiple load balancer types (found under the EC2 service console), ALBs provide several unique features.

Application load balancers route traffic at Layer 7 (HTTP/HTTPS). Because of this, they can take advantage of dynamic host port mapping when you use them in front of Amazon ECS clusters. Remember that whether your tasks run on a cluster consisting of EC2 instances or on the more abstracted Fargate, many will need to listen on ports that are, in turn, exposed by the compute layer. When multiple tasks are scheduled on the same underlying compute instance, they cannot both be exposed on the same port, lest a conflict occur. In this case, ECS will dynamically map container ports to distinct host ports. When fronting an ECS service, ALBs use their Layer 7 capabilities to participate in this dynamic port mapping, ensuring that the right traffic goes to the right port, no matter how many services may be using the same port behind the load balancer.

Scheduled Tasks

If you increase the number of instances in an Amazon ECS cluster, it does not automatically increase the number of running tasks as well. When you configure a service, the service scheduler determines how many tasks run on one or more clusters and automatically starts replacement tasks should any fail. This is especially ideal for long-running tasks such as web servers. If you configure it to do so, the service scheduler will ensure that tasks register with a load balancer.

You can also run a task manually with the RunTask action, or you can run them on a cron-like schedule (such as every N minutes on Tuesdays and Thursdays). This works well for tasks such as log rotation, batch jobs, or other data aggregation tasks.

To dynamically adjust the run task count, use Amazon CloudWatch Alarms in conjunction with Application Auto Scaling to increase or decrease the task count based on alarm status. You can use two approaches for automatically scaling Amazon ECS services and tasks: target tracking policies and step scaling policies.

Target Tracking Policies

Target tracking policies determine when to scale the number of tasks based on a target metric. If the metric is above the target, such as CPU utilization being above 75 percent, Amazon ECS can automatically launch more tasks to bring the metric below the desired value. You can specify multiple target tracking policies for the same service. In the case of a conflict, the policy that would result in the highest task count wins.

Step Scaling Policies

Unlike target tracking policies, *step scaling policies* can continue to scale in or out as metrics increase or decrease. For example, you can configure a step scaling policy to scale out when CPU utilization reaches 75 percent, again at 80 percent, and one final time at 90 percent. With this approach, a single policy can result in multiple scaling activities as metrics increase or decrease.

Task Placement Strategies

Regardless of the method you use, *task placement strategies* determine on which instances tasks launch or which tasks terminate during scaling actions. For example, the spread task placement strategy distributes tasks across multiple AZs as much as possible. Task placement strategies perform on a best-effort basis. If the strategy cannot be honored, such as when there are insufficient compute resources in the AZ you select, ECS will still try to launch the task(s) on other cluster instances. Other strategies include `binpack` (uses CPU and memory on each instance at a time) and `random`.

Task placement strategies associate with specific `attributes`, which are evaluated during task placement. For example, to spread tasks across availability zones, the placement strategy to use is as follows:

```
"placementStrategy": [
    {
        "field": "attribute:ecs.availability-zone",
        "type": "spread"
    }
]
```

Task Placement Constraints

Task placement constraints enforce specific requirements on the container instances on which tasks launch, such as to specify the instance type as `t3.micro`:

```
"placementConstraints": [
    {
        "expression": "attribute:ecs.instance-type == t3.micro",
        "type": "memberOf"
    }
]
```

Amazon ECS Service Discovery

Amazon ECS Service Discovery allows you to assign Amazon Route 53 DNS records automatically for tasks your service manages. To do so, you create a private service namespace for each Amazon ECS cluster. As tasks launch or terminate, the private service namespace updates to include DNS records for each task. A service directory maps DNS records to available service endpoints. Amazon ECS Service Discovery maintains health checks of containers, and it removes them from the service directory should they become unavailable.

To use public namespaces, you must purchase or register the public hosted zone with Amazon Route 53.

Private Image Repositories

Amazon ECS can connect to private image repositories with basic authentication. This is useful to connect to Docker Hub or other private registries with a username and password.

To do so, you must set the ECS_ENGINE_AUTH_TYPE and ECS_ENGINE_AUTH_DATA environment variables with the authorization type and actual credentials to connect. However, you should not set these properties directly. Instead, store your container instance configuration file in an Amazon S3 bucket and copy it to the instance with userdata.

Amazon ECS Container Agent

The *Amazon ECS Agent* is responsible for monitoring the status of tasks that run on cluster instances. If a new task needs to launch, the container agent will download the container images and start or stop containers. If any containers fail health checks, the container agent will replace them. Since the Fargate launch type uses AWS-managed compute resources, you do not need to configure the agent.

To register an instance with an Amazon ECS cluster, you must first install the Amazon ECS agent. This agent installs automatically on Amazon ECS-optimized AMIs.

Users who do not use an ECS-optimized AMI have a few options for installing the agent, such as scripting the installation in EC2 user data or installing it manually and creating a new AMI. However, AWS Systems Manager provides a great option for automating this work. Search the AWS Management Console for **Distributor**, and you will find a service that lets you select a set of EC2 instances and push certain packages to them. Distributor is a great way to install AWS-supplied support software, such as the CodeDeploy agent and ECS agent.

The Amazon ECS container agent updates regularly and can update on your instance(s) without any service interruptions. To perform updates to the agent, replace the container instance entirely or use the Update Container Agent command on ECS-optimized AMIs.

> You cannot perform agent updates on Windows instances using these methods. Instead, terminate the instance and create a new server in its absence.

Using Amazon ECS with AWS CodePipeline

When you select Amazon ECS as a deployment provider, there is no option to create the cluster and service as part of the pipeline creation process. This must be done ahead of time. After the cluster creates, select the appropriate cluster and service names in the AWS Code-Pipeline console, as shown in Figure 9.4.

You must provide an image filename as part of this configuration. This is a JSON-formatted document inside your code repository or archive or as an output build artifact, which specifies the service's container name and image tag. We recommend that the cluster contain at least two Amazon EC2 instances so that one can act as primary while the other handles deployment of new containers.

FIGURE 9.4   Amazon ECS as a deployment provider

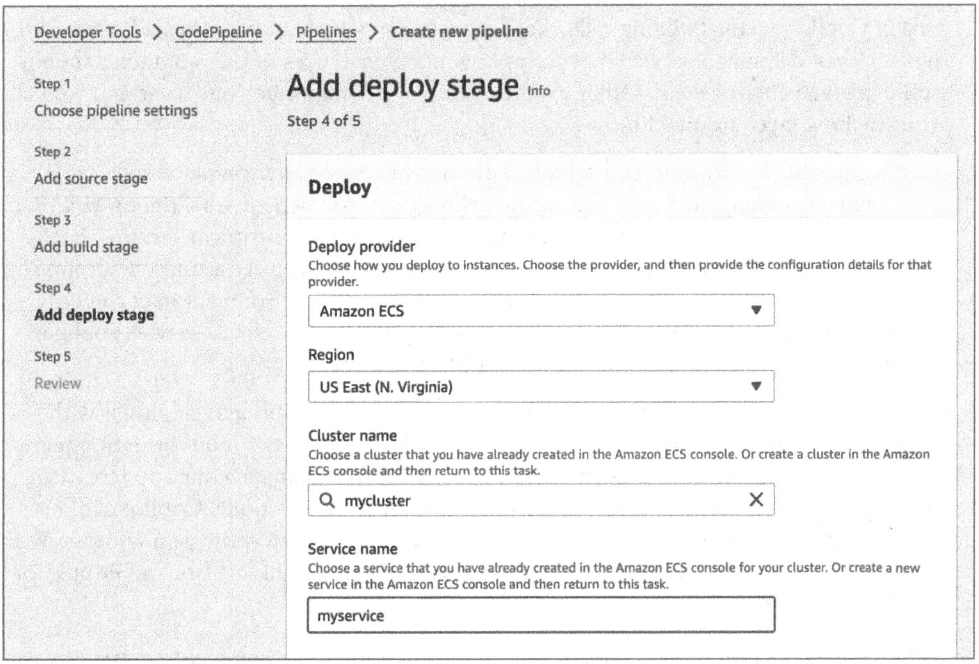

Amazon Copilot

With v2 of its command-line interface for ECS, AWS has taken a new "application-focused" approach, which they have called *AWS Copilot*. AWS Copilot is a command-line experience whose aim is to simplify the deployment of ECS-based applications to its most fundamental elements.

Copilot provides wizards and default infrastructure choices to get you started on a variety of architectures, such as Request-Driven Web Service, Load Balanced Web Service, and Worker Service.

Detailed documentation can be found on AWS's GitHub space at `https://aws .github.io/copilot-cli`.

AWS Copilot Basic Concepts

Copilot is designed to abstract some of the complexity of container-based deployments and let you focus on building apps. To this end, it is an "opinionated" framework. If you learn to conceive of your app in Copilot terms, it can be very helpful in standing up applications and automating deployments quickly. Here are the basic concepts of Copilot:

Applications   An application is the logic container (not to be confused with a Docker container) encapsulating everything about your app. Your application may consist of multiple services running in multiple environments.

Services   A Copilot service is the definition of a container workload, mapping directly to ECS services. For instance, your application may require a database service. Defining this in Copilot means building a Docker image to run your database (say, a PostgreSQL image), then defining a service that states how many instances of that container should run in a given environment. Other examples of services might be your front-end web UI, your caching layer, or an API.

Environments   Environments are logical divisions between environments such as development, staging, and production. By defining environments with Copilot, you're able to deploy multiple versions of your application and its constituent services. Each may have a different configuration, access rules defined by security groups, environment variables, and data. For example, while your development environment may run only one PostgreSQL container, your production environment can define a service configuration that ensures high availability of this critical component.

Pipelines   Once you have established a Copilot application, you may deploy it with Copilot command-line tools. Behind the scenes, AWS constructs CloudFormation templates to stand up the necessary infrastructure, letting you manage your app (creating, tearing down, and scaling) as one unit via Copilot. After this is done, Copilot can initialize pipelines for you, using CodePipeline to further automate your deployments. With Copilot Pipelines, you can easily stand up deployments that kick off from a Git push or pull request merge.

Each of these concepts is clearly relayed in the Copilot interface, which offers friendly step-by-step wizards and helper text, as shown in Figure 9.5.

AWS Copilot Installation

Copilot can be installed through Homebrew, a popular Mac- or Linux-based package manager available at `https://brew.sh`. With Homebrew installed, type the following at a command line:

```
$ brew install aws/tap/copilot-cli
```

Further details, including Windows installation steps, are available at `https://aws .github.io/copilot-cli/docs/getting-started/verify`.

To configure the tool to authenticate as a particular AWS user, set up a named profile as described in Chapter 1, "Introduction to Amazon Web Services," in the section "CLI Named Profiles." Suppose you have a profile named `copilot_user`. Commands can be appended with `--profile copilot_user`; alternatively, you can run `export AWS_ PROFILE=copilot_user` for all Copilot (or CLI) commands in that terminal session to use the `copilot_user` profile.

AWS Copilot Commands and Configuration

Many of the commands in Copilot kick off guided wizards that will ask you questions, helping you configure your application from the commend line.

FIGURE 9.5   Amazon Copilot for ECS

```
● ● ●                        apps — -zsh — 90×29
> copilot
🏮 Launch and manage containerized applications on AWS.

Commands
  Getting Started ⚓
    init        Create a new ECS or App Runner application.
    docs        Open the copilot docs.

  Develop ☼
    app         Commands for applications.
                Applications are a collection of services and environments.
    env         Commands for environments.
                Environments are deployment stages shared between services.
    svc         Commands for services.
                Services are long-running ECS or App Runner services.
    job         Commands for jobs.
                Jobs are tasks that are triggered by events.
    task        Commands for tasks.
                One-off Amazon ECS tasks that terminate once their work is done.
    run         Run the workload locally.

  Release 🚀
    pipeline    Commands for pipelines.
                Continuous delivery pipelines to release services.
    deploy      Deploy one or more Copilot jobs or services.

  Extend 🛢
    storage     Commands for working with storage and databases.
    secret      Commands for secrets.
```

Note that when you create a service or environment, Copilot creates a *manifest* file, a YAML-formatted document that contains all the configurations of a particular application, service, or environment. These files can be checked into version control, then edited and redeployed with Copilot command-line commands or Copilot Pipelines to update your app.

The command copilot app init establishes a new application definition. Not much happens until you take the next step, copilot init, which will prompt you to specify an architecture (such as Load Balanced Web Service), a Dockerfile, and an environment name. This step creates the basic starting point for a Copilot application.

The command copilot env init asks you about how you'd like to deploy your application, then stands up all the necessary AWS infrastructure for it. It also creates the environment manifest file in your code base. It can be useful to run this command before running copilot app init so that you establish the environment manifest and can configure it before attempting your first deployment.

Once your application and environment are ready, copilot svc deploy builds your Docker image locally, pushes to ECR, and deploys it to ECS in keeping with your configuration choices.

The command copilot secret init can be used to manage application secrets, such as API keys or database passwords, using AWS Secrets Manager. Copilot takes care of creating those secrets and making sure they are available as environment variables to your running service. These values can be defined individually or via a YAML file you create that contains multiple environment variables.

Copilot apps can be deployed either to an AWS-managed VPC (the default) or into your private VPC. If you choose the latter, you'll need to follow several more configuration steps to specify the correct VPC, subnets, and network communication configuration.

Once you have successfully deployed an app from the command line, `copilot pipeline init` can walk you through the steps of configuring a CodePipeline deployment.

Copilot can be a great way to get started with container-based application deployments quickly, using some common idioms familiar to application developers.

Amazon Elastic Kubernetes Service

Kubernetes is a widely adopted open source platform for deploying and managing container-based workloads. With Elastic Kubernetes Service (EKS), Amazon gives AWS users a way to rapidly deploy managed Kubernetes environments while taking advantage of many AWS-native tools, such as the use of IAM for managing permissions between services, security groups for controlling network accessibility, CloudWatch for centralized logging, and AWS Secrets Manager for storing and provisioning sensitive values. As a fully Kubernetes-compliant system, EKS is compatible with all existing Kubernetes tooling and is a simple migration target for Kubernetes workloads run locally or on other cloud providers.

EKS Foundational Concepts

Kubernetes deployment environments are logically divided into two layers: the *control plane* and the *worker nodes*. The control plane manages the worker nodes, schedules (deploys) containers (as groups called "pods," similar to ECS tasks or services), and responds to events in the worker nodes, such as the unexpected termination of a container. Its job is to make sure the Kubernetes environment always matches your desired configuration in terms of what is deployed and how it is scaled. It is also the layer that runs foundational administrative components like `kube-apiserver` (the Kubernetes API) and `etcd`, the key-value store that provides the data store for cluster management and configuration.

Control Plane

Out of the box, EKS provides a fully managed, serverless control plane for EKS. This means that you can leave the creation, scaling, and administration of the control plane—and all those foundational components—to AWS. EKS's managed control plane is spread over three availability zones, ensuring high availability. This is the layer that exposes the Kubernetes API, with which administrative tools and the worker nodes communicate to manage cluster activities.

Worker Nodes

The other critical layer of a Kubernetes deployment is a cluster of worker nodes—the infrastructure on which pods are deployed. As with ECS, this cluster can be deployed on your own Auto Scaling Group or in a fully serverless configuration with Fargate. The nodes in this layer can use security groups to govern network accessibility, just like any compute on EC2.

The EKS cluster can be configured with multiple node types:

- **AWS Fargate:** As with ECS, in this mode, compute is hidden, fully managed by Amazon.
- **Self-managed nodes:** Similar to ECS's EC2-based clusters, in this type, you provide the compute and manage your own scaling. This type can be based on an Auto Scaling Group, which will let you automate some of the scaling policies.
- **Managed node groups:** In this mode, the compute layer is still on EC2, but it is launched, managed, patched, and scaled by AWS.

These node types can be mixed to create a cluster with heterogeneous management and scaling behavior.

EKS on Spot

When running on EC2, the worker node layer can use *spot instances*. *Spot instances* are EC2 instances that Amazon makes available when an availability zone has slack capacity. To maximize the utilization of compute, AWS incentivizes customers to purchase spot instances by offering them at a much cheaper than on-demand per-hour cost. This can mean a fraction of the normal run-rate of EC2 purchases. The only downside is that spot instances are susceptible to termination at a moment's notice. This makes them incompatible with many traditional workloads, but quite viable as a compute layer for distributed applications that can handle the loss of an individual node.

Container-based workloads like those run on EKS, therefore, can be a great match; your Kubernetes configuration defines a desired number of pods to replicate, and the control plane ensures that number of containers are always running, even if one happens to terminate because its spot instance has terminated.

The EKS control plan and worker nodes make up the EKS cluster, as shown in Figure 9.6. The control plane, managed by AWS, presents the Kubernetes API, through which users may deploy and manage the cluster with the AWS Management Console or multiple different command-line tools. `eksctl`, `kubectl`, and EKS add-ons are described in the following sections.

EKS Console

The EKS Console provides a web-based front end to the EKS-managed control plane, which provides the API for Kubernetes administration. The EKS Console is accessible from the AWS Management Console and lets EKS administrators monitor the state of the cluster, the distribution of pods, the status of nodes, and more. It also provides an interface for managing the configuration of your deployments and the cluster itself.

FIGURE 9.6   Amazon EKS architecture

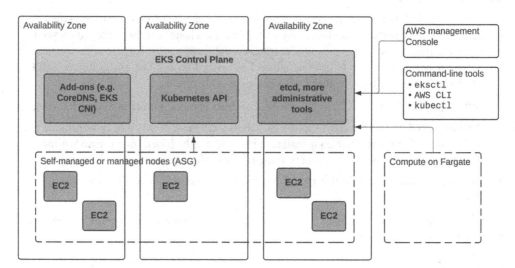

Command-Line Tool *eksctl*

While the AWS CLI provides many commands for interacting with EKS, AWS provides a more robust, specific tool for managing your EKS infrastructure with eksctl. Available at http://eksctl.io, this tool is the "official CLI for Amazon EKS" and lets you do everything from creating clusters to managing nodes to deploying pods.

EKS Add-ons

In addition to basics like etcd and kube-apiserver, EKS allows you to preconfigure your control plane with add-ons. The list is limited, including commonly used tools like kube-proxy, CoreDNS, and the EKS CNI (Container Network Infrastructure plug-in, described in a moment), all three installed by default in a new cluster. In addition to these add-ons, EKS lets you optionally install the EKS Pod Identity Agent, which enables the use of IAM roles to manage AWS resource-based permissions for pods running on your cluster, and an add-on for *AWS GuardDuty*, which provides security monitoring for your worker nodes.

Networking

EKS is fully Kubernetes compliant and compatible with all Kubernetes plug-ins. AWS maintains the Amazon VPC Container Network Infrastructure (CNI) plug-in to allow Kubernetes to assign each pod a unique IP address and enable pods to communicate with each other and other services within the VPC. Worker node network accessibility is managed by security groups, just like any EC2 instance.

Security Groups for Pods

Security groups on nodes offer a coarse-grained approach to network security that, while useful, may present difficulties when you are running diverse workloads that should not all share the same level of access. To achieve distinct security behavior, you may be forced to segment your pods across different purpose-built nodes with distinct security groups, which can be inefficient and costly; after all, you get the best utilization when your pods are packed onto as few nodes as possible. What you need is pod-level security. Adding the AWS-managed IAM policy `AmazonEKSVPCResourceController` to your cluster's IAM role will allow you to assign security groups at the pod level, letting you think less about instances and more about your applications.

Storage

When using Fargate-managed or EC2-based worker nodes, you may mount EFS filesystems for storage on your pods. When using EC2 only, EBS volumes are also an option for persistent storage. To help provision and attach EBS volumes to your pods, AWS provides another plug-in: the Amazon Elastic Block Store (EBS) Container Storage Infrastructure (CSI) driver, which can be installed as a container in your cluster.

Configuring *kubectl*

kubectl is the Kubernetes native command-line tool. This tool can be configured to work with an EKS cluster, letting you continue to use familiar Kubernetes tooling with EKS.

To point it to your EKS installation, begin by updating your kubeconfig file to include the EKS cluster details. Run the following command with the AWS CLI:

```
aws eks update-kubeconfig --region YOUR_REGION --name YOUR_CLUSTER_NAME
```

This command fetches the cluster details and updates the kubeconfig file, typically located at ~/.kube/config. With the updated kubeconfig file, you can now use kubectl to interact with your EKS cluster. Verify the configuration by running kubectl get svc, which should display the services running in the cluster.

Scaling EKS

EKS supports multiple ways to scale your applications in response to load or resource demand:

Cluster Autoscaler   The Cluster Autoscaler operates at the node level, manipulating the Auto Scaling configuration of your cluster to automatically adjust the number of worker nodes based on resource usage. The Cluster Autoscaler works only with EC2-based clusters, since they are managed with Auto Scaling Groups (ASGs), unlike Fargate, where the management is abstracted from you. To work, this tool must be deployed to your cluster as an add-on pod, and you must configure IAM permissions to allow this pod to manipulate the Auto Scaling Group.

Horizontal Pod Autoscaler   The Horizontal Pod Autoscaler (HPA) is a standard Kubernetes tool that works at the level of pods, automatically scaling the number of pod replicas based on observed CPU utilization or other custom metrics. To start using it, you must ensure that the Kubernetes metric server is running; otherwise, there are no installation steps. You configure the autoscaler with `kubectl`; for details, see `https://docs.aws.amazon.com/eks/latest/userguide/horizontal-pod-autoscaler.html`.

Vertical Pod Autoscaler   The Vertical Pod Autoscaler (VPA) also operates at the pod level, updating the CPU and RAM resources allocated to a pod based on observed CPU utilization or other custom metrics. The Horizontal Autoscaler is deployed as a Kubernetes add-on; for details, see `https://docs.aws.amazon.com/eks/latest/userguide/vertical-pod-autoscaler.html`.

Registering an Existing Cluster

EKS allows you to register existing Kubernetes clusters with the EKS service. In this scenario, you bring your own environment running on existing infrastructure, whether directly on EC2 or deployed using a service like Rancher or Red Hat OpenShift. AWS does not provision a managed control plane because your cluster is already expected to have one. However, by registering your cluster with EKS, you gain the ability to integrate with all the AWS services available to native EKS clusters, such as integration with ECR as an image store, IAM permissions, EBS and EFS storage, security groups, and CloudWatch.

Other Container Deployment Options

ECS and EKS are not the only ways to run containers on AWS. While these two options provide full-fledged orchestration and are therefore ideal for persistent container-based applications that must scale and have high availability, there are a few other ways to run containers on AWS.

Containers on EC2

With the OS-level access provided by a simple EC2 instance, it's easy to install Docker and run containers directly on EC2. You can even fully manage your own cluster on any orchestration system you prefer, from Docker Swarm to Kubernetes itself—but you'll oversee all the server and configuration management that is handled by the higher-order services of ECS and EKS.

Containers on Lambda

AWS Lambda, which we cover in depth in Chapter 12, "Serverless Compute," allows you to deploy and run code directly on AWS without provisioning any infrastructure. In addition to the out-of-the-box runtimes provided by Lambda, such as Java and Python, AWS allows you to deploy functions in containers. This lets developers run code in a serverless way using any language or framework they desire, whether or not it's natively supported by Lambda. In addition, this option allows you to deploy larger functions to Lambda; container-based functions can be up to 500 MB, while zipped packages can only be 250 MB unzipped (50 MB zipped).

Containers on Beanstalk

We previously discussed how AWS Elastic Beanstalk lets developers deploy web applications on a number of predefined stacks. Similar to Lambda, Beanstalk has a container-based deployment option that can deploy to EC2 or ECS. In both cases, this allows developers to use the Beanstalk tooling for runtimes that are not natively supported by the service. With the ECS option, developers have a way to automate deployments to ECS, though the integrations with CodePipeline (or the ones created by Copilot) described earlier are better long-term solutions, integrating your deployments with version control.

Summary

This chapter took you into the details of managing configuration and secrets on Parameter Store and AWS Secrets Manager, two tools that make it possible to manage application data in a secure, centralized manner.

We also explored container-based deployments and the services AWS provides to enable highly available, scalable, and managed deployments with ECS and EKS.

Amazon ECS supports Docker containers, and it allows you to run and scale containerized applications on AWS. ECS eliminates the need to install and operate your own container orchestration software, manage and scale a cluster of virtual machines, or schedule containers on those virtual machines.

AWS Fargate reduces management further as it deploys containers to serverless architecture and removes cluster management requirements. To create a cluster and deploy services, you configure the resource requirements of containers and availability requirements. ECS manages the rest through an agent that runs on cluster instances. Fargate requires no agent management.

ECS clusters are the foundational infrastructure components on which containers run. Clusters consist of Amazon EC2 instances in your Amazon VPC. Each cluster instance has an agent installed that is responsible for receiving scheduling/shutdown commands from the ECS service and reporting the current health status of containers (restart or replace).

Amazon Elastic Kubernetes Service (EKS) is a managed Kubernetes service that makes it easy for you to run Kubernetes on AWS without needing to install, operate, and maintain your own Kubernetes control plane. EKS is certified Kubernetes compliant, meaning that existing applications running on Kubernetes are compatible with EKS. This service provides a highly available and secure Kubernetes control plane that runs across multiple AWS availability zones to eliminate a single point of failure.

EKS worker nodes can be deployed on compute in several modes, from serverless with Fargate to self-managed on EC2 to AWS-managed EC2 clusters. Incorporating spot instances into your worker nodes can provide a great way to drive down costs for workloads that are resilient to node failure. You can connect EKS to your existing Kubernetes clusters on site, if you choose. Whether fully in the cloud or running on-premises, EKS brings the advantage of AWS-managed services and integration with common AWS concepts such as IAM role permissions and security groups.

Exam Essentials

Know the components of an Amazon ECS cluster. A cluster is the foundational infrastructure component on which containers are run. Clusters are made up of one or more Amazon EC2 instances, or they can be run on AWS-managed infrastructure using AWS Fargate. A task definition is a JSON file that describes what containers to launch on a cluster, compute, networking, and storage requirements. A service launches on a cluster and specifies the task definition and number of tasks to maintain. If any containers become unhealthy, the service is responsible for launching replacements.

Know the difference between Amazon ECS and AWS Fargate launch types. The Fargate launch type uses AWS-managed infrastructure to launch tasks. As a customer, you are no longer required to provision and manage cluster instances. With Fargate, each cluster instance is assigned a network interface in your VPC. ECS launch types require a cluster in your account, which you must manage over time.

Know how to scale running tasks in a cluster. Changing the number of instances in a cluster does not automatically cause the number of running tasks to scale in or out. You can use target tracking policies and step scaling policies to scale tasks automatically based on target metrics. A target tracking policy determines when to scale based on metrics such as CPU utilization or network traffic. Target tracking policies keep metrics within a certain boundary. For example, you can launch additional tasks if CPU utilization is above 75 percent. Step scaling policies can continuously scale as metrics increase or decrease. You can configure a step scaling policy to scale tasks out when CPU utilization reaches 75 percent and again at 80 percent and 90 percent. A single step scaling policy can result in multiple scaling activities.

Know how images are stored in Elastic Container Registry (ECR).   ECR is a Docker registry service that is fully compatible with existing Docker tools. ECR supports resource-level permissions for private repositories, and it allows you to maintain a secure registry without the need to maintain additional instances/applications.

Understand Elastic Kubernetes Service (EKS) cluster architecture.   EKS distinguishes between the control plane, managed by AWS, and the data plane, which consists of worker nodes provisioned within your account. The control plane is responsible for running essential Kubernetes components, whereas the data plane encompasses the EC2 instances that execute your pod workloads.

Know how to leverage EKS add-ons and integrated AWS services.   While EKS provides a standard Kubernetes control plane, it also offers add-ons like the AWS VPC CNI plugin for integrating Kubernetes networking with your VPC. Other add-ons enable using AWS services like IAM roles for pod identity and GuardDuty for security monitoring of worker nodes.

Exercises

EXERCISE 9.1

Launching an Amazon ECS Fargate Cluster

1.   Navigate to the Elastic Container Service section of AWS.

2.   Click Create Cluster.

3.   For Cluster Name, type **DemoCluster**.

4.   Keep all defaults, including Fargate for infrastructure.

5.   Click Create.

EXERCISE 9.2

Creating an ECR Repo and Pushing an Image to It

To complete this demo, you must have Docker installed on your computer. Instructions can be found at `https://docs.docker.com`. You must also have the AWS CLI installed and configured with a user who has permissions on ECR.

1.   Navigate to the Elastic Container Registry section of AWS.

2.   Note your AWS region in the top menu bar; for this demo, we'll use **us-east-1**.

3. Click Create Repository.

4. Under Repository Name, after the pregenerated prefix, enter **wordpress**.

5. Keep all other defaults and click Create Repository.

6. You'll be taken to the list of repositories. Copy the URI of your repo.

7. From a command line on a computer with Docker installed and running, type

```
docker pull wordpress
aws ecr get-login-password --region us-east-1 | docker login --username AWS
--password-
        stdin <YOUR_REPO_URI>
```

8. These steps retrieve the off-the-shelf WordPress image from Docker Hub and establish a login connection to your ECR repo. Now, you will tag the image (using the tag latest, which could be anything) and push it to ECR:

```
docker tag wordpress <YOUR_REPO_URI>:latest
docker push <YOUR_REPO_URI>:latest
```

9. Back in your browser, click into your repo and observe that the image has been pushed with the tag latest.

10. Click Copy URI to put the repo URI in your clipboard for the next exercise.

EXERCISE 9.3

Creating a Task Definition

1. Navigate to the Elastic Container Service section of AWS.

2. In the left-hand menu, click Task Definitions.

3. Click Create New Task Definition and choose the first option, Create New Task Definition.

4. For Task Definition Family Name, enter **WordPress**.

5. Keep the defaults. Launch Type should be Fargate.

6. (Optional) Modify the CPU and memory allocated to this task definition.

7. (Optional) Add environment variables (not needed for this exercise). These values can be overridden when you actually launch a task.

Note that when you leave Task Role blank, AWS will autogenerate one with the permissions necessary for ECS to launch tasks.

8. (Optional) Provide a Task Execution Role (not needed for this exercise), which will allow code in the container to interact with AWS services via the SDK or CLI.

9. Scroll to the Container - 1 section.

10. For Name, enter **WordPress** and for URI, enter the ECR repo URI from the previous exercise. It should end with **:latest**.

11. Leave Port Mappings at the default. The basic settings will map port 80 inside the container to an assigned port number outside.

12. Scroll down and click Create.

EXERCISE 9.4

Launching a Task

1. Navigate to the Elastic Container Service section of AWS.

2. Click Clusters and click the link labeled "DemoCluster" to view details of your cluster.

3. Scroll down and click the Tasks tab.

4. Click Run New Task.

5. Scroll to Deployment Configuration and for Family, select Wordpress.

6. Expand the Networking section and select your account's VPC and at least one public subnet.

7. Under Security Group, choose Create A New Security Group. Rename it **http-from-world**.

8. For Port Range, enter **80**.

9. For Source, select Anywhere. Note that this will make this container task accessible to anyone in the world and may not be a suitable security group for a non-exercise scenario.

10. Ensure Public IP is toggled on.

11. (Optional) Override the default Task Definition settings (e.g., Environment Variables under Container Overrides).

12. Click Create.

13. Back on the details page for DemoCluster, click the Tasks tab to view running Tasks.

14. Click the task ID of your running task. Under Configuration, note the Public IP, and click Open Address.

EXERCISE 9.4 *(continued)*

You should now be seeing WordPress running in your browser.

To clean up:

15. Go to Clusters, and click your DemoCluster.

16. Click Tasks, then Stop ➤ Stop All. Follow the directions to stop all tasks.

17. Still on the Cluster Details page, click Delete Cluster.
    Keep your ECR repo for the next exercise.

EXERCISE 9.5

Creating an IAM Role for EKS

1. Navigate to the Identity and Access Management (IAM) section of AWS.

2. In the left-hand menu, click Roles, then Create Role.

3. Keep Trusted Entity Type as AWS Service.

4. Under Use Case, select EKS.

5. In the resulting set of choices, select EKS - Cluster.

6. Click Next.

7. Review the permissions given to this role: AmazonEKSClusterPolicy.

8. Click Next.

9. On the next page, enter the name **MyEKSClusterPolicy**.

10. Click Create Role.

EXERCISE 9.6

Creating an EKS Cluster with *eksctl*

This exercise assumes you have already installed and configured the AWS CLI with credentials that have permissions for the EKS service.

1. Follow the directions at http://eksctl.io to download and install the command-line tool eksctl.

2. Run the following command to create a new cluster:

```
eksctl create cluster --name DemoCluster --region us-east-1 --managed
```

The managed keyword tells EKS to deploy a managed EC2 cluster. This creates a cluster of worker nodes based on EC2 that AWS manages for you.

EXERCISE 9.7

Configuring *kubectl*

This exercise assumes you have installed kubectl on your local computer. For more information, see http://kubernetes.io.

1. From a terminal with kubectl and the AWS CLI configured with a user with EKS permissions, enter the following:

```
aws eks update-kubeconfig --region us-east-1 --name DemoCluster
```

If you see "Cluster status is creating," wait and run this command after your cluster is in the Active state.

2. Confirm the connection with **kubectl get svc**.

EXERCISE 9.8

Deploying WordPress to EKS

1. Create a file named **wordpress-deployment.yml**.

2. Enter the following code, being sure to replace the ECR repo URI with your own, including the latest tag:

```
apiVersion: apps/v1
kind: Deployment
metadata:
  name: wordpress
spec:
  replicas: 1
  selector:
    matchLabels:
      app: wordpress
  template:
```

```
  metadata:
    labels:
      app: wordpress
  spec:
    containers:
    - name: wordpress
      image: <YOUR_ECR_REPO_URI_HERE>
      ports:
      - containerPort: 80
```

3. Apply the deployment with kubectl:

```
kubectl apply -f wordpress-deployment.yaml
```

4. Observe that the wordpress pod has been created by going to the EKS Cluster in your web browser and looking at the Resources tab. You will see a pod with a name similar to wordpress-c99bf9f19-6vg7j.

5. Create an ingress service to allow access to this wordpress pod.

6. Enter the following code into a new file called **wordpress-service.yml**:

```
apiVersion: v1
kind: Service
metadata:
  name: wordpress
spec:
  type: LoadBalancer
  ports:
  - port: 80
    targetPort: 80
  selector:
    app: wordpress
```

7. Apply the service with **kubectl apply -f wordpress-service.yaml**.

Validating WordPress and Cleaning Up

1. Discover the URI of the load balancer service with kubectl get services. You will see output like this:

```
NAME        TYPE        CLUSTER-IP      EXTERNAL-IP
kubernetes  ClusterIP   10.100.0.1      <none>
```

```
wordpress    LoadBalancer    10.100.211.64    adbxyz-<acctnum>.us-east-
1.elb.amazonaws.com
```

2. Copy the `external-ip` value of the `wordpress LoadBalancer` and enter it into a web browser. Note that while the containers come online, you may need to wait a few moments for the page to load.

3. Verify WordPress has loaded.

4. To clean up:

   a. Navigate to the EKS Console and select Clusters.

   b. Click the link labeled "DemoCluster" to see details of your cluster.

   c. Select the Compute tab, scroll to Node Groups, then select and delete any node groups found.

   d. When all node groups have disappeared, click Delete Cluster.

Review Questions

1. When using AWS Fargate with Amazon ECS, which of the following are you responsible for managing?

   A. The underlying EC2 instances

   B. The container orchestration engine

   C. The task definitions and services

   D. Restarting failed tasks within a service

2. When configuring an Amazon ECS service, what does the `minimumHealthyPercent` parameter control?

   A. The minimum number of tasks that must be running during a deployment

   B. The minimum percentage of tasks that must be healthy during a deployment

   C. The threshold number of container instances that must be available in the cluster before a scaling event is triggered

   D. The threshold of tasks that must be running before AWS billing kicks in for ECS

3. You have an Amazon ECS cluster that runs on a single service with one task. The cluster currently contains enough instances to support the containers you define in your task, with no additional compute resources to spare (other than those needed by the underlying OS and Docker). Currently the service is configured with a maximum in-service percentage of 100 percent and a minimum of 100 percent. When you attempt to update the service, nothing happens for an extended period of time, as the replacement task appears to be stuck as it launches. How would you resolve this? (Choose two.)

   A. The current configuration prevents new tasks from starting because of insufficient resources. Add enough instances to the cluster to support the additional task temporarily.

   B. The current configuration prevents new tasks from starting because of insufficient resources. Modify the configuration to have a maximum in-service percentage of 200 percent and a minimum of 0 percent.

   C. Configure the cluster to leverage an AWS Auto Scaling Group and scale out additional cluster instances when CPU utilization is over 90 percent.

   D. Submit a new update to replace the one that appears to be failing.

4. Which party is responsible for patching and maintaining underlying clusters when you use the AWS Fargate launch type?

   A. The customer

   B. Amazon Web Services (AWS)

   C. Docker

   D. Independent software vendors

5. What component is responsible for stopping and starting containers on an Amazon Elastic Container Service (ECS) cluster instance?

    A. The Amazon ECS agent running on the instance

    B. The Amazon ECS service role

    C. AWS Systems Manager

    D. The customer

6. What is service-oriented architecture (SOA)?

    A. The use of multiple AWS services to decouple infrastructure components and achieve high availability

    B. A software design practice where applications divide into discrete components (services) that communicate with each other in such a way that individual services do not rely on one another for their successful operation

    C. Involves multiple teams to develop application components with no knowledge of other teams and their components

    D. Leasing services from different vendors instead of doing internal development

7. How many containers can a single task definition describe?

    A. 1

    B. Up to 3

    C. Up to 5

    D. Up to 10

8. When using Amazon ECS, which of the following is the most secure way to store and provide access to sensitive data that your containers need at runtime?

    A. Store the sensitive data in the task definition.

    B. Store the sensitive data in the container image.

    C. Store the sensitive data in AWS Systems Manager Parameter Store and access it via the ECS agent.

    D. Store the sensitive data in AWS Secrets Manager and inject it into the container as environment variables.

9. You have a web proxy application that you would like to deploy in containers with the use of Amazon Elastic Container Service (ECS). Typically, your application binds to port 80 on the instance on which it runs. How can you use an application load balancer to run more than one proxy container on each instance in your cluster?

    A. Do not configure the container to bind to port 80. Instead, configure application load balancing (ALB) with dynamic host port mapping so that a random port is bound. The ALB will route traffic coming in on port 80 to the port on which the container is listening.

    B. Configure a port address translation (PAT) instance in Amazon Virtual Private Cloud (VPC).

    C. You can't; if the container binds to a specific port, only one copy can launch per instance.

    D. Configure a classic load balancer to use dynamic host port mapping.

10. Which Amazon Elastic Container Service (ECS) task placement policy ensures that tasks are distributed as much as possible in a single cluster?

   A. `spread`

   B. `binpack`

   C. `random`

   D. `least cost`

11. Your application requires many different values to be set at runtime, including sensitive values like database passwords and nonsensitive values like API base URLs. Each one varies whether the application is deployed in development, staging, or production mode. What is the best approach to managing all these values?

   A. Store each value in Parameter Store as either `String` or `SecureString` types. Give each parameter a name like `ENV_VALUE_NAME`, and allow your code permissions to loop through all system parameters, comparing environment names to fetch the right ones.

   B. Store all values as a JSON array and place them in Secrets Manager. Give each secret a name like `MYAPP_ENV_ALL_SECRETS` and parse the JSON bundle in your app.

   C. Containerize your application. Hard-code the secrets into your application image, building a distinct image for each environment, and uploading to an ECR repo that is set as Encrypted.

   D. Use a combination of services. Store nonsensitive values in Parameter Store with names like `/myapp/env/secret_value`, and use hierarchical fetch to grab all `/myapp/env/*` values at once. Maintain sensitive values in Secrets Manager.

12. When using Amazon ECS with Fargate, which of the following networking modes is required for containers?

   A. Bridge

   B. Host

   C. awsvpc

   D. None

13. You are deploying a Python app via ECS that connects to an RDS database. The RDS username and password must be changed regularly to comply with information security policy in your organization. What is the best approach?

   A. Include the username and password as environment variables in your ECS task definition and coordinate with database administrators to deploy a new version whenever they update the password.

   B. Store the username and password as `SecureString` values in Parameter Store and fetch them in your Python code before connecting to the database.

   C. Configure RDS password rotation via Secrets Manager and fetch the values from your Python code before connecting to the database.

   D. Configure RDS password rotation via Secrets Manager and omit the username and password from your Python code; AWS automatically injects the right values.

14. In an Amazon EKS cluster, which component is responsible for assigning a unique IP address to each pod?

A. The EKS control plane

B. The worker nodes (depending on whether EC2 is configured to auto-assign public IPs)

C. The Amazon VPC Container Network Interface (CNI) plug-in

D. The Kubernetes API server

15. You are running a Kubernetes application on EKS. Your cluster is based on EC2. When trying to add a new pod, you receive errors indicating there are insufficient CPU resources in the cluster. Which are your best options? (Choose two.)

A. Configure the Vertical Pod Autoscaler to reduce the resource demand of idle pods.

B. Configure the Horizontal Pod Autoscaler to allow your new pod to be balanced over multiple nodes.

C. Install the Cluster Autoscaler to make sure your cluster can add new nodes for your pods.

D. Switch to Fargate.

Chapter

10

Authentication and Authorization

**THE AWS CERTIFIED DEVELOPER –
ASSOCIATE EXAM TOPICS COVERED IN
THIS CHAPTER MAY INCLUDE, BUT ARE
NOT LIMITED TO, THE FOLLOWING:**

✓ **Domain 2: Security**

- Task Statement 1: Implement authentication and/or
  authorization for applications and AWS services

Authentication is the process or action that verifies the identity of a user or process. *Authorization* is a security mechanism that determines access levels or permissions related to system resources, including files, services, computer programs, data, and application features. The authentication and authorization process grants or denies user access to network resources based on the identity.

AWS Identity and Access Management (IAM) allows you to create identities (users, groups, or roles) and control access to various AWS Cloud services using policies. IAM serves as an *identity provider (IdP)*.

As an IdP, AWS is responsible for storing identities and providing the mechanism for authentication. You can use AWS as an IdP for the following:

- AWS Cloud services
- Applications running on AWS infrastructure
- Applications running on non-AWS infrastructure, such as web or mobile applications

There are multiple benefits for using AWS as the IdP. AWS provides a managed service, eliminates single points of failure, is highly available, and can scale as needed. AWS also provides a number of tools, such as Amazon CloudWatch and AWS CloudTrail to manage, control, and audit this service.

Using a third party to provide identity services is known as *federation*.

In this chapter, you learn the various ways to integrate existing identity providers into AWS and how to use AWS as an identity provider to control access to applications, both inside and outside the AWS infrastructure.

Authentication and Authorization in AWS

As the Shared Responsibility Model reminds us, AWS is responsible for the security *of* the cloud, ensuring that their services are physically secure, separate from other accounts, and capable of compliance-driven features like encryption at rest. Meanwhile, developers are responsible for security *in* the cloud: namely, how they use the security capabilities offered by AWS. We've learned about features like encryption and security groups that provide data and network security, but more than that, security in the cloud means controlling who has access to services, when, and to what extent. Understanding developers' responsibility in this domain begins with the distinct but related concepts of authentication and authorization.

Identity and Access Management Concepts

Authentication and authorization are core to any discussion of access management. Authentication, sometimes abbreviated authN, asks and answers "Who are you?" This process confirms your identity in the system. Authorization, sometimes called authZ, asks and answers "What can you do?" This process confirms your permissions in the system.

AWS establishes identity in several different ways, as shown in Table 10.1.

TABLE 10.1   AWS identity

Name	Identifier	Credential
Root user	Email	Password
User	Email	Password
User, group, or role	Access key ID	Secret access key
API	Access key ID	Secret access key

In AWS, policies are JSON documents that define a set of permissions, specifying the exact actions that the recipient of the policy can and cannot take. Policies are stand-alone documents that take effect when applied to users, roles, or groups. Each of these entities may have multiple policies attached.

Every policy document contains one or more *statements,* each of which includes three attribute-value pairs: effect, action, and resource.

Effect may have the value ALLOW or DENY. The entity is either granted the permission to execute a particular API action or is denied the permission to execute that action.

Actions specify those actions, and they may refer to either an individual API call or a group of calls using a wildcard (for example, S3:ListBuckets refers to a single action, whereas S3:* includes all Amazon S3 API calls).

Resource specifies the resources on which the action is defined. For example, with Amazon S3, you can allow the execution of an API in a particular bucket, object, or particular group of objects (using the wildcard *).

The following example has two statements. The "Sid" attribute (short for "Statement ID") is an identifier that describes the author's intention. Statement IDs have no other purpose; they can be whatever alphanumeric value you wish, but may not contain spaces.

The first statement, DenyAllS3Actions, uses an explicit Deny Effect to restrict all S3 actions by the use of the asterisk wildcard in the value "s3:*". This denies every possible action under S3, and by specifying "Resource" to be "*" this denial is applied to every possible resource to which that call could be made (i.e., all S3 buckets).

The second statement, `AllowReadOnlyOnMyBucket`, overrules the blanket denial in statement 1 with affirmative permissions allowing `GetObject` and `ListBucket` actions on a single bucket named `demo_bucket`. The Resource section lists both the top-level bucket path, and, using the asterisk, includes all possible paths underneath it.

```
{
    "Version": "2012-10-17",
    "Statement": [
        {
            "Sid": "DenyAllS3Actions",
            "Effect": "Deny",
            "Action": "s3:*",
            "Resource": "*"
        },
        {

            "Sid": "AllowReadOnlyOnMyBucket",
            "Effect": "Allow",
            "Action": [
                "s3:GetObject",
                "s3:ListBucket"
            ],
            "Resource": [
                "arn:aws:s3:::my_bucket",
                "arn:aws:s3:::my_bucket/*"
            ]
        }
    ]
}
```

A policy can be made up of many statements both allowing and denying actions on many resources. A best practice for AWS developers is to create policies that encompass the permissions of a particular user, role, application, or service, and name the policy descriptively. For example, you might bundle all the permissions needed by a production "orders" service as a policy called `ReadProductionOrderData`, granting permissions to not just one resource, but anything needed to fulfill the concept implied by the same. Maybe this policy gives access not only to items details in a DynamoDB table, but also to an SQS topic where another system submits order messages.

This policy can then be applied in many different contexts, such as an individual user or an EC2 instance profile. No matter where it is applied, because it encapsulates one conceptual set of permissions, you can reuse it and add, modify, or revoke permissions for all policyholders simply by editing the one policy JSON document.

This approach helps centralize the management of permissions in your AWS account, and enhances security because it reduces the number of policies you must edit when making changes. With just one policy to update, you can be assured that you have not accidentally neglected to update permissions because you missed a policy.

> Though the order of the three attribute-value pairs has no impact on their execution, use the acronym EAR to remember the three attribute-value pairs: effect, action, and resource (EAR).

Federation Defined

In a federated identity configuration, administrators outsource the management of identity and authentication to another service.

Your *identity provider* (often abbreviated IdP) stores identities, provides a mechanism for authentication, and provides a course level of authorization. An *identity consumer* stores a reference to the identity, providing authorization at a greater granularity than the identity provider.

For instance, if your organization already uses Okta or Sailpoint for directory and login services, federation lets users log in to AWS with their existing username and password. Alternatively, AWS may act as your IdP, letting you manage users and authentication for AWS and other services using AWS.

Federation with AWS

Federation with AWS allows for two things. First, it allows you to use AWS as an IdP to gain access to both AWS and non-AWS resources. *Amazon Cognito* is an AWS service that acts as an IdP. Second, you can use non-AWS resources like Security Assertion Markup Language (SAML) 2.0, OpenID Connect (OIDC), or Microsoft Active Directory as the IdP to facilitate single sign-on (SSO).

With federation, you can retain (or adopt) central management of your corporate or institutional identities in a dedicated system, integrating with AWS via standards such as SAML or OIDC to exchange identity and security information between an IdP and an application.

The five mechanisms that the AWS federation can facilitate are as follows:

- Custom build an IdP
- Cross-account access
- SAML
- OIDC
- Microsoft Active Directory

Custom Build an Identity Provider

Custom builds were the original method of federation within AWS, but they have since been supplanted by SAML, OIDC, and Microsoft Active Directory. With SAML, you can build a custom IdP that verifies users and their identities. Though building a custom IdP offers a high degree of customization, it is a complex process, and most customers now use standard solutions.

Cross-Account Access

When you need to access resources across multiple AWS accounts, *cross-account access* lets you grant users access resources in different accounts without having to maintain multiple user entities, and your users do not have to remember multiple passwords. Users can access the resources they need in AWS accounts by switching AWS roles. Access is permitted by the policies attached to each role. There are two accounts in cross-account access: the account in which the user resides, or *source account*, and the account with the resources to which the user wants access, or *target account*.

The target account has an IAM role that includes two components: a permissions policy and a trust policy. The *permissions policy* controls access to AWS services and resources, while the *trust policy* determines who can assume the role.

The source account is given an IAM role (AssumeRole) with a permissions policy that allows you to assume this role. The target account issues short-term credentials to the AssumeRole, which allows access to AWS Cloud services and the resources you specify in this credential.

Use cross-account access when you own either the target account or the source account and require no more than coordination between the owners of the source account and the target account. Cross-account access allows users to access the AWS Management Console, AWS APIs, and the AWS CLI.

Security Assertion Markup Language

Security Assertion Markup Language (SAML) provides federation between an IdP and a service provider (SP) when you are in an AWS account and a trust relationship has been established between the IdP and the SP. The IdP and the SP exchange metadata in an XML file that contains both the certificates and attributes that form the basis of the trust relationship between the IdP and the SP.

You interact only with the IdP, and all authentication and authorization occurs between you and the IdP. Based on a successful authentication and authorization, the IdP makes an assertion to the service provider. Based on the previously established trust relationship, the service provider accepts this assertion and provides access.

Use SAML to provide access to the AWS Management Console, AWS APIs, and the AWS CLI. SAML can also access Amazon Cognito to control access to cloud services that exist outside AWS, such as software as a service (SaaS) applications.

OpenID Connect

OpenID Connect (OIDC) is the successor to SAML. It simplifies communication between systems by relying on passing tokens rather than more complicated assertions. Most use cases for OIDC involve external versus internal users.

With OIDC, the *OpenID provider (OP)* uses a *relying party* (RP) trust to track the service provider. OP and RP exchange metadata by focusing on the OP providing information to the RP about the location of its endpoints. The RP must register with the OP and then receive a client ID and a client secret. This exchange establishes a trust relationship between the OP and the RP.

Because you interact only with the OP, all authentication and authorization occur only between you and the OP. The OP issues a token to the service provider, which accepts this token and provides access. OIDC includes three different types of tokens:

- The *ID token* establishes a user's identity.

- The *access token* provides access to APIs.

- The *refresh token* allows you to acquire a new access token when the previous one expires.

Companies such as Google, Twitter, Facebook, and Amazon can also establish their own OpenID provider.

After authentication and authorization occur, you can access numerous services, including the AWS Management Console, AWS APIs, and AWS CLIs. You can use OIDC to grant access to AWS Cloud services, including Amazon Cognito, Amazon AppStream 2.0, and Amazon Redshift. You can also use OIDC to grant access to SaaS applications outside of AWS.

Planes of Control

When thinking of how to control access to AWS resources, consider two different levels, or "planes" of management: the control plane and data plane.

First, the *control plane* governs access to operations on particular AWS resources, such as the ability to create or terminate an EC2 instance or S3 bucket. Configuration of these permissions is typically performed through the AWS Management Console, CLI, or SDK. Control plane operations are authenticated and authorized using AWS IAM roles, policies, and permissions.

In contrast, the *data plane* permits access to the application or data that exists on AWS resources. Examples include permission to log into an EC2 instance via SSH or to access individual objects within an S3 bucket. The data plane also extends to parts of your application stack not directly within AWS control, such as access to the administrative functions of a custom-built web application. Data plane operations may, at times, also be secured by IAM policies, but often use different mechanisms and credentials specific to the service being accessed.

The control and data planes typically use different paths, different protocols, and different credentials; however, for several AWS services, the control and data planes are identical. Amazon DynamoDB allows you to stop and start the compute instances (control plane) and stop and start the database (data plane) using an AWS API.

Managing the Data Plane with Microsoft Active Directory

Microsoft Active Directory (AD) is the identity provider for a majority of corporations. You use the *Active Directory forest trusts* to establish trust between an AD domain controller and AWS Directory Service for Microsoft Active Directory. For Microsoft Active Directory, the domain controller is on-premises or in the AWS Cloud.

In the Microsoft Active Directory setup, the Active Directory domain controller defines the user. However, you add users to the groups that you define in the AWS Directory Service for Microsoft Active Directory. Access to services depends on membership within these groups.

Use Microsoft Active Directory to provide data plane access to EC2 instances running Windows, RDS instances running SQL Server, Amazon WorkSpaces, Amazon WorkDocs, Amazon WorkMail, and, with limitation, the AWS Management Console.

AWS Identity Center

Formerly known as *AWS Single Sign-On* (AWS SSO), AWS Identity Center is an AWS service that provides a unified interface to manage user identities and their access to AWS accounts and applications, using its own directory or leveraging existing corporate identities. You can have multiple permission sets, allowing for greater granularity and control over access.

Identity center can act as its own IdP with its own user directory and ability to enforce standard IdP security features like multi-factor authentication. Alternatively, Identity Center users can federate user management and authentication out to third parties, making Identity Center the front door for AWS access by identities managed outside of AWS.

AWS CLI Access

Because AWS Identity Center enables signing into AWS and related service with one's existing corporate ID, you may wonder how users authenticate when using the CLI or an AWS SDK. One particularly useful feature of AWS Identity Center is that it provides temporary command-line credentials that developers and other command-line users can copy and paste into their terminal to establish access.

These AWS CLI credentials automatically expire after 60 minutes to prevent unauthorized access to AWS accounts. After this, users need only refresh the Identity Center page in their browser to fetch new credentials.

Management with AWS Organizations

For those managing multiple accounts through AWS Organizations, AWS Identity Center provides administration of SSO access and user permissions. Identity Center creates the necessary permissions in each account for you to centrally manage user provisioning to any subaccount.

Identity Center also gives you a thorough audit trail of both user and administrative activities. It records all user activity logins with AWS CloudTrail, letting you review in detail which users are accessing which accounts and when. Changes made by administrators in the Identity Center console are also recorded in AWS CloudTrail.

Integration with Other Identity Providers

AWS Identity Center integrates with Microsoft AD through the AWS Directory Service, enabling you to sign into the user portal using your Active Directory credentials. With the Active Directory integration, you can manage SSO access to your accounts and applications for users and groups in your corporate directory. For instance, when you add DevOps Active

Directory users to your production AWS group, you are granted access to your production AWS accounts automatically. This makes it easier to onboard new users and gives existing users SSO access so they can quickly access new accounts and applications.

Identity Center can also federate authentication and user management to external providers such as Okta or Sailpoint. This can allow you to manage AWS users in the same system you use for non-AWS access in your organization and gain the benefit of already-configured policies, such as multi-factor requirements.

Figure 10.1 shows the various AWS Identity Center options.

FIGURE 10.1   AWS Identity Center use cases model

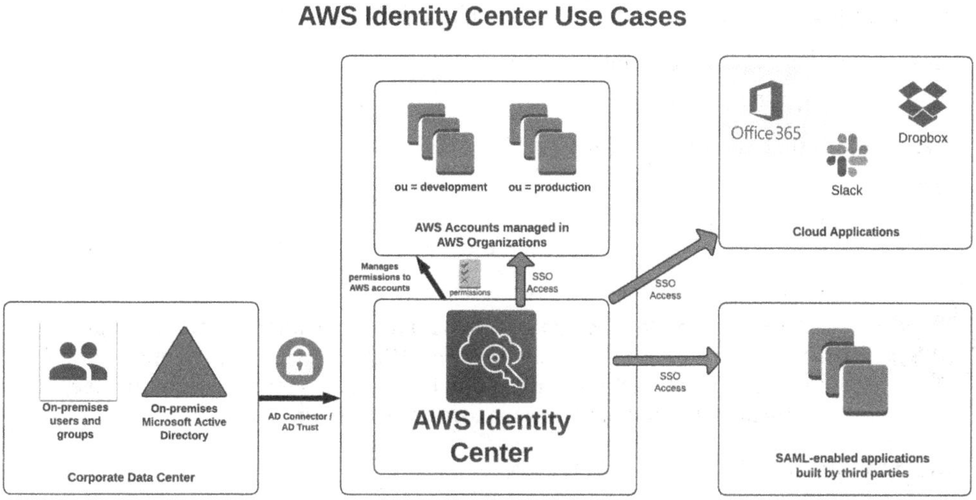

AWS Identity Center Use Cases

AWS Security Token Service

AWS Security Token Service (AWS STS) creates temporary security credentials and provides trusted users with those temporary security credentials. The trusted users then access AWS resources with those credentials. Temporary security credentials work similarly to long-term access key credentials, but with the following differences:

- Temporary security credentials consist of an *access key ID*, a *secret access key*, and a *security token*.

- Temporary security credentials are short-term, and you configure them to remain valid for a duration between a few minutes to several hours. After the credentials expire, AWS no longer recognizes them or allows any kind of access from API requests made with them.

- Temporary security credentials are generated dynamically and provided to you upon request. Users can request new credentials before or after the temporary security credentials expire, if they still have permissions to do so.

Because of these differences, temporary credentials offer the following advantages:

- You do not have to distribute or embed long-term AWS security credentials with an application.
- You can provide users access to your AWS resources without defining an AWS identity for them. Temporary credentials are the basis for AWS roles and identity federation.
- The temporary security credentials have a limited lifetime. You do not have to rotate or explicitly revoke them when the user no longer requires them.
- After temporary security credentials expire, they cannot be reused. You can specify how long the credentials are valid, up to a maximum limit.

AWS STS IdPs come from different sources, including the following:

- IAM users from another account
- Microsoft Active Directory
- Users of IdPs that are SAML 2.0–based
- Web IdPs
- Customer identity brokers

 Amazon Cognito helps you implement authentication for mobile applications and supports the same IdPs as STS. However, it also supports unauthenticated (guest) access and provides a means for synchronizing user data between multiple devices owned by the same user.

AWS STS supports the following APIs:

AssumeRole   This API provides a set of temporary security credentials to access AWS resources. AssumeRole lets a user *assume,* or temporarily take on, the privileges of a particular IAM role. Callers of AssumeRole must state the IAM role they wish to assume. Use AssumeRole to grant access to existing IAM users who have identities in other AWS accounts. By default, the maximum duration of the credentials that this API issues is 60 minutes.

 The default maximum duration for AssumeRole APIs is 60 minutes. However, you can change the maximum duration to 12 hours (720 minutes) for a specific role.

AssumeRoleWithSAML   AssumeRoleWithSAML provides a set of temporary security credentials (consisting of an *access key ID,* a *secret access key,* and a *security token*) to access AWS resources. Use this API when you are using an identity store or directory that is SAML-based, rather than having an identity from an IAM user in another AWS account. This API does not support multifactor authentication (MFA).

AssumeRoleWithWebIdentity AssumeRoleWithWebIdentity provides a set of temporary security credentials that you use to access AWS resources. Use this API when users have been authenticated in a mobile or web application with a web IdP, such as Amazon Cognito, or log in with Amazon, Facebook, Google, or any OIDC-compatible identity provider. This API does not support MFA. Cognito Identity Pools is an alternative to this approach for giving temporary AWS credentials to web users.

DecodeAuthorizationMessage DecodeAuthorizationMessage decodes additional information about the authorization status of a request from an encoded message returned in response to an AWS request. The message is encoded to prevent the requesting user from seeing details of the authorization status, which can contain privileged information.

The decoded message includes the following:

- Whether the request was denied because of an explicit deny or because of the absence of an explicit allow
- Principal who made the request
- Requested action
- Requested resource
- Values of condition keys in the context of the user's request

GetCallerIdentity The GetCallerIdentity API returns details about the IAM identity whose credentials call the API.

GetFederationToken The GetFederationToken API provides a set of temporary security credentials to access AWS resources. For example, a typical use is within a proxy application that retrieves temporary security credentials on behalf of distributed applications inside a corporate network.

The permissions for the temporary security credentials returned by GetFederation Token are a combination of the policy or policies that are attached to the IAM user, whose credentials call the GetFederationToken, and the policy passes as a parameter in the call.

Because the call for the GetFederationToken action uses the long-term security credentials of an IAM user, this call is appropriate in contexts where credentials can be safely stored. The API credentials can have a duration of up to 36 hours. This API does not support MFA.

Remember that in IAM policy documents, the most restrictive policy is the one enforced. So, if you have a user who has a policy that ALLOWS access to an API but a policy is passed as a parameter that DENIES access to that API, the result is a DENY.

GetSessionToken   GetSessionToken provides a set of temporary security credentials to access AWS resources. You normally use GetSessionToken to enable MFA to protect programmatic calls to specific AWS APIs like Amazon EC2 StopInstances.

MFA-enabled IAM users call GetSessionToken and submit an MFA code that is associated with their MFA device. Using the temporary security credentials that return from the call, IAM users can then make programmatic calls to APIs that require MFA authentication.

User Authentication with Amazon Cognito

User authentication is a critical component to secure your web and mobile applications, whether you are running a banking site or a blog service. *Amazon Cognito* allows for simple and secure user sign-up, sign-in, and access control mechanisms designed to handle web application authentication.

Amazon Cognito includes the following features:

- Amazon Cognito user pools, which are secure and scalable user directories
- Amazon Cognito identity pools (federated identities), which offer social and enterprise identity federation
- Standards-based Web Identity Federation Authentication through Open Authorization (OAuth) 2.0, Security Assertion Markup Language (SAML) 2.0, and OpenID Connect (OIDC) support
- Multifactor authentication
- Encryption for data at rest and data in transit
- Access control with Identity and Access Management (IAM) integration
- Easy application integration (prebuilt user interface)
- iOS Object C, Android, iOS Swift, and JavaScript
- Adherence to compliance requirements such as Payment Card Industry Data Security Standard (PCI DSS)

Amazon Cognito User Pools

Cognito user pools is the service that acts as an IdP, letting you register users and authenticate them over the web. Cognito handles all aspects of user sign-in, including registration, password standards, forgotten password flows, email or phone verification, and MFA, all of which are configurable options in user pools.

Cognito users pools can be deployed based on an internal database of users, or it can federate out to other identity providers, such as Facebook, Apple, or Amazon.

Any administrative activity performed in Cognito User Pools, such as creating or deleting accounts, is tracked in CloudTrail. You can also configure CloudWatch alarms for certain activity and trigger SNS or email notifications as a result.

In addition, Cognito can be configured to trigger a lambda for many different parts of the authentication process, such as pre-authentication, post-authentication, pre-registration, post-registration, and pre-token grant. This feature allows you to override or augment any of the default functionality of Cognito.

Finally, Cognito provides an optional web UI experience for login, letting you skip coding a login user interface and simply direct your users to AWS's implementation, which provides a simple web page with controls for registering, logging in, and retrieving forgotten passwords.

User pools provide the following:

- Sign-up and sign-in services.

- A built-in, customizable web user interface (UI) to sign in users.

- Social sign-in with Facebook, Google, and Amazon, and sign-in with SAML identity providers from your user pool.

- User directory management and user profiles.

- Security features, such as MFA, that check for compromised credentials, account takeover protection, and phone and email verification.

- Customized workflows and user migration through AWS Lambda triggers.

- After successfully authenticating a user, Cognito issues *JSON Web Tokens* (JWT) that you can use to secure and authorize access to your own APIs or exchange them for AWS credentials.

With Cognito, you can choose how you want your users to sign in: with a username, an email address, and/or a phone number. Additionally, user pools allow you to select *attributes*. Attributes are properties that you want to store about your end users, with standard attributes that are created for you, if you enable the option. You can also develop custom attributes.

The standard attributes are as follows:

- address
- birthdate
- email
- family name
- gender
- given name
- locale

- middle name
- name
- nickname
- phone number
- picture
- preferred username
- profile
- zoneinfo
- updated at
- website

Password Policies

In addition to attributes, you can configure *password policies*. You can determine the minimum length and defining requirements around the inclusion of numbers, special characters, uppercase letters, and lowercase letters. Furthermore, you can either allow users to sign up and enroll themselves or allow only administrators to create users. If administrators create the account, you can also set the account to expire if it remains unused for a specified period of time.

Multifactor Authentication

Multifactor authentication (MFA) prevents anyone from signing into a system without authenticating through two different sources, such as a password and a mobile device–generated token. With Cognito, you can enable MFA to secure your application further. To enable this option with Cognito, create a role that enables Cognito to send Short Message Service (SMS) messages to users.

Besides MFA, you can customize your SMS verification messages, email verification messages, and user invitation messages. For example, you could send your end users a welcome message when they verify their account.

Device Tracking and Remembering

If you enable MFA, this increases the security of an application to require a second authentication challenge from the user. However, this does require a new two-factor sign-in after a prolonged absence of activity, even when the user device has not been signed out or shut off.

With device tracking and remembering, you can save that user's device and remember it so they do not have to provide a token again, as the application has already seen this specific device. Figure 10.2 shows how to enable this feature.

FIGURE 10.2 Device tracking

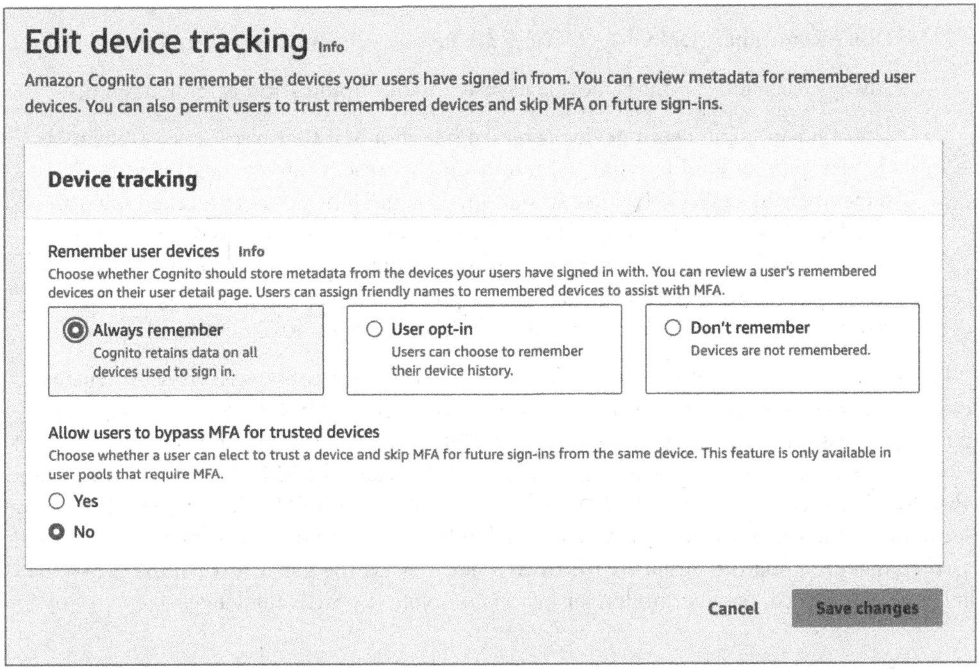

Edit device tracking Info

Amazon Cognito can remember the devices your users have signed in from. You can review metadata for remembered user devices. You can also permit users to trust remembered devices and skip MFA on future sign-ins.

Device tracking

Remember user devices | Info

Choose whether Cognito should store metadata from the devices your users have signed in with. You can review a user's remembered devices on their user detail page. Users can assign friendly names to remembered devices to assist with MFA.

- ⦿ **Always remember**
  Cognito retains data on all devices used to sign in.
- ○ **User opt-in**
  Users can choose to remember their device history.
- ○ **Don't remember**
  Devices are not remembered.

Allow users to bypass MFA for trusted devices

Choose whether a user can elect to trust a device and skip MFA for future sign-ins from the same device. This feature is only available in user pools that require MFA.

- ○ Yes
- ⦿ No

Cancel   Save changes

The specifics of the configuration terminology include the following:

Tracked A *tracked device* is assigned a set of device credentials and consists of a *key* and *secret key pair*. You can view all tracked devices for a specific user on the Users screen of the Cognito console. In addition, you can view the device's metadata (whether it is remembered, time it began being tracked, last authenticated time, and such) and the device's usage.

Remembered A *remembered device* is also tracked. During user authentication, the key and secret pair assigned to a remembered device authenticates the device to verify that it is the same device the user previously used to sign into the application. You can view remembered devices in the Cognito console.

Not Remembered A *not-remembered device*, while still tracked, is treated as if it was never used during the user authentication flow. The device credentials are not used to authenticate the device. The new APIs in the *AWS Mobile SDK* do not expose these devices, but you can see them in the Cognito console.

The first configuration setting reads "Do you want to remember devices?" and has the following options:

Don't Remember (Default)   Devices are neither remembered nor tracked.

Always Remember   Every device used with your application is remembered.

User Opt-In   The user's device is remembered only if that user opts to remember the device. This enables your users to decide whether your application should remember the devices they use to sign in, though all devices are tracked regardless of which setting they choose. This is a useful option when you require a higher security level, but the user may sign in from a shared device. For example, if a user signs in to a banking application from a public computer at a library, the user requires the option to decide whether their device is to be remembered.

The second configuration option is whether to "allow users to bypass MFA for trusted devices." It appears when you select either Always or User Opt-In for the first configuration option. The second factor suppression option enables your application to use a remembered device as a second factor of authentication, and it suppresses the SMS-based challenge in the MFA flow. This feature works together with MFA, and it requires MFA to be enabled for the user pool. The device must first be remembered before it can be used to suppress the SMS-based challenge. Upon the initial sign-in with a new device, the user must complete the SMS challenge. Afterward, the user no longer has to complete the SMS challenge.

User Interface Customization

An Amazon Cognito user pool includes a prebuilt *user interface (UI)* that you can use inside of your application to build a user authentication flow quickly, as shown in Figure 10.3.

You can modify the UI with the AWS Management Console, the AWS CLI, or the API. You can also upload your own custom logo with a maximum file size of 100 KB. The *CSS classes* you can customize in the prebuilt UI are as follows:

- `background-customizable`
- `banner-customizable`
- `errorMessage-customizable`
- `idpButton-customizable`
- `idpButton-customizable:hover`
- `inputField-customizable`
- `inputField-customizable:focus`
- `label-customizable`
- `legalText-customizable`
- `logo-customizable`
- `submitButton-customizable`
- `submitButton-customizable:hover`
- `textDescription-customizable`

FIGURE 10.3   Cognito prebuilt UI

You can customize the UI and CLI with two commands: `get-ui-customization` to retrieve the customization settings and `set-ui-customization` to set the UI customization, as shown in the following example code:

```
aws cognito-idp get-ui-customization
aws cognito-idp set-ui-customization --user-pool-id <your-user-pool-id>
--client-id
<your-app-client-id> --image-file <path-to-logo-image-file> --css ".label-
customizable{ color: <color>;}"
```

Cognito Identity Pools

With *Cognito Identity Pools,* you can grant web and mobile users direct, temporary access to AWS resources without having to embed AWS credentials into the web or mobile application. For instance, let's say you want to give mobile users access to data in a DynamoDB table. You can have your users register and authenticate with Cognito User Pools. Then, you can use the token provided from that login and pass it to Cognito Identity Pools. Identity Pools then validates the token and responds with temporary tokens based on an IAM role you define. With these short-lived tokens, your web or mobile app can then make SDK calls directly to AWS resources on behalf of the user—such as querying that DynamoDB table.

Roles issued by Cognito Identity Pools are defined at multiple levels. You may define default roles for all unauthenticated users as well as for all authenticated users. With the latter, you may optionally use variables in your IAM policy, such as the user's ID, to scope access in your policy document. With this capability, you could provide security access to data, such as giving mobile users the ability to read S3 objects in subfolders prefixed with their user ID, and no other data. Cognito Identity Pool roles can also be associated with specific users or groups.

Cognito SDK

You can start developing for Cognito using the *AWS Mobile SDK*. Cognito currently supports the following SDKs through the AWS Mobile SDK:

- JavaScript SDK
- iOS SDK
- Android SDK

In addition to using the higher-level mobile and JavaScript SDKs, you can also use the lower-level APIs available via the following AWS SDKs to integrate all Cognito functionality in your applications:

- Java SDK
- .NET SDK
- Node.js SDK
- Python SDK
- PHP SDK
- Ruby SDK
- User Authentication with Amazon Cognito

Active Directory on AWS

Microsoft's Active Directory is a popular choice for identity management in many enterprises. AWS enables your organization to work with Active Directory in the cloud with services that make it easy to manage and scale AD installations.

Microsoft AD as Identity Provider

Many enterprises already use Microsoft AD as their identity store. The ability to integrate your existing Active Directory, rather than configuring a new identity store, simplifies administrative overhead. *AWS Directory Service*, also known as *AWS Managed Microsoft*

AD, provides multiple ways to use Amazon Cloud Directory and Microsoft AD with other AWS Cloud services.

Directories store information about users, groups, and devices, which administrators use to manage access to information and resources. AWS Directory Service provides multiple directory choices for customers who want to use existing Microsoft Active Directory– or *Lightweight Directory Access Protocol* (LDAP)–aware applications in the cloud. It also offers those same choices to developers who need a directory to manage users, groups, devices, and access.

There are four different ways to implement Microsoft AD in an AWS infrastructure:

- Run Microsoft AD on Amazon EC2 with an AWS account.
- Use Active Directory Connector to connect AWS Cloud services with an on-premises Microsoft Active Directory.
- Create a Simple Active Directory that provides basic Active Directory compatibility.
- Deploy AWS Managed Microsoft AD.

AWS publishes a number of Quick Start reference deployment guides, including a deployment guide for Active Directory Domain Services. For more information, see https://docs.aws.amazon.com/quickstart/ latest/active-directory-ds/youlcome.html.

Microsoft AD on EC2 with AWS Account

Active Directory Domain Services (AD DS) and *Domain Name System* (DNS) are essential Windows services used in enterprise solutions like Microsoft SharePoint, Exchange, and .NET applications. When deploying AD DS yourself using EC2, you are responsible for configuring high availability, backing up the directory, and setting up fault tolerance. You can deploy AD DS as either a primary or secondary domain controller and have the option to use Amazon Machine Images (AMIs) or import your own virtual machine images.

Active Directory Connector

Active Directory Connector (AD Connector) links your on-premises Microsoft Active Directory to AWS applications like Amazon WorkSpaces, QuickSight, WorkMail, and EC2 for Windows. Acting as a proxy, AD Connector lets you use your existing AD without needing directory synchronization or complex federation infrastructure.

When you add users to AWS applications, AD Connector reads your AD to pull users and groups for AWS applications, and when users sign in, it forwards authentication requests to your on-premises AD domain controllers. This makes integrating AWS services with your existing AD simple and cost-effective.

AD Connector is not compatible with Amazon Relational Database Service (RDS) SQL Server.

While managing access to cloud resources, you can continue using and managing your existing Active Directory exactly as you do now, with the same familiar tools. This allows you to centrally enforce enterprise policies, such as password requirements and account expirations, without any changes to your current workflow.

AD Connector enables you to access the AWS Management Console and manage AWS resources by signing in with your existing Active Directory credentials.

You can use the AD Connector to enable MFA for your AWS application users by connecting it to your existing RADIUS-based MFA infrastructure. This provides an additional layer of security when users access AWS applications.

Simple Active Directory

Simple Active Directory is a Microsoft AD that is compatible with AWS Directory Service and is powered by Samba 4. Simple AD is a stand-alone directory in the cloud, where you create and manage identities and manage access to applications. You can use many familiar Active Directory–aware applications and tools that require basic AD features.

Simple AD supports common AD features like user accounts, group memberships, Kerberos-based SSO, and group policies. However, it lacks advanced capabilities like trust relationships, multi-factor authentication, schema extensions, and compatibility with SQL Server. It also doesn't support some management features like PowerShell AD cmdlets or FSMO role transfer.

You can use Simple AD accounts to sign in to the AWS Management Console, but with its limited compatibility, Simple AD is hard to recommend over the next, full-featured offering: AWS Directory Service.

AWS Directory Service

AWS Directory Service is a fully-managed implementation of Microsoft AD that gives you an ideal landing zone for migrating existing Active Directory or AD-compatible services to the cloud. AWS Directory Service works with Microsoft SharePoint, Microsoft SQL Server Always-On Availability Groups, and many .NET applications, as well as any application that works with AD or LDAP.

Figure 10.4 illustrates AWS Directory Service and its relation to AWS applications and services: Amazon EC2, Active Directory–aware workloads, cloud applications, and on-premises Active Directory.

AWS Directory Service includes features that enable you to extend your schema, manage password policies, and enable secure LDAP communications through Secure Socket Layer (SSL)/Transport Layer Security (TLS).

With AWS Directory Service, you can use all your existing Active Directory tools while gaining cloud capabilities like the ability to horizontally scale by adding more domain controllers.

FIGURE 10.4 AWS Directory Service chart

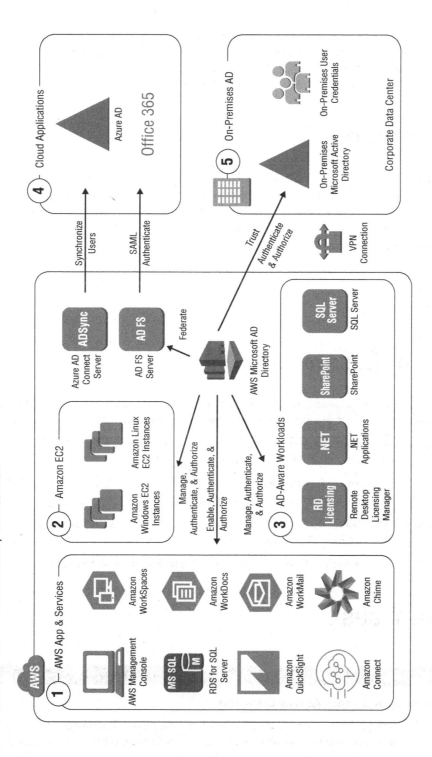

AWS provides monitoring, daily snapshots, and recovery as part of the service. You can establish a trust relationship between AWS Directory Service and an on-premises Active Directory, allowing you to use on-premises credentials. The service supports one-way (both inbound and outbound) and two-way trust relationships.

Summary

This chapter discussed the concepts of identity and authorization and how you can use AWS services to provide them. You learned the difference between authentication and authorization. Finally, you learned about the various AWS Cloud services and where you use identity and authorization, including the following:

- AWS Identity Center
- AWS STS
- Amazon Cognito
- AWS Directory Service

Exam Essentials

Understand what federation is.   Know the difference between federation and SSO. Understand when you would use federation and when you would use SSO.

Understand the role of an identity provider (IdP).   Know what an IdP does, how it operates, and how it interacts with an identity consumer.

Know the federation services that AWS offers.   Understand which services act as IdPs, which act as identity consumers, and which act as SSO.

Understand AWS Directory Service options.   Know the use cases for Microsoft Active Directory, Amazon Cloud Directory, and Amazon Cognito.

Know how policies work.   Know the structure of policies and how to apply them.

Exercises

EXERCISE 10.1

Setting Up a Simple Active Directory

In this exercise, you will set up an AWS Simple Active Directory. Simple AD is a standalone directory that is powered by a Samba 4 Active Directory Compatible Server. Because it's a stand-alone managed directory, you do not have to manage user accounts and group memberships. This is achieved through the Microsoft Active Directory.

Step 1: Creating a Virtual Private Cloud

In this step, you will use the Amazon VPC wizard in the Amazon VPC console to create a virtual private cloud. The wizard steps create a VPC with a /16 IPv4 CIDR block and attaches an Internet gateway to the VPC.

1. In the AWS Management Console navigation pane, select VPC and then click Create VPC.

2. Select VPC And More.

3. Under Name Tag Auto-generation, enter something memorable, like `simple-ad-demo`.

4. In the configuration options below, change Number Of Availability Zones (AZs) to **1** and Number Of Private Subnets to **0**.

5. Change VPC Endpoints to 0.

    To communicate with an Active Directory outside of AWS, you must create the Simple AD directory in a public subnet.

6. Click Create VPC.

    You have launched a VPC that has a public subnet, an Internet gateway attached to it, and the necessary route table and security group configurations to allow traffic to flow between the subnet and the Internet gateway. However, because Simple AD is a highly available service, you must create a second public subnet on this VPC.

7. Navigate to the VPC dashboard and select Subnets.

8. Click Create Subnet.

9. On the next page, enter the following settings:

    a. Select your VPC from the drop-down menu.

    b. Type in a name tag like `public-subnet-2`.

    c. Choose an availability zone that is different from the one selected in the previous steps.

    d. For the IPv4 Subnet CIDR Block, enter `10.0.16.0/20`.

10. Click Create Subnet.

    You have created a VPC that has two public subnets. When you create a Simple AD directory, each node will be located in a different availability zone.

Step 2: Creating Your Simple AD Instance in AWS

Create your AWS Managed Microsoft AD directory using the AWS Management Console:

1. Navigate to the Directory Service section of AWS.

2. On the front page, under Set Up Directory, select Simple AD and then click Set Up Directory. On the next page, click Next.

3. On the Enter Directory Information page, provide the following:

   a. Directory Size (Small or Large).

   b. Directory DNS Name. For this exercise, this does not need to be a real domain. You can use **yourname.example.com**.

   c. (Optional) Directory NetBIOS Name (**CORP**, for example). If one is not provided, a name is created by default.

   d. An administrator password, which must be from 8 through 24 characters in length. It must also contain at least one character from three of the following four categories: uppercase letters, lowercase letters, numbers, or nonalphanumeric characters.

   e. Confirm the password.

   f. (Optional) Description of the directory. This is useful in tracking your services within AWS.

   g. Click Next.

4. On the VPC And Subnets page, provide the following information, and click Next.

   a. For VPC, select the VPC you created earlier.

   b. Under Subnets, select the two subnets you created for the domain controllers.

5. Review your settings and click Create Directory.

   It takes 5–10 minutes to create your directory. You may need to refresh the page. When the directory creation is complete, the Status value changes to Active.

When the status changes to Active, the AWS Managed Microsoft AD directory is ready to do the following:

- Manage the AWS applications and services available to users

- Perform various maintenance activities, such as creating Amazon Simple Notification Service (Amazon SNS) email or text messages to inform you of changes in status to your directory, performing a point-in time backup (snapshot) of your directory, and modifying the schema of your AWS Managed AD directory

EXERCISE 10.2

Setting Up an AWS Managed Microsoft AD

In this exercise, you will set up an AWS Managed Microsoft AD. Because this is an Active Directory managed by AWS, you do not have to consider the size or type of compute instances that will be running on this Active Directory. You will, however, have to choose the Amazon VPC that this service will run on.

This service is designed for high availability, so two domain controllers are created. Therefore, two corresponding subnets are used.

To simplify the installation, you will use the VPC and subnets created in Exercise 10.1.

Step 1: Creating Your AWS Managed Microsoft AD Directory in AWS

Create your AWS Managed Microsoft AD directory by using the AWS Management Console.

1. In the AWS Directory Service console navigation pane, select Directories and then click Set Up Directory.

2. On the Select Directory Type page, select AWS Managed Microsoft AD and click Next.

3. On the Enter Directory Information page, provide the following information and then click Next.

   a. For **Edition**, select either **Standard Edition** or **Enterprise Edition**. For more information about editions, see AWS Directory Service for Microsoft Active Directory at: https://docs.aws.amazon.com/directoryservice/latest/admin-guide/what_is.html#microsoftad

   b. For this exercise, select Standard Edition.

   c. For Directory DNS Name, enter **corp.example.com**.

   d. For Directory NetBIOS Name, enter **corp**.

   e. For Directory Description, enter **AWS DS Managed**.

   f. For Admin Password, enter the password that you want to use for this account, following the password rules shown on screen.

   g. In Confirm Password, enter the password again.

4. On the Choose VPC And Subnets page, choose the same VPC and subnets you used in Exercise 10.1.

5. On the Review & Create page, review the directory information and make any necessary changes. When the information is correct, click Create Directory.

Creating the directory takes from 20 to 40 minutes. After the directory is created, the Status value changes to Active.

After AWS Managed Microsoft AD is set up, you are able to perform the following maintenance and management operations:

- Manage the AWS applications and services available to users

- Share directories, see the availability zone and subnet of existing controllers, and add additional controllers

- Create trust relationships, establish IP routing, enable log forwarding, and use multi-factor authentication

- Create Amazon Simple Notification Service (SNS) email or text messages to inform you of changes in status to your directory, perform a point-in time backup (snapshot) of your directory, and modify the schema of your AWS Managed AD directory

Setting Up an Amazon Cloud Directory

In this exercise, you will set up an Amazon Cloud Directory. Cloud Directory is a highly available multitenant directory-based store where AWS is responsible for scaling. AWS manages the directory infrastructure while the administrators focus on building the directories and the applications that use those directories.

Step 1: Creating a Directory

Amazon Cloud Directory requires that you create a schema to attach to the directory. You may create one under Schemas, or you can use one provided by AWS while creating the Cloud Directory, which is how we'll do it in this exercise.

1. Navigate to Directory Service. In the lefthand menu, under Cloud Directory, click Directories.

2. Click Set Up Cloud Directory.

3. Assign the name **test-cloud-directory.**

4. Under Select A Schema Option That Fits Your Needs, select Managed Schema.

5. Select the schema named QuickStartSchema, then click Next.

6. Review the directory information and click Create.

You have successfully created an Amazon Cloud Directory. You can modify and delete the directory, including the schema associated with the directory.

Setting Up Amazon Cognito

In this exercise, you will set up Amazon Cognito, which is the service that provides authentication, authorization, and user management for web and mobile applications.

The two main components of Cognito are user pools and identity pools. A user pool is a user directory that provides sign-up and sign-in services. Identity pools are used to provide access to other AWS services.

You can use identity pools and user pools separately or together. In this exercise, you will set up a user pool.

1. Navigate to the Cognito service console by searching in the top navigation bar of the AWS Management Console.

2. Click Create User Pool.

3. Under Cognito User Pool Sign-in Options, select User Name, and then click Next.

4. For this exercise, select No MFA. Otherwise, retain the default settings and choose Next.

   Note that you can set MFA as optional or required. After a user pool is configured, you cannot change the MFA setting. Cognito uses Amazon SNS to send SMS messages. If MFA is enabled, you must assign a role with the correct policy to send SMS messages.

5. On the Configure Sign-up Experience page, keep the default settings and click Next.

6. On the Configure Message Delivery page, select Send Email With Cognito and click Next. This allows you to skip the configuration of Simple Email Service (SES).

7. Provide a name for your user pool. For this exercise, enter **admin-group**.

8. (Optional) Click Use The Cognito Hosted UI and configure your application domain. This enables the use of Cognito's prebuilt login page with your app.

9. Enter an **App Client Name**. For this exercise, use **demo-app.**

10. On the **Review** page, review your configurations, and click Create User Pool.

You have successfully created a user pool in Amazon Cognito.

Review Questions

1. You need to grant a user, who is outside your AWS account, access to an object in an Amazon Simple Storage Service (Amazon S3) bucket. Which is the best way to provide access?

    A. Create a role and assign that role to the user.

    B. Create a user ID within Identity and Access Management (IAM) and assign the user ID a policy that allows access.

    C. Create a new AWS account, assign that user to the account, and then give the account cross-account access.

    D. Have the user create a user ID using a third-party identity provider (IdP), and based on that user ID, assign a policy that permits access.

2. Which of the following is the purpose of an identity provider (IdP)?

    A. To control access to applications

    B. To control access to the AWS infrastructure

    C. To minimize the opportunity to assign the incorrect policy

    D. To answer the question "Who are you?"

3. Which of the following is the best way to minimize misuse of AWS credentials?

    A. Set up multifactor authentication (MFA).

    B. Embed the credentials in the bastion host and control access to the bastion host.

    C. Put a condition on all of your policies that allows execution only from your corporate IP range.

    D. Make sure you have a limited number of credentials and limit the number of people who can use them.

4. Which of the following is not a valid identity provider (IdP) for Amazon Cognito?

    A. Google

    B. Microsoft Active Directory

    C. Your own identity store

    D. A Security Assertion Markup Language (SAML) 1.0–based IdP

5. Which of the following is one benefit of using AWS as an identity provider (IdP) to access non-AWS resources?

    A. AWS cannot be used as an IdP for non-AWS services.

    B. Using AWS as an IdP allows you to use Amazon CloudWatch to monitor activity.

    C. Using AWS as an IdP allows you to use AWS CloudTrail to audit who is using the service.

    D. Using AWS as an IdP allows you to assign policies to non-AWS resources.

6. Which of the following are benefits from using the Active Directory Connector (AD Connector)? (Choose two.)

   A. Easy setup

   B. Ability to connect to multiple Active Directory domains with a single connection

   C. Ability to configure changes to Active Directory on your existing Active Directory console

   D. Ability to support authentication to non-AWS services

7. Which of the following is a prerequisite for using AWS Identity Center (aka AWS SSO)?

   A. Set up AWS Organizations and enable all features.

   B. Configure Cognito identity pools.

   C. Deploy AWS Simple Active Directory.

   D. Use DynamoDB to set up a user data schema.

8. AWS Security Token Service (AWS STS) supports a number of different tokens. Which token would you use to establish a longer-term session?

   A. `AssumeRole`

   B. `GetUserToken`

   C. `GetFederationToken`

   D. `GetSessionToken`

9. Which of the following is not a service that AWS Managed Microsoft AD provides?

   A. Daily snapshots

   B. Ability to manage the Amazon EC2 instances that AWS Managed Microsoft AD is running on

   C. Monitoring

   D. Ability to sync with on-premises Active Directory

10. You are using an existing RADIUS-based multifactor authentication (MFA) infrastructure. Which AWS service is your best choice?

    A. Active Directory Connector (AD Connector)

    B. AWS Managed Microsoft AD

    C. Simple Active Directory

    D. No AWS service would be suitable.

11. Your mobile application needs to integrate with AWS services like DynamoDB, requiring both authenticated and guest user access with different levels of permissions. Which AWS service is best suited to manage these identity and authentication requirements?

    A. AWS Identity Center

    B. Amazon Cognito user pools

    C. Amazon Cognito identity pools

    D. AWS Directory Service

Refactoring
to Microservices

**THE AWS CERTIFIED DEVELOPER—
ASSOCIATE EXAM TOPICS COVERED IN
THIS CHAPTER MAY INCLUDE, BUT ARE
NOT LIMITED TO, THE FOLLOWING:**

✓ **Domain 1: Development with AWS Services**

- Task Statement 3: Use data stores in application development

✓ **Domain 4: Troubleshooting and Optimization**

- Task Statement 2: Instrument code for observability

- Task Statement 3: Optimize applications by using AWS
  services and features

As applications grow, they become harder to manage and maintain. When application components are tightly coupled with each other, the failure of one component can cause the failure of the whole application.

In a *microservices* architecture, developers build software applications as a suite of modular services, each of which performs a specific functional task and communicates with the others through API interfaces. A key advantage of this architecture is that each service can be deployed, scaled, and maintained independently of the others.

To *refactor to microservices* is to separate application components into separate microservices so that each has its own data store, scales independently, and deploys on its own infrastructure. AWS provides the infrastructure that enables your microservices to communicate with each other asynchronously.

This section describes the different services AWS provides to support microservice architectures.

Amazon Simple Queue Service

Amazon Simple Queue Service (SQS) is a fully managed message queuing service that allows *producers* to broadcast and publish data to multiple message *consumers*, also known as *message subscribers*.

With Amazon SQS, application components communicate *asynchronously*, sending messages to each other without having to wait for a response. Queues act as a buffer between services. This allows for much more resilient software, because unlike in a synchronous communication scenario (such as an HTTP call), the caller is not affected by the response time or uptime of the recipient. If you call a web server and that server is down, you'll receive an error. If, instead, you place a message on a queue for a service to pick up asynchronously, your message can be processed whenever that service is online and ready to handle requests. This pattern is shown in Figure 11.1.

FIGURE 11.1   Amazon Simple Queue Service flow

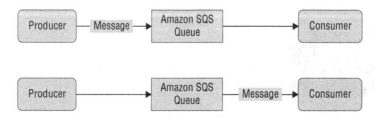

The *producer* is the component that *sends* the message. The *consumer* is the component that *pulls* the message off the queue. The queue passively stores messages and does not notify you of new messages. When you poll the *SQS queue*, the queue *responds* with messages that it includes, as shown in Figure 11.2.

FIGURE 11.2   SQS queue

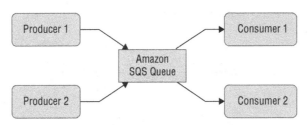

Each *Amazon Simple Queue Service queue* allows multiple producers to write messages and one or more consumers to work together to process messages. Each message can be consumed only once and is deleted after it is processed. If the amount of work on the queue exceeds the capacity for a single consumer, you can add more consumers to help the process. For information on creating a one-to-many system where multiple consumers can react to the same message, see the section below titled "Fan-Out Pattern: Combining SNS and SQS," or head to the Chapter 15 section "EventBridge."

Figure 11.3 illustrates the way the Amazon SQS queue interacts with both Amazon EC2 and the process servers.

FIGURE 11.3   Amazon Simple Queue Service

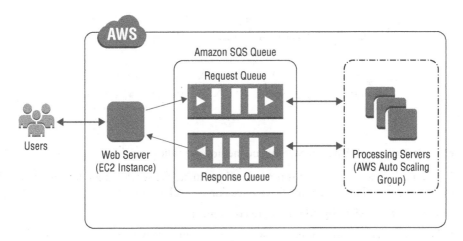

As shown in Figure 11.4, a sign-in service run on a single *log server* is dependent on the reliability of the log server to send and receive messages. If the log server experiences any issues, the sign-in service can go offline.

FIGURE 11.4   Log server

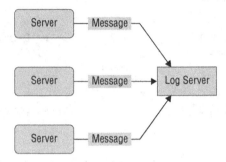

If you replace the log server with an Amazon SQS queue with multiple log servers, you can remove this point of failure. As the other servers in your application send their sign-in messages to the queue, the sign-in server can pull messages off the queue and process them, as shown in Figure 11.5.

FIGURE 11.5   Amazon SQS queue

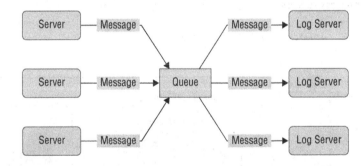

Benefits to using the Amazon SQS queue include the following:

- If you need to take a service offline for maintenance, the service does not interrupt. Messages remain in the queue until the service comes back online.

- You can *scale* services by adding more consumers.

- SQS automatically scales to handle an increase in incoming messages.

- Messages can be sent to the dead-letter queue.

- Messages have a visibility timeout, a message retention period, and a receive-message wait time.
- Messages can have a long polling interval or a short polling interval (default).

SQS is a *distributed cluster of servers*. There is no limit on the number of producers that can write to the queue, and there is no limit on the number of messages that the queue can store.

Amazon SQS Parameters

An Amazon SQS message has three states:

1. Sent to a queue by a producer
2. Received from the queue by a consumer
3. Deleted from the queue

When a message has been sent and is waiting in a queue to be received (i.e., it is between states 1 and 2), it is said to be *stored*. AWS allows unlimited messages to be stored on a queue. When a message has been consumed but not yet deleted (i.e., while it is being processed by a consumer), that message is referred to as *in-flight*.

For most *standard queues*, there can be a maximum of approximately 120,000 in-flight messages. To avoid receiving the resulting OverLimit error message, delete messages from the queue after they are processed.

For *first-in, first-out* (FIFO) queues, you can have a max of 20,000 messages in-flight. If you hit this limit, short-polling consumers will see an OverLimit error, while long-polling clients simply won't receive any messages until the number of in-flight messages subsides.

ReceiveMessage

Clients use the function ReceiveMessage to poll for a message, which has the following configuration options:

VisibilityTimeout   The VisibilityTimeout parameter is the duration (in seconds) that received messages are hidden from subsequent retrieve requests after being retrieved by a ReceiveMessage request. This value defaults to 30 seconds, but can be set as low as 0 seconds or as high as 12 hours.

This window allows consumers time to process messages and delete them without concern that another consumer may receive the same message and act on it. Try to tune the value to the maximum time you believe your consumer may take to process a message.

Note that if the consumer fails and this window elapses, the message may be received by another consumer. This helps guarantee that every message is eventually processed.

WaitTimeSeconds   WaitTimeSeconds is the duration (in seconds) for which a ReceiveMessage call waits for a message to arrive in the queue before returning. If a message is available, the call returns immediately. This is the consumer-side equivalent of ReceiveMessageWaitTimeSeconds.

A wait time of 0 means that requests for new messages return immediately. This *short polling* can result in many, frequent calls to SQS that return no messages, which means overall higher usage and higher bills for you. In contrast, *long polling* helps reduce the cost of Amazon SQS by setting a higher wait time, resulting in fewer calls with no data to process. Long polling also allows you to receive multiple messages per call so that you can process messages in batches. This can increase your overall throughput if your downstream recipients (such as a Lambda function) can handle multiple inputs at once.

ReceiveMessageWaitTimeSeconds   ReceiveMessageWaitTimeSeconds is the SQS-side equivalent of a consumer's WaitTimeSeconds value. If set, the client-side value takes precedence.

ChangeMessageVisibility   This option lets you alter the VisibilityTimeout of the messages received by this call to differ from the queue's default. Clients may set it anywhere from 0 seconds to 12 hours. This call can be useful whenever a client knows it will need additional time to process a message successfully. If this need is consistent, consider changing the queue's default VisibilityTimeout setting for all messages.

> Be aware that SQS does not allow the overall visibility timeout of a message to exceed 12 hours. If you use ChangeMessageVisibility and set a value that would put the message's invisibility time beyond this, SQS will return an error.

DelaySeconds   DelaySeconds is the length of time, in seconds, for which to delay a specific message. Valid values range from 0 seconds to 15 minutes. Messages with a positive DelaySeconds value become available for processing after the delay period is finished. If you do not specify a value, the default value for the queue applies.

This value can be set at the queue level or used by producers to deliberately delay processing on a specific message.

> When you set FifoQueue, you cannot set DelaySeconds per message. You can set this parameter only on a queue level.

MessageRetentionPeriod   MessageRetentionPeriod is how long an SQS message can stay in the queue (i.e., in the *stored* state). The default is four days; this option allows you to set it anywhere from 60 seconds to 14 days.

DeleteMessage

It's the client's responsibility to delete messages from the queue after processing them. Pass the ReceiptHandle of a message to the DeleteMessage function to have SQS delete it from the queue. If you do nothing, the message is returned to the queue after the visibility timeout elapses, and, if left unprocessed, will expire from the queue after the message retention period.

Refer to Table 11.5 to view the differences between the Amazon Simple Notification Service and Amazon SQS event-driven solutions.

SQS Queue Types

Standard queues prioritize *scalability* and *throughput*. To achieve this, they trade off two qualities:

- Order is not guaranteed.
- Messages can appear twice.

FIFO (or "first in, first out") queues deliver messages in the order they receive them. *Message groups* also follow this order so that when you publish messages to different message groups, each message group preserves the messages' internal order.

Be aware that FIFO queues have lower limits on concurrent in-flight messages than standard queues; plan accordingly to make sure consumers don't hold on to messages any longer than needed.

Dead-Letter Queue

Sometimes a message cannot be processed. This could occur due to bad data coming from the producer, a problem on the consumer side, or some other misconfiguration causing a message to result in an error. To help you troubleshoot, SQS lets you define *dead-letter queues* to store failed messages for later investigation or re-processing.

To set up a dead-letter queue, first create a normal, second queue that will act as the DLQ. You can then define an SQS RedrivePolicy to automatically move failed messages to that secondary queue after a message's ReceiveCount exceeds the queue's maxReceiveCount. The secondary queue then acts as a dead-letter queue, not by any specific configuration or setting, but by how it is used.

Use a dead-letter queue to:

- Configure an alarm for any messages delivered to a dead-letter queue
- Examine logs for exceptions that might have caused messages to be delivered to a dead-letter queue
- Analyze the contents of messages delivered to a dead-letter queue to diagnose issues
- Determine whether you have given your consumer sufficient time to process messages

Note that in high-volume scenarios where many messages may fail processing, you can improve throughput by having consumers manually move failed messages to the dead letter queue rather than waiting for the message to repeatedly fail and expire out.

Like any queue, dead-letter queues have a retention period. A message will expire from the dead-letter queue once its lifetime (the sum of its time in the original queue and dead-letter queue) exceeds that retention period. *Thus, AWS recommends that you set the retention period of a dead-letter queue to be longer than the retention period of the original queue.*

Dead-letter queues must match the type of the primary queue; use FIFO for FIFO queues and standard for standard queues.

When to Use a Dead-Letter Queue

Use dead-letter queues with SQS standard queues when your application does not depend on the order of messages and you want to closely inspect the contents of failed messages to understand and resolve bugs in your pipeline.

Dead-letter queues necessarily limit the number of retries on a message. If failures in your system tend to occur due to issues or wait times from downstream systems, and your requirements dictate strict message-processing dependencies, you may be better off setting long message expiration times and letting messages attempt to re-try for long periods.

If it's essential to avoid breaking message order in a FIFO queue, make sure you are not re-processing failed messages from a dead-letter queue; you can still use one for investigation of failure states after the fact.

SQS Attributes, Dead-Letter Queue Settings, and Server-Side Encryption Settings

Tables 11.1, 11.2, and 11.3 provide all the details of the SQS message attributes, dead-letter queue settings, and server-side encryption (SSE) settings.

TABLE 11.1 Amazon SQS message attributes

Attribute	Default	Meaning
Default Visibility Timeout	30 seconds	How long a message is hidden while it is processed. Maximum limit is 12 hours.
Message Reten-tion Period	4 days	How long a queue retains a message before deleting it. Can be from 1 hour to 14 days.

Attribute	Default	Meaning
Maximum Message Size	256 KB	Maximum size of a message with 10 items maximum.
Delivery Delay	0 seconds	How long to delay before publishing the message to the queue. *Delay queues* let you schedule messages for later.
Receive Message Wait Time	0 seconds	Maximum time consumer receives call waits for new messages.

Large Messages

To send a message larger than 256 KB, use SQS to save the file in Amazon S3 and then send a link to the file via SQS.

TABLE 11.2 Dead-letter queue settings

Setting	Meaning
Use Redrive Policy	Send messages to the dead-letter queue if consumers keep failing to process it.
Dead-Letter Queue	Name of dead-letter queue.
Maximum Receives	Maximum number of times a message is received before it is sent to the dead-letter queue.

TABLE 11.3 Server-Side Encryption (SSE) settings

Setting	Meaning
Use SSE	SQS encrypts all messages sent to this queue.
AWS Key Management Service (AWS KMS) Customer Key	The AWS KMS customer key that encrypts the data keys used to encrypt messages.
Data Key Reuse Period	Length of time to reuse a data key before a new one regenerates.

Monitoring SQS Queues Using CloudWatch

Amazon CloudWatch monitors your AWS resources and the applications you run on AWS in real time, collecting and tracking metrics you can use for troubleshooting.

CloudWatch alarms send notifications or automatically make changes to the resources you monitor based on rules that you define, such as when a message is sent to the dead-letter queue.

The AWS/Events namespace includes the DeadLetterInvocations metric, as shown in Table 11.4. The DeadLetterInvocations metric uses Count as the unit, so Sum and SampleCount are the most useful statistics.

TABLE 11.4   CloudWatch dead-letter queue

Metric	Description
DeadLetterInvocations	Measures the number of times a rule's target is not invoked in response to an event. This includes invocations that would result in triggering the same rule again, causing an infinite loop. Valid dimensions: RuleName Units: Count

Amazon Simple Notification Service

Amazon Simple Notification Service (SNS) is a flexible, fully managed *publisher/subscriber* (pub/sub) messaging service that coordinates the delivery of messages to subscribing endpoints and clients. In contrast to SQS, in which consumers explicitly "pull" data by polling for messages, SNS is a "push" mechanism, delivering messages automatically to subscribed services.

SNS messages are added to *topics* by publishers in a fire-and-forget, or asynchronous, manner. From there, multiple subscribers can listen and consume the messages via a diverse selection of protocols such as HTTPS, email, and SMS (text messages). You can even subscribe SQS queues to SNS topics or have messages trigger Lambda functions, as shown in Figure 11.6.

The sequence of operations in Amazon SNS includes the following:

1.   The administrator creates a topic.

2.   Users subscribe to the topic by using email addresses, SMS numbers, SQS queues, and other endpoints.

3.   The administrator publishes a message on the topic.

4.   The subscribers to the topic receive the message that was published.

FIGURE 11.6 Amazon SNS

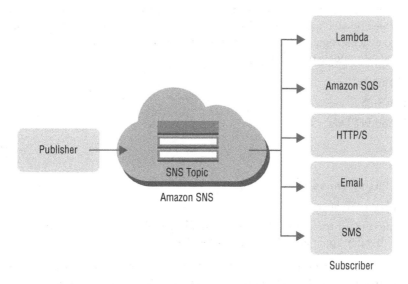

If a user subscribes to the topic after a message was published, the user will *not* receive the message. A subscriber receives messages that are published only after they have subscribed to the topic. The topics do not buffer messages.

SQS and SNS can be used in conjunction to create asynchronous processes that notify users when they are complete. Figure 11.7 depicts such a flow, where users drop files into an S3 bucket, which are then transformed by some process (e.g., a Lambda function). The Lambda can then use SNS to notify users of the job's completion via channels such as email or text message.

FIGURE 11.7 Combined SQS and SNS workflow

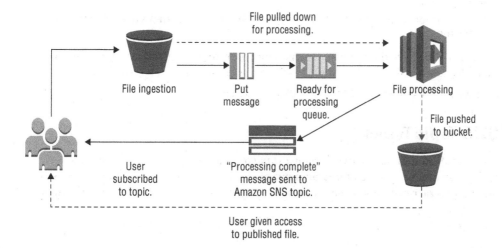

For example, a brokerage website may use a pub/sub pattern when stock prices fluctuate. When a change occurs, the site must update user dashboards to indicate the new price and update the value of each user's portfolio to reflect the new price. In addition, all users who subscribed to a stock topic can receive a notification on the new prices.

Amazon SNS supports the following endpoints:

- AWS Lambda
- Amazon SQS
- HTTP and HTTPS
- Email
- SMS
- Mobile `PushRecords`
- Kinesis Data Firehose
- Application platform endpoints (used for sending mobile-native push notifications to systems like the Apple Push Notification Service)

Amazon SNS retries sending messages for HTTPS endpoints as a REST call to these end-points. You can configure the number of retries and the delay between them.

Features and Functionality

Amazon SNS topic names have a limit of 256 characters. Topic names must be unique within an AWS account and can include alphanumeric characters plus hyphens (-) and underscores (_). After you delete a topic, you can reuse the topic name. When a topic is created, SNS assigns a unique Amazon Resource Name (ARN) to the topic, which includes the service name (SNS), AWS region, AWS ID of the user, and topic name.

SNS clients use the ARN address to identify the right topic:

```
aws sns publish --topic-arn <TOPIC_ARN> --message "ORDER_DETAILS_HERE"
--message-attributes
'{"destination_department":{"DataType":"String","StringValue":"order_
processing"}}'
```

Topic ARNs have the following format, incorporating the region (us-east-1) in this example, account ID (1234567890123456) and the topic name (my_topic):

```
arn:aws:sns:us-east-1:1234567890123456:my_topic
```

SNS Topic Types

Like SQS, SNS topics have two variants: *standard* and *first-in, first-out (FIFO)*. Standard topics may occasionally send messages out of order, and sometimes duplicate messages. FIFO topics sacrifice some scalability and throughput to achieve exactly once, deduplicated delivery.

Deduplication is achieved either via a user-supplied message ID, which SNS will guarantee not to replicate, or by examining the content of the messages themselves. In the absence of a message ID, SNS will calculate a hash of each message's payload to confirm that the hashed message has not been sent before.

When subscribing SQS queues to SNS, you must match the type. Only FIFO queues can subscribe to FIFO topics; the same applies to standard topics and queues.

Transport Protocols

Amazon SNS supports notifications over multiple transport protocols. You can select transports as part of the subscription requests.

- **HTTP, HTTPS:** Subscribers specify a URL as part of the subscription registration; notifications deliver through an HTTP POST to the specified URL.

- **Email, Email-JSON:** Messages are sent to registered addresses as email. Email-JSON sends notifications as a JSON object, while Email sends text-based email.

- **SQS:** Users specify an SQS standard queue as the endpoint. SNS enqueues a notification message to the specified queue (which subscribers can then process with SQS APIs, such as `ReceiveMessage` and `DeleteMessage`). SQS does not support FIFO queues.

- **SMS:** Messages are sent to registered phone numbers as AWS SMS text messages.

SNS Mobile Push Notifications

SNS also has the ability to send mobile push notifications to platforms such as Android and iOS. By sending messages to a mobile endpoint on one of these platforms, you can trigger alerts, notification badges, or sounds on a user's mobile device.

The following push notification services are supported:

- Amazon Device Messaging (ADM)

- Apple Push Notification Service (APNS) for both iOS and macOS

- Baidu Cloud Push (Baidu)

- Google Cloud Messaging for Android (GCM)

- Microsoft Push Notification Service for Windows Phone (MPNS)

- Windows Push Notification Services (WNS)

When a mobile device user opts in to push notification from an app, the platform holder's push services (such as APNS and GCM) create a unique token to represent that individual app on that specific device. SNS uses these app/device tokens to create a destination endpoint to which it can send messages to the device. To authorize SNS to do this, you're required to configure SNS with your credentials to the push notification service.

You can also use SNS to send messages to mobile endpoints subscribed to a topic, just like any other endpoint. Figure 11.8 shows this scenario. The mobile endpoint communicates with push notification services, whereas the other endpoints do not.

FIGURE 11.8   SNS mobile endpoint subscriber

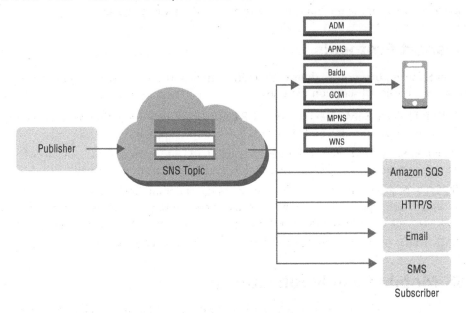

Fan-Out Pattern: Combining SNS and SQS

One of the more powerful architectural patterns for using SNS and SQS together is the "fan-out" pattern, which combines the publisher-subscriber model of SNS with the queueing behavior of SQS. In a fan-out design, one SNS topic has multiple SQS subscribers. With this approach, you can have one publisher pushing out events that may be consumed by any number of receivers, as shown in Figure 11.9.

FIGURE 11.9   Fan-out pattern with SNS and SQS

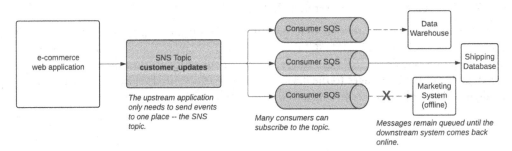

While SNS alone can have many subscribers, it is possible for a subscriber to miss a message, after which it cannot be retrieved. However, if that subscriber is an SQS queue, the missed message will be retained in SQS until the consuming application is able to pull it. Later, more applications can subscribe new SQS queues to the topic, and the publisher never has to change to accommodate these new consumers.

Billing, Limits, and Restrictions

SNS includes a Free Tier that makes the first 1 million SNS requests free and does not charge for the first 100,000 notifications over HTTP. It also does not charge for the first 100 notifications over SMS, nor the first 1,000 notifications over email.

With SNS, there is no minimum fee, and you pay only for what you use. You pay $0.50 per 1 million Amazon SNS requests, $0.06 per 100,000 notification deliveries over HTTP, and $2 per 100,000 notification deliveries over email. *For SMS messaging, users can send 100 free notification deliveries and, for subsequent messages, charges vary by destination country.*

By default, Amazon SNS offers 10 million subscriptions per topic and 100,000 topics per account. To request a higher limit, contact AWS Support.

 SNS supports the same attributes and parameters as SQS. For more information, refer to Tables 11.2, 11.3, and 11.4.

There several differences between the SNS and SQS event-driven solutions, as shown in Table 11.5.

TABLE 11.5   SNS and SQS feature comparison

Features	SNS	SQS
Message persistence	Not persisted	Persisted
Delivery mechanism	Push (passive)	Pull (active)
Producer/consumer	Publish/subscribe (1 to N)	Send/receive (1 to 1)

Amazon Kinesis Data Streams

The *Amazon Kinesis Data Streams* feature allows you to ingest and process large amounts of data. It is designed to handle high-throughput and real-time analytics use cases, where data needs to be processed as soon as it arrives.

With Kinesis Data Streams, producers are responsible for continuously pushing data into the service, while consumers read and process the data.

Amazon Kinesis is built around the concept of streams, which are highly scalable and durable real-time data transportation pipelines. These streams can handle data from hundreds of thousands of producers simultaneously, continuously ingesting vast amounts of information. Each stream is composed of one or more shards, which are the fundamental units of parallelism and data distribution within a stream. Shards allow for efficient processing and enable Kinesis to handle massive throughput.

Data records sent to a Kinesis stream are automatically distributed across shards based on a partition key. This partitioning strategy ensures that records with the same partition key are always routed to the same shard, guaranteeing that these records are processed in strict order within each partition key. This design allows for both high scalability and ordered processing of related data points.

One of the key advantages of Kinesis Data Streams is its ability to support multiple consumers reading from the same stream simultaneously, similar to the SNS/SQS fan-out pattern described earlier, but with higher overall throughput capacity and better cost scaling at high levels of demand.

Unlike traditional messaging systems, data records in Kinesis Data Streams are not deleted after being consumed; instead, consumers maintain their own checkpoints, allowing them to restart processing from a specific point in the stream if needed. In addition, Kinesis offers long-term (up to 365 days) data retention, and the ability to perform stream analytics.

Figure 11.10 illustrates the high-level architecture of Kinesis Data Streams. Producers continually push (`PushRecords`) data to Kinesis Data Streams, and consumers (such as a custom application running on EC2, Lambda functions, or an Amazon Kinesis Data Firehose delivery stream) can send results to an AWS service such as DynamoDB, Amazon Redshift, or S3.

FIGURE 11.10   Amazon Kinesis Data Streams

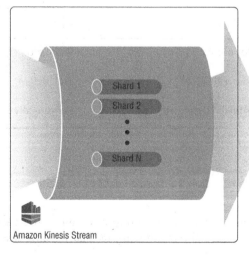
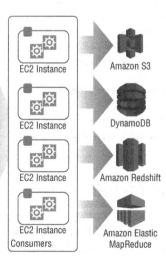

To place (PutRecords) data into the stream, producers specify the name of the stream and an item to place on the stream. Items have two attributes: a *partition key* and the *data blob* to add to the stream. The partition key is an identifier for the record and, as with DynamoDB, determines the shard in the stream to which the data record will be added.

All data in each shard is sent to the same worker that processes the shard, which may be a Lambda function, a Kinesis Data Firehose, or a client built with the SDK or Kinesis Client Library.

High Throughput

Amazon Kinesis uses shards to configure and support high throughput. When you create an Amazon Kinesis data stream, you specify a baseline number of shards, which you can then increase or decrease via API calls or management console configuration changes.

On the producer side, the shard supports 1 MB per second of ingest, or 1,000 transactions per second. Producers can write up to 1 MB per second of data, or 1,000 writes.

On the consumer side, each shard supports 2 MB per second of reads, or 5 transactions per second. Amazon Kinesis Data Streams support twice as much data for reads as they do for writes (2 MB per second of read versus 1 MB per second of write) per shard. This allows multiple applications to read from a stream to enable more reads. Because the same records might be read by multiple applications, you require more throughput on the read side.

This throughput model is now called "classic." For an additional provisioning fee, your data stream can be set to "enhanced" mode, wherein that 2 MB per second capacity is provisioned to *each consumer*, rather than being split among all consumers.

Amazon Kinesis Data Streams support 5,000 transactions per second for writes, but only five transactions per second for reads per shard. Reads frequently acquire many records at once. When a read request asks for all the records that came in after the last read, it acquires a large number of records. Because of this, five transactions per second per shard is sufficient to handle reads.

In addition to using "enhanced" mode, another way to increase your throughput capacity is to reshard the stream to adjust the number of shards.

Real-Time Analytics

Unlike SQS, Amazon Kinesis Data Streams enable *real-time analytics*, which produce metrics from incoming data as it arrives. The alternative is batch analytics in which data accumulates for a period, such as 24 hours, and then is analyzed as a batch job. Real-time analytics allow you to detect patterns in your data as it arrives, with a delay of only a few seconds to a few minutes.

From here, you will want to observe the behavior of your environment to establish a baseline for expected performance, comparing your Kinesis Data Streams output with historical data to identify any anomalous behavior in the future.

Open Source Tools

Open source tools like Fluentd and Flume can publish messages to Kinesis Data Streams. Custom applications running on EC2 instances can process this data using open source deep-learning algorithms or third-party Kinesis-integrated apps, either in real-time or batch mode.

Producer Options

Here are options for you to build producers that can write into Kinesis Data Streams:

Amazon Kinesis Agent   The Kinesis Agent is a stand-alone Java application that can monitor files (such as application logs) and write them directly to a stream. This agent handles file rotation and retries for you, and also sends data to CloudWatch metrics to help you monitor your ingestion process.

Amazon Kinesis Data Steams API   With this approach, your application uses the AWS SDK, CLI, or API to directly call `PutRecord` on your stream and add items.

Amazon Kinesis Producer Library (KPL)   The KPL gives you a higher-level interface over the low-level Kinesis Data Streams API. It has the logic to retry failures and to buffer and batch-send multiple messages together.

Consumer Options

Consumers also have multiple options for reading Kinesis Data Streams:

Amazon Kinesis Data Streams API   Consumers may use the Kinesis Data Streams API directly or via the SDK or CLI to read data from a stream. To scale this to process large volumes of data, you should create a shard in your stream for each consumer. With this approach, it is your job to write code that handles failures and ensures that all shards are consumed by exactly one consumer.

Amazon Kinesis Client Library (KCL)   The Kinesis Client Library handles the complexity of coordinating between different consumers that read from different shards in a stream. It ensures that *no shard is ignored*, and *no shard is processed by two consumers*. The library creates a table in Amazon DynamoDB with the same name as the application name and uses this table to coordinate between the different consumers.

AWS Lambda   AWS Lambda functions can be configured to poll Kinesis on a regular basis for events. When Kinesis and Lambda are integrated, AWS automatically coordinates the two such that a single function instance always pulls data from the same shard. As a Kinesis consumer, Lambda can scale and handle fault tolerance automatically. It does not require the use of the KCL.

Amazon Kinesis Data Firehose

Amazon Kinesis Data Firehose is a service whose primary function is to take in large quantities of data, such as those generated by Kinesis Data Streams or other services like CloudWatch, and get that data into downstream AWS services, such as S3, Redshift, and Elasticsearch, as well as third-party applications like Splunk and Dynatrace, as rapidly as possible. For those use cases, Firehose can be easier to use than Kinesis Data Streams, as it does not require you to write a consumer application.

Kinesis Data Firehose also handles dynamically scaling the underlying shards of the stream based on the amount of traffic.

Kinesis Data Firehose buffers the data before it writes it to S3, with a delayed reaction to real-time data based on the length of the buffer, as detailed in Table 11.6.

TABLE 11.6   Amazon Kinesis Data Firehose buffers

Parameter	Min	Max	Description
Buffer size	1 MB	128 MB	How much data Kinesis Data Firehose buffers
Buffer interval	60 seconds	900 seconds	How long to buffer data

With Kinesis Data Firehose, you do not need to write consumer applications or manage resources. Configure data producers to send data to Kinesis Data Firehose, and it will automatically deliver the data to the destination you specify. You can also configure Kinesis Data Firehose to transform your data before you deliver it. For example, say you run a news site, and you analyze the stream of clicks from users who read the articles on your site. You want to use this analysis to move the most popular articles to the top of the page to capture news stories that are going viral. It is simple to verify that a story acquires a large number of hits, with a lag of only a few minutes.

Amazon Kinesis Data Analytics

Database developers are well-acquainted with the power of Structured Query Language, or SQL. *Amazon Kinesis Data Analytics* lets you use SQL not only to query and analyze streaming data, but to perform advanced operations like time-series analytics. Kinesis Data Analytics supports ingesting from either Amazon Kinesis Data Streams or Amazon Kinesis Data Firehose, and it continuously reads and processes streaming data. You can configure destinations where Kinesis Data Analytics sends the results, as shown in Figure 11.11. Kinesis Data Analytics supports the following destinations:

- Amazon Kinesis Data Firehose
- Amazon S3
- Amazon Redshift
- Amazon Elasticsearch
- Splunk
- AWS Lambda
- Amazon Kinesis Data Streams

FIGURE 11.11 Amazon Kinesis Data Analytics flow

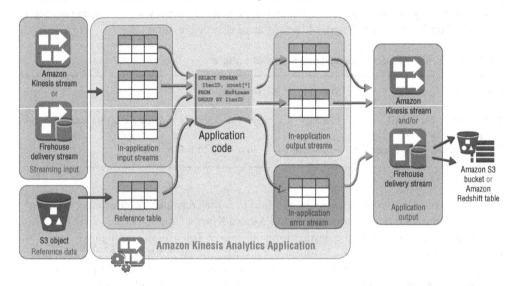

Use cases for Amazon Kinesis Data Analytics include the following:

Generate Time-Series Analytics You can calculate metrics over time windows and stream values to S3 or Redshift through a Firehose delivery stream.

Feed Real-Time Dashboards You can send aggregated and processed streaming data results downstream to feed real-time dashboards.

Create Real-Time Metrics You can create custom metrics and triggers for use in real-time monitoring, notifications, and alarms.

Amazon DynamoDB Streams

The *Amazon DynamoDB Streams* feature allows you to publish a message any time a change is made in a DynamoDB table. Every insert, delete, or update produces an *event*, which publishes it to Amazon DynamoDB Streams, as shown in Figure 11.12. To use this table-level feature, enable Amazon DynamoDB Streams on the table.

FIGURE 11.12   Amazon DynamoDB Stream

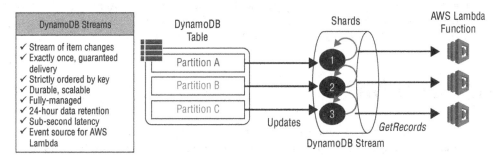

DynamoDB Stream Use Case

DynamoDB Streams is a database trigger for DynamoDB tables that you can use in any situation in which you continuously poll the database to indicate if a variable changes. For example, within an online application, a customer publishes a vote in a DynamoDB table called votes. With DynamoDB Streams, you can automatically track that change in both the votes table and in the consumer table to update the aggregate votes counted.

DynamoDB Stream Consumers

DynamoDB Streams (like Kinesis Firehose) can be integrated with AWS Lambda functions, allowing you to execute function code in response to every insert, update, and delete on a table. In this pattern, your Lambda function continually polls the DynamoDB stream for events, executing on events in batches. Events in DynamoDB streams are published in order, only once.

Using DynamoDB streams with Lambda functions allows you to create the equivalent of *triggers* on a traditional relational database. Just like in an RDBMS, having the ability to execute code in response to changes in data creates powerful opportunities to do things like record events to audit logs, notify users, or trigger workflow events. Unlike traditional databases, these sorts of triggers are asynchronous, and don't risk locking your database while they operate. Other use cases include replicating every DynamoDB record to persistent storage or updating another table in response to activity in the source table. One example of the latter might be maintaining a "high score" table in a game application, updating the leaderboard whenever a user posts a new game score.

Because the polling of DynamoDB Streams is initiated by Lambda, your function must have an execution role capable of reading the stream. You'll read more about this asynchronous "pull" model of Lambda event streaming in the next chapter, "Serverless Compute."

DynamoDB Streams Concurrency and Shards

DynamoDB is designed for scale and can handle a significant number of concurrent writes. To accommodate this kind of load when using DynamoDB Streams, AWS divides the outgoing event flows into multiple *shards*. These shards correspond to the underlying partitions in the DynamoDB table, as described in Chapter 4, "AWS Database Services." When a Lambda function acts as the target for DynamoDB streams, each invocation of the function will deal exclusively with events from a single shard, allowing your stream processing to handle loads just as seamlessly as the DynamoDB database itself.

Amazon MQ

ActiveMQ is a popular open-source message broker from Apache. It allows users to set up and manage queues with many subscribers and is the backbone of many production-grade real-time integrations. It can be configured for high availability and failover, but this requires a significant operational investment in managing multiple nodes and shared storage.

Amazon MQ is AWS's solution to this management overhead, providing a fully-managed ActiveMQ environment that handles scaling and failover for you. AWS manages the instances, the operating system, and the Apache ActiveMQ software stack. You place these instances in your VPC and control access to them through security groups.

Amazon MQ provides endpoints for queues called brokers.

A *single-instance broker* is the least fault-tolerant configured, running in one availability zone, whereas an *active/standby broker for high availability* places two synchronized brokers across two different availability zones.

Similar to RDS, you can have Amazon MQ automatically install minor version upgrades issued by Apache on the broker engine. These upgrades occur during a two-hour mainte-nance window that you define.

Comparison of MQ and SQS or SNS

MQ is a managed message broker service that provides compatibility with many popular message brokers. AWS recommends MQ to migrate applications from current message bro-kers that rely on compatibility with APIs such as JMS or protocols like Advanced Message Queuing Protocol (AMQP), MQTT, OpenWire, and STOMP.

SQS (queues) and SNS (topics) offer high scalability and simplicity without message bro-kers. AWS recommends them for new apps needing virtually unlimited scale and easy APIs.

AWS Step Functions

AWS Step Functions is a service that lets you build workflows that coordinate actions trig-gered by events in AWS or manual execution with powerful-yet-simple mechanisms for conditional logic, parallel processing, and flow control. Step functions are an excellent way to build automation into your AWS environment using either code or a convenient drag-and-drop interface. Figure 11.13 displays the AWS Step Functions service.

FIGURE 11.13   AWS Step Functions

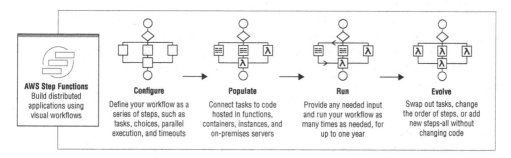

State Machine

The *state machine* is the workflow template that is made up of a collection of states. Each time you launch a workflow, you provide it with an input. Each state that is part of the state machine receives the input, modifies it, and passes it to the next state.

You can use AWS Step Functions as event sources to trigger AWS Lambda. Figure 11.14 is an example of using the AWS Step Functions service.

FIGURE 11.14   State machine code and visual workflow

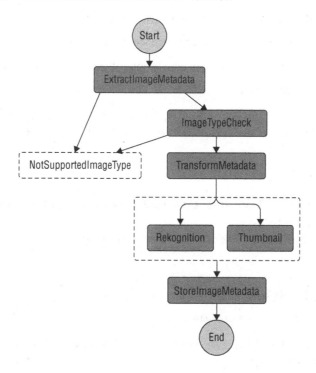

AWS Step Functions manages state, checkpoints, and restarts; built-in try/catch, retry, and rollback capabilities deal with errors and exceptions automatically.

AWS Step Functions manages the logic of your application for you, and it implements basic primitives such as branching, parallel execution, and timeouts.

A finite state machine defines a set of states, their relationships, and their input and output. AWS Step Functions lets you define a workflow as a finite state machine written in the *Amazon States Language*. Each state (or "step") has a particular input, an action that it performs or decision that it makes, and a particular output that feeds into the next state. The *Step Functions console* provides a graphical representation of that state machine to help visualize your application logic.

Names identify states, which can be any string, but must be unique within the state machine specification. Otherwise, it can be any valid string in JSON text format.

 NOTE An instance of a state exists until the end of its execution.

States can perform a variety of functions in your state machine:

Task state: Performs work in your state machine

Choice state: Makes a choice between branches of execution

Fail or Succeed state: Stops an execution with a failure or success

Pass state: Passes inputs to outputs or injects corrected data

Wait state: Provides a delay for a certain amount of time or until a specified time/date

Parallel state: Begins parallel branches of execution

In this example of a Task state, we invoke a Lambda function called HelloWorld, specified by its ARN. This state runs the Lambda, then hands off execution to the next state called MyNextState.

```
"HelloWorld": {
  "Type": "Task",
  "Resource": "arn:aws:lambda:us-east-1:123456789012:function:HelloWorld",
  "Next": "MyNextState",
  "Comment": "Executes HelloWorld and then continues"
}
```

Common State Fields

These fields are common within each state:

Type (Required): One of the state types described above, such as Task or Wait. Determines the state's behavior.

Next: Specifies the next state to which to transition after this one completes. Some states, such as Choice, allow multiple next states.

End: If reached, states with the End value true terminate the step function. Some state types, such as Choice, do not support or use the End field, since their purpose is to conditionally advance the workflow to another state.

Comment (Optional): Allows you to annotate the state with a description of its purpose.

InputPath (Optional): Each state receives input, often in JSON, from the previous state. InputPath specifies which part of the input to pass to the state's processing (e.g., to the Lambda function on a Task state). If you use the value $, you will pass along the entire value, but you may use JSONPath to drill in and extract more specific values. For more on JSONPath, see https://docs.aws.amazon.com/kinesisanalytics/latest/dev/about-json-path.html

OutputPath (Optional): Similar to InputPath, OutputPath allows you to use JSONPath syntax to specify what part of the output will be passed to the next state. By default, this is $, or the entire value.

To see the Amazon Function State Language, refer to Figure 11.15.

FIGURE 11.15   Amazon Function State Language

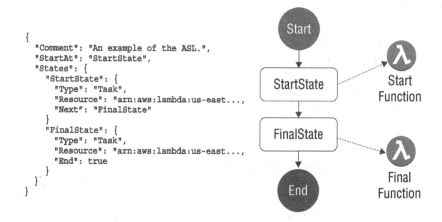

Task State

Task states perform some compute action on your input. They are divided into multiple possible Task Types.

Task Types

Tasks support the following actions:

- Lambda invocations
- HTTP calls
- Supported AWS service calls
- Activities

The type of task state is determined by the Resource field.

Lambda   For a Lambda invocation, you might expect Resource to be the Lambda name or ARN. While this is possible to do, the more flexible option requires you to use the value arn:aws:states:::lambda:invoke with the Lambda ARN given as a parameter, like so:

```
{
  "ProcessData": {
    "Type": "Task",
    "Resource": "arn:aws:states:::lambda:invoke",
    "Parameters": {
      "FunctionName": "arn:aws:lambda:REGION:ACCOUNT_ID:function:
FUNCTION_NAME",
      "Payload": {
        "input.$": "$"
      }
    },
    "ResultPath": "$.lambdaResult",
    "Next": "NextState"
  }
}
```

Alternatively, using the ARN for the Resource type, while more concise, limits output to just the function result, and prevents you from using waitForTaskToken. This directive is part of a callback pattern very similar to CloudFormation WaitConditions. When you specify the Resource value arn:aws:states:::lambda:invoke.waitForTaskToken, you may pass along the token value found on the input at $$.Task.Token, and it is the responsibility of your external processing code to call back to Step Functions with that token to resolve processing. Like WaitConditions, this lets you implement any kind of asynchronous wait, including those that implement human approval steps.

HTTP endpoints   For an HTTP call, you use Resource type arn:aws:states:::http:invoke, as shown in this example where we invoke a third-party API:

```
{
    "Type": "Task",
    "Resource": "arn:aws:states:::http:invoke",
    "Parameters": {
      "ApiEndpoint": "https://some-third-party.com/api/example",
      "Authentication": {
        "ConnectionArn": "arn:aws:events:us-east-2:123456789012:connection/
MyService/CONNECTION_ID"
      },
      "Method": "POST"
    },
    "End": true
  }
```

As you will observe, rather than providing credentials to the API directly in the Step Function configuration, we reference a `ConnectionARN`. Connections like these are defined in the AWS EventBridge service ahead of time so you can avoid hard-coding sensitive values. For more on this, see `https://docs.aws.amazon.com/eventbridge/latest/userguide/eb-target-connection.html`.

AWS Service Calls   Next, some AWS services may be invoked directly from Step Functions. You can find a list of available actions at `https://docs.aws.amazon.com/step-functions/latest/dg/supported-services-awssdk.html` or by calling the CLI function `aws stepfunctions list-supported-services`. Alternatively, these are provided as a drop-down when you create Step Functions through the AWS web console. In this example, the Task calls `PutItem` on a DynamoDB table:

```
{
    "DynamoDBPutItem": {
      "Type": "Task",
      "Resource": "arn:aws:states:::dynamodb:putItem",
      "Parameters": {
        "TableName": "MyTable",
        "Item": {
          "PK": {"S.$": "$.userId"},
          "SK": {"S.$": "$.timestamp"},
          "Data": {"S.$": "$.someData"}
        }
      },
      "ResultPath": "$.dynamoDBResult",
      "Next": "NextState"
    }
  }
```

Activities   Finally, an *activity* is a fully asynchronous invocation of a function hosted outside of Step Functions, such as a process that runs on EC2 or ECS. When you create a definition for an activity in Step Functions (either via the web console or the `CreateActivity` API), you do not specify what the activity will actually be; rather, you are simply given a freshly-generated activity ARN and nothing else. It is the responsibility of your external service to poll the Step Functions service for work using the API function `GetActivityTask`. Here's a brief example of how an external Python script would poll for work and return a value to a Step Function:

```python
import boto3
import json

def main():
    client = boto3.client('stepfunctions')

    while True:
        try:
            # Poll for task in a loop
            task = client.get_activity_task(activityArn="YOUR_
ACTIVITY_ARN")

            if 'taskToken' in task:
                # Get input data from task
                input_data = json.loads(task['input'])
                result = do_something()

                # Send success
                client.send_task_success(
                    taskToken=task['taskToken'],
                    output=json.dumps(result)
                )
            else:
                # No task, wait before polling again
                time.sleep(1)
        except Exception as e:
            print(f"Error: {e}")
```

A Task state must either set the End field to `true` if the state ends the execution or provide a state in the `Next` field that runs upon completion of the Task state. Here's an example:

```json
"ActivityState": {
  "Type": "Task",
  "Resource": "arn:aws:states:us-east-1:123456789012:activity:HelloWorld",
```

```
"TimeoutSeconds": 300,
"HeartbeatSeconds": 60,
"Next": "NextState"
}
```

In this example, `ActivityState` invokes an activity called `HelloWorld`. Your external processor (e.g., a Python script on an EC2 instance) must poll Step Functions to know that this Activity has been invoked, at which point it should run, perform its wok, and respond back with output. When `HelloWorld` completes, the Next state (`NextState`) runs.

If this task fails to complete within 300 seconds or it does not send heartbeat notifications in intervals of 60 seconds, then the task is marked as `failed`. Set a `Timeout` value and a `HeartbeatSeconds` interval for long-running activities.

In addition to the common state fields, Task state fields include the following:

Resource (Required): The resource identifier of the specific Task type, as described above.

Retry (Optional): Used to define the retry behavior of this tat

Catch (Optional): Used to define actions that take place when a task fails, but the retries have been exhausted or they are not defined.

TimeoutSeconds (Optional): Determines the length of time, in seconds, before the state times out and the Step Function fails with a `States.Timeout` error. The default value is 99999999.

HeartbeatSeconds (Optional): Useful for long-running tasks that risk silently failing, this option lets you fail with `States.Timeout` if the task's external processor fails to send a heartbeat signal within the specified recurring timeframe.

Specify Resource Amazon Resource Names in Tasks

To specify the `Resource` field's ARN, use the syntax:

`arn:partition:service:region:account:task_type:name`

where:

- `partition` is the AWS Step Functions partition to use, most commonly `aws`.
- `service` indicates the AWS service that you use to execute the task, which is one of the following values:
  - `states` for an activity
  - `lambda` for an AWS Lambda function
- `region` is the AWS region in which the Step Functions activity/state machine type or AWS Lambda function has been created.
- `account` is your Account ID.

- `task_type` is the type of task to run. It is one of the following:
  - `activity`: An activity
  - `function`: An AWS Lambda function
- `name` is the registered resource name (activity name or AWS Lambda function name).

Choice State

The *Choice state* enables control flow between several different paths based on the input you select. In a Choice state, you place a *condition* on the input. The state machine evaluates the condition, and it follows the path of the first condition that is true about the input.

 A Choice state may have more than one `Next`, but only one within each Choice rule. A Choice state cannot use `End`.

A Choice state (`"Type"`: `"Choice"`) adds branch logic to a state machine. Other Choice state fields include the following:

Choices (Required)   An array of Choice rules that determines which state the state machine transitions to next

Default (Optional, Recommended)   The name of the state to transition to if none of the transitions in `Choices` is taken.

 Choice states do not support the `End` field. They also use `Next` only inside their `Choices` field.

 You must specify the `$.type` field. If the state input does not contain the `$.type` field, the execution fails, and an error displays in the execution history.

This is an example of a Choice state and other states to which it transitions:

```
"ChoiceStateX": {
  "Type": "Choice",
  "Choices": [
    {
      "Not": {
        "Variable": "$.type",
        "StringEquals": "Private"
      },
      "Next": "Public"
```

```
    },
    {
      "Variable": "$.value",
      "NumericEquals": 0,
      "Next": "ValueIsZero"
    },
    {
      "And": [
        {
          "Variable": "$.value",
          "NumericGreaterThanEquals": 20
        },
        {
          "Variable": "$.value",
          "NumericLessThan": 30
        }
      ],
      "Next": "ValueInTwenties"
    }
  ],
  "Default": "DefaultState"
},

"Public": {
  "Type" : "Task",
  "Resource": "arn:aws:lambda:us-east-1:123456789012:function:Foo",
  "Next": "NextState"
},

"ValueIsZero": {
  "Type" : "Task",
  "Resource": "arn:aws:lambda:us-east-1:123456789012:function:Zero",
  "Next": "NextState"
},

"ValueInTwenties": {
  "Type" : "Task",
  "Resource": "arn:aws:lambda:us-east-1:123456789012:function:Bar",
  "Next": "NextState"
},
```

```
"DefaultState": {
  "Type": "Fail",
  "Cause": "No Matches!"
}
```

In this example, the state machine starts with the input `value`:

```
{
  "type": "Private",
  "value": 22
}
```

Step Functions transitions to the `ValueInTwenties` state, based on the `value` field.

If there are no matches for the Choice state's `Choices`, the state in the `Default` field runs instead. If there is no value in `DefaultState`, the execution fails with an error.

Choice Rules

A Choice state must have a `Choices` field whose value is a nonempty array and whose every element is an object called a Choice rule. A Choice rule contains the following:

Comparison   Two fields that specify an input variable to compare, the type of comparison, and the value to which to compare the variable.

Next Field   The value of this field must match a `state` name in the state machine.

This example checks whether the numerical value is equal to 1:

```
{
  "Variable": "$.foo",
  "NumericEquals": 1,
  "Next": "FirstMatchState"
}
```

This example checks whether the string is equal to `MyString`:

```
{
  "Variable": "$.foo",
  "StringEquals": "MyString",
  "Next": "FirstMatchState"
}
```

This example checks whether the string is greater than `MyStringABC`:

```
{
  "Variable": "$.foo",
  "StringGreaterThan": "MyStringABC",
  "Next": "FirstMatchState"
}
```

This example checks whether the timestamp is equal to `2024-01-01T12:00:00Z`:

```
{
  "Variable": "$.foo",
  "TimestampEquals": "2024-01-01T12:00:00Z",
  "Next": "FirstMatchState"
}
```

Step Functions examines each of the Choice rules in the order that they appear in the `Choices` field and transitions to the state you specify in the `Next` field of the first Choice rule in which the variable matches the value equal to the comparison operator.

The comparison supports the following operators:

- And
- BooleanEquals
- Not
- NumericEquals
- NumericGreaterThan
- NumericGreaterThanEquals
- NumericLessThan
- NumericLessThanEquals
- Or
- StringEquals
- StringGreaterThan
- StringGreaterThanEquals
- StringLessThan
- StringLessThanEquals
- TimestampEquals
- TimestampGreaterThan
- TimestampGreaterThanEquals
- TimestampLessThan
- TimestampLessThanEquals

For each of these operators, the value corresponds to the appropriate type: string, number, Boolean, or timestamp. Step Functions do not attempt to match a numeric field to a string value. However, because timestamp fields are logically strings, you can match a timestamp field by a `StringEquals` comparator.

For interoperability, do not assume that numeric comparisons work with values outside the magnitude or precision that the IEEE 754-2008 binary64 data type represents. In particular, integers outside of the range [–253+1, 253–1] might fail to compare in the way that you would expect.

Timestamps (for example, `2016-08-18T17:33:00Z`) must conform to RFC3339 profile ISO 8601, with the following further restrictions:

- An uppercase `T` must separate the date and time portions.
- An uppercase `Z` must denote that a numeric time zone offset is not present.

To understand the behavior of string comparisons, see the Java `compareTo` documentation here:

`https://docs.oracle.com/javase/8/docs/api/java/lang/String`
`.html#compareTo-java.lang.String-`

The values of the `And` `Or` operators must be nonempty arrays of Choice rules that do not themselves contain `Next` fields. Likewise, the value of a `Not` operator must be a single Choice rule with no `Next` fields.

You can create complex, nested Choice rules using `And`, `Not`, and `Or`. However, the `Next` field can appear only in a top-level Choice rule.

Parallel State

The *Parallel state* enables control flow to execute several different execution paths at the same time in parallel. This is useful if you have activities or tasks that do not depend on each other, can execute in parallel, and can help your workflow complete faster.

You can use the Parallel state (`"Type": "Parallel"`) to create parallel branches of execution in your state machine.

In addition to the common state fields, Parallel states introduce these additional fields:

Branches (Required)   An array of objects that specify state machines to execute in parallel. Each such state machine object must have the fields `States` and `StartAt` and mean the same as those in the top level of a state machine.

ResultPath (Optional)   Specifies where in the input to place the output of the branches. The `OutputPath` field (if present) filters the input before it becomes the state's output.

Retry (Optional)   An array of objects, called *retriers*, that define a retry policy in case the state encounters runtime errors.

Catch (Optional)   An array of objects, called *catchers* that define a fallback state that executes in case the state encounters runtime errors and you do not define the `retry` policy or it has been exhausted.

A Parallel state causes AWS Step Functions to execute each branch. The state starts with the name of the state in that branch's `StartAt` field, as concurrently as possible, and waits until all branches terminate (reaches a terminal state) before it processes the Parallel state's `Next` field. Here's an example:

```
{
  "Comment": "Parallel Example.",
```

```
"StartAt": "LookupCustomerInfo",
"States": {
  "LookupCustomerInfo": {
    "Type": "Parallel",
    "End": true,
    "Branches": [
      {
        "StartAt": "LookupAddress",
        "States": {
          "LookupAddress": {
            "Type": "Task",
            "Resource":
              "arn:aws:lambda:us-east-1:123456789012:function:AddressFinder",
            "End": true
          }
        }
      },
      {
        "StartAt": "LookupPhone",
        "States": {
          "LookupPhone": {
            "Type": "Task",
            "Resource":
              "arn:aws:lambda:us-east-1:123456789012:function:PhoneFinder",
            "End": true
          }
        }
      }
    ]
  }
}
}
```

In this example, the LookupAddress and LookupPhone branches execute in parallel. Figure 11.16 displays the workflow in the Step Functions console.

Each branch must be self-contained. A state in one branch of a Parallel state must not have a Next field that targets a field outside of that branch, nor can any other state outside the branch transition into that branch.

FIGURE 11.16   Parallel state visual workflow

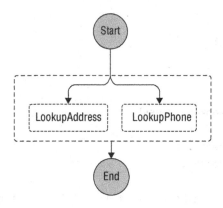

Parallel State Output

A Parallel state provides each branch with a copy of its own input data (InputPath). It generates output, which is an array with one element for each branch that contains the output from that branch. There is no requirement that all elements be of the same type.
Here's an example:

```
{
  "Comment": "Parallel Example.",
  "StartAt": "FunWithMath",
  "States": {
    "FunWithMath": {
    "Type": "Parallel",
    "End": true,
    "Branches": [
      {
        "StartAt": "Add",
        "States": {
          "Add": {
            "Type": "Task",
            "Resource": "arn:aws:swf:us-east-1:123456789012:task:Add",
            "End": true
          }
        }
      },
      {
        "StartAt": "Subtract",
        "States": {
```

```
      "Subtract": {
        "Type": "Task",
        "Resource": "arn:aws:swf:us-east-1:123456789012:task:Subtract",
        "End": true
      }
    }
   }
  ]
 }
 }
}
```

If the FunWithMath state was given the array [3, 2] as input, then both the Add and Subtract states receive that array as input. The output of Add would be 5, that of Subtract would be 1, and the output of the Parallel state would be an array:

```
[ 5, 1 ]
```

Error Handling

If any branch fails, because of an unhandled error or by a transition to a Fail state, the entire Parallel state fails, and all of its branches stop. If the error is not handled by the Parallel state itself, Step Functions stops the execution with an error.

 When a Parallel state fails, invoked AWS Lambda functions continue to run, and activity workers that process a task token do not stop.

To stop long-running activities, use heartbeats to detect whether Step Functions has stopped its branch, and stop workers that are processing tasks. If the state has failed, calling SendTaskHeartbeat, SendTaskSuccess, or SendTaskFailure generates an error.

You cannot stop AWS Lambda functions that are running. If you have implemented a fallback, use a Wait state so that cleanup work happens after the AWS Lambda function finishes.

End State

A state machine completes its execution when it reaches an *End state*. Each state defines either a Next state or an End state, and the End state terminates the execution of the step function.

Input and Output

Each execution of the state machine requires an input as a JSON object and passes that input to the first state in the workflow. The state machine receives the initial input by the process initiating the execution. Each state modifies the input JSON object that it receives and injects its output into this object. The final state produces the output of the state machine.

Individual states receive JSON as the input and usually pass JSON as the output to the next state. Understand how this information flows from state to state and learn how to filter and manipulate this data to design and implement workflows in AWS Step Functions effectively.

In the Amazon States Language, three components filter and control the flow of JSON from state to state: `InputPath`, `OutputPath`, and `ResultPath`.

Figure 11.17 shows how JSON information moves through a Task state. `InputPath` selects which components from the input to pass to the task of the Task state, for example, an AWS Lambda function. `ResultPath` then selects what combination of the state input and the task result to pass to the output. `OutputPath` can filter the JSON output to limit further the information that passes to the output.

FIGURE 11.17   Input and output processing

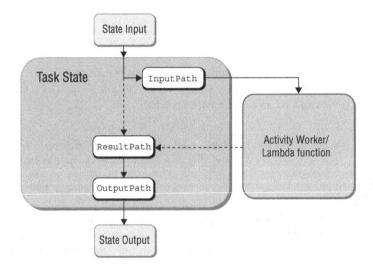

`InputPath`, `OutputPath`, and `ResultPath` each use paths to manipulate JSON as it moves through each state in your workflow.

  ResultPath uses reference paths, which limit scope so that it can identify only a single node in JSON.

Paths and Reference Paths

In this section, you will learn how to use paths and reference paths to process inputs and outputs.

Paths In Amazon States Language, a *path* is a string that begins with $ that you can use to identify components within JSON text. Paths follow the JsonPath syntax.

Reference Paths A *reference path* is a path whose syntax can identify only a single node in a JSON structure.

You can access object fields with only a dot (.) and square brackets ([ ]) notation.

Paths and reference paths do not support the operators @ .. , : ? * and functions such as length().

For example, state input data contains the following values:

```
{
    "foo": 123,
    "bar": ["a", "b", "c"],
    "car": {
        "cdr": true
    }
}
```

In this case, the reference paths return the following:

```
$.foo => 123
$.bar => ["a", "b", "c"]
$.car.cdr => true
```

Certain states use paths and reference paths to control the flow of a state machine or configure a state's options.

Paths in *InputPath, ResultPath,* and *OutputPath* Fields

To specify how to use part of the state's input and what to send as output to the next state, you can use InputPath, OutputPath, and ResultPath.

For InputPath and OutputPath, you must use a path that follows the JsonPath syntax.

For ResultPath, you must use a reference path.

InputPath The InputPath field selects a portion of the state's input to pass to the state's task to process. If you omit the field, it receives the $ value, which represents the entire input. If you use null, the input is not sent to the state's task, and the task receives JSON text representing an empty object {}.

A path can yield a selection of values. Here's an example:

{ "a": [1, 2, 3, 4] }

If you apply the path $.a[0:2], the result is as follows:

[1, 2]

ResultPath If a state executes a task, the task results are sent along as the state's output, which becomes the input for the next task.

If a state does not execute a task, the state's own input is sent, unmodified, as its output. However, when you specify a path in the `value` of a state's `ResultPath` and `OutputPath` fields, different scenarios become possible.

The `ResultPath` field takes the results of the state's task that executes and places them in the input. Next, the `OutputPath` field selects a portion of the input to send as the state's output. The `ResultPath` field might add the results of the state's task that executes to the input, overwrites an existing part, or overwrites the entire input:

- If the `ResultPath` matches an item in the state's input, only that input item is overwritten with the results of executing the state's task. The entire modified input becomes available to the state's output.

- If the `ResultPath` does not match an item in the state's input, an item adds to the input. The item contains the results of executing the state's task. The expanded input becomes available to the state's output.

- If the `ResultPath` has the default value of $, it matches the entire input. In this case, the results of the state execution overwrite the input entirely, and the input becomes available to pass along.

- If the `ResultPath` is `null`, the results of executing the state are discarded, and the input remains the same.

 ResultPath field values must be reference paths.

OutputPath If the `OutputPath` matches an item in the state's input, only that input item is selected. This input item becomes the state's output:

- If the `OutputPath` does not match an item in the state's input, an exception specifies an invalid path.

- If the `OutputPath` has the default value of $, this matches the entire input completely. In this case, the entire input passes to the next state.

- If the `OutputPath` is `null`, JSON text represents an empty object, {}, and is sent to the next state.

The following example demonstrates how `InputPath`, `ResultPath`, and `OutputPath` fields work in practice. Consider this input for the current state:

```
{
  "title": "Numbers to add",
  "numbers": { "val1": 3, "val2": 4 }
}
```

In addition, the state has the `InputPath`, `ResultPath`, and `OutputPath` fields:

```
"InputPath": "$.numbers",
"ResultPath": "$.sum",
"OutputPath": "$"
```

The state's task receives only the `numbers` object from the input. In turn, if this task returns 7, the output of this state equals the following:

```
{
  "title": "Numbers to add",
  "numbers": { "val1": 3, "val2": 4 }
  "sum": 7
}
```

You can modify the `OutputPath` as follows:

```
"InputPath": "$.numbers",
"ResultPath": "$.sum",
"OutputPath": "$.sum"
```

As before, you use the state input data:

```
{
  "numbers": { "val1": 3, "val2": 4 }
}
```

However, now the state output data is 7.

AWS Step Functions Use Case

You can use state machines to process long-running workflows. For example, if a customer orders a book and it requires several different events, use the state machine to run all the events. When the customer orders the book, the state machine creates a credit card transaction, generates a tracking number for the book, notifies the warehouse to ship the order, and then emails the tracking number to the customer. The Step Functions service runs all these steps.

The benefit of Step Functions is that it enables the compute to be stateless. The Lambda functions and the EC2 instances provide compute to the state machine to execute in a stateless way. Lambda functions and EC2 do not have to remember the information about the state of the current execution. The Step Functions service remembers the information about the state of the current execution.

Summary

This chapter covered the different services to refactor larger systems into smaller components that can communicate with each other through infrastructure services. To be successful, the refactoring infrastructure must exist, which enables the different components to communicate with each other. You also now know about the infrastructure communication services that AWS provides for different use cases.

Exam Essentials

Know how refactoring to microservices is beneficial and what services it includes. This includes the use of the Amazon Simple Queue Service, Amazon Simple Notification Service, Amazon Kinesis Data Streams, Amazon Kinesis services, Amazon DynamoDB Streams, Amazon Message Query, and AWS Step Functions.

Know the purpose of the Amazon Simple Queue Service. Know that the Amazon Simple Queue Service is a fully managed message queuing service that makes it easy to decouple and scale microservices, distributed systems, and serverless applications. Know about dead-letter queues and how to use them to troubleshoot issues. Recall that SQS operates on a "pull" pattern for consumers.

Be able to describe the Amazon Simple Notification Service. Familiarize yourself with the Amazon Simple Notification Service and how it is a flexible, fully managed producer/consumer (publisher/subscriber) messaging and mobile notifications web service for coordinating the delivery of messages to subscribing endpoints and clients. SNS coordinates and manages the delivery or sending of messages to subscriber endpoints or clients. Recall that SNS operates on a "push" model, sending data to subscribers as soon as they are published to a topic.

Know about Amazon Kinesis Data Streams. Study how Amazon Kinesis Data Streams is a service for ingesting large amounts of data in real time and for performing real-time analytics on the data. Producers write data into Amazon Kinesis Data Streams, and consumers read data from it. Be familiar with the use of multiple applications, high throughput, real-time analytics, and open source tools that Kinesis supports. Know about producer and consumer options on the exam.

Know the purpose of Amazon Kinesis Data Firehose. Familiarize yourself with Amazon Kinesis Data Firehose and its latency behavior. Data Firehose scales a stream's shards based on the amount of traffic. This service can be used to deliver streaming data to destinations such as S3, Redshift, OpenSearch, or third-party analytics tools, making it an excellent choice for scenarios where you need to continuously move large volumes of data into storage or analytics platforms for further processing and analysis.

Know the purpose of Amazon Kinesis Data Analytics. Know how Amazon Kinesis Data Analytics enables you to process and analyze streaming data with standard SQL. Make sure that you know which destinations it supports.

Be able to describe Amazon DynamoDB Streams. Remember that DynamoDB Streams allows DynamoDB to publish a message every time a change is made in a table. When you insert, update, or delete an item, DynamoDB produces an event that publishes it to the DynamoDB Streams. Familiarize yourself with tables, consumers, concurrency, and streams.

Be able to describe Amazon MQ. Know that the primary use for Amazon MQ is to enable customers who use Apache Active MQ to migrate to the cloud. A message broker allows software applications and components to communicate with various programming languages, operating systems, and formal messaging protocols. Know how the SQS and SNS differ from Amazon MQ.

Understand AWS Step Functions. Have a thorough understanding of AWS Step Functions. Ensure that you know each step in the state machine: Task state, Choice state, Parallel state, and End state. Remember the inputs and outputs in the Step Functions.

Know how state information flows and how to filter that data. Understand how this information flows from state to state and learn how to filter and manipulate this data to design and implement workflows effectively in AWS Step Functions.

Exercises

EXERCISE 11.1

Creating an Amazon SQS Queue, Add Messages, and Receive Messages

In this exercise, you will use the AWS SDK for Python (Boto) to create an Amazon SQS queue, and then you will put messages in the queue. Finally, you will receive messages from this queue and delete them.

1. Make sure that you have AWS administrator credentials set up in your account.

2. Install the AWS SDK for Python (Boto).

    Refer to https://aws.amazon.com/sdk-for-python.

3. Enter the following code into your development environment for Python or the IPython shell. This is the code that you downloaded at the beginning of the exercises.

```
# Test SQS.
import boto3

# Pretty print.
import pprint
pp = pprint.PrettyPrinter(indent=2)

# Create queue.
sqs = boto3.resource('sqs')
queue = sqs.create_queue(QueueName='test1')
print(queue.url)
```

```
# Get existing queue.
queue = sqs.get_queue_by_name(QueueName='test1')
print(queue.url)

# Get all queues.
for queue in sqs.queues.all():
    print(queue)

# Send message.
response = queue.send_message(MessageBody='world')
pp.pprint(response)

# Send batch.
response = queue.send_messages(Entries=[
    { 'Id': '1', 'MessageBody': 'world' },
    { 'Id': '2', 'MessageBody': 'hello' } ])
pp.pprint(response)

# Receive and delete all messages.
for message in queue.receive_messages():
    pp.pprint(message)
    message.delete()

# Delete queue.
queue.delete()
```

4. Run the code. This creates a queue, sends messages to it, receives messages from it, deletes the messages, and then deletes the queue.

5. To experiment with the queue further, add a hash sign to comment out queue .delete() from the last line, which deletes the queue.

6. After you are satisfied with your changes, delete the queue.

Creating an Amazon Kinesis Data Stream and Write/Read Data

In this exercise, you will create an Amazon Kinesis data stream, put records on it (write to the stream), and then get those records back (read from the stream). At the end, you will delete the stream.

1. Enter this code into your development environment for Python or the IPython shell. This is the code that you downloaded at the beginning of the exercises.

```python
import boto3
import random
import json

# Create the client.
kinesis_client = boto3.client('kinesis')

# Create the stream.
kinesis_client.create_stream(
  StreamName='donut-sales',
  ShardCount=2)

# Wait for stream to be created.
waiter = kinesis_client.get_waiter('stream_exists')
waiter.wait(StreamName='donut-sales')

# Store each donut sale using location as partition key.
location = 'california'
data = b'{"flavor":"chocolate","quantity":12}'
kinesis_client.put_record(
    StreamName='donut-sales',
    PartitionKey=location, Data=data)
print("put_record: " + location + " -> " + str(data))

# Next lets put some random records.

# List of location, flavors, quantities.
locations = ['california', 'oregon', 'washington', 'alaska']
flavors = ['chocolate', 'glazed', 'apple', 'birthday']
quantities = [1, 6, 12, 20, 40]

# Generate some random records.
for i in range(20):

    # Generate random record.
    flavor = random.choice(flavors)
    location = random.choice(locations)
    quantity = random.choice(quantities)
```

```
        data = json.dumps({"flavor": flavor, "quantity": quantity})

        # Put record onto the stream.
        kinesis_client.put_record(
            StreamName='donut-sales',
            PartitionKey=location, Data=data)
        print("put_record: " + location + " -> " + data)

    # Get the records.

    # Get shard_ids.
    response = kinesis_client.list_shards(StreamName='donut-sales')
    shard_ids = [shard['ShardId'] for shard in response['Shards']]
    print("list_shards: " + str(shard_ids))

    # For each shard_id print out the records.
    for shard_id in shard_ids:

        # Print current shard_id.
        print("shard_id=" + shard_id)

        # Get a shard iterator from this shard.
        # TRIM_HORIZON means start from earliest record.
        response = kinesis_client.get_shard_iterator(
            StreamName='donut-sales',
            ShardId=shard_id,
            ShardIteratorType='TRIM_HORIZON')
        shard_iterator = response['ShardIterator']

        # Get records on shard and print them out.
        response = kinesis_client.get_records(ShardIterator=shard_iterator)
        records = response['Records']
        for record in records:
            location = record['PartitionKey']
            data = record['Data']
            print("get_records: " + location + " -> " + data.decode('utf-8'))

    # Delete the stream.
    kinesis_client.delete_stream(
```

```
    StreamName='donut-sales')

    # Wait for stream to be deleted.
    waiter = kinesis_client.get_waiter('stream_not_exists')
    waiter.wait(StreamName='donut-sales')
```

2. Run the code.

Observe the output and how all the records for a specific location occur in the same shard. This is because they have the same partition keys. All records with the same partition key are sent to the same shard.

Creating an AWS Step Functions State Machine 1

In this exercise, you will create an AWS Step Functions state machine. The state machine will extract price and quantity from the input and inject the billing amount into the output. This state machine will calculate how much to bill a customer based on the price and quantity of an item they purchased.

1. Sign into the AWS Management Console and navigate to the Step Functions console.

2. Select Get Started.

3. On the resulting pop-up, select Create Your Own. If this is not your first Step Function, select Blank.

4. Edit the name by clicking the pencil next to the autogenerated function name; enter **order-machine**. It is not necessary to save the Step Function at this point.

5. Near the pencil, change the view from Design to Code.

6. Enter the code for the state machine definition. This is the code that you downloaded at the beginning of the exercises, copied below.

```
{
  "StartAt": "CreateOrder",
  "States": {
    "CreateOrder": {
      "Type": "Pass",
      "Result": {
        "Order" : {
          "Customer" : "Alice",
          "Product" : "Coffee",
```

```
            "Billing" : { "Price": 10.0, "Quantity": 4.0 }
        }
      },
      "Next": "CalculateAmount"
    },
    "CalculateAmount": {
      "Type": "Pass",
      "Result": 40.0,
      "ResultPath": "$.Order.Billing.Amount",
      "OutputPath": "$.Order.Billing",
      "End": true
    }
  }
}
```

You'll see the visual representation of the Step Function update. The state machine consists of two states: CreateOrder and CalculateAmount. They are both Pass types and pass hard-coded values.

You can also use this view to debug ResultPath and OutputPath. ResultPath determines where in the input to inject the result. OutputPath determines what data passes to the next state.

7. In the top right, click Create, and then Confirm.

8. Click Start Execution.

9. In Input type, enter {}.

10. Click Start Execution.

11. Once the function has completed, click Execution Input And Output. The output should look like the following:

```
{
  "Price": 10,
  "Quantity": 4,
  "Amount": 40
}
```

In CalculateAmount, "ResultPath": "$.Order.Billing.Amount" injected Amount under Billing under Order. Then in the same element, "OutputPath": "$.Order.Billing" threw away the rest of the input and passed only the contents of the Billing element forward. This is why the output contains only Price, Quantity, and Amount.

12. (Optional) Experiment with different values of `ResultPath` to understand how it affects where the result of a state inserts into the input.

13. (Optional) Experiment with different values of `OutputPath` to understand how it affects what part of the data passes to the next state.

EXERCISE 11.4

Creating an AWS Step Functions State Machine 2

In this exercise, you will create an AWS Step Functions state machine. The state machine will contain a conditional branch. It will use the Choice state to choose which state to transition to next.

The state machine inspects the input and based on it decides whether the user ordered green tea, ordered black tea, or entered invalid input.

1. Sign into the AWS Management Console and navigate to the Step Functions console.

2. Click Create State Machine.

3. When asked to Choose A Template, select Blank.

4. Click the pencil icon to edit the name to **tea-machine**.

5. Click Code to change the view from Design to Code. Enter the following code, which is the code that you downloaded at the beginning of the exercises.

```
{
  "Comment" :
    "Input should look like {'tea':'green'} with double quotes instead of
single.",
  "StartAt": "MakeTea",
  "States" : {
    "MakeTea": {
      "Type": "Choice",
      "Choices": [
        {"Variable":"$.tea","StringEquals":"green","Next":"Green"},
        {"Variable":"$.tea","StringEquals":"black","Next":"Black"}
      ],
      "Default": "Error"
    },
    "Green": { "Type": "Pass", "End": true, "Result": "Green tea" },
    "Black": { "Type": "Pass", "End": true, "Result": "Black tea" },
    "Error": { "Type": "Pass", "End": true, "Result": "Bad input" }
  }
}
```

You will see the visual representation of the state machine update. The MakeTea state is a Choice state. Based on the input it receives, it will branch out to Green, Black, or Error.

6. In the top right, click Create, then click Confirm.

7. Click Start Execution.

8. In the Input section, enter this value:

    ```
    { "tea" : "green" }
    ```

9. Click Start Execution.

10. Once the execution is successful, click Execution Input And Output. The output should look like this:

    ```
    "Green tea"
    ```

11. (Optional) Experiment with different inputs to the state machine. For example, try the following inputs:

    a. For Input, enter **black tea**. This input works.

        ```
        { "tea" : "black" }
        ```

    b. For Input, enter **orange tea**. The execution succeeds, but this input produces an error output message.

        ```
        { "tea" : "orange" }
        ```

12. Change the state machine so that orange tea also works.

Review Questions

1. When a user submits a build into the build system, you want to send an email to the user, acknowledging that you have received the build request, and start the build. To perform these actions at the same time in a Step Function, what type of a state should you use?

   A. Choice

   B. Parallel

   C. Task

   D. Wait

2. Suppose that a standard SQS queue has no consumers. The queue has a maximum message retention period of 14 days. After 14 days, what happens?

   A. After 14 days, the messages are deleted and move to the dead-letter queue.

   B. After 14 days, the messages are deleted and do not move to the dead-letter queue.

   C. After 14 days, the messages are not deleted.

   D. After 14 days, the messages become invisible.

3. What is the maximum size of an Amazon Simple Queue Service message?

   A. 256 KB

   B. 128 KB

   C. 1 MB

   D. 5 MB

4. You want to send a 1 GB file through Amazon Simple Queue Service. How can you do this?

   A. This is not possible.

   B. Save the file in Amazon S3 and then send a link to the file on SQS.

   C. Use AWS Lambda to push the file.

   D. Bypass the log server so that it does not get overloaded.

5. What is the maximum size of an Amazon Simple Notification Service message?

   A. 256 KB

   B. 128 KB

   C. 1 MB

   D. 5 MB

6. You have an Amazon Kinesis Data Stream with one shard and one producer. How many consumer applications can you consume from the stream?

   A. One consumer

   B. Two consumers

   C. Limitless number of consumers

   D. Limitless number of consumers as long as all consumers consume fewer than 2 MB and five transactions per second

7. A company has a website that sells books. It wants to find out which book is selling the most in real time. Every time a book is purchased, it produces an event. What service can you use to provide real-time analytics on the sales with a latency of 30 seconds?

A. Amazon Simple Queue Service

B. Amazon Simple Notification Service

C. Amazon Kinesis Data Streams

D. Amazon Kinesis Data Firehose

8. A company sells books in the 50 states of the United States. It publishes each sale into an Amazon Kinesis Data Stream with two shards. For the partition key, it uses the two-letter abbreviation of the state, such as WA for Washington, WY for Wyoming, and so on. Which of the following statements is true?

A. The records for Washington are all on the same shard.

B. The records for both Washington and Wyoming are on the same shard.

C. The records for Washington are on a different shard than the records for Wyoming.

D. The records for Washington are evenly distributed between the two shards.

9. What are the options for Amazon Kinesis Data Streams producers?

A. Amazon Kinesis Agent

B. Amazon Kinesis Data Steams API

C. Amazon Kinesis Producer Library (KPL)

D. Open source tools

E. All of these are valid options.

10. Your organization is building a microservices-based application where one service generates updates about system health, and multiple other services need to react to these updates in different ways. The system must be scalable and able to handle a high volume of messages, and receivers must be able to process every message, even if they temporarily go offline. What is the best approach to implementing this requirement?

A. Have the status service publish messages to SNS and use SQS to subscribe multiple queues to the SNS topic.

B. Have the status service push updates to a Kinesis Data Stream and have each receiving service subscribe with the Kinesis Consumer Library.

C. Configure an Amazon SQS FIFO queue for each subscriber service to ensure messages are received in order.

D. Deploy AWS Step Functions to orchestrate the distribution of health updates to each service.

11. An application in your organization receives message from a user registration form via a standard SQS queue. You notice that the same message is sometimes processed more than once, causing duplicate user entries. Which feature of Amazon SQS should be adjusted to minimize this issue?

    A. Increase the message retention period in the SQS queue settings.

    B. Decrease the message visibility timeout for the SQS queue.

    C. Convert the standard SQS queue to a FIFO SQS queue.

    D. Enable Long Polling on the SQS queue.

Serverless Compute

**THE AWS CERTIFIED DEVELOPER –
ASSOCIATE EXAM TOPICS COVERED IN
THIS CHAPTER MAY INCLUDE, BUT ARE
NOT LIMITED TO, THE FOLLOWING:**

✓ **Domain 1: Development with AWS Services**

  ▪ Task Statement 2: Develop code for AWS Lambda

✓ **Domain 2: Security**

  ▪ Task Statement 3: Manage sensitive data in application code

✓ **Domain 3: Deployment**

  ▪ Task Statement 1: Prepare application artifacts to be
    deployed to AWS

  ▪ Task Statement 2: Test applications in development
    environments

  ▪ Task Statement 3: Automate deployment testing

  ▪ Task Statement 4: Deploy code using AWS CI/CD services

✓ **Domain 4: Troubleshooting and Optimization**

  ▪ Task Statement 1: Assist in a root cause analysis

  ▪ Task Statement 2: Instrument code for observability

  ▪ Task Statement 3: Optimize applications by using AWS ser-
    vices and features

Serverless compute allows you to deploy functions to the cloud without the need to provision or maintain server infrastructure.

AWS Lambda lets you write functions in a variety of programming languages, such as Python, Java, or Go, and invoke them via API, through SDK calls, or by triggers from other AWS services. Pricing is based on invocations and resources consumed. You only pay when your functions are run, making Lambda a highly elastic service.

The term "serverless" is a bit of a misnomer, as AWS certainly runs your code on server infrastructure somewhere in the stack. However, this complexity is entirely hidden from the user, who must only be concerned with writing and deploying code.

Sometimes called *function-as-a-service* (FaaS), AWS Lambda executes code whenever the function triggers, and no EC2 instances need to be spun up in your infrastructure. Lambda functions are highly scalable, as you may invoke many instances of the same function in parallel.

With the use of AWS Lambda and other AWS Cloud services, you can begin to decouple the application, which allows you to improve your ability to both scale horizontally and create asynchronous systems.

Where Did the Servers Go?

Serverless computing still requires servers, but the complexities of server provisioning, management, and capacity planning are all hidden from view, fully managed by the Lambda service. Serverless code can provide the compute in a microservice architecture, take action in response to events, or serve web applications as part of a fully serverless framework.

When a Lambda function is triggered, AWS launches a *container* to run your code. The first time the container is launched is referred to as a *cold start*. Once a function container has run, it remains active for several minutes before it terminates. If another function invocation occurs while a container is already available, your code will run on that *warm container*.

By default, AWS Lambda runs containers inside the AWS environment, and not within your personal AWS account. However, you can also run AWS Lambda inside your VPC. Figure 12.1 displays the execution flow process.

FIGURE 12.1 AWS Lambda execution flow

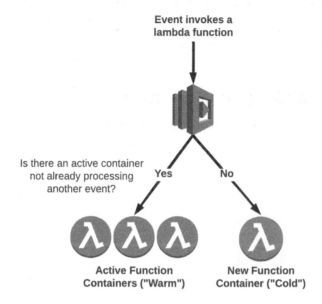

Lambda does not simply provision one container per invocation. Based on usage patterns, Lambda may pre-provision several containers to meet expected future demand.

Monolithic vs. Microservices Architecture

As discussed in Chapter 11, *microservices* are an architectural approach to software development wherein small independent services communicate over well-defined application programming interfaces (APIs). Small, self-contained teams can own and manage these services independently.

In contrast, many applications are developed as *monolithic* architectures. With monolithic architectures, all processes are tightly coupled and run as a single service. If one process of the application experiences a spike in demand, you must scale the entire architecture. Changing a monolithic application becomes more complicated as the code base grows. This complexity limits experimentation and makes it difficult to implement new ideas. Monolithic architectures increase the risk for application availability, as many dependent and tightly coupled processes increase the impact of a single process failure.

Microservices are more agile, scalable, and flexible than monolithic applications. You can deploy new portions of your code faster and with less disruption to the system. With AWS Lambda and other services like SNS and SQS, you can build a microservice architecture for your applications.

AWS Lambda Functions

This section discusses how to create, secure, trigger, debug, monitor, improve, and test AWS Lambda functions.

Languages AWS Lambda Supports

AWS Lambda functions currently support the following languages:

- C# .NET
- PowerShell
- Go
- Ruby
- Java
- Node.js
- Python

Creating an AWS Lambda Function

There are several ways to create a Lambda function:

AWS Management Console   Use the web console; the Lambda service has a built-in code editor appropriate for small-scale or proof-of-concept deployments. This method is not advised as a way to maintain production functions, since it cannot tie into version control systems like GitHub.

AWS Command-Line Interface (AWS CLI)   Build your functions locally on your own machine, then use the AWS CLI Lambda commands to push them to AWS for execution.

AWS Software Development Kit (AWS SDK)   Use SDK libraries Java, .NET, Node.js, PHP, Python, Ruby, Go, Browser, and C++ to create Lambda functions and deploy code.

AWS CloudFormation   Use the resource type `AWS::Lambda::Function` to deploy either inline function code or zip-compressed packages stored in S3.

AWS Serverless Application Model   Discussed in Chapter 14, the Serverless Application Model is an extension of CloudFormation that simplifies the deployment of serverless architecture components like Lambda functions and API endpoints. Use it to manage not just Lambdas, but multiple, connected components of serverless apps.

In this chapter, you will create an AWS Lambda function and properties with the AWS Management Console. In the Exercises section, you will use the AWS CLI and the Python SDK for the AWS Lambda function.

Launch the AWS Management Console, select Services, then search for Lambda, as shown in Figure 12.2. It can also be found by clicking the Compute section.

FIGURE 12.2 AWS Management Console

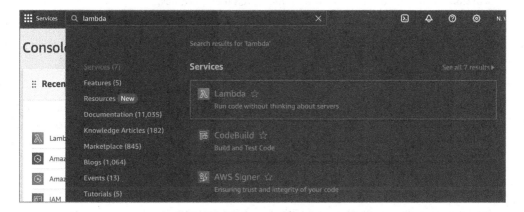

When you create an AWS Lambda function, there are three options:

Author from Scratch   Manually create all settings and options.

Blueprints   Select a preconfigured template that you can modify.

Container Image   Deploy a container that runs your function.

When authoring from scratch, you must provide a few details to create an AWS Lambda function:

Name   The name of the AWS Lambda function.

Runtime/Architecture   The language in which the AWS Lambda function is written. You may also need to specify the architecture, such as x86 or arm64, of the environment in which your code will run.

Execution Role   You may accept the default basic permissions, which Lambda will provision as a new IAM role, or you may provide your own role to the function.

Execution Methods/Invocation Models

There are three distinct invocation models for AWS Lambda:

Synchronous   When a client makes a synchronous call to a Lambda function, it waits until it receives a response or the function times out. Examples include CLI or SDK invocations made with invocation type RequestResponse and instances where Lambdas provide the implementation for API Gateway endpoints, such as an HTTP GET or POST.

Asynchronous (Push Model)   Many AWS services can be configured to invoke a Lambda function when something occurs in that service. For instance, S3 can trigger a Lambda when an object is created or deleted, SNS can call AWS Lambda whenever a message is published on a topic, or EventBridge can invoke a Lambda function on a schedule or in response to observed CloudWatch metric values.

In each of these cases, the Lambda function is invoked *asynchronously*, meaning that instead of waiting for a response, the calling service takes a "fire and forget" approach, placing its request on an internal queue monitored by AWS Lambda. The Lambda function receives an event object containing information about the incoming request, but it does not provide a response back to the caller.

Be aware that in this model, AWS Lambda may retry processing an event up to three times if it somehow fails in its execution. Be sure your Lambda functions are coded to handle the possibility of seeing duplicate events!

CLI or SDK users can also invoke Lambda functions in this manner by using the invocation type `Event`.

With a "push model" event source, a service such as Amazon S3 invokes the Lambda function each time an event occurs with the bucket you specify.

Figure 12.3 illustrates the push model flow.

FIGURE 12.3   Amazon S3 push model

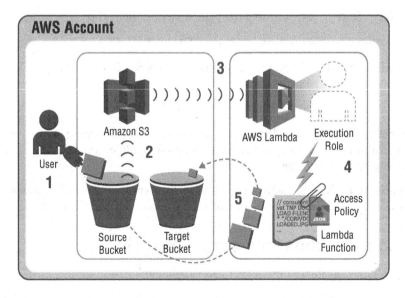

1.   You create an object in a bucket.

2.   S3 detects the `object created` event.

3. S3 invokes your Lambda function according to the event source mapping in the bucket configuration.

4. AWS Lambda verifies the permissions policy attached to the function to ensure that S3 has the necessary permissions to call it.

5. AWS executes the Lambda function, passing in the event as a parameter.

Asynchronous (Pull Model, aka Event Streaming)   Event streaming sources are those AWS services that generate significant amounts of data, such as Amazon Kinesis or DynamoDB streams. In these cases, Lambda functions configured to respond to this data do not monitor a queue, but rather poll the source themselves to determine which events are available to process. This approach is known as *event source mapping* and can be used with several AWS services:

- Amazon DocumentDB
- Amazon DynamoDB
- Amazon Kinesis
- Amazon MQ
- Amazon Managed Streaming for Apache Kafka (MSK)
- Self-managed Apache Kafka
- Amazon Simple Queue Service (SQS)

From the perspective of the event source, this is an asynchronous invocation; for example, DynamoDB does not wait for the Lambda function to complete. On the Lambda side, the functional call is synchronous, in the sense that an invocation must finish before AWS Lambda will poll for more events.

With a *pull model* invocation, AWS Lambda polls a stream and invokes the function upon detection of new records on the stream. Amazon Kinesis uses the pull model.

Figure 12.4 illustrates the sequence for a pull model.

1. A custom application writes records to an Amazon Kinesis stream.

2. AWS Lambda continuously polls the stream or streams specified in your event source mapping configuration. When it detects new records on the stream, AWS Lambda invokes your function.

3. After verifying the permissions of Kinesis to invoke the function, the Lambda service executes the function.

Figure 12.4 uses an Amazon Kinesis stream, but the same principle applies when you work with an Amazon DynamoDB stream.

FIGURE 12.4 Kinesis pull model

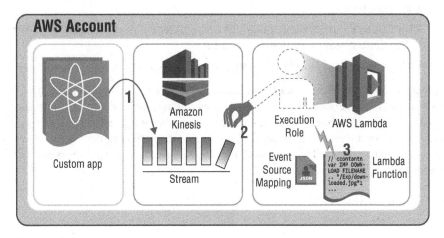

Dry Run

As mentioned earlier, the InvocationType parameter determines in what mode a Lambda function will be executed when called by the CLI or SDK. This parameter has a third option, DryRun, which tests that the caller has permissions to call the function but does not execute it.

Invocation Sources

There are many ways to invoke an AWS Lambda function. You can use the push or pull method, use a custom application, or use a schedule and event to run an AWS Lambda trigger. AWS Lambda supports the following AWS services as event sources:

- Amazon S3
- Amazon DynamoDB
- Amazon Kinesis Data Streams
- Amazon Simple Notification Service
- Amazon Simple Email Service
- Amazon Cognito
- AWS CloudFormation
- Application Load Balancers
- Amazon CloudWatch Logs
- Amazon EventBridge (includes schedules)
- AWS CodeCommit
- AWS Config
- Amazon Alexa

- Amazon Lex
- Amazon API Gateway
- AWS IoT Button
- Amazon CloudFront
- Amazon Kinesis Data Firehose
- Manually invoking a Lambda function on demand

Invoking Lambda Through the CLI or SDK

Running a Lambda function from the CLI is quite straightforward. Using the CLI, call the `invoke` method of the Lambda service:

```
aws lambda invoke \
    --function-name helloWorld \
    --cli-binary-format raw-in-base64-out
    --payload '{ "first": "John", "last": "Doe", "age": "27"}' \
        response_data.json
```

In this example, we invoke a function in our account named `helloWorld` and provide it with some incoming event data in the form of a JSON payload. This payload is explained in detail in the upcoming section "Event Object." The return value of the function is written to the output filename provided in the last parameter; in this case, `response_data.json`. For a testing shortcut, assign the name **/dev/stdout** on Mac or Linux machines to route return data to the console.

To do the same via the AWS SDK for Python (Boto3), run the following:

```
import boto3
import json

# Create a Lambda client
client = boto3.client('lambda')

# Define the payload
payload = {
    "first": "John", "last": "Doe", "age": "27"
}

# Invoke the Lambda function
response = client.invoke(
    FunctionName='helloWorld',
    InvocationType='RequestResponse',
    Payload=json.dumps(payload).encode('utf-8')
)
```

```
# Read the response
response_payload = response['Payload'].read().decode('utf-8')
response_data = json.loads(response_payload)
```

You may refer to the Lambda function by its ARN or its function name. Using the function name by itself will execute the latest deployed version of the code; to run a specific version number, append that number with a colon, like `helloWorld:2`. Versions are described in detail in the upcoming section "Lambda Deployment and Testing."

Running Lambda Functions on a Schedule

To run Lambda functions on a schedule, you can use Amazon EventBridge (formerly known as CloudWatch Events). EventBridge allows you to create rules that trigger your Lambda functions at specified times or intervals. First, create an EventBridge rule, defining the schedule via the GUI or with cron syntax. Then, set the target of this rule to your Lambda function.

This setup enables your Lambda function to execute automatically based on the defined schedule, allowing for tasks like regular data processing, backups, or periodic maintenance without manual intervention.

Invoking Lambda Functions Through Amazon API Gateway

An often-used and powerful pattern for building cloud-native applications in AWS is to use Amazon API Gateway to build APIs whose functionality is implemented by AWS Lambda. For instance, you might create a simple blog application whose backend is a REST API with two endpoints: `GET /articles` and `POST /article`. Each of these URLs can expose functionality implemented in a Lambda function. Amazon API Gateway and this architectural pattern are discussed in detail in Chapter 13, "Serverless Applications."

Securing AWS Lambda Functions

AWS Lambda functions include two types of permissions:

- *Execution permissions* enable the AWS Lambda function to access other AWS resources in your account. For example, if the Lambda function needs access read data in S3, you grant permissions through an AWS IAM role called a Lambda *execution role*.

- *Invocation permissions* are the permissions that an event source needs to invoke your Lambda function. Depending on the invocation model (push or pull), you can either update the access policy you associate with your Lambda function (push) or update the Lambda execution role (pull). The former is called a "resource-based" permission, and AWS often creates this policy for you whenever you configure an event invocation, such as an S3 event trigger.

AWS Lambda provides several managed policies for Lambda execution roles, including:

LambdaBasicExecutionRole   Grants permissions only for CloudWatch. Use this policy if your Lambda function does not access any other AWS resources except writing logs.

LambdaKinesisExecutionRole   Grants permissions for Kinesis Data Stream and CloudWatch log actions. If you are writing a Lambda function to process Kinesis stream events, attach this permissions policy.

LambdaDynamoDBExecutionRole   Grants permissions for DynamoDB stream and CloudWatch log actions. If you are writing a Lambda function to process DynamoDB stream events, attach this permissions policy.

LambdaVPCAccessExecutionRole   Grants permissions for Amazon EC2 actions to manage elastic network interfaces. If you are writing an AWS Lambda function to access resources inside the Amazon VPC service, attach this permissions policy. The policy also grants permissions for CloudWatch log actions to write logs.

Inside the AWS Lambda Function

AWS Lambda is all about executing your code quickly and efficiently without the need to provision servers. You can use any libraries, artifacts, or compiled native binaries you need within the runtime environment provided by Lambda's supported platforms. As the runtime environment is a Linux-based *Amazon Machine Image (AMI)*, always compile and test your components within the matching environment. To accomplish this, use the AWS Serverless Application Model (SAM) CLI to test AWS Lambda functions locally (`https://github.com/awslabs/aws-sam-cli`).

Function Package

The *function package* contains everything needed for your function to execute. At minimum, it contains your function code, but it may also contain other assets, imports, or libraries that your code references upon execution. For instance, if you are writing a Lambda function in JavaScript/Node and require certain npm packages, those packages (i.e., the files in the `node_modules/` folder) must be part of the function package you provide to Lambda.

Some common dependencies, such as the AWS SDK, are preinstalled in the runtime environment for each language. For instance, there is no need to package the AWS Python SDK, Boto, with a Python Lambda function.

You provide the function package as a ZIP file, which you may upload directly to Lambda or upload to S3 and provide as an S3 file path. The maximum size of a function package is 50 MB compressed and 250 MB extracted/decompressed.

You can create a Lambda function by using the AWS Management Console, SDK, or CLI. Use the AWS CLI to create a function with these commands:

```
aws lambda create-function \
--region us-east-2 \
--function-name MyCLITestFunction \
--role arn:aws:iam:account-id:role/role_name \
--runtime python3.12 \
--handler MyCLITestFunction.my_handler \
--zip-file fileb://path/to/function/file.zip
```

You may also edit Lambda code directly in the Lambda section of the AWS Management Console, as shown in Figure 12.5.

FIGURE 12.5 Editing Lambda code in the Management Console

Function Handlers

Lambda code execution starts with the *function handler*, the function or method that acts as the entry point for your code. Handler syntax depends on the language you use for the function.

For Python, a handler is written as follows:

```
def handler_name(event, context):
    return some_value
```

For Node.js, a handler is written as follows:

```
exports.handler = async (event, context) => {
}
```

For other languages, consult the AWS documentation, or just create a new function in the AWS console: Lambda will autogenerate the boilerplate you need.

The handler is just the starting point; your code can call other methods and functions within other files and classes stored in the ZIP archive. Your code can also interact with other AWS services and make third-party API requests to web services with which it might need to interact.

Improve Performance with Code Outside the Handler

As we have discussed, AWS executes your Lambda functions inside a container. After your function executes, these containers are not immediately discarded but may be used for subsequent Lambda invocations within a short period of time (estimates vary, but some have measured this at around 10 minutes). These *warm containers* increase throughput and performance by avoiding the cost of launching a container from scratch.

In addition, developers may take advantage of Lambda container reuse to avoid reexecuting costly application logic. For example, if your Lambda code establishes a database connection before taking action, you can make sure that any warm execution skips this step. To achieve this, place reusable setup code *outside your handler*. In pseudocode:

```
database_connection = get_connection_from_db_pool()

def handler_name(event, context):
    // use database_connection here
```

The code will still be executed, but only once per container launch. If you take care that your code handles both code and warm executions, placing code outside the handler can be a valuable optimization for your Lambda functions.

Event Object

Lambda functions receive two parameters when they are invoked: the *event* and *context*. You can see each in the handler examples shown earlier; the first parameter is the incoming event.

This event contains information from the caller, which will vary by invocation method. For instance, an event parameter from an S3 PUT invocation will contain information about the newly created or updated S3 object.

 If you use API Gateway to invoke your Lambda function, the event contains details of the HTTPS request that was made by the API client, including values such as the path, query string, and request body, are within the event object.

Context Object

The second object that you pass to the handler is the `context` object. This parameter contains data about the AWS Lambda function invocation itself. The context and structure of the object vary based on the AWS Lambda function language. Here are three data points that the `context` object always contains:

AWS RequestId   A unique identifier for a specific invocation of a Lambda function, the RequestId (`context.aws_request_id` in Python) is important for tracking error reports or when you need to contact AWS Support. Be aware that when event-based invocations fail, they will retry up to three times; each of these invocations has the same RequestId.

Remaining Time   Amount of time in milliseconds that remain before your function timeout occurs. AWS Lambda functions can run a maximum of 900 seconds (15 minutes) as of this writing, but you can configure a shorter timeout. Because the remaining time is always changing, this value is obtainable by calling a method on the context. For example in Python, this method is rendered `ontext` `.get_remaining_time_in_millis()`.

Logging   Each language runtime provides the ability to stream log statements to CloudWatch Logs. The context object contains information about which CloudWatch Log stream your log statements are sent to, such as `context.log_group_name`.

Testing Your Function with Event Data

You can get a closer look at how the context and event objects work by configuring a test event and invoking the function. This sample function uses Node.js to output the structure of both objects:

```
exports.handler = async (event, context) => {
    console.log('Received event:', JSON.stringify(event, null, 2));
    console.log('Received context:', JSON.stringify(context, null, 2));
    return "Execution Complete";
};
```

In the Lambda code editor, the Test button includes an option Configure Test Event. In the dialog box, you can configure a JSON object to simulate an event passed in by any of the invocation methods we have discussed. As an example, we'll give a simple object:

```
{
  "first": "John",
  "last": "Doe",
  "age": "35"
}
```

Then, being sure to deploy the latest version of your code first, click Test and choose your new testing object. The output will show all the details received by Lambda, which contains not only your testing object, but all the metadata in the context:

Test Event Name
MyTestEvent

Response
"hello world"

Function Logs
```
START RequestId: 2f1e65fc-386d-46fe-a273-572651e6808e Version: $LATEST
2024-08-11T11:48:59.994Z2f1e65fc-386d-46fe-a273-572651e6808e INFO Received
event: {
  "first": "John",
  "last": "Doe",
  "age": "35"
}
2024-08-11T11:48:59.994Z 2f1e65fc-386d-46fe-a273-572651e6808e INFO  Received
context: {
  "callbackWaitsForEmptyEventLoop": true,
  "functionVersion": "$LATEST",
  "functionName": "helloWorld",
  "memoryLimitInMB": "128",
  "logGroupName": "/aws/lambda/helloWorld",
  "logStreamName": "2024/08/11/[$LATEST]2eacd63f0e4a424eb49d7573fceeeb56",
  "invokedFunctionArn": "arn:aws:lambda:us-east-1:031878740168:function:
helloWorld",
  "awsRequestId": "2f1e65fc-386d-46fe-a273-572651e6808e"
}
END RequestId: 2f1e65fc-386d-46fe-a273-572651e6808e
REPORT RequestId: 2f1e65fc-386d-46fe-a273-572651e6808e Duration: 83.07 ms
Billed Duration: 84 ms Memory Size: 128 MB Max Memory Used: 68 MB
```

Request ID
2f1e65fc-386d-46fe-a273-572651e6808e

The output under Function Logs is the same output you can see in the CloudWatch logs of your function execution; in fact, any console output created by your function will appear in CloudWatch. Testing your function with sample events is an essential way to validate the behavior of your function.

Optimizing with Lambda Layers

When packaging your code for execution by AWS Lambda, you must download and zip all your code's dependencies. For instance, a Node function likely depends on many npm packages. Before packaging your code, you need to run `npm install` in your local environment, which installs all dependencies in your `package.json` file, and include the resulting `node_modules` folder in your function package.

This necessary step can lead to complications. As we've mentioned, the size limit of a function package is 250 MB uncompressed. What if your dependencies are too large? This is one of the use cases of Lambda layers. With layers, you can package up dependencies like the aforementioned node modules and upload them separately to AWS Lambda as a layer. Then, any function can reference a layer, which is then incorporated into the function's runtime environment without counting against its size limits. This can also make it easier to work with your function in the AWS Management Console, as the built-in Lambda code editor won't function if your package size is too large.

Many functions can reference the same layer, making it an easy way to decompose complex code. It also allows you to manage parts of your code independently; you can update a layer and point functions to the newest version without necessarily having to update the primary function code that references it.

Finally, because layers let you install anything you need into the function's runtime, they are also a way to transcend the fixed number of runtimes provided by AWS. If you need to run a Lambda function in lisp or FORTRAN, Lambda layers can give you a clean way to package the dependencies you need to make that work.

Running Containers on Lambda

Another way to go beyond the Python, Java, Node.js, and other stock runtimes provided by Lambda is to deploy a container using the Docker runtime.

When running a Lambda with Docker, AWS expects you to provide the URI of an image in an ECR repository. This image should be based on one of several AWS-provided base images. Images based on the existing Lambda runtimes (such as Python) are maintained at this location: `https://gallery.ecr.aws/lambda`. For all other situations, including when you want to execute code for a runtime not supported by Lambda, start your Dockerfile with one of the OS-only base images located here: `https://gallery.ecr.aws/lambda/provided`. Of course, your container image will want to extend the functionality of the base images in whatever way you need by providing your own unique OS package installs, custom configuration, and custom initialization steps.

Another advantage of running your Lambda as a Docker container is package size. Just as using a Lambda layer can give you more space to work with for large deployments, a container can as well. Lambda supports containers of up to 10 GB in size—significantly higher than the 250 MB limit of non-container function packages.

Running your Lambda functions as containers can give you all the benefits of Docker—full flexibility to define your environment and the knowledge that code that runs on your machine will run in the cloud—along with the rapid, highly scalable, low-cost execution behavior of Lambda.

Configuring an AWS Lambda Function

This section details how to configure AWS Lambda functions.

Memory and CPU

You can allocate anywhere from 128 MB to 10,240 MB (about 10 GB) of RAM to your function. While you cannot explicitly set the CPU and network resources available to your function, these values scale with greater memory allocation. If your function requires additional CPU resources, increase your function's RAM; CPU can currently increase to 6 vCPUs.

Timeout

The timeout value determines how long the Lambda function will execute before terminating prematurely. The default timeout value is three seconds; however, you can specify a maximum of 900 seconds (15 minutes), the longest timeout value. You should not automatically set this function for the maximum value for your AWS Lambda function, as AWS charges based on execution time in 100 ms increments. There are many cases where a quick failure is preferable to a longer, unsuccessful function invocation.

After the execution of an AWS Lambda function completes or a timeout occurs, the response returns and all execution ceases. This includes any processes, subprocesses, or asynchronous process that your AWS Lambda function may have spawned during its execution.

Network Configuration

By default, Lambda functions execute from outside your VPC. From this context, they can reach the public Internet and communicate with services like S3 and DynamoDB, but they are unable to reach resources deployed inside your VPC, such as EC2 instances or RDS databases.

Alternatively, you can configure Lambda to run functions in VPC mode. This approach provisions an *Elastic Network Interface (ENI)*, inside your VPC, allowing the Lambda to reach resources within the VPC network. From there, you may treat the ENI like any other VPC resource, assigning it security groups to govern what it can access on the network.

Unlike in default networking mode, VPC Lambdas do not come configured with outbound Internet access. To enable this, you must deploy them to a subnet that includes a Network Address Translation (NAT) instance.

If your Lambda function does not need to connect to any privately deployed resources, select the default networking option, as the VPC option requires you to manage more details when implementing an Lambda function. These details include the following:

- Selecting an appropriate number of subnets, while you keep in mind the principles of high availability and availability zones
- Allocating enough Internet Protocol (IP) addresses for each subnet

- Implementing a VPC network design that permits your AWS Lambda function to have the correct connectivity and security to meet your requirements

- Configuring a NAT (instance or gateway) to enable outbound Internet access

If you deploy a Lambda function with access to your VPC, use the following formula to estimate the ENI capacity:

```
Projected peak concurrent executions * (Memory in GB / 3GB)
```

> If you had a peak of 400 concurrent executions, use 512 MB of memory. This results in about 68 network interfaces. You therefore need an Amazon VPC with at least 68 IP addresses available. This provides a /25 network that includes 128 IP addresses, minus the 5 that AWS uses. Next, you subtract the AWS addresses from the /25 network, which gives you 123 IP addresses.

AWS Lambda easily integrates with *AWS CloudTrail*, which records and delivers log files to your Amazon S3 bucket to monitor API usage inside your account. With CloudTrail, you can see what actions are being taken in your account, when, and by whom, and respond to any event with a Lambda execution.

Concurrency

Though AWS allows you to scale infinitely; AWS recommends that you fine-tune your concurrency options. By default, the account level concurrency is set to 50 simultaneous function executions. This limit increases as your concurrency increases; however, you can also request a limit increase for concurrent executions from the AWS Support Center.

To view the account-level setting, use the `GetAccountSettings` API and view the `AccountLimit` object and the `ConcurrentExecutions` element.

For example, run this command in the AWS CLI:

```
aws lambda get-account-settings
```

This returns the following:

```
{
    "AccountLimit": {
        "CodeSizeUnzipped": number,
        "CodeSizeZipped": number,
        "ConcurrentExecutions": number,
        "TotalCodeSize": number,
        "UnreservedConcurrentExecutions": number
    },
    "AccountUsage": {
        "FunctionCount": number,
        "TotalCodeSize": number
    }
}
```

Concurrency Limits

The concurrency limit is an account-level restriction. Once this amount is exceeded, Lambda executions will fail with the error `TooManyRequestsException: Rate Exceeded`. Any functions that fail in this way will continue to attempt execution for the next 6 hours, employing an exponential backoff approach so as not to overwhelm the system.

Because the concurrency limit is account-wide, it's important to take steps the ensure a single high-demand function cannot deny capacity to other Lambda functions that may be running in your account. To achieve this, AWS Lambda allows you to set function-level concurrent execution limits.

Setting the *concurrent execution limit* for an individual function not only ensures that one function cannot consume all the concurrency capacity for your account, but it can be necessary for other reasons. For instance, if your Lambda function makes a call out to an external API or connects to a database, setting the per-function concurrency limit can make sure that Lambda doesn't scale so quickly that it overwhelms those external resources.

When you set a concurrency limit on a function, AWS Lambda ensures that the allocation applies individually to that function, regardless of the number of traffic-processing remaining functions. If that limit is exceeded, the function is throttled. How that function behaves when throttled depends on the event source.

Dead-Letter Queues

All applications and services experience failure. Reasons that an AWS Lambda function can fail include (but are not limited to) the following:

- Function times out while trying to reach an external endpoint
- Function fails to parse input data successfully
- Function experiences resource constraints, such as out-of-memory errors or other timeouts

If any of these failures occur, your function generates an exception. While Lambda's basic execution role ensures these exceptions will appear in CloudWatch logs, by configuring your function with a dead-letter queue (DLQ), you can more easily monitor, troubleshoot, and even retry failed invocations.

A DLQ is either an Amazon SNS or SQS queue that you configure as the destination for all failed invocation events.

For asynchronous event sources (`InvocationType` is a declared event), after two retries with automatic backoff between the retries, the event enters the DLQ. After you enable DLQ on a Lambda function, a CloudWatch metric (`DeadLetterErrors`) is available. The metric increments whenever the dead letter message payload cannot be sent to the DLQ at any time.

A dead-letter queue can be a valuable way to alert you if, for instance, your Lambda function encounters a new type of input that its code does not properly handle. With a DLQ, you can fix the bug in Lambda, deploy an update to your function, and reprocess the events saved in the DLQ.

Lambda Destinations

Lambda destinations are a way to handle successes and failures by routing Lambda results to various AWS services. When an asynchronous invocation terminates, the results can be sent to SQS, SNS, EventBridge, or another Lambda function. With event streaming functions (such as those used by DynamoDB streams), Lambda destinations can target SQS or SNS on failure only.

AWS suggests that Lambda destinations are preferable to DLQs for handling failure conditions, as they contain not only the failed event, but details of the Lambda function's original response. Whereas a DLQ can only store failed events and require you to implement other means to pull and analyze those events, Lambda destinations allow you to take action immediately with another Lambda.

Environment Variables

It is always a good idea to separate configuration values from your code. One good way is to use *environment variables* for these values. Environment variables are key-value pairs that you set as part of your Lambda configuration and that are then accessible in your code. For instance, to fetch an environment variable called `connection_string` via Python, use the following:

```
import os
connection_string = os.environ.get("connection_string")
```

By default, environment variables are encrypted at rest, using a default KMS key of `aws/lambda`. Environment variables in Lambda have a maximum size of 4 KB.

While it is possible to use environment variables for secret values such as database passwords, consider instead using a service like AWS Secrets Manager to store these values and fetch them as needed in your Lambda function code. In this Python example, we use the AWS SDK for Python (Boto3) to fetch a secret named `'myapp/prod/database_password'` from Secrets Manager in region `us-east-1`. The Lambda execution role needs the permission `secretsmanager:GetSecretValue` on the secret or a wildcard that includes this secret:

```
import boto3
client = boto3.client(
    service_name='secretsmanager',
    region_name='us-east-1'
)
secret_response = client.get_secret_value( SecretId="myapp/prod/database_password" )
database_password = secret_response['SecretString']
```

For Lambda functions that will be invoked frequently, you may wish to save costs by reducing the number of times that Secrets Manager is queried. One way is to place this code outside the handler, as described earlier in the section "Improve Performance with Code Outside the Handler." As long as your Lambda function container stays warm, this code will not be reexecuted.

Another optimization involves Lambda layers. Amazon provides a layer called the "AWS Parameters and Secrets Lambda Extension," which enables some caching of secrets in memory. Both this and the "outside the handler" method rely on keeping the secrets in memory and therefore require a warm container execution. However, the AWS extension has a few extra features built in, such as automatically refreshing the secret after a specified time-to-live duration. For more on the AWS Parameters and Secrets Lambda Extension, see:

```
https://docs.aws.amazon.com/secretsmanager/latest/userguide/
retrieving-secrets_lambda.html
```

Finally, although you can store non-secret values in Secrets Manager, you can save on costs by keeping nonsensitive configuration values like database URLs in Parameter Store. By using hierarchical parameter names, you can maintain all the configuration values for a single environment's deployment in the same place. For instance, for a Lambda function called `process_order`, you might store the following values:

- `/lambda/process_order/development/database_url`
- `/lambda/process_order/development/product_api_base_url`
- `/lambda/process_order/staging/database_url`
- `/lambda/process_order/staging/product_api_base_url`
- `/lambda/process_order/production/database_url`
- `/lambda/process_order/production/ product_api_base_url`

Fetching all parameters under `/lambda/process_order/development` can get you everything you need to run your Lambda function in the development environment.

Lambda Deployment and Testing

AWS gives you many tools to manage how you update and deploy your Lambda functions. To begin, let's examine the concepts of function versions and aliases, which will help you coordinate deployments as you make changes to your code.

Versioning Your Function

You can publish one or more *versions* and *aliases* for your Lambda functions. Versioning allows you to tag your function at a certain point in time, which can be useful for keeping history of past function behavior or for rolling back in the event that the current version fails. Each Lambda function version has a unique *Amazon Resource Name (ARN)*. After you publish a version, the code is immutable, and you cannot change it.

Lambda version numbers are autogenerated integers that count up from 1. You may add a version description, but AWS determines the number by taking the next in the sequence. In addition, AWS always maintains a unique version of your code called $LATEST, representing, of course, the latest published version of your function. Because numbered versions are immutable, $LATEST is the only version whose code can change over time.

Creating an Alias

After you create a version of an AWS Lambda function, you *could* use that version number in the ARN to reference that exact version of the function. However, if you release an update to the Lambda function, you must then locate all the places where you call that ARN inside the application and change the ARN to the new version number. Lambda aliases can simplify things significantly.

Aliases allow you to apply labels to certain versions (one or more, as detailed in a moment). For example, you might have an alias called prod that you ensure always points to the most recently deployed version of your function.

Weighted Aliases

Applying an alias to multiple versions enables a unique feature of Lambda: weighted deployments. Imagine you have just completed coding a few version of your code, which you label 2, intending it to replace the current version 1. With aliases, you can point your prod label to both versions 2 and 1 with a weight assigned to each. For instance, you might give a weight of 90 percent to version 1 and just 10 percent to version 2. This will ensure that invocations to this Lambda function are served by the new version 10 percent of the time, giving you the chance to monitor logs for success or failure. When you are satisfied, you can update the weights to shift all your traffic to the new version. In this way, Lambda aliases enable both "canary" deployment types (those where only a small percent of executions run the update until a sufficient number complete without error) and A/B deployments (those where you compare the efficacy of multiple versions at once by serving different versions to different audiences).

Using weighted aliases is one way to do a controlled code rollout from the management console. Read on to discover how to package and deploy new code and how to fully automate the process.

Packaging and Deploying Your Function

When using the code editor in the AWS Management Console, simply clicking Deploy on your function will update the $LATEST version, therefore updating the functionality of any invocation that does not specifically call a past version.

Of course, many functions will have dependencies—like npm packages for Node.js or pip libraries for Python—that must be part of the deployment, or the function will not work. In this case, you'll work from the command line, and you'll need to take a few steps to package up your code before deploying it using the AWS CLI. Let's look at a short Python example.

This function makes an API call and returns the result to the caller. To do that, it needs the Python package `requests`:

```python
# my_function.py
import requests


def lambda_handler(event, context):
    response = requests.get('https://api.example.com')
    return {
        'statusCode': response.status_code,
        'body': response.text
    }
```

Even though it's just one package, let's put it in a `requirements.txt` file so we can install it easily with pip (adding any future required packages to this file):

```
# requirements.txt
Requests
```

Now we're ready to package the code using the AWS CLI. We'll install the dependency into a subfolder called `package`, and then copy the main Python file in there as well. From there, we zip up the entire contents:

```
pip install -r requirements.txt -t package/
cp my_function.py package/
cd package
zip -r ../function.zip .
cd ..
```

The resulting file `function.zip` is our Lambda deployment package. To create it as a new function in Lambda, run the following code. For this to work, your environment must be configured with the AWS credentials of a user who is allowed to create Lambda functions. You also need to provide the ARN of a Lambda execution role:

```
aws lambda create-function \
    --function-name myFunction \
    --runtime python3.12 \
    --role arn:aws:iam::account-id:role/execution-role \
    --handler my_function.lambda_handler \
    --zip-file fileb://function.zip
```

Any time you update the function code locally, you must create a new package (`updated-function.zip` in this example) and push the change to Lambda with the `update-function` CLI call:

```
aws lambda update-function-code \
    --function-name  myFunction \
    --zip-file fileb://updated-function.zip
```

These commands deploy the package as a direct upload, which is limited to a size of 50 MB. Alternatively, you can upload code to an S3 bucket, where the package can be up to 250 MB (unzipped). Doing this requires two steps. First, the upload (assuming the bucket already exists):

```
aws s3 cp function.zip s3://bucket-name/path/to/function.zip
```

Then, the deployment, with the `code` parameter referencing this location:

```
aws lambda create-function \
    --function-name myFunction \
    --runtime python3.12 \
    --role arn:aws:iam::account-id:role/execution-role \
    --handler my_function.lambda_handler \
    --code S3Bucket=bucket-name,S3Key=path/to/function.zip
```

To update the function, overwrite the S3 object with a new package and then run the following code. As you can see, the update call has parameters to explicitly reference S3 locations:

```
aws lambda update-function-code \
    --function-name myFunction \
    --s3-bucket bucket-name \
    --s3-key path/to/function.zip
```

With these commands, it's relatively easy to script and automate the packaging and deployment of a single function. However, the best practice would be to automate code changes not by writing custom scripts, but by creating a pipeline that can react to changes you push to version control. One AWS-native way to do this is using CodeDeploy.

Automating Deployments with CodeDeploy

When we previously delved into AWS CodeDeploy, it was through the lens of code running on traditional server-based compute environments. However, CodeDeploy also allows developers to choose AWS Lambda as a deploy target, giving you the ability to automate your Lambda releases.

After you create a CodeDeploy application with compute type AWS Lambda, you then create a deployment group. Unlike with EC2 deployments, there are no instances to select, as the destination is the Lambda service itself. However, you still select the deployment configuration—the pattern of how your new code will roll out. You have three categories from which to choose: canary, linear, or all-at-once, as shown in the following selected examples:

CodeDeployDefault.LambdaCanary10Percent5Minutes   For five minutes, CodeDeploy will route 10 percent of invocations to your new code before cutting all traffic over entirely. This window gives you time to monitor CloudWatch logs and cancel the deployment if any errors occur. This can be done manually or through a post-deployment hook in your `appspec.yml` file.

`CodeDeployDefault.LambdaLinear10PercentEvery10Minutes` CodeDeploy will ramp up the number of invocations that are handled by the new code, starting at 10 percent and increasing by an additional 10 percent every 10 minutes, until all traffic is handled by the newest version.

CodeDeployDefault.LambdaAllAtOnce All invocations of your Lambda function will immediately be handled by the newest code version.

As discussed in previous chapters, CodeDeploy can be made part of a fully automated CodePipeline flow.

Continuous Delivery with CodePipeline

To create an end-to-end automation, first create a CodePipeline whose Source stage is your Lambda code repository (e.g., GitHub).

Your Build stage can be a CodeBuild project that packages your code using the same CLI commands shown earlier. You can use S3-based packages, or if doing a direct upload, you may pass the `function.zip` package from the Build stage to the Deploy stage as a pipeline artifact, as shown in this `buildspec.yml` file:

```
version: 0.2

phases:
  install:
    runtime-versions:
      python: 3.12
    commands:
      - echo "Installing dependencies..."
      - pip install -r requirements.txt -t package/
  build:
    commands:
      - echo "Building the Lambda function..."
      - cp lambda_function.py package/
  post_build:
    commands:
      - echo "Packaging Lambda function..."
      - cd package
      - zip -r ../lambda_function.zip .
      - cd ..
      - echo "Build completed on `date`"
```

```
artifacts:
  files:
    - lambda_function.zip
```

From there, your Deploy stage should be a CodeDeploy project that deploys that packaged ZIP file. This `appspec.yml` file updates the `production` alias from version 1 to version 2. Special life cycle hooks allow you to run other Lambda functions to validate traffic before and after the deployment:

```
version: 0.0
Resources:
  - myLambdaFunction:
      Type: AWS::Lambda::Function
      Properties:
        Name: "myFunction"
        Alias: "production"
        CurrentVersion: "1"
        TargetVersion: "2"
Hooks:
  - BeforeAllowTraffic: "Some_pre_deploy_function"
  - AfterAllowTraffic: "Some_post_deploy_function "
```

AWS offers additional ways to build, package, and deploy Lambda functions. The AWS Serverless Application Model is a command-line framework that abstracts many of the steps needed to create and deploy functions, giving you more options for automation. For more on AWS SAM, see the section "AWS Serverless Application Model" in Chapter 14.

Automating Lambda Testing

Once you have established a pipeline that includes a Build stage, you can execute automated tests in the CodeBuild execution environment prior to deployment. This can be done with custom code or by using your framework of choice for the runtime language of the function, such as jest for Node.js or pytest for Python.

When testing, be sure to submit event JSON representing the full range of possible input conditions for your function. Include all possible classes of correct input along with events representing failure states: bad data, missing data, malformed input, and the like.

If all these tests pass during the Build stage, you can proceed with confidence to deployment. From there, approaches like canary deployments and post-deployment integration tests can further solidify the quality of your release.

Monitoring AWS Lambda Functions

As with all AWS services and all applications, it is critical to monitor your environment and application. With AWS Lambda, there are two primary tools to monitor functions to ensure that they are running correctly and efficiently: *Amazon CloudWatch* and *AWS X-Ray*.

Using Amazon CloudWatch

By default, Lambda tracks the following metrics in CloudWatch: invocation count, invocation duration, invocation errors, throttled invocations, iterator age, and DLQ errors.

You can create custom CloudWatch alarms that watch any of these metrics and perform one or more actions based on the value of the metric. The action can be an Amazon EC2 action, an Amazon EC2 Auto Scaling action, or a notification sent to an Amazon SNS topic.

The AWS Lambda namespace includes, but is not limited to, the metrics shown in Table 12.1.

TABLE 12.1 AWS Lambda CloudWatch metrics

Metric	Description
Invocations	Measures the number of times a function is invoked in response to an event or invocation API call.
	Replaces the deprecated `RequestCount` metric.
	Includes successful and failed invocations but does not include throttled attempts. This equals the billed requests for the function.
	You may view or request this metric in intervals of 1 minute, 5 minutes, or 1 hour. AWS aggregates the number of invocations at each resolution; the count is reset with every new interval. For instance, if a Lambda function is invoked 20 times over 2 hours, you might observe the values 11 and 9 for those two one-hour intervals.
	Counts are retained for 1-minute, 5-minute, and 1-hour intervals for 15 days, 63 days, and 455 days, respectively.
	AWS Lambda sends these metrics to CloudWatch only if they have a nonzero value.
	Units: Count
Errors	Measures the number of invocations that failed as the result of errors in the function (response code 4XX).
	Replaces the deprecated `ErrorCount` metric. Failed invocations may trigger a retry attempt that succeeds. This includes the following:
	▪ Handled exceptions (for example, `context.fail(error)`)
	▪ Unhandled exceptions causing the code to exit
	▪ Out-of-memory exceptions
	▪ Timeouts
	▪ Permissions errors This does not include invocations that fail because invocation rates exceeded default concurrent limits (error code 429) or failures resulting from internal service errors (error code 500).
	Units: Count

TABLE 12.1 AWS Lambda CloudWatch metrics *(continued)*

Metric	Description
DeadLetterErrors	Incremented when AWS Lambda is unable to write the failed event payload to DLQs that you configure. This could be because of the following: ▪ Permissions errors ▪ Throttles from downstream services ▪ Misconfigured resources ▪ Timeouts Units: Count

Using AWS X-Ray

AWS X-Ray is a service that provides visibility into your application's performance and behavior by tracking requests and mapping their flow across your architecture. It collects data about requests served by your application, as well as calls made to downstream components like AWS resources, microservices, databases, and HTTP web APIs. This data allows you to analyze and troubleshoot performance bottlenecks and identify optimization opportunities within your application.

There are three main parts to the X-Ray service:

- **Your application code:** When you include the AWS X-Ray SDK, available for Node.js, Java, .NET, Ruby, Python, and Go, in your application, you can configure it to start collecting telemetry on your application such as request times and error information.

- **X-Ray daemon:** This application listens for traffic on User Datagram Protocol (UDP) port 2000, gathers raw segment data, and relays it to the AWS X-Ray API. The daemon is available for Linux, Windows, and macOS, and it's included on AWS Elastic Beanstalk and Lambda platforms.

- **AWS X-Ray console:** The X-Ray web console provides a user interface for reviewing application insights in the AWS Management Console.

With the SDK, you integrate X-Ray into the application code. The SDK records data about incoming and outgoing requests and sends it to the X-Ray Daemon, which relays the data in batches to X-Ray. For example, when your application calls Amazon DynamoDB to retrieve user information from a table, the X-Ray SDK records data from both the client request and the downstream call to DynamoDB.

X-Ray then generates a detailed service graph of your application showing the client, your front-end service, and backend services that your front-end calls to process requests and persist data. You then use the service graph to identify bottlenecks, latency spikes, and other issues to improve the performance of your applications.

With X-Ray and the service map, as shown in Figure 12.6, you can visualize how your application is running and troubleshoot any errors.

FIGURE 12.6   AWS X-Ray service map

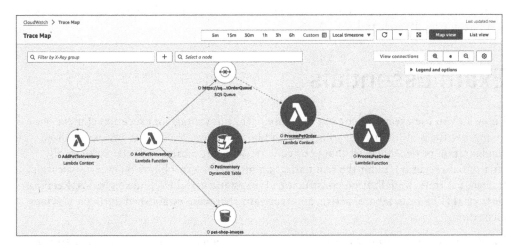

Configuring X-Ray tracing for Lambda functions is simple: You just enable it in the function configuration. There is no need to bundle the SDK with your code or manage the SDK daemon. To configure your function to use X-Ray:

1. Open the Lambda service page and select or create a function.

2. On the Configuration tab, find the section Monitoring And Operations Tools.

3. Click Edit.

4. In the X-Ray section, select Active Tracing.

5. Click Save.

In addition, your Lambda execution role needs permission to write data to the X-Ray service. Adding the managed IAM policy `AWSXRayDaemonWriteAccess` will let Lambda talk to X-Ray, allowing detailed trace data to appear in the X-Ray console. With X-Ray, you can quickly discover the performance or logic errors in your code, along with details to help you eliminate them. We'll discuss X-Ray in more detail in Chapter 15, "Monitoring and Troubleshooting."

Summary

In this chapter, you learned about serverless compute, explored what it means to use a serverless service, and took an in-depth look at AWS Lambda. With Lambda, you learned how to create a function with the AWS Management Console and AWS CLI and how to scale Lambda functions by specifying appropriate memory allocation settings and properly defining timeout values. Additionally, you took a closer look at the Lambda function handler, the event object, and the context object to use data from an event source with AWS Lambda. Finally, you looked at how to invoke Lambda functions by using synchronous, asynchronous, and event streaming functions. We wrapped up the chapter with a brief look at Amazon CloudWatch and AWS X-Ray.

Exam Essentials

Know how to use execution context for reuse.   Take advantage of execution context reuse to improve the performance of your AWS Lambda function. Verify that any externalized configuration or dependencies that your code retrieves are stored and referenced locally after initial execution. Limit the reinitialization of variables or objects on every invocation. Instead, use static initialization/constructor, global/static variables, and singletons. Keep connections (HTTP or database) active, and reuse any that were established during a previous invocation.

Know how to use environment variables.   Use environment variables to pass operational parameters to your Lambda functions. For example, if you are writing to an Amazon S3 bucket, instead of hard-coding the bucket name to which you are writing, configure the bucket name as an environment variable.

Know how to control the dependencies in your function's deployment package.   In addition to the base platform like Node.js libraries, the AWS Lambda execution environment you choose may contain support libraries such as the AWS SDK. Lambda periodically updates these libraries to stay up-to-date with features and security patches. These updates may introduce subtle changes to the behavior of your AWS Lambda function. To maintain full control of your function's dependencies, you can include everything your application needs with your deployment package.

Be able to minimize your deployment package size to its runtime necessities.   Minimizing your deployment package size reduces the amount of time that it takes for your deployment package to download and unpack ahead of invocation. For functions authored in Java or .NET Core, it is best not to upload the entire AWS SDK library as part of your deployment package. Instead, select only the modules that include components of the SDK you need, such as Amazon DynamoDB, S3 SDK modules, and Lambda core libraries. For larger or shared dependencies, use Lambda layers.

Know how memory works.   Performing Lambda function tests is a crucial step to ensure that you choose the optimum memory size configuration. Any increase in memory size triggers an equivalent increase in CPU that is available to your function. The memory usage for your function is determined per invocation, and it displays in the Amazon CloudWatch Logs.

Know how to load-test your AWS Lambda function to determine an optimum timeout value. It is essential to analyze how long your function runs to determine any problems with a dependency service. Dependency services may increase the concurrency of the function beyond what you expect. This is especially important when your AWS Lambda function makes network calls to resources that may not handle Lambda's scaling.

Describe how permissions for IAM policies work. Use the most restrictive permissions when you set AWS IAM policies. Understand the resources and operations that your AWS Lambda function needs, and limit the execution role to these permissions.

Know how to use AWS Lambda metrics and Amazon CloudWatch alarms. Use AWS Lambda metrics and Amazon CloudWatch alarms (instead of creating or updating a metric from within your AWS Lambda function code). This is a much more efficient way to track the health of your AWS Lambda functions, and it allows you to catch issues early in the development process. For instance, you can configure an alarm based on the expected duration of your AWS Lambda function execution time to address any bottlenecks or latencies attributable to your function code.

Know how to capture application errors. Leverage your log library and AWS Lambda metrics and dimensions to catch application errors, such as ERR, ERROR, and WARNING.

Be able to create and use dead-letter queues (DLQs). Create and use DLQs to address and replay asynchronous function errors.

Exercises

Code Examples for Exercises

To complete these exercises, download the AWS Certified Developer – Associate Exam code examples for Chapter 12, Chapter12_Code.zip, from Resources at www.wiley.com/go/sybextestprep.

For these exercises, you are a developer for a shoe company. The shoe company has a third-party check processor who sends checks, pay stubs, and direct deposits to the shoe company's employees. The third-party service requires a JSON document with the employee's name, the number of hours they worked for the current week, and the employee's hourly rate. Unfortunately, the shoe company's payroll system exports this data only in CSV format. Devise a serverless method to convert the exported CSV file to JSON.

EXERCISE 12.1

Creating an Amazon S3 Bucket for CSV Ingestion

1. To solve this, create two Amazon S3 buckets (CSV ingestion and JSON output) and an AWS Lambda function to process the file.

2. After you export the CSV file, upload the file to Amazon S3. First, create an Amazon S3 bucket with the following Python code:

   ```
   import boto3
   # Variables for the bucket name and the region we will be using.
   # Important Note: s3 Buckets are globally unique, as such you need to change
   the name of the bucket to something else.
   # Important Note: If you would like to use us-east-1 as the region, when
   making the s3.create_bucket call, then do not specify any region.
   bucketName = "shoe-company-ingestion-csv-demo"
   bucketRegion = "us-west-1"

   # Creates an s3 Resource; this is a higher level API type service for s3.
   s3 = boto3.resource('s3')

   # Creates a bucket
   bucket = s3.create_bucket(ACL='private',Bucket=bucketName,CreateBucket
   Configuration={'LocationConstraint': bucketRegion})
   ```

   This Python code creates a resource for interacting with the Amazon S3 service.

3. After the resource is created, you can call the function `.create_bucket` to create a bucket.

4. After executing this Python code, verify that the bucket has been successfully created inside the Amazon S3 console. If it is not successfully created, the most likely cause is that the bucket name is not unique; therefore, renaming the bucket should solve the issue.

EXERCISE 12.2

Creating an Amazon S3 Bucket for Final Output JSON

1. To create the second bucket for final output, run the following:

   ```
   import boto3
   # Variables for the bucket name and the region we will be using.
   ```

```
# Important Note: s3 Buckets are globally unique, as such you need to change
the name of the bucket to something else.
    # Important Note: If you would like to use us-east-1 as the region, when
making the s3.create_bucket call, then do not specify any region.
bucketName = "shoe-company-final-json-demo"
bucketRegion = "us-west-1"


# Creates an s3 Resource; this is a higher level API type service for s3.
s3 = boto3.resource('s3')


# Creates a bucket
bucket = s3.create_bucket(ACL='private',Bucket=bucketName,CreateBucket
Configuration={'LocationConstraint': bucketRegion})
```

2. In the first exercise, you created the initial bucket for ingestion of the CSV file. This
    bucket will be used for the final JSON output. Again, if you see any errors here, look at
    the error logs. Verify that the bucket exists inside the Amazon S3 console. You will verify
    the buckets programmatically in the next exercise.

EXERCISE 12.3

Verifying List Buckets

1. To verify the two buckets, use the Python 3 SDK and run the following:

```
    import boto3
# Variables for the bucket name and the region we will be using.
# Important Note: Be sure to use the same bucket names you used in the
previous two exercises.
bucketInputName = "shoe-company-ingestion-csv-demo"
bucketOutputName = "shoe-company-final-json-demo"


# Creates an s3 Resource; this is a higher level API type service for s3.
s3 = boto3.resource('s3')


# Get all of the buckets
bucket_iterator = s3.buckets.all()


# Loop through the buckets
```

EXERCISE 12.8 *(continued)*

```
for bucket in bucket_iterator:
    if bucket.name == bucketInputName:
        print("Found the input bucket\t:\t", bucket.name)
    if bucket.name == bucketOutputName:
        print("Found the output bucket\t:\t", bucket.name)
```

Here, you are looping through the buckets, and if the two that you created are found, they are displayed. If everything is successful, then you should see output similar to the following:

```
Found the output bucket    : shoe-company-final-json-demo
Found the input bucket     : shoe-company-ingestion-csv-demo
```

EXERCISE 12.4

Preparing the AWS Lambda Function

1. To perform the conversion using the AWS CLI and the Python SDK, create the AWS Lambda function. The AWS CLI creates the AWS Lambda function. The Python SDK processes the files inside the AWS Lambda service.

2. In the following code, change the bucket names to bucket names you defined. The `lambda_handler` function passes the event parameter. This allows you to acquire the Amazon S3 bucket name.

```
import boto3
import csv
import json
import time
# The csv and json modules provide functionality for parsing
# and writing csv/json files. We can use these modules to
# quickly perform a data transformation
# You can read about the csv module here:
# https://docs.python.org/2/library/csv.html
# and JSON here:
# https://docs.python.org/2/library/json.html

# Create an s3 Resource: https://boto3.readthedocs.io/en/latest/guide/
resources.html
s3 = boto3.resource('s3')
```

```
csv_local_file = '/tmp/input-payroll-data.csv'
json_local_file = '/tmp/output-payroll-data.json'

# Change this value to whatever you named the output s3 bucket in the previous
exercise
output_s3_bucket = 'shoe-company-final-json-demo'

def lambda_handler(event, context):

    # Need to get the bucket name
    bucket_name = event['Records'][0]['s3']['bucket']['name']
    key = event['Records'][0]['s3']['object']['key']

    # Download the file to our AWS Lambda container environment
    try:
        s3.Bucket(bucket_name).download_file(key, csv_local_file)
    except Exception as e:
        print(e)
        print('Error getting object {} from bucket {}. Make sure they exist
and your bucket is in the same region as this function.'.format(key,
bucket_name))
        raise e

    # Open the csv and json files
    csv_file = open(csv_local_file, 'r')
    json_file = open(json_local_file, 'w')

    # Get a csv DictReader object to convert file to json
    dict_reader = csv.DictReader( csv_file )

    # Create an Employees array for JSON, use json.dumps to pass in the string
    json_conversion = json.dumps({'Employees': [row for row in dict_reader]})

    # Write to our json file
    json_file.write(json_conversion)

        # Close out the files
    csv_file.close()
    json_file.close()
```

EXERCISE 12.4 *(continued)*

```
# Upload finished file to s3 bucket
try:
    s3.Bucket(output_s3_bucket).upload_file(json_local_file, 'final-
output-payroll.json')
except Exception as e:
    print(e)
    print('Error uploading object {} to bucket {}. Make sure the file
paths are correct.'.format(key, bucket_name))
    raise e

    print('Payroll processing completed at: ', time.asctime( time.localtime
(time.time()) ) )
    return 'Payroll conversion from CSV to JSON complete.'
```

3. Save this code to a file called `lambda_function.py`, then compress the file.

   You can use a descriptive filename; however, remember to update the handler code in Exercise 12.6. Your zip filename needs to match the python filename.

   ```
   zip lambda_function.zip lambda_function.py
   ```

4. Upload this file to Amazon S3 with the AWS CLI:

   ```
   aws s3 cp lambda_function.zip s3://shoe-company-ingestion-csv-demo
   ```

   If the following command successfully executed, you should see something similar to the following printed to the console:

   ```
   upload: .\lambda_function.zip to s3://shoe-company-ingestion-csv-demo/lambda_
   function.zip
   ```

   You may also verify that the file has been uploaded by using the AWS Management Console inside the Amazon S3 service.

EXERCISE 12.5

Creating AWS IAM Roles

In this exercise, you'll create an AWS IAM role so that the AWS Lambda function has the correct permissions to execute the function with the AWS CLI.

1. Create a JSON file of the trust relationship, which allows the AWS Lambda service to assume this particular IAM role with the Security Token Service.

2. Create a policy document. A predefined policy document was distributed in the code example that you downloaded in Exercise 12.1. However, if you prefer to create the file manually, you can do so. The following is required for the exercise to work correctly:

```
lambda-trust-policy.json
{
    "Version": "2012-10-17",
    "Statement": [
        {
            "Effect": "Allow",
            "Principal": {
                "Service": "lambda.amazonaws.com"
            },
            "Action": "sts:AssumeRole"
        }
    ]
}
```

3. After the `lambda-trust-policy.json` document has been created, run the following command to create the IAM role:

```
aws iam create-role --role-name PayrollProcessingLambdaRole \
                    --description "Provides AWS Lambda with access to s3 and
cloudwatch \
                            to execute the PayrollProcessing function" \
                            --assume-role-policy-document file://lambda-
trust-policy.json
```

4. A JSON object returns. Copy the RoleName and ARN roles for the next steps.

```
{
    "Role": {
        "AssumeRolePolicyDocument": {
            "Version": "2012-10-17",
            "Statement": [
                {
                    "Action": "sts:AssumeRole",
                    "Effect": "Allow",
                    "Principal": {
                        "Service": "lambda.amazonaws.com"
                    }
                }
            ]
```

```
        },
        "RoleId": "roleidnumber",
        "CreateDate": "2024-05-19T17:30:05.020Z",
        "RoleName": "PayrollProcessingLambdaRole",
        "Path": "/",
        "Arn": "arn:aws:iam::accountnumber:role/PayrollProcessingLambdaRole"
    }
}
```

5. After you create an AWS role, attach a policy to the role. There are two types of AWS policies: AWS managed and customer managed. Amazon creates predefined policies that you can use called AWS managed policies. You may create customer managed policies specific to your requirements.

   For this example, you will use an AWS managed policy built for AWS Lambda named AWSLambdaExecute. This provides AWS Lambda with access to CloudWatch Logs and S3 GetObject and PutObject API calls:

   ```
   aws iam attach-role-policy --role-name PayrollProcessingLambdaRole --policy-arn
     arn:aws:iam::aws:policy/AWSLambdaExecute
   ```

   This command both creates the role PayrollProcessingLambdaRole and attaches the custom policy at the same time. If this command successfully executes, it does not return results.

6. To verify that the IAM role has been properly configured, from the AWS Management Console, go to the IAM service. Click Roles, and search for PayrollProcessing LambdaRole. On the Permissions tab, verify that the AWSLambdaExecute policy has been attached. On the Trust Relationships tab, verify that the trusted entities state the following: "The identify provider(s) lambda.amazonaws.com."

   You have successfully uploaded the Python code that has been compressed to S3, and you created an IAM role. In the next exercise, you will create the Lambda function.

Creating the AWS Lambda Function

1. In this exercise, create the AWS Lambda function. You can view the AWS Lambda API reference here:

   ```
   https://docs.aws.amazon.com/cli/latest/reference/lambda/index
   .html
   ```

2. Be sure that for the --handler parameter, you specify the name of the PY file you created in Exercise 12.4. Also, ensure that for the S3Key parameter, you specify the name of the compressed file inside the Amazon S3 bucket.

3. Run this AWS CLI command:

```
aws lambda create-function --function-name PayrollProcessing \
                           --runtime python3.12 \
                           --role arn:aws:iam::<YOUR_ACCOUNT_NUM>:role/Payroll
ProcessingLambdaRole \
                           --handler lambda_function.lambda_handler \
                           --description "Converts Payroll CSVs to JSON and
puts the results in an s3 bucket." \
                           --timeout 3 \
                           --memory-size 128 \
                           --code S3Bucket=shoe-company-ingestion-csv-demo,
S3Key=lambda_function.zip \
                           --region us-west-1
```

If the command was successful, you'll receive a JSON response similar to the following:

```
{
    "FunctionName": "PayrollProcessing",
    "FunctionArn": "arn:aws:lambda:us-east-2:accountnumber:function:Payroll
Processing",
    "Runtime": "python3.7",
    "Role": "arn:aws:iam::accountnumber:role/PayrollProcessingLambdaRole",
    "Handler": "payroll.lambda_handler",
    "CodeSize": 1123,
    "Description": "Converts Payroll CSVs to JSON and puts the results in an
s3 bucket.",
    "Timeout": 3,
    "MemorySize": 128,
    "LastModified": "2024-12-10T06:36:27.990+0000",
    "CodeSha256": "NUKm2kp/fLzVr58t8XCTw6YGBmxR2E1Q9MHuW11QXfw=",
    "Version": "$LATEST",
    "TracingConfig": {
        "Mode": "PassThrough"
    },
    "RevisionId": "ae30524f-26a9-426a-b43a-efa522cb1545"
}
```

4. You have successfully created the AWS Lambda function. Verify this from the AWS Management Console and navigate to the AWS Lambda page.

EXERCISE 12.7

Giving Amazon S3 Permission to Invoke an AWS Lambda Function

1. Use the AWS Lambda CLI add-permission command to allow S3 to invoke the AWS Lambda function. Be sure to replace yourawsaccountnumber with your actual account number:

```
aws lambda add-permission --function-name PayrollProcessing \
                          --statement-id lambdas3permission \
                          --action lambda:InvokeFunction \
                          --principal s3.amazonaws.com \
                          --source-arn arn:aws:s3:::shoe-company-ingestion-
csv-demo \
                          --source-account YOUR_ACCT_NUM \
                          --region us-west-1
```

After you run this command and it is successful, you should receive a JSON response that looks similar to the following:

```
{
    "Statement": {
        "Sid": "lambdas3permission",
        "Effect": "Allow",
        "Principal": {
            "Service": "s3.amazonaws.com"
        },
        "Action": "lambda:InvokeFunction",
        "Resource": "arn:aws:lambda:us-east-2:accountnumber:function:Payroll
Processing",
        "Condition": {
            "StringEquals": {
                "AWS:SourceAccount": "accountnumber"
            },
            "ArnLike": {
                "AWS:SourceArn": "arn:aws:s3:::shoe-company-ingestion-csv-
demo"
            }
        }
    }
}
```

2. This provides a function policy to the AWS Lambda function that allows the S3 bucket that you created to call the action `lambda:InvokeFunction`. You can verify this by navigating to the AWS Lambda service inside the AWS Management Console. In the Configuration section, click Permissions, and under Resource-Based Policy Statements, you will see the policy you just created.

EXERCISE 12.8

Adding the Amazon S3 Event Trigger

1. In this exercise, you'll add the trigger for Amazon S3 using the AWS CLI for the s3api commands. The `notification-config.json` file was provided in the exercise files. Its contents are as follows:

```
{
    "LambdaFunctionConfigurations": [
        {
            "Id": "s3PayrollFunctionObjectCreation",
            "LambdaFunctionArn": "arn:aws:lambda:us-west-1:accountnumber:
function:PayrollProcessing",
            "Events": [
                "s3:ObjectCreated:*"
            ],
            "Filter": {
                "Key": {
                    "FilterRules": [
                        {
                            "Name": "suffix",
                            "Value": ".csv"
                        }
                    ]
                }
            }
        }
    ]
}
aws s3api put-bucket-notification-configuration --bucket shoe-company-
ingestion-csv-demo --notification-configuration file://notification-
config.json
```

EXERCISE 12.8 *(continued)*

2. If the execution is successful, no response is sent. To verify that the trigger has been added to the AWS Lambda function, navigate to the AWS Lambda console inside the AWS Management Console, and verify under Function Overview that there is now an Amazon S3 trigger. This will be displayed visually when you select the Diagram view.

EXERCISE 12.9

Testing the AWS Lambda Function

1. To test the AWS Lambda function, use the AWS CLI to upload the CSV file to the Amazon S3 bucket; then check whether the function transforms the data and puts the result file in the output bucket.

```
aws s3 cp input-payroll-data.csv s3://shoe-company-ingestion-csv-demo
```

2. If everything executes successfully, in the output bucket that you created, you should see the transformed JSON file. You accepted input into one Amazon S3 bucket as a CSV, transformed it to serverless by using AWS Lambda, and then stored the resulting JSON file in a separate S3 bucket. If you do not see the file, retrace your steps through the exercises. It is a good idea to view the Lambda CloudWatch Logs, which can be found on the Monitoring tab in the Lambda console. This way, you can determine whether there are any errors.

Review Questions

1. A company currently uses a serverless web application stack, which consists of Amazon API Gateway, Amazon Simple Storage Service (Amazon S3), Amazon DynamoDB, and AWS Lambda. They would like to make improvements to their AWS Lambda functions but do not want to impact their production functions. How can they accomplish this?

   A. Create new AWS Lambda functions with a different name, and update resources to point to the new functions when they are ready to test.

   B. Copy their AWS Lambda function to a new region where they can update their resources to the new region when ready.

   C. Create a new AWS account, and re-create all their serverless infrastructure for their application testing.

   D. Publish the current version of their AWS Lambda function, and create an alias PROD. Then, assign PROD to the current version number, update resources with the PROD alias ARN, and create a new version of the updated AWS Lambda function and assign an alias of $DEV.

2. What is the maximum amount of memory that you can assign an AWS Lambda function?

   A. AWS runs the AWS Lambda function; it is a managed service, so you do not need to configure memory settings.

   B. 10 GB

   C. 1,000 MB

   D. 950 MB

3. What is the default timeout value for an AWS Lambda function?

   A. 3 seconds

   B. 10 seconds

   C. 15 seconds

   D. 25 seconds

4. A company uses a third-party service to send checks to its employees for payroll. The company is required to send the third-party service a JSON file with the person's name and the check amount. The company's internal payroll application supports exporting only to CSVs, and it currently has cron jobs set up on their internal network to process these files. The server that is processing the data is aging, and the company is concerned that it might fail in the future. It is also looking to have the AWS services perform the payroll function. What would be the best serverless option to accomplish this goal?

   A. Create an Amazon Elastic Compute Cloud (Amazon EC2) and the necessary cron job to process the file from CSV to JSON.

   B. Use AWS Import/Export to create a virtual machine (VM) image of the on-premises server and upload the Amazon Machine Images (AMI) to AWS.

   C. Use AWS Lambda to process the file with Amazon Simple Storage Service.

   D. There is no way to process this file with AWS.

5. You have established a trigger in S3 to invoke a Lambda function that processes incoming files. This processing is very CPU-heavy and can take anywhere from 10-20 minutes depending on the input file. You are noticing occasional timeouts with this function; which answer will NOT help you eliminate the problem?

   A. Increase the Lambda function timeout to maximum.

   B. Decompose the process into multiple steps that can be handled by more than one Lambda process, then coordinate with Step Functions.

   C. Increase the Lambda's RAM allocation.

   D. Configure a dead letter queue and write another Lambda to re-invoke failures.

6. Which language is *not* natively supported for AWS Lambda functions?

   A. Rust

   B. Python

   C. Node.js

   D. C# (.NET Core)

7. How can you increase the limit of AWS Lambda concurrent executions?

   A. Use the Support Center page in the AWS Management Console to open a case and send a Server Limit Increase request.

   B. AWS Lambda does not have any limits for concurrent executions.

   C. Send an email to limits@amazon.com with the subject "AWS Lambda Increase."

   D. You cannot increase concurrent executions for AWS Lambda.

8. A company is receiving *permission denied* after its AWS Lambda function is invoked and executes and has a valid trust policy. After investigating, the company realizes that its AWS Lambda function does not have access to download objects from Amazon Simple Storage Service. Which type of policy do you need to correct to give access to the AWS Lambda function?

   A. Function policy

   B. Trust policy

   C. Execution policy

   D. None of the above

9. A company wants to be able to send event payloads to an Amazon Simple Queue Service queue if the AWS Lambda function fails. Which of the following configuration options does the company need to be able to do this in AWS Lambda?

   A. Enable a dead-letter queue (DLQ).

   B. Define an Amazon Virtual Private Cloud network.

   C. Enable concurrency.

   D. AWS Lambda does not support such a feature.

10. What is the best approach for passing configuration values to AWS Lambda functions at execution time?

   A. Use dead-letter queues.

   B. Enter the values as environment variables so the function has them in memory.

   C. Enter the configuration values as hierarchical parameters in Parameter Store, and fetch all the ones related to your function.

   D. None of the above.

11. Your company is using AWS Lambda to run data transformation jobs on files stored in S3, which are then loaded into a DynamoDB table. The process is triggered on a schedule using Amazon EventBridge. The company wants to minimize the latency of file processing upon arrival while managing costs effectively. What is the most effective way to configure the Lambda's triggers and resources to meet this requirement? (Choose two.)

   A. Set up the Lambda function to be triggered directly by S3 event notifications instead of an EventBridge schedule.

   B. Increase the function's memory (and therefore CPU) to process files faster overall.

   C. Implement a batching process in the Lambda function to handle multiple files per invocation.

   D. Update EventBridge to trigger the function more frequently.

12. You want to design an application that sends a status email every morning to system administrators. Which option will work?

   A. Create an Amazon SQS queue. Subscribe all the administrators to this queue. Set up an Amazon EventBridge event to send a message on a daily cron schedule into the Amazon SQS queue.

   B. Create an Amazon SNS topic. Subscribe all the administrators to this topic. Set up an EventBridge event to send a message on a daily cron schedule to this topic.

   C. Create an Amazon SNS topic. Subscribe all the administrators to this topic. Set up an EventBridge event to send a message on a daily cron schedule to an AWS Lambda function that generates a summary and publishes it to this topic.

   D. Create an AWS Lambda function that sends out an email to the administrators every day directly with SMTP.

Chapter 13

Serverless Applications

**THE AWS CERTIFIED DEVELOPER –
ASSOCIATE EXAM TOPICS COVERED IN
THIS CHAPTER MAY INCLUDE, BUT ARE
NOT LIMITED TO, THE FOLLOWING:**

✓ **Domain 1: Development with AWS Services**

   ■ Task Statement 1: Develop code for applications
      hosted on AWS

   ■ Task Statement 2: Develop code for AWS Lambda

   ■ Task Statement 3: Use data stores in application development

✓ **Domain 2: Security**

   ■ Task Statement 1: Implement authentication and/or authoriza-
      tion for applications and AWS services

✓ **Domain 4: Troubleshooting and Optimization**

   ■ Task Statement 2: Instrument code for observability

   ■ Task Statement 3: Optimize applications by using AWS
      services and features

In the previous chapter, you learned about AWS Lambda and how you can write functions that run in a serverless manner. Now, we'll take this concept several steps further. Serverless applications move beyond individual functions and provide full-stack user experiences built on serverless technologies. These apps are entirely cloud-native, using pay-as-you-go services that can be built using CloudFormation, skipping the infrastructure management and allowing developers to focus on delivering functionality. They typically revolve around Lambda functions, but also incorporate data storage, front-end user interfaces, authentication and authorization, and APIs using cloud servers, often tied together asynchronously with SQS queues or SNS notifications.

Serverless applications have three main benefits:

- No server management
- Flexible scaling
- Automated high availability

Without server management, you no longer have to provision or maintain servers. Infrastructure can spin up rapidly and be torn down just as quickly for truly agile development, and you almost never have to be concerned about leaving on EC2 instances or other resources that cost you money while they're idle.

With flexible scaling, you no longer have to disable EC2 instances to scale them vertically or manage CloudWatch alarms to drive Auto Scaling events. With Lambda, you adjust the desired resources (such as RAM), and AWS scales the next invocation appropriately.

Finally, serverless applications have built-in availability and fault tolerance. You do not need to architect for these capabilities, as the services that run the application provide them by default.

In previous chapters, we saw many patterns that allow developers to build serverless functionality by integrating AWS services, such as triggering Lambda executions from S3 or queuing failed Lambda events to a dead-letter queue for automatic reprocessing.

Later in this book, you'll encounter even more services that help you build serverless applications: Chapter 14 shows how the AWS Serverless Application Model (SAM) makes serverless architecture easy to define and deploy; Chapter 15 details how EventBridge helps you build sophisticated event-driven architectures.

Before we get to that, in this chapter we'll extend our understanding of how other AWS services can contribute to the architecture of serverless applications, exploring static content delivery with S3 and CloudFront, and API integration of services with API Gateway and AWS AppSync.

Web Server with Amazon S3 (Presentation Layer)

A typical three-tier web application architecture consists of a *presentation layer*, which handles front-end interactions for a web or mobile user; an *application layer*, which processes requests to retrieve or update data; and a *data layer*, which handles the persistent storage of application and user information. In addition, most applications integrate with some service to provide authentication and authorization. Serverless applications implement the capabilities of each layer with pay-as-you-go, serverless components.

Running your front-end code in a serverless model can take a few forms. Applications whose presentation and application layers comprise a single codebase, such as a Python Django web application, need a runtime engine to function. In AWS, your best serverless option for this may be to run the app in a container on ECS or EKS, where Fargate can eliminate the need to run EC2 servers.

In contrast, some applications' front end can be run fully client-side on users' browsers. These applications have presentation layers that use HTML, CSS, and JavaScript only, communicating with the application layer purely through API calls. For such applications, S3 can store all these files in an S3 bucket and host the website like a traditional web server, with no need to run any virtual machines.

In fact, many popular JavaScript frameworks, such as Angular, React, or Vue.js, allow you to build apps with a *Model-View-Controller* (MVC) architecture that brings many elements of full-stack applications to the client side, such as routing, caching, and data management.

Still, most applications will need to implement functionality that doesn't run on the client's browser. After all, the user has complete control over the browser; it is not a secure environment, and inputs received from a client should always be validated. This is why you want to implement both user authentication and authorization, available via Cognito, and backend functionality via APIs, which are HTTP services you build to provide data retrieval and remote procedure invocations via the web. When combined, Cognito and AWS's various API services let you build secure applications with functionality authorized only for those with the correct permissions.

One of the most popular styles of API today is called REST, or Representational State Transfer. *Amazon API Gateway* lets developers define REST endpoints that connect to Lambda functions or other AWS services, allowing the application to save and retrieve data dynamically and perform other critical backend functionality.

A popular alternative to REST-style APIs is *GraphQL*, an HTTP API approach that allows consumers to query data using a structured query language. AWS's AppSync service makes it easy to build and serve GraphQL-compatible APIs over your data, giving you another serverless option for your application architecture.

Let's start with the presentation layer and see what it takes to configure S3 for static web hosting.

Static Website Hosting with S3

 For the remainder of this chapter, the example bucket's name is
examplebucket. This is for illustration purposes only, as Amazon S3
bucket names must be globally unique.

To create an S3 static website, start by creating a bucket. Name the bucket something
meaningful, such as **examplebucket**. Your bucket name will be part of the URL used to
access the website, so keep this in mind. You may also have noticed that S3 bucket names
must comply with the character restrictions of web URLs; this is why. Later in this chapter,
you will see how to configure a custom domain name using Amazon Route 53.

When hosting content in S3 buckets with Secure Sockets Layer (SSL), the SSL wildcard
certificate only matches buckets that do *not* contain periods. To work around this, you must
write your own certificate verification logic, so it's not recommended to use periods (.) in
bucket names when using virtual hosted–style buckets.

After you create your Amazon S3 bucket, you must enable and configure it to use static
website hosting, index documents, error documents, and redirection rules (optional) by
choosing AWS Management Console ➤ Amazon S3 Service. Use this examplebucket bucket
to host a website. For the lowest latency, choose the region closest to where your users will
primarily be located.

Although S3 web hosting can support complex client-side single-page applications (SPAs)
such as those written in React or Angular, the simplest demonstration involves as few as one
file. Upload your index document (typically index.html) along with an optional custom
error page such as error.html. As with many of the Amazon services, you can make these
changes with the AWS Command-Line Interface (CLI) or in a software development kit
(SDK). To enable this option with the CLI, run the following command:

```
aws S3 website s3://examplebucket/ --index-document index.html --error-
document error.html
```

After you enable the Amazon S3 static website hosting feature, your website will be available for browsing at a URL incorporating the bucket name and region. For our purposes,
that URL is examplebucket.s3-website.us-east-1.amazonaws.com.

Configuring S3 Logging

Whether you are using web hosting or operating a standard bucket for storage, Amazon
S3 allows you to configure logging to capture every detail of how users interact with your
object data.

When hosting a website, this logging can be used to discern information such as the
number of visitors who access your website. To enable logs, create a new S3 bucket to be the
log destination. Continuing our example, create a logs-examplebucket-com bucket, and
inside of that bucket, create a folder called logs/ (or any name you choose). Use this folder
to store your logs.

On the primary bucket, navigate to the Configuration ➤ Logging section and enter the name of your log destination bucket. It may take several minutes (or longer) for logs to begin to appear. When they do, they will have a format similar to the following:

```
79a59df900b949e55d96a1e698fbacedfd6e09d98eacf8f8d5218e7cd47ef2be my-bucket
[13/Sep/2024:10:00:01 +0000] 198.51.100.23
79a59df900b949e55d96a1e698fbacedfd6e09d98eacf8f8d5218e7cd47ef2be
A1206F460EXAMPLE REST.PUT.OBJECT examplefile1.txt "PUT /my-
bucket/examplefile1.txt HTTP/1.1" 200 - - 34567 567 22 "-" "S3Console/0.4" -
BNaBsXZQQDbssi6xMBdBU2sLt+Yf5kZDmeBUP35sFoKa3sLLeMC78iwEIWxs99CRUrbS4n11234=
SigV4 ECDHE-RSA-AES128-GCM-SHA256 AuthHeader my-bucket.s3.us-west-
1.amazonaws.com TLSV1.2 - Yes


79a59df900b949e55d96a1e698fbacedfd6e09d98eacf8f8d5218e7cd47ef2be my-bucket
[13/Sep/2024:10:01:10 +0000] 192.0.2.89
79a59df900b949e55d96a1e698fbacedfd6e09d98eacf8f8d5218e7cd47ef2be
7B4A0FABBEXAMPLE REST.GET.OBJECT examplefile1.txt "GET /my-
bucket/examplefile1.txt HTTP/1.1" 200 - 34567 4567 18 "-" "S3Console/0.4" -
Ke1bUcazaN1jWuUlPJaxF64cQVpUEhoZKEG/hmy/gijN/I1DeWqDfFvnpybfEseEME/u7ME1234=
SigV4 ECDHE-RSA-AES128-GCM-SHA256 AuthHeader my-bucket.s3.us-west-
1.amazonaws.com TLSV1.2 - Yes
```

Because they are so complex, this example depicts just two lines, but you can see the bucket name, timestamp, object name, and API call (such as GET or PUT) that was made. Once logging is configured, it's a good idea to set life cycle rules on the logging bucket, using deletion policies to establish a retention period for logs. S3 life cycle rule configuration is discussed in Chapter 3, "AWS Data Storage."

Be careful! Never configure S3 logging to write its logs back into the source bucket, as this creates a recursive situation where log writes trigger more log writes, and so on, causing quickly escalating storage consumption and costs.

We have used the term *folder* when describing logs; however, the Amazon S3 data model is a flat structure that allows you to create a bucket, and the bucket stores objects. There is no hierarchy of sub-buckets or subfolders; nevertheless, you can infer a logical hierarchy using key name prefixes and delimiters (like forward slashes), and this idiom is reinforced by the Amazon S3 console, which visually displays folders. Despite this, as a developer, you should know that there is technically no such thing as an Amazon S3 folder—a "file path" consisting of folders and subfolders is simply a key.

When configuring the static website–hosted bucket (`examplebucket`) to log files to bucket `logs-examplebucket-com`, you may also specify a target prefix to send log files to a particular prefix key only. Depending on the needs of your organization, it may be beneficial to establish a single bucket to be a centralized, shared log target, where each source bucket uses prefixes that separate bucket logs into distinct folders. For instance, you might specify the prefix in this example to be `examplebucket-logs` while configuring another bucket to target the same log bucket with prefix `anotherbucket-logs`. The log bucket in such a scenario would therefore look a bit like this

```
my-<orgname>-log-bucket/
    source-application-bucket-1/
        log1.txt
        log2.txt
    source-application-bucket-2/
        log1.txt
        log2.txt
```

To enable this feature with the CLI, create an access control list that provides access to the log files that you want to create and then apply the `logging` policy. Here's an example:

```
aws s3api put-bucket-acl --bucket examplebucket --grant-write
'URI="http://acs.amazonaws.com.cn/groups/s3/LogDelivery"' --grant-read-acp
'URI="http://acs.amazonaws.com.cn/groups/s3/LogDelivery"'

aws s3api put-bucket-logging --bucket examplebucket --bucket-logging-status
file://logging.json
```

Here's the file `logging.json`:

```
{
  "LoggingEnabled": {
    "TargetBucket": "examplebucket",
    "TargetPrefix": "examplebucket/",
    "TargetGrants": [
      {
        "Grantee": {
          "Type": "AmazonCustomerByEmail",
          "EmailAddress": "user@example.com"
        },
        "Permission": "FULL_CONTROL"
      },
      {
        "Grantee": {
          "Type": "Group",
          "URI": "http://acs.amazonaws.com/groups/global/AllUsers"
```

```
        },
        "Permission": "READ"
      }
    ]
  }
}
```

Creating Custom Domain Names with Amazon Route 53

Amazon Route 53 is a highly available and scalable cloud Domain Name System (DNS) web service. It is designed to give developers and businesses an extremely reliable and cost-effective way to manage and configure DNS, translating names like www.amazon.com into numeric IP addresses like 52.94.236.248 that computers use to connect to each other. Amazon Route 53 is fully compliant with IPv6 as well.

You may not want to use the Amazon S3 endpoint such as bucket-name.s3-website-region.amazonaws.com. Instead, you may want a more user-friendly URL such as myex amplewebsite.com. To accomplish this, purchase a domain name with Amazon Route 53.

 You can purchase your domain from another provider and then update the name servers to use Amazon Route 53, letting you use AWS tooling to manage your DNS configuration.

Amazon Route 53 effectively connects user requests to infrastructure running in AWS—such as Amazon EC2 instances, Elastic Load Balancing load balancers, or Amazon S3 buckets—and can route users to infrastructure outside of AWS. You can use Amazon Route 53 to configure DNS health checks to route traffic to healthy endpoints or to monitor independently the health of your application and its endpoints. Amazon Route 53 Traffic Flow makes it easy for you to manage traffic globally through a variety of routing types, including latency-based routing, geolocation, geoproximity, and weighted round-robin, all of which can be combined with DNS failover to enable a variety of low-latency, fault-tolerant architectures.

Using Amazon Route 53 Traffic Flow's simple visual editor, you can easily manage how your end users are routed to your application's endpoints—whether in a single AWS region or distributed around the globe. Amazon Route 53 also offers domain name registration. You can purchase and manage domain names such as example.com, and Amazon Route 53 will automatically configure DNS settings for your domains.

Speeding Up Content Delivery with Amazon CloudFront

Minimizing *latency* is essential when you deliver web applications to the end user, as you always want your user to have an efficient, responsive experience on your website. Increased latency can result in both decreased customer satisfaction and decreased sales. One way to decrease latency is to use *Amazon CloudFront* to move your content closer to your end users.

CloudFront is a content distribution network (CDN) whose responsibility is to replicate your web assets to nodes (called "edge locations") around the world, so that when clients request content such as HTML, CSS, or JavaScript, it can be delivered from a location as close to them as possible, reducing overall download time.

As a web developer seeking to optimize web performance, your goal is always to deliver up-to-date data to users while minimizing the frequency with which your application and data layer are hit. Any time a client request can be served out of cache—especially one that is located geographically close to the client—you avoid redundant requests, reduce load on your backend application, and deliver content back to the user faster. CloudFront can be a valuable part of a multilayered caching strategy, caching client-side assets in a global network, while server-side data responses are cached in another system, such as ElastiCache.

Amazon CloudFront has two delivery methods to deliver content. The first is a web distribution for storing HTML, CSS, and other static files such as graphics. CloudFront also allows you to create RTMP distributions to speed up distribution of streaming media files using Adobe Flash Media Server's RTMP protocol. An RTMP distribution allows an end user to begin playing a media file before the file has finished downloading from a Cloud-Front edge location.

Configuring a CloudFront Distribution

To use Amazon CloudFront with your Amazon S3 static website, perform these tasks:

1. Choose a delivery method. In our example, we will be using Amazon S3 to store a static web page; thus, we will be using the web distribution delivery method. However, as mentioned previously, you could also use RTMP for streaming media files.

2. Specify the cache behavior. A cache behavior lets you configure a variety of CloudFront functionality for a given URL path pattern for files on your website.

3. Choose the distribution settings and network that you want to use. For example, you can use all edge locations or only U.S., Canada, and Europe locations.

You then provide an origin for the content that CloudFront will deliver: your S3 bucket. The resulting CloudFront distribution has a DNS name that you can swap in for the base URL of assets in your application. Note that this approach—serving static assets from CloudFront—works equally well if your application is a website fully hosted on S3 or a dynamic web application built on Kubernetes. You can sync your content to S3, associate that location with CloudFront, and then direct all requests for static content to CloudFront.

Managing CloudFront Caching Behavior

CloudFront does not immediately distribute your S3 content to its global network of nodes; rather, it operates on a "lazy loading" approach in which contents are only fetched and cached when explicitly requested by a user. The first time a client issues a request for a file, CloudFront fetches it from the origin (your S3 bucket) and distributes it to edge locations that are geographically close to the requester. CloudFront doesn't distribute content globally by default; rather, it waits until it receives requests from different localities. This is more efficient, but be aware that even for the same object, users in different parts of the globe may incur that initial fetch latency as the CloudFront cache is updated.

After that first hit, the second, third, and n[th] requests pull from the Amazon CloudFront's cache at a lower latency and cost, as shown in Figure 13.1.

FIGURE 13.1   Amazon CloudFront cache

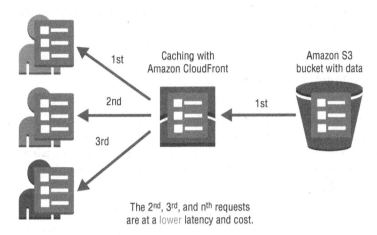

Lazy loading is described in greater detail in the section "Amazon Elasticache" further in this chapter. Because of this mechanism, developers need to engage in some active cache management to ensure fresh content is delivered to users.

There are two ways in which your content may be updated in CloudFront: when an object's *time-to-live (TTL) value* expires, or when the cache is explicitly invalidated. Time-to-live values say how long an object should remain active in the cache. This can be set at the CloudFront distribution level, or on a per-object basis by setting S3 object metadata. The following CLI call sets this value to 1 hour (3,600 seconds) on an object by setting a Cache-Control metadata value:

```
aws s3 cp s3://mybucket/style.css s3://mybucket/style.css --metadata-directive
REPLACE --cache-control "max-age=3600"
```

CloudFront distributions may be explicitly invalidated, clearing the cache for all data or for specific paths. To do this with the CLI, run the following:

```
aws cloudfront create-invalidation --distribution-id <MY_DISTRIBUTION_ID> --
paths <PATHS>
```

A common practice for developers is to issue a CloudFront invalidation any time you deploy your web application, ensuring that clients don't get any old, cached content. The first request to each object will be a cache miss, causing a request to S3 that fills the cache for subsequent requests.

Optimizing CloudFront Performance

The *cache hit ratio* is the proportion of client requests that CloudFront can serve from edge caches versus all requests. The higher this ratio, the better the latency experience for your users.

You can view the percentage of viewer requests that are hits, misses, and errors in the Cloud-Front console.

Several factors affect the cache hit ratio. These include how you configure cache keys, the TTL settings for your cached objects, and how you handle query strings, URL parameters, and headers in your requests. You can adjust your CloudFront distribution configuration to improve the cache hit ratio.

Focus initially on the makeup of your cache key. Cache keys are the strings that uniquely identify a resource to be saved in your cache. For instance, consider the request below:

```
GET /products/outdoor/camping?q=sleeping+bag
```

This request no doubt returns a list of sleeping bag products from an online store's inventory. If we are to cache the result, what should we make the key? Remember that subsequent requests will receive the cached data. If we include the URL pattern `/products/outdoor/camping` but exclude the query parameter `sleeping+bag`, hoping to match more requests and create a higher cache hit ratio, the cache would serve information about sleeping bags for a similar, but very different request for camp stoves:

```
GET /products/outdoor/camping?q=camp+stoves
```

Therefore, you need to include in your cache key any element that affects the actual response of a request. The query parameter q is crucial, but another query parameter indicating the user's customer ID would not be. These two requests should serve the same data:

```
GET /products/outdoor/camping?q=backpacks&customer_id=123
GET /products/outdoor/camping?q=backpacks&customer_id=456
```

If you included `customer_id` in the cache key, you'd end up wasting space with redundant cache data. In this case, the `customer_id` doesn't matter; every customer sees the same inventory of backpacks.

Time-to-live is also important. You might get a noticeable performance hit by caching the following request with a long TTL:

```
GET /product_categories
```

If you know what product categories rarely change, this TTL could be measured in days. On the other hand, data that changes frequently should have a short TTL so that updates reach consumers sooner. Cache hit ratio and page load time don't mean much if your cache is showing users an item in stock that just sold out.

With CloudFront, you can improve the already impressive performance of S3 content hosting with geographically proximate edge locations and sophisticated caching to decrease your application's latency and costs, and to provide a better user experience.

Amazon API Gateway (Logic or App Layer)

Amazon API Gateway is one of AWS's most well-conceived services, providing robust, managed tools for building HTTP APIs that invoke Lambda functions, proxy backend

HTTP services, or execute any AWS service API available in the AWS Cloud. API Gateway's many features make it easy to create REST API services backed by AWS compute and to design, version, configure, and deploy APIs both in the web console or as templated code.

API Gateway has tight integration with the OpenAPI 3.0 spec, which API developers use to design and document their APIs. With this integration, not only can you document your APIs in a structured way, but those documents can include extensions that define the configuration of the Amazon API Gateway itself. Moreover, you can import an OpenAPI document into API Gateway to automatically construct the corresponding API.

The first step in using API Gateway is to define an API, which can be one of the following formats:

REST API   REST APIs are API Gateway's most full-featured offering. They are built around the API design pattern known as *Representative State Transfer (REST)*, which is detailed in the next section. API Gateway REST APIs can connect to Lambda functions, HTTP backends (e.g., your own custom-built APIs on running EC2, Beanstalk, or ECS), or AWS services (e.g., an S3 PUT). They have the broadest range of deployment modes, including Edge-Optimized, which enables low-latency access across regions. They allow deep configuration of user access authorization and rate limiting, sophisticated deployment options, extensive caching capabilities, and deep system tracing with X-Ray.

HTTP API   HTTP APIs are a simpler, cheaper form of the REST API, lacking many of its features at a more attractive cost. HTTP APIs may only invoke Lambda and HTTP backends. Unlike REST APIs, they are only deployable in Regional mode, which means that users in other regions may experience additional latency. They have fewer options for security than REST APIs as well, supporting only mutual TLS authentication.

However, despite their diminished feature list compared to REST APIs, HTTP APIs have a few unique capabilities, such as their ability to integrate natively with OpenID Connect for authorization using JSON Web Tokens (JWTs). This is a common method of accessing APIs that must be implemented via custom code when working with REST APIs.

WebSocket APIs   WebSocket APIs enable persistent two-way communication between clients and servers over a single, long-lived connection. They are ideal for applications that require real-time updates, such as chat applications, live dashboards, and multiplayer games. Systems that provide responses from Large Language Models can enhance the user experience by using WebSocket APIs to stream tokens to the client, rather than waiting for a lengthy response to be rendered all at once. API Gateway WebSocket APIs support integration with Lambda functions, HTTP backends, and AWS services.

WebSocket APIs also offer features like connection management, message broadcasting, and support for authorization using IAM roles or custom authorizers. However, they lack some of the more advanced features of REST APIs, such as extensive caching and deployment modes.

Use Amazon API Gateway to safely expose AWS resources and backend services to other systems.

Endpoints

There are three types of *endpoints* for Amazon API Gateway. This selection determines the overall accessibility of each URL defined in your API.

Regional Endpoints   Deployed inside a specific AWS region, such as us-west-2, Regional endpoints may experience additional latency when called by clients outside the region.

Edge-Optimized Endpoints   Edge-optimized endpoints leverage Amazon CloudFront's network of global distribution points to provide connection points for clients so that wherever your consumers are in the world, they can access your API with an endpoint that is geographically close and low-latency.

Private Endpoints   Private endpoints live only inside a *virtual private cloud* (VPC) and can only be accessed by consumers within that VPC. This is an ideal choice when you need to build internal APIs that are not to be accessed outside your organization.

Your choice of endpoint type can determine the total response time of your API. You can improve the performance of specific API requests with Amazon API Gateway by caching responses in an optional in-memory cache. This not only provides performance benefits for API repeated requests, but it also reduces backend executions, which helps to reduce overall costs.

API endpoints created in AWS API Gateway can be a default host name or a custom domain name that you supply via Route 53. The default host name format is as follows:

{api-id}.execute-api.{region}.amazonaws.com

Understanding REST

API Gateway's default operating model is the REST API. REST is a popular style of API interaction proposed by Roy Fielding in 2000. In contrast to the then-prevalent SOAP API pattern, which requires requests and responses to be formatted in XML, REST APIs use JSON, and are overall a much lighter-weight implementation approach.

The key innovation of REST is that HTTP APIs should hew closely to the design concepts of HTTP itself, taking advantage of URLs, a mechanism to describe resources and hierarchical relationships, and using HTTP verbs (such as GET, POST, and DELETE) to act on those resources. A common illustration of this concept is a pet store. In the pet store example, a URL defines a resource called pets, which represents the list of pets in the pet store. This list is retrievable via an HTTP GET request:

```
GET /pets
```

That request may respond with JSON describing many pets in the store, along with unique identifiers, like so:

```
[
    {
```

```
        pet_id: 1,
        species: "dog",
        breed: "Golden Retriever"
    },
    {
        pet_id: 1,
        species: "cat",
        breed: "British Shorthair"
    }
]
```

Remember, REST is a design pattern only; the specific URLs, parameters, and return data will vary from implementation to implementation. In this response, you can see identifiers for reach record. A single record may then be retrieved by providing that ID in the URL like so:

```
GET /pets/1
```

When a pet is adopted, it can be deleted from the store's inventory with a DELETE request:

```
DELETE /pets/1
```

As you can see, the implementation is very HTTP-native. To create a new pet record, you would issue a POST to the same /pets endpoint, this time including a JSON representation of a new pet in the HTTP body.

While a complete exploration of REST could fill many more pages, this overview should give you enough context to understand more about what Amazon API Gateway is doing when it asks you to define things like resources and methods, discussed next.

Resources

An API Gateway REST API consists of resources and methods. As in the previous example, a *resource* is an object that provides operations you use to interact with it, implemented as HTTP commands such as GET, POST, or DELETE. The combination of a resource path and a specific operation on that resource is called a *method*. Users can call API methods to obtain controlled access to resources and to receive a response.

You define *mappings* between the method and the backend to control the flow of data and any transformations that you may wish to implement along that flow (i.e., in the request or response). You can create *mapping templates* that apply these changes between the API's front end façade and its backend implementation.

In the Amazon API Gateway service, you expose addressable *resources* as a tree of *API Resources* entities, with the root resource (/) at the top of the hierarchy. All endpoints are prefixed by the API's base URL, which consists of the API endpoint plus a *stage name*. Stages, discussed in the next section, can define things like environments (e.g., dev, test, or prod) or versions (e.g., v1, v2) and become part of a method's URL. In the API Gateway console, the base URL is referred to as the *Invoke URL*, and it displays in the API's stage editor after the API deploys.

As an example, if you own a pizza restaurant and run a website to display your menu options, you can create a *root resource* called menu (for production) at URL /menu with a GET method that returns a JSON representation of your entire menu. When individuals visit your website and navigate to the menu, your application code can invoke the API to fetch all this data, which you then display to the user.

For example, the following:

```
{api-id}.execute-api.region.amazonaws.com/menu
```

will return the dataset through the Amazon API Gateway service:

```
[
 {
     "id": 1,
     "menu-item": "cheese pizza",
     "price": "14.99"
 },
 {
     "id": 2,
     "menu-item": "pepperoni pizza",
     "price": "17.99"
 }
]
```

With resources, you create paths such as /menu, /specials, and /orders to interact with different datasets via HTTP methods.

HTTP Verbs

As we've discussed, API Gateway creates REST-style APIs using HTTP verbs. The following methods are supported:

- GET
- HEAD
- POST
- PUT
- PATCH
- OPTIONS
- DELETE

When your REST interface is well defined, these verbs, acting on resources that accurately model your business data, comprise a programming interface that should be discernible not just to your code, but to a reader.

The combination of a particular verb, such as GET or POST, along with a specific API resource (such as /pets or /orders) defines a single API method. This is how API Gateway refers to a single call that a client can make on an API.

Backend Integrations

Of course, a method definition alone is not enough—it has to actually do something. To configure your methods to take action, you must associate it with an *integration*. API Gateway offers several different integration types, giving you lots of flexibility for how to fulfill your API's contract with backend services.

Lambda Function   The most common backend implementation used by AWS developers, it takes only a few clicks to connect an API method to a Lambda, giving you fully serverless functionality along with the flexibility of Lambda to implement business logic in a variety of languages.

HTTP   Lambda is not the only approach; you can connect API Gateway methods to any service running on HTTP in your account. For instance, this could be another API running on an EC2 instance, an ECS service, or Elastic Beanstalk. Because API Gateway allows you to transform incoming requests and outgoing responses with custom configurations, this backend HTTP service can even be a non-REST API. In fact, you can use an HTTP integration to build a RESTful façade over a SOAP backend, translating SOAP requests and XML responses to the format desired by REST clients. Initial configuration of an HTTP backend is easy—you just provide another URL.

Mock Integration   With a mock backend, you provide a static, hard-coded response to callers. Mock integrations are useful during testing of new API endpoints, when the implementation may still be in flux, but you'd like to allow consumers to build client-side code using real requests. Mock endpoints let those clients work with fake responses that conform to the style and format that the real API will ultimately have, speeding up and parallelizing development efforts.

AWS Service   The AWS Service integration type allows you to directly connect an API method to almost any AWS service. This integration type is powerful for scenarios where your API needs to interact with AWS resources like DynamoDB, S3, or Step Functions. Recall that all interactions with AWS resources are implemented as APIs, such as S3's PutObject API. With this integration type, you may directly map an Amazon API Gateway REST endpoint to one of these types of service calls, involving no code or custom infrastructure whatsoever.

VPC Link   The VPC Link integration type enables secure and scalable connectivity between your API Gateway and backend services hosted within a VPC. This setup is ideal for APIs that need to access private resources such as EC2 instances, RDS databases, or services deployed on ECS or EKS within your VPC. By configuring a VPC Link, API Gateway can securely route incoming API requests to these private resources without exposing them to the Internet. Setting up a VPC Link involves creating a VPC Link resource in API Gateway, associating it with one or more network load balancers in your VPC, and then integrating your API methods with this VPC Link. This ensures secure and reliable communication between your API Gateway and backend services.

Stages

Once you have defined your resources, methods, and their specific backend integrations, you must deploy the API before you can use it. When deploying your API, you may define and choose a *stage* for that deployment. Stages are named logical groupings for your deployments that become part of the endpoint URL.

Because each stage can be configured with its own access rules, rate limiting, and environment variables, common use cases for stages are to separate environments or API versions. For example, when performing your first deployment of an API, you might name a dev stage. The resulting endpoint URL has this format:

```
{api-id}.execute-api.{region}.amazonaws.com/{stage}/{method}
```

In the pets example, when deploying to a stage called dev, the URL to retrieve all pets would look like this:

```
GET q83ij7fn1.execute-api.us-east-1.amazonaws.com/dev/pets
```

When you create a stage, your API is deployed and accessible to whomever you grant access. Note that all API endpoints are deployed at once; it is not possible to deploy some methods and omit others. An advisable API strategy is to create stages for each of your environments such as DEV, TEST, and PROD, so that you can continue to develop and update your API and applications without affecting production.

Many options can be set at the stage level, including caching, customized request throttling, logging configuration, and stage variables.

Using Stage Variables for Dynamic Backend References

Stage variables allow you to parameterize certain elements of your deployment with values set at the stage level. One use case described by AWS is making your backend function references dynamic such that different stages refer to different function versions. Recall that a Lambda function can be tagged with version labels or aliases, which can be specified with a colon at the end of its ARN:

```
arn:aws:lambda:{region}:{account-id}:function:{function-name}:{version-or-alias}
```

If you wish, you can have an API method refer to its backend Lambda using a stage variable so that each stage can point to a distinct Lambda version or alias. Stage variables use the format ${stageVariables.variable_name}, where stageVariables is fixed and variable_name is your choice. If you point your method to a Lambda ARN with a stage variable at the end, you can make the function version dependent on a value set at the stage:

```
arn:aws:lambda:us-east-1:123456789012:function:my-backend-
function:${stageVariables.lambda_version}
```

After doing this, you will find that your stage configuration has a new input for a value called lambda_version. Whatever you enter here will fill the value above.

This approach allows you a significant amount of control over the release of functionality in your API, as you can deploy changes to the backend functionality by altering Lambda versions, letting you test potential changes in a controlled manner.

When referring to Lambda aliases or versions, your API Gateway must have IAM permissions to execute that specific alias or version. When you configure a Lambda reference using stage variables, the AWS Management Console alerts you to this fact and prompts you with instructions on creating the required permissions.

Testing Changes with Canary Deployments

Another powerful API deployment strategy is the *canary release*. In software deployment, a *canary* is a code update that is deployed only to a small fraction of the full user base so that developers can assess a change without impacting every user at once. Canary deployments are often used in production, with code that has otherwise been fully tested; they are an exercise in caution, allowing you to slowly roll out a change before committing to a full release.

In practical terms, a canary operates much like a sub-stage of the stage on which it is used. You can define a single canary configuration on a given stage; that canary has all the configuration options of a full-fledged stage, such as caching settings, logging, and stage variables. You define a percentage of that stage's traffic to route to the canary (say, 5 or 10 percent). When this takes effect, you can monitor logging, and when you are satisfied that the release is working effectively, you may "promote" the canary, at which point its configuration takes over its parent stage's configuration.

Authorizers

There are multiple ways to configure user authorization in API Gateway, each with different levels of control and complexity.

IAM Authorizers

The simplest and least flexible form of API Gateway authorization is the IAM authorizer, in which API Gateway expects incoming requests to be signed with actual AWS account credentials (i.e., the root user or an IAM user). Consumers use an AWS-proprietary protocol called SigV4 to encode their credentials, then pass this value with their API call. The IAM authorizer then maps these credentials to a known user in the AWS account and applies the IAM policies associated with that user to determine whether the API endpoint can be called. SigV4 is not just used in API Gateway; it can be used for other services like S3. For more on SigV4, visit:

https://docs.aws.amazon.com/AmazonS3/latest/API/sig-v4-authenticating-requests.html

Lambda Authorizers

Formerly known as "custom authorizers," Lambda authorizers route every request to an API gateway endpoint through an AWS Lambda function that you have written. Your Lambda must respond with a JSON-templated IAM policy document that authorizes the caller for specific endpoints (i.e., combinations of an HTTP verb and a URL). In the following example, the policy document allows access to a certain endpoint:

```
{
  "Version": "2012-10-17",
  "Statement": [
    {
      "Action": "execute-api:Invoke",
      "Effect": "Allow",
      "Resource": "arn:aws:execute-api:us-west-2:123456789012:example/prod/
GET/my_resource"
    }
  ]
}
```

The Effect may be "Allow" or "Deny". Note that the Resource value can be defined all the way down to a single endpoint by including the verb and resource names; however, you may specify rules at a higher level using asterisks. For example, this value would control access to the entire API:

```
"Resource": "arn:aws:execute-api:<region>:<account_id>:<api_id>/*"
```

While building a Lambda authorizer requires the most work, this approach is the most flexible, because your Lambda can take any action necessary, or call out to any service needed, to make an authorization decision.

For instance, a popular API authorization flow requires consumers to authenticate end users with a third-party identity provider (IdP) such as Okta or Sailpoint, which then grants the client a token in the form of a JWT. The token contains *scopes*—user attributes that you may use to represent API permissions. A Lambda authorizer is the way to enable API Gateway REST APIs to validate this token with the third-party provider and to interpret its scopes as IAM permissions. This pattern is depicted in Figure 13.2.

FIGURE 13.2   API Gateway Authorizer validating a client's JSON web token with an issuing identity provider

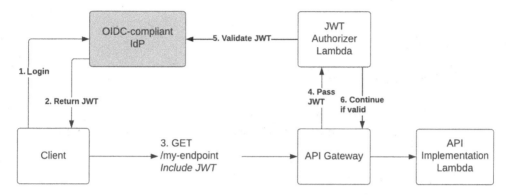

This is the one area in which API Gateway HTTP APIs have a distinct advantage over REST APIs—they natively support JWT authorizers without the use of a custom Lambda. For more on this configuration, visit:

https://docs.aws.amazon.com/apigateway/latest/developerguide/http-api-jwt-authorizer.html

Cognito Authorizers

In this method, applications that leverage Cognito user pools for end-user authentication may configure API Gateway to consult Cognito for authorization decisions. This is essentially an AWS-native implementation of the JWT flow described earlier. Cognito issues JWTs to authenticated users, who pass the value along to API Gateway whenever making an API request. However, unlike when using a third-party IdP, Cognito JWT authorization can be configured without the use of a custom Lambda. You configure API Gateway with the scopes and claims that are allowed for each endpoint, and AWS takes care of the JWT validation and mapping of the user's scopes to API permissions automatically.

Resource Policies

Like S3 buckets, API Gateway APIs may be configured with resource policies. These JSON documents can constrain who is able to call the API and from where. The following sources may be explicitly allowed or denied:

- Specified AWS accounts
- Source IP ranges (CIDR blocks)
- Source VPCs or VPC endpoints

In the following example, incoming calls to a specific endpoint are restricted to IPs coming from two /24 blocks, which together encompass 512 addresses:

```
{
    "Version": "2012-10-17",
    "Statement": [
        {
            "Effect": "Allow",
            "Principal": "*",
            "Action": "execute-api:Invoke",
            "Resource": "arn:aws:execute-api:<region>:<account_id>:<api_id>/
<stage>/<method>/<resource>",
            "Condition": {
                "IpAddress": {
                    "aws:SourceIp": [
                        "192.168.0.0/24",
                        "203.0.113.0/24"
                    ]
                }
            }
        }
    ]
}
```

Resource policies can work together with authorizers to apply access controls at both coarse- and fine-grained levels.

Resource policies can only be applied to REST APIs, not HTTP APIs.

API Keys and Usage Plans

API Gateway can generate *API keys* to provide access to your API for external users using the API call apikey:create to create an API key.

API keys may be enabled on your API, at which point every incoming request must contain a valid key in the X-API-Key HTTP header. When using an authorizer, the authorizer may return the key in its IAM policy response in this format:

usageIdentifierKey:{api-key}

Do not rely on API keys for authenticating or authorizing users; instead, use them in conjunction with the authorization approaches described earlier.

A unique use case for API keys is associating them with *usage plans*. API Gateway usage plans allow you to set throttling rules and quotas on the consumption of your endpoints. With usage plans, you can configure rate limiting on your endpoints, specifying, say, the number of calls per minute that are allowed on a certain endpoint, along with a maximum number of calls allowed per day. In this way, you can shape the demand on your backend resources to optimize performance for all your clients.

Cross-Origin Resource Sharing

To help prevent malicious requests and denial-of-service attacks, modern browsers restrict clients' ability to make requests from one domain to another. This is called the *same-origin policy*, and it's a fundamental component of Internet security. However, modern web applications often host their front end at one domain and their backend services (such as your API Gateway endpoints) on another, so it's essential that some valid traffic be exempted from this policy. *Cross-origin resource sharing (CORS)* allows developers to explicitly allow specified non-matching domains to make incoming calls to a service. You can read the specification at www.w3.org/TR/cors.

CORS allows you to set certain HTTP headers to enable cross-origin access to call APIs or services to which you need access. The HTTP headers include the following:

- `Access-Control-Allow-Origin`
- `Access-Control-Allow-Credentials`
- `Access-Control-Allow-Headers`
- `Access-Control-Allow-Methods`
- `Access-Control-Expose-Headers`
- `Access-Control-Max-Age`
- `Access-Control-Request-Headers`
- `Access-Control-Request-Method`
- `Origin`

When your browser makes a call that crosses domains, it first issues a "pre-flight" call to the remote service to validate that this traffic is allowed. If the incoming domain is allowed, the CORS configuration on the backend service will respond affirmatively.

To use Amazon API Gateway, you must enable the CORS *resource* in the Amazon API Gateway console so that your web application makes calls to the Amazon API Gateway service successfully. Without CORS, any calls made to the Amazon API Gateway service will fail.

Reduce Latency with Caching

As with web applications, APIs can optimize performance significantly with the strategic use of caching. In API Gateway, you can configure caching automatically at the stage level of an

API; with this setting enabled, responses to your stage's endpoints will be saved and replayed back to users for as long as the time-to-live setting you specify. This saved response can be sent to the caller much more quickly than it often takes to generate a fresh response from the backend, giving your users a faster experience and saving you on backend compute costs.

The TTL for your cache defaults to 300 seconds (5 minutes) and can be assigned a range from 0 seconds to 3,600 seconds (1 hour). You may manually invalidate the cache at any time, and clients with appropriate permissions may also bust the cache by setting the HTTP header to `Cache-Control: max-age=0`.

Stage-level caching settings may also be overridden at the individual endpoint level, on the method configuration. In this way, you can set a longer TTL for more slowly changing data.

Finally, it's important to consider the way API's cache key will be constructed. This is the value that associates an incoming request with a cached response. For instance, although both of the following URLs use the same API resource and method, you would not want to cache the same response for each:

```
GET /pets?type=dog
GET /pets?type=cat
```

To make API Gateway aware of the distinction, edit your method configuration; each parameter or header value will have an option to include it in the cache key. In this way, you can set distinct caches for distinct user requests.

> API Gateway's caching is a fairly naïve approach, in that it is not aware when backend data changes. Combine Gateway-level caching with a strategy implemented on your backend (such as write-through caching with ElastiCache in front of your persistence layer) to achieve the optimal balance between data freshness and response times.

Implementing WebSocket APIs

WebSockets allow you to create persistent connections with web and mobile clients, establishing two-way communication that is ideal for real-time systems such as chat applications.

A WebSocket API has just one URL, but within that URL, you define *routes* for individual actions. Think of these a bit like resource endpoints in a REST API or as "commands" for your WebSocket. Clients connect to the WebSocket and can then both listen for messages or send data to routes. For instance, a WebSocket used for chat may send messages representing each new chat message while advertising a route called `"postMessage"` that the client can use to send its own message to other clients connected on the WebSocket. The WebSocket itself defines how clients request routes. There is no hard-and-fast standard, but a common approach is for clients to send messages as JSON, where one of the fields indicates the desired route. For example, if the WebSocket is looking for routes on `$request.body .action`, a client might send a `"postMessage"` command whose payload looks like this:

```
{
    "action": "postMessage",
```

```
    "messageContent": "hello world!"
}
```

It is fully up to the developer of the WebSocket API to determine which routes to implement and how clients should send data to them. API Gateway just helps define how these routes will be implemented. Like REST API endpoints, each route has a backend implementation, such as a Lambda function, another HTTP endpoint, or a Mock. You can mix-and-match all of these types in a single WebSocket API. In addition to user-defined routes, AWS optionally defines three special routes for WebSocket APIs:

- $connect: This route is invoked whenever a client first connects to the Web-Socket URL.

- $disconnect: This route is invoked whenever a client explicitly terminates the Web-Socket connection.

- $default: This route is invoked whenever a client requests a route that does not exist.

If you map the $connect route to a Lambda, you can then use that Lambda to conduct user authorization or any other initial steps needed before a client uses the WebSocket API.

By taking care of the infrastructure and simplifying the job of defining routes, AWS API Gateway makes it easy to build real-time communication in your serverless apps.

Monitoring Amazon API Gateway with AWS CloudWatch

Amazon API Gateway integrates with AWS CloudWatch, which provides preconfigured metrics to help you monitor your APIs and build both dashboards and alarms. As of this writing, there are nine metrics available by default with AWS CloudWatch, as shown in Table 13.1.

TABLE 13.1   AWS CloudWatch Metrics

Metric	Description
4XXError	The number of client-side errors captured in a specified period. The Sum statistic represents this metric, namely, the total count of the 4XXError errors in the given period. The Average statistic represents the 4XXError error rate, namely, the total count of the 4XXError errors divided by the total number of requests during the period. The denominator corresponds to the Count metric. Unit: Count
5XXError	The number of server-side errors captured in a given period. The Sum statistic represents this metric, namely, the total count of the 5XXError errors in the given period. The Average statistic represents the 5XXError error rate, namely, the total count of the 5XXError errors divided by the total number of requests during the period. The denominator corresponds to the Count metric. Unit: Count

TABLE 13.1 AWS CloudWatch Metrics *(continued)*

Metric	Description
CacheHitCount	The number of requests served from the API cache in a given period. The Sum statistic represents this metric, namely, the total count of the cache hits in the specified period. The Average statistic represents the cache hit rate, namely, the total count of the cache hits divided by the total number of requests during the period. The denominator corresponds to the Count metric. Unit: Count
CacheMissCount	The number of requests served from the back end in a given period, when API caching is enabled. The Sum statistic represents this metric, namely, the total count of the cache misses in the specified period. The Average statistic represents the cache miss rate, namely, the total count of the cache hits divided by the total number of requests during the period. The denominator corresponds to the Count metric. Unit: Count
Count	The total number API requests in a given period. The SampleCount statistic represents this metric. Unit: Count
IntegrationLatency	The time between when Amazon API Gateway relays a request to the backend and when it receives a response from the backend. Unit: Millisecond
Latency	The time between when Amazon API Gateway receives a request from a client and when it returns a response to the client. The latency includes the integration latency and other Amazon API Gateway overhead. Unit: Millisecond

See Figure 13.3 for a sample dashboard.

If you use Amazon CloudWatch with Amazon API Gateway, you can monitor your application from an API standpoint to see whether any issues occur as the application is being used. Particularly, you can view metrics such as CacheMissCount and Latency to keep an eye on the user experience. Each metric can be filtered by API name, stage name, resource, or method.

FIGURE 13.3   Sample dashboard for Amazon API Gateway using Amazon CloudWatch

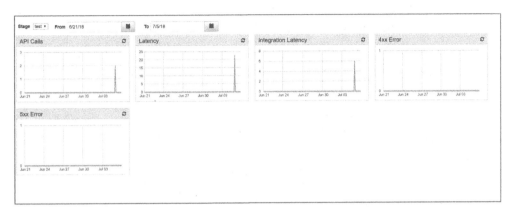

Integration with OpenAPI Docs

One of the most popular ways to document REST APIs is using the OpenAPI specification. Originally developed by SmartBear and known as Swagger, the OpenAPI spec was made open source in 2015. Since then, the Swagger name lives on in reference to tools released by SmartBear to work with and display OpenAPI documents. OpenAPI's most recent release is 3.0.

OpenAPI lets you document REST APIs via either JSON or YAML. With it, you can capture every element on an API's design, from methods and resources to parameters and response bodies. Most tools for displaying OpenAPI docs convert them into friendly web pages, complete with a UI for testing out the API, whether directly via the browser or by generating the appropriate cURL command for the terminal. OpenAPI docs are very powerful and easy to write, if somewhat verbose. This YAML snippet depicts an API with just one GET endpoint, no parameters, and a single "200 OK" success response:

```
openapi: 3.0.0
info:
  title: Pet Store API
  description: API for a pet store
  version: 1.0.0
servers:
  - url: https://api.petstore.com/v1
paths:
  /pets:
    get:
      summary: List all pets
      description: Retrieve a list of all pets in the store
      responses:
        '200':
          description: A list of pets
          content:
```

```
    application/json:
      schema:
        type: array
        items:
          type: object
          properties:
            id:
              type: integer
              example: 1
            name:
              type: string
              example: "Fluffy"
            type:
              type: string
              example: "cat"
```

For the complete OpenAPI spec, visit www.openapis.org. When visualized (in this case, via the official OpenAPI extension for VSCode), the document looks like the screen shown in Figure 13.4.

FIGURE 13.4 Swagger (OpenAPI) documentation rendered with a user interface

OpenAPI docs are not only an excellent way to communicate the interface of existing APIs to consumers, they are also a fantastic design and even development aid. APIs can be rapidly prototyped "on paper" via OpenAPI docs and reviewed by team members for their adherence to RESTful design and to your team's own style and behavior standards. Then, many tools can work with these docs directly to accelerate implementation.

Amazon API Gateway is one such tool. By uploading an OpenAPI specification, you can direct API Gateway to construct and configure the necessary API resources, methods, and parameters for your endpoints automatically; you need only supply the backend implementation. What's more, Amazon supports proprietary extensions to the OpenAPI spec so that you can use an OpenAPI file not only to document your API, but to indicate to API Gateway how to configure AWS-specific values such as caching settings, CORS configurations, and integration details. An exhaustive list of these extensions is available here:

https://docs.aws.amazon.com/apigateway/latest/developerguide/api-gateway-swagger-extensions.html

GraphQL APIs with AWS AppSync (Logic or App Tier)

Amazon API Gateway makes it easy to build REST APIs in the cloud. However, REST is not the only style of API that developers use to build client-facing apps. GraphQL is an API pattern developed by Facebook in 2012 and open sourced in 2015. As the name suggests, GraphQL APIs enable developers to ask for data using a structured query language, giving clients more flexibility in how to ask for and join data than is afforded by REST APIs.

Basics of GraphQL

With REST, filtering or combining data resources is most often done on the client side; server-side filters are limited to those designed and implemented by the individual API builder, sometimes varying on an endpoint-to-endpoint basis. With GraphQL, querying, filtering, sorting, and joining data is built into the premise of the API style.

GraphQL APIs use a JSON-like syntax to define a schema for resources that is published to consumers. Compute instances called *resolvers* then serve as interface points for clients to query these schemas. Here is a simple example of a schema that depicts the pet store example we used for REST:

```
type Query {
  pets: [Pet]
  pet(id: ID!): Pet
}

type Mutation {
  addPet(input: NewPet!): Pet
```

```
    deletePet(id: ID!): Pet
}

type Pet {
  id: ID!
  name: String!
  type: String!
}

input NewPet {
  name: String!
  type: String!
}
```

This snippet defines the "Pet" type that will be stored in the backend database, along with a set of *query* and *mutation* definitions. Queries retrieve data; mutations alter it. This schema shows two queries: one to retrieve an array of all Pets, and another to retrieve a single Pet by ID. It also provides two mutations, or functions, to update the data: addPet, which accepts a NewPet type (just a Pet that doesn't have an ID yet) and deletePet.

To fetch the ID and name of the pet with ID 3, a client would invoke the second query like so:

```
query {
  pet(id: "3") {
    id
    name
  }
}
```

Note how the client can specify a subset of fields, in this case, by including id and name but omitting type. This is a core feature of GraphQL.

To respond to queries and act on mutations, a GraphQL API needs an implementation layer in the form of *resolvers*. Resolvers are code snippets that take in requests and return responses or partial responses. For instance, the basic outline of a resolver written in Java Script looks like this:

```
export function request(ctx) {
    // process the incoming request
}

export function response(ctx) {
    // Return data or error values
}
```

In the Pets example, you might have a resolver whose entire purpose is to query a back-end database and return formatted Pet data. Alternatively, resolvers can handle subsets of models. Imagine your Pets schema had a section that described a pet's history of veterinarian visits by returning an array of VetVisit objects:

```
type VetVisit{
  visit_date: Date!
  purpose: String!
}


type Pet {
  id: ID!
  name: String!
  type: String!
  vet_history: [VetVisit]!
}
```

You might implement a distinct resolver for the pet's vet history that consults a different database:

```
// File Query.pet.js - this resolver get pets from DynamoDB table PetTable
export function request(ctx) {
  return {
    operation: 'GetItem',
    key: {
      id: { S: ctx.args.id }
    },
    tableName: 'PetTable'
  };
}

export function response(ctx) {
  return ctx.result;
}


// File Pet.vet_history.js - this resolver gets vet history
export function request(ctx) {
  // pseudocode - ctx.source.id represents the parent's ID
  // (in this case, the "Pet" queried). This code could pull vet history
  // from a different source outside of AWS.
  return getVetHistoryFromExternalService(ctx.source.id)
  };
}
```

```
export function response(ctx) {
  return ctx.result.items;
}
```

Resolvers are a powerful aspect of GraphQL that allows them to combine heterogeneous backend data sources into a single, coherent API.

AWS AppSync

AWS AppSync makes it easy to construct GraphQL APIs for your web or mobile applications. AWS manages the entire stack, from data backend to resolvers to API interface points, and as with API Gateway, gives you multiple options for access control.

When creating a new AppSync GraphQL API, you may use either existing DynamoDB or Amazon Aurora tables as the backend database, or, if you choose to design your schema from scratch, AWS can automatically create the persistence layer as a set of DynamoDB tables. AWS creates a basic set of queries, mutations, and resolvers based on your initial configuration. From there, you may further expand your schema with additional fields, resources, data sources, and resolvers.

Resolvers

Resolvers map GraphQL operations (queries, mutations, and subscriptions) to the corresponding data source operations. They can be defined at the field level, allowing for fine-grained control over how data is fetched or manipulated. AppSync resolvers can be written to run in APPSYNC_JS, a JavaScript-like environment that implements most of ECMAScript 6.0, or you can use VTL (Velocity Template Language), an AWS proprietary language. AWS recommends the former, APPSYNC_JS.

Data Sources

Data sources in AppSync can come in various forms, including DynamoDB tables, Lambda functions, OpenSearch Service domains, HTTP/HTTPS endpoints, and relational databases through RDS. Setting up a data source in AppSync makes it available for use within your GraphQL API. In some cases, such as creating a schema from scratch based on DynamoDB, or when configuring Lambda data sources, AWS will create resolvers for you. Whether you generate the resolver or write it by hand, the data sources you configure will be available as an abstraction in your resolver code.

Offline Data

AppSync forms the backend data layer of a service called Amplify DataStore, which enables applications to interact with local, on-device storage that is synced in an eventually consistent manner back to DynamoDB via AppSync GraphQL APIs. AWS Amplify is addressed in the next chapter, "Modern AWS Deployment Frameworks."

Caching

AppSync APIs can be configured to optimize performance by caching responses. *Full request caching* stores content based on values in the context (namely in $ctx.arguments and $ctx.identity), meaning that data is cached per request, per user. In contrast, *per resolver caching* puts the control in your hands, letting you configure resolvers with details specify which keys to cache. The default cache TTL is 60 seconds, and cache data can be optionally encrypted both at rest and in transit.

AppSync Access Control

As with API Gateway, AWS AppSync provides multiple methods for authorizing users to your GraphQL API:

Lambda Authorization   The most fully customizable method, Lambda authorization allows you to write a custom Lambda function, where you can inspect any details passed in with the request or consult external services to determine the caller's permissions on your API.

IAM Authorization   With this method, signed requests resolve to IAM principles (i.e., users or roles) whose IAM permissions must allow access to the API.

Cognito User Pools   This method leverages your existing Cognito user pools; consumers pass in a token associated with a user, at which point you may consult that user's Cognito attributes and groups to make authorization decisions.

OpenID Connect   Allows you to integrate with any service that is OIDC compliant so that users can obtain a JWT token, which you can validate and inspect to make authorization decisions.

Also like API Gateway, API keys can be used to apply rate limiting and throttling on top of authorization implemented in one of these ways. Finally, you may always apply your own fine-grained access logic in the code you write at the resolver layer.

Other Features of AppSync

AppSync features more capabilities than just implementing GraphQL API schemas, queries, and mutations.

GraphQL Subscriptions

For apps that require real-time notifications when data changes or to optimize data integrations by processing changes only, rather than entire batches, AWS AppSync offers GraphQL Subscriptions. Subscriptions can be declared by annotating your GraphQL schema with subscription details. Clients are then able to view and subscribe to these subscription objects, receiving updates via WebSocket whenever the targeted data changes.

Merged APIs

It can be challenging to manage large GraphQL APIs with many data elements, data sources, and resolvers. In order to break up the complexity of expansive APIs and enable teams to manage their GraphQL more smoothly, AppSync allows merged APIs. A merged API is an AppSync GraphQL interface that presents as a single GraphQL API to consumers, but whose backend comprises a heterogeneous set of multiple AppSync APIs, potentially from different AWS accounts, whose team ownership, deployment life cycle, and maintenance can all run independently of each other.

Standard Three-Tier vs. the Serverless Stack

This chapter has introduced serverless services and their benefits. Now that you know about some of the serverless services that are available in AWS, let's compare a traditional three-tier application against a serverless application architecture. Figure 13.5 shows a typical three-tier web application.

This architecture uses these components and services:

- **Routing:** Amazon Route 53
- **Content distribution network (CDN):** Amazon CloudFront
- **Static data:** Amazon S3
- **High availability/decoupling:** Application load balancers
- **Web servers:** Amazon EC2 with Auto Scaling
- **App servers:** Amazon EC2 with Auto Scaling
- **Database:** Amazon RDS in a multi-AZ configuration

Route 53 lets you map your own domain name to this application. CloudFront reduces latency by distributing static content, such as HTML, CSS, and JavaScript, to edge locations worldwide. CloudFront sources that content from an S3 bucket. Figure 13.6 depicts a web application that provides a front-end web experience, user authentication, and backend data access using AWS serverless technologies.

Application load balancers distribute traffic across availability zones (AZs) to your Amazon EC2 servers, which run your web application with a service such as Apache or Nginx.

Application servers are responsible for performing business logic and for storing the data in a database server run on *Amazon Relational Database Service* (RDS).

RDS is the managed database server, and it can run an Amazon Aurora, Microsoft SQL Server, Oracle SQL Server, MySQL, PostgreSQL, or the MariaDB database server.

FIGURE 13.5 Standard three-tier web infrastructure architecture

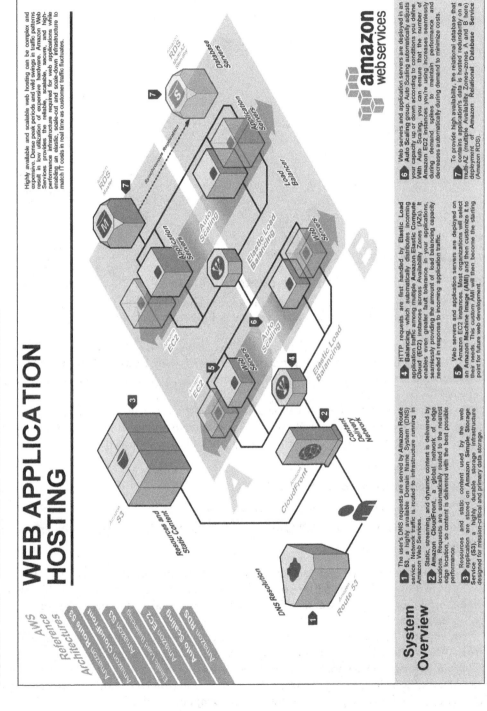

WEB APPLICATION HOSTING

Highly available and scalable web hosting can be complex and expensive. Dense peak periods and wild swings in traffic patterns result in low utilization of expensive hardware. Amazon Web Services provides the reliable, scalable, secure, and high-performance infrastructure required for web applications while enabling an elastic, scale-out and scale-down infrastructure to match IT costs in real time as customer traffic fluctuates.

System Overview

1 The user's DNS requests are served by Amazon Route 53, a highly available Domain Name System (DNS) service. Network traffic is routed to infrastructure running in Amazon Web Services.

2 Static, streaming, and dynamic content is delivered by Amazon CloudFront, a global network of edge locations. Requests are automatically routed to the nearest edge location, so content is delivered with the best possible performance.

3 Resources and static content used by the web application are stored on Amazon Simple Storage Service (S3), a highly durable storage infrastructure designed for mission-critical and primary data storage.

4 HTTP requests are first handled by Elastic Load Balancing, which automatically distributes incoming application traffic among multiple Amazon Elastic Compute Cloud (EC2) instances across Availability Zones (AZs). It enables even greater fault tolerance in your applications, seamlessly providing the amount of load balancing capacity needed in response to incoming application traffic.

5 Web servers and application servers are deployed on Amazon EC2 instances. Most organizations will select an Amazon Machine Image (AMI) and then customize it to their needs. This custom AMI will then become the starting point for future web development.

6 Web servers and application servers are deployed in an Auto Scaling group. Auto Scaling automatically adjusts your capacity up or down according to conditions you define. With Auto Scaling, you can ensure that the number of Amazon EC2 instances you're using increases seamlessly during demand spikes to maintain performance and decreases automatically during demand to minimize costs.

7 To provide high availability, the relational database that contains application's data is hosted redundantly on a multi-AZ (multiple Availability Zones–zones A and B here) deployment of Amazon Relational Database Service (Amazon RDS).

AWS Reference Architectures

Amazon Route 53
Amazon CloudFront
Amazon S3
Elastic Load Balancing
Amazon EC2
Auto Scaling
Amazon RDS

FIGURE 13.6   Serverless web application architecture

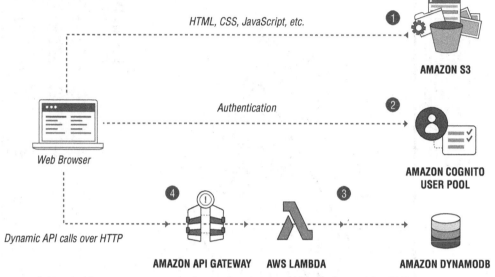

Source: https://aws.amazon.com/getting-started/projects/build-
serverless-web-app-lambda-apigateway-s3-dynamodb-cognito

While this architecture is a robust and highly available service, there are several down-sides, including the fact that you must manage servers. You are responsible for patching those servers, preventing downtime associated with those patches, and properly scaling the servers.

In a typical serverless web application architecture, you also run a web application, but you have zero servers that run inside your AWS account, as shown in Figure 13.6.

Serverless web application architecture services include the following:

- **Routing:** Amazon Route 53

- **Web front-end/static data:** Amazon S3

- **User authentication:** Amazon Cognito user pools

- **Backend services:** Amazon API Gateway with AWS Lambda or AppSync GraphQL APIs

- **Database:** Amazon DynamoDB

Amazon Route 53 is your DNS, and you can use Amazon CloudFront for your CDN.

You can also use Amazon S3 for your web servers. In this architecture, you use Amazon S3 to host your entire static website. You use JavaScript to make API calls to the Amazon API Gateway service.

For your business or application servers, you use Amazon API Gateway in conjunction with AWS Lambda. This allows you to retrieve and save data dynamically.

You use Amazon DynamoDB as a serverless database service, and you do not provision any Amazon EC2s inside your Amazon VPC account. Amazon DynamoDB is also a great database service for storing session state for stateful applications.

If you need a relational database, you can use RDS; however, most RDS database engines require a persistent compute instance and are not truly serverless in the same way that DynamoDB is. *Amazon Aurora Serverless* is RDS's one exception. Serverless is a full RDS MySQL- or PostgreSQL-compatible service that scales up and down in response to demand. See the next section for more details.

By using Amazon Cognito user pools for user authentication, you can provide a secure user directory that can scale to hundreds of millions of users with no servers to manage. While user authentication was not shown in Figure 13.6, use your web server tier to talk to a user directory such as *Lightweight Directory Access Protocol* (LDAP) for user authentication.

Taking advantage of the AWS global network, you can develop fully scalable, highly available web applications—all without having to worry about maintaining or patching servers.

Amazon Aurora Serverless

Amazon Aurora Serverless is an on-demand, autoscaling configuration of Amazon Aurora, AWS's fully PostgreSQL- or MySQL-compatible RDS database. This allows you to run a traditional SQL database in the cloud without needing to manage any infrastructure or instances.

With Amazon Aurora Serverless, you also get the same high availability as traditional Amazon Aurora, which means that you get six-way replication across three availability zones inside a region to protect against data loss.

Because it scales up and down in response to demand, Aurora Serverless is great for infrequently used applications, new applications, variable workloads, unpredictable workloads, development and test databases, and multitenant applications. You can both avoid server maintenance and drive down costs at the same time.

Amazon ElastiCache

Amazon ElastiCache is a web service that makes it easy to set up, manage, and scale distributed in-memory cache environments on the AWS Cloud. It provides a high-performance, resizable, and cost-effective in-memory cache while removing the complexity associated with deploying and managing a distributed cache environment.

As you've seen, in order to horizontally scale applications, you must ensure that no essential data is stored on the compute layer. For instance, when using an EC2 Auto Scaling Group, instances may be created or terminated regularly; relying on those instances to store session data would mean potentially losing the user's state.

ElastiCache is an ideal solution to store application state. Applications often store session data in memory, but this approach does not scale well. To address scalability and provide a shared data storage for sessions that can be accessible from any individual web server, you can abstract the HTTP sessions from the web servers themselves. As an *in-memory key-value* store, ElastiCache supports the following open source in-memory caching engines:

- *Memcached*, an open source, high-performance, distributed memory object caching system that is widely adopted by and protocol-compliant with Amazon ElastiCache.

- *Redis*, an open source, in-memory data structure store that you can use as a database cache and message broker. Amazon ElastiCache supports multi-AZ replication that you can use to achieve cross-AZ redundancy.

Amazon ElastiCache is an in-memory cache. Caching frequently used data is one of the most important performance optimizations that you can make in your applications. Compared to retrieving data from an in-memory cache, querying a database is a much more expensive operation. By storing frequently accessed data in memory, you can greatly improve the speed and responsiveness of read-intensive applications. For instance, application state for a web application can be stored in an in-memory cache, as opposed to storing state data in a database.

Although accessing a system like ElastiCache data does incur network latency and has a cost associated with it, key-value data stores are fast and provide submillisecond reads. Plus, these systems can cache any data, not only HTTP sessions, which gives you many options to boost the overall performance of your applications.

Considerations for Choosing a Distributed Cache

One consideration when choosing a distributed cache for session management is determining the number of nodes necessary to manage the user sessions. You can determine this number by how much traffic is expected and how much risk is acceptable. In a distributed session cache, the sessions are divided by the number of nodes in the cache cluster. In the event of a failure, only the sessions that are stored on the failed node are affected. If reducing risk is more important than cost, adding additional nodes to reduce the percentage of stored sessions on each node may be preferable—even when fewer nodes are sufficient for your traffic.

Another consideration may be whether the sessions must be replicated. Some key-value stores offer replication through read replicas. If a node fails, the sessions are not entirely lost. Whether replica nodes are important in your individual architecture may inform as to which key-value store you should use. ElastiCache for Redis supports replication, while ElastiCache for Memcached does not. To avoid losing track of data, Memcached uses a kind of "sticky session" feature to make sure a user's requests always go to the same node in the cluster.

There are many ways to store sessions in key-value stores. Many application frameworks provide libraries that can abstract some of the integration required to Get/Set those sessions in memory. For example, web developers using the Python framework Django can install the django-redis library to let Django automatically manage saving and retrieving session data to Redis or Redis-compliant ElastiCache. This starts with configuration in the settings.py file:

```
CACHES = {
    'default': {
        'BACKEND': 'django_redis.cache.RedisCache',
        'LOCATION': 'redis://<your_redis_endpoint_url>:6379/1',
        'OPTIONS': {
            'CLIENT_CLASS': 'django_redis.client.DefaultClient',
        }
    }
}
```

```
SESSION_ENGINE = 'django.contrib.sessions.backends.cache'
SESSION_CACHE_ALIAS = 'default'
```

By setting SESSION_ENGINE and SESSION_CACHE_ALIAS, you can simply interact with a request's session object, while behind the scenes, this configuration uses Redis as its backing store. For example, let's say you're storing a user's preference for the UI's light or dark mode in session. Once django-redis is configured, you can get and set this value directly, knowing that the framework is handling all interactions with Redis:

```
request.session['dark_mode'] = true
```

Similar libraries exist for many other languages, both for Redis and Memcached. In other cases, you can write your own session handler to persist the sessions directly.

ElastiCache makes it easy to deploy, operate, and scale an in-memory cache in the cloud. When choosing between the two available engines, consider the following.

Use Memcached if you need to:

- Use a simple data model
- Run large nodes with multiple cores or threads
- Scale out or scale in
- Partition data across multiple shards
- Cache complex objects, such as a database

Use Redis if you need to:

- Work with complex data types
- Sort or rank in-memory datasets
- Persist the key store
- Replicate data from the primary to one or more read replicas for read-intensive applications
- Automate failover if the primary node fails
- Publish and subscribe (pub/sub): the client is informed of events on the server
- Back up and restore data

Use Table 13.2 to determine which product best fits your needs.

TABLE 13.2 Memcached or Redis

Capability	Memcached	Redis
Simple cache to offload DB burden	✓	✓
Ability to scale horizontally	✓	
Advanced data types		✓
Sorting/ranking datasets		✓
Pub/Sub capability		✓
Multi-AZ with Auto Failover		✓
Persistence		✓

Amazon ElastiCache Terminology

This section describes some of the key terminology that Amazon ElastiCache uses.

Nodes

A *node* is the smallest building block of an ElastiCache deployment. A node is a fixed-size chunk of secure, network-attached RAM. Each node runs an instance of Memcached or Redis, depending on which you select when you create the cluster.

Clusters

Each Amazon ElastiCache deployment consists of one or more nodes in a *cluster*. When you create a cluster, you may choose from many different nodes based on the requirements of both your solution case and your capacity. One Memcached cluster can be as large as 60 nodes. Redis clusters consist of a single node; however, you can group multiple clusters into a Redis replication group.

The individual node types are derived from a subset of the Amazon EC2 instance type families, such as t2, m3, and r3. The *t2* cache node family is ideal for development and low-volume applications with occasional bursts, but certain features may not be available. The *m3* family is a mix of memory and compute, whereas the *r3* family is optimized for memory-intensive workloads. Each cache node type is designed for use with ElastiCache and is pre-fixed with the word *cache*, such as cache.t3.micro.

Based on your requirements, you may decide to have a few large nodes or many smaller nodes in your cluster or replication group. As demand for your application fluctuates, you may add or remove nodes over time. Each node type has a preconfigured amount of memory, with a small portion of that memory reserved for both the caching engine and operating system.

Though it is unlikely, always plan for the possible failure of an individual cache node. For a Memcached cluster, decrease the impact of the failure of a cache node by using a larger number of nodes with a smaller capacity instead of a few large nodes. Recall that unlike Redis, Memcached data is not replicated between nodes, so your application should always be prepared for the possibility of a failure to retrieve cache data.

If Amazon ElastiCache detects the failure of a node, it provisions a replacement and then adds it back to the cluster. During this time, your backend data sources, previously insulated from load by having requests handled by the cache, will experience increased load. For Redis clusters, Amazon ElastiCache detects failures and replaces the primary node. If you enable a multi-AZ replication group, a read replica automatically promotes to primary.

Replication Group

A *replication group* is a collection of Redis clusters with one primary read/write cluster and up to five secondary, read-only clusters called *read replicas*. Each read replica maintains a copy of the data from the primary cluster. Asynchronous replication mechanisms keep the read replicas synchronized with the primary cluster. Applications can read from any cluster in the replication group. Applications can write only to the primary cluster. Read replicas enhance scalability and guard against data loss.

Endpoint

An *endpoint* is the unique address your application uses to connect to an ElastiCache node or cluster. Memcached and Redis have the following characteristics with respect to endpoints:

- A Memcached cluster has its own endpoint and a configuration endpoint.
- A stand-alone Redis cluster has an endpoint to connect to the cluster for both reads and writes.
- A Redis replication group has two types of endpoints:
  - The *primary endpoint* connects to the primary cluster in the replication group.
  - The *read endpoint* points to a specific cluster in the replication group.

ElastiCache Serverless

In addition to defining clusters with pre-provisioned capacity, AWS offers ElastiCache serverless, an automatically scaling cache for Redis versions 7.1 or newer and Memcached 1.6 or newer.

Building an ElastiCache Serverless cache requires many fewer decisions than what AWS now terms the "design your own cache" approach. For instance, you don't need to estimate your application's required cache size or projected traffic; AWS monitors your app's demand and scales the cache accordingly.

To avoid cost overruns, you may set a ceiling for the cache size. Upon reaching that threshold, ElastiCache will start to expire the cached items with the oldest time-to-live values.

Similarly, you can set compute limits such that requests will be throttled when they start to approach your stated thresholds.

AWS gives developers a migration path to serverless from existing clusters. To initialize your serverless cluster with existing data, you may choose an ElastiCache-owned backup or any existing backup file in `rdb` format stored in an S3 bucket location.

Cache Scenarios

ElastiCache caches data as key-value pairs. An application can retrieve a value corresponding to a specific key. An application can store an item in the cache by a specific key, value, and an expiration time. TTL is an integer value that specifies the number of seconds until the key expires.

A *cache hit* occurs when an application requests data from the cache, the data is both present and not expired in the cache, and it returns to the application. A *cache miss* occurs if an application requests data from the cache, and it is not present in the cache (returning a null). In this case, the application requests and receives the data from the database and then writes the data to the cache.

Strategies for Caching

Your strategy for populating and maintaining data in the cache depends on what you are caching and the access patterns to that data. For example, you would likely not want to use the same strategy for both a top-10 leaderboard on a gaming site, Facebook posts, or trending news stories, each of which has a different rate of change and requirement for data freshness. While the top 10 may be fine to lag by a few minutes, trending news stories must be updated as quickly as possible.

Lazy Loading

Lazy loading loads data into the cache only when necessary. Whenever your application requests data, it first makes the request to the ElastiCache cache. If the data exists in the cache and it is current, ElastiCache returns the data to your application. If the data does not exist in the cache or the data in the cache has expired, your application requests the data from your data store, which returns the data to your application. Your application then writes the data received from the store to the cache so that it can be retrieved more quickly the next time that it is requested.

Advantages of lazy loading are:

- Only requested data is cached. Because most data is never requested, lazy loading avoids filling up the cache with data that is not requested.

- Node failures are not fatal. When a new, empty node replaces a failed node, the application continues to function, though with increased latency. As requests are made to the new node, each missed cache results in a query of the database and adding the data copy to the cache so that subsequent requests are retrieved from the cache.

Disadvantages of lazy loading are:

- There is a cache miss penalty. Each cache miss results in three trips:
    1. Initial request for data from the cache

2. Querying of the database for the data

3. Writing the data to the cache

   This can cause a noticeable delay in data getting to the application.

- The application may receive stale data because another application may have updated the data in the database behind the scenes.

Write-Through

The *write-through* strategy adds data or updates data in the cache whenever data is written to the database.

Advantages of write-through are:

- The data in the cache is never stale. Because the data in the cache updates every time it is written to the database, the data in the cache is always current.

   Disadvantages of write-through are:

- Write penalty. Every write involves two trips: a write to the cache and a write to the database.

- Missing data. When a new node is created either to scale up or replace a failed node, the node does not contain all data. Data continues to be missing until it is added or updated in the database. In this scenario, you might choose to use a lazy caching approach to repopulate the cache.

- Unused data. Because most data is never read, there can be a lot of data in the cluster that is never read.

- Cache churn. The cache may be updated often if certain records are updated repeatedly.

Data Access Patterns

Retrieving a flat key from an in-memory cache is faster than the most performance-tuned database query. Analyze the access pattern of the data before you determine whether you should store it in an in-memory cache.

Cache Static Elements

A good candidate for caching data is a list of products in a catalog. For a high-volume web application, the list of products could be returned thousands of times per second. Though it may seem like a good idea to cache the most frequently requested items, your application may also benefit from caching items that are not frequently accessed.

You should not store certain data elements in an in-memory cache. For instance, if your application produces a unique page on every request, you probably do not want to cache the page results. However, though the page is different every time, it makes sense to cache the aspects of the page that are static.

Scaling Your Environment

As your workloads evolve over time, you can use Amazon ElastiCache to change the size of your environment to meet the requirements of your workloads. To meet increased levels of write or read performance, expand your cluster horizontally by adding cache nodes. To scale your cache vertically, select a different cache node type.

Scale Horizontally   Amazon ElastiCache functionality enables you to scale the size of your cache environment horizontally. This functionality differs depending on the cache engine you select. With Memcached, you can partition your data and scale horizontally to 20 nodes or more. A Redis cluster consists of a single cache node that handles read and write transactions. You can create additional clusters to include a Redis replication group. Although you can have only one node handle write commands, you can have up to five read replicas handle read-only requests.

Scale vertically   The Amazon ElastiCache service does not directly support vertical scaling of your cluster. You can create a new cluster with the desired cache node types and begin redirecting traffic to the new cluster.

To hand off scaling decisions to AWS, use ElastiCache Serverless.

Replication and Multi-AZ

Replication is an effective method for providing speedy recovery if a node fails and for serving high quantities of read queries beyond the capacities of a single node. Amazon ElastiCache clusters running Redis support both. In contrast, cache clusters running Memcached are stand-alone in-memory services that do not provide any data redundancy–protection services. Cache clusters running Redis support the notion of replication groups. A *replication group* consists of up to six clusters, with five of them designated as read replicas. By using a replication group, you can scale horizontally by developing code in the application to offload reads to one of the five replicas.

Multi-AZ Replication Groups

With Amazon ElastiCache, you can provision a *multi-AZ replication group* that allows your application to raise the availability and reduce the loss of data. Multi-AZ streamlines the procedure of dealing with a failure by automating the replacement and failover from the primary node.

If the primary node goes down or is otherwise unhealthy, multi-AZ selects a replica and promotes it to become the new primary; then a new node is provisioned to replace the failed one. Amazon ElastiCache updates the DNS entry of the new primary node to enable your application to continue processing without any changes to the configuration of the application and with only minimal disruption. ElastiCache replication is handled asynchronously, meaning that there will be a small delay before the data is available on all cluster nodes.

Backup and Recovery

Amazon ElastiCache clusters that run Redis support *snapshots*. Use *snapshots* to persist your data from your in-memory key-value stores to disk. Each snapshot is a full clone of the data that you can use to recover to a specific point in time or to create a copy for other purposes. Snapshots are not available to clusters that use the Memcached caching engine. This is because Memcached is a purely in-memory, key-value store, and it always starts empty. Amazon ElastiCache uses the native backup capabilities of Redis and generates a standard Redis database backup file, which is stored in Amazon S3.

Snapshots need memory and compute resources to perform, and this can possibly have a performance impact in heavily used clusters. Amazon ElastiCache attempts different backup techniques depending on the amount of memory currently available. As a best practice, set up a replication group and perform the snapshot against one of the read replicas instead of creating the snapshot against the primary node. You can automate snapshots to create on a schedule, or you can manually initiate a snapshot. Additionally, you can configure a window for the snapshot to complete and then configure how many days of backups you want to save. Manual snapshots are stored indefinitely until you delete them.

It doesn't matter whether the snapshot was created manually or automatically. You can use the snapshot to provision a new cluster. The new cluster has the same configuration as the source cluster by default, but you can override these settings. You can also restore a snapshot from the RDB file that generates from any other Redis compatible cluster. The Redis RDB file is a binary representation of the in-memory store. This binary file is sufficient to restore the Redis state completely.

Control Access

As with many AWS services, controlling access to your ElastiCache cluster happens at two layers: network access and resource permissions.

ElastiCache nodes are deployed inside your VPC to subnets of your choosing; each one is assigned a private IP and is not accessible from the internet or other VPCs. Securing network access within your VPC works just like an EC2 instance: You configure and attach security groups that control the inbound and outbound traffic. Similarly, network access control lists between subnets can give you coarse-grained control over which networks can reach your cluster.

Access to manage the configuration and infrastructure of the cluster is controlled separately from network access to the actual Memcached or Redis service endpoint. Using the IAM service, you can define policies that control which AWS users or roles can manage the Amazon ElastiCache infrastructure using API permissions such as `elasticache:ModifyCacheCluster` and `elasticache:CreateReplicationGroup`.

Summary

In this chapter, we covered the AWS serverless core services, how to store your static files inside of Amazon S3, how to use Amazon CloudFront in conjunction with Amazon S3, and how to deploy and scale your API quickly and automatically with Amazon API Gateway. You also saw how to create GraphQL APIs using AppSync and how to enhance your application's performance with caching provided by ElastiCache.

Serverless applications have three main benefits: no server management, flexible scaling, and automated high availability. Without server management, you no longer have to provision or maintain servers. With AWS Lambda, you upload your code, run it, and focus on your application updates. With flexible scaling, you no longer have to disable EC2 instances to scale them vertically, groups do not need to be auto-scaled, and you do not need to create CloudWatch alarms to add them to load balancers. Finally, serverless applications have built-in availability and fault tolerance. When periods of low traffic occur, you do not spend money on EC2 instances that do not run at their full capacity.

You can use an Amazon S3 web server to host your presentation tier. Within an Amazon S3 bucket, you can store HTML, CSS, and JavaScript files. JavaScript can make HTTP requests to Representational State Transfer (REST) endpoints on Amazon API Gateway, which allows the application to save and retrieve data dynamically by triggering a Lambda function. Alternatively, you can have it communicate with a GraphQL API built in AWS AppSync, interacting via a query language with a schema backed by Lambda-based resolvers.

Use Amazon API Gateway authorizers with Amazon Cognito user pools to validate access to Lambda functions, enabling you to secure your APIs.

After you create your Amazon S3 bucket, you configure it to use static website hosting in the AWS Management Console and enter an endpoint that reflects your AWS region.

S3 allows you to configure web traffic logs to capture information, such as the number of visitors who access your website in the S3 bucket.

One way to decrease latency and improve your performance is to use Amazon CloudFront with Amazon S3 to move your content closer to your end users. Amazon CloudFront is a serverless service.

You can use Amazon Route 53 to create a more user-friendly domain name instead of using the default host name (Amazon S3 endpoint). To support two subdomains, you create two Amazon S3 buckets that match your domain name and subdomain.

You saw how to use ElastiCache in Redis or MemoryDB mode for a high-performance in-memory cache and learned about its features and configuration options. Additionally, you learned the differences between the standard three-tier web applications and the AWS serverless stack.

Exam Essentials

Know serverless applications' three main benefits.   The benefits are as follows:

- No server management
- Flexible scaling
- Automated high availability

Know what no server management means.   Without server management, you no longer have to provision or maintain servers. With AWS Lambda, you upload your code, run it, and focus on your application updates.

Know what flexible scaling means.   With flexible scaling, you no longer have to disable Amazon Elastic Compute Cloud (Amazon EC2) instances to scale them vertically, groups do not need to be autoscaled, and you do not need to create Amazon CloudWatch alarms to add them to load balancers. With AWS Lambda, you adjust the units of consumption (memory and execution time), and AWS adjusts the rest of the instances appropriately.

Define serverless applications.   Serverless applications have built-in availability and fault tolerance. You do not need to architect for these capabilities, as the services that run the application provide them by default. Additionally, when periods of low traffic occur on the web application, you do not spend money on Amazon EC2 instances that do not run at their full capacity.

Know what services are serverless.   On the exam, it is important to understand which Amazon services are serverless and which ones are not. The following services are serverless:

- Amazon API Gateway
- Amazon AppSync
- AWS Lambda
- Amazon SQS
- Amazon SNS
- Amazon Kinesis
- Amazon Cognito
- Amazon Aurora Serverless
- Amazon S3
- Amazon ElastiCache Serverless

Know how to host a serverless web application.   Hosting a serverless application means that you need to have Amazon S3 to host your static website; this is your HTML, JavaScript, and CSS files. For your database infrastructure, you can use DynamoDB or Amazon Aurora

Serverless. For your business logic tier, you can use AWS Lambda. For DNS services, you can use AWS Route 53. If you need the ability to host an API, you can use API Gateway. Finally, if you need to decrease latency to portions of your application, you can utilize services like Amazon CloudFront, which allows you to host your content at the edge.

Know how to use Amazon ElastiCache.   Improve the performance of your application by deploying Amazon ElastiCache clusters as a part of your application and offloading read requests for frequently accessed data. Use the lazy loading caching strategy in your solution to first check the cache for your query results before checking the database.

Understand when to choose one specific cache engine over another.   Amazon ElastiCache provides two open source caching engines. You are responsible for choosing the engine that meets your requirements. Use Redis when you must persist and restore your data, you need multiple replicas of your data, or when you are seeking advanced features and functionality, such as sort and rank or leaderboards. Redis supports these features natively. Alternatively, you can use Memcached when you need a simpler, in-memory object store that can be easily partitioned and horizontally scaled.

Understand the core concepts of AWS AppSync and GraphQL.   AWS AppSync is a managed service that lets you define a GraphQL API interface with implementations provided by various backend sources, including DynamoDB, Lambda, and HTTP endpoints. Remember the fundamentals of GraphQL—including schemas, queries, mutations, and subscriptions. Be able to describe how AppSync uses resolvers to map GraphQL operations to data sources and how it enables real-time data synchronization and offline capabilities for mobile and web applications.

Exercises

Code Examples for Exercises

To complete these exercises, download the AWS Certified Developer – Associate Exam Code examples, Chapter13_Code.zip, at xxxx.html.

EXERCISE 13.1

Hosting a Website with Amazon S3

In this exercise, you'll create a simple website and host it using S3. You'll be using the AWS CLI, so you need to have that tool installed and configured with sufficient credentials—at minimum, with full S3 access.

To start, you'll create an Amazon S3 bucket for your website. Make sure to give it a unique name and use that name throughout the exercise.

1. Create an Amazon S3 bucket.

    ```
    aws s3 mb s3://my-bucket-name --region us-east-1
    ```

    If the command was successful, you should see output similar to the following, which means the bucket has been created:

    ```
    make_bucket: my-bucket-name
    ```

2. Next, let's create a simple website. In a folder, create a file called `index.html` with these contents:

    ```
    <html>
    <head>
        <title>Hello World</title>
        <style>
            body { font-family: Arial; text-align: center; padding: 50px;
    background: #f0f0f0; }
            p { color: #666; }
        </style>
    </head>
    <body>
    <h1>Hello, World!</h1>
        <p>This is a simple HTML page deployed on AWS S3.</p>
    </body>
    </html>
    ```

3. Upload the file to the bucket:

    ```
    aws s3 cp index.html s3://my-bucket-name
    ```

4. Before we can enable website hosting on this bucket, we need to override some default protections that prevent buckets from being made public. This is a good security measure by AWS, but in order to host web content, we need to bypass it.

    ```
    aws s3api put-public-access-block --bucket my-bucket-name --public-
    access-block-
    configuration BlockPublicAcls=false,IgnorePublicAcls=false,BlockPublicPolicy=
    false,RestrictPubli
    cBuckets=false
    ```

5. Next, we need to apply a bucket policy that actually enables the public access. Create a file called `bucket-policy.json` with these contents:

```
{
  "Version": "2012-10-17",
  "Statement": [
    {
      "Sid": "MakeWebsiteDataPublic",
      "Effect": "Allow",
      "Principal": "*",
      "Action": "s3:GetObject",
      "Resource": "arn:aws:s3:::my-bucket-name/*"
    }
  ]
}
```

6. Apply the policy to the bucket with the CLI:

```
aws s3api put-bucket-policy --bucket my-bucket-name --policy file://bucket-policy.json
```

7. You can confirm this configuration with the following command:

```
aws s3api get-bucket-policy-status --bucket my-bucket-name
```

You should see the following output:

```
{
    "PolicyStatus": {
        "IsPublic": true
    }
}
```

8. Finally, enable website hosting on the bucket configuration:

```
aws s3 website s3://wiley-chapter-13/ --index-document index.html
```

Now you can navigate to the public website via your browser at this URL, making sure to substitute your bucket name:

```
http://my-bucket-name.s3-website-us-east-1.amazonaws.com
```

EXERCISE 13.2

Creating a REST API with API Gateway

In this exercise, we'll create the classic Pet Store example API by importing an OpenAPI 3.0 (Swagger) API spec.

1. Download the `petstore_api_swagger.yml` file from the Chapter 13 exercise files.

   Note the AWS-specific extensions `x-amazon-gateway-integration`. This nonstandard tag will initialize your AWS API Gateway with a backend implementation for each endpoint; in this case, pointing to a real HTTP API run by AWS.

2. Navigate to the API Gateway console at `https://us-east-1.console.aws.amazon.com/apigateway`.

3. Click Create API.

4. Scroll to REST API and click Import.

5. Under API Details, click Choose File and select the `petstore.yaml` file you downloaded.

6. Click Create API.

7. Click Deploy API.

8. For Stage, select *New Stage*.

9. For Stage Name, enter **Dev**.

10. Click Deploy.

11. The API is now available at the Invoke URL. Copy it into your browser and append **/pets** to invoke the `list pets` operation. You will see mocked-up data supplied by the AWS HTTP backend of this endpoint.

EXERCISE 13.3

Adding a Lambda Backend Integration

In this exercise, we'll add an implementation of our own to the GET /pets resource using a Lambda function that pulls data from DynamoDB.

You'll use the file `create_dynamo_and_lambda.yml` from the exercise files. This Cloud-Formation template creates a DynamoDB table for recording pets and a Lambda function that returns the pet listing as JSON. It also includes the IAM permission to enable Lambda to read the table.

1. From a terminal, run the following CLI command:

   ```
   aws cloudformation create-stack --stack-name PetsApp --template-body file://
   create_dynamo_and_lambda.yml --capabilities CAPABILITY_NAMED_IAM CAPABILITY_
   IAM CAPABILITY_AUTO_EXPAND
   ```

2. Monitor the progress with **aws cloudformation describe-stacks --stack-name PetsApp**.

3. When StackStatus is CREATE_COMPLETE, continue.

4. Enter a few records into the DynamoDB table with these commands:

   ```
   aws dynamodb put-item \
       --table-name Pets \
       --item '{"name": {"S": "Beckett"}, "species": {"S": "Cat"}}'

   aws dynamodb put-item \
       --table-name Pets \
       --item '{"name": {"S": "Benjamin"}, "species": {"S": "Rabbit"}}'
   ```

5. Back in the AWS console, navigate to API Gateway at https://us-east-1
   .console.aws.amazon.com/apigateway.

6. From the left-hand menu, select APIs.

7. Click PetStore.

8. From the left-hand menu, select Resources.

9. In the main panel of the screen, expand the resource tree and click GET under /pets.

10. Copy the ARN of this endpoint and paste it into the following command:

    ```
    aws lambda add-permission \
      --function-name GetPetsFunction \
      --statement-id APIGatewayInvokePermission \
      --action lambda:InvokeFunction \
      --principal apigateway.amazonaws.com \
      --source-arn "<YOUR_ENDPOINT_ARN>"
    ```

11. Run the command in the terminal to grant API Gateway permission to call
    your Lambda.

12. Back in the API Gateway console, select the Integration Request tab.

13. Click Edit.

14. Change the integration type from HTTP to Lambda Function.

15. Under Lambda Function, search for GetPetsFunction. If you see an "invalid Lambda"
    warning, ignore it!

16. Click Save.

17. Click Deploy API.

18. In a browser, open your /pets URL again. It may take a moment to clear your cache, but you will see the records from your DynamoDB.

You have just fully integrated an API Gateway REST API with AWS Lambda and DynamoDB. To see how the Serverless Application Model makes this process much simpler, check out Chapter 14, "Modern AWS Deployment Frameworks."

To clean up, delete your API Gateway through the console (selecting Delete API under API Actions) and tear town your CloudFormation with this command:

```
aws cloudformation delete-stack --stack-name PetsApp
```

EXERCISE 13.4

Creating an Amazon ElastiCache Cluster Running Memcached

In this exercise, you will create an Amazon ElastiCache cluster using the Memcached engine.

1. Sign in to the AWS Management Console, and open the Amazon ElastiCache console at https://console.aws.amazon.com/elasticache.

2. To create a new Amazon ElastiCache cluster, click Get Started and choose Memcached from the drop-down menu.

3. Under "Choose a cluster creation method," select the deployment option Design Your Own Cache and Easy Create. At low usage, the ElastiCache Serverless option can be more expensive than the lowest on-demand rate.

4. Under Configuration, select Demo for the smallest instance size.

5. Under Cluster Info, name your cluster **memcached-demo**.

6. Under Connectivity, select Create A New Subnet Group and give it the name **memcached-demo-subnet-group**.

7. Under VPC ID, select your account's default VPC. Subnets will be automatically selected, but if you wish to change them, you can do so by clicking Manage.

8. Expand View Default Settings to review the cluster configuration. This wizard creates a cluster with three nodes. To edit this information, switch from Easy Create to Standard Create. Otherwise, click Create.

9. Connect to the cluster with any Memcached client from inside your VPC by using the DNS name of the cluster.

EXERCISE 13.5

Connecting to Your Memcached Cluster

The default security group for your cluster allows all incoming traffic, but the cluster only has a private IP. This means the following steps must be done from an instance in your VPC. For more on creating and logging into an instance in your VPC, see Chapters 1 and 2.

1. Locate the endpoint URL for your cluster by navigating to the ElastiCache console.

2. Click Dashboards, then Memcached Caches.

3. Click Memcached-demo.

4. Under Cluster Details, find Configuration Endpoint and copy the value.

5. Connect to your VPC instance to execute the following:

```
sudo yum install -y python3 python3-pip
pip3 install python-memcached
```

6. Create and run the following script, making sure to plug in your endpoint value:

```
import memcache

# Replace with your ElastiCache endpoint
memcached_endpoint = '<your-cluster-config-url>:11211'

# Connect to Memcached
client = memcache.Client([memcached_endpoint], debug=0)

# Set a value in the cache
result = client.set('message', 'Hello world!', time=900)
print("Set value in cache with key 'message'" )


# Retrieve the value from the cache
value = client.get('message')
print('Cache hit -- fetched value from Memcached:', value)
```

You should see output similar to this:

```
Set value in cache with key 'message'
Cache hit -- fetched value from Memcached: Hello world!
```

You have now created and connected to your first Amazon ElastiCache cluster.

EXERCISE 13.6

Expanding the Size of a Memcached Cluster

In this exercise, you will expand the size of an existing Amazon ElastiCache Memcached cluster.

1. Navigate to the Amazon ElastiCache dashboard, and view the configuration of your existing cluster.

2. View the list of nodes that are currently being used, and then click Add Nodes.

3. For Number Of Nodes, enter **1**.

4. Under Availability Zone, select No Preference.

5. Apply the changes to the configuration, and wait for the new node to finish provisioning.

6. Confirm that the new node has been provisioned, and connect to the node using a Memcached client.

You have horizontally scaled an existing Amazon ElastiCache cluster by adding a new cache node.

EXERCISE 13.7

Deleting the Memcached Cluster

1. Use the Services search bar to navigate to the ElastiCache console.

2. Select Dashboard from the left-hand menu.

3. Under Resource Overview, click Memcached Caches.

4. Check the radio button next to memcached-demo, then click Actions and select Delete.

Review Questions

1. What option do you need to enable to call Amazon API Gateway endpoints from another server or service?

   A. You do not need to enable any options. Amazon API Gateway is ready to use as soon as it's deployed.

   B. Enable cross-origin resource sharing (CORS).

   C. Deploy a stage.

   D. Deploy a resource.

2. A company is considering moving to the AWS serverless stack. What are two benefits of serverless stacks? (Choose two.)

   A. No server management.

   B. It costs less than Amazon Elastic Compute Cloud (Amazon EC2).

   C. Flexible scaling.

   D. There are no benefits to serverless stacks.

3. Can you create HTTP (port 80) endpoints with Amazon API Gateway?

   A. Yes. You can create HTTP endpoints with Amazon API Gateway.

   B. No. API Gateway creates FTP endpoints.

   C. No. API Gateway only supports SSH endpoints.

   D. No. API Gateway is a secure service that only supports HTTPS.

4. A company is moving to a serverless application, using Amazon S3, AWS Lambda, and Amazon DynamoDB. They are currently using Amazon CloudFront for their content delivery network (CDN). They are concerned that they can no longer use Amazon Cloud-Front because they will have no Amazon EC2 instances running. Is their concern valid?

   A. Their concerns are valid: CloudFront only supports EC2.

   B. Their concerns are valid because all serverless applications are fully dynamic and contain no static information; thus, CloudFront does not support serverless applications.

   C. Their concerns are not valid. CloudFront supports serverless applications with S3 as an origin.

   D. Their concerns are valid. CloudFront does support serverless applications; however, it does not support S3.

5. A company wants to use a serverless application to run its dynamic website that is currently running on EC2 instances behind an application load balancer. Currently, the application uses HTML, CSS, and React, and the database is a NoSQL flavor. You are the adviser—is this possible?

   A. No. This is not possible, because there is no way to run React in AWS. React is a Facebook technology.

   B. No. This is not possible, because you need an Amazon EC2 to run the web server.

    C. No. This is not possible, because there is no way to load balance a serverless application.

    D. Yes. This is possible; however, some refactoring will be required.

6. Which of the following objects are good candidates to store in a cache? (Choose three.)

    A. Session state

    B. Shopping cart

    C. Product catalog

    D. Bank account balance

7. Which of the following cache engines does Amazon ElastiCache support? (Choose two.)

    A. Redis

    B. MySQL

    C. Couchbase

    D. Memcached

8. How many nodes can you add to an Amazon ElastiCache cluster that is running Redis?

    A. 100

    B. 5

    C. 60

    D. 1

9. What feature does Amazon ElastiCache provide?

    A. A highly available and fast indexing service for querying

    B. An Amazon EC2 instance with a large amount of memory and CPU

    C. A managed in-memory caching service

    D. An Amazon EC2 instance with Redis and Memcached already installed

10. You are building a GraphQL API using AWS AppSync and want to use a DynamoDB table as the backend data store. What role do resolvers play in this process?

    A. Resolvers define the schema for the GraphQL API.

    B. Resolvers use code to implement GraphQL operations by connecting to data sources such as DynamoDB.

    C. Resolvers are responsible for caching the query results.

    D. Resolvers handle security and access permissions for the API.

11. When using Amazon S3 to host a static website, what is the correct method to ensure the website can use a custom domain name instead of the S3 bucket URL?

    A. Enable S3 website hosting and configure Amazon Route 53 to use a custom domain.

    B. Create an Amazon CloudFront distribution and use its URL instead.

    C. Use an application load balancer (ALB) to forward traffic to the S3 bucket.

    D. Configure an API Gateway to handle domain forwarding to the S3 bucket.

12. What is an advantage that API Gateway HTTP APIs have over REST APIs?

    A. HTTP APIs support WebSockets, whereas REST APIs do not.

    B. HTTP APIs provide a built-in, configurable option for authorizing requests by validating JSON Web Tokens (JWTs).

    C. HTTP APIs support direct integration with AWS Lambda, whereas REST APIs do not.

    D. REST APIs are less expensive to use compared to HTTP APIs.

13. Performance of your most heavily trafficked API Gateway stage is beginning to degrade. Watching CloudWatch metrics, you see that latency is high on endpoints in the stage. You recognize that these endpoints are frequently accessed, but serve data that is infrequently updated. What is your best next step?

    A. Enable caching on the API Gateway stage to serve responses without the need to hit the backend service.

    B. Look at improving the backend Lambda performance by increasing their RAM allocation.

    C. Deploy a private API endpoint inside a VPC for faster performance on a shared network.

    D. Enable Cross-Origin Resource Sharing (CORS) to horizontally scale the responses.

14. How does AWS AppSync handle real-time data updates for subscribed clients?

    A. By creating a client-side loop that issues HTTP GET requests at regular intervals, updating data reactively on the page

    B. By using WebSocket APIs to continuously stream data to clients

    C. By using subscriptions that automatically push data to clients when it changes

    D. By using issuing calls to a webhook whenever data changes

15. When using Amazon ElastiCache, which is a good reason to choose Redis over Memcached? (Choose two.)

    A. Redis automatically scales horizontally with additional nodes, whereas Memcached must be pre-provisioned.

    B. Redis supports complex data types and data persistence.

    C. You need the ability to sort and rank in your data queries.

    D. You need the simplest possible deployment.

16. You need to restrict access to an API Gateway endpoint to a specific range of IP addresses. What is the best way to configure this restriction while ensuring the API remains publicly accessible for those IPs?

    A. Use Amazon Cognito to authenticate and limit access based on IP addresses.

    B. Configure an API Gateway resource policy that includes an `IpAddress` condition specifying the allowed IP range.

    C. Attach a VPC endpoint to API Gateway to ensure that traffic only comes from specified IP addresses.

    D. Use AWS Web Application Firewall (WAF) to filter traffic based on the IP addresses.

Modern AWS Deployment Frameworks

THE AWS CERTIFIED DEVELOPER – ASSOCIATE EXAM TOPICS COVERED IN THIS CHAPTER INCLUDE, BUT ARE NOT LIMITED TO, THE FOLLOWING:

✓ **Domain 1: Development with AWS Services**

- Task Statement 1: Develop code for applications hosted on AWS

- Task Statement 2: Develop code for AWS Lambda

✓ **Domain 2: Security**

- Task Statement 1: Implement authentication and/or authorization for applications and AWS services

✓ **Domain 3: Deployment**

- Task Statement 1: Prepare application artifacts to be deployed to AWS

- Task Statement 4: Deploy code by using AWS CI/CD services

So far, we have explored the power of AWS to take previously difficult tasks and simplify them tremendously. Software-defined infrastructure transforms challenging manual work—from racking servers to running network connections to configuring firewalls and load balancers—into scripts that can be version controlled, peer reviewed, and automated. From there, many AWS services build on fundamental cloud concepts to apply helpful abstractions: Fargate hides the complexity of container cluster management; S3 intelligent tiering automates decisions about the object storage life cycle; CloudFormation abstracts many individual API calls into comprehensible templates.

In this chapter, we head even higher up the abstraction stack, exploring three technologies that provide some of AWS's most useful abstractions. First, we delve into *Cloud Developer Kit (CDK)*, an infrastructure-as-a-service tool that gives you the power of CloudFormation in the form of your favorite programming language, complete with time-saving helper functions and classes. Next, we look at the Serverless Application Model, a transformation of standard CloudFormation that introduces convenient shortcuts to defining applications that use Lambda, API Gateway, and other serverless architectural conceits. Finally, we explore *AWS Amplify*, an all-in-one developer experience that lets you define complex backend infrastructure in just a few lines of TypeScript, while giving you easy-to-use tools to connect those backends to client-side web and mobile experiences.

Just as these services build on underlying cloud concepts, so will your understanding rely on what you have seen before. Let's dive in to understand these powerful and fun-to-use tools.

AWS Cloud Development Kit

As we discussed in Chapter 8, "Infrastructure as Code," when talking about CloudFormation, infrastructure-as-code (IaC) is a powerful concept enabled by running your resources in the cloud. Having software-defined resources gives you an excellent way not just to quickly build things like networks, virtual machines, and databases, but to make sure that infrastructure is trackable, testable, and auditable.

CloudFormation is powerful, but its JSON or YAML templates declare your intentions in a more-or-less static way. Outside of a few options to implement conditional logic or assign values from dynamic mapping, CloudFormation was deliberately designed to avoid concepts like variables and control structures. What if you had an option to build infrastructure using tools that are more dynamic and more familiar—more like writing a script or a web application?

Enter Cloud Development Kit (CDK). With CDK, you write infrastructure not as templates in a domain-specific language, but with a choice of your favorite programming languages, like NodeJS or Python. With CDK, you can use all your preferred tooling, from code editors to version control systems and more, to write scripts that combine all the power of CloudFormation with the flexibility of traditional code syntax. This means the freedom to use variables, arrays, `if` statements, and `while` loops, and to structure your logic into modules, functions, and classes. CDK gives you as many ways to structure and streamline your code as your preferred language allows, which it then transpiles to CloudFormation templates, ensuring that your IaC is compliant with everything you've learned already.

Unlike compiling, which converts high-level code like Java into machine code, *transpiling* refers to the process of converting one programming language into another. Transpiling is often used to implement languages that add additional features to an existing language, as TypeScript does for Javascript, or to create a new syntactical experience for programmers, as CDK does for CloudFormation.

Why CDK?

There are many reasons you may want to write your infrastructure in CDK. First, there's no new language to learn; you can start right away in NodeJS, TypeScript, Python, Java, C#, or Go.

Improved Tooling   While editor plug-ins and extensions work well to make writing CloudFormation fast and efficient, writing in a language like Java or Python offers many very helpful capabilities, including the ability to use your preferred IDE with type-ahead and code completion features.

Familiar Testing Frameworks   CDK applications automatically initialize with standard boilerplate code that includes scaffolding for automated tests in your chosen language. For example, starting up a JavaScript CDK project gives you the beginning of tests using the Jest testing framework.

Your IDE is also able to detect code issues just like you would be alerted to in a normal programming setting, flagging problems like misspelling parameters or making calls to functions that don't exist.

Clearer Relationships   When writing CDK code, relationships between your resources can be easier and clearer to express, because you're calling functions that explicitly join the two. Suppose your CDK code already has a variable representing an EC2 instance, `myInstance`, and a variable called `allowSSHFromWorld`, which is a security group you created earlier. Attaching the security group to the instance is simple:

```
myInstance.addSecurityGroup( allowSSHFromWorld )
```

Helper Functions   As the previous example shows, CDK is full of functions that simplify AWS concepts in a way that may be more understandable to developers. In fact, some helper functions offer an even greater abstraction than the security group example. For instance, assume `myDynamoTable` and `myLambdaFunction` are two resources already created in your code. Consider this line:

```
myDynamoTable.grantReadWriteData( myLambdaFunction )
```

Very readable, right? This single line of code not only creates the entire IAM policy needed to let your Lambda function read your table, but also creates the association between the policy and the function. In CloudFormation, this could easily take a dozen lines of code and never be as quick to understand as this one line of CDK code.

Easy Fan-outs   In CloudFormation, we've seen how StackSets and nested stacks allow you to deploy similar infrastructure across accounts and regions. With CDK, it's arguably simpler, as the same CDK code can be deployed to multiple regions simply by referencing it more than once with different parameters.

More Concise Code   There are just some things that are much easier to do in a full-fledged programming language. Imagine you need to create 50 sequentially named S3 buckets for a large parallel data process. Would you rather code 50 identical `AWS::S3::Bucket` resource blocks into CloudFormation via YAML, or would you rather just write this

```
for (var i = 1; i <= 50; i++) {
    new s3.Bucket(this, `DataProcessingBucket${i}`,
            { bucketName: `data-processing-bucket${i}`
    });
}
```

Valuable Abstractions   As you will see, while CDK code encapsulates resources similar to those you'd define in CloudFormation, CDK "constructs" often come with convenient abstractions that prevent you from needing to understand the fine-grained details of each resource you want to use. In some cases, these abstractions bring together higher-level concepts that deploy multiple resources at once. This can be a significant benefit over CloudFormation. Constructs are elaborated upon in the next section.

Community Sharing   Users of CDK who create some reusable snippet of code often share that code back to the community. Third-party hubs exist online where developers share constructs that others can pick up and use. One such hub exists at `https://constructs.dev` and features code shared by well-known entities such as HashiCorp and Datadog, in addition to AWS themselves.

Now that you understand some of the benefits of using CDK, let's look at the main concepts that you need to know in order to use it.

CDK Concepts

In this section, we'll explore the three foundation concepts of CDK: constructs, stacks, and apps.

Constructs

Constructs are the central concept of CDK, roughly equivalent to a resource in CloudFormation. Unlike CloudFormation, however, CDK constructs have multiple levels of abstraction. Let's explore.

Level 1 Constructs

Level 1 constructs are those CDK objects that are lowest-level with the least abstraction. They are essentially language-specific SDK wrappers over CloudFormation resource types, and they expose all the same underlying parameters. These objects typically have the prefix cfn, standing for CloudFormation, and are useful only when you want maximum control over the properties of the object. cfnInstance is a good example; this object is a wrapper over AWS::EC2::Instance. One benefit to Level 1 constructs is that because they adhere closely to CloudFormation, they are always up-to-date with the latest changes in how resources are built.

Level 2 Constructs

Level 2 constructs, known also as "curated" constructs, are the most commonly used objects in CDK. Like Level 1 constructs, they tend to correspond to a single resource; however, they offer higher-level abstraction by simplifying the parameters needed to create them. This is accomplished by CDK supplying default values to many attributes that you'd otherwise need to configure in a cfn construct.

Level 2 constructs are the ones that work with the helper functions described in the previous section, offering well-named, clear ways of doing things like granting permissions, creating associations, and configuring behavior. With Level 2 constructs, AWS does its best to hide the complexity of building resources and gives you methods in plain language that accomplish several related steps at once. The goal is for things to "just make sense."

Level 3 Constructs

Level 3 constructs pack much more functionality under the hood of a single object than Level 1 or 2. Referred to as "patterns," Level 3 constructs create many related resources at once, often reflecting popular architecture patterns. For instance, the Level 3 construct ecsPatterns.ScheduledFargateTask is a single object that creates an ECS task definition and run schedule, along with all necessary configurations and relationships.

Stacks

Stacks are logical groupings of constructs, literally equivalent to a CloudFormation stack. CDK projects let you define multiple stacks targeting, such as additional regions or accounts, and include resource definitions from elsewhere in the project. One use case is to replicate identical infrastructure to other places; another is to logically group resources into layers such as "web tier" and "data tier."

Apps

Apps are the primary logical container for your CDK resources. Every CDK project is an app, which may contain one or more stacks.

The structure of your CDK application's code will vary somewhat depending on the language you choose to use, but these elements will be present no matter what.

CDK Example

The following example demonstrates several CDK concepts in a JavaScript script that deploys two instances running the web server nginx. First, it uses built-in functions to fetch details about a VPC (referenced with a placeholder ID), then uses another built-in helper function to fetch all the associated public subnets. The script then creates a security group using the Level 1 construct `ec2.SecurityGroup`. The code then iterates over a list of instance types so that it can create an EC2 instance in each size using the object `ec2.Instance`. Notice additional helper functions like `ec2.MachineImage.latest AmazonLinux2`, which fetches the AMI ID of the latest Amazon Linux. Finally, outside the loop, we iterate over the instances themselves to attach a user data script, demonstrating that CDK objects are not one-time use, but can be modified over the course of a script.

```javascript
const { Stack } = require('aws-cdk-lib');
const ec2 = require('aws-cdk-lib/aws-ec2');

class CdkJavascriptDemoStack extends Stack {
  constructor(scope, id, props) {
    super(scope, id, props);

    // Use an existing VPC by specifying the VPC ID
    const vpc = ec2.Vpc.fromLookup(this, 'MyVpc', {
      vpcId: 'vpc-your_id_here'
    });

    // Helper function selects your public subnets -- very convenient
    const publicSubnets = vpc.selectSubnets({
      subnetType: ec2.SubnetType.PUBLIC
    });

    // Create a security group that allows inbound traffic on port 80 from
anywhere
    const sg = new ec2.SecurityGroup(this, 'MySecurityGroup', {
```

```
      vpc,
      description: 'Allow inbound traffic on port 80 from anywhere',
      allowAllOutbound: true    // Allow all outbound traffic
    });
    sg.addIngressRule(ec2.Peer.anyIpv4(), ec2.Port.tcp(80), 'Allow inbound
HTTP');

    // All the instance sizes we want to create
    const instanceSizes = ['t3.micro', 't3.small'];

    // Keep an array to hold the instance objects we're about to create
    const instances = []

    // Loop over these instance sizes with standard javascript
    instanceSizes.forEach((instanceSize, index) => {

      // create an instance for each with a dynamic instance Name tag
      const instance = new ec2.Instance(this, `MyInstance${index}`, {
        vpc,
        // instance type needs an object, so the next line instantiates one
with the size string
        instanceType: new ec2.InstanceType(instanceSize),

        // helper function provides the latest Amazon Linux AMI ID
        machineImage: ec2.MachineImage.latestAmazonLinux2(),

        // attach our security group by referencing the object created above
        securityGroup: sg,

        // associate with subnet. You may specify one, as this code does,
        // but if you pass in the array, CDK will pick one.
        vpcSubnets: {
          subnets: [publicSubnets.subnets[0]]
        },

        associatePublicIpAddress: true  // Explicitly associate a public IP
      });

      instances.push(instance)
    });
```

```
    // Attach user data to each instance. This shows how you can manipulate
    // resource constructs after creating them. This works because CDK is
transpiled
    // to CloudFormation, so all your code is read and understood by CDK
before creating the stack.
    instances.forEach((instance) => {
      instance.addUserData('#!/bin/bash', 'yum install -y nginx', 'service
nginx start');
    });


  }
}


module.exports = { CdkJavascriptDemoStack }
```

You can also see the three central concepts of apps, stacks, and constructs in this example. This file declares and exports a class that extends `Stack`, which is filled with code-defining constructs like EC2 instances. That export is then imported into an `App` object in another file:

```
#!/usr/bin/env node
const cdk = require('aws-cdk-lib');
const { CdkJavascriptDemoStack } = require('../lib/cdk_javascript_
demo-stack');


const app = new cdk.App();
new CdkJavascriptDemoStack(app, 'CdkJavascriptDemoStack', {
  env: { account: '<your_account_id>>', region: 'us-east-1' },
});
```

The syntax will vary from language to language, but the concepts and structure are the same. Deploying this code will result in CDK creating a CloudFormation template that implements the intended resources as a new stack.

Working with the CDK CLI

The command-line interface for CDK can be installed via npm:

```
npm install -g aws-cdk
```

Note that you must use npm to install the tool even if you intend to write your CDK scripts in a language other than JavaScript. Afterward, all CDK commands can be accessed with the cdk keyword on your terminal. The CDK CLI depends on the AWS CLI and uses the same account credentials; see Chapter 1, "Introduction to Amazon Web Services," for details on how to set those values. Now, let's take a look at the CDK CLI commands you'll use most often to work with your code.

cdk synth   This command transpiles your CDK project code and outputs the equivalent CloudFormation template. This is the exact stack your CDK project will deploy, so this is a great way to understand how CDK works and to review your work before attempting a deployment.

cdk deploy   Transpiles and packages your code into CloudFormation, then deploys the stack.

cdk destroy   Tears down your infrastructure by deleting the underlying CloudFormation stack.

cdk watch   Monitors the files in your CDK project for changes and updates the CloudFormation stack automatically in response.

Additional CDK Considerations

CDK has many benefits for developers looking for efficient ways to write infrastructure as code. Still, there are some caveats to consider.

CloudFormation's simplicity (and yes, rigidity) can be a strength. It is designed to be declarative. Introducing conditions and variables in CDK means that it can be harder for a reader to tell at a glance what the outcome of running it will be.

In addition, CDK may introduce more complex troubleshooting. CDK is good at flagging problems in your scripts early, but because those scripts are transpiled to CloudFormation before they are run and deployed, you may still find yourself needing to debug the underlying CloudFormation. If you have adopted CDK to avoid needing to understand CloudFormation itself, this could be challenging.

Choosing which to use and when may come down to personal preference or organizational standards. If your colleagues all use CloudFormation or all use CDK, use the standard tool! You can be very effective in both. The important thing is to take advantage of all that IaC offers by using it as much as possible, avoiding manual changes, instituting code reviews, using version control, and triggering updates automatically. With these practices in place, you will be well on your way to mature, efficient operational practices in the cloud.

AWS Serverless Application Model

The *AWS serverless application model (AWS SAM)* allows you to create and manage resources in your serverless application with AWS CloudFormation to define your serverless application infrastructure as a SAM template. A *SAM template* is a JSON or YAML configuration file that describes the AWS Lambda functions, API endpoints, tables, and other resources in your application. With simple commands, you upload this template to Cloud-Formation, which creates the individual resources and groups them into an *AWS Cloud-Formation stack* for ease of management. When you update your AWS SAM template, you redeploy the changes to this stack. CloudFormation updates the individual resources for you.

AWS SAM Templates

AWS SAM is an extension of CloudFormation (implemented with CloudFormation Transforms, as described in Chapter 8) that adds special syntax, resources, and configuration properties to let you define and deploy serverless applications quickly and concisely. The following example shows the power of the SAM templating language. Using just one template, we can define an API Gateway endpoint whose backend is a Lambda function, all in many fewer lines than it would take in pure CloudFormation. Not only that, but you can write the Lambda function as its own file, and SAM takes care of packaging it appropriately at deploy time. First is the SAM template (`template.yml`), then the Lambda code (`index.js`):

```
# template.yml
AWSTemplateFormatVersion: '2010-09-09'
Transform: AWS::Serverless-2016-10-31
Resources:
  HelloWorldFunction:
    Type: AWS::Serverless::Function
    Properties:
      Handler: index.handler
      Runtime: nodejs18.x
      CodeUri: .
      Events:
        HelloWorldApi:
          Type: Api
          Properties:
            Path: /hello_world
            Method: get

Outputs:
  HelloWorldApiUrl:
    Description: "API Gateway endpoint URL for Hello World function"
    Value: !Sub "https://${ServerlessRestApi}.execute-api.${AWS::Region}
.amazonaws.com/Prod/hello_world"

# index.js
exports.handler = async (event) => {
    return {
```

```
            statusCode: 200,
            body: JSON.stringify('Hello, World!'),
        };
};
```

This example shows how trivial SAM makes it to deploy a Lambda using the resource type `AWS::Serverless::Function`, which can reference an external file using `CodeUri`, then specifying the `Handler` and `Runtime`—that's it. Nothing else is required to deploy a basic Lambda function with SAM. This snippet deploys the code in `index.js`—a simple "hello world" response with a 200 OK status code.

Then, in just a few lines, SAM lets us expose this functionality as an API. The remaining properties of the function define an `Event` with type `Api`. From there, the `Path` and `Method` properties are all that is needed to create a simple unauthenticated `GET` endpoint that invokes the previously defined Lambda.

From just these two files, you can build and deploy working infrastructure with the SAM command-line interface commands `sam build` and `sam deploy`, described in the next section.

AWS SAM code is similar to CloudFormation, with a few key differences, as shown in the second line:

```
Transform: 'AWS::Serverless-2016-10-31'
```

This important line of code transforms the AWS SAM template into an AWS CloudFormation template. Without it, the AWS SAM template will not work.

Like CloudFormation, SAM templates have a `Resources` property where you define infrastructure to provision. The difference is that you provision serverless services with a new `Type` called `AWS::Serverless::Function`. This provisions an AWS Lambda function and all its related configuration options. AWS Lambda includes `Properties`, such as `MemorySize`, `Timeout`, `Role`, `Runtime`, and `Handler`, among others.

While you can create an AWS Lambda function with Amazon CloudFormation using `AWS::Lambda::Function`, the benefit of AWS SAM lies in a property called `Event`, where you can tie in a trigger to an AWS Lambda function, all from within the `AWS::Serverless::Function` resource. This `Event` property makes it simple to provision an AWS Lambda function and configure it with an Amazon API Gateway trigger. If you use Amazon CloudFormation, you would have to declare an Amazon API Gateway separately with `AWS::ApiGateway::Resource`.

AWS SAM allows you to provision serverless resources more rapidly with less code by extending AWS CloudFormation.

AWS SAM CLI

AWS SAM CLI is a tool that allows developers to iterate quickly on their serverless applications from the command line. You'll see how to create and test an AWS Lambda function locally in the "Exercises" section near the end of this chapter. Let's take a quick look at some of the most essential SAM CLI commands.

`sam init` initializes a new SAM application in your current folder, walking you through the setup by offering you a choice of several templates. Among the many prebuilt starter projects, you'll find a basic "hello world" app, a scheduled task using Lambda, and a GraphQL API with AppSync. It also allows you to select your Lambda runtime and optionally enable X-ray tracing and CloudWatch Insights.

`sam local` lets you run your serverless app on your own computer with emulators provided by AWS. Remember to have Docker installed and running before using this command.

`sam build` packages your template for deployment, just like packaging a CloudFormation template.

`sam deploy` runs the CloudFormation package that deploys or updates the stack associated with your SAM application. Use the `--guided` flag to get a command-line wizard that steps you through several choices associated with your deployment.

`sam sync` deploys your application, then monitors your application folder for changes. Using CDK commands (as opposed to full CloudFormation template deployments), SAM keeps the remote AWS deployment up-to-date with the changes you make locally, pushing changes as you edit and save your SAM template.

This can be a powerful alternative to using `sam local`, since you will be using live AWS resources while developing and have no need to run Docker locally or spend any time troubleshooting issues with the local configuration that may never appear in a real deployment. Use `sam sync` to develop with nonproduction data; then, when you're ready to go live to customers, deploy your stack with its production configuration.

AWS Serverless Application Repository

The *AWS serverless application repository* enables you to deploy code samples, components, and complete applications quickly for common use cases, such as web and mobile backends, event and data processing, logging, monitoring, Internet of Things (IoT), and more. Each application is packaged with an AWS SAM template that defines the AWS resources. Publicly shared applications also include a link to the application's source code.

You can also use the serverless application repository to publish your own applications and share them within your team, across your organization, or with the community at large. The serverless application repository can be a great resource to start a new project quickly, share ideas, or learn from what others have built.

Amazon Amplify

AWS Amplify is a powerful tool for full-stack development that packs multiple tools into one offering. It takes many of the cloud-native app development concepts we have learned thus far and wraps them in a single user-friendly UI and CLI experience that makes it easy to define your cloud architecture not in terms of infrastructure, but in terms of the data your application needs.

First, it provides static website hosting; this option lets you get client-side applications like those written in VueJS, React, or Angular deployed to the web in minutes.

Second, Amplify lets developers define cloud-based, serverless backend infrastructure using TypeScript. With only a few lines of code, you define data schemas. Behind the scenes, Amplify deploys your schema as a GraphQL API that uses DynamoDB to store your data. This is achieved by Level 3 CDK constructs, but you don't need to know any of this. You just write TypeScript, deploy, and start using your data.

Beyond data models, Amplify's backend functionality extends to authentication and authorization (backed by Amplify), storage (backed by S3), REST APIs (provided by API Gateway), and more. All of these can be defined in TypeScript and deployed with a simple git push.

Third, Amplify is a set of AWS-developed JavaScript libraries that let you easily use those backend resources on the front end. You can develop your code in a variety of popular JavaScript frameworks, including React, VueJS, and Angular. Beyond JavaScript, Amplify supports front-end code in Dart, Java, Kotlin, and Swift. With Amplify's client-side libraries, accessing your data model or integrating Cognito-backed authentication is made very simple.

Amplify's goal is to provide a great developer experience for those who want to deploy client-side applications with serverless backends. Let's take a closer look at how it works.

Amplify Hosting

Before you get into any of Amplify's infrastructure-building features, you can use Amplify as an extremely simple way to deploy client-side code to static hosting. Amplify can take your git repo (hosted in GitHub, Bitbucket, CodeCommit, or GitLab) and deploy it to a public URL. Although this deployment no doubt uses S3 and CloudFront distributions, you won't see them in your account; Amplify is a fully managed service, and this all takes place behind the curtain.

Amplify Hosting provides a web console that lets you manage build scripts, redirects, and custom domains; not only that, but it gives you a monitoring dashboard with telemetry on your front-end application's performance. This slimmed-down CloudWatch experience offers historical graphs, the ability to set alarms, and access to your app's access logs. Figure 14.1 shows how this appears in the web UI.

Backend Resources

Beyond just hosting, Amplify is designed to get you building client-side apps with AWS backend resources as quickly as possible. To do this, it provides a way for you to define backend services using TypeScript. These TypeScript files are then translated behind the scenes into Level 3 CDK constructs that are deployed whenever you deploy your application. The two primary backend resources you can build in this way are data resources and authentication/authorization resources.

FIGURE 14.1 Amplify Hosting monitoring dashboard

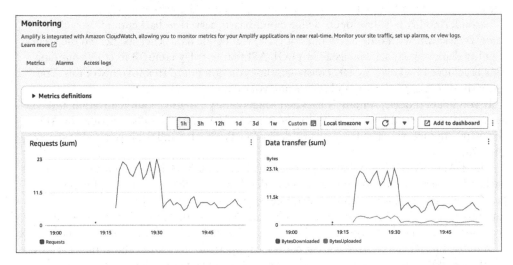

Data   The data layer of an Amplify app is an AppSync GraphQL API that provides an interface to data stored in DynamoDB tables. You define the schema of this data layer in a file called `amplify/data/resources.ts`. Building your data backend requires you to import the library `@aws-amplify/backend`.

```
import { type ClientSchema, a, defineData } from "@aws-amplify/backend";
const schema = a.schema({
  Pet: a.model({
      name: a.string()
      species: a.string()
    })
});

export type Schema = ClientSchema<typeof schema>;

export const data = defineData({
  schema
});
```

This example builds a very simple data model for pets. The export of type `Schema` makes the data model available to the front end for use on the client side; see the next section, "Working with Data on the Front End."

Auth   The file `amplify/auth/resources.ts` allows you to customize the authentication experience for your users. After importing `@aws-amplify/backend`, you use code to define how users will register and log in to your application. In the following example, we define the most basic authentication scheme possible: email login. When deployed, this simple configuration tells Cognito to create a user pool for your application that allows email-based registration and authentication.

As you can see, the code is geared very much toward the aspects that are relevant to front-end developers, while Amplify (again, powered here by CDK/CloudFormation) abstracts away all unnecessary complexity.

```
import { defineAuth } from '@aws-amplify/backend';

export const auth = defineAuth({
  loginWith: {
    email: true,
  },
});
```

In the later section "Adding Authentication on the Front End," you'll see how Amplify gives you an easy way to build a login screen for your apps based on this configuration.

This code can be extended with many different configuration options, from password format requirements to a phone login option. You can also configure third-party login from here, such as "Sign on with Facebook" functionality. Essentially, Amplify lets you configure anything you might want to do with Cognito user pools using TypeScript—without the need for any infrastructure management whatsoever. For a more comprehensive look at your options for auth, see AWS docs at `https://docs.amplify.aws/react/build-a-backend/auth/set-up-auth`.

Please note that although it is beyond the scope of this book to explore in detail, Amplify's data and auth libraries work together to allow you to define authorization rules that govern who can access data and when. To learn how to use TypeScript to annotate your data resources with authorization rules, see `https://docs.amplify.aws/react/build-a-backend/data/customize-authz`.

Working with Data on the Front End

The Amplify framework provides an easy way to interact with your Amplify backend in the front-end language and framework of your choice. First, import `generateClient` from `aws-amplify/data`, then import your `Schema`, which we exported in the `amplify/data/resource.ts` file.

```
import { generateClient } from "aws-amplify/data";
import type { Schema } from "@/amplify/data/resource";
```

From there, you can call `generateClient` on the `Schema` object, which creates a `client` object with fields corresponding to your own data schema:

```
const client = generateClient<Schema>();
```

```
// list all Pet records
const { all_pets } = await client.models.Pet.list();

// create a new Pet record
await client.models.Pet.create({
  name: 'Beckett',
  species: 'cat'
});
```

This is a major feature of AWS Amplify: the ability to generate a client to interact with your data as native JavaScript. Remember, the actual implementation of Amplify's backend is a GraphQL API that uses DynamoDB as its backend, but with the AWS's Amplify JavaScript framework, you don't need to understand how to interact with either service; you only need to know how to work with data objects in JavaScript.

Adding Authentication on the Front End

Once the backend auth services are configured, import front-end Amplify libraries to add a drop-in login UI that implements that configuration. The specific import differs based on the front end you choose. For VueJS developers, you'd use @aws-amplify/ui-vue. The following code imports the Authenticator VueJS UI component along with some CSS (Cascading Style Sheets) definitions that determine its visual look:

```
import { Authenticator } from "@aws-amplify/ui-vue";
import "@aws-amplify/ui-vue/styles.css";
```

Specific syntax will vary by your chosen language, but in this VueJS code, you can wrap your content in the authenticator tags. If the user is not signed in, this entire snippet will be replaced in the user's browser by a login/registration screen. If the user is signed in, they will see a welcome message, followed by a Sign Out button. In this example, a bit of VueJS code—@click—assigns the click action to a user-defined method called signOut.

```
<authenticator>
  <template v-slot="{ user, signOut }">
    <h1>Welcome {{user?.signInDetails?.loginId}}!</h1>
    <button @click="signOut">Sign Out</button>
  </template>
</authenticator>
```

Figure 14.2 shows the default sign-in user interface supplied by Amplify.

Local Development Environments

Developers rely on local environments to code, test, and iterate on their personal machines before pushing changes. This isolation prevents accidental disruptions to users and other developers. However, because Amplify applications depend on cloud services, "local" development environments for Amplify apps cannot run completely on a laptop. Instead, Amplify provides tools to help you stand up a version of the app using cloud infrastructure that is completely isolated from others.

FIGURE 14.2   Amplify default login/registration UI

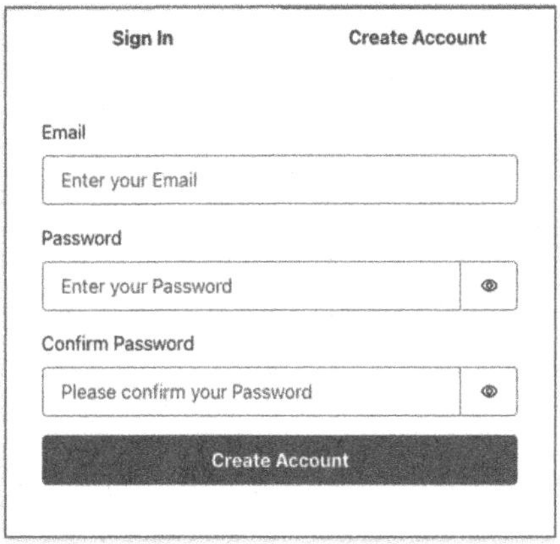

amplify_outputs.json

When you create your backend with Amplify, you build resources in AWS that are needed by your front end. Before it can talk to these resources, your front end needs details, including authentication information (such as a Cognito user pool ID) and API endpoints (such as your AppSync GraphQL API URL). After these resources are built by Amplify, you can download a JSON file containing information about all these backend resources to enable a local copy of your front end to reach them. Because Amplify does not provide local emulators for backend resources such as these, the amplify_outputs.json file is a crucial piece of configuration data that enables local copies of the Amplify app to interact with backend systems in AWS.

Cloud Sandboxes

With the command npm ampx sandbox, Amplify can create an alternate copy of the backend AWS infrastructure for exclusive use by a certain developer on a certain branch. These development environments can give multiple app developers the ability to work on an Amplify app at the same time, running their front-end code on localhost and each interacting with distinct cloud infrastructure for their backend data and auth services. This helps ensure that no one will overwrite or disrupt the app's cloud infrastructure as different developers make changes. This deployment also updates the amplify_outputs.json file with details on the alternate infrastructure so that Amplify can switch backend contexts whenever you switch git branches.

The Amplify Build Process

Amplify's build and deployment settings are stored in a file called `amplify.yml`. This file contains sections very similar to those used by CodeBuild (`buildspec.yml`) and CodeDeploy (`appspec.yml`). Its structure is as follows:

```
version: 1
env:
  variables:
    key: value
backend:
  phases:
    preBuild:
      commands:
    build:
      commands:
    postBuild:
        commands:
frontend:
  buildpath:
  phases:
    preBuild:
      commands:
        - cd your-app
        - npm ci
    build:
      commands:
        - npm run build
  artifacts:
    files:
        - file1
        - file2
    discard-paths: yes
    baseDirectory: location
  cache:
    paths:
        - path
        - path
test:
  phases:
    preTest:
```

```
      commands:
    test:
      commands:
    postTest:
      commands:
  artifacts:
    files:
        - file1
        - file2
    configFilePath:
    baseDirectory:
```

As you can see, the four major sections of the file are env, frontend, backend, and test. The environment section lets you define environment variables for your app.

The frontend and backend sections allow you to inject any commands you need to happen during the build phases of each. On the backend, you have access to three life-cycle hooks—preBuild, build, and postBuild—that let you run arbitrary commands at these stages. Similarly, frontend defines preBuild and build hooks. In this example, JavaScript developers will see that the front-end build phase includes the ubiquitous npm run build to build their client-side application. This would be the place to add any other commands needed for your build.

Finally, the test section allows you to run any automated tests you may have for your application. A failure here would suspend the deployment of a new application so that you can be sure never to deploy code that doesn't 100 percent pass your tests.

Handling Secrets

Amplify allows you to set application secrets that can be accessed by your application. For developer sandboxes, this command will prompt you to set the value for my_password:

```
npx ampx sandbox secret set my_password
```

For secrets affecting other branches or your production environment, use the Amplify console. The resulting value is kept in a hierarchical Parameter Store key-value pair using the SecretString value type. These values can be accessed in your backend-implementing TypeScript files by using the secret function from @aws-amplify/backend:

```
import { secret } from '@aws-amplify/backend';
...
secret('my_password')// access secrets by name
```

This could be used, for instance, in the integration of single sign-on from your OpenID Connect (OIDC)-compatible IdP. Of course, these values are not accessible from the front end, as you wouldn't want users to be able to access your secrets from their browsers!

Secret values can also be accessed from amplify.yml, where they are made available via the special variable $secret. This variable is a JSON representation of all the secrets you've stored using Amplify, so you must use a JSON parsing tool such as `jq` to access values by name. To get the value of the key stored earlier, you'd do this:

```
echo $secrets | jq -r '.my_password'
```

Between environment variables and secrets management, Amplify simplifies many of the ways you need to configure your applications.

Deploying and Managing Amplify Apps

Deploying your Amplify application requires logging into the AWS console, navigating to Amplify, and initializing a new app. This is required so that you can authenticate your GitHub (or BitBucket or GitLab) account with AWS, giving it permission to listen for pushes to your branches to trigger deployments. Figure 14.3 shows all the options you have for connecting your app to version control systems.

FIGURE 14.3   Amplify version control options

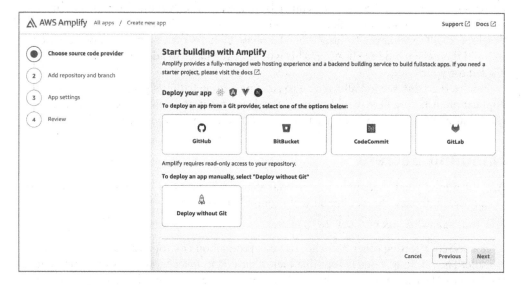

Your initial deployment will create all the backend infrastructure your app declares in your AWS account. From there, Amplify's continuous integration/continuous deployment capabilities mean that it will monitor the git branches you specified and deploy changes whenever a push occurs. To exert more control over this process, edit your desired steps, commands, and quality checks into the build process via `amplify.yml`.

Amplify also lets you provision and manage multiple environments tied to distinct git branches; similar to cloud sandboxes, these environments allow you to set up fully isolated cloud infrastructure, giving you the ability to create dev, staging, and test environments where you can push changes for evaluation before updating production.

There is much more that could be written about AWS Amplify's wide range of features. For in-depth documentation, see `https://docs.amplify.aws`.

Summary

In this chapter, we took a close look at three AWS tools that significantly streamline the building of cloud infrastructure and serverless applications.

Cloud Developer Kit (CDK) extends the power of CloudFormation by giving you a way to build infrastructure-as-code in your language of choice, including Python, JavaScript, C#, and more. CDK goes beyond the relatively static, declarative JSON or YAML templates of CloudFormation to enable procedural logic, conditional statements, variables, and functions—all the control you'd have coding in your preferred programming language. It then allows you to deploy using a command-line interface, either on-demand through the `cdk deploy` command or continuously with `cdk watch`.

CDK resources, known as "constructs," are divided into three levels. Level 1 constructs are thin wrappers around CloudFormation resources with all the same names, parameters, and configuration options exposed. Level 2 constructs provide scores of helper functions, such as those that abstract complex IAM policy creation and attachment behind functions that "just make sense" in context. Finally, Level 3 constructs, or "patterns," abstract larger, related sets of resources that express common architectures, such as the combination of a load balancer, target group, autoscaling template, and Auto Scaling Group to create a horizontally scalable EC2 deployment. Developers have created online hubs to share the CDK constructs they've built with the community.

The AWS serverless application model (AWS SAM) allows you to create and manage resources for serverless applications using a transformed version of CloudFormation templates. The directive `Transform: 'AWS::Serverless-2016-10-31'` in a SAM template alerts CloudFormation to convert it into an AWS CloudFormation template.

Using SAM, you get the declarative clarity of CloudFormation with a syntax that makes standing up serverless architectures much more straightforward than the vanilla tool. You can declare a Lambda function in a few lines, maintaining its code in a separate file that is packaged up automatically by command-line command `sam build`. With a few more lines, you can expose that endpoint as a REST API using AWS API Gateway, declare a DynamoDB table with its indices, or map triggering events from sources like S3. Deploy it all as a Cloud-Formation stack with `sam deploy` for a powerful and simple way to get started with serverless application patterns.

The AWS serverless application repository enables you to deploy code samples, components, and complete applications for common use cases. Each application is packaged with an AWS SAM template that defines the AWS resources.

AWS Amplify is a powerful and flexible framework for developing full-stack applications. With it, you use TypeScript to declare your desired backend data schema and authentication/authorization wishes. Amplify translates these into GraphQL APIs and AWS Cognito user pool configurations, respectively. It then provides JavaScript libraries for you to incorporate data handling and authentication seamlessly into front-end code built into web or mobile frameworks such as VueJS, React, Angular, Kotlin, and Swift. For building infrastructure-as-code and serverless architectures, Amplify is the most abstracted of the three tools discussed in this chapter, letting developers focus on data and the user experience, not on cloud infrastructure.

In addition, Amplify integrates tightly with git to create development sandboxes for teams, letting you and your colleagues work on copies of the same infrastructure. With this feature, you can build and change as much as you want in your own full production-like deployment environment without disrupting your teammates' work. Use version control and pull requests to coordinate code merges for deployment in Amplify's git-based deployment automation.

Exam Essentials

Know the advantages of programming in CDK.   Using your preferred programming languages lets you work with familiar code and tooling (such as editors), and gives you access to all the power of traditional coding structures.

Understand the differences between CDK construct levels.   Level 1 constructs wrap CloudFormation resources and leave all the configuration decision-making to you. Level 2 constructs provide a higher level of abstraction with sensible defaults for parameter values and many helper functions that achieve complex ideas with just a few lines of code. Finally, Level 3 constructs abstract entire architectural patterns.

Know the use cases for the Serverless Application Model.   Any time you are deploying Lambda functions, especially when they will be triggered by API Gateway, Step Functions, or event sources like S3, is a good opportunity to save time with SAM.

Understand how Amplify enables full-stack developers to build serverless backend resources.   Amplify lets you use TypeScript to define backend data sources that are implemented in GraphQL (via AppSync) and DynamoDB, then provide powerful helper functions to let you work with this data in JavaScript. It also lets you define login, registration, and authorization rules to be implemented by Cognito.

Recognize when to use CDK, SAM, or Amplify based on your requirements.   Choose CDK for complex, customizable cloud architectures using familiar programming languages; opt for SAM when focusing on serverless applications, particularly those built around Lambda and API Gateway; select Amplify for full-stack development with seamless front-end-backend integration, especially when using modern frameworks like React or Vue.js, and prioritizing rapid prototyping or multiplatform support.

Exercises

Defining an AWS SAM Template

In this exercise, you will develop a Lambda function locally and then test that Lambda function using the AWS SAM CLI. To perform this exercise successfully, you must have AWS SAM CLI installed. For information on how to install the AWS SAM CLI, review the following documentation: `https://github.com/awslabs/aws-sam-cli`. The following steps assume you have a working AWS SAM CLI installation.

1. Once you have installed AWS SAM CLI, open your favorite integrated development environment (IDE) and define an AWS SAM template.

2. Enter the following in your template file:

```
AWSTemplateFormatVersion: '2010-09-09'
Transform: AWS::Serverless-2016-10-31

Description: Welcome to the Pet Store Demo

Resources:
  PetStore:
    Type: AWS::Serverless::Function
    Properties:
      Runtime: nodejs20.x
      Handler: index.handler
```

3. Save the file as **template.yaml**.

At this point, all you have done is create the SAM template and save the file locally. In the subsequent exercises, you will use this information to execute an AWS Lambda function.

Define an AWS Lambda Function Locally

Now that you have a valid SAM template, you can define your AWS Lambda function locally. In this example, we use Nodejs 8.10, but you can use any AWS Lambda-supported language.

1. Open your favorite IDE, and type the following Nodejs code:

```
'use strict';
```

```
//A simple Lambda function
exports.handler = (event, context, callback) => {

    console.log('This is our local lambda function');
    console.log('Creating a PetStore service');
    callback(null, "Hello " + event.Records[0].dynamodb.NewImage.Message.S +
"! What kind of
pet are you interested in?");
}
```

2. Save the file as **index.js**.

   At this point, you should have two files: index.js and the SAM template. In the next exercise, you will generate an event source that will be used as the trigger for the Lambda function.

Generating an Event Source

Now that you have a valid SAM template and a valid AWS Lambda Nodejs 8.10 function, you can generate an event source.

1. Inside your terminal, type the following to generate an event source:

   ```
   sam local generate-event dynamodb update > event.json
   ```

   This will generate an Amazon DynamoDB update event. For a list of all of the event sources, type the following:

   ```
   sam local generate-event -help
   ```

2. Modify the event source JSON file (event.json). On line 17, change New Item! to your first and last names.

   ```
   "S": "John Smith"
   ```

You have now configured the three pieces you need: the AWS SAM template, the Lambda function, and the event source. In the next exercise, you will be able to run the AWS Lambda function locally.

EXERCISE 14.4

Running the AWS Lambda Function

Now you can trigger and execute the Lambda function.

1. In your terminal, type the following to execute the Lambda function:

   ```
   sam local invoke "PetStore" -e event.json
   ```

   You will see the following message:

   Hello Casey Gerena! What kind of pet are you interested in?

   What is happening here is that the Lambda Docker image is downloaded to your local environment, and the event.json serves as all of the data that will be received as an event source to the Lambda function. Inside the SAM template, you will have given this function the name of PetStore; however, you can define as many functions as you need to in order to build your application.

EXERCISE 14.5

Modifying the SAM Template to Include an API Locally

Now, to make your pet store into an API, modify template.yaml.

1. Open the template.yaml file, and modify it to look like the following:

   ```yaml
   AWSTemplateFormatVersion: '2010-09-09'
   Transform: AWS::Serverless-2016-10-31


   Description: Welcome to the Pet Store Demo


   Resources:
     PetStore:
       Type: AWS::Serverless::Function
       Properties:
         Runtime: nodejs20.x
         Handler: index.handler
         Events:
           PetStore:
             Type: Api
   ```

```
        Properties:
          Path: /
          Method: any
Outputs:
  ApiUrl:
    Description: "API Gateway endpoint URL"
    Value: !Sub "https://${ServerlessRestApi}.execute-api.${AWS::Region}
.amazonaws.com/Prod/"
```

2. Save the `template.yaml` file.

You have now modified the SAM template to connect an API Gateway event for any method (GET, POST, and so on) to the AWS Lambda function. In the next exercise, you will modify the AWS Lambda function to work with the API.

Modifying Your AWS Lambda Function for the API

Now that you defined an API, you need to modify your AWS Lambda function.

1. Open the `index.js` file, and make the following changes:

```
'use strict';

//A simple Lambda function
exports.handler = (event, context, callback) => {

    console.log('DEBUG: This is our local lambda function');
    console.log('DEBUG: Creating a PetStore service');

    callback(null, {
        statusCode: 200,
        headers: { "x-petstore-custom-header": "custom header from petstore
service" },
        body: '{"message": "Hello! Welcome to the PetStore. What kind of Pet
are you interested in?"}'
    })

}
```

2. Save the `index.js` file.

Now you have modified the AWS Lambda function to respond to an API REST request. At this point, though, you have not actually executed anything—you will do that in the next exercise.

EXERCISE 14.7

Running API Gateway Locally

Now that you have everything defined, run API Gateway locally.

1. Open a terminal and type the following:

sam local start-api

You will see output that looks like the following. Take note of the URL.

```
2018-10-11 23:05:25 Mounting PetStore at http://127.0.0.1:3000/hello [GET]
2018-10-11 23:05:25 You can now browse to the above endpoints to invoke your functions. You
do not need to restart/reload SAM CLI while working on your functions changes will be
reflected instantly/automatically. You only need to restart SAM CLI if you update your AWS
SAM template
2018-10-11 23:05:25  * Running on http://127.0.0.1:3000/ (Press CTRL+C to quit)
```

2. Open a web browser, and navigate to the previous URL.

You will see the following message:

```
Message: "Hello! Welcome to the Pet Store. What kind of Pet are you interested in?"
```

When you navigate to the URL, the local API Gateway forwards the request to AWS Lambda, which is also running locally, provided by index.js. You can now build serverless applications locally and then deploy them to the AWS Cloud with AWS SAM when you are ready to deploy to a real development or production environment. This allows developers to iterate through their code quickly and make improvements locally.

EXERCISE 14.8

Deploying the API to AWS

Now that the API is running locally, you can deploy it to AWS.

1. Open a terminal to the folder with your template and Lambda function, then type the following:

   `sam build`

2. Type **sam deploy --guided** to initiate the deployment wizard. Answer the questions like so:

   Stack Name [pet-api]:

   AWS Region [us-east-1]:

   #Shows you resources changes to be deployed and require a 'Y' to initiate deploy

   Confirm changes before deploy [Y/n]: Y

   #SAM needs permission to be able to create roles to connect to the resources in your template

   Allow SAM CLI IAM role creation [Y/n]: Y

   #Preserves the state of previously provisioned resources when an operation fails

   Disable rollback [y/N]: N

   PetStore has no authentication. Is this okay? [y/N]: y

   Save arguments to configuration file [Y/n]: Y

   SAM configuration file [samconfig.toml]:

   SAM configuration environment [default]:

3. Confirm the change set when prompted.

4. You'll see output similar to this. Copy the URL into your browser:

   ```
   ------------------------------------------------------------------------
   Outputs
   ------------------------------------------------------------------------

   Key           ApiUrl
   Description   API Gateway endpoint URL
   Value         https://f2gjypuly9.execute-api.us-east-1.amazonaws.com/
                 Prod/
   ------------------------------------------------------------------------
   ```

5. Navigate to the URL; you will see the `PetStore` greeting again.

6. Back on your terminal, tear down the stack with **sam delete**. Answer yes to all prompts to fully clean up what you deployed.

You have just used the Serverless Application Model and SAM CLI to test and deploy a Lambda-powered API to AWS!

EXERCISE 14.9

Working with CDK

In this exercise, you will write and deploy infrastructure with CDK using Python. Observe how the Level 2 constructs in this example simplify steps that would take many more lines of code in CloudFormation.

1. Make sure CDK is installed using **npm install -g aws-cdk**. The AWS CLI is a prerequisite; make sure it is installed and configured with credentials that can create and configure S3 buckets and Lambda functions.

2. In a new folder, initialize a Python CDK app with the following command:

```
cdk init app --language python
```

3. Run the following commands to start a new virtual environment and use pip3 to install the libraries in the newly generated `requirements.txt` file – aws-cdk-lib and constructs. Python users may be familiar with the process of setting up virtual environments, but if you want to know more, visit https://realpython.com/python-virtual-environments-a-primer.

```
python3 -m venv .venv
source .venv/bin/activate
pip3 install -r requirements.txt
```

4. Copy into this folder the two Python scripts from the Chapter 14 code: app.py and lambda_stack.py. The former is brief; it is the entry point for CDK. The infrastructure logic is in lambda_stack.py.

Note a few things about this script. First, that it includes the inline definition of a Lambda function, so there is an element of Python-within-Python. Read carefully to understand which part is the Lambda declaration.

Second, note the actual functionality of the script: It creates two S3 buckets and gives permissions on both to the Lambda function via the helper methods grant_read and grant_write. These two short lines encompass several steps you'd need to take if you were setting this up manually. The script also uses add_event_notification to trigger the Lambda whenever a file hits the input bucket, at which point a corresponding file is written to the output.

Finally, notice that it declares two parameters that will need filling: InputBucketName and OutputBucketName.

5. Using unique names for your buckets, run the CDK script. You'll see a preview of all the changes it will make; type **y** to confirm.

```
cdk deploy --parameters InputBucketName=your-input-bucket --parameters Output
BucketName=your-
output-bucket
```

6. Now test the functionality by first observing that the output bucket is empty:

```
aws s3 ls s3://your-output-bucket
```

7. Next, create a file to upload to the input bucket:

```
echo "hello" > hello.txt
aws s3 cp hello.txt s3://your-input-bucket
```

8. Now we can check the output and download the processed file:

```
aws s3 ls s3://your-output-bucket
aws s3 cp s3://your-output-bucket/processed-hello.txt
```

9. Print it out to see the result:

```
cat processed-hello.txt
File processed by Lambda!
```

10. To clean everything up, run **cdk destroy** and confirm the teardown by typing **y**.

Review Questions

1. Which templating engine can you use to deploy infrastructure inside of AWS that is built for serverless technologies?

   A. AWS CloudFormation

   B. DynamoDB

   C. AWS Systems Manager

   D. AWS Serverless Application Model (AWS SAM)

2. What is the property name that you use to connect an AWS Lambda function to the Amazon API Gateway inside an AWS Serverless Application Model (AWS SAM) template?

   A. events

   B. handler

   C. context

   D. runtime

3. Which are advantages of using Cloud Development Kit (CDK) over CloudFormation? (Choose two.)

   A. CDK allows the use of familiar programming languages and tools such as Java, C#, or Python.

   B. CDK lets you design infrastructure with a simple drag-and-drop interface.

   C. CDK lets you build with higher-level abstractions than CloudFormation.

   D. CDK uses YAML templates, which are easier to read than JSON.

4. Which AWS Amplify feature allows multiple developers to work on different versions of the same app infrastructure without overwriting each other's changes?

   A. Amplify Hosting

   B. Cloud sandboxes

   C. Staging environments

   D. StackSets

5. Why would you run the cdk synth command when programming with CDK?

   A. To sync code between your local environment and AWS

   B. To watch your local files for changes that are then automatically deployed

   C. To create the CloudFormation template out of your CDK code, validating that it builds correctly

   D. To synthesize a new architecture scaffolding based on an existing template

6. You are tasked with migrating an existing microservice from an EC2-based architecture to a fully serverless setup. The microservice exposes a REST API with routes that create and retrieve data in a DynamoDB table. What is the optimal AWS tool for the developer to use to migrate this functionality to a serverless architecture?

   A. Elastic Container Service

   B. AWS Serverless Application Model (AWS SAM)

   C. AWS CDK

   D. AWS Amplify

7. Which CloudFormation feature enables the AWS Serverless Application Model to provide syntax specific to launching serverless architectures?

   A. Change sets

   B. Transform

   C. Metadata

   D. StackSets

8. You have an AWS SAM template that deploys a Lambda function. You need to add Amazon DynamoDB as a data store for the Lambda function without modifying the function code. What changes would you make to the SAM template?

   A. Add a DynamoDB table as a resource and configure a managed policy in the Lambda function to allow read and write access.

   B. Define the DynamoDB table and pass its ARN to the Lambda function using environment variables.

   C. Use an inline policy in the SAM template to allow the Lambda function to interact with the DynamoDB table.

   D. Manually create the DynamoDB table and update the Lambda function's role to include access.

9. Which of the following steps of building a Lambda-backed REST API is *not* abstracted by AWS SAM?

   A. Configuring the Lambda as an integration point for the API

   B. Packaging the Lambda function code

   C. Creating the permissions for API Gateway to call the Lambda

   D. Setting a custom domain for the API

10. You're tasked with standing up a proof-of-concept (POC) for a new application being designed by your organization. It needs to be serverless and use infrastructure-as-code, built with a REST API as its backend so that other internal services can eventually interact with the data maintained by web and mobile users of the app. The POC needs to be accessible to a subset of your colleagues only, including some not using your company VPN. What is the best tool to use?

    A. AWS Serverless Application Model

    B. AWS Cloud Developer Kit

    C. AWS Amplify

    D. AWS Elastic Beanstalk

Monitoring and Troubleshooting

**THE AWS CERTIFIED DEVELOPER –
ASSOCIATE EXAM TOPICS COVERED IN
THIS CHAPTER MAY INCLUDE, BUT ARE
NOT LIMITED TO, THE FOLLOWING:**

✓ **Domain 1: Development with AWS Services**

  ▪ Task Statement 1: Develop code for applications
    hosted on AWS

✓ **Domain 4: Troubleshooting and Optimization**

  ▪ Task Statement 1: Assist in a root cause analysis

  ▪ Task Statement 2: Instrument code for observability

  ▪ Task Statement 3: Optimize applications by using AWS
    services and features

Monitoring the applications and services you build is vital to the success of any information technology (IT) organization. With AWS, monitoring your resources can drive business decisions such as what resources to create, improve, optimize, and secure.

Traditional approaches to monitoring do not scale for cloud architectures. Large systems can be difficult to set up, configure, and scale. These efforts are compounded by the trend away from monolithic installations to service-oriented architecture (SOA), microservices, and serverless architectures. Monitoring modern IT systems is proportionally difficult. When working on a monolithic application, you can add logging statements and troubleshoot with breakpoints. However, applications today are spread across multiple systems over large networks that make it difficult to track the health of systems and react to issues. For example, using logging statements to monitor execution time and error rates of AWS Lambda functions can become difficult as your infrastructure grows and spreads across multiple AWS regions.

Fortunately, AWS has built logging and monitoring into nearly every aspect of its services, giving you powerful out-of-the-box, turnkey-yet-customizable capabilities to monitor every aspect of your cloud infrastructure, no matter how complex. In this chapter, you'll explore Amazon CloudWatch, OpenSearch, AWS CloudTrail, Athena, and AWS X-Ray, services that combine to give you comprehensive visibility into your cloud resources. Figure 15.1 shows the AWS monitoring services available.

FIGURE 15.1 Various monitoring services on AWS

Amazon CloudWatch   AWS CloudTrail   AWS X-Ray

Monitoring Basics

Before you explore these services, consider why they are essential. As a developer, you are designing systems to provide IT or business solutions to a customer. Success is measured by the effective application of software to business objectives. What are some of the metrics that you must track over time to ensure that these objectives are being met?

Choosing Metrics

Start with the customer in mind, tracing the underlying components that affect the customer's experience. This provides a foundation for identifying which metrics to monitor, as they correlate directly to the customer experience. Frequently, the top characteristics that directly affect the customer experience are performance and cost—assuming your cloud costs are passed on to your users. Changes to either have a direct impact on how customers perceive the software they use.

Deciding which metrics to monitor requires that you answer several crucial questions.

Performance and Cost

Question: "Are your customers having a good experience with the services or systems that you provide?"

The phrase *good experience* can then be broken down into measurable metrics, such as request latency, time to first byte, error rates, and more. Metrics such as instance CPU utilization or network bytes in/out may not be directly representative of the customer experience, yet they often indicate conditions that translate into noticeable measures like the responsiveness of page loads, the speed of data processing, and the wait time for business-facing events like order notifications and shipping.

The second question to ask is, "What is the overall cost of my system?" Increases in performance often correlate directly to increases in cost. With unlimited money, it would be easy to design a system that scales infinitely in response to customer usage. However, this is never a reality. Instead, you need to measure the performance of your system to determine what is acceptable performance based on the usage at any point in time.

Trends

Question: "How can you use monitoring to predict changes in customer demand?"

Monitoring and measuring customer demand over time allows you to scale your infrastructure predictively to meet changes in customer demand without having to purchase more resources than are necessary. For example, suppose that you have a web application that runs on three EC2 instances during the day. In the evenings, demand increases significantly for several hours before decreasing again late at night. On weekends, your application sees almost no traffic. With historical information obtained through monitoring, you can design your application to scale out across more instances during the evenings and scale in on the weekends when there is little demand. Predictive scaling occurs before customer demand changes, ensuring a smooth experience while new resources are created and brought online.

Troubleshooting and Remediation

Question: "Where do problems occur?"

As Werner Vogels, VP and CTO of AWS, once said, "Everything fails all the time." No system is impervious to failure. By gathering potentially relevant information ahead of time, it becomes easier to determine causes for failure. By collecting this information, you can reduce mean time between failure (MTBF), mean time to resolution (MTTR), and other key operational performance metrics.

Learning and Improvement

Question: "Can you detect or prevent problems in the future?"

By evaluating operational metrics over time, you can reveal patterns and common issues in your systems. Machine learning algorithms can begin to understand how your systems normally behave, then alarm proactively when they notice unusual changes in those metrics.

When choosing metrics, align them closely to your business processes to provide a better customer experience. For example, suppose that you have an application running in AWS Elastic Beanstalk. Unbeknownst to you, the application has a memory leak. Without tracking memory utilization over time, you will not have insight into why customers are experiencing degraded performance. If your Elastic Beanstalk environment is configured to scale out based on CPU utilization, it is possible that no new instances are launched to serve customer requests. In this case, the memory leak prevents new requests from being processed, causing a drop in CPU utilization. Without comprehensive tracking of system performance, issues such as this can go unnoticed until systemwide outages occur.

These factors impact what is referred to as the health of your systems. As a developer and contributor, you are not only responsible for the code that you develop but also for the operational health of these services. It is vital to align operational and health metrics properly with customer expectations and experiences.

Amazon CloudWatch

Amazon CloudWatch is a monitoring and metrics service that provides you with a fully managed system to collect, store, and analyze your metrics and logs. By using CloudWatch, you can create notifications on changes in your environment.

Typical use cases include the following:

- Infrastructure monitoring and troubleshooting
- Resource optimization
- Application monitoring
- Logging analytics
- Error reporting and notification

CloudWatch enables you to collect and store monitoring and operations data from logs, metrics, and events from AWS and on-premises resources. To ensure that your applications run smoothly, you can use CloudWatch to perform the following tasks:

- Set alarms
- Visualize logs and metrics
- Automate recovery from errors
- Troubleshoot issues
- Discover insights that enable you to optimize your resources

How Amazon CloudWatch Works

CloudWatch acts as a *metrics repository*, storing metrics and logs from various sources. These metrics can come from AWS resources using built-in or custom metrics. Figure 15.2 illustrates the role of CloudWatch in operational health.

FIGURE 15.2   Diagram of Amazon CloudWatch

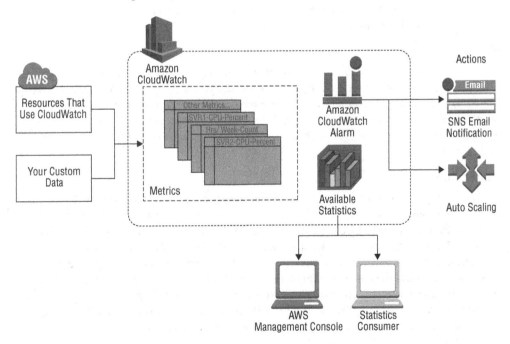

CloudWatch can process these metrics into statistics that are made available through the Amazon CloudWatch console, AWS APIs, the AWS Command-Line Interface (AWS CLI), and

AWS Software Development Kits (AWS SDKs). Using CloudWatch, you can display graphs, create alarms, or integrate with third-party solutions.

Amazon CloudWatch Metrics

To better understand CloudWatch, and especially how data is collected and organized, review the following terms.

Built-In Metrics

A *metric* is a set of time-series data points that you publish to CloudWatch—for example, a commonly monitored metric for Amazon EC2 instances is CPU utilization. Data points can come from multiple systems, both AWS and on-premises. You can also define custom metrics based on data specific to your system. A metric is identified uniquely by a namespace, a name, and zero or more dimensions.

Namespace

A *namespace* is a collection of metrics or a container of related metrics. Namespaces used by AWS offerings or services all start with AWS; for example, EC2 uses the AWS/EC2 namespace. As a developer, you can create namespaces for different components of your applications, such as front-end, backend, and database components.

Name

A *name* for a given metric defines the attribute or property that you are monitoring. For example, within the AWS/EC2 namespace, CPU Utilization for EC2 is called CPUUtilization. The AWS/EC2 namespace contains many other metrics that are important to monitoring the health of EC2 resources, such as Disk I/O, Network I/O, or Status Check. You can also create custom metrics for attributes, such as request latency, HTTP 400/500 response codes, and throttling.

Dimension

A *dimension* is a name/value pair used to define a metric uniquely. Each metric may have up to 30 dimensions. You can think of dimensions as attributes or metadata on a metric. For example, for the metric CPUUtilization in the AWS/EC2 namespace, examples of dimensions are InstanceId and AvailabilityZone. Often, you will want to query metrics by filtering for specific dimension values; supplying a specific instance ID as a filter on InstanceId would drill into the CPU Utilization of a single instance. Other times, you might want an aggregate picture of your resource behavior. Omitting any dimension value would give you the overall average of CPU utilization for all instances, while specifying only an availability zone (AZ) would aggregate the measure for every instance in an AZ.

When creating metrics, consider defining namespaces that align with your services and assigning dimensions to important metrics that describe the health of that service. For example, if you have a front-end web fleet running nginx servers, then dimensions such as requests-per-second, response time, active connections, and response codes could help you determine what configuration changes would optimize system performance.

Data Points

When data is published to CloudWatch, it is pushed in sets of data points. Each data point contains information such as the timestamp, value, and unit of measurement.

Timestamp

Timestamps are dateTime objects with the complete date and time, for example, 2024-10-31T23:59:59Z. Although not required, AWS recommends formatting times as Coordinated Universal Time (UTC).

Value

The *value* is the measurement for the data point.

Unit

A *unit* of measurement is used to label your data. This offers a better understanding of what the value represents. Example units include Bytes, Seconds, Count, and Percent. If you do not specify a unit in CloudWatch, your data point units are designated as None.

CloudWatch stores this data based on the *retention period*, which is the length of time to keep data points available. Data points are stored in CloudWatch based on how often the data points are published.

- Data points with a published frequency less than 60 seconds are available for 3 hours. These data points are high-resolution custom metrics.

- Data points with a published frequency of 60 seconds (1 minute) are available for 15 days.

- Data points with a published frequency of 300 seconds (5 minutes) are available for 63 days.

- Data points with a published frequency of 3,600 seconds (1 hour) are available for 455 days (15 months).

From these data points, CloudWatch can calculate statistics to provide you with insight into your application, service, or environment. In the next section, you will discover how CloudWatch calculates and organizes these statistics.

Statistics

CloudWatch provides statistics based on metric data provided to the service. *Statistics* are aggregations of data points over specified periods of time for specified metrics. A *period* is the length of time, in seconds. Periods can be defined in values of 1, 5, 10, 30, or any multiple of 60 seconds (up to 86,400 seconds, or 1 day). The available statistics in Amazon CloudWatch include the following:

- `Minimum` (Min), the lowest value recorded over the specified period
- `Maximum` (Max), the highest value recorded over the specified period
- `Sum`, the total value of the samples added together over the specified period
- `Average` (Avg), the `Sum` divided by the `SampleCount` over the specified period
- `SampleCount`, the number of data points used in the calculation over the specified period
- `pNN`, percentile statistics for tracking metric outliers

Statistics can be used to gain insight into the health of your application and to help you determine the correct settings for various configurations.

Aggregations

CloudWatch aggregates metrics according to the period of time you specify when retrieving statistics. When you request this statistic, you also can have CloudWatch filter the data points based on the dimensions of the metrics. For example, in Amazon DynamoDB, metrics are fetched across all DynamoDB operations. You can specify a filter on the dimension `operations` to exclude specific operations, such as `GetItem` requests. CloudWatch does not aggregate data across regions.

CloudWatch metrics, statistics, and aggregations provide a powerful way to process large amounts of data at scale and present insights that are easy to consume. Now that you understand how CloudWatch metrics work and are organized, let's explore some of the metrics available.

Available Metrics

Table 15.1 displays available metrics for Elastic Load Balancing resources. These metrics encompass application load balancers as well as the older elastic (now "Classic") load balancers. To discover all the available metrics, refer to the AWS documentation.

TABLE 15.1   Elastic load balancing metrics

Namespace	AWS/ELB
	AWS/ApplicationELB
	AWS/NetworkELB
Dimensions	LoadBalancerName: Name of the load balancer
Key metrics	• HealthyHostCount: Number of responding backend servers. Applies to target groups, so make sure to pay attention to the TargetGroup dimension.
	• RequestCount: Number of IPv4 and IPv6 requests. Filter by dimensions like LoadBalancer or LoadBalancer + TargetGroup.
	• ActiveConnectionCount: Total number of concurrent active connections from clients at the load balancer level.

Table 15.2 displays available Amazon EC2 metrics.

TABLE 15.2   Amazon EC2 metrics

Namespace AWS/EC2

Dimensions InstanceId: Identifier of a particular Amazon EC2 instance

InstanceType: Type of Amazon EC2 instance, such as t2.micro, m4.large

Key metrics ■   CPUUtilization: Percentage of vCPU utilization on the instance

■   DiskReadOps, DiskWriteOps: Number of operations per second on attached disk

■   DiskReadBytes, DiskWriteBytes: Volume of bytes to transfer on attached disk

■   NetworkIn, NetworkOut: Number of bytes sent or received by network interfaces

■   NetworkPacketsIn, NetworkPacketsOut: Number of packets sent or received by network interfaces

EC2 does not report memory utilization to CloudWatch. This is because memory is allocated in full to an instance by the underlying host. Memory consumption is visible only to the guest operating system (OS) of the instance. However, you can report memory utilization to Cloud-Watch using the CloudWatch agent.

Table 15.3 displays the AWS Auto Scaling Group metrics.

TABLE 15.3   AWS Auto Scaling Groups

Namespace AWS/AutoScaling

Dimensions AutoScalingGroupName: Name of the Auto Scaling Group

Key metrics ■   GroupMinSize, GroupMaxSize, GroupDesiredCapacity: Minimum, maximum, and desired size of the Auto Scaling Group

■   GroupInServiceInstances: Number of instances up and running in the Auto Scaling Group

■   GroupTotalInstances: Total number of instances in the Auto Scaling Group, regardless of state

Table 15.4 displays the Amazon Simple Storage Service (Amazon S3) metrics.

TABLE 15.4   Amazon S3 Metrics

Namespace	`AWS/S3`
Dimensions	`BucketName`: Name of a specific S3 bucket
	`StorageType`: The S3 storage class (STANDARD, STANDARD_IA, and GLACIER storage classes) of the bucket
Key metrics	▪ `BucketSizeBytes`: Total size, in bytes, of data stored in an S3 bucket
	▪ `NumberOfObjects`: Total number of objects stored in an S3 bucket
	▪ `AllRequests`: Total number of requests made to an S3 bucket

Table 15.5 displays the Amazon DynamoDB metrics.

TABLE 15.5   Amazon DynamoDB Metrics

Namespace	`AWS/DynamoDB`
Dimensions	`TableName`: Name of Amazon DynamoDB table
	`Operation`: Limits metrics to either a particular operation (`PutItem`, `GetItem`, `UpdateItem`, `DeleteItem`, `Query`, `Scan`, `BatchGetItem`) or `BatchWriteItem`
Key metrics	▪ `ConsumedReadCapacityUnits`, `ConsumedWriteCapacityUnits`: Total number of read and write capacity units consumed
	▪ `ThrottledRequests`: Requests to DynamoDB that exceed the provisioned throughput limits on a resource (such as a table or an index)
	▪ `ReadThrottleEvents`: Requests to DynamoDB that exceed the provisioned read capacity units for a table or a global secondary index
	▪ `WriteThrottleEvents`: Requests to DynamoDB that exceed the provisioned write capacity units for a table or a global secondary index
	▪ `ReturnedBytes`: Size of response returned in request
	▪ `ReturnedItemCount`: Number of items returned in request

Table 15.6 displays the Amazon API Gateway metrics.

TABLE 15.6 Amazon API Gateway Metrics

Namespace	AWS/ApiGateway
Dimensions	ApiName: Filters out metrics for a particular API
	ApiName, Method, Resource, Stage: Filters out metrics for a particular API, method, resource, and stage
	ApiName, Stage: Filters out metrics for a particular deployed stage of an API
Key metrics	▪ 4XXError: Number of HTTP 400 errors
	▪ 5XXError: Number of HTTP 500 errors
	▪ Latency: Time between when API Gateway receives a request and when it responds to the client

Table 15.7 displays the AWS Lambda metrics.

TABLE 15.7 AWS Lambda Metrics

Namespace	AWS/Lambda
Dimensions	FunctionName: Name of your AWS Lambda function
Key metrics	▪ Invocations: Number of executions of your Lambda function
	▪ Errors: Number of executions in which your Lambda function failed
	▪ Duration: Total time for each execution of your Lambda function

Table 15.8 displays the Amazon Simple Queue Service (Amazon SQS) metrics.

TABLE 15.8 Amazon SQS Metrics

Namespace	AWS/SQS
Dimensions	QueueName: Name of the Amazon SQS queue
Key metrics	▪ ApproximateNumberOfMessagesVisible: Number of messages currently available for retrieval
	▪ ApproximateNumberOfMessagesNotVisible: Number of messages currently being processed, or messages that are in-flight (Visibility Timeout is still active)
	▪ NumberOfMessagesDeleted: Number of messages that have been deleted

Amazon SQS does not report the total number of messages in the queue. You can find this value by adding `ApproximateNumberOf MessagesVisible` and `ApproximateNumberOfMessagesNotVisible`. As you can tell from these names, SQS message counts are approximations attempting to aggregate totals over all the nodes in a very distributed, dynamic system.

Table 15.9 displays the Amazon Simple Notification Service (Amazon SNS) metrics.

TABLE 15.9   Amazon SNS Metrics

Namespace	`AWS/SNS`
Dimensions	`TopicName`: Name of the Amazon SNS topic
Key metrics	• `NumberOfMessagesPublished`: Number of messages sent to an SNS topic • `NumberOfNotificationsDelivered`: Number of messages that were successfully delivered to subscribers • `NumberOfNotificationsFailed`: Number of messages that were unsuccessfully delivered to subscribers

Custom Metrics

In addition to the built-in metrics that AWS provides, CloudWatch supports custom metrics that you can publish from your systems. This section includes some commands that you can use to publish metrics to Amazon CloudWatch.

High-Resolution Metrics

With custom metrics, you have two options for resolution (the time interval between data points). You can use *standard resolution* for data points that have a granularity of one minute or *high resolution* for data points that have a granularity of less than one second. By default, most metrics delivered by AWS services have standard resolution.

Publishing Metrics

Amazon CloudWatch supports multiple options when you publish metrics. You can publish them as single data points, statistics sets, or zero values. Single data points are optimal for most telemetry. However, statistics sets are recommended for values with high-resolution data points in which you are sampling multiple times per minute. *Statistics sets* are sets of calculated values, such as minimum, maximum, average, sum, and sample count, as opposed to individual data points. The value zero is for applications that have periods of inactivity, where no data is sent. The following are some sample scripts using the AWS CLI to publish data points.

Using the AWS CLI to Publish Single Data Points

The following commands each publish a single data point under the Metric Name PageViewCount to the Namespace MyService with respective values and timestamps. You are not required to create a metric name or namespace. CloudWatch is aware of the data points to a metric or creates a new metric if it does not exist.

```
aws cloudwatch put-metric-data \
     --metric-name PageViewCount \
     --namespace MyService \
     --value 2 \
     --timestamp 2024-10-20T12:00:00.000Z

aws cloudwatch put-metric-data \
     --metric-name PageViewCount \
     --namespace MyService \
     --value 4 \
     --timestamp 2024-10-20T12:00:01.000Z

aws cloudwatch put-metric-data \
     --metric-name PageViewCount \
     --namespace MyService \
     --value 5 \
     --timestamp 2024-10-20T12:00:02.000Z
```

Using the AWS CLI to Publish Statistics Sets

The following command publishes a statistic set to the metric-name PageViewCount to the namespace MyService, with values for various statistics (Sum 11, Minimum 2, Maximum 5), and SampleCount 3 with the corresponding timestamp:

```
aws cloudwatch put-metric-data \
     --metric-name PageViewCount \
     --namespace MyService \
     --statistic-values Sum=11,Minimum=2,Maximum=5,SampleCount=3 \
     --timestamp 2024-10-14T12:00:00.000Z
```

Using the AWS CLI to Publish the Value 0

The following command publishes a single data point with the value 0 to the metric-name PageViewCount to the namespace MyService with the corresponding timestamp:

```
aws cloudwatch put-metric-data \
     --metric-name PageViewCount \
     --namespace MyService \
```

```
--value 0 \
--timestamp 2024-10-14T12:00:00.000Z
```

Publishing Metrics Using SDK Methods

In addition to using the CLI, CloudWatch supports the `PutMetricData` API command through its various SDKs. Here, we publish the aggregated statistic for `PageViewCount` using the Python library `boto3`:

```python
# Get a handle to the cloudwatch service
cloudwatch = boto3.client('cloudwatch')

# Put the metric data via python
response = cloudwatch.put_metric_data(
    Namespace='MyService',
    MetricData=[
        {
            'MetricName': 'PageViewCount',
            'Timestamp': datetime(2024, 10, 14, 12, 0, 0),
            'StatisticValues': {
                'SampleCount': 3,
                'Sum': 11,
                'Minimum': 2,
                'Maximum': 5
            }
        },
    ]
)
```

This is the right approach when publishing data from existing Python code, such as in a Python-based Lambda function.

Retrieving Statistics for a Metric

After you publish data to CloudWatch, you may want to retrieve statistics for a specified metric of a given resource.

Using the AWS CLI to Retrieve Statistics for a Metric

This command retrieves the `Sum`, `Max`, `Min`, `Average`, and `SampleCount` statistics for the `metric-name` `PageViewCount` to the `namespace` `MyService` with a `period` interval of `60` seconds between the `start-time` and `end-time`. This means that CloudWatch will aggregate data points in one-minute intervals to calculate statistics.

```
aws cloudwatch get-metric-statistics \
    --namespace MyService \
```

```
--metric-name PageViewCount \
--statistics "Sum" "Maximum" "Minimum" "Average" "SampleCount" \
--start-time 2024-10-20T12:00:00.000Z \
--end-time 2024-10-20T12:05:00.000Z \
--period 60
```

Example output from this command displays a single data point for the `Metric Page VieweCount`:

```
{
    "Datapoints": [
        {
            "SampleCount": 3.0,
            "Timestamp": "2024-10-20T12:00:00Z",
            "Average": 3.6666666666666665,
            "Maximum": 5.0,
            "Minimum": 2.0,
            "Sum": 11.0,
            "Unit": "None"
        }
    ],
    "Label": "PageViewCount"
}
```

CloudWatch Embedded Metric Format

AWS provides another method to ship metric data to CloudWatch—one that doesn't require any CLI, SDK, or API calls of any kind. Called the CloudWatch Embedded Metric Format, this approach involves nothing more than including specially formatted JSON embedded in the same logs that you send to CloudWatch normally.

The Embedded Metric Format includes two primary sections: one for metadata, and one for the metric data itself.

Structure of an Embedded Metric in CloudWatch

Let's examine the basic structure of a CloudWatch embedded metric and observe its required fields:

```
{
  "_aws": {
    "Timestamp": <timestamp>,
    "CloudWatchMetrics": [
      {
        "Namespace": "MyService",
        "Dimensions": [
```

```
        ["MyDimension"]
      ],
      "Metrics": [
        {
          "Name": "MyMetric",
          "Unit": "Count"
        }
      ]
    }
  ]
},
"MyDimension": "MyDimensionValue",
"MyMetric": 1
}
```

It's a little wordy, but it expresses everything CloudWatch needs to know to recognize your input.

The Metadata Section

First, the metadata section with key _aws contains two elements: Timestamp and CloudWatchMetrics. The former is just what it sounds like: a timestamp, required to be the number of milliseconds since the Unix epoch (i.e., January 1, 1970). This is a common timestamp format. In Python, you can fetch it using the time import:

```
int(time.time()*1000)
```

In JavaScript, it's even simpler:

```
new Date().valueOf()
```

After the timestamp is the CloudWatchMetrics section. This part of the JSON defines the schema of the metric whose value you'll define later in the code. As you can see from the example, we must define Namespace, Dimensions, and Metrics.

Note that you can give only one Namespace value and that while Dimensions is an array (of strings), it is not nested under Metrics; all dimensions you specify will be expected to apply to all metrics. If you need to write a different metric with different dimensions, you'll have to write another one of these JSON documents to your logs.

Finally, the Metrics section is an array of JSON objects containing two elements: Name and Unit, which, as you have learned, together define a single metric.

The Metric Section

On the same level as the _aws metadata section must come your dimensions and metric value, matching the values you described in the CloudWatchMetrics section earlier.

Embedded Metric Example

Let's see how we'd use this to set the `PageViewCount` metric we set earlier with the CLI and SDK:

```json
{
  "_aws": {
    "Timestamp": 1728907200000,
    "CloudWatchMetrics": [
      {
        "Namespace": "MyService",
        "Dimensions": [
          ["ServiceName"]
        ],
        "Metrics": [
          {
            "Name": "PageViewCount",
            "Unit": "Count"
          }
        ]
      }
    ]
  },
  "ServiceName": "MyService",
  "PageViewCount": {
    "SampleCount": 3,
    "Sum": 11,
    "Min": 2,
    "Max": 5
  }
}
```

By writing this to your logs as you would any other output heading to CloudWatch, you tell the CloudWatch service to grab this data and add new metric values. Writing logs to CloudWatch is detailed in the next section, "Amazon CloudWatch Logs."

 When using EKS or ECS, you must use the CloudWatch agent to send embedded metrics in your logs.

While it's good to understand the Embedded Metric Format, AWS has made it even easier to write this format by supplying libraries for many popular languages. For instance, Node.js programmers can use the npm package `aws-embedded-metrics` to write this format with a simplified function call.

Writing metrics in this way can be easier and less error-prone than other methods. Unlike making a synchronous API call to `PutMetricData`, which itself may need error handling, you can ship plaintext out in an asynchronous, fire-and-forget approach. For complete documentation of the Embedded Metric Format, visit the following URL:

```
https://docs.aws.amazon.com/AmazonCloudWatch/latest/monitoring/
CloudWatch_Embedded_Metric_Format_Specification.html
```

Amazon CloudWatch Logs

Though most commercial standard applications already produce some form of logging, most modern applications are deployed in distributed or service-oriented architectures. Collecting and processing these logs can be a challenge as a system grows and expands across multiple regions. Centralized logging using CloudWatch Logs can overcome this challenge. With CloudWatch Logs, you can set up a central log storage location to ingest and process logs at scale.

Log Aggregation

Setting up centralized logging with CloudWatch Logs is a straightforward process. The first step is to install and configure the CloudWatch agent, which is used to collect custom logs and metrics from EC2 instances or on-premises servers. You can choose which log files you want to ingest by pointing to the locations using a JSON configuration file. The second step is to configure AWS Identity and Access Management (IAM) roles or users to grant permission for the agent to publish logs into CloudWatch. In addition to the CloudWatch agent, you can send metrics to CloudWatch using the AWS CLI, AWS SDK, or AWS API.

Because you are collecting logs from multiple sources, CloudWatch organizes your logs into three conceptual levels: groups, streams, and events.

Log Groups

A *log group* is a collection of log streams. For example, if you have a service consisting of a cluster of multiple machines, a log group would aggregate the logs from each of the individual instances.

Log Streams

A *log stream* is a sequence of log events, such as a single log file from one of your instances.

Log Events

A *log event* is a record of some activity from either an application, process, or service. This is analogous to a single line in a log file.

CloudWatch stores log events based on your retention settings, which are assigned at the log group. The default configuration is to store log data in CloudWatch Logs indefinitely. You are charged for any data stored in CloudWatch Logs in addition to data transferred out of the service. You can export CloudWatch Logs to Amazon S3 for long-term storage, which is valuable when regulations require long-term log retention. Long-term retention can be combined with S3 life cycle policies to archive data to S3 Glacier for additional cost savings.

Log Searches

With centralized logging on CloudWatch Logs, you do not need to search through hundreds of individual servers to find a problem. After logs are ingested into CloudWatch Logs, you can search for logs through a central location using metric filters.

Metric Filters

A *metric filter* is a text pattern used to parse log data for specific events. As an example, consider the logs in Table 15.10.

TABLE 15.10 Example logs

Line	Log event
1	[ERROR] Caught IllegalArgumentException
2	[ERROR] Unhandled Exception
3	Another message
4	Exiting with ERRORCODE: -1
5	[WARN] Some message
6	[ERROR][WARN] Some other message

To look for occurrences of the ERROR event, you use ERROR as your metric filter, as illustrated in Table 15.11. CloudWatch will search for that term across the logs.

TABLE 15.11 Example metric filters

Metric filter	Description
" "	Matches all log events.
"ERROR"	Matches logs events containing the term ERROR. Based on the events in the example log in Table 15.10, this metric filter would find lines 1–3 and 6.
"ERROR" – "EXITING"	Matches any log events containing the term ERROR minus any events containing the word EXITING. Based on the events in the example log in Table 15.10, this metric filter would find lines 1, 2, and 6.

TABLE 15.11 Example metric filters *(continued)*

Metric filter	Description
"ERROR Exceptions"	Matches log events containing both terms ERROR and Exceptions. This filter is an AND function.
	Based on the events in the example log in Table 15.10, this metric filter would find lines 1 and 2.
"?ERROR ?WARN"	Matches log events containing either ERROR or WARN. This filter is an OR function.
	Based on the event in the example log in Table 15.10, this metric filter would find lines 1, 2, 4, and 6.

If your logs are structured in JSON format, Amazon CloudWatch can also filter object properties. Consider the following example JSON log.

Example AWS CloudTrail JSON Log Event

```
{
    "user": {
        "id": 1,
        "email": "Admin@example.com"
    },
    "users": [
        {
        "id": 2,
        "email": "John.Doe@example.com"
        },
        {
        "id": 3,
        "email": "Jane.Doe@example.com"
        }
    ],
    "actions": [
        "GET",
        "PUT",
        "DELETE"
    ],
    "coordinates": [
        [0, 1, 2],
        [4, 5, 6],
        [7, 8, 9]
    ]
}
```

You can create a metric filter that selects and compares certain properties of this event, as shown in Table 15.12.

TABLE 15.12   Example JSON metric filters

JSON metric filter	Description
{ ($.user.id = 1) && ($.users[0].email = "John.Doe@ example.com") }	Check that the property user.id equals 1 and the first user's email is John.Doe@example.com. The preceding log event would be returned.
{ ($.user.id = 2 && $.users[0]. email = "John.Doe@exmple.com") || $.actions[2] = "GET" }	Check that the property user.id equals 2 and the first user's email is John.Doe@example.com or the second action is GET. The preceding example would not be returned because the second action is PUT, not GET.

This format is similar to JSON-querying formats like JSONPath, but is actually a proprietary syntax of AWS's creation. For a complete reference on syntax for filtering CloudWatch logs via pattern matching, regular expression, JSON parsing, and more, visit:

https://docs.aws.amazon.com/AmazonCloudWatch/latest/logs/
FilterAndPatternSyntax.html

Log Processing

Instead of having to write additional code to add monitoring to your application, Cloud-Watch can process logs that you already generate and provide valuable metrics. Using the example from the previous section, the same metric filter can be used to generate metrics corresponding to the number of occurrences of the term ERROR in your logs.

Amazon CloudWatch Alarms

After data points are established in CloudWatch, either as metrics or as logs (from which you generate metrics), you can set *alarms* to monitor your metrics and trigger actions in response to changes in state. CloudWatch alarms have three possible states: OK, ALARM, and INSUFFICIENT_DATA. Table 15.13 defines each alarm state.

TABLE 15.13   Alarm states

State	Description
OK	The metric or expression is within the defined threshold.
ALARM	The metric or expression is outside of the defined threshold.
INSUFFICIENT_DATA	The alarm has just started, the metric is not available, or not enough data is available for the metric to determine the alarm state.

An ALARM state may not indicate a problem. It means that the given metric is outside the defined threshold. For example, you have two alarms for Auto Scaling Groups: one for high CPU utilization and one for low CPU utilization. During normal use, both alarms should be OK, indicating that you have adequate capacity to handle the current workload. If your workload changes, the high CPU utilization metric threshold may be breached, sending the corresponding alarm into the ALARM state. With an Auto Scaling Group, the alarm's state change triggers a scale-out event, adding capacity to your infrastructure. An ALARM state for low CPU utilization can be configured to trigger the opposite: a reduction in instances.

Using CloudWatch Alarms

When you create an alarm, specify three settings that determine when the alarm should change states: the threshold, period, and data points on which you want to notify, as described in Table 15.14.

TABLE 15.14   Alarm settings

Setting	Description
Period	The length of time (in seconds) to evaluate the metric or expression to create each individual data point for an alarm. If you choose one minute as the period, there is one data point every minute.
Evaluation Period	The number of the most recent periods, or data points, to evaluate when determining alarm state.
Data Points to Alarm	The number of data points within the evaluation period that must breach the specified threshold to cause the alarm to go to the ALARM state. These data points do not have to be consecutive.

Figure 15.3 illustrates how an alarm works based on configuration settings.

The figure illustrates a threshold configured to the value 3 (the horizontal line at value 3), a period set to 3, and a series of captured CloudWatch data points (the graph line). Vertical lines indicate the difference of each data point from the threshold. Notice how the settings drive the alarm occurrence. Even though the data points breach the threshold after the third period, it is not sustained for the required three periods to be in an ALARM state. Only after the fifth period would the alarm change to an ALARM state (the upper threshold is breached for three periods). Between the fifth and sixth period, the data points drop below the threshold. However, because the state has not dropped below the threshold for three periods, it does not change to an OK state until the eighth period. It remains in the OK state past the ninth period because three consecutive periods exceeding the threshold are necessary for the alarm state to change.

FIGURE 15.3 Alarm evaluation

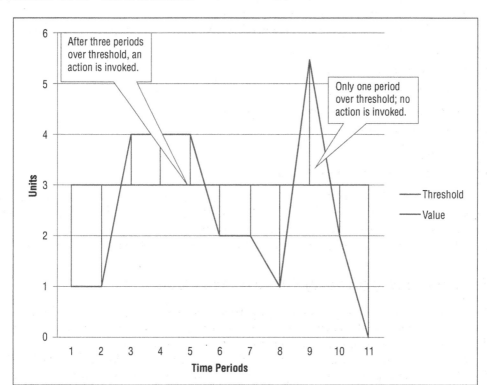

Alarms can trigger EC2 actions and EC2 Auto Scaling actions. CloudWatch can leverage SNS or SQS for alarm state notifications, both of which provide numerous integrations with other AWS services.

Exercise caution when creating email notifications for alarms in your environment. This can lead to many unnecessary emails to you or your team. Ultimately, these notifications get filtered as spam or result in "notification fatigue." Evaluate your alarms and the metrics you are monitoring to determine whether notifications are necessary. If they are only status updates, set notifications sparingly.

Triggering Actions from CloudWatch Alarms

CloudWatch allows you to trigger a variety of actions when a CloudWatch alarm enters the ALARM state.

For instance, EC2 Auto Scaling Groups (ASGs) are closely integrated with CloudWatch alarms. From the Auto Scaling Group configuration screen, you can set thresholds for CloudWatch metrics that trigger scale-in and scale-out events on your ASG. You might set a trigger to add new instances whenever CloudWatch detects high CPU usage for a sustained period of time and have it remove instances when CPU usage subsides.

CloudWatch alarms integrate with many other AWS services. In response to a CloudWatch alarm, you may:

- Invoke a Lambda function
- Send an SNS message
- Trigger an EC2 action such as a reboot or shutdown
- Run a Step Function
- Scale an ECS Task
- Take actions with AWS Systems Manager

With CloudWatch alarms monitoring the state of compute resources or even custom metrics submitted by your application code, AWS provides a powerful way to take action based on the state of your system. Scale services, attempt self-healing, or send notifications; you have the power to automate operations tasks for any metric that CloudWatch can track.

EventBridge (formerly CloudWatch Events)

EventBridge, formerly known as CloudWatch Events, is a full-featured event bus designed to facilitate connections between AWS services, SaaS applications, and your own custom-developed apps by routing JSON-based notifications of events between them.

While CloudWatch alarms let you take action when metric thresholds are breached, and CloudTrail (described later in this chapter) allows for automated responses when someone makes an AWS API call, these services alone do not provide a comprehensive set of tools for acting on events. Whereas AWS has long offered event-driven integrations on some specific services (such the ability to trigger a Lambda based on an S3 PUT event), EventBridge gives you the ability to trigger actions on almost anything that happens inside—and outside—your account.

Event-Driven Architecture

Many traditional service and data integration approaches rely on batch processing. For instance, you might write a job that queries your customer database every night, bundles up each one's contact information, and syncs that information to a marketing application. Batch processing can be effective, but it is not efficient; you are always sending all the data, all the time. The goal of such a batch process is to make sure that changes in the source system are reflected in the target, so why not design a system that reacts only to changes?

Likewise, what if you could react to more than just data changes? We have talked about the benefits of loosely coupled, asynchronous application patterns. What if we could invoke a Lambda when an order ships, or scale up an ECS service right before a marketing email goes out?

This approach is *event-driven architecture*: application design oriented not around batch data movement, but around reacting to events as they happen. This is the kind of application-building that EventBridge was made to facilitate.

At the heart of EventBridge is the concept of the *event bus*. An event bus is a stream of data objects—in this case, JSON objects—that describe events. These events can be placed by any AWS service, internal application, or, if you allow, a third party, such as a SaaS vendor. Then, events may be read asynchronously by many consumers that take some action.

Figure 15.4 depicts the EventBridge event bus. Note that multiple rules may match a single JSON event, and vice versa.

FIGURE 15.4   Event-driven architecture in EventBridge

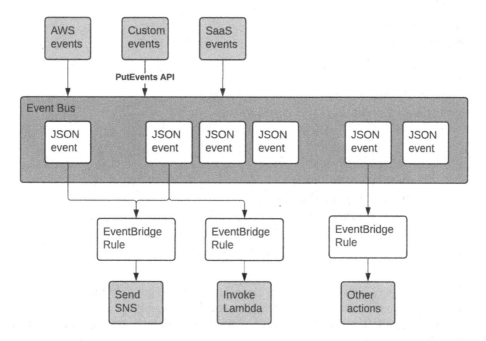

You pay a small amount for events whenever they match a rule and take some action. This event-driven architecture allows you to automate responses to almost any action that takes place in AWS.

Event Buses

AWS provides a default event bus on which it publishes many native events that occur in your account: S3 changes, Lambda invocation events, CodePipeline status events, and more.

You can add events to this bus or create your own custom buses.

Where Do Events Come From?

In addition to native events, any code with IAM permissions on the EventBridge PutEvents API may place a JSON event on a bus, as shown in this Python example:

```python
import boto3
import json

# Initialize a boto3 client for EventBridge
eventbridge_client = boto3.client('events')

# Create the custom event payload
my_event = {
    "key": "value",
    "key2": "value2",
}

# Use the PutEvents API to send the custom event
response = eventbridge_client.put_events(
    Entries=[
        {
            'Source': 'MyApp',
            'DetailType': 'MyCustomEvent',
            'Detail': json.dumps(my_event),
            'EventBusName': 'default',
        }
    ]
)
```

This code places a custom event on the event bus called `default`. `DetailType` and `Source` are custom metadata label for the event—fields that can be used by EventBridge rules to match against. If successful, the `put_events` call will receive a response similar to this, showing an event ID:

```python
{
    'FailedEntryCount': 0,
    'Entries': [
        {
            'EventId': '12345678-1234-5678-9123-abcdef123456'
        }
    ]
}
```

Other sources for EventBridge events can be SaaS integrations like those offered by Datadog or Zendesk. After configuring the connection in the AWS console, these partners are able to send events from your SaaS subscription directly to EventBridge. For instance, with Zendesk, you can react directly to customer messages with automations in your AWS account, such as a Step Function or Lambda.

Events may also be added via webhooks that you can set up in EventBridge for external users or apps. The third party can perform an HTTP POST to this webhook to send JSON events to your bus.

Finally, EventBridge Pipes (discussed in a moment) can make the bus a target for events.

Event Details

Events are always JSON documents. Events stay on the bus about 24 hours and are then deleted; any rule that matches an event at its creation time will fire. Custom events can be up to 256 KB in size.

EventBridge Rules

EventBridge rules define consumers for events that appear on the event bus. These rules define a pattern to match against events in the bus along with a trigger action or destination for the event. These targets include the following:

- Lambda functions
- CodePipeline actions
- API Gateway (to send events outside your account)
- Amazon SNS
- Amazon SQS
- EC2 Actions
- Step Functions
- Systems Manager
- Another event bus

There are many more options. For the complete list, see `https://docs.aws.amazon .com/eventbridge/latest/userguide/eb-targets.html`.

By itself, an EventBridge rule does nothing. Only once an event appears that matches the rule's pattern will the rule trigger its action. Multiple rules can, and often do, match a single event. This allows EventBridge to provide a one-to-many or many-to-many integration between rule sources and consumers. We previously discussed how SNS and SQS can work together to form a "fan-out" pattern; EventBridge takes that a step further, with less infrastructure to manage.

Event Patterns

With EventBridge rules, you specify a pattern that matches events as they appear. These patterns are written in JSON. In the following example, the pattern looks for S3 object creation events of type PDF placed in a bucket called my-bucket.

```
{
  "source": ["aws.s3"],
  "detail-type": ["Object Created"],
  "detail": {
    "bucket": {
      "name": ["my-bucket"]
    },
    "requestParameters": {
      "key": [{
        "suffix": ".pdf"
      }]
    }
  }
}
```

To understand these patterns and familiarize yourself with the event structure of AWS-native events, see AWS documentation or read the upcoming section, "EventBridge Schema Registry." In that service, AWS provides a catalog for your custom event patterns, as well as its own.

Event Matching and Retries

When an event hits the bus, all rules are evaluated at once, and the actions for any matching rules are executed. If a rule's action cannot be completed successfully (e.g., a Lambda invocation times out), EventBridge will attempt to retry the delivery up to 185 times using an exponential backoff strategy to avoid overwhelming the destination. After exhausting these retry attempts, EventBridge can then route the event to a dead-letter SQS queue for later inspection.

Note that although events may remain on the bus up to 24 hours, new rules never match past events; they only begin to be triggered by events that are placed on the bus after they are created.

EventBridge Pipes

EventBridge Pipes are a point-to-point integration between an event source and a target. A pipe is an asynchronous, fire-and-forget automatic conveyance of events to targets. In contrast to using SQS, an EventBridge Pipe does not require a sender to put data onto a queue; rather, the pipe is configured to scan for events in your AWS account and send them immediately to a destination. The pipe may apply filtering before deciding which events to convey, and it may optionally enrich the data by calling out to an API.

Among the destinations available to pipes are EventBridge buses, giving you a way to add events to a bus after enriching it with external data. Because of this feature, pipes are great for adding events from AWS sources that don't natively publish to EventBridge, such as SQS queues and DynamoDB streams.

Input Transformations

EventBridge pipes allow you to define JSONPath-esque queries that transform the JSON in place. These transforms can change the structure of a document or add details using natively available variables such as the Pipe ID. If you want to add more external data to an object, see the upcoming section, "Event Enrichment." For full details on EventBridge Pipes input transformation syntax, visit:

https://docs.aws.amazon.com/eventbridge/latest/userguide/eb-pipes-input-transformation.html

Event Filters

EventBridge pipes also provide a syntax for filtering events that come from your source so that you can take some, but not all, of your intended events. This option can allow you to, for instance, split customer orders that appear in a DynamoDB table into multiple streams that you place on distinct event buses. In this example, we filter incoming DynamoDB events based on the category field of the record:

```
{
  "eventName": ["INSERT", "MODIFY"],
  "dynamodb": {
    "NewImage": {
      "category": {
        "S": ["electronics"]
      }
    }
  }
}
```

Complete syntax for pipe event filters is available here:

https://docs.aws.amazon.com/eventbridge/latest/userguide/eb-pipes-event-filtering.html

Event Enrichment

Event enrichment in EventBridge pipes involves sending event JSON objects to an external source, then receiving back a transformed version of that object before passing it to its destination. For instance, you might configure a pipe to consume product order events from an SQS queue, then call an enrichment service that calculates how many customer loyalty points should be attached to the purchase.

Enrichment can be done by passing the event to multiple services, including Lambda functions, external APIs, Amazon API Gateway APIs, and Step Functions (Express Workflows only). These external services are then responsible for returning the transformed JSON object.

EventBridge Schedules

Not every data or service integration can rely on a triggering event; sometimes you just need to schedule a job. *EventBridge schedules* allow you to create one-time or recurring schedules, defined using either explicit times or with the Unix-based `cron` format.

The target can be any AWS API at all, giving you many powerful options to schedule actions in your account. A very common scenario is to schedule a recurring Lambda function execution, but you can take any action allowed by the API, such as deleting S3 objects, writing to a DynamoDB table, or kicking off a CodeBuild project. To help you get started, AWS offers many prebuilt templates for invoking actions.

EventBridge Schema Registry

The EventBridge Schema Registry lets you browse the event structure for any AWS-native event. In addition, it can automatically detect the schema of custom events you have placed on the bus (or you can manually write the schema yourself).

This registry not only creates a central repository you can share with developers to show what events are available, but it goes a significant step further by allowing you to download code bindings for a schema in Python, Java, TypeScript, or Go—code libraries that allow you to interact with registry event types as if they were native code objects, rather than pure JSON. This enables your code to do type-checking and other convenience measures to reduce errors in your EventBridge-interacting code.

Contrast with Other AWS Services

EventBridge has a few things in common with AWS's most long-lived service: Simple Queue Service (SQS). Let's look at some of the distinctions that make EventBridge a more sophisticated, cleaner abstraction—and a few ways in which SQS may be preferable for some use cases.

First, realize that SQS requires you to both create a queue and make explicit pushes of data to it. Then, consumers must explicitly pull messages from those queues to act on them. With EventBridge, the default bus already publishes many AWS-native events, and you need only to start writing rules to send them to targets.

Second, recall that creating a "fan-out" publisher/subscriber pattern requires an SNS topic and many SQS queues, each of which needs IAM permissions for the consumer. EventBridge achieves the same one-to-many pattern by default, since events can be delivered to multiple consumers at once.

Third, SQS acts as a "dumb" pipe, offering no ability to alter the messages that run on its queues, but EventBridge pipes can filter and enrich data, giving them more control over the contents of messages.

However, SQS queues do have one significant advantage over EventBridge: they queue messages. With SQS, if a consumer goes offline, messages on the queue will remain and be consumable up to a configurable 14 days. With EventBridge, if a consumer is offline more than 24 hours, the event will be missed.

Finally, you may wonder if EventBridge obviates the need for previously existing event integrations such as those enabling S3 events to trigger Lambda functions directly. In some ways, yes, because most use cases covered by this older integration style will work in Event-Bridge, and having a unified design pattern (i.e., the event bus) underpinning many different integrations is desirable. However, direct integration between S3 and Lambda does skip the asynchronous EventBridge bus, resulting in lower latency overall. If speed is absolutely critical, fall back to the more direct integration; otherwise, go with EventBridge.

Amazon Logs Anomaly Detection

Your job as a cloud developer is to think ahead, creating metrics and alarms for those states that are most relevant to the proper functioning of your application.

But what about the situations you can't anticipate? It would be great to be able to watch your logs all the time, taking note of their typical patterns and investigating only when unusual activity takes place. Unfortunately, the volume of log data in modern applications makes this untenable; fortunately, this kind of monitoring is very well suited to machine learning algorithms.

Amazon Logs Anomaly Detection can take a log group and analyze the past two weeks of output, creating a machine learning model that understands its typical patterns of behavior. You can then set an evaluation frequency from 5 minutes to 60 minutes. Each Anomaly Detector you create looks at your live logs on this interval and matches the current output against the established historical patterns. If something looks amiss, you can set a Cloud-Watch alarm to notify you or take action.

CloudWatch Anomaly Detection is best used with log groups whose logs present a fairly consistent set of recognizable patterns. Web logs from servers like nginx or Apache work well, as do logs from web frameworks like Django or Rails. CloudWatch Insights, the query engine for CloudWatch described later in this chapter, includes an option to view detected patterns in your logs. AWS recommends Anomaly Detection as suitable for any log that exhibits fewer than 300 distinct patterns. This tool can be a good way to determine ahead of time if Anomaly Detection will work for your use case.

Amazon CloudWatch Dashboards

Amazon CloudWatch offers a convenient way to observe operational metrics for all your applications. *CloudWatch dashboards* are customizable pages in the Amazon CloudWatch console that you can use to monitor resources in a single view (see Figure 15.5).

CloudWatch dashboards provide customizable status pages in the CloudWatch console. These status pages can be used to monitor resources across multiple regions and on-premises in a consolidated view using widgets. Each widget can be customized to present information in CloudWatch in a user-friendly way so that educated decisions can be made based on the current status of your system.

FIGURE 15.5   Amazon CloudWatch dashboard

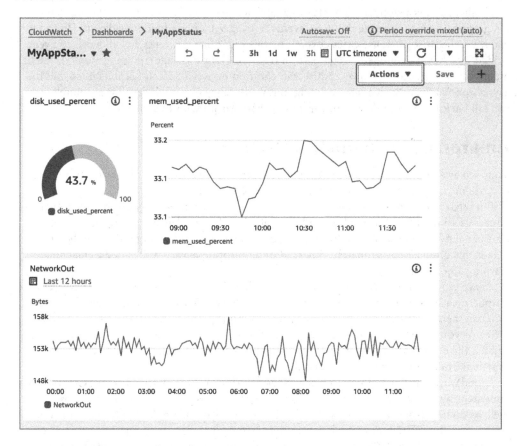

CloudWatch Logs Insights

CloudWatch Logs Insights offers AWS users a way to query, filter, aggregate, and join log data from one or more logs using a query language. CloudWatch discovers recognizable fields in many log types, making them available as individual columns that your query can reference in the returned data, formulas, or conditional logic. In Figure 15.6, you can see that CloudWatch has discovered multiple fields from VPC flow logs.

With the fields, you use the CloudWatch Logs Insights query language to drill into your logs and visualize the results. Here's a basic example, in which the first line names a set of the discovered fields to return, the second specifies a sort column and sorting order, and the last limits the number of returned records:

```
fields @timestamp, @srcAddr, @dstAddr, @action
| sort @timestamp desc
| limit 20
```

FIGURE 15.6   VPC flow logs analyzed by CloudWatch Insights

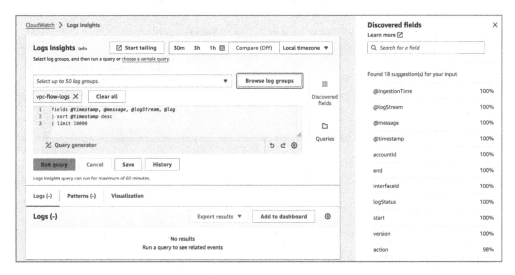

Pipe characters separate clauses (i.e., commands) in Insights queries. The @ sign is used to denote discovered fields. You may also show Insights how to recognize fields it has not automatically discovered using the parse command. This command, unfortunately, does not result in a persistent mapping, but allows you to reference parsed fields only within the query itself. For more flexibility on mapping fields, see the upcoming section "Amazon Open-Search." To understand parse, consider the following:

```
INFO 2024-08-18 12:34:56 - User: john.doe logged in
INFO 2024-08-18 12:34:56 - User: sam.jones logged in
```

Let's say you want to capture the username value john.doe, but username was not discovered by CloudWatch insights. The following query uses the asterisk as a wildcard to capture the characters between User: and logged in. The as username directive allows you to reference this parsed field and filter for any lines where a specific user has logged in.

```
fields @message
| parse @message "User: * logged in" as username
| filter username = "sally.smith"
| display @message
```

There is much more to the parse command; to learn more, visit:

https://docs.aws.amazon.com/AmazonCloudWatch/latest/logs/CWL_
QuerySyntax-Parse.html

Insights also allows us to filter the results on any of the known columns. For instance, if you wanted to look for any traffic coming from a certain host that is not HTTPS, Figure 15.7 demonstrates how to filter the results by a certain source IP and look for records where the destination port is any value other than the HTTPS port 443.

FIGURE 15.7   Querying VPC flow logs with CloudWatch Insights

Going further, Insights allows you to query aggregated values, as in this query, where we sum the number of bytes transferred over HTTP port 80:

```
fields @timestamp, srcPort, dstPort, bytes, action
| filter dstPort = 80 and action = "ACCEPT"
```

```
| stats sum(bytes) as totalBytes by srcAddr
| sort totalBytes desc
```

For a complete reference to the Insights query language, visit:

https://docs.aws.amazon.com/AmazonCloudWatch/latest/logs/
CWL_QuerySyntax.html

Any Insights query or visualization can be added to a CloudWatch dashboard, giving you wide flexibility to define ways to understand your AWS account data and monitor changes over time.

CloudWatch Synthetics

Developers integrate quality checks into their application at many stages of the software development life cycle. Unit tests that run during the development phase can catch errors early; integration tests and user acceptance testing help identity problems before deployment; and at runtime, CloudWatch metrics and alarms can alert you to issues before users encounter them.

However, there is another class of testing and monitoring that depends on users interactively engaging with your application through a web browser. These kinds of tests typically require a user to navigate to your application, sometimes log in, and perform actions through the user interface. This kind of test can be great for regression-testing the user experience after an update or evaluating an application's overall availability and responsiveness.

Synthetic tests use a headless web browser to emulate just those kinds of human interactions. Using a software library like Selenium or Puppeteer, developers can define actions that can traverse a UI, enter text, click on page elements, and more.

CloudWatch Synthetics is just such a system. Depending on your choice of Node.js or Python, CloudWatch Synthetics uses Google-developed Puppeteer or Selenium, respectively. In either case, scripts made using CloudWatch synthetics use a chromium-based browser to perform actions much like a human would. These tests, called "canaries" (not to be confused with canary deployment styles in CodeDeploy or Lambda), can simulate straightforward website visits or execute a series of steps that a user may take, such as registering or purchasing a product.

Types of CloudWatch Synthetics

CloudWatch Synthetics offers several different blueprints of canary tests for different use cases. Each one comes with a script that you can manually edit, if you so choose. Each Synthetic also has a few standard options, which enable you to:

- Trigger an SNS message or a CloudWatch alarm
- Run inside a VPC to access private resources
- Set a run schedule with your desired frequency
- Take screenshots of what the canary sees while running

You'll configure an S3 bucket to store artifacts such as screenshots taken by your scripts. You can also enable active tracing courtesy of X-Ray, a service discussed later in this chapter.

Let's take a look at the blueprints offered by CloudWatch Synthetics.

Heartbeat Monitoring

One of the first and most essential things that a synthetic test can assess is application uptime. After all, if your website is inaccessible, nothing else matters! Sometimes, your infrastructure alarms can tell you when you app is inaccessible, but not every reason for downtime can be detected by resource metrics. Only a front-end user can tell you for sure. To make sure you know about downtime before your users, AWS offers the simplest form of CloudWatch Synthetic canaries: the heartbeat monitor.

This canary takes up to five individual URLs and checks to see if they are responsive by performing an HTTP GET. If any of the sites is unreachable, you can trigger a CloudWatch Alarm or send an SNS message directly from Synthetics.

API Canary

API canaries work similarly to heartbeat monitors in that they are based on HTTP requests made to a certain endpoint. However, API canaries have some additional features: they can do POST as well as GET requests, they can carry an HTTP body payload and parameters, and they can be optionally ordered into a sequence of multiple API calls that is tested all at once.

When testing APIs built in AWS API Gateway, Synthetics API canaries offer a few additional configuration options: primarily, the ability to upload your API spec in Swagger 3.0 format, which simplifies the process of defining how to call your API endpoints.

If your organization runs private APIs that have no public accessibility, enable VPC traffic to monitor them without the need to expose them to external traffic.

Broken Link Checker

This option isn't about checking your application for accessibility; rather, it's about making sure that all the links on your site work. It's a fact of Internet life that links, especially those to external sites, occasionally go out of date as the content is moved or the hosting goes offline. The Broken Link Checker canary crawls your target website and gathers information about broken links so that you can fix them, creating a better experience for your web users.

Canary Recorder

This option requires you to install the AWS Synthetics Recorder Chrome Plugin. Once installed, you can start a recording, load a website, and have the plug-in record your inputs, button clicks, and page loads. This activity is captured and transformed into a Synthetics script. As of this writing, only Puppeteer scripts are supported by the recorder plug-in. This approach can be an excellent way to engage end users in creating tests that developer or cloud operations team members can translate into automated, recurring tests.

GUI Workflow Builder

The GUI Workflow Builder offers a level of abstraction for creating tests that is not quite as easy as the Chrome Plugin, but is still less hands-on than writing Python or Node.js code directly. This tool lets you define actions like *click* or *input text* with drop-down menus, targeting specific page elements with a syntax that can target HTML tags using standard DOM (Domain Object Model) selectors like IDs and CSS classes.

Visual Monitor

The last blueprint on offer is a bit different from the others. Rather than running a script and verifying that the steps can be completed fully, the Visual Monitor takes screenshots and compares them to ones taken during the last completed run. If the screenshot differs by more than the percentage you specify, the canary will fail, resulting in whatever action you have configured to occur, such as triggering a CloudWatch alarm.

Why might this be useful? There may be cases where you want to test for the existence of page elements that are hard to verify with mouse and keyboard inputs. For instance, maybe you want to make sure that images load properly, or that recent CSS changes have not overly impacted the visual layout of the page. The Visual Monitor can do this for you.

Additional Notes on Synthetics

CloudWatch Synthetics are a great addition to a robust monitoring solution. There are just a few additional items to keep in mind. First, canaries only work over HTTPS; you will not be able to test HTTP endpoints. Second, canaries output their own CloudWatch metrics, so you can keep track of their results on a historical basis, and even set up alarms should they deviate from expectations over time. Finally, if your Selenium or Puppeteer script requires the use of secret values such as passwords, upload it to S3 first as a zip file, which Synthetics can then reference. Pasting scripts with secrets directly to CloudWatch may result in those secrets leaking through CloudTrail. As always with sensitive values, it's best to write scripts that fetch secrets at runtime from AWS Secrets Manager.

Amazon OpenSearch

For developers to get the most out of their logs, it is often not enough to simply have them available to read and search for output. This so-called "log diving" can be a tedious and fruitless endeavor without tools to make it easier to search and derive insights from your data.

A popular way for developers to store and analyze log data is known as the *ELK stack*. This acronym refers to the combination of three open source technologies: Elasticsearch, Logstash, and Kibana. Working together, these products can ingest logs from a wide variety of sources, recognize the structure of many common log formats, and provide developers with deep query capabilities and dashboards.

Understanding the ELK Stack

The three parts of the ELK stack are Elasticsearch, Logstash, and Kibana.

Elasticsearch is a distributed, highly scalable search engine based on Apache Lucene. It stores JSON documents, which it indexes, identifying document structure and important fields to enable deep search and filtering functionality. In addition to powering the search features of many websites, Elasticsearch can act as the foundation of data search and analytics for developers.

Logstash is an ingestion engine, offering adapters to get many popular data sources into Elasticsearch without the need for custom code. Logstash has plug-ins for a wide variety of sources, such as Apache or nginx web logs, database data via JDBC, logs in the log4j format, data from SQS, and Salesforce data, just to name a few.

Logstash integrates tightly with Elasticsearch but can be used to feed other destinations; for instance, running the Logstash service on an EC2 instance can be a good way to get application logs into CloudWatch. At the same time, other AWS services like Kinesis Data Firehose can be used to send data into Elasticsearch.

Kibana is the analysis and visualization layer of the ELK stack. It provides a web interface for users to query logs and create custom dashboards that surface the most important information for their applications.

Originally providing managed versions of these open source apps, AWS now offers this same set of tools in a service collectively called *OpenSearch*.

History of OpenSearch

In 2015, AWS launched Amazon Elasticsearch Service, a managed version of Elasticsearch. Like other managed services on AWS (such as Amazon MQ), Elasticsearch Service offered a popular open source product as a complete, plug-and-play option. Users could spin up an instance, configure it, and start using it in seconds; AWS took care of the uptime, scaling, and patching.

In early 2021, Elastic NV, the company behind Elasticsearch, decided to change the terms under which the product could be licensed. In response, Amazon created a fork of both Elasticsearch and Kibana, which it named OpenSearch and OpenSearch Dashboards, respectively. This split took place when both open source products were on version 7.10.2. As a result, Amazon's newly renamed OpenSearch Service offers managed Elasticsearch up to version 7.10.2, after which newer launches run on Amazon's forked version.

In 2024, AWS completed its suite of ELK stack alternatives with the release of Amazon OpenSearch Ingestion, a managed service that replaces the need to use a tool like Logstash to pull data into the OpenSearch system.

OpenSearch Basics

To start using OpenSearch, you need a compute layer. This is the infrastructure on which your OpenSearch *indexes* (the basic unit of an OpenSearch deployment) will run. Like ECS, OpenSearch allows you a choice of a managed cluster, consisting of EC2 instances run by AWS in your account, or a serverless option, in which servers are fully managed behind the scenes, without you seeing them. In the former setup, indexes belong to *domains*; in the latter, they are members of a *collection*.

Neither configuration requires you to "bring your own" instances. In an EC2 cluster, OpenSearch asks you for parameters on the size and scale of the cluster, then spins up and manages an Auto Scaling Group to accommodate. A managed domain gives you more control over how the cluster functions. In a serverless setup, you manage nothing on the compute layer; your collections run on AWS-managed, behind-the-scenes compute that automatically scales in response to demand.

OpenSearch Serverless is billed in *OpenSearch Compute Units* (OCUs). An OCU is a logical unit of compute resources needed to run a query on your data. Data indexing and search are calculated separately.

Unlike other services designated "serverless" in AWS, OpenSearch Serverless does not scale to zero when there is no activity. Instead, you will always pay a minimum ongoing rate after the service is spun up. Production instances bill a minimum of two OCUs/hour; "dev" sized services bill at 0.5 OCUs/hour. As of this writing, an OCU-hour costs 24 cents. You are also billed for the storage, which lives in S3 and charges a more modest 2.4 cents per gigabyte per month. OpenSearch emits CloudWatch metrics on OCUs so that you can monitor, observe trends, and alert on your OCU usage.

The underlying storage for OpenSearch is based on EBS volumes, where OpenSearch keeps its active, or "hot" data. To help you lower costs with minimal impact on performance, AWS offers a tier of storage called Ultrawarm. Whereas "warm" storage typically refers to storage that is not active but is kept ready to be swapped in for a live service in the event of a failure, Ultrawarm storage is actively used as part of the live OpenSearch infrastructure. However, by using cheaper S3 bucket storage and caching strategies, it lowers your overall cost.

OpenSearch Serverless does not scale to zero when there is no activity, but always bills you for a baseline amount of compute per hour. Keep this behavior in mind when budgeting for OpenSearch.

OpenSearch Ingestion

Amazon OpenSearch Ingestion simplifies the process of streaming and ingesting data into OpenSearch, eliminating the need for other tools like Logstash. It is designed to handle high-throughput scenarios, such as ingesting logs from thousands of servers or IoT devices, with minimal latency. OpenSearch Ingestion integrates with other AWS offerings like Kinesis Data Streams and Amazon S3, providing data pipelines that connect to these sources and let you stream, filter, and transform data as it makes its way into OpenSearch.

OpenSearch Dashboards

OpenSearch Dashboards, AWS's fork of Kibana, is the visualization component of OpenSearch. It lets users interact with their log data using bar charts, heat maps, line graphs, and more. Because it is based on Kibana, it also supports many of the plug-ins from the Kibana ecosystem. As the name suggests, OpenSearch Dashboards let you assemble visualizations and report snippets into dashboards that you can share with others, giving developers and operations staff a single place to understand the full status of your application ecosystem. OpenSearch Dashboards was forked from Kibana 7.10.2.

Comparison with CloudWatch

Given CloudWatch's logging, analysis, and dashboard creation capabilities, you may wonder when to use CloudWatch versus OpenSearch. CloudWatch's unique strength is in operational monitoring of AWS services and infrastructure, and the broad, often one-click support found throughout AWS for sending logs to CloudWatch. Use it any time you're working with an AWS service that can be automatically configured to log to CloudWatch and integrate custom data whenever that input is closely aligned with operational monitoring. For instance, it makes sense to send EC2 memory usage stats to CloudWatch so you can use one service to track and alarm on closely related metrics like CPU, RAM, and storage.

OpenSearch, on the other hand, excels at processing and analyzing large-scale data input from a variety of sources beyond AWS resources. You can send application logs, web server logs, database statistics, user behavior, and more to OpenSearch and use its powerful tools to mine rich insights from the data. For example, you might use OpenSearch to analyze user clickstreams from a web application to identify usage patterns that will inform UI/UX improvements.

In short, the two services complement each other. Use CloudWatch for real-time monitoring and alerting on AWS-native resources, and use OpenSearch for in-depth analysis of both AWS and non-AWS data streams, especially when you need to derive business value from complex data sets.

AWS CloudTrail

All actions in your AWS account are composed of API calls, regardless of the origin (the AWS Management Console or programmatic/scripted actions via CLI or SDK). As you create resources in your account, API calls are being made to AWS services in different regions around the world. *AWS CloudTrail* is a fully managed service that continuously monitors and records API calls and stores them in Amazon S3. You can use these logs to troubleshoot and resolve operational issues, meet and verify regulatory compliance, and monitor or alarm on specific events in your account. CloudTrail supports most AWS services, making it easy for IT and security administrators to analyze activity in accounts. IT auditors can also use log files as compliance aids.

CloudTrail helps answer five key questions about monitoring access:

- Who made the API call?
- When was the API call made?

- What was the API call?
- Which resources were acted upon in the API call?
- Where was the origin of the API call?

AWS CloudTrail Events

An *AWS CloudTrail event* is any single API activity in an AWS account. This activity can be an action triggered by any of the following agents or actions:

- AWS IAM user
- AWS IAM role
- AWS service

CloudTrail tracks two types of events: management events and data events. Events are recorded in the region where the action occurred, except for global service events.

Management Events

Management events give insight into operations performed on AWS resources, such as the following examples:

Configuring security: An example is attaching a policy to an IAM role.

Configuring routing rules: An example is adding inbound security group rules.

Data Events

Data events give insight into operations that store data in (or extract data from) AWS resources, such as the following examples:

Amazon S3 object activity: Examples are GetObject and PutObject operations.

AWS Lambda function executions: These use the InvokeFunction operation.

By default, AWS CloudTrail tracks the last 90 days of API history for management events. The following is an example output for an AWS CloudTrail event:

```
{
    "Records": [{
        "eventVersion": "1.01",
        "userIdentity": {
            "type": "IAMUser",
            "principalId": "AIDAJDPLRKLG7UEXAMPLE",
```

```
        "arn": "arn:aws:iam::123456789012:user/Alice",
        "accountId": "123456789012",
        "accessKeyId": "AKIAIOSFODNN7EXAMPLE",
        "userName": "Alice",
        "sessionContext": {
            "attributes": {
                "mfaAuthenticated": "false",
                "creationDate": "2024-03-18T14:29:23Z"
            }
        }
    },
        "eventTime": "2024-03-18T14:30:07Z",
        "eventSource": "cloudtrail.amazonaws.com",
        "eventName": "StartLogging",
        "awsRegion": "us-west-2",
        "sourceIPAddress": "198.162.198.64",
        "userAgent": "signin.amazonaws.com",
        "requestParameters": {
            "name": "Default"
        },
        "responseElements": null,
        "requestID": "cdc73f9d-aea9-11e3-9d5a-835b769c0d9c",
        "eventID": "3074414d-c626-42aa-984b-68ff152d6ab7"
    },
... additional entries ...
]
```

This event provides the following information:

- The user who made the request from the userIdentityField. In this example, it is the IAM user Alice.

- When the request was made (the eventTime). In this case, it is 2024-03-18T14:30:07Z.

- Where the request was made (the sourceIPAddress). In this case, it is 198.162.198.64.

- The action the request is trying to perform (the eventName). In this case, it is the StartLogging operation.

As a security precaution, you can use events such as this example to configure alerts when an IAM user attempts to sign in to the AWS Management Console too many times.

Global Service Events

Some AWS services allow you to create, modify, and delete resources from any region. These are referred to as *global services*. Examples of global services include the following:

- IAM
- AWS Security Token Service
- Amazon CloudFront
- Amazon Route 53

Global services are logged as occurring in US East (N. Virginia) Region. Any trails created in the CloudTrail console log global services by default, which are delivered to the Amazon S3 bucket for the trail.

Trails

If you need long-term storage of events (for example, for compliance purposes), you can configure a trail of events as log files in CloudTrail. A trail is a configuration that enables delivery of CloudTrail events to an S3 bucket, CloudWatch Logs, and CloudWatch Events. When you configure a trail, you can filter the events that you want to be delivered.

Amazon Athena

Organizations spend a lot of time thinking about how to stream, format, and store their data to enable search and analytics. Keeping valuable data in a data warehouse can facilitate a wide variety of analytics capabilities; still, this approach often requires careful planning, dedicated infrastructure, and custom data intake jobs. Sometimes, you just wish you could query data where it lives without first needing to get it into a purpose-built analytics environment.

That is the purpose of *Amazon Athena*. Based on the open source Apache Presto engine, Athena is a serverless AWS service that enables you to query data in Amazon S3 with standard ANSI SQL (Structured Query Language). Because SQL is familiar to users of relational databases everywhere, Athena can be a quick way to enable developers to pull insights from data without the need to learn specialized tooling or reporting software. Athena supports querying a wide variety of file formats, including CSV, JSON, Parquet, and ORC. It can also be run against AWS-generated logs such as CloudWatch and CloudTrail logs.

Because Athena uses standard SQL queries, you can use it to connect your AWS data to visualization tools via JDBC or ODBC.

A more recent offering of Athena is the ability to query the same underlying S3 data with Apache Spark—specifically, PySpark and Spark SQL.

AWS X-Ray

The services covered so far are centered on the concept of using logs as monitoring and troubleshooting tools. Developers often write code, test the code, and inspect the logs. If there are errors, they may add breakpoints, run the test again, and add additional log statements. This works well in small cases, but it becomes cumbersome as teams, software, and infrastructure grow. Traditional troubleshooting and debugging processes do not work well at scaling across multiple services. Troubleshooting cross-service, cross-region applications can be especially difficult when different systems use varying log formats.

AWS X-Ray is a service that collects data about requests served by your application and provides tools you can use to view, filter, and gain insights into that data to identify issues and opportunities for optimization.

AWS X-Ray Use Cases

AWS X-Ray helps developers build, monitor, and improve applications. Use cases include the following:

- Identifying performance bottlenecks
- Pinpointing specific service issues
- Identifying errors
- Identifying impact to users

AWS X-Ray integrates with the AWS SDK, adding traces to track your application requests as they are generated and received from various services.

Tracking Application Requests

To better understand how AWS X-Ray works, consider the example service shown in Figure 15.8. In this service, the front-end fleet relies on a backend API, which is built using API Gateway, acting as proxy to Lambda. Lambda then uses Amazon DynamoDB to store data.

AWS X-Ray can track a user request using a trace, a segment, and a subsegment:

Trace   A *trace* is the path of a request through your application. Each trace tracks the detailed steps of an end-to-end request from the client—from its entry into your environment to the backend and back to the user. A trace ID is passed through the AWS services with each user request so that AWS X-Ray can collate related segments.

Segment   A trace is made up of many *segments*, each of which depicts the request's interaction with a particular service. In the example microservice shown in Figure 15.8, two segments correspond to two services: the front-end service and the backend API.

Subsegment   A *subsegment* identifies the underlying API calls made from a particular service. In this scenario, the Lambda invoked by the backend API sends requests to Amazon DynamoDB and Amazon SQS. Each of those calls is a subsegment within the Lambda segment of the overall request.

FIGURE 15.8   Microservice example

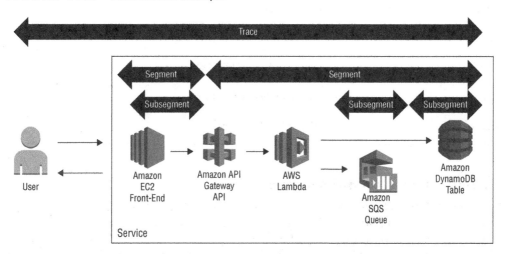

From these components of a request, AWS X-Ray compiles the traces into a service graph that describes the components and their interactions that comprise a request. A *service graph* is a visual representation of the services and resources that make up your application. Figure 15.9 shows an example of a service graph.

FIGURE 15.9   Example service graph for an application

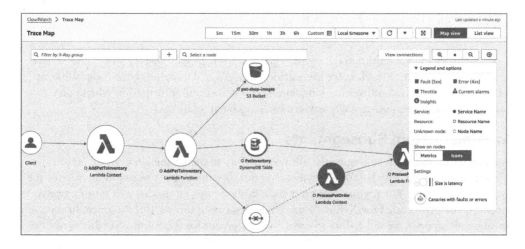

The service graph provides an overview of the health of various aspects of your system such as average latencies and request rates between your services and dependent resources. The colored circles also show the ratio of different response codes, as listed in Table 15.15.

TABLE 15.15   AWS X-Ray service graph status codes

Color	Status code
Purple	Throttling or HTTP 5XX codes
Orange	Client-side or HTTP 4XX codes
Red	Fault application failure
Green	OK or HTTP 2XX codes

Enabling Tracing on Subsegments

By default, X-Ray is able to trace requests through services like API Gateway and AWS Lambda. To gain further visibility into your application's interactions with AWS services, however, you'll need to use the AWS X-Ray into your code. The X-Ray library for Python allows you to instrument subsegments—that is, the individual calls out to AWS services like SQS or DynamoDB you may make in your code. To initialize this library, use pip to install aws-ray-sdk:

```
pip install aws-xray-sdk
```

Then, use it in your code by patching the boto3 AWS SDK library:

```
from aws_xray_sdk.core import import patch

# Instrument all supported AWS SDK libraries (like boto3)
patch(['boto3'])
```

With this enabled, additional data will begin to appear in your X-Ray traces and service map, as X-Ray starts to track every invocation of an AWS SDK call in your code. Without this step (or the equivalent in other languages), you will see no information when your Lambda makes calls to other AWS services such as DynamoDB.

Tracking Custom Subsegments

You can track your own subsegments, allowing X-Ray to depict the latency and error rate of code that does not involve AWS services. For this, use the xray_recorder feature of the Python X-Ray SDK. When you wrap your code in the xray_recorder.in_subsegment function, you give a label for X-Ray to use when describing this part of the trace. In the following code snippet, we tell X-Ray to create a subsegment for a custom validate_order method using the label OrderValidation. With this in place, we will be able to observe the latency and error rate of this function in the service graph.

```
from aws_xray_sdk.core import xray_recorder
with xray_recorder.in_subsegment('OrderValidation'):
        validate_order(order)
```

AWS provides an X-Ray SDK for multiple languages. For instance, in Java, you must import the X-Ray TracingHandler object and use it with each call. Please note that for brevity, this snippet skips the lines of code that initialize the AWS SDK:

```
import com.amazonaws.xray.AWSXRay;
import com.amazonaws.xray.handlers.TracingHandler;

        AmazonDynamoDB dynamoDB = AmazonDynamoDBClientBuilder.standard()
                .withRequestHandlers(new TracingHandler(AWSXRay.getGlobal
Recorder())))
                .build();
```

Likewise, Node.js developers can type npm install aws-xray-sdk and start using X-Ray in their code this way:

```
const AWSXRay = require('aws-xray-sdk');

// equivalent to patching boto; automatically instruments AWS calls
const AWS = AWSXRay.captureAWS(require('aws-sdk'));

const s3 = new AWS.S3();
```

Capturing custom subsegments in Node.js is a little different than in Python; with JavaScript, you must manually create those subsegments and close them when you are done. All code invoked in between is traced:

```
// Get the current segment
const segment = AWSXRay.getSegment();

// explicitly add a subsegment into the current segment object
const subsegment = segment.addNewSubsegment('OrderProcessing');

// optionally add metadata for later viewing / filtering in X-Ray
subsegment.addAnnotation('user_id', user_id);
subsegment.addMetadata('order_detail', { order_id: order_id, total: total });

// do some custom logic
processOrder()

// explicitly close the segment
subsegment.close();
```

This example illustrates a feature available to any language working with X-Ray subsegments: the ability to annotate the data. By attaching metadata for the user_id and order_detail, you may later see this information when viewing the trace in the X-Ray console.

AWS X-Ray can be a powerful way to add traceability to your applications. The X-Ray console integrates tightly with CloudWatch, letting you visually observe the behavior of individual requests, click on a step (such as a Lambda invocation) for more detail, and immediately drill in from there to the CloudWatch logs associated with that invocation. These tools give you the ability to observe, tune, enhance, and troubleshoot your serverless apps quickly from a single, comprehensive view of the system.

Summary

AWS provides multiple options for monitoring and troubleshooting your applications. As you have discovered, AWS services help you manage logs from various systems, either running on the cloud or on-premises; create triggers that notify you about application health and issues in your infrastructure; and build applications with modern debugging tools for distributed applications. CloudWatch gives you many choices for logging, analyzing, and testing the behavior of your cloud services and applications. OpenSearch provides an AWS-native take on the ELK stack for sophisticated data analytics and searching that can give you actionable log insights. CloudTrail helps you audit all the changes that take place in your AWS accounts—and who performed them. Athena lets you search logs in S3 using SQL queries. X-Ray gives you a "single pane of glass" on your applications to offer in-depth understanding of how your application is behaving. Together, these services overcome the difficulties of creating a centralized logging solution, giving you operational insights that can lead to a better experience for you and your users.

Exam Essentials

Know what Amazon CloudWatch is and why it is used.   Amazon CloudWatch is the service used to aggregate, analyze, and alert on metrics generated by other AWS services. It is used to monitor the resources you create in AWS and the on-premises infrastructure. You can use Amazon CloudWatch to store logs from your applications and trigger actions in response to events.

Know what common metrics are available for Amazon Elastic Compute Cloud (Amazon EC2) in Amazon CloudWatch.   Amazon EC2 metrics in Amazon CloudWatch include the following:

- CPUUtilization
- DiskReadOps

- `DiskReadBytes`
- `DiskWriteOps`
- `DiskWriteBytes`
- `NetworkIn`
- `NetworkOut`
- `StatusCheckFailed`

Amazon EC2 does not report OS-level metrics such as memory utilization.

Understand the difference between high-resolution and standard-resolution metrics.   High-resolution metrics are delivered in a period of less than one minute. Standard-resolution metrics are delivered in a period greater than or equal to one minute.

Know what AWS CloudTrail is and why it is used.   AWS CloudTrail is used to monitor API calls made to the AWS Cloud for various services. CloudTrail helps IT administrators, IT security administrators, DevOps engineers, and auditors enable compliance and the monitoring of access to AWS resources within an account.

Know what AWS CloudTrail tracks automatically.   By default, AWS CloudTrail tracks the last 90 days of activity. These events are limited to management events with create, modify, and delete API calls.

Understand the difference between AWS CloudTrail management and data events. Management events are operations performed on resources in your AWS account. Data events are operations performed on data stored in AWS resources. Examples are creating or deleting objects in Amazon S3 and inserting or updating items in an Amazon DynamoDB table.

Know what CloudWatch Logs Insights is for and how to use it.   With this service, you can search your logs with a powerful query syntax that lets you select attributes, filter values, and compute aggregations across one or more log groups. CloudWatch Logs Insights can also scan your logs for patterns, which can help you understand which log groups are best suited for Anomaly Detection.

Understand CloudWatch Anomaly Detection and when you would use it.   Anomaly Detection uses machine learning algorithms to derive patterns from the last two weeks of a log group's output, then lets you raise a CloudWatch alarm if the behavior deviates significantly from established patterns. This can be an excellent way to monitor web or other service logs for sporadically occurring issues or for situations that you cannot anticipate.

Know how CloudWatch Synthetics work to test your applications.   CloudWatch Synthetics offer the ability to execute automated client-side testing using scripts written in Node.js with the Puppeteer framework or Python plus Selenium. Stock blueprints offer heartbeat testing, manually input DOM actions, and the ability to monitor changes in screenshots. The Synthetics Recorder Chrome Plugin lets you generate Selenium scripts based on your mouse and keyboard input. CloudWatch Synthetics are great for any tests that might otherwise need human interaction to run.

Understand the ELK stack and how it is represented via OpenSearch services.   ELK stands for ElasticSearch, Logstash, and Kibana. These services provide log storage and search, log ingestion, and data visualization, respectively, and work together to provide comprehensive log analytics to operations staff. AWS offers OpenSearch, OpenSearch Ingestion, and OpenSearch Dashboards as cloud-based offerings for this stack. OpenSearch can be run in a serverless mode, though it does not scale to zero.

Understand the relationship between OpenSearch services and ElasticSearch and Kibana. OpenSearch is a fork of ElasticSearch started at version 7.10.2, and can be run in a mode compatible with all plug-ins as of that version. Newer iterations of OpenSearch may diverge and are not guaranteed to keep working with third-party tools. Likewise, OpenSearch Dashboards is derived from Kibana 7.10.2 and has similar caveats. Both services are open source and licensed under Apache License, Version 2.0.

Know the purpose of Amazon Athena.   Amazon Athena lets you load S3 with unstructured data in JSON, CSV, or columnar formats like Parquet, then apply a schema to it, which may be searched with standard ANSI SQL.

Know what AWS X-Ray is and why it is used.   AWS X-Ray is a service that collects data about your application requests, including the various subservices or systems that perform tasks to complete a request. X-Ray is commonly used to help developers find bottlenecks in distributed applications and monitor the health of various components in their services.

Know the basics of AWS X-Ray and how it helps troubleshoot applications.   AWS X-Ray records requests by initiating a trace ID with the origin of the request. This trace ID is added as a header to the request that propagates to various services. If you enable the AWS X-Ray SDK in your applications, AWS X-Ray submits telemetry and the request as segments for each service and subsegments for downstream services upon which you depend. Using these traces, X-Ray collates the data to view request performance metrics, such as latency and error rates. The data can then be used to create a graph of your application and its dependencies and the health of any requests your application might make.

Understand EventBridge and event-based architecture.   EventBridge places JSON-based event messages on an event bus, allowing you to define rules that match against these events and take some action. Events include native AWS events like S3 object actions or custom actions placed by your custom `PutEvents` API calls or SaaS integrations. EventBridge Pipes are point-to-point integrations that can filter and enrich events before sending them to a destination. EventBridge Scheduler allows you to invoke any AWS API on a schedule you define.

Exercises

Creating an Amazon CloudWatch Alarm on an Amazon S3 Bucket

It is common to monitor the storage usage of your Amazon S3 buckets and trigger notifications when there is a large increase in storage used. In this exercise, you will use the AWS CLI to configure an Amazon CloudWatch alarm to trigger a notification when more than 1 KB of data is uploaded to an Amazon S3 bucket.

If you need directions while completing this exercise, see "Using Amazon CloudWatch Alarms" here:

https://docs.aws.amazon.com/AmazonCloudWatch/latest/monitoring/Alarm
ThatSendsEmail.html

1. Create an Amazon S3 bucket in your AWS account.

   a. Log into the AWS Management Console.

   b. Use the search bar to search for **S3** and click into the S3 console.

   c. Click Create Bucket.

   d. Provide a bucket name using only lowercase letters and hyphens, such as my-demo-bucket, but remember to make your bucket name unique.

   e. Keep all other settings at default, scroll down, and click Create Bucket.

2. Use the search bar to search for **CloudWatch**, then click CloudWatch to open the Cloud-Watch console.

3. Select Alarms ➤ All Alarms ➤ Create Alarm.

4. Choose Select Metric.

   a. In the search bar, type **S3**.

   b. In the results, find and click S3 > Storage Metrics.

   c. Select the checkbox next to the metric where BucketName matches the name of the Amazon S3 bucket that you created and where Metric Name is BucketSizeBytes.

5. Choose Select Metric.

6. Under Alarm Details:

   a. Under Conditions, keep Threshold Type as Static.

   b. For the comparator, select >= (greater than or equal to).

    c. Set the value to **1000** for 1 KB.

    d. Click Next.

7. Under Notification:

    a. Keep Alarm State Trigger as In Alarm.

    b. Under Send A Notification To The Following SNS Topic, choose Create New Topic.

    c. Enter a new topic name and provide your email address under Email Endpoints.

    d. Click Create Topic.

8. Optionally expand and add Lambda, Auto Scaling, EC2, or Systems Manager actions.

9. Click Next.

10. For Alarm Name, enter **S3 Storage Alarm**.

11. Click Next.

12. Review your settings, then click Create Alarm.

The alarm is created in your account. If you already have data in your Amazon S3 bucket, it is switched from the Insufficient Data to the Alarm state. Otherwise, try uploading several files to your bucket to monitor changes in the alarm state.

To delete the alarm, follow these steps:

1. Open the Amazon CloudWatch console.

2. Click All Alarms.

3. Select the alarm you want to delete.

4. For Actions, select Delete.

In this exercise, you created an Amazon CloudWatch alarm to notify administrators when large files are uploaded to Amazon S3 buckets in your account.

Enabling an AWS CloudTrail Trail on an Amazon S3 Bucket

1. In this exercise, you will set up access logs to an Amazon S3 bucket in your account to monitor activity. Follow the steps from Exercise 15.1 to create one in your account.

2. Use the search bar to search for CloudTrail, then click CloudTrail to open the CloudTrail console.

3. Click Create Trail.

4. Set Trail Name to **s3_logs**.

5. Under Storage Location, for Create A New S3 bucket, select Yes.

6. For Name, enter a name for the Amazon S3 bucket that will store your CloudTrail logs. This should be a different bucket than the one to be monitored by CloudTrail.

7. Under Log File SSE-KMS Encryption, deselect Enabled. This will leave your CloudTrail logs in plaintext, which is suitable for this exercise; in production, leave this selected according to your security requirements.

8. Click Next.

9. Under Events, make sure the Management Events option is selected and that Data Events and Insights Events are not selected.

10. Under Management Events, select Read and Write.

11. Click Next.

12. Review your choices, then click Create Trail.

In this exercise, you enabled AWS CloudTrail to record data events and store corresponding logs to an Amazon S3 bucket.

EXERCISE 15.3

Creating an Amazon CloudWatch Dashboard

In this exercise, you will create an Amazon CloudWatch dashboard to see graphed metric data.

1. Use the search bar to search for **CloudWatch**, then click CloudWatch to open the Cloud-Watch console.

2. In the left-hand menu, click Dashboards.

3. Click Create Dashboard.

4. For Dashboard Name, enter a name for your dashboard.

5. Click Create Dashboard.

6. In the Add Widget pop-up window, select the Line graph.

7. Click Next.

8. From the available metrics, select one or more metrics that you want to monitor.

9. Click Create Widget.

10. To add more widgets, click Add Widget and repeat steps 6 through 9 for other widget types.

11. Click Save Dashboard.

In this exercise, you created an Amazon CloudWatch dashboard to create graphs of important metric data for resources in your account.

EXERCISE 15.4

Creating a Serverless Application with SAM for Analysis with X-Ray

In this exercise, you will stand up a small serverless app using the AWS Serverless Application Model. See details in Chapter 14 on setting up SAM and the SAM CLI.

Note: To avoid unwanted charges, make sure to follow the directions to the end of exercise 15.5 so that you can delete this stack. This demo creates a public API endpoint that can write to a DynamoDB table, so it is important that you do not leave it exposed after you are done.

1. Download the zip file `blog_comments.zip` and unzip into a folder. Make sure you have configured AWS CLI credentials for an administrative user. Inside that folder, run the following:

   ```
   cd blog-comment-lambda
   ```

2. Run the following command to install the X-Ray SDK alongside the Lambda code. Note the dot at the end.

   ```
   aws-xray-sdk -t .
   ```

3. Return to the parent directory by typing **cd ...**

4. Run **sam build**.

5. Run **sam validate**.

6. Run **sam deploy --guided**.

7. When prompted, provide the following answers:

   ```
   Setting default arguments for 'sam deploy'
   =========================================
   Stack Name [blog-comments]: blog-comments
   AWS Region [us-east-1]: <press enter to accept default>
   Confirm changes before deploy [Y/n]: Y
   ```

```
Allow SAM CLI IAM role creation [Y/n]: Y
Disable rollback [y/N]: N
AddCommentFunction has no authentication. Is this okay? [y/N]: y
Save arguments to configuration file [Y/n]: Y
SAM configuration file [samconfig.toml]: <press enter to accept default>
SAM configuration environment [default]: <press enter to accept default>
```

Note that if you run this step more than once, you will need to enter a different stack name, as the previous one may still exist or be in a still-deleting state.

8. After a moment, confirm the deployment:

```
Deploy this changeset? [y/N]: y
```

9. Take note of the API Gateway endpoint URL in the terminal output:

```
---------------------------------------------------------------------------
Outputs
---------------------------------------------------------------------------
Key            ApiUrl
Description    API Gateway endpoint URL
Value          <URL_will_appear_here>
---------------------------------------------------------------------------
```

10. We can POST comments to this endpoint using curl:

```
curl -X POST <your-api-url-here> \
  -d '{"comment": "This is my comment!"}'
```

The Lambda function is written to introduce random latency into the flow, so some responses may be quicker than others. To simulate more traffic:

11. Edit the script simulate_traffic.sh with your API URL as the value for API_URL.

12. Save and exit.

13. Run **bash simulate_traffic.sh** to invoke the Lambda 20 times. Your output will look similar to this:

```
Response 1: Status Code: 200, Body: {"message": "Comment added successfully",
"sleep_time": 4.260677795242143}
Response 2: Status Code: 200, Body: {"message": "Comment added successfully",
"sleep_time": 4.595475824371987}
```

EXERCISE 15.5

Observing Application Traces with AWS X-Ray

This exercise requires that you have completed Exercise 15.4.

1. Open the AWS Management Console and navigate via the search bar to CloudWatch.

2. Under X-Ray, click Traces.

3. Under Query Refiners, choose Node next to Refine Query By.

4. Select the checkboxes next to AddBlogComment (both the Lambda function and Lambda context) and next to BlogComments (the DynamoDB table). If you don't see these values, extend the time window at the top of the page or run **simulate_traffic .sh** again to get fresh data.

5. Click Add To Query, then Run Query.

6. Scroll down to the results under Traces and click the first Trace ID.

7. Observe the visual representation of the trace from Lambda to DynamoDB.

8. Under the Legend And Options menu, change the nodes to show Metrics instead of Icons. This will show you details of latency on this individual request.

9. Click into an individual node to see details of its execution.

10. Click Go To Trace Map to see aggregated data across many traces.

11. Click the Lambda Function node for AddBlogComment, then scroll down and view metrics. If you click Analyze Traces, you will see a graph depicting its very inconsistent response times!

12. After you have viewed everything, return to the command line and run **sam delete** to delete the infrastructure you built.

Review Questions

1. You are required to set up dynamic scaling using Amazon CloudWatch alarms. Which of the following metrics could you monitor to trigger Auto Scaling events to scale out and scale in your instances?

   A. High CPU utilization to trigger scale-in action, and low CPU utilization to trigger scale-out action

   B. High CPU utilization to trigger scale-out action, and low CPU utilization to trigger scale-in action

   C. High latency to trigger a scale-in action, and low latency to trigger a scale-out action

   D. None of the above

2. What is the length of time that metrics are stored for a data point with a period of 300 seconds (5 minutes) in Amazon CloudWatch?

   A. The data point is stored for 3 hours.

   B. The data point is stored for 15 days.

   C. The data point is stored for 30 days.

   D. The data point is stored for 63 days.

   E. The data point is stored for 455 days (15 months).

3. You must set up centralized logging for an application and create a cost-effective way to archive logs for compliance purposes. Which is the best solution?

   A. Install the Amazon CloudWatch agent on your servers to ingest the logs and store them indefinitely.

   B. Configure Amazon CloudWatch to ingest logs from your application servers.

   C. Install the Amazon CloudWatch agent on your servers to ingest the logs and set a new retention period for logs with regular exports to Amazon S3 for archival.

   D. None of the above.

4. Which of the following options allow logs and metrics to be ingested into Amazon CloudWatch? (Choose three.)

   A. Install the Amazon CloudWatch agent and configure it to ingest logs.

   B. Execute API operations to push metrics to Amazon CloudWatch.

   C. Configure Amazon CloudWatch to pull logs from servers.

   D. Use the AWS CLI to push metrics to Amazon CloudWatch.

5. The following are Apache HTTP access logs.

   Which filter pattern would select events matching 404 errors?

   ```
   127.0.0.1 - - [24/Sep/2024:11:49:52 -0700] "GET /index.html HTTP/1.1" 404 287
   127.0.0.1 - - [24/Sep/2024:11:49:52 -0700] "GET /index.html HTTP/1.1" 404 287
   ```

```
127.0.0.1 - - [24/Sep/2024:11:50:51 -0700] "GET /~test/ HTTP/1.1" 200 3
127.0.0.1 - - [24/Sep/2024:11:50:51 -0700] "GET /favicon.ico HTTP/1.1" 404 308
127.0.0.1 - - [24/Sep/2024:11:50:51 -0700] "GET /favicon.ico HTTP/1.1" 404 308
127.0.0.1 - - [24/Sep/2024:11:51:34 -0700] "GET /~test/index.html
HTTP/1.1" 200 3
```

    A. 4xx

    B. 400

    C. 404

    D. None of the above

6. You build an application and enable AWS X-Ray tracing. You analyze the service graph and determine that the application requests to Amazon DynamoDB are not performing well and a majority of the issues are purple.

    What kind of problem is your application experiencing?

    A. Throttling

    B. Error

    C. Faults

    D. OK

7. Which AWS service enables you to monitor resources and gather statistics, such as CPU utilization, from a single "pane of glass" interface?

    A. AWS CloudTrail logs

    B. Amazon CloudWatch alarms

    C. Amazon CloudWatch dashboards

    D. Amazon CloudWatch Logs

8. By default, what is the number of days of AWS account activity that you can view, search, and download from the AWS CloudTrail event history?

    A. 30 days

    B. 60 days

    C. 75 days

    D. 90 days

9. In AWS CloudTrail, which of the following are management events? (Choose two.)

    A. Adding a row to an Amazon DynamoDB table

    B. Modifying an Amazon S3 bucket policy

    C. Uploading an object to an Amazon S3 bucket

    D. Creating an Amazon Relational Database Service (Amazon RDS) database instance

    E. Sending a notification to Amazon Simple Notification Service (Amazon SNS)

10. Suppose that you have a custom web application running on an Amazon Elastic Compute Cloud (Amazon EC2) instance. What steps are needed to configure this instance to send custom application logs to Amazon CloudWatch Logs? (Choose three.)

    A. Install the Amazon CloudWatch Logs agent.

    B. Attach an Elastic IP address to your Amazon EC2 instance.

    C. Configure the agent to send specific logs.

    D. Start the agent.

    E. Install the AWS Systems Manager agent.

11. Which of the following Amazon EC2 metrics is not directly available through Amazon CloudWatch metrics?

    A. CPU utilization

    B. Network traffic in/out

    C. Disk I/O

    D. Memory (RAM) utilization

12. Which of the following is the correct Amazon CloudWatch metric namespace for Amazon EC2 instances?

    A. `AWS/EC2`

    B. `Amazon/EC2`

    C. `AWS/EC2Instance`

    D. `Amazon/EC2Instance`

13. Your organization runs a serverless application that needs to process messages from multiple third-party services. Each service sends events in different formats. You want to route these events to a specific Lambda function based on the event content. What is the most efficient way to achieve this?

    A. Create a single EventBridge rule with an event pattern that matches all possible event formats and sends them to the Lambda function.

    B. Set up multiple EventBridge event buses, one for each third-party service, and create rules to route all events to the Lambda function.

    C. Create multiple EventBridge rules, each with one of the specific event patterns that matches specific attributes from the events of each submitting service.

    D. Use AWS Step Functions to process the incoming events and determine the Lambda function to which to route each event.

14. You want to limit the number of log results returned by CloudWatch Log Insights to the top 100 entries. Which command allows you to do this?

    A. `filter`

    B. `limit`

    C. `max`

    D. `sort`

15. What feature of Amazon OpenSearch Service helps lower your storage costs while preserving query performance by storing less frequently accessed data on a lower-cost service?

    A. OpenSearch Infrequent Access

    B. Blue/green architecture

    C. EBS (Elastic Block Store) volumes

    D. Ultrawarm storage

Chapter

16

Optimization

**THE AWS CERTIFIED DEVELOPER –
ASSOCIATE EXAM TOPICS COVERED IN
THIS CHAPTER MAY INCLUDE, BUT ARE
NOT LIMITED TO, THE FOLLOWING:**

✓ **Domain 1: Development with AWS Services**

  ▪ Task Statement 1: Develop code for applications
    hosted on AWS

✓ **Domain 4: Troubleshooting and Optimization**

  ▪ Task Statement 1: Assist in a root cause analysis

  ▪ Task Statement 2: Instrument code for observability

  ▪ Task Statement 3: Optimize applications by using AWS
    services and features

Creating a software system is a lot like constructing a building. If the foundation is not solid, structural problems can undermine the integrity and function of the building. If you've made it this far in the book, you have a solid understanding of all the AWS services most relevant to application developers and have become familiar with how they work together to create dynamic, robust, and scalable architectures. You know enough to start building, but how do you ensure your foundation is secure?

Now it's time to delve into the operations side of things and discuss not just *what* you can build, but *how* you can build (and monitor, and scale, and adjust) your cloud resources to achieve the optimal balance between cost and performance. This chapter covers some of the best practices and considerations you can use to design systems that are cost-effective and performant, automating as much as possible in response to real-time feedback from your environment.

Cost Optimization: Everyone's Responsibility

All teams help manage cloud costs, and cost optimization is everyone's responsibility. Make sure that costs are known from beginning to end, at every level, and from executives to engineers. Ensure that project owners/budget holders know both up-front and ongoing costs. Business decision makers must track costs against budgets and understand return on investment (ROI).

Encourage everyone to track their cost optimization daily so that they can establish a habit of efficiency and see the daily impact of their cost savings over time.

Every engineer can be a cost engineer. Engineers should design their solutions to consume resources only when needed, control the utilization, build sizing into architecture, and tag the resources to optimize usage.

Enforce Tagging

Tagging your AWS resources assigns custom metadata to instances, images, and other resources. For example, you can categorize resources by owner, purpose, or environment, which helps you organize them and establish cost responsibilities. When you apply tags to your AWS resources and activate them via the AWS Cost and Billing Management console, AWS adds this information to Cost and Usage reports.

Follow Mandatory Cost Tagging

An effective tagging strategy gives you improved visibility and monitoring, helps you create accurate chargeback/showback models, and extracts more granular and precise insights about usage and spending by applications and teams. The following tag categories help you achieve these goals:

Environment   Distinguishes among development, test, and production infrastructure. Specifying an environment tag reduces analysis time, post-processing, and the need to maintain a separate mapping file of production versus nonproduction accounts.

Application ID   Identifies resources that are related to a specific application for easy tracking of spending changes and that turn off at the end of projects.

Automation Opt-In/Opt-Out   Indicates whether a resource should be included in an automated activity such as starting, stopping, or resizing instances.

Cost Center/Business Unit   Identifies the cost center or business unit associated with a resource, typically for cost allocation and tracking.

Owner   Used to identify who is responsible for the resource. This is typically the technical owner. If needed, you can add a separate business owner tag. You can specify the owner as an email address. Using email addresses supports automated notifications to both the technical and business owners as required.

Tag on Creation

You can make tagging a part of your build process and automate it with AWS management tools, such as AWS Elastic Beanstalk and/or Systems Manager.

The following AWS CLI sample adds two tags, `CostCenter` and `environment`, for an Amazon Machine Image (AMI) and an instance.

```
aws ec2 create-tags --resources ami-1a2b3c4d i-1234567890abcdef0 --tags
Key=CostCenter,Value=123   Key=environment,Value=Production
```

You can execute management tasks at scale by listing resources with specific tags and then executing the appropriate actions. For example, you can list all the resources with the tag and value of `environment:test`; then, for each of the resources, delete or terminate the resource. This is useful for automating shutdown or removal of a test environment at the end of the working day. Running reports on tagged and, more importantly, untagged resources enables greater compliance with internal cost management policies.

Enforce Tag Use

Using IAM policies, you can enforce tag use to gain precise control over access to resources, ownership, and accurate cost allocation.

The following example policy allows a user to create an Amazon Elastic Block Store (Amazon EBS) volume only if the user applies the tags (`Costcenter` and `environment`) that are defined in the policy using the qualifier `ForAllValues`. If the user applies any tag that is not included in the policy, the action is denied. To enforce case sensitivity, use the condition `aws:TagKeys`.

```
Effect: Allow
Action: 'ec2:CreateVolume'
Resource: 'arn:aws:ec2:us-east-1:123456789012:volume/*'
Condition:
    StringEquals:
        'aws:RequestTag/costcenter': '115'
        'aws:RequestTag/environment': prod
    'ForAllValues:StringEquals':
        'aws:TagKeys':
            - Costcenter
            - environment
```

Tagging Tools

The following tools help you manage your tags:

AWS Tag Editor: Finds resources with search criteria (including missing and misspelled tags) and enables you to edit tags from the AWS Management Console

AWS Config: Identifies resources that do not comply with tagging policies

Capital One's Cloud Custodian (open source): Ensures tagging compliance and remediation

Minimize Resource Usage

Set a continuous practice to review your consumption of AWS resources, and understand the factors that contribute to cost. Use various AWS monitoring tools to provide visibility, control, and cost optimization. Following the DevOps phase, use dashboards to view the estimated costs of your AWS usage, top services that you use most, and the proportion of your costs to which each service contributed. If your monthly bill increases, make sure that it is for the right reason (business growth) and not the wrong reason (waste).

Delete Unnecessary EBS Volumes

Stopping an EC2 instance leaves any attached EBS volumes operational. You continue to incur charges for these volumes until you delete them.

Stop Unused Instances

Stop instances used in development and production during hours when these instances are not in use and then start them again when their capacity is needed. Assuming a 50-hour workweek, you can save 70 percent of costs by automatically stopping dev/test/production instances during nonbusiness hours. A scheduled Lambda can work well for this.

Update Outdated Resources

As AWS releases new services and features, it is a best practice to review your existing architectural decisions to ensure that they remain cost effective and stay evergreen. As your requirements change, be aggressive in decommissioning resources, components, and workloads that you no longer require.

Delete Unused Keys

Each customer key that you create in AWS Key Management Service (AWS KMS), regardless of whether you use it with KMS-generated key material or key material imported by you, incurs a cost until you delete it. After making certain you no longer need a specific key, schedule the key deletion. This begins a waiting period of 30 days (by default, configurable down to 7) before which the key will be fully deleted.

This countdown is a necessary safeguard against data loss, since any data encrypted by this key will be unrecoverable without the key. Be sure the keys you target for deletion were either never used or that the data they were used to encrypt has been appropriately decrypted first.

Manage EBS Snapshot Life Cycle

Costs associated with retaining EBS snapshots can add up quickly, especially if you are taking snapshots at daily intervals. Use the AWS Backup service to create a layered backup approach. This service will let you define multiple backup and retention schedules (e.g., 6 months of monthly backups and 1 week of daily) while automating the purging of costly backup retention.

Right Sizing

Right sizing is the process of matching instance types and sizes to performance and capacity requirements at the lowest possible cost. To achieve cost optimization, right sizing must become an ongoing process within your organization. Many inexperienced cloud practitioners, worried that they will hit capacity, tend to hedge their bets and overprovision resources with more RAM, CPU, or disk than is needed. Over time, this leads to significant waste as idle resources drive up cost. On the other hand, if you are constantly underprovisioned, you will pay for it in poor business outcomes.

AWS provides APIs, SDKs, and features that allow resources to be modified as demands change.

The following are examples of how you can change the instance type to match performance and capacity requirements:

- On Amazon Elastic Compute Cloud (Amazon EC2), you can perform a stop-and-start to allow a change of instance size or instance type.

- On Amazon EBS, you can increase volume size or adjust performance while volumes are still in use to improve performance through increased input/output operations per second (IOPS) or throughput or to reduce cost by changing the type of volume.

Select the Right Use Case

As you monitor current performance, identify the following usage needs and patterns so that you can take advantage of potential right-sizing options:

Steady State   The load remains constant over time, making forecasting simple. Consider using Savings Plans (discussed in the next section) to gain significant savings.

Variable, but Predictable   The load changes on a predictable schedule. Consider using Auto Scaling.

Dev/Test/Production   Development, testing, and production environments can usually be turned off outside of work hours.

Temporary   Temporary workloads that have flexible start times and can be interrupted are good candidates for Spot Instances instead of On-Demand Instances.

Select the Right Instance Family

When you launch an instance, the instance type that you specify determines the hardware of the host computer used for your instance. Each instance type offers different compute, memory, and storage capabilities, and they are grouped in instance families based on these capabilities. Depending on the AWS offering, you can determine the right instance family for your infrastructure.

Amazon Elastic Cloud Compute

Amazon EC2 provides a wide selection of instances that give you flexibility to right-size CPU and memory needs for your compute resources to match capacity needs at the lowest cost. Following are the different options for CPU, memory, and network resources:

General Purpose (Includes A1, T4g, T2, M6i, and M7g Instance Types)   A1 and T4g instances deliver significant cost savings and are ideally suited for scale-out workloads, such as web servers, containerized microservices, caching fleets, and distributed data stores. T3 instances offer a low-cost option, providing baseline CPU resources that can burst when needed. They are ideal for lower throughput applications, such as administrative tools or low-traffic websites. M6i and M7g instances provide a balance of CPU, memory, and network resources, making them ideal for running small and midsize databases, memory-intensive processing, caching fleets, and backend servers. Instance types ending in "g" use ARM-based AWS Graviton processors, while those ending in "i" use Intel Xeon processors.

Compute Optimized (Includes the C6i, C7g, and C6gn Instance Types)   This family has a higher ratio of virtual CPUs to memory than the other families and the lowest cost per virtual CPU of all of the EC2 instance types. Consider compute-optimized instances first if you are running CPU-bound, scale-out applications, such as front-end fleets for high-traffic websites, on-demand batch processing, distributed analytics, web servers, video encoding, and high-performance science and engineering applications.

Memory Optimized (Includes the X2idn, R6i, and R7g Instance Types)   Designed for memory-intensive applications, these instances have the lowest cost per GB of RAM of all EC2 instance types. Use these instances if your application is memory-bound.

Storage Optimized (Includes the I4i and Im4gn Instance Types)   Optimized to deliver tens of thousands of low-latency, random input/output (I/O) operations per second (IOPS) to applications. Storage-optimized instances are ideal for large deployments of NoSQL databases and high I/O workloads. I4i instances are designed for I/O-intensive applications, equipped with high-performance NVMe SSD storage, and can deliver up to 30 GB/second of disk throughput. Im4gn instances are specialized for dense storage workloads, such as Hadoop, distributed computing, data warehousing, and log processing.

Accelerated Computing (Includes the P4d, G5, and F1 Instance Types)   Provides access to hardware-based compute accelerators, such as graphics processing units (GPUs) or field programmable gate arrays (FPGAs). Accelerated-computing instances enable more parallelism for higher throughput on compute-intensive workloads.

Amazon Relational Database Service

Like Amazon EC2 instances, Amazon Relational Database Service (Amazon RDS) provides options to choose from database instances that are optimized for memory, performance, and I/O.

Standard Performance   Designed for general-purpose database workloads that do not run many in-memory functions. This family has the most options for provisioning increased IOPS.

Burstable Performance   For workloads that require burstable performance capacity.

Memory Optimized   Optimized for in-memory functions and big data analysis.

Use Reserved Instances and Savings Plans

Amazon EC2 provides several purchasing options to enable you to optimize your costs based on your needs.

AWS Pricing for Reserved Instances

With EC2 reserved instances, you can achieve up to 72 percent lower EC2 costs than On-Demand pricing by committing to a one-year or three-year duration at the time of purchase.

There are three payment options for Reserved Instances (RIs).

No Up-front No up-front payment is required, and Reserved Instances are billed monthly. This requires a good payment history with AWS.

Partial Up-front A portion of the cost is paid up-front, and the remaining hours in the term are billed at a discounted hourly rate, regardless of whether the RI is being used.

All Up-front Full payment is made at the start of the term, with no other costs or additional hourly charges incurred for the remainder of the term, regardless of hours used.

EC2 Reservations

EC2 Reserved Instances both lower costs and reserve capacity (hence the name) within a particular availability zone and region. Applications with predictable steady-state resource demands can benefit significantly from reserved instances.

- For applications that have steady state or predictable usage, Reserved Instances can provide significant savings compared to using On-Demand Instances, without requiring a change to your workload.

Convertible Reserved Instances

Convertible Reserved Instances are provided for a one-year or three-year term, and they enable conversion to different families, new pricing, different instance sizes, different platforms, or tenancy during the period. Use Convertible Reserved Instances when you are uncertain about instance needs in the future, but you are still committed to using EC2 instances for a three-year term in exchange for a significant discount.

Suppose that you own an EC2 Reserved Instance for a `c4.8xlarge` for three years. This Reserved Instance applies to any usage of a Linux/Unix c4 instance with shared tenancy in the same region as the Reserved Instance, such as one `c4.8xlarge` instance, two `c4.4xlarge` instances, or 16 `c4.large` instances, during this term. This adds flexibility to match the new needs of your workloads.

- There are no limits to how many times you perform an exchange, as long as the target Convertible Reserved Instance is of an equal or higher value than the Convertible Reserved Instances that you are exchanging.

- Exchanging Convertible Reserved Instances is free of charge, but you might need to pay a true-up cost if the value is lower than the value of the Reserved Instances for which you're exchanging. For example, you can convert C3 Reserved Instances to C4 Reserved Instances to take advantage of a newer instance type, or you can convert C4 Reserved Instances to M4 Reserved Instances if your application requires more memory. You can also use Convertible Reserved Instances to take advantage of EC2 price reductions over time.

Reserved Instance Marketplace

Use the *Reserved Instance Marketplace* to sell your unused Reserved Instances and buy Reserved Instances from other AWS customers. As your needs change throughout the course of your term, the AWS Marketplace provides an option to buy Reserved Instances for shorter terms and with a wider selection of prices.

RDS Reservations

Reserved database instances are not physical instances; they are a billing discount applied to the use of certain on-demand DB instances in your account. Discounts for reserved DB instances are tied to instance type and AWS region.

All Reserved Instance types are available for Aurora, MySQL, MariaDB, PostgreSQL, Oracle, and SQL Server database engines.

- Reserved Instances can also provide significant cost savings for mission-critical applications that run on multi-AZ database deployments for higher availability and data durability. Reserved Instances can minimize your costs up to 69 percent over On-Demand rates when used in steady state.

- Most production applications require database servers to be available 24/7. Consider using Reserved Instances to gain substantial savings if you are currently using On-Demand stances.

- Any usage of running DB instances that exceeds the number of applicable Reserved Instances you have purchased are charged the On-Demand rate. For example, if you own three Reserved Instances with the same database engine and instance type (or instance family, if size flexibility applies) in a given region, the billing system checks each hour to determine how many total instances you have running that match those parameters. If it is three or fewer, you are charged the Reserved Instance rate for each instance running that hour. If more than three are running, you are charged the On-Demand rate for the additional instances.

- With size flexibility, your Reserved Instance's discounted rate is automatically applied to usage of any size in the instance family (using the same database engine) for the MySQL,

MariaDB, PostgreSQL, and Amazon Aurora database engines and the "Bring your own license" (BYOL) edition of the Oracle database engine. For example, suppose that you purchased a db.m4.2xlarge MySQL Reserved Instance in US East (N. Virginia). The discounted rate of this Reserved Instance can automatically apply to two db.m4.xlarge MySQL instances without you needing to do anything.

- The Reserved Instance discounted rate also applies to usage to both single-AZ and multi-AZ configurations for the same database engine and instance family.

  Suppose that you purchased a db.r3.large PostgreSQL Single-AZ Reserved Instance in EU (Frankfurt). The discounted rate of this Reserved Instance can automatically apply to 50 percent of the usage of a db.r3.large PostgreSQL multi-AZ instance in the same region.

Savings Plans

Offering the same level of discount with greatly increased flexibility and a wider range of resources covered, Savings Plans are an excellent supplement (or outright replacement) for Reserved Instances. Like RIs, Savings Plans operate on a 1-year or 3-year commitment and offer the same three payment plans. In both cases, when you exceed your plan, your costs revert to normal on-demand pricing.

However, Savings Plans are reckoned by dollars spent, not by instance time, and they allow a lot more mobility and resources covered. If you are just getting into AWS, Savings Plans are the way to go. Let's look at the two types and how they differ from RIs.

EC2 Savings Plans

Very similar to EC2 Reserved Instances, EC2 savings plans differ from RIs by allowing you to switch between Regions and between instance types in the same family (e.g., m1.medium to m1.large).

Compute Savings Plans

Here's where Savings Plans really start to become attractive: Compute Plans extend to both Fargate compute clusters and Lambda execution time. Not only that, but they can apply very generally to EC2, giving you savings regardless of region, OS, family, or size. If you have a Compute Savings Plan in effect, you can migrate a workload from EC2 to Lambda and still retain the up to 66 percent savings offered by the plan. It's quite flexible!

It's important to note that unlike RIs, Savings Plans do not actually reserve capacity; a Savings Plan on an in-demand instance type doesn't mean you'll be able to spin one up. However, you can join your Savings Plan with On-Demand Capacity Reservations to achieve a similar effect.

Use Spot Instances

Amazon EC2 Spot Instances offer spare compute capacity in the AWS Cloud at steep discounts compared to On-Demand Instances.

You can use Spot Instances to save up to 90 percent on stateless web applications, big data, containers, CI/CD, HPC, and other fault-tolerant workloads. Or, scale your workload throughput by up to 10X and stay within the existing budget.

Spot Fleets

Spot Fleets let you request and manage multiple Spot Instances automatically, which provides the lowest price per unit of capacity for your cluster or application, such as a batch-processing job, a Hadoop workflow, or an HPC grid computing job. You can include the instance types that your application needs and define a target capacity based on your application requirements (in units, including instances, vCPUs, memory, storage, or network throughput) and update the target capacity after the fleet is launched. Spot Fleets enable you to launch and maintain the target capacity and to request resources automatically to replace any that are disrupted or manually terminated.

The most useful feature of Spot Fleets is the ability to include On-Demand instance capacity in your Spot Fleet request. If there is capacity, the On-Demand request is fulfilled. If there is capacity and availability, the balance of the target capacity is fulfilled as Spot. This gives you a way to deploy on low-cost Spot instances while maintaining a baseline of on-demand compute that cannot be revoked.

The following example specifies the desired target capacity as 10, of which 5 must be On-Demand capacity. Spot capacity is not specified; it is implied that any non-On-Demand instances should be fulfilled by Spot. If there is available Amazon EC2 capacity and availability, Amazon EC2 launches 5 capacity units as On-Demand and 5 capacity units (10 – 5 = 5) as Spot.

```
{
"IamFleetRole":"arn:aws:iam::1234567890:role/aws-ec2-spot-fleet-tagging-role",
"AllocationStrategy":"capacity-optimized",
"TargetCapacity":10,
"SpotPrice":null,
"ValidFrom":"2024-04-04T15:58:13Z",
"ValidUntil":"2025-04-04T15:58:13Z",
"TerminateInstancesWithExpiration": true,
"LaunchSpecifications":[],
"Type":"maintain",
"OnDemandTargetCapacity":5,
"LaunchTemplateConfigs":[
    {
"LaunchTemplateSpecification":{
"LaunchTemplateId": "lt-0dbb04d4a6abcabcabc",
"Version": "2"
    },
"Overrides": [
        {
```

```
"InstanceType": "t2.medium",
"WeightedCapacity": 1,
"SubnetId": "subnet-d0dc51fb"
        }
    ]
  }
 ]
}
```

Design for Continuity

With Spot Instances, you never pay more than the maximum price you specify when purchasing the instance. If the Spot price for that instance type rises higher than your max or if overall EC2 demand surges such that capacity is no longer available, your instance will be terminated automatically (or stopped/hibernated, if you opt for this behavior on a persistent request).

Spot offers features such as termination notices, persistent requests, and spot block duration to help you better track and control when Spot Instances can run and terminate (or stop/hibernate).

Using Termination Notices

If you need to save state, upload final log files, or remove Spot Instances from a load balancer before interruption, you can use termination notices, which are issued two minutes before interruption.

When your instance is targeted for termination, the notice is written to the instance's metadata two minutes before its termination time. From your EC2 instance, the notice is accessible at http://169.254.169.254/latest/meta-data/spot/termination-time and includes the time when the shutdown signal will be sent. If your time is up, that endpoint will return data; otherwise, it's absent, and you'll get an HTTP 404 Not Found.

Monitoring Spot termination from inside the instance itself requires continuous polling of the metadata endpoint. Spot termination notifications can also trigger CloudWatch alarms; if the action you need to take can be handled by an EC2 action or a Lambda, you may consider implementing this as an external monitor, rather than relying on application code.

Using Persistent Requests

Using persistent requests, you can set Spot requests to remain open so that a new instance is launched to replace any terminated instance. You can also have your Amazon EBS–backed instance stopped upon interruption and restarted when Spot has capacity at your preferred price.

Minimizing the Impact of Interruptions

Because AWS may terminate Spot Instances at any time, it is any applications you run on Spot instances must be resilient to interruption. Many tasks can be run in parallel over multiple instances and are resilient to node failures by default. For other workloads, some ways to build in resilience to terminated instances include the following:

Adding Checkpoints   Add checkpoints that save your work periodically—for example, to an Amazon EBS volume. Another approach is to launch your instances from Amazon EBS–backed AMI.

Splitting up the work   By using Amazon Simple Queue Service (Amazon SQS), you can queue up work increments and track work that has already been done.

Use Auto Scaling

Auto Scaling can be used to reduce cost and maintain performance by automatically increasing the number of resources during the demand spikes and decreasing capacity when demand lulls. Auto Scaling is well suited for applications that have stable demand patterns and for ones that experience hourly, daily, or weekly variability in usage. Auto Scaling is useful for applications that show steady demand patterns and that experience frequent variations in usage.

Amazon EC2 Auto Scaling

Amazon EC2 Auto Scaling helps you scale your EC2 instances and Spot Fleet capacity up or down automatically according to conditions that you define. Auto Scaling is generally used with AWS Load Balancers to distribute incoming application traffic across multiple EC2 instances in an Auto Scaling Group. Auto Scaling is triggered using scaling plans consisting of policies that define how to scale (manual, schedule, and demand spikes) and the metrics and alarms to monitor in Amazon CloudWatch.

CloudWatch metrics are used to trigger the scaling event. These metrics can be standard Amazon EC2 metrics, such as CPU utilization, network throughput, Application Load Balancer observed request/response latency, and even custom metrics that might originate from application code on your EC2 instances.

You can use EC2 Auto Scaling to increase the number of EC2 instances automatically during demand spikes to maintain performance and decrease capacity during lulls to reduce costs.

Dynamic Scaling

The *dynamic scaling* capabilities of EC2 Auto Scaling refers to the functionality that automatically increases or decreases capacity based on load or other metrics. For example, if your CPU spikes above 80 percent (and you have an alarm set up), EC2 Auto Scaling can add a new instance dynamically, reducing the need to provision Amazon EC2 capacity manually in advance. Alternatively, you can set a target value by using the `Request CountPerTarget` metric from an Application Load Balancer. EC2 Auto Scaling will then automatically adjust the number of EC2 instances as needed to maintain your target.

Predictive Scaling

With *predictive scaling*, AWS uses machine learning to analyze past traffic patterns, forecasting load, and adjusting capacity as needed. This scaling configuration can automatically achieve cost savings and good performance by anticipating your scaling needs.

Scheduled Scaling

Schedule-based scaling allows you to plan ahead, anticipating known periods of load with additional instances provisioned in advance. For instance, you might scale up every day at the start of business hours, thus ensuring that resources are available when users arrive, or you might scale down a development environment outside of office hours, when no one is working.

In addition to horizontal scaling (e.g., increasing the number of instances that work together), you can also vertically scale by increasing the power of a single compute resource. For example, you could scale up a production EC2 system by changing the instance size or class. This can be achieved by stopping and starting the instance and selecting the different instance size or class. You can also apply this technique to other resources, such as EBS volumes, which can be modified to increase size, adjust performance (IOPS), or change the volume type while in use.

Instances Purchasing Options

With EC2 Auto Scaling, you can provision and automatically scale instances across purchase options, availability zones, and instance families. For instance, you can include Spot Instances with On-Demand and Reserved Instances in a single Auto Scaling Group to save up to 90 percent on compute. You have the option to define the desired split between On-Demand and Spot capacity, select which instance types work for your application, and specify preferences for how EC2 Auto Scaling should distribute the Auto Scaling Group capacity within each purchasing model.

Golden Images

A *golden image* is a snapshot of a particular state of a resource, such as an EC2 instance, Amazon EBS volumes, and Amazon RDS DB instance. When horizontally scaling a web application on EC2, it's important for new instances to spin up and reach healthy status as soon as possible. If you create a golden image from a fully configured instance, save that image as an AMI (Amazon Machine Image), and then use that AMI as the base image for your Auto Scaling launch template, you can significantly improve scaling response time, because new instances won't have to waste time installing software that is already baked into the golden image. Just remember to regularly patch and rebuild your AMIs so that your EC2 instances remain secure.

AWS Auto Scaling

When most people think about Auto Scaling in AWS, they think of EC2; however, AWS allows you to automatically scale other resources as well. *AWS Auto Scaling* can scale resources on ECS, DynamoDB, Aurora, EC2 Spot Fleets, and more.

If your app uses these scalable resources and has spiky traffic with periods of heavy load, AWS Auto Scaling is a great choice. A good example would be an e-commerce web application that receives variable traffic throughout the day. It follows a standard three-tier architecture with an Application Load Balancer for distributing incoming traffic, EC2 for the compute layer, and DynamoDB for the data layer. In this case, AWS Auto Scaling can scale the EC2 Auto Scaling groups and DynamoDB tables powering the application in response to the demand curve.

AWS Auto Scaling bases its scaling recommendations on the most popular scaling metrics and thresholds used for Auto Scaling and provides sensible defaults to let you start scaling with little initial configuration.

Predictive Scaling

Predictive scaling for AWS Auto Scaling uses machine learning to analyze current past metric patterns and automatically adjust thresholds for scaling resources up and down. This can be a great option for applications whose traffic patterns tend to be regular but change over time, perhaps seasonally. Predictive scaling can help you avoid needing to anticipate your load ahead of time.

DynamoDB Auto Scaling

DynamoDB automatic scaling automatically adjusts provisioned throughput capacity (i.e., Write Capacity Units and Read Capacity Units) in response to observed traffic patterns. This lets your tables increase their provisioned read and write capacity to handle sudden increases in traffic without throttling.

Amazon Aurora Auto Scaling

Amazon Aurora automatic scaling dynamically adjusts the number of Aurora Replicas provisioned for an Aurora DB cluster. When the connectivity or workload decreases, Aurora automatic scaling removes unnecessary Aurora Replicas so that you don't pay for unused provisioned DB instances.

Amazon Aurora Serverless is an on-demand, automatic scaling configuration for Amazon Aurora. An Aurora Serverless DB cluster automatically starts up, shuts down, and scales capacity up or down based on your application's needs.

Use Containers

As we discussed in Chapter 9, "Secure Configuration and Container Management," containers build everything your applications need to run into a self-contained, portable, replicable image. Containers share resources with the host operating system but run on top of a Docker runtime. Running Docker locally as your development environment means that you can validate almost everything about how the app will run in production before deploying it, since all its dependencies are within the container.

Containers provide process isolation that lets you granularly set CPU and memory utilization for better use of compute resources.

Containerize Everything

Containers are lightweight and provide a consistent, portable software environment for applications to run and scale effortlessly anywhere.

Amazon Elastic Container Service (Amazon ECS) enables you to use containers as building blocks for your applications by eliminating the need for you to install, operate, and scale your own cluster management infrastructure.

ECS tasks are well suited for ad hoc or scheduled (but finite) job runs, such as batch data transfers, while ECS services turn tasks into resilient, long-running apps that are suitable for cases such as building a highly available e-commerce site.

ECS is integrated with familiar features like Application Load Balancing, EBS volumes, VPC, and IAM.

Containers without Servers

AWS Fargate is an ECS launch type that provisions a cluster without your needing to create or manage the underlying instances. Not only that, you do not have to worry about task placement strategies, such as binpacking or host spread, and tasks are automatically balanced across availability zones.

For developers who require more granular, server-level control over the infrastructure, Amazon ECS EC2 launch type enables you to manage a cluster of servers and schedule placement of containers on the servers.

Use Serverless Approaches

Serverless architectures are ideal for applications for which load can vary dynamically. Using a serverless approach means no compute costs are incurred when there is no user traffic, while still offering instant scale to meet high demand, such as a flash sale on an e-commerce site or a social media mention that drives a sudden wave of traffic.

Benefits gained by using AWS serverless services include the following:

- No need to manage servers
- No need to ensure application fault tolerance, availability, and explicit fleet management to scale to peak load
- No charge for idle capacity

You can focus on product innovation and rapidly construct these applications:

- Amazon S3 offers a simple hosting solution for static content.
- AWS Lambda, with Amazon API Gateway, supports dynamic API requests using functions.

- Amazon DynamoDB offers a simple storage solution for session and per-user state.
- Amazon Cognito provides a way to handle user registration, authentication, and access control to resources.
- AWS SAM can be used by developers to describe the various elements of an application.
- AWS CodePipeline can set up a CI/CD toolchain with a few clicks.
- AWS Amplify lets you quickly spin up backend infrastructure for use on front-end apps hosted in AWS.

Compared to traditional infrastructure approaches, an application is also often less expensive to develop, deliver, and operate when it is architected in a serverless fashion. The serverless application model is generic, and it applies to almost any type of application from a start-up to an enterprise.

Optimize Lambda Usage

AWS Lambda lets you run code for virtually any type of application or backend service, all with zero administration. A variety of events can trigger Lambda functions, enabling developers to build reactive, event-driven systems that only run code when needed. Not only that, but under load, Lambda is designed to scale by firing up as many instances of your function code as needed, so your compute is always right-sized to your need. With Lambda, there's no need to pre-scale or even auto-scale, because AWS launches exactly as much compute as needed at a given time.

Consider the following recommendations for optimizing Lambda functions:

Optimal Memory Size   The memory usage for your function is determined per invocation and can be viewed in CloudWatch Logs. By analyzing the MaxMemoryUsed field in the Invocation report, you can determine whether your function needs more memory or whether you over-provisioned the function's RAM.

Language Runtime Performance   If your application use case is both latency-sensitive and susceptible to incurring the initial invocation cost frequently (spiky traffic or infrequent use), then consider using one of the interpreted languages, such as Node.js or Python.

Optimizing Code   Much of the application performance depends on your logic and dependencies. Pay attention to reusing the objects and using global/static variables by defining them outside the handler function.

Avoiding Recursion   Be wary of the possibility of creating infinite loops in AWS. For instance, if you set up an S3 bucket to trigger a Lambda and that Lambda writes back to the same bucket, your code will be invoked continuously, running up your bill. To help avoid this, Lambda tracks "chains of requests," which are invocations originating with the same event. If you exceed approximately 16 invocations from the same event, Lambda will start to block invocations from that source. If you have a dead-letter queue set up on the function, the blocked event will be sent to it for review.

Optimize Storage

AWS storage services are optimized for different scenarios. When evaluating your storage requirements, consider data storage options for each workload separately.

To optimize the storage, you must first understand the performance levels of your workloads. Conduct a performance analysis to measure input/output operations per second (IOPS), throughput, quick access to your data, durability, sensitivity, size, and budget.

Amazon offers three broad categories of storage services: object, block, and file storage. Each offering is designed to meet a different storage requirement, which gives you flexibility to find the solution that works best for your storage scenarios.

Optimize Amazon S3

Identifying the right storage class and moving less-frequently-accessed Amazon S3 data to cheaper storage tiers yields considerable savings. For example, by moving data from the STANDARD to the STANDARD_IA storage class, you can save up to 60 percent (on a per-gigabyte basis) of Amazon S3 pricing. By moving data that is at the end of its life cycle and accessed on rare occasions from Amazon S3 Glacier, you can save up to 80 percent of S3 pricing.

Storage Management Tools/Features

The following sections describe some of the tools that help you determine when to transition data to another storage class.

Cost Allocation S3 Bucket Tags

To track the storage cost or other criteria for individual projects or groups of projects, label your S3 buckets using cost allocation tags. A *cost allocation tag* is a key-value pair that you associate with an S3 bucket that tells you who should pay for the storage costs—a useful bit of metadata when calculating chargeback for customers sharing resources on a central AWS account.

Amazon S3 Analytics: Storage Class Analysis

This feature analyzes storage access patterns to help you decide when to transition the right data to the right storage class.

After storage class analysis observes the infrequent access patterns of a filtered set of data over time, you can use the analysis results to help you improve your life cycle policies. You can configure storage class analysis to analyze all the objects in a bucket at once, or you can configure filters to group objects together for analysis by common prefix or tags. Filtering by object groups is often the best way to benefit from storage class analysis.

You can use the Amazon S3 console, the `s3:PutAnalyticsConfiguration` REST API, or the equivalent from the AWS CLI or AWS SDKs to configure storage class analysis.

Amazon S3 Inventory

S3 Inventory runs a weekly or monthly audit report on your objects' replication and encryption status. It produces CSV files containing object metadata and allows multiple inventory lists per bucket, organized by S3 metadata tags. For advanced analysis, you can query these inventories using SQL through various analytics platforms like Amazon Athena, Redshift Spectrum, Presto, Hive, and Spark, giving you deep insights into your S3 data.

Amazon S3 Select

Amazon S3 Select lets you use SQL to query inside an S3 object. Contrast this with Athena, whose purpose is to let you use SQL to query across many objects.

The following is a Python sample code snippet that shows how to retrieve columns from a CSV file stored as an S3 object. This code queries the city and airport code where country name is similar to "United States." If you have column headers and you set FileHeader Info to Use, you can identify columns by name in the SQL expression.

```
result = s3.select_object_content(
        Bucket=example-bucket-us-west-2',
        Key='sample-data/airportCodes.csv',
        ExpressionType='SQL',
        Expression="select s.city, s.code from s3object s where" \
                "s.\"Country (Name)\" like '%United States%'",
        InputSerialization = {'CSV': {"FileHeaderInfo": "Use"}},
        OutputSerialization = {'CSV': {}},
    :
```

Optimize Amazon EBS

With Amazon EBS, you are paying for provisioned capacity and performance—even if the volume is unattached or has low write activity. Optimizing EBS means actively deleting unattached volumes and unneeded snapshots and monitoring for overprovisioned volumes that may be able to work with a lower storage allocation or IOPS rating.

Check Configuration

There are a few behaviors of EBS snapshots and volumes you should know about in order to get the best performance out of them:

- New EBS volumes achieve maximum performance immediately, as soon as they are attached. On the other hand, volumes restored from snapshots take some time to initialize as they fetch their archived data from S3, resulting in higher initial per-block latency when writing to each block.

- To counter the slow start of snapshot-based volumes, you have two options. First, you may write some code to force a read on every block of the volume; second, you may use the Fast Snapshot Restore option on individual snapshots in your account. This toggle prompts AWS to pre-warm the snapshot so there is no initialization penalty. Maintaining this option can be pricey, as you're billed $0.75 / hour for every hour it is enabled. Employ this in circumstances where immediate I/O performance is essential.

- To achieve a higher level of performance for a filesystem than you can provision on a single volume, create a RAID 0 (zero) array. Consider using RAID 0 when I/O performance is more important than fault tolerance. For example, you could use it with a heavily used database where data replication is already set up separately.

Use Monitoring Tools

AWS offers tools that help you optimize block storage.

Amazon CloudWatch

Amazon CloudWatch automatically collects a range of data points for EBS volumes, and you can then set alarms on volume behavior.

Consider the following important metrics:

BurstBalance   When your burst allocation is depleted, volume I/O credits (for gp3 volumes) or volume throughput credits (for st1 and sc1 volumes) are throttled to the baseline. Check the `BurstBalance` value to determine whether your volume is being throttled for this reason.

VolumeQueueLength   If your disk latency is too high, check `VolumeQueueLength`, which will indicate whether your application is hitting a ceiling on IOPS. If so, try switching to a larger gp3 volume with higher baseline IOPS ratings or do an io2 volume with Provisioned IOPS.

VolumeReadBytes, VolumeWriteBytes, VolumeReadOps, VolumeWriteOps
HDD-based volumes work best when they are moving data close to the 1MB maximum I/O size. `VolumeWriteBytes` and `VolumeWriteOps` are two metrics that can tell you, on average, the size of your disk operations. If the average size is below 64 KB, performance may be improved by configuring your OS to increase the size of the I/O operations.

AWS Trusted Advisor

AWS Trusted Advisor is another way for you to analyze your infrastructure to identify unattached, underutilized, and overutilized EBS volumes.

Delete Unattached Amazon EBS Volumes

Storing EBS volumes in your account costs money. To lower your bills, check frequently for volumes in the "available" state, which indicates they are not attached to any instance. You can do this manually by sorting volumes in the EBS web console or by writing a script that uses the CLI or SDK to scan your whole account, across regions, and report on volumes that are eligible for deletion.

If necessary, take a snapshot before you delete a volume so that you can restore it later. Snapshots cost less over time than volumes—but they do accumulate. Make sure to regularly sweep your account of unneeded snapshots as well.

Resize or Change the EBS Volume Type

Observe CloudWatch metrics to find EBS volumes that are underutilized, and scale those volumes down to a more appropriate level.

Follow these tips:

- Some volumes can be resized dynamically, without detaching them from their instances. For details on when this option is available, see `https://docs.aws.amazon.com/ebs/latest/userguide/requesting-ebs-volume-modifications.html`.

- For General Purpose SSD gp3 volumes, focus on how much data you're actually storing, since you pay for capacity.

- With Provisioned IOPS SSD io2 volumes, you pay for IOPS utilization, so watch that you are not overprovisioned. A ceiling of 10–20 percent should be sufficient; anything else, and you should reduce your IOPS request to avoid overpaying.

- For large volumes (say, over 500 GB), an HDD sc1volume may help you save—if the I/O performance is acceptable.

Optimize Data Transfer

Optimizing data transfer ensures that you minimize data transfer costs. Review your user presence if global or local and how the data gets located in order to reduce the latency issues.

- Use Amazon CloudFront to push content to edge locations that are physically nearer your customers, reducing latency for a better user experience while driving down overall data transfer costs.

- *Amazon S3 transfer acceleration* helps you optimize the transfer of data into S3 by using the CloudFront distribution network. It is a great way to improve data upload speeds when you are migrating to AWS.

- When uploading large files, use *multipart uploads* maximize throughput by breaking your files apart before transfer. They give the following advantages:

  - *Improved throughput*: You can upload parts in parallel to improve throughput.

  - *Quick recovery from any network issues*: Smaller part size minimizes the impact of restarting a failed upload due to a network error.

- *Pause and resume object uploads*: You can upload object parts over time. After you initiate a multipart upload, there is no expiry; you must explicitly complete or abort the multipart upload.

- *Begin an upload before you know the final object size*: You can upload an object as you are creating it.

- Using Amazon Route 53, you can reduce latency for your users by serving their requests from the AWS region for which network latency is lowest. Amazon Route 53 latency-based routing lets you use Domain Name System (DNS) to route user requests to the AWS region that will give your users the fastest response.

Monitoring Costs

Managing costs in AWS is a continuous process. Amazon makes many tools available to you to track your spend and identify overprovisioned resources. Monitoring these indicators and taking action to adjust your cloud infrastructure appropriately can help lower your bill, but it must be a constant effort, as changes in user behavior can easily shift demand over time. AWS offers the following services to help you stay on top of this ever-changing utilization landscape.

Cost Management Tools

AWS offers a variety of tools for understanding, tracking, and managing your resource costs. Let's delve into some of these tools and how they can help.

AWS Trusted Advisor

AWS Trusted Advisor follow AWS best practices by analyzing your environment and providing recommendations that can help you avoid waste and save money.

Here are some Trusted Advisor checks that help you determine how to reduce your bill:

- Low utilization of Amazon EC2 instances
- Idle resources, such as load balancers and Amazon RDS DB instances
- Underutilized Amazon EBS volumes and Amazon Redshift clusters
- Unassociated Elastic IP addresses
- Optimization, lease expiration—Amazon Reserved Instances
- Inefficiently configured Amazon Route 53 latency record sets

AWS Cost Explorer

AWS Cost Explorer is a tool that helps you understand your overall account bill by breaking the charges down into individual services and resources. Cost Explorer helps you nail down the drivers of your cloud spend and observe trends over time.

Cost Explorer gives you sophisticated business analysis reports for your AWS resource usage. Choose from a drop-down menu to view costs through the lens of such dimensions as resource type, availability zone, region, or even individual API calls such as S3's `PutObject`. This level of detail gives you tremendous insight into exactly what influences your bill at the end of the month.

Cost Explorer also lets you slice and filter reports by tag values, showing once again the many advantages of tagging your resources not only with names, but with meaningful metadata such as the associated project, application, or team. Being able to filter costs by these dimensions can be very helpful in assessing the overall cost of a particular organizational unit or initiative; indeed, it's essential if your organization conducts any sort of internal accounting, billing divisions or units for their cloud costs.

AWS Cost Explorer built-in reports include the following:

Monthly Costs by AWS Service   Allows you to visualize the costs and usage associated with your top five cost-accruing AWS services and gives you a detailed breakdown on all services in the table view. The reports let you adjust the time range to view historical data going back up to 12 months to gain an understanding of your cost trends.

EC2 Monthly Cost and Usage   Lets you view all AWS costs over the past two months, in addition to your current month-to-date costs. From there, you can drill down into the costs and usage associated with particular linked accounts, regions, tags, and more.

Monthly Costs by Linked Account   Allows you to view the distribution of costs across your organization.

Monthly Running Costs   Provides an overview of all running costs over the past three months and provides forecasted numbers for the coming month with a corresponding confidence interval. This report gives you good insight into how your costs are trending and helps you plan ahead.

AWS Cost Explorer Reserved Instance Reports include the following:

RI Utilization Report   Visualizes the degree to which you are using your existing resources and identifies opportunities to improve your Reserved Instance cost efficiencies. The report shows how much you saved by using Reserved Instances, how much you overspent on Reserved Instances, and your net savings from purchasing Reserved Instances during the selected time range. This helps you to determine whether you have purchased too many Reserved Instances.

RI Coverage Report   Discovers how much of your overall instance usage is covered by Reserved Instances so that you can make informed decisions about when to purchase or modify a Reserved Instance to ensure maximum coverage. These show how much you spent on On-Demand Instances and how much you might have saved had you purchased more reservations. The report enables you to determine whether you have under-purchased Reserved Instances.

AWS Cost Categories

Cost Categories is a feature of the Billing and Cost Management console that lets you create arbitrary groupings of resources for use in cost analysis. While tagging can be a great way to group resources (say, by a "project" tag), cost categories gives you the flexibility to define groups governed by tag, resource type, availability zone, and many other criteria. These categories then appear elsewhere, such as in cost report filters, to let you easily observe cost metrics around the group you defined.

AWS Budgets

With *AWS Budgets*, you can set alarms to let you know when your costs or usage exceed (or are forecasted to exceed) your budgeted amount. You can also use AWS Budgets to set Reserved Instance utilization or coverage targets and receive alerts when your utilization drops below the threshold you define. Key features include:

- Tracking at monthly, quarterly, or yearly levels with customizable time frames
- Refined budget tracking across multiple dimensions (e.g., AWS service, linked account, tags)
- Thresholds to alert you before your budgets are exceeded (e.g., alerts that occur at 80 percent of your target spend amount)

With AWS Budget alarms, you can make sure to stay in-the-know on your costs so that you can take action before getting an expectedly high bill.

AWS Cost and Usage Report

The *AWS Cost and Usage Report* tracks your AWS usage and provides estimated charges associated with that usage. You can configure this report to present the data hourly or daily. It is updated at least once a day until it is finalized at the end of the billing period. The AWS Cost and Usage report gives you the most granular insight possible into your costs and usage, and it is the source of truth for the billing pipeline. It can be used to develop advanced custom metrics using business intelligence, data analytics, and third-party cost optimization tools. Figure 16.1 shows how the Cost and Usage Report breaks down your monthly spend by resource type.

The AWS Cost and Usage report is delivered automatically to an S3 bucket that you specify, and it can be downloaded directly from there (standard Amazon S3 storage rates apply). It can also be ingested into Amazon Redshift or uploaded to Amazon QuickSight.

Cost Anomaly Detection

AWS Cost Anomaly Detection is a machine learning–powered feature of Cost Explorer that continuously monitors your AWS cost and usage to detect spending anomalies. When you set up anomaly monitoring around individual AWS services, you set subscriptions that alert you via email or SNS when charges occur that are inconsistent with the observed past behavior of your account.

FIGURE 16.1   The Cost and Usage Report showing resource spend as a stacked bar chart

Unexpected charges can come from anywhere: out-of-control SDK scripts, malicious actors with access to your account, or simple misconfigurations that spin up costlier resources than expected. Cost Anomaly Detection is a valuable tool in your toolbox to help you quickly respond to and mitigate these kinds of unexpected cost spikes.

AWS Cost Optimization Monitor

AWS Cost Optimization Monitor is an automated reference deployment solution that processes detailed billing reports to provide granular metrics that you can search, analyze, and visualize in a customizable dashboard. The solution uploads detailed billing report data automatically to Amazon Elasticsearch Service (Amazon ES) for analysis and leverages its built-in support for Kibana, enabling you to visualize the first batch of data as soon as it's processed.

The default dashboard is configured to show specific costs and usage metrics. All of these metrics, as listed here, were selected based on best practices observed across AWS customers:

- EC2 Instances Running per Hour
- Total Cost
- Cost by Tag Key: Name
- Cost by EC2 Instance Type
- EC2 Elasticity
- EC2 Hours per Dollar Invested

Cost Optimization: AWS Compute Optimizer

AWS Compute Optimizer is an automated AWS reference deployment solution that analyzes past utilization data (typically the last two weeks) to provide detailed recommendations for right-sizing many cloud resources, such as EC2 instances, RDS databases, ECS services, EBS volumes, and Lambda functions. Compute Optimizer provides recommendations only; you are responsible for taking action as a result.

Monitoring Performance

After you have implemented your architecture, it's important to monitor its performance so that you can remediate any issues before your customers are aware of them. Use monitoring metrics to raise alarms when thresholds are breached. The alarm can trigger automated action to work around any components with poor performance.

Tools

AWS provides tools that you can use to monitor the performance, reliability, and availability of your resources on the AWS Cloud.

Amazon CloudWatch

Amazon CloudWatch is essential to performance efficiency, which provides systemwide visibility into resource utilization, application performance, and operational health.

You can create an alarm to monitor any CloudWatch metric in your account. For example, you can create alarms on an EC2 instance CPU utilization, Elastic Load Balancing request latency, DynamoDB table throughput, or SQS queue length.

In the following example, AWS CLI is used to create an alarm to send an Amazon SNS email message when CPU utilization exceeds 70 percent:

```
aws cloudwatch put-metric-alarm --alarm-name cpu-mon --alarm-description
"Alarm when CPU exceeds 70 percent" --metric-name CPUUtilization --namespace
```

```
AWS/EC2 --statistic Average --period 300 --threshold 70 --comparison-operator
GreaterThanThreshold  --dimensions "Name=InstanceId,Value=i-12345678" --
evaluation-periods 2 --alarm-actions arn:aws:sns:us-east-
1:111122223333:MyTopic --unit Percent
```

Here are a few examples of when and how alarms are sent:

- Sends an email message using SNS when the average CPU use of an EC2 instance exceeds a specified threshold for consecutive specified periods
- Sends an email when an instance exceeds 10 GB of outbound network traffic per day
- Stops an instance and sends a text message (SMS) when outbound traffic exceeds 1 GB per hour
- Stops an instance when memory utilization reaches or exceeds 90 percent so that application logs can be retrieved for troubleshooting

AWS Trusted Advisor

AWS Trusted Advisor inspects your AWS environment and makes recommendations that help to improve the speed and responsiveness of your applications.

The following are a few Trusted Advisor checks to improve the performance of your service. The Trusted Advisor checks your service limits, ensuring that you take advantage of provisioned throughput, and monitors for overutilized instances.

- Amazon EC2 instances that are consistently at high utilization can indicate optimized, steady performance, but this check can also indicate that an application does not have enough resources.
- EC2 security groups with a large number of rules.
- EC2 instances that have a large number of security group rules.
- Amazon EBS magnetic volumes (standard) that are potentially overutilized and might benefit from a more efficient configuration.
- CloudFront distributions for alternate domain names with incorrectly configured DNS settings.
- Some HTTP request headers, such as Date or User-Agent, significantly reduce the cache hit ratio. This increases the load on your origin and reduces performance because CloudFront must forward more requests to your origin.

Summary

Achieving an optimized system that balances performance and cost is a continual process. Engineers must know the cost of deploying resources and how to architect for cost optimization. Practice eliminating waste and build accountability into every step of the build process. Use mandatory cost tags on all your resources to gain precise insights into usage. Define

IAM policies and AWS Config to enforce tag usage, and use tagging tools, such as AWS Config and AWS Tag Editor to manage tags. Be cost conscious, reduce usage by terminating unused instances, and delete old snapshots and unused keys.

Right-size your infrastructure by matching instance types and sizes; set periodic checks to ensure that your initial scale remains appropriate as your business changes over time.

Compute Savings Plans can give you significant cost savings compared to On-Demand Instance pricing. Despite the need to commit to 1- or 3-year terms, these plans provide you with significant flexibility to migrate to alternate EC2 instances types or families, changing availability zone or region as needed. Compute Savings Plans even let you carry your discount over to ECS and Lambda compute costs.

Spot Instances provide an additional option for obtaining instance time at a reduced cost by bidding on underutilized EC2 capacity. Spot Fleets enable you to launch and maintain the target capacity and to request resources automatically to replace any that are disrupted or manually terminated. Fleets can also be composed of a combination of on-demand and spot instances, giving you a safety net for workloads that cannot sustain full termination of all nodes. Using termination notices and persistent requests in your application design help to maintain continuity as the result of interruptions.

AWS Auto Scaling automatically scales if your application experiences variable load and uses one or more scalable resources, such as ECS, DynamoDB, Aurora, EC2 Spot requests, and EC2 scaling groups. Predictive Scaling uses machine learning models to forecast daily and weekly patterns. EC2 Auto Scaling enables you to scale in response to demand via CloudWatch alarms and in advance on known load schedules. It supports the provisioning of scale instances across purchase options, availability zones, and instance families to optimize performance and cost.

Containers provide process isolation and improve resource utilization. ECS lets you easily build all types of containerized applications and launch thousands of containers in seconds. With AWS Fargate, you can deploy containers without having to provision or manage servers for your cluster.

AWS Lambda runs code in response to events from other services or via direct invocations with no need to manage servers. Serverless services have built-in automatic scaling, availability, and fault tolerance.

AWS storage services are optimized to meet different storage requirements. Use Amazon S3 analytics to analyze storage access patterns and help you decide when to transition your data to other storage classes that match required availability with the best possible price. Monitor Amazon EBS volumes periodically to identify ones that are unattached or appear to be underutilized and adjust provisioning to match actual usage.

Optimizing data transfer means minimizing data transfer costs. Use options such as CloudFront, S3 transfer acceleration, and Route 53 geoproximity features to lower latency, eliminate unnecessary data requests, and reduce overall transfer costs.

AWS provides several tools to help you identify cost-saving opportunities and keep your resources right-sized. AWS Trusted Advisor inspects your AWS environment to identify idle and underutilized resources and provides real-time insight into service usage to help you improve system performance and save money. CloudWatch collects and tracks metrics, monitors log files, sets alarms, and reacts to changes in AWS resources automatically. AWS Cost Explorer checks patterns in AWS spend over time, projects future costs, identifies areas that need further inquiry, and provides Reserved Instance and Savings Plan recommendations.

Optimization is an ongoing process. It can be a challenge to keep up, but using the tools described in this chapter to continually assess your architecture will ensure it remains cost effective.

Exam Essentials

Know the importance of tagging.   By using tags, you can assign metadata to AWS resources. This tagging makes it easier to manage, search for, and filter resources in billing reports, automation activities, and when setting up access controls.

Know about various tagging tools and how to enforce the tag rules.   With AWS Tag Editor, you can add tags to multiple resources at once, search for the resources that you want to tag, and then add, remove, or edit tags for the resources in your search results. AWS Config identifies resources that do not comply with tagging policies. You can use IAM policies conditions to force the usage of tags while creating the resources.

Know the fundamental practices of reducing cloud spend.   Follow best practices of cost optimization in every step of your build process, such as turning off unused resources, spinning up instances only when needed, and spinning them down when not in use. Use tagging to help with the cost allocation. Use Amazon EC2 Spot Instances, Amazon EC2, and Reserved Instances where appropriate, and use alerts, notifications, and cost-management tools to stay on track.

Know the various instance families for right-sizing and the corresponding use cases.   EC2 provides a wide selection of instances to match capacity needs at the lowest cost and comes with different options for CPU, memory, and network resources. The families include General Purpose, Compute Optimized, Memory Optimized, Storage Optimized, and Accelerated Computing.

Know EC2 Auto Scaling benefits and how this feature can make your solutions more optimized and highly available.   AWS Auto Scaling is a fast, easy way to optimize the performance and costs of your applications. It makes smart scaling decisions based on your preferences, automatically maintaining performance even when your workloads are periodic, unpredictable, and continuously changing.

Know how to create a single Auto Scaling Group to scale instances across different purchase options.   You can provision and automatically scale EC2 capacity across different EC2 instance types; availability zones; and On-Demand, Reserved Instances, and Spot purchase options in a single Auto Scaling Group. You can define the desired split between On-Demand and Spot capacity, select which instance types work for your application, and specify preference for how EC2 Auto Scaling should distribute the Auto Scaling Group capacity within each purchasing model.

Know how block, object, and file storages are different.   Block storage is commonly dedicated, low-latency storage for each host, and it is provisioned with each instance. Object storage is developed for the cloud, has vast scalability, is accessed over the web, and is not directly attached to an instance. File storage enables accessing shared files as a file system.

Know key CloudWatch metrics available to measure the Amazon EBS efficiency and how to use them.   CloudWatch metrics are statistical data that you can use to view, analyze, and set alarms on the operational behavior of your volumes. Depending on your needs, set alarms and response actions that correspond to each data point. For example, if your I/O latency is higher than you require, check the metric VolumeQueueLength to make sure that your application is not trying to drive more IOPS than you have provisioned. Review and learn more about the available metrics that help optimize the block storage.

Know tools and features that help in efficient data transfer.   Using Amazon CloudFront, you can locate data closer to users and reduce administrative efforts to minimize data transfer costs. Amazon S3 Transfer Acceleration enables fast data transfer over an optimized network path. Use the Multipart Upload File option while uploading a large file to improve network throughput.

Know the AWS Cost Management tools and their features.   AWS provides tools to help you manage, monitor, and, ultimately, optimize your costs. Use AWS Cost Explorer for deeper dives into the cost drivers. Use AWS Trusted Advisor to inspect your AWS infrastructure to identify overutilized or idle resources. AWS Budgets enables you to set custom cost and usage budgets and receive alerts when budgets approach or exceed the limits. There are a wide range of tools to explore, such as AWS Cost Optimization – EC2 Right Sizing, and monitoring tools to identify additional savings opportunities.

Know how the AWS Trusted Advisor features help in saving costs and improving the performance of your solutions.   AWS Trusted Advisor scans your AWS environment, compares it to AWS best practices, and makes recommendations for saving money, improving system performance, and more. Cost Optimization recommendations highlight unused and underutilized resources. Performance recommendations help to improve the speed and responsiveness of your applications.

Know how to evaluate the reporting details in the AWS Cost Explorer default reports.   Cost Explorer provides built-in reports like Cost and Usage reports and Savings Plans utilization and coverage reports. The Cost and Usage reports display your daily and monthly costs by service, highlighting the top five services. These reports can help assess whether you've optimized your spend with Savings Plans. The Savings Plans Coverage reports show how many of your compute hours are covered by Savings Plans, how much you're spending on On-Demand usage, and how much you could save by adjusting your Savings Plan commitment. This helps you determine if you're under-utilizing your Savings Plans.

Know Amazon CloudWatch metrics and how to set alarms.   With Amazon CloudWatch, you can observe CPU utilization, network throughput, and disk I/O, and match the observed peak metrics to a new and cheaper instance type. You choose a CloudWatch metric and threshold for the alarm to watch. The alarm turns into the ALARM state when the metric breaches the threshold for a specified number of evaluation periods. Use the Amazon CloudWatch console, AWS CLI, or AWS SDKs for creating or managing alarms.

Know how AWS Lambda integrates with other AWS serverless services to build cost-effective solutions.   AWS Lambda provides the cloud-logic layer and integrates seamlessly with the other serverless services to build virtually any type of application or backend service. For example, Amazon S3 can automatically trigger Lambda functions when an object is created, copied, or deleted. Lambda functions can process Amazon SQS messages. EventBridge allows you to trigger many different actions whenever activity occurs in your account, including invoking Lambda functions.

Exercises

 Before you begin this task, you must first create an SNS topic (name: myHighCpuAlarm) and subscribe to it via email.

EXERCISE 16.1

Setting Up a CPU Usage Alarm Using AWS CLI

In this exercise, you will use the AWS CLI to create a CPU usage alarm that sends an email message using Amazon SNS when the CPU usage exceeds 70 percent.

1. Set up an SNS topic with the name **myHighCpuAlarm** and subscribe to it. For more information, see this article:

   https://docs.aws.amazon.com/AmazonCloudWatch/latest/monitoring/
   Notify_Users_Alarm_Changes.html#US_SetupSNS

2. Create an alarm using the put-metric-alarm command as follows. Note that for this exercise, the EC2 instance ID can remain fake, but you must replace SNS_TOPIC_ARN with your real SNS topic ARN.

   ```
   aws cloudwatch put-metric-alarm \
       --alarm-name cpu-mon \
       --metric-name CPUUtilization \
       --namespace "AWS/EC2" \
       --statistic Average \
   ```

EXERCISE 16.1 *(continued)*

```
--period 300 \
--threshold 70 \
--comparison-operator GreaterThanThreshold \
--dimensions Name=InstanceId,Value=i-12345678 \
--evaluation-periods 2 \
--alarm-actions <SNS_TOPIC_ARN> \
--unit Percent
```

3. Test the alarm by forcing an alarm state change using the `set-alarm-state` command.

   a. Change the alarm state from `INSUFFICIENT_DATA` to OK.

   ```
   aws cloudwatch set-alarm-state --alarm-name cpu-mon --state-reason
   "initializing" --state-value OK
   ```

   b. Change the alarm state from OK to ALARM.

   ```
   aws cloudwatch set-alarm-state --alarm-name cpu-mon --state-reason
   "initializing" --state-value ALARM
   ```

   c. Check that you have received an email notification about the alarm.

Using AWS CLI, you created a CPU alarm that sends an email notification when CPU usage exceeds 70 percent. You tested it by manually changing its alarm state to ALARM.

 For Windows, replace the backslash (\) Unix continuation character at the end of each line with a caret (^).

EXERCISE 16.2

Creating an AWS Config Rule

In this exercise, using the AWS Management Console, you will create an AWS Config rule to monitor whether Elastic IP addresses are attached to EC2 instances.

1. Create an Elastic IP address to be used as part of this exercise, but do not attach it to any EC2 instance. Please note that there is a small charge for keeping an Elastic IP provisioned; make sure to delete it (known as "releasing" the IP) when the exercise is complete. To create the EIP, see the following for instructions:

   https://docs.aws.amazon.com/AWSEC2/latest/UserGuide/working-with-eips
   .html#using-instance-addressing-eips-allocating

2. Open the AWS Config console at https://console.aws.amazon.com/config.

3. Click Get Started.

4. On the Settings page, for Recording Strategy, select All Resource Types With Customizable Overrides.

5. Scroll to Delivery Method, and select Create A Bucket. Enter a unique bucket name or remember the dynamically generated name. This will be the Amazon S3 bucket to which AWS Config sends configuration history and configuration snapshot files.

6. Under Amazon SNS Topic, select Stream Configuration Changes And Notifications To An Amazon SNS Topic.

7. For Topic Name, type a name for your SNS topic. If you wish to see a notification for the config rule you're currently creating, open a new tab, navigate to the SNS console, and subscribe your email address to it. Remember to confirm your subscription via the link SNS sends to your inbox.

8. Click Next.

9. On the Rules page, in the search bar, enter **eip** to filter the list of AWS-provided rules.

10. Select the eip-attached rule.

11. Click Next and then Confirm.

    AWS Config will run this rule against your resources. The rule flags the unattached EIP as noncompliant.

12. Delete the AWS Config rule.

13. Release the Elastic IP address. See the following for instructions:

    https://docs.aws.amazon.com/AWSEC2/latest/UserGuide/using-instance-addressing-eips-releasing.html

From the AWS Config console, you used AWS Config to create a rule to determine whether an Elastic IP address is attached to an EC2 instance.

EXERCISE 16.3

Creating a Launch Template and Auto Scaling Group, and Scheduling a Scaling Action

In this exercise, using AWS Management Console, you will create a launch configuration, Auto Scaling policy, and verify the scheduled scaling action.

1. To create a launch template, complete the following steps:

   a. Open the Amazon EC2 console at `https://console.aws.amazon.com/ec2`.

   b. On the navigation pane, under Instances, select Launch Templates. Click Create Launch Template.

   c. Enter a name for your launch template.

   d. For Application And OS Images (Amazon Machine Image), search for **Amazon** and press Enter. On the results page, select Amazon Linux 2023 AMI.

   e. Back on the Launch Template configuration page, under Instance Type page, select a low-cost instance type such as t3.nano.

   f. Under Key Pair, you can keep the setting Don't Include In Launch Template. There is no need to SSH to these instances.

   g. Under Network Settings, optionally add an existing Security Group or create a new one.

   h. Expand Advanced Network Configuration.

   i. Click Add Network Interface. In the resulting fields, set Auto-Assign Public IP to Enable.

   j. Review your choices and click Create Launch Template.

2. To create an Auto Scaling Group, complete the following steps:

   a. Under Create An Auto Scaling Group From Your Template, select Create Auto Scaling Group.

   b. On the Create Auto Scaling Group page, follow these steps:

      i. For Group Name, enter a name for your Auto Scaling Group. Your launch template from the previous step is preselected.

      ii. Click Next.

      iii. On the Choose Instance Launch Options page, under vCPUs, set both Minimum and Maximum to 1. Under Memory, enter 8 for both. Note that under Instance Purchase Options, you may choose to launch a percentage of this group on Spot Instances.

      iv. Under Network, choose at least one of your VPC's subnets. Choosing more will distribute the Auto Scaling Group over these subnets.

      v. Click Next.

      vi. On the Configure Advanced Options – Optional page, keep all values at the defaults.

      vii. Click Next.

    viii. On the Configure Group Size And Scaling – Optional page, you can keep the defaults, or set a group size other than 1 by adjusting Desired Capacity.

    ix. Click Next.

    x. On the Add Notifications – Optional page, click Next.

    xi. On the Add Tags – Optional page, click Next.

    xii. On the Review page, click Create Auto Scaling Group.

3. The group will begin to launch instances up to your desired capacity. To schedule an additional Auto Scaling action and verify that it's working, complete the following steps:

    a. Select your Auto Scaling group.

    b. On the Automatic Scaling tab, scroll to Schedule Actions and click Create Scheduled Action.

    c. On the Schedule Action page, follow these steps:

        i. For Name, type the name of the action (i.e., **addTwoInstances**).

        ii. For Max, type **2**.

        iii. For Desired Capacity, type **2**.

        iv. For Start Time, select the current day in Date (UTC), and type the current UTC time + 2 minutes.

        v. Click Save.

        vi. Select the Instances tab, refresh the tab in the next two minutes, and observe that a new EC2 instance was created.

In this exercise, you created a launch template and an Auto Scaling Group using the launch group that you just created. To test whether automatic scaling is working, you added a Scaling action to launch a new EC2 instance by increasing capacity. You also verified that a new instance was added to the current capacity.

To clean up and avoid unnecessary charges, return to the Auto Scaling Groups list.

1. Select your Auto Scaling Group.

2. Click Actions and then Delete.

3. Type the word **delete** to confirm and click Delete.

Review Questions

1. You are developing an application that will run across dozens of instances. It uses some components from a legacy application that requires some configuration files to be copied from a central location and held on a volume local to each of the instances. You plan to modify your application with a new component in the future that will hold this configuration in Amazon DynamoDB. Which storage option should you use in the interim to provide the lowest cost and the lowest latency for your application to access the configuration files?

   A. Amazon S3

   B. Amazon EBS

   C. Amazon EFS

   D. Amazon EC2 instance store

2. AWS Trusted Advisor offers a rich set of best practice checks and recommendations across five categories: cost optimization, security, fault tolerance, performance, and service limits. Which of the following checks is *not* under Cost and Performance categories?

   A. Amazon EBS Provisioned IOPS (SSD) volume attachment configuration

   B. Amazon CloudFront header forwarding and cache hit ratio

   C. Amazon EC2 Availability Zone balance

   D. Unassociated Elastic IP address

3. You are developing an application that consists of a set of EC2 instances hosting a web layer and a database hosting a MySQL instance. You are required to add a layer that can be used to ensure that the most frequently accessed data from the database is fetched in a faster and more efficient manner. Which of the following can be used to store the frequently accessed data?

   A. Amazon Simple Queue Service (Amazon SQS) queue

   B. Amazon Simple Notification Service (Amazon SNS) topic

   C. Amazon CloudFront distribution

   D. Amazon ElastiCache instance

4. You have an application deployed to the AWS platform that makes requests to an S3 bucket. After monitoring CloudWatch metrics, you notice that the number of GET requests has suddenly spiked. Which of the following can be used to optimize S3 cost and performance?

   A. Add Amazon ElastiCache in front of the S3 bucket.

   B. Use Amazon DynamoDB instead of Amazon S3.

   C. Place an Amazon CloudFront distribution in front of the S3 bucket.

   D. Place an Elastic Load Balancing load balancer in front of the S3 bucket.

5. A developer is migrating an on-premises web application to the AWS Cloud. The application currently runs on a 32-processor server and stores session state in memory. On Mondays, the server runs at 80 percent CPU utilization, but at only about 5 percent CPU utilization at other times. How should the developer change the code to optimize running in the AWS Cloud?

   A. Store session state on the EC2 instance store.

   B. Encrypt the session state in memory.

   C. Store session state in an Amazon ElastiCache cluster.

   D. Compress the session state in memory.

6. A company is using an ElastiCache cluster in front of their Amazon RDS instance. The company would like you to implement logic into the code so that the cluster retrieves data from Amazon RDS only when there is a cache miss. Which strategy can you implement to achieve this?

   A. Error retries

   B. Lazy loading

   C. Exponential backoff

   D. Write-through

7. You just developed code in AWS Lambda that uses recursive functions. You see some throttling errors in the metrics. Which of the following should you do to resolve the issue?

   A. Use API Gateway to call the recursive code.

   B. Use versioning for the recursive function.

   C. Place the recursive function in a separate package.

   D. Avoid using recursive code in your function.

8. You have an application that uploads objects to Amazon S3 between 200 and 500 MB. The process takes longer than expected, and you want to improve the performance of the application. Which of the following would you consider?

   A. Enable versioning on the bucket.

   B. Use the multipart upload API.

   C. Write the items in batches for better performance.

   D. Create multiple threads to upload the objects.

9. Your application requires several dependencies to be installed before it will work. This process is slowing down your ability to scale up healthy instances in your EC2 Auto Scaling Group. What is the best way to optimize this process?

   A. Create a Lambda function to install the script.

   B. Place a scheduled task on the instance that starts on boot.

   C. Create a "golden image" AMI that contains the dependencies and use it as the basis for instances in the ASG.

   D. Place the script in the instance metadata.

10. Your team is tasked with managing AWS costs for a large-scale application. You want to ensure that unused resources, such as idle EC2 instances and unattached EBS volumes, are identified and decommissioned regularly. Which AWS service or tool can best assist with this task?

    A. AWS CloudTrail

    B. AWS Trusted Advisor

    C. Amazon Inspector

    D. AWS Systems Manager

11. You are configuring your AWS environment to ensure resources are only consumed when necessary and are correctly allocated to their respective departments for accurate cost tracking. Which AWS best practices should you implement? (Choose two.)

    A. Enable AWS CloudTrail logging.

    B. Use AWS Systems Manager to manage resource groups.

    C. Enforce mandatory tagging of resources.

    D. Enable AWS Config rules for resource compliance.

12. Your application is experiencing expensive spikes in traffic during peak hours due to high demand. You are tasked with evaluating and recommending an AWS strategy to optimize costs without impacting application performance. What should you recommend?

    A. Switch to a fleet of Spot Instances.

    B. Use an Auto Scaling Group with a mix of Spot and On-Demand instances.

    C. Purchase a Compute Savings Plan.

    D. Containerize your application and run it on ECS.

13. Your organization has numerous S3 buckets containing various data types with different access patterns. What action should you take to optimize the storage costs based on the access frequency of the data?

    A. Use S3 Standard for all buckets.

    B. Migrate infrequently accessed data to S3 Glacier.

    C. Configure S3 life cycle policies to move data between storage classes as access patterns change.

    D. Consolidate all data into a single S3 bucket to streamline management.

14. Your AWS account is experiencing sudden cost increases, and you suspect unauthorized changes are being made to your resources. What action should you take to monitor and control these changes?

    A. Create AWS Config rules to detect non-compliant changes to resources.

    B. Set up AWS Budgets on your account to alert you before costs exceed your defined threshold.

    C. Check CloudTrail to determine who is making unauthorized changes.

    D. Regularly monitor AWS Cost Explorer to track unauthorized spending.

    E. All of the above.

15. Your company has workloads that run on EC2 across multiple AWS regions. Your developers are interested in exploring container-based deployments or perhaps switching to a Lambda-based architecture. Your goal is to keep costs low, no matter which route is chosen. Which AWS pricing model should you choose to maximize both savings and flexibility?

A. Convertible Reserved Instances

B. Spot Instances

C. Compute Savings Plans

D. On-Demand Instances

ppendix

Answers to Review Questions

Chapter 1: Introduction toAmazon Web Services

1. **B.** The specific credentials include the access key ID and secret access key. If the access key is valid only for a short-term session, the credentials also include a session token.

   AWS uses the username and passwords for working with the AWS Management Console, not for working with the APIs. Data encryption uses the AWS KMS key, not API access.

2. **C.** Most AWS API services are regional in scope. The service is running and replicating your data across multiple availability zones within an AWS region. You specify the region either in your default configuration or by explicitly setting a location for your API client.

3. **A.** The AWS SDK relies on access keys, not passwords. The best practice is to use AWS Identity and Access Management (IAM) credentials and not the AWS account credentials. Comparing IAM users or IAM roles, only IAM users can have long-term security credentials.

4. **C.** Although you can generate IAM users for everyone, this introduces management overhead of a new set of long-term credentials. If you already have an external directory of your organization's users, use IAM roles and identity federation to provide short-term, session-based access to AWS.

5. **A.** The permissions for the `DynamoDBFullAccess` managed policy grant access to *all* Amazon DynamoDB tables in your account. Write a custom policy to scope the access to a specific table. You can update the permissions of a user independently from the life cycle of the table. DynamoDB does not have its own concept of users, but it uses the AWS API and relies on IAM.

6. **B.** You can view or manage your AWS resources with the console, AWS CLI, or AWS SDK. The core functionality of each SDK is powered by a common set of web services on the backend. Most AWS services are isolated by AWS region.

7. **B.** If you look closely at the URL, the AWS region string is incorrectly set as `us-east-1a`, which is specific to the availability zone. An AWS region string ends in a number, and the correct configuration is `us-east-1`. If the error was related to your credentials, you would receive a more specific error related to credentials, such as `AccessDenied`.

8. **B.** This policy allows access to the `s3:ListBucket` operation on `example_bucket` as a specific bucket. This does not grant access to operations on the objects within the bucket. IAM is granular. The date in the `Version` attribute is a specific version of the IAM policy language and not an expiration.

9. **D.** The long-term credentials are not limited to a single AWS region. IAM is a global service, and IAM user credentials are valid across different AWS regions. However, when the call is made, a signing key is derived from the long-term credentials, and that signing key is scoped to a region, service, and day.

10. D. AWS maintains managed policies (designated by an orange cube icon in the console) automatically as services change. Option A is incorrect because managed services update on their own. Option B is incorrect because policy changes are automatically reflected in the permissions of users with that policy. Option C is incorrect because extending managed policies is not necessary; AWS will update them without your intervention.

11. D. The `DynamoDBReadOnlyAccess` policy is a built-in policy that applies to the resource * wildcard, which means that it applies to any and all DynamoDB tables accessible from the account regardless of when those tables were created. Because IAM policies are related to the IAM user, not the access key, rotating the key does not affect the policy. IAM policies are also global in scope, so you do not need a custom one per AWS region. You can add IAM users to IAM groups but not IAM roles. Instead, roles must be assumed for short-term sessions.

12. B. The IAM trust policy defines the principals who can request role credentials from the AWS STS. Access policies define what API actions can be performed with the credentials from the role.

13. C. You can define an IAM user for your new team member and add the IAM user to an IAM group to inherit the appropriate permissions. The best practice is *not* to use *AWS account root user* credentials. Though you can use AWS Directory Service to track users, this answer is incomplete, and the AWS KMS is not related to permissions. Roles can be assumed only for short-term sessions—there are no long-term credentials directly associated with the role.

14. D. The AWS API backend is accessed through web service calls and is operating system– and programming language–agnostic. You do not need to do anything special to enable specific programming languages other than downloading the appropriate SDK.

15. B. The primary latency concern is for customers accessing the data, and there are no explicit dependencies on existing infrastructure in the United States. Physically locating the application resources closer to these users in Australia reduces the distance that the information must travel and therefore decreases the latency.

Chapter 2: Introduction to Compute and Networking

1. B. You launch Amazon Elastic Compute Cloud (Amazon EC2) instances into specific subnets that are tied to specific availability zones. You can look up the availability zone in which you have launched an Amazon EC2 instance. While an availability zone is part of a region, "region" is not the most specific answer. You do not get to choose the specific data center, and edge locations do not support EC2.

2. B. When you stop an Amazon EC2 instance, its public IP address is released. When you start it again, a new public IP address is assigned. If you require a public IP address to be persistently associated with the instance, allocate an Elastic IP address. SSH key pairs and security group rules do not have any built-in expiration, and SSH is enabled as a service by default. It is available even after restarts. Security groups do not expire.

3. A. A restricted rule that allows RDP from only certain IP addresses may block your request if you have a new source IP address because of your location. Because you are trying to connect to the instance, verify that an appropriate inbound rule is set as opposed to an outbound rule. For many variants of Windows, RDP is the default connection mechanism, and it defaults to enabled even after a reboot.

4. D. The NAT gateway allows outbound requests to the external API to succeed while preventing inbound requests from the Internet. Configuring the security group to allow only inbound requests from your web servers allows outbound requests to succeed because the default rule for the security group allows outbound requests to the APIs that your web service needs. Option B is incorrect because security group rules cannot explicitly deny traffic; they can only allow it. Option C is incorrect because network ACLs are stateless, and this rule would prevent all of the replies to your outbound web requests from entering the public subnet.

5. C. You are in full control over the software on your instance. The default user that was created when the instance launched has full control over the guest operating system and can install the necessary software. Instance profiles are unrelated to the software on the instance.

6. D. You can query the Amazon EC2 metadata service for this information. Networking within the Amazon Virtual Private Cloud (Amazon VPC) is based on private IP addresses, so this rules out options A and B. Because the metadata service is available, you are not required to use a third-party service, which eliminates option C.

7. A. You can implement user data to execute scripts or directives that install additional packages. Even though you can use Amazon Simple Storage Service (Amazon S3) to stage software installations, there is no special bucket. You have full control of EC2 instances, including the software. AWS KMS is unrelated to software installation.

8. A. Amazon EC2 instances are resizable. You can change the RAM available by changing the instance type. Option B is incorrect because you can change this attribute only when the instance is stopped. Although option C is one possible solution, it is not required. Option D is incorrect because the RAM available on the host server does not change the RAM allocation for your EC2 instance.

9. A. AWS generates the default password for the instance and encrypts it by using the public key from the Amazon EC2 key pair used to launch the instance. You do not select a password when you launch an instance. You can decrypt this with the private key. IAM users and IAM roles are not for providing access to the operating system on the Amazon EC2 instance.

10. A, E, B. For an instance to be directly accessible as a web server, you must assign a public IP address, place the instance in a public subnet, and ensure that the inbound security group rules allow HTTP/HTTPS. A public subnet is one in which there is a direct route to an Internet gateway. Option C defines a private subnet. Because security groups are stateful, you are not required to set the outbound rules—the replies to the inbound request are automatically allowed.

11. A, D. You can use an AMI as a template for launching any number of Amazon EC2 instances. AMIs are available for various versions of Windows and Linux. Option B is false

because AMIs are local to the region in which they were created unless they are explicitly copied. Option C is false because, in addition to AWS-provided AMIs, there are third-party AMIs in the marketplace, and you can create your own AMIs.

12. B, D. Option B is true; Amazon EBS provides persistent storage for all types of EC2 instances. Option D is true because hardware accelerators, such as GPU and FGPA, are accessible depending on the type of instance. Option A is false because instance store is provided only for a few EC2 instance types. Option C is incorrect because EC2 instances can be resized after they are launched, provided they are stopped during the resize. Hardware accelerators, such as GPU and FGPA, are accessible depending on the type of instance.

13. B, D. Only instances in the running state can be started, stopped, or rebooted.

14. D. Both the web server and the database are running on the same instance, and they can communicate locally on the instance. Option A is incorrect because security groups apply to only network traffic that leaves the instance. Option C is incorrect because network ACLs apply only to traffic leaving a subnet. Similarly, option B is incorrect because the public IP address is required for inbound requests from the Internet but is not necessary for requests local to the same instance.

15. C. A public subnet is one in which there is a route that directs Internet traffic (0.0.0.0/0) to an Internet gateway. None of the other routes provides a direct route to the Internet, which is required to be a public subnet.

16. D. A private subnet that allows outbound Internet access must provide an indirect route to the Internet. This is provided by a route that directs Internet traffic to a NAT gateway or NAT instance. Option C is incorrect because a route to an Internet gateway would make this a public subnet with a direct connection to the Internet. The remaining options do not provide access to the Internet.

17. D. Amazon VPC Flow Logs have metadata about each traffic flow within your Amazon VPC and show whether the connection was accepted or rejected. The other responses do not provide a log of network traffic.

18. C. Amazon CloudWatch is the service that tracks metrics such as CPU utilization for an EC2 instance. The other services are not responsible for tracking metrics.

19. B. EBS volumes provide persistent storage for an Amazon EC2 instance. The data is persisted until the volume is deleted and therefore persists on the volume when the instance is stopped.

20. F. You can install any software you want on an Amazon EC2 instance, including any interpreters required to run your application code.

21. B, C. Web requests are typically made on port 80 for HTTP and port 443 for HTTPS. Because security groups are stateful, you must set only the inbound rule. Options A and D are unnecessary because the security group automatically allows the outbound replies to the inbound requests.

22. B, D. The customer is responsible for the guest operating system and above. Options C and E fall under AWS's responsibility. AWS is responsible for the virtualization layer, underlying host machines, and all the way down to the physical security of the facilities.

Chapter 3: AWS Data Storage

1. A. In this scenario, create a life cycle policy that moves cooler data to infrequent access after 30 days, then to Glacier after 90. Option B is incorrect because cold data will continue to incur the same costs as hot. Option C is incorrect because uploading frequently accessed data to Glacier would cause longer retrieval times and a poor user experience. Option D does not retain your data, so it is not a valid plan for this scenario.

2. C, D. Objects are stored in buckets and contain both data and metadata.

   Option A is incorrect because Amazon S3 is object storage, not block storage.

   Option B is incorrect because objects are identified by a URL generated from the bucket name, service region endpoint, and key name.

3. B. The volume is created immediately, but the data is loaded lazily, meaning that the volume can be accessed upon creation, and if the data being requested has not yet been restored, it will be restored upon first request.

   Options A and C are incorrect because it does not matter what the size of the volume is or the amount of the data that is stored on the volume. Lazy loading will get data upon first request as needed while the volume is being restored.

   Option D is incorrect because an Amazon EBS–optimized instance provides additional, dedicated capacity for Amazon EBS I/O. This minimizes contention, but it does not increase or decrease the amount of time before the data is made available while restoring a volume.

4. A, B, D. Option C is incorrect because while it is possible to mount S3 as a file system, this is not native functionality and requires the use of additional software.

   Option E is incorrect because, unlike EBS volumes, storage in a bucket does not need to be preallocated and can grow in a virtually unlimited manner.

5. A, C. Amazon S3 Glacier is optimized for long-term archival storage and is not suited to data that needs immediate access or short-lived data that is erased within 90 days.

6. B. Option B is correct because presigned URLs allow you to grant time-limited permission to download objects from an S3 bucket.

   Option A is incorrect because static web hosting requires world-read access to all content.

   Option C is incorrect because AWS IAM policies do not know who the authenticated users of your web application are, as these are not IAM users.

   Option D is incorrect because logging can help track content loss, but not prevent it.

7. A, C. Option A is correct because the data is automatically replicated within an availability zone.

   Option C is correct because EBS volumes are automatically encrypted at creation.

   Option B is incorrect. There are no tapes in the AWS infrastructure.

   Option D is incorrect because EBS volumes persist when the instance is stopped.

8. C. The Max I/O performance mode is optimized for applications where tens, hundreds, or thousands of EC2 instances are accessing the file system. It scales to higher levels of aggregate throughput and operations per second with a trade-off of slightly higher latencies for file operations.

Option A is incorrect because the General-Purpose performance mode in EFS is appropriate for most file systems, and it is the mode selected by default when you create a file system. However, when you need concurrent access from 10 or more instances to the file system, you may need to increase your performance.

Option B is incorrect. This is an option to increase I/O throughput for Amazon EBS volumes by connecting multiple volumes and setting up RAID 0 to increase overall I/O.

Option D is incorrect. Changing to a larger instance size will increase your cost for compute, but it will not improve the performance for concurrently connecting to your EFS file system from multiple instances.

9. A, B, D. Options A, B, and D are required, and optionally you can also set a friendly CNAME to the bucket URL.

Option C is incorrect because S3 does not support FTP transfers.

Option E is incorrect because HTTP does not need to be enabled.

10. C. A short period of heavy traffic is exactly the use case for the bursting nature of general-purpose SSD volumes—the rest of the day is more than enough time to build up enough IOPS credits to handle the nightly task.

Option A is incorrect because to set up a provisioned IOPS SSD volume to handle the peak would mean overprovisioning and spending money for more IOPS than you need during off-peak time.

Option B is incorrect because instance stores are not durable.

Option D is incorrect because magnetic volumes cannot provide enough IOPS.

11. C, D, E. Depending on the chosen tier, Glacier objects may take hours to restore. Glacier Instant Retrieval offers immediate access for an additional cost. In fact, all Glacier tiers have some fee for retrieval, making option D a correct answer as well. Finally, AWS does continue to offer Glacier as a stand-alone service with different features from S3 Glacier tiers.

Option A is incorrect because objects may be uploaded directly into Glacier tiers.

Option B is incorrect because any object can be stored in S3 Glacier tiers.

12. A. Amazon EFS supports one to thousands of Amazon EC2 instances connecting to a file system concurrently.

Options B and C are incorrect because EBS and EC2 instance stores can be mounted only to a single instance at a time.

Option D is incorrect because Amazon S3 does not provide a file system connection but rather connectivity over the web. It cannot be mounted to an instance directly.

13. B. There is no impact to volume availability when commencing a snapshot.

Options A and C are incorrect because the size of the volume or the amount of the data that is stored on the volume does not matter. The volume will be available immediately.

Option D is incorrect because an EBS-optimized instance provides additional, dedicated capacity for EBS I/O. This minimizes contention, but it does not change the fact that the volume will still be available while taking a snapshot.

14. B, C, E. Amazon S3 bucket policies can specify a request IP range, an AWS account, and a prefix for objects that can be accessed.

Options A and D are incorrect because bucket policies cannot be restricted by company name or country of origin.

15. B, D. Option B is not an appropriate use case for S3, as it is object storage. For boot volumes, you would typically use EBS or instance store volumes.

Option D is incorrect because S3 should not serve as primary database storage because it is object storage, not transactional block-based storage. Databases are generally stored on disk in one or more large files. If you needed to change one row in a database, the entire database file would need to be updated in S3, and every time you needed to access a record, you'd need to download the whole database.

16. B, C, E. Option A is incorrect because static web hosting does not restrict data access. You can host a website on Amazon S3, but the bucket must have public read access so everyone in the world will have read access to this bucket.

Option B is correct because creating a presigned URL for an object optionally allows you to share objects with others.

Option C is correct because S3 access control lists (ACLs) enable you to manage access to buckets and objects, defining which AWS accounts or groups are granted access and the type of access.

Option D is incorrect because using an S3 life cycle policy does not restrict data access. Life cycle policies can be used to define actions for Amazon S3 to take during an object's lifetime (for example, transition objects to another storage class, archive them, or delete them after a specified period of time).

Option E is correct because a bucket policy is a resource-based AWS IAM policy that allows you to grant permission to your S3 resources for other AWS accounts or IAM users.

17. C, E. Option A is incorrect because even though you get increased redundancy using cross-region replication, that does not protect the object from being deleted.

Option B is incorrect because vault locks are a feature of S3 Glacier, not a feature of S3.

Option D is incorrect because a life cycle policy would move the object to cheaper cold storage without preventing it from being deleted once it arrives in S3 Glacier.

Options C and E are correct. Versioning protects data against inadvertent or intentional deletion by storing all versions of the object, and MFA Delete requires a one-time code from a multifactor authentication (MFA) device to delete objects.

18. C. To track requests for access to your bucket, enable access logging. Each access log record provides details about a single access request, such as the requester, bucket name, request time, request action, response status, and error code (if any). Access log information can be useful in security and access audits. It can also help you learn about your customer base and understand your Amazon S3 bill.

19. A, B, D. Option A is correct because cross-region replication allows you to replicate data between distance AWS regions to satisfy these requirements.

Option B is correct because this can minimize latency in accessing objects by maintaining object copies in AWS regions that are geographically closer to your users.

Option D is correct because you can maintain object copies in both regions, allowing lower latency by bringing the data closer to the compute.

Option C is incorrect because cross-region replication does not protect against accidental deletion.

Option E is incorrect because S3 is designed for 11 nines of durability for objects in a single region. A second region does not significantly increase durability.

20. C. If data must be encrypted before being sent to S3, client-side encryption must be used.

Options A, B, and D are incorrect because they use server-side encryption. This will only encrypt the data at rest in Amazon S3, not prior to transit to S3.

21. B. Data is automatically replicated across at least three availability zones within a single region.

Option A is incorrect because you can optionally choose to replicate data to other regions, but that is not done by default.

Option C is incorrect because versioning is optional, and data in S3 is durable regardless of turning on versioning.

Option D is incorrect because there are no tapes in the AWS infrastructure.

Chapter 4: AWS Database Services

1. B, D, E. Amazon RDS manages the work involved in setting up a relational database, from provisioning the infrastructure capacity to installing the database software. After your database is up and running, RDS automates common administrative tasks, such as performing backups and patching the software that powers your database. Option A is incorrect. Because RDS provides native database access, you interact with the relational database software as you normally would. This means that you're still responsible for managing the database settings that are specific to your application. Option C is incorrect. You need to build the relational schema that best fits your use case and are responsible for any performance tuning to optimize your database for your application's workflow and query patterns.

2. A. RDS can automatically apply minor upgrades at scheduled maintenance windows with no intervention from the user. Major upgrades require manual intervention, since they can impact your existing schema or code. Option B, though recommended, is incorrect because snapshots do not update your database. Option C is incorrect because not only is Lambda not necessary in this situation, but boto (or the SDK in general) cannot patch your database. Option D is incorrect because it is not a cost-effective or efficient way to patch the database when that functionality is automated by RDS.

3. B. NoSQL databases, such as DynamoDB, excel at scaling to hundreds of thousands of requests with key-value access to user profile and session. Option A is incorrect because the session state is typically suited for small amounts of data, and DynamoDB can scale more effectively with this type of dataset. Option C is incorrect because Redshift is a data warehouse service that is used for analytical queries on petabyte scale datasets, so it would not be a good solution. Option D is incorrect because DynamoDB provides scale, whereas MySQL on EC2 eventually becomes bottlenecked. Additionally, NoSQL databases are much faster and more scalable for this type of dataset.

4. A. 1 RCU = One strongly consistent read per second of 4 KB.

   15 KB is four complete chunks of 4 KB ($4 \times 4 = 16$).

   So you need $25 \times 4 = 100$ RCUs.

5. C. 1 RCU = Two eventually consistent reads per second of 4 KB.

   15 KB is four complete chunks of 4 KB ($4 \times 4 = 16$).

   So you need $(25 \times 4) / 2 = 50$ RCUs.

6. D. 1 WCU = 1write per second of 1 KB (1024 bytes).

   512 bytes uses one complete chunk of 1 KB ($512/1024 = 0.5$, rounded up to 1).

   So you need $100 \times 1 = 100$WCUs.

7. B. Amazon DynamoDB Accelerator (DAX) is a write-through caching service that quickly integrates with DynamoDB with a few quick code changes. DAX will seamlessly intercept the API call, and your caching solution will be up and running in a short amount of time. Option A is incorrect because although you could implement your own solution, this would likely take a significant amount of development time. Option C is incorrect because your company would like to get the service up and running quickly. Implementing Redis on EC2 to meet your application's needs would take additional time. Option D is incorrect for many of the same reasons as option C, as time is a factor here. Additionally, your company would like to refrain from managing more EC2 instances, if possible.

8. B. With ElastiCache, only Redis can be run in a high-availability configuration. Option A is incorrect because this would add complexity to your architecture. It would also likely introduce additional latency, as the company is already using RDS. Option C is incorrect because ElastiCache for Memcached does not support a high-availability configuration. Option D is incorrect because DAX is a caching mechanism that is used for DynamoDB, not RDS.

9. B. Aurora automatically scales the storage as needed and can handle intense read traffic by allowing up to 15 read replicas with sub-second replication lag. Its fault-tolerant architecture

can also reduce failover times significantly compared to standard RDS. You should consider Aurora any time you are working with a compatible engine—MySQL or Postgres.

Option A is a reasonable second choice, as it would enhance both read performance and failover times, but not as much as moving to Aurora. Option C would help with reads for frequently read data, but would not help universally, nor enhance failover. Option D involves quite a bit of manual work for a solution that is automated by managed services like Aurora.

10. A. Scans are less efficient than queries. When possible, always use queries with DynamoDB. Option B is incorrect because doing nothing isn't a good solution; the problem is unlikely to go away. Option C is incorrect because a strongly consistent read would actually be a more expensive query in terms of compute and cost. Strongly consistent reads cost twice as much as eventually consistent reads. Option D is incorrect because the concern is with reading data, not writing data. WCUs are write capacity units. Option E is incorrect because while adding RCUs would increase the overall read throughput of the table (allowing more concurrent reads), it does not address the inefficiency of using a scan over a query.

Chapter 5: Encryption on AWS

1. B, D, E. Option A is incorrect because data can be encrypted in any location (on-premises or in the AWS Cloud). Option C is incorrect because encryption keys should be stored in a secured hardware security module (HSM). Option B is correct because there must be data to encrypt in order to use an encryption system. Option D is correct because tools and a process must be in place to perform encryption. Option E is correct because encryption requires a defined algorithm.

2. A, C. Option B is incorrect because KMI does not have a concept of a data layer. Option D is incorrect because KMI does not have a concept of an encryption layer. Option A is correct because the storage layer is responsible for storing encryption keys. Option C is correct because the management layer is responsible for allowing authorized users to access the stored keys.

3. A, C, D. Option A is correct because this is a common method to off-load the responsibility of key storage while maintaining customer-owned management processes. Option C is correct because customers can use this approach to fully manage their keys and KMI. Option D is correct because AWS Key Management Service (AWS KMS) supports both encryption and KMI. Option B is incorrect because this would imply significant overhead to manage the storage while not providing customer benefits.

4. D. Option A is incorrect; with SSE-S3, S3 is responsible for encrypting the objects, not KMS. Option B is incorrect because the customer provides the key to the S3 service. Option C is incorrect because the question specifically states that server-side encryption is used. Option D is correct because none of the other options listed server-side encryption with KMS (SSE-KMS), whereby KMS manages the keys.

5. D. Option D is the correct choice because both KMS and CloudHSM support asymmetric and symmetric encryption. Options C is incorrect.

6. A, B. Option A is correct because AWS KMS uses AES-256 as its encryption algorithm. Option B is correct because CloudHSM supports a variety of symmetric encryption options. Options C and D are incorrect because KMS and CloudHSM support symmetric encryption options.

7. C. Option A is incorrect because the organization does *not* want to manage any of the encryption keys. With AWS KMS, it will have to create customer KMS keys. Option B is incorrect because by using customer-provided keys, the organization would have to manage the keys. Option C is correct because S3 manages the encryption keys and performs rotations periodically. Option D is incorrect because SSE-S3 provides this option.

8. C. Option A is incorrect because KMS provides a centralized key management dashboard; however, this feature does not leverage CloudHSM. Option B is incorrect because you want to use KMS *with* CloudHSM and not use it as a replacement for KMS. Option C is correct because custom key stores allow KMS to store keys in a CloudHSM cluster. Option D is incorrect because S3 DistCp is a feature for Amazon Redshift, whereby it copies data from S3 to the cluster.

9. A. Option A is correct because KMS provides the simplest solution with little development time to implement encryption on an EBS volume. Option B is incorrect because even though you can use open source or third-party tooling to encrypt volumes, there would be some setup and configuration involved. Using CloudHSM would also require some configuration and setup, so option C is incorrect. Option D is incorrect because KMS enables you to encrypt EBS volumes.

10. D. Options A, B, and C are incorrect because KMS integrates with all these services.

Chapter 6: Deployment Strategies

1. D. AWS CodePipeline is a continuous delivery service for fast and reliable application updates. It allows the developer to model and visualize the software release process. Code-Pipeline automates your build, test, and release process when there is a code change.

   Option A is incorrect because AWS CodeCommit is a secure, highly scalable, managed source control service that hosts private GIT repositories.

   Option B is incorrect because AWS CodeDeploy automates code deployments to any instance and handles the complexity of updating your applications.

   Option C is incorrect because AWS CodeBuild compiles source code, runs tests, and produces ready-to-deploy software packages.

2. A. Option A is correct because as a platform-as-a-service, Elastic Beanstalk handles the details of capacity, load balancing, and monitoring. Option B is incorrect because Beanstalk stands up infrastructure for you, such as EC2 instances and load balancers, via

CloudFormation. Option C is incorrect because Elastic Beanstalk supports multiple programming languages, including Java, .NET, PHP, Node.js, Python, Ruby, and Go. Option D is incorrect; one of Beanstalk's chief advantages is its tight integration with other AWS services.

3. C. Elastic Beanstalk supports Java, Node.js, and Go, so options A, B, and D are incorrect. It does not support Objective C, so option C is the correct answer.

4. A. Elastic Beanstalk deploys application code and the architecture to support an environment for the application to run.

5. C. Option C is correct; the fastest spin-up time for a new instance is best achieved by baking dependencies into the AMI (though it is advisable to perform package updates frequently). Options A and B would both work, but would incur time installing packages before the app can be installed, the health check passes, and the instances can be added to the load balancer's pool of instances. Option D also incurs this time penalty, and requires pre-placement of packages on S3—not very helpful when you may as well use a package manager.

6. A, B, C. Elastic Beanstalk can run EC2 instances, build queues with SQS, and deploy to ECS tasks.

7. A, B. Elastic Beanstalk can access S3 buckets and connect to RDS databases. It cannot install GuardDuty agents or create or manage Amazon WorkSpaces.

8. C. By using IAM policies, you can control access to resources attached to users, groups, and roles.

9. B, C. Elastic Beanstalk creates a service role to access AWS services and an instance role to access instances.

10. C. Elastic Beanstalk runs at no additional charge. You incur charges only for services deployed.

11. C. Option A is incorrect because an Auto Scaling group on its own is not sufficient, within a VPC or not, for horizontal scaling. Option B is incorrect because although half of the solution—the application load balancer—is present, DNS configuration through Route 53 is not necessary. Option D, like option A, is half a correct answer. The Internet gateway is necessary for public traffic to reach the ALB, but does not assist in scaling. Only Option C, having both the load balancer and the Auto Scaling group to target, can achieve horizontal scaling on EC2.

Chapter 7: Deployment as Code

1. A. Options B and D are incorrect because the deployment is already in progress, and this would not be possible if the CodeDeploy agent had not been installed and running properly. The CodeDeploy agent sends progress reports to the CodeDeploy service. The service does not attempt to query instances directly, and the EC2 API does not interact with instances at the operating system level. Thus, option C is incorrect, and option A is correct.

2. B. Option B is correct because the `ApplicationStop` life cycle event occurs before any new deployment files download. For this reason, it will not run the first time a deployment occurs on an instance. Option C is incorrect, as this is a valid life cycle event. Option A is incorrect. Option D is incorrect because life cycle hooks are not aware of the current state of your application. Life cycle hook scripts execute any listed commands.

3. A. Option B requires precise timing that would be overly burdensome to add to a CI/CD workflow. Option C would not include edge cases where both sources are updated within a small time period and would require separate release cadences for both sources. Option D is incorrect, as CodePipeline supports multiple sources. When multiple sources are configured for the same pipeline, the pipeline will be triggered when any source is updated.

4. C. Option A is incorrect because storing large binary objects in a Git-based repository can incur massive storage requirements. Any time a binary object is modified in a repository, a new copy is saved. Comparing cost to S3 storage, it is more expensive to take this approach. By building the binary objects into an Amazon Machine Image (AMI), you are required to create a new AMI any time changes are made to the objects; thus, option B is incorrect. Options D and E introduce unnecessary cost and complexity into the solution. By using both a CodeCommit repository and an S3 archive, the lowest cost and easiest management is achieved.

5. C. Option A is incorrect because even though you scale up to 2x and then only update half the instances, remember your load balancer would still route to all instances until health checks fail. It is certainly possible that user requests could get routed to an instance with a failed deployment during this time, causing downtime to your app. Option B is incorrect because even if you add additional instances, the AllAtOnce strategy risks downtime of the whole ASG if a deployment fails. Option D is incorrect as this approach still requires manual coordination and doesn't automate switching between Auto Scaling groups. Only Option C spins up new compute and confirms the health of the new deployment before users are exposed to it. Blue/green deploys allow CodeDeploy to automate all the steps of spinning up new instances in an alternate target group and ensuring application health before cutting over the load balancer to use the new deployment. You can determine the amount of time to preserve the old group to tune fallback options and cost.

6. D. Option C is incorrect because S3 does not have a concept of service roles. When a pipeline is initiated, it is done in response either to a change in a source or when a previous change is released by an authorized AWS IAM user or role. However, after the pipeline has been initiated, the CodePipeline service role is used to perform pipeline actions. Thus, option A is incorrect. Option D is correct, rather than option B because it is the CodeDeploy agent on each deployment group instance—not the CodePipeline service—that initiates the call to download an S3 bundle.

7. B. Option A is incorrect because this output is used only in the CodeBuild console. Option D is incorrect because CodeBuild natively supports this functionality. Though option C would technically work, CodeBuild supports output artifacts in the `buildspec.yml` specification. The BuildSpec file includes a `files` directive to indicate any files from the build environment that will be passed as output artifacts. Thus, option B is correct.

8. C. Option A is incorrect because a custom build environment would expose the secrets to any user able to create new build jobs using the same environment. Option B is also incorrect. Though uploading the secrets to S3 would provide some protection, administrators with S3 access may still be able to view the secrets. Option D is incorrect because AWS does not recommend storing sensitive information in source control repositories, as it is easily viewed by anyone with access to the repository. Option C is correct. By storing encrypted secrets in Secrets Manager, you ensure that the values are protected both at rest and in transit. Only AWS IAM users or roles with permissions to the Secrets Manager secret would have access to the information.

9. A. Options B, C, D, and E are incorrect. Lambda functions can execute as part of a pipeline only with the Invoke action type.

10. A, B. Options D and E are incorrect because FIFO/LIFO are not valid pipeline action configurations. Option C is incorrect because pipeline stages support multiple actions. Pipeline actions can be specified to occur both in series and in parallel within the same stage. Thus, options A and B are correct.

11. A. Options B, C, and D are all possible actions you may take in an `appspec.yml` file. The correct answer is option A, as the `appspec.yml` file cannot directly control infrastructure.

12. D. Option A is incorrect. CodeCommit is fully compatible with existing Git tools, and it also supports authentication with AWS Identity and Access Management (IAM) credentials. Options B and C are incorrect. These are the only protocols over which you can interact with a repository. You can use the CodeCommit credential helper to convert an IAM access key and secret access key to valid Git credentials for SSH and HTTPS authentication. Thus, option D is correct.

13. C. Options A, B, and D are all valid SNS notification event sources for CodeCommit repositories. Option C is correct because SNS notifications cannot be configured to send when a commit is made to a repository.

14. C, E. Options A, B, and D are incorrect because these action types do not support CodeBuild projects. Options C and E are correct because CodeBuild projects can be executed in a pipeline as part of build and test actions.

15. C. Each of the options is technically feasible, but only one is optimal. Option A is incorrect because it tightly couples the build and deploy phases, reducing your ability to manage and troubleshoot the two independently. Option B is not optimal because it does not automate the deploy step. Option D is incorrect because it involves manual processing steps. Option C is correct because it takes the most advantage of the automation services provided by AWS, linking distinct CodeBuild and CodeDeploy projects into a continuous delivery pipeline via CodePipeline.

16. A. Because AWS does not have the ability to create or destroy infrastructure in customer data centers, options B, C, and D are incorrect. Option A is correct because on-premises instances support only in-place deployments.

17. C. Options A and B are incorrect because CodeDeploy will not modify files on an instance that were not created by a deployment. Option D is incorrect because this approach could result in failed deployments because of missing settings in your configuration file. Option C is correct. By default, CodeDeploy will not remove files that it does not manage. This is maintained as a list of files on the instance.

18. C. Option A is incorrect because function versions cannot be modified after they have been published. Option B is also incorrect because function version numbers cannot be changed. Aliases can be used to point to different function versions; however, the alias itself cannot be overwritten (it is a pointer to a function version). Thus, option D is incorrect. Lambda does not support in-place deployments. This is because after a function version has been published, it cannot be updated. Option C is correct.

19. C. CodePipeline requires that every pipeline contain a source stage and at least one build or deploy stage. Thus, the minimum number of stages is 2.

20. C. Option A, while true, is not the problem in this scenario, since the pipeline successfully passed the Source stage to reach the Deploy stage. Option B is incorrect because while the browser cache may need refreshing after an update, it exists on the client-side and would not cause a deployment to fail. Option D, again true, is not the issue; otherwise the CodeDeploy job would not be able to initiate at all. The correct answer is option C. The Source stage reads from CodeCommit, then bundles the application revision into a location on S3. In order to deploy using this artifact, the instances in the deployment group (i.e., the instances where the CodeDeploy agent pulls down and runs deployment jobs) needs to be able to access the pipeline's S3 bucket.

Chapter 8: Infrastructure as Code

1. D. Only the `Resources` section of a template is required. If this section is omitted, Cloud-Formation has no resources to manage. However, a template does not require `Parameters`, `Metadata`, or `AWSTemplateFormatVersion`. Thus, options A, B, C, and E are incorrect.

2. E. Option E correctly concatenates a fully functioning URL by joining `https://` and `login.php` with the domain name of the ALB, fetched via the `GetAtt` function. The return value of the `Ref` intrinsic function for an `AWS::ElasticLoadBalancingV2::Load Balancer` resource is the load balancer ARN, which is not valid in a URL, so option A is incorrect. Since the application server instances are in a private subnet, neither will have a public DNS name; thus, option B is incorrect. Option C uses incorrect syntax for the `Ref` intrinsic function. Option D attempts to output a URL for the database instance. Thus, option E is correct.

3. A, C, D. If account limits were preventing the launch of additional instances, the stack creation process would fail as soon as CloudFormation attempts to launch the instance (the EC2 API would return an error to CloudFormation in this case). Thus, option B is incorrect. Any issues preventing the instance from calling `cfn-signal` and sending a success/failure message to CloudFormation would cause the creation policy to time out. Thus, options A, C, and D are correct answers.

4. C, E. Only C and E are correct—Lambda functions and SNS topics can be triggers for CloudFormation custom resources. Step Functions, though often used to orchestrate work-flows that include Lambda, are not callable by CloudFormation custom resources, so A is incorrect. Similarly, though ECS tasks are suitable for one-time invocations of work, they cannot be invoked by a custom resource, so D is incorrect. SQS is often used to invoke jobs asynchronously, but not from CloudFormation, so B is incorrect.

5. A. Option A is correct. If the custom resource function is executed but does not provide a response to the CloudFormation service endpoint, the resource times out with the aforemen-tioned error. Custom resource function permissions are obtained by a function execution role, not the service role invoking the stack update, thus, option B is incorrect. When the Lambda function corresponding to a custom resource no longer exists, the custom resource will fail to update immediately, thus, option C is incorrect.

6. A. Option A is correct because `AWS::Serverless` is a special transform that turns SAM syntax into native CloudFormation. Option B is wrong because SAM mappings are not stored in S3. Although transformations may rely on Lambda code, option C is not correct, as transforms do not require custom resources. Option D is incorrect, as `WaitConditions` are used to sync and coordinate actions outside the template, and are not required by transforms.

7. A. Option A is correct; each of these functions and attributes contributes to forming the rela-tionship and dependency graph that CloudFormation internally uses to determine resource creation order. Option B is incorrect because these functions can be used at any time, in any resource. Option C is incorrect because `Ref`, `GetAtt`, and `DependsOn` are all valid Cloud-Formation options. Option D is incorrect because none are required for a Transform to execute.

8. A. The `cfn-init` helper script is used to define which packages, files, and other configura-tions will be performed when an instance is first launched. The `cfn-signal` helper script is used to signal back to CloudFormation when a resource creation or update has completed, so options B and C are incorrect. Option D is incorrect because `cfn-update` is not a valid helper script. The `cfn-hup` helper script performs updates on an instance when its parent stack is updated. Thus, option A is correct.

9. C. Wait conditions accept only one signal and will not track additional signals from the same resource, thus, options A and B are incorrect. `WaitCount` is an invalid option type, so option D is incorrect. Option C is correct because creation policies enable you to specify a count and a timeout.

10. A. Option A is correct. Options B and C will affect resources in your account. Option D would let you see the syntax differences between two template versions, but this does not indicate what type of updates will happen on the resources themselves, thus, option D is incorrect. Change sets create previews of infrastructure changes without actually executing them. After reviewing the changes that will be performed, the change set can be executed on the target stack.

11. B. Option B is correct, as it uses intrinsic functions to access resource properties in the same manner as any other stack resource. Option A is incorrect, as this is a supported feature of nested stacks. Option C creates a circular dependency between the parent and child stacks (the parent stack needs to import the value from the child stack, which cannot be created until the parent begins creation). Option D is incorrect because as cross-stack references are not possible without exporting and importing outputs.

12. B. Option B is the correct answer. CloudFormation does not assume full administrative control on your account, and it requires permissions to interact with resources you own. CloudFormation can operate using a service role; however, this must be explicitly passed as part of the stack operation. Otherwise, it will execute with the same permissions as the user performing the stack operation.

13. C. Option C is correct. Because the reference to the DynamoDB table is made as part of an arbitrary string (the function code), CloudFormation does not recognize this as a dependency between resources. To prevent any potential errors, you would need to declare explicitly that the function depends on the table.

14. E. Option E, all of the above, is correct. Replacing updates results in the deletion of the original resource and the creation of a replacement. CloudFormation creates the replacement first with a new physical ID and verifies it before deleting the original.

15. B, C. Options B and C are correct. Option A is incorrect, as it states that no interruption will occur. Options D and E are not valid update types. Replacing updates delete the original resource and provision a replacement. Updates with some interruption have resource downtime, but the original resource is not replaced.

16. A. The stack cannot be deleted until any other stacks that import the value remove the import. Thus, option A is correct. The export does not need to be removed from the stack before it can be deleted, so option B is incorrect. Options C and D are also incorrect, as the stack does not need to be deleted.

17. B. Old resources that are no longer required are removed during the cleanup phase. Thus, option B is correct. Because the stack status shows the update has completed, you know that the update did not fail. This means that options A and D are incorrect. When a stack updates and resources are created, they will not be deleted unless the update fails. Thus, option C is incorrect.

18. A, C. Options A and C are correct. CloudFormation currently supports JSON and YAML template formats only.

19. E. CloudFormation provides a number of benefits over procedural scripting. The risk of human error is reduced because templates are validated by CloudFormation before deployment. Infrastructure is repeatable and versionable using the same process as application code development. Individual users provisioning infrastructure need a reduced scope of permissions when using CloudFormation service roles. Thus, option E is correct.

20. B. SNS topics and Lambda functions can act as recipients to custom resource requests. Thus, option B is correct. Option C is incorrect because, though on-premises servers can be part of a custom resource's workflow, they do not receive requests directly. Options D and E are incorrect because specific actions are not declared in custom resource properties. Option A is incorrect because AWS services themselves do not process custom resource requests.

21. C. Option C is correct because any data that is declared in a custom resource response is accessible to the remainder of the template using the `Fn::GetAtt` intrinsic function. Options A and B are incorrect because they would require interacting with other AWS services using the AWS CLI. For certain situations, such as running arbitrary commands in EC2 instance user data scripts, this would work. However, not all resource types have this ability. Option D is incorrect, as this is a built-in functionality of CloudFormation.

Chapter 9: Secure Configuration and Container Management

1. C. When using AWS Fargate, you are responsible for defining the task definitions and services, which specify the container images to run and their resource requirements. Option A is incorrect because Fargate abstracts the underlying compute infrastructure; you only manage EC2 instances when you choose to run your own cluster. Option B is incorrect because ECS acts as the container orchestration engine, choosing how to place containers in the cluster. Option D is incorrect because ECS services are designed to always maintain your desired number of tasks, and will start new ones if one fails.

2. B. The `minimumHealthyPercent` parameter specifies the minimum percentage of tasks that must remain in the Running state during a deployment. This ensures that your desired level service availability is maintained while updates are being applied. Option A is incorrect because the parameter is expressed as a percentage, not an absolute number of tasks. Option C is incorrect because the parameter applies to tasks, not container instances. Option D is incorrect because while ECS billing depends on your overall compute utilization, there is no configurable threshold that determines billing.

3. A, B. Option C is incorrect because changing the cluster capacity will not affect service scaling. Option D is incorrect because submitting a replacement will result in the same behavior. If there are insufficient resources to launch replacement tasks when a service updates, Amazon Elastic Container Service (ECS) will continue to attempt to launch the tasks until it is able to do so. If you increase the cluster size, additional resources add to the pool to allow the new task to start. After it has done so, the old task will terminate. After it terminates, the cluster can scale back to its original size. If the downtime of this service does not concern you, set the minimum in-service percentage to 0 percent to allow ECS to terminate the currently running task before it launches the new one.

4. B. Options A, C, and D are incorrect because no other parties have access to the underlying clusters in Fargate. When you use the Fargate launch type, AWS provisions and manages underlying cluster instances for your containers. You do not need to manage maintenance and patching.

5.   A. The Amazon ECS agent is responsible for all on-instance tasks such as downloading container images and starting or stopping containers. Option B is incorrect because the Amazon ECS service role is used to create and manage AWS resources on behalf of the customer. Option C is incorrect because AWS Systems Manager is not part of Amazon ECS. Option D is incorrect because Amazon ECS automates the process of stopping and starting containers within a cluster.

6.   B. Service-oriented architecture involves using containers to implement discrete application components separately from one another to ensure availability and durability of each component. Option A is incorrect. Though high availability is a tenet of SOA, it is not a requirement. Option C is incorrect because SOA does not define how development teams are organized. Option D is incorrect because SOA does not define what should or should not be procured from vendors.

7.   D. A single task definition can describe up to 10 containers to launch at a time. To launch more containers, you need to create multiple task definitions. Task definitions should group containers by similar purpose, life cycle, or resource requirements.

8.   D. The most secure way to store and access sensitive data in Amazon ECS is to use AWS Secrets Manager. You can store the sensitive data as secrets in Secrets Manager and then inject them into the container as environment variables at runtime. This ensures that the sensitive data is not stored in the task definition (option A) or the container image (option B), which could potentially be accessed by unauthorized users. While AWS Systems Manager Parameter Store (option C) can also be used to store sensitive data, injecting the data as environment variables using Secrets Manager is a more direct and secure approach.

9.   A. Option A is correct because the application load balancer is responsible for mapping requests on one port to each container's specific port. Option B is incorrect because PAT cannot be configured within your VPC (it must be configured using a proxy instance of some kind). Option C is incorrect because containers can be configured to bind to a random port instead of a specific one. Dynamic host port mapping allows you to launch multiple copies of the same container listening on different ports. Classic load balancers do not support dynamic host port mapping; thus, option D is incorrect.

10.   A. The `spread` policy distributes tasks across multiple availability zones and cluster instances. Thus, option A is correct. Options B and C are incorrect because they do not consider the availability zone of each cluster instance when placing tasks. Option D is incorrect because `least cost` is not a valid placement policy.

11.   D. Parameter Store's hierarchical fetch features make it easier to store and retrieve many related parameters at once, and Secrets Manager is the best option for sensitive values. Option A was viable before the introduction of Secrets Manager; however, Secrets Manager has more robust features for encrypting sensitive values. Option B could work, but it's not optimal to store nonsensitive values in Secrets Manager, as it will incur higher costs. This option also introduces additional application overhead of JSON parsing in your application. Option C is not correct; even with encrypted images, it is never a good idea to hard-code secret values. There is a risk of leaking secrets to version control, and updating the secrets requires a full rebuild and redeployment of your application.

12. C. Fargate can only be configured with the awsvpc network mode, which provides each task with its own elastic network interface (ENI) and a private IP address within the VPC, enabling the task to have networking capabilities similar to an EC2 instance. Options A and B are incorrect; neither bridge mode nor host mode, which allows containers to share the same network namespace as the host instance, is supported by Fargate. They are only available on EC2 clusters. Option D is incorrect because the none networking mode disables networking for the container and is not suitable for most use cases with Fargate.

13. C. Using Secrets Manager's tight integration with RDS means that neither you nor a database administrator needs to be directly involved with credential rotation; it can happen automatically, and your Python code simply needs to fetch the values. Option A is not ideal because including sensitive information directly in the ECS task definition is not a best practice for secret management, and requiring a deployment with each change means additional error-prone process coordination must take place between teams. Option B, using Parameter Store to manage secrets is a good approach, but this service lacks the built-in automatic rotation feature that Secrets Manager provides. Option D is incorrect because AWS does not automatically inject secrets into the application. Secrets Manager stores the credentials and applications are responsible for fetching them.

14. C. The Amazon VPC Container Network Interface (CNI) plug-in is responsible for assigning a unique IP address from the VPC's address space to each pod in the EKS cluster. This allows pods to communicate with each other and other services within the VPC. Options A and D are incorrect because the EKS control plane and its Kubernetes API server are not directly involved in IP address assignment. Option B is incorrect because worker nodes run the pods but do not assign IP addresses themselves, nor does the networking configuration of individual EC2 instances in the cluster determine pod networking options.

15. C, D. The best answers are C and D; however, there are benefits to each answer. Given that the cluster is already established on EC2, installing the Cluster Autoscaler will help alleviate the immediate problem by adding new nodes via Auto Scaling. Option D is also a good choice. However, it is a more involved option that requires you to migrate your EKS cluster capacity from EC2 to Fargate. This can be done incrementally, and so could be a good choice if the additional cost of Fargate is not a concern. Option B incorrectly describes the Horizontal Pod Autoscaler. EKS already distributes pods across nodes by default; the Horizontal Autoscaler only helps scale the number of pods distributed up and down. This is a good thing, but it will not help the current resource constraint situation. Option A, while potentially helpful in that idle resources could be freed up, does not directly address the need for scalable cluster resources.

Chapter 10: Authentication and Authorization

1. D. You need to use a third-party IdP as the confirmation of identity. Based on that confirmation, a policy can be assigned. Option A is incorrect because roles cannot be assigned to users outside of your account. Option B is incorrect because you cannot assign an IAM user ID to a user that is external to AWS. Option C is incorrect because it makes provisioning an identity a manual process.

2. D. An identity provider (IdP) answers the question, "Who are you?" Based on this answer, policies are assigned. Those policies control the level of access to the AWS infrastructure and applications (if using AWS for managed services).

Option A is incorrect; it is one of the functions of a service provider—to control access to applications. Option B is incorrect; policies are used to control access to APIs, which is how access to the AWS infrastructure is controlled. Option C is incorrect; identity providers do no error checking on policy assignments.

3. A. Where possible, using multifactor authentication (MFA) minimizes the impact of lost or compromised credentials. Option B is incorrect in that embedding credentials is both a security risk and makes credential administration much more difficult. Option C would decrease the opportunity for misuse. It would not address any misuse that was a result of internal users. Option D is a good step but not as secure as option A.

4. D. If you want to use Security Assertion Markup Language (SAML) as an identity provider (IdP), use SAML 2.0. With Amazon Cognito, you can use Google (option A), Microsoft Active Directory (option B), and your own identity store (option C) as identity providers.

5. C. By using AWS Cloud services, such as Cognito, you are able to view the API calls in CloudTrail. CloudWatch Logs are generated if you are using Cognito to control access to AWS resources. Option A is incorrect as AWS can act as an IdP for non-AWS services. Option B is incorrect in that CloudWatch allows you to monitor the creation and modification of identity pools. It will not show activity. Option D is incorrect because the service provider assigns the policies, not the identity provider (IdP).

6. A, C. AD Connecter is easy to set up, and you continue to use the existing AD console to do configuration changes on Active Directory. Option B is incorrect because you cannot connect to multiple Active Directory domains with AD Connector, only a single one. AD Connector requires a one-to-one relationship with your on-premises domains. You can use AD Connector for AWS-created applications and services. Option D is incorrect because AD Connector is used to support AWS services.

7. A. Option A is correct. Setting up AWS Organizations and enabling all features is a prerequisite for using AWS Identity Center. This setup allows for centralized management across multiple AWS accounts, which is a fundamental requirement for implementing Identity Center. Option B is incorrect; Cognito identity pools give you a way to issue IAM roles to mobile or web users, which is not a prerequisite for Identity Center. Option C is incorrect because Identity Center does not require the deployment of Simple AD. It can integrate with AWS Managed Microsoft AD or use AD Connector for connecting to an existing on-premises Microsoft Active Directory, but Simple AD is not supported. Option D is incorrect—using Amazon DynamoDB to set up a user data schema is not required for Identity Center.

8. C. Option C is correct because `GetFederationToken` returns a set of temporary security credentials (consisting of an access key ID, a secret access key, and a security token) for a federated user. You call the `GetFederationToken` action using the long-term security credentials of an IAM user. This is appropriate in contexts where those credentials can be safely stored, usually in a server-based application. Option D is incorrect because

GetSessionToken provides only temporary security credentials. Option A is incorrect because AssumeRole is shorter lived (the default is 60 minutes, and can be extended to 720 minutes). However, it is still possible to refresh these tokens regularly, making it a viable option for long-lived clients that can automate that refresh. Options B and D are incorrect because GetUserToken and GetSessionToken are nonexistent APIs.

9. B. Because it is a managed service, you are not able to access the EC2 instances directly running AWS Managed Microsoft AD. AWS Managed Microsoft AD provides for daily snapshots, monitoring, and the ability to sync with an existing on-premises Active Directory.

10. A. Amazon Active Directory Connector (AD Connector) allows you to use your existing RADIUS-based multifactor authentication (MFA) infrastructure to provide authentication.

11. C. Amazon Cognito identity pools is the best choice as it allows the application to offer temporary IAM credentials for both authenticated and logged-in users. Option B is incorrect; Cognito user pools are used for managing user identities but don't directly support issuing AWS credentials for resource access. Option A is incorrect; Identity Center is about managing federated access for AWS administrators, not handling mobile app user authentication, and AWS Directory Service helps with managed Active Directory services.

Chapter 11: Refactoring to Microservices

1. B. Option B is correct because a Parallel state enables you to execute several different execution paths at the same time in parallel. This is useful if you have activities or tasks that do not depend on each other and can execute in parallel. This can make your workflow complete faster. Option A is incorrect because it executes only one of the branches, not all. Option C is incorrect because it can execute one task, not multiple. Option D is incorrect because it waits and does not execute any tasks.

2. B. The correct answer is B: the messages move to the dead-letter queue if they have met the Maximum Receives parameter (the number of times that a message can be received before being sent to a dead-letter queue) and have not been deleted. Option A is incorrect; messages only move to dead-letter queues when there is an error in processing, not when their timeout expires. Option C is incorrect because the messages will be deleted. Option D is incorrect because messages only become invisible when they are within the retention period and within the visibility timeout window after being received by a consumer.

3. A. Amazon SQS attributes support 256KB messages. Refer to Tables 11.2, 11.3, and 11.4.

4. B. Option B is correct because to send a message larger than 256KB, you use SQS to save the file in S3 and then send a link to the file on SQS. Option A is incorrect because using the technique in option B, this is possible. Option C is incorrect because AWS Lambda cannot push messages to SQS that exceed the size limit of 256KB. Option D is incorrect because it does not address the question.

5. A. Amazon SNS supports the same attributes and parameters as Amazon SQS. Refer to Tables 11.2, 11.3, and 11.4.

6. D. Option D is correct because there is no limit on the number of consumers as long as they stay within the capacity of the stream, which is based on the number of shards. For a single shard, the capacity is 2MB of read or five transactions per second. Options A and B are incorrect because there is no limit on the number of consumers that can consume from the stream. Option C is incorrect because together the consumers can consume only 2MB per second or five transactions per second.

7. C. Option C is correct because Amazon Kinesis Data Streams is a service for ingesting large amounts of data in real time and for performing real-time analytics on the data. Option A is not correct because you use SQS to ingest events, but it does not provide a way to aggregate them in real time. Option B is incorrect because SNS is a notification service that does not support ingesting. Option D is incorrect because Kinesis Data Firehose provides analytics; however, it has a latency of at least 60 seconds.

8. A. Options B, C, and D are incorrect because there are no guarantees about where the records for Washington and Wyoming will be relative to each other. They could be on the same shard, or they could be on different shards. Option A is correct because the records for Washington will not be distributed across multiple shards.

9. E. Options A, B, C, and D are all valid options for writing Amazon Kinesis Data Streams producers.

10. A. The correct answer is A. This describes the "fan-out" pattern that combines pub-sub functionality of SNS with the queuing behavior of SQS, offering the best combination of scalability, decoupling, and flexibility for the microservices architecture. Option B is incorrect because Kinesis Data Streams, while suitable for high-volume data streaming, is more complex than needed for this scenario. Option C is incorrect because, used alone, SQS queues lack the fan-out capability of option A. The publisher would have to push a message individually to each queue. Option D is incorrect because Step Functions are better suited for orchestrating complex workflows rather than simple message distribution.

11. C. Option C is the most effective solution. Converting from a standard SQS queue to an SQS FIFO queue ensures that messages are processed exactly once and in the order they were sent. Option A is incorrect because message retention only affects how long a message will stay queued before any consumer gets it. Option B is incorrect because the while message visibility timeout ensures that a message cannot be re-delivered for a period of time while being processed, it does not provide the same exactly once guarantee that a FIFO queue does. Option D is incorrect because Long Polling optimizes message retrieval from the queue but does not address duplicate processing.

Chapter 12: Serverless Compute

1. D. Option D is correct because it enables the company to keep their existing AWS Lambda functions intact and create new versions of the AWS Lambda function. When they are ready to update the Lambda function, they can assign the PROD alias to the new version. Option A is possible; however, this adds a lot of unnecessary work because developers would have to update all of their code everywhere. Option B is incorrect because moving regions would require moving all other services or introducing latency into the architecture, which is not the best option. Option C is possible; however, creating new AWS accounts for each application version is not a best practice, and it complicates the organization of such accounts unnecessarily.

2. B. As of this writing, the maximum amount of memory for a Lambda function is 10GB.

3. A. As of this writing, the default timeout value for a Lambda function is 3 seconds. However, you can set this to as little as 1 second or as long as 900 seconds.

4. C. Option D is incorrect, as several methods in AWS can achieve this functionality. Options A and B are both viable answers; however, the question asks what is the best *serverless* option. Lambda is the only serverless option in this scenario; therefore, option C is the best answer.

5. D. Option D is the only answer that is not a valid step to fully eliminate the problem. If the Lambda is receiving events from an SQS queue, a dead-letter queue can alert you to issues and even let you retry executions, but if the processing time is just too long, a retry will not fix it. Options A and C are your best initial steps. Option A will make sure you are not unnecessarily limiting your runtime with a too-low timeout configuration. Of course, to keep costs low, you really want to reduce the actual time necessary to process files. Option C can help by quickly determining whether the function is indeed CPU-bound. How? Remember that although Lambda functions' CPU cannot be increased directly, increasing RAM also increases CPU. Since the processing time is related to CPU, it is possible you may drive down your average processing time enough to eliminate the errors. Finally, option B is a good overall practice. Lambda's maximum processing time is 900 seconds, or 15minutes, meaning that long-running processes over that limit will never successfully complete. Breaking the process into steps can avoid timeout errors and give you better overall insight into the behavior and performance of your processing steps. Step Functions can work quite well in this case to orchestrate.

6. A. As of this writing, Rust is not supported for Lambda functions.

7. A. As of this writing, the default limit for concurrent executions with Lambda is set to 1,000. This is a soft limit that can be raised. To do this, you must open a case through the AWS Support Center page and send a Server Limit Increase request.

8. C. There are two types of policies with Lambda: a function policy and an execution policy, or AWS role. A function policy defines which AWS resources are allowed to invoke your function. The execution role defines which AWS resources your function can access. Here, the function is invoked successfully, but the issue is that the Lambda function does not have access to process objects inside Amazon S3. Option A is not correct because a function policy is responsible for invoking or triggering the function; here, the function is invoked and executes properly. Option B is not correct, as the scenario states that the trust policy is valid. The execution policy or AWS role is responsible for providing Lambda with access to other services; thus, the correct answer is option C.

9. A. Option A is correct because Lambda automatically retries failed executions for asynchronous invocations. You can also configure Lambda to forward payloads that were not processed to a DLQ, which can be an Amazon SQS queue or Amazon SNS topic. Option B is incorrect because a VPC network is an AWS service that allows you to define your own network in the AWS Cloud. Option C is incorrect because this is dealing with concurrency issues, and here you have no problems with Lambda concurrency. Additionally, concurrency is enabled by default with Lambda. Option D is incorrect because Lambda does support SQS.

10. C. Option C is correct because using Parameter Store with hierarchical values lets your application fetch many configuration items at once, and this approach remains flexible in that you can always add more values in the hierarchy. Option A is not correct because dead-letter queries are used for events that could not be processed by Lambda and need to be investigated later. Option B is not correct because while manually entered environment variables are suitable for nonsensitive configuration values, you should centralize the administration of such configuration in a service like Parameter Store. Option D is incorrect because there are multiple ways to accomplish this task.

11. A, C. Options A and C are correct. Option A ensures that the function is triggered as soon as input is available, whereas the EventBridge schedule may fire when there is nothing to do. Therefore, the function is invoked a minimal number of times. Option C may result in unnecessary invocations, but with the right balance of invocations to batching, you may increase efficiency by doing more work with fewer executions. Option B is incorrect; while it might reduce processing time, it doesn't directly address latency or cost. Option D may reduce latency somewhat but is less efficient than directly responding to S3 events.

12. C. Option C is correct if you need to send messages to other users. Create an Amazon SNS topic and subscribe all the administrators to this queue. Configure an Amazon EventBridge event to send a message on a daily cron schedule into the Amazon SNS topic. Option A is not correct because Amazon SQS queues do not support subscriptions. Option B is not correct because the message is sent without any status information. Option D is not correct because AWS Lambda does not allow sending outgoing email messages on port 22. Email servers use port 22 for outgoing messages. Port 22 is blocked on Lambda as an antispam measure.

Chapter 13: Serverless Applications

1. B. Option B is correct. CORS is responsible for allowing cross-site access to your APIs. Without it, you will not be able to call the Amazon API Gateway service. You use a stage to deploy your API, and a resource is a typed object that is part of your API's domain. Each resource may have an associated data model and relationships to other resources and can respond to different methods. Option A is incorrect because you do need to enable CORS. Option C is incorrect, as deploying a stage allows you to deploy your API. Option D is incorrect—a resource is where you can define your API, but it is not yet deployed to a stage and "live."

   For more information on CORS, see https://developer.mozilla.org/en-US/docs/Web/HTTP/CORS.

2. A, C. There are three benefits to serverless stacks: no server management, flexible scaling, and automated high availability. Costs vary case by case. For these reasons, options A and C are the best answers.

3. D. Option D is correct. Option A is incorrect; API Gateway only supports HTTPS endpoints. Option B is incorrect because API Gateway does not support creating FTP endpoints. Option C is incorrect; API Gateway does not support SSH endpoints. API Gateway only creates HTTPS endpoints.

4. C. Option A is incorrect because CloudFront supports a variety of sources, including S3. Option B is incorrect because serverless applications contain both static and dynamic data. Additionally, CloudFront supports both static and dynamic data. Option C is correct because CloudFront supports a variety of origins. For the serverless stack, it supports Amazon S3. Option D is incorrect because Amazon S3 is a valid origin for CloudFront.

5. D. Option D is correct. You can run a fully dynamic website in a serverless fashion. You can also use JavaScript frameworks such as Angular and React. The NoSQL database may need to be refactored to run in Amazon DynamoDB. Option A is incorrect. You can run React in an AWS service. Option B is incorrect. You can run your web server with Amazon S3. With option C, you do not need to load-balance Lambda functions because Lambda scales automatically.

6. A, B, C. Options A, B, and C are all good candidates to cache because multiple users are more likely to access them repeatedly, although you could also cache the bank account balance for shorter periods if the database query is not performing well. Option D is incorrect because when compared to the other options, a bank balance is not likely to be stored in a cache; it is probably not data that is retrieved as frequently as the others are fetched, and it's critical that the value is never out of date.

7. A, D. Options A and D are correct because Amazon ElastiCache supports both the Redis and Memcached open source caching engines. Option B is incorrect because MySQL is not a caching engine—it is a relational database engine. Option C is incorrect because Couchbase is a NoSQL database and not one of the caching engines that ElastiCache supports.

8. C. Option C is correct because the default limit is 60 nodes per cluster.

9. C. Option C is correct; ElastiCache is a managed in-memory caching service. Option A is incorrect because the description aligns more closely to the Elasticsearch Service. Option B is incorrect because this is not an accurate description of the ElastiCache service. Option D is incorrect because, as a managed service, ElastiCache does not manage EC2 instances.

10. B. Option B is correct. Resolvers map GraphQL operations, such as queries and mutations, to data sources like DynamoDB. Option A is incorrect because the schema defines the structure of the API, not the resolvers. Option C is incorrect because resolvers do not handle caching. Option D is incorrect because security and access control are managed separately, typically using IAM or Cognito.

11. A. Option A is correct. To use a custom domain with an S3-hosted static website, you can configure Amazon Route 53 to manage the DNS and direct the custom domain to the S3 bucket. Option B is incorrect because CloudFront can enhance performance but does not inherently configure custom domains. Option C is incorrect because an ALB is unnecessary for static website hosting on S3, and while it has its own domain name, it would not be your custom domain. Option D is incorrect because API Gateway is used for API management, not for static website domain forwarding.

12. B. Option B is correct. Though REST APIs broadly offer more advanced features, such as edge-optimized endpoints, request validation, and full integration with services like AWS X-Ray, only HTTP APIs currently support an out-of-the-box authorization integration with JWTs. Option A is incorrect because WebSockets are a third type of API supported by API Gateway outside of HTTP and REST APIs. Option C is incorrect because both REST and HTTP APIs support AWS Lambda integration. Option D is incorrect as HTTP APIs are generally less expensive than REST APIs.

13. A. Option A is correct. Enabling caching on an API Gateway stage allows frequently accessed responses to be stored and quickly replayed, reducing backend processing time and improving performance. Option B is incorrect because increasing Lambda memory may affect function execution time; it is not as effective as caching, which reduces the amount the Lambda must be invoked at all. Option C is incorrect because private endpoints are for security, not performance optimization, and it is unlikely your consumer traffic is coming exclusively from inside your VPC. Option D is incorrect because CORS is for security, not performance enhancement.

14. C. Option C is correct. Subscriptions are GraphQL's built-in mechanism for pushing data updates to clients in real time. Option A is incorrect because clients do not need to initiate regular API queries if they are using subscriptions. Option B is incorrect because WebSockets are a form of persistent HTTP API that functions quite differently from GraphQL or GraphQL subscriptions. Option D is incorrect because GraphQL cannot initiate calls to webhooks, which are a server-side concept anyway, not something that can update the client.

15. B, C. Options B and C are correct. Redis is a good choice over Memcached when you need **support for complex data types** like lists, sets, and hashes, and **data persistence**, which Memcached does not offer. Additionally, Redis allows you to **sort and rank data** in queries, whereas Memcached does not. Option A is incorrect because Redis does not scale horizontally by adding additional nodes in the same way as Memcached; Redis uses replication for scaling reads, but it is not designed for partitioning data across multiple nodes automatically. Option D is incorrect because Redis, with its additional features, is more complex to deploy than Memcached, which is designed for simpler, in-memory caching use cases.

16. B. **Option B** is correct. An API Gateway resource policy can be used to restrict access based on IP addresses by setting an `IpAddress` condition. Option A is incorrect because Amazon Cognito handles user authentication, not IP-based filtering. Option C is incorrect because VPC endpoints are not suitable for filtering traffic from specific external IPs. Option D is incorrect because although AWS WAF can filter IPs, API Gateway resource policies are a simpler, more direct method for controlling access based on IP addresses.

Chapter 14: Modern AWS Deployment Frameworks

1. D. Option D is correct: AWS SAM is an open source framework that you can use to build serverless applications on AWS. Option A is incorrect—although AWS CloudFormation can help you provision infrastructure, AWS Serverless Application Model (AWS SAM) is optimized for deploying AWS serverless resources by making it easy to organize related components and resources that operate on a single stack; therefore, option A is not the best answer. Option B is incorrect because DynamoDB, though serverless, is a NoSQL database engine. Option C is incorrect because AWS Systems Manager is a service that helps manage compute instances at scale.

2. A. Option A is correct because the `events` property allows you to assign Lambda to an event source. Option B is incorrect because `handler` is the function handler in a Lambda function. Option C is incorrect because `context` is the context object for a Lambda function. Option D is incorrect because `runtime` is the language that your Lambda function runs as.

3. A, C. Options A and C are correct. CDK lets you program infrastructure-as-code with traditional programming languages, and it includes abstractions, such as helper functions, that encapsulate complex infrastructure ideas into single commands. Option B is incorrect because CDK does not include a graphical designer interface like the one described. Option D is incorrect because although YAML may be easier to read than JSON, neither is used by developers writing CDK code.

4. B. Option B is correct; cloud sandboxes let Amplify developers deploy an alternate, personal version of the app's backend infrastructure for use while they are running the front end locally. Option A, Amplify Hosting, is a real feature of Amplify, but it is for serving the static assets of a client-side app, not for managing developer environments. Option C is not technically a feature of Amplify. Though you could declare a branch of your git repository to act as a staging environment, doing so would not explicitly be for managing dev environments. Option D is incorrect, as StackSets are a feature of CloudFormation for deploying the same infrastructure to multiple accounts or regions with central management.

5. C. Option C is correct. cdk synth attempts to generate the CloudFormation that results from your CDK code. Performing this step can validate that your code has no "compile time" (technically, "transpile time") errors and can alert you to issues before you try to deploy. Option A is incorrect; sync is just a similar word, and there's nothing in CDK that syncs code to AWS in this way (outside of CloudFormation templates when they are deployed, of course). Option B is incorrect because watching for file changes is the job of cdk watch. Finally, D is incorrect. CDK has no command that scaffolds architecture in this way, but Level 3 constructs do give you a way to build complex, multi-resource architecture quickly.

6. B. Option B is correct. In just a few lines of a SAM template, you can create AWS API Gateway routes backed by Lamba functions that access DynamoDB data. Option A is incorrect because although it would work (and the cluster can be serverless with Fargate), it is still a heavier-weight solution that just using SAM and Lambda/API Gateway. Option C is incorrect for similar reasons. It could stand up the infrastructure you need, but is not purpose-built for the task in the way SAM is. Finally, Option D is incorrect. Even though Amplify can stand up data resources quickly (even REST APIs using API Gateway), it is geared primarily toward providing backend services for front-end applications.

7. B. Option B is correct. The Transform feature of CloudFormation empowers individuals to send all or part of a CloudFormation template to an external Lambda for processing. This enables you to support syntax that is not native to CloudFormation; this is how SAM works. Option A is incorrect. Although SAM does take advantage of change sets to give you a choice before deploying new updates, change sets are not the technology that enables SAM syntax. Option C is incorrect for similar reasons; CloudFormation metadata annotates templates but does not transform the syntax. Finally, option D is incorrect, as StackSets are designed for deploying infrastructure across multiple accounts and regions.

8. A. Option A is correct. You can add a DynamoDB table as a resource and configure a managed policy to allow the Lambda function to read and write data without modifying the code. Option B is incorrect because environment variables alone do not grant permissions. Option C is incorrect because using inline policies is not the best practice in this case; managed policies are more flexible and maintainable. Option D is incorrect because creating the table manually breaks the automation SAM provides.

9. D. Option D is correct: SAM does not assist with domain configuration for API Gateway, but it does simplify all the other steps mentioned in options A, B, and C.

10. C. Option C is correct because Amplify fulfills all the requirements in a single package. Amplify lets you define serverless backends, including API Gateway-powered REST APIs, using TypeScript, so serverless infrastructure-as-code is covered. Amplify also gives you the tools to build, deploy, and host web and mobile front ends using popular frameworks like React and VueJS. Finally, to fulfill the last requirement about accessibility, Amplify provides login capabilities through Cognito so that you can scope access to a subset of users. Option A is incorrect; SAM does handle the REST API but not the front end or user authentication. Option B is incorrect because, similar to SAM, CDK can handle the infrastructure, but does not help build and deploy a web application. Option D is also incorrect; Beanstalk does help you stand up and deploy apps, but they are not serverless by default, nor does it make adding authentication simple the way that Amplify does.

Chapter 15: Monitoring and Troubleshooting

1. **B.** Option B is correct because scaling out should occur when more resources are being consumed than normal, and scaling in should occur when fewer resources are being consumed. Option A is incorrect because you do not want to scale in to reduce your capacity when you are experiencing a high load. Option C is incorrect because you do not want to scale in to reduce your capacity when your application is taking a long time to respond. Option D is incorrect because metrics are required for triggering AWS Auto Scaling events.

2. **D.** Option D is correct. Data points with a period of 300 seconds are stored for 63 days in Amazon CloudWatch.

3. **C.** Option C is correct because archiving logs from CloudWatch to Amazon S3 reduces overall data storage costs. Option A would work; however, it is not the most cost-effective way because logs stored in CloudWatch cost more than logs stored in Amazon S3. Option B is incorrect because CloudWatch cannot ingest logs without access to your servers.

4. **A, B, D.** Option C is incorrect because CloudWatch has no way to access data in your applications or servers. You must push the data either by using the CloudWatch SDK or AWS CLI or by installing the CloudWatch agent. Option A is correct because the CloudWatch agent is required to send operating system and application logs to CloudWatch. Option B is also correct because metrics logs are sent to CloudWatch using the `PutMetricData` and `PutLogEvents` API actions. Option D is also correct because the AWS CLI can be used to send metrics to CloudWatch using the `put-metric-data` and `put-log-events` commands.

5. **C.** Options A and B are incorrect because the strings must match a filter pattern equal to 404. Option C is correct because 404 matches the error code present in the example logs.

6. **A.** AWS X-Ray color-codes the response types you get from your services. For 4XX, or client-side errors, the circle is orange. Thus, option B is incorrect. Application failures or faults are red, and successful responses, or 2XX, are green. Thus, options C and D are incorrect. For throttling, or 5XX series errors, the circle is purple. Thus, option A is correct.

7. **C.** Option C is the correct answer. Use CloudWatch dashboards to create a single interface where you can monitor all the resources. Option A is incorrect because CloudTrail logs list security-related events and do not provide a dashboard feature. Option B is incorrect because CloudWatch alarms are used to notify you when something isn't operating based on your specifications. Option D is incorrect because Amazon CloudWatch Logs are for sending and storing server logs to the CloudWatch service; however, you could use these logs to create a metric and then place it on the CloudWatch dashboard.

8. **D.** CloudTrail stores the CloudTrail event history for 90 days; however, if you would like to store this information permanently, you can create an CloudTrail trail, which stores the logs in Amazon S3.

9. B, D. Options B and D are correct. Management events are operations performed on resources in your AWS account. Data events are operations performed on data stored in AWS resources. For example, modifying an object in Amazon S3 would qualify as a data event, and changing a bucket policy would qualify as a management event. Because options A, C, and E involve sending or receiving data, not modifying or creating AWS resources, they are data events.

10. A, C, D. When installing the CloudWatch Logs agent, no additional networking configuration is required as long as your instance can reach the CloudWatch API endpoint. Therefore, option B is incorrect. You can use AWS Systems Manager to install and start the agent, but it is not required to install the Systems Manager agent alongside the CloudWatch Logs agent; thus, option E is incorrect. When installing the agent, you must configure the specific logs to send. The agent must be started before new log data is sent to CloudWatch Logs.

11. D. CPU, network, and disk activity are metrics that are visible to the underlying host for an instance. Thus, options A, B, and C are incorrect. Because memory is allocated in a single block to an instance and is managed by the guest OS, the underlying host does not have visibility into consumption. This metric would have to be delivered to CloudWatch as a custom metric by using the agent. Thus, option D is correct.

12. A. No namespace starts with an Amazon prefix; therefore, options B and D are incorrect. Option C is incorrect because namespaces are specific to a service (Amazon EC2), not a resource (an instance). Option A is correct because the Amazon EC2 service uses the AWS prefix, followed by EC2.

13. C. Option C is correct. Creating multiple EventBridge rules with custom event patterns allows for flexible routing based on the specific details of each event type. This approach ensures that only relevant events are sent to the Lambda function. Option A is incorrect because trying to match all possible formats in a single rule is overly complex and unnecessary. Similarly, option B is too complex. Multiple event buses are not required; EventBridge rules can match multiple event sources. Option D is incorrect because Step Functions cannot be invoked by heterogenous events on its own; in fact, you'd need EventBridge for this in the first place.

14. B. Option B is correct. The limit command restricts the number of log events returned by CloudWatch Log Insights, in this case, to the top 100.

15. D. Option D is correct. Ultrawarm uses S3 buckets to give you lower-cost storage for less frequently accessed data. Option A is incorrect; infrequent access is a storage tier of S3. Option B is incorrect as it describes a pattern for zero-downtime deployments, not storage. Option C is incorrect; it refers to EBS volumes, which are used for OpenSearch's active "hot" storage.

Chapter 16: Optimization

1. D. Amazon EC2 instance store is directly attached to the instance, which gives you the lowest latency between the disk and your application. Instance store is also provided at no additional cost on instance types that have it available, so this is the lowest-cost option.

Additionally, because the data is being retrieved from somewhere else, it can be copied back to an instance as needed. Option A is incorrect because Amazon S3 cannot be directly mounted to an Amazon EC2 instance. Options B and C are incorrect because Amazon EBS and Amazon EFS would be higher-cost options, with a higher latency than an instance store.

2. C. Option C is a fault-tolerance check. By launching instances in multiple availability zones in the same region, you help protect your applications from a single point of failure. Options A and B are performance checks. Provisioned IOPS volumes in the Amazon EBS are designed to deliver the expected performance only when they are attached to an EBS optimized instance. Some headers, such as Date or User-Agent, significantly reduce the cache hit ratio (the proportion of requests that are served from a CloudFront edge cache). This increases the load on your origin and reduces performance because CloudFront must forward more requests to your origin. Option D is a cost check. Elastic IP addresses are static IP addresses designed for dynamic cloud computing. A nominal charge is imposed for an Elastic IP address that is not associated with a running instance.

3. D. Option A is incorrect because SQS is a messaging service. Option B is incorrect because SNS is a notification service. Option C is incorrect because CloudFront is a web distribution service. Option D is correct because ElastiCache improves the performance of your application by retrieving data from high throughput and low latency in-memory data stores. For details, see `https://aws.amazon.com/elasticache`.

4. C. Option C is correct because CloudFront optimizes performance if your workload is mainly sending `GET` requests. There are also fewer direct requests to Amazon S3, which reduces cost. For details, see `https://docs.aws.amazon.com/AmazonS3/latest/dev/request-rate-perf-considerations.html`.

5. C. Option A is incorrect because EC2 instance store is too volatile to be optimal. Option B is incorrect because this is a security solution and will not impact performance positively. Option C is correct because ElastiCache is ideal for handling session state. You can abstract the HTTP sessions from the web servers by using Redis and Memcached. Option D is incorrect because compression is not the optimal solution given the choices. For details, see `https://aws.amazon.com/caching/session-management`.

6. B. Option B is correct because lazy loading only loads data into the cache when necessary. This avoids filling up the cache with data that isn't requested. Options A, C, and D are incorrect because they do not match the requirements of the question. For details, see `https://docs.aws.amazon.com/AmazonElastiCache/latest/mem-ug/Strategies.html`.

7. D. Options A, B, and C are incorrect because they are not recommended best practices. Option D is correct because it is one of the recommendations in the best practices documentation, "Avoid using recursive code." For details, see `https://docs.aws.amazon.com/lambda/latest/dg/best-practices.html`.

8. B. Options A, C, and D are incorrect because they are not optimal for handling large object uploads to Amazon S3. Option B is correct because a multipart upload enables you to upload large objects in parts to Amazon S3. For details, see `https://docs.aws.amazon.com/AmazonS3/latest/dev/mpuoverview.html`.

9. C. Option C is correct because any advanced provisioning you can bake into the base image is work that does not have to be done on boot. Just make sure that you update your AMI periodically to ensure your dependencies stay up-to-date. Option A is incorrect because this is not the optimal approach for bootstrapping. Option B is incorrect because, though possible, pre-baking the dependencies is optimal. Option D is incorrect because bootstrapping is done in instance user data, not instance metadata.

10. B. Option B is correct; AWS Trusted Advisor inspects your AWS environment and identifies unused or underutilized resources, providing recommendations on actions that can reduce costs. Option A is incorrect because AWS CloudTrail is used for logging API calls. Option C is incorrect because Amazon Inspector is a security assessment service. Option D is incorrect because AWS Systems Manager is primarily used for operational data and automation.

11. C, D. Option C is correct because enforcing mandatory tagging allows you to track and manage resources by owner, environment, or project, which helps in cost allocation and optimization. Option D is also correct because AWS Config rules can help ensure that your resources have the required tags on them. Option A is incorrect because CloudTrail logs API calls but does not help with resource tagging. Option B is incorrect because AWS Systems Manager does not enforce tagging policies.

12. B. Option B is correct. An Auto Scaling Group with a mix of On-Demand and Spot Instances can give you significant savings along with the responsive scaling behavior of ASGs. Spot instances can be cost as little as 10 percent of On-Demand prices, while keeping On-Demand instances in the pool helps ensure your app stays online. On that note, Option A is incorrect because using Spot Instances exclusively would risk downtime for your app, should all the Spot Instances be terminated at the same time. Option C is incorrect because while Savings Plans would allow you to save money on the compute in this scenario (and they are relatively flexible), they do not, by themselves, offer any solution to the spikiness of the app's load. That's what Auto Scaling can provide. Similarly, Option D is incorrect because while this approach can reduce operational overhead significantly, and ECS Services can auto-scale like EC2 ASGs, they do not provide the level of cost savings that Spot can provide. If cost is paramount, Spot is hard to beat.

13. C. **Option C is correct** because using S3 life cycle policies allows you to automatically transition data between different storage classes based on access patterns, optimizing costs while ensuring your data availability aligns with your usage requirements. Option A is incorrect because as its name indicates, S3 Standard is the standard option, tuned for general purpose use and conferring no particular discount. It's for commonly used data, not for infrequently accessed data. Option B is incorrect because S3 Glacier is suitable only for archival purposes, not merely infrequently accessed data. Option D is incorrect because consolidating your objects would not address access frequency or cost optimization.

14. E. All of the above options work together to help you combat this problem. Your first move should be option D. Looking at Cost Explorer reports, you can see a detailed breakdown of your bill and observe changes over time. This will help you know which resources or services are causing the newly spiked charges. Follow this up with option C. AWS CloudTrail provides detailed logs of API calls made within your account, letting you track who made changes, what they did, and when they did it. Because you know which services to focus on from your Cost Explorer reports, you can likely determine which user or process is responsible for the charges. From there, implement option B, setting AWS Budgets so that you are not caught off-guard by unexpected charges in the future. Finally, try option A. AWS Config rules monitor compliance with predefined rules that can help you know immediately when an out-of-compliance change is made in your environment, which may help catch unexpected changes in the future.

15. C. Option C is correct: Compute Savings Plans offer up to 66 percent cost savings while allowing you the flexibility to switch between EC2 (regardless of instance family or type), Fargate, and Lambda, changing regions as needed. This makes them ideal in this scenario, as they will not limit your deployment options. Option A is incorrect because, although Convertible Reserved Instances are not tied to specific EC2 configurations and regions, they do not extend to ECS deployments or Lambda. Option B is incorrect because Spot Instances, while cheaper, are not guaranteed and are best for fault-tolerant tasks. Option D is incorrect because On-Demand Instances offer flexibility but at a higher cost compared to Savings Plans.

Index

C

S

Online Test Bank

To help you study for your AWS Certified Developer exam, register to gain one year of FREE access after activation to the online interactive test bank—included with your purchase of this book!

To access our learning environment, simply visit www.wiley.com/go/sybex testprep, follow the instructions to register your book, and instantly gain one year of FREE access after activation to:

- Hundreds of practice test questions, so you can practice in a timed and graded setting
- Flashcards
- A searchable glossary